BUILDING AND PLANNING FOR INDUSTRIAL STORAGE AND DISTRIBUTION

Second Edition

Jolyon Drury is a logistics and materials handling consultant with more than 25 years experience of specialist practice. He is a Chartered Architect and Fellow of the Institute of Logistics and Transport where he is a member of the Public Policy Committee and a leading member of their Europe Forum.

Peter Falconer was a Fellow of the Royal Institute of British Architects who spent a lifetime working as architect and consultant on buildings for industrial storage and distribution. He pioneered the use of 'big box' warehouses in the U.K. forming one of the first dedicated materials handling consultancies in parallel with his architectural practice that revolutionised handling in breweries and in steel stockholding. He died in February 2003.

BUILDING AND PLANNING FOR INDUSTRIAL STORAGE AND DISTRIBUTION

Second Edition

Jolyon Drury and Peter Falconer

Architectural Press
AMSTERDAM   BOSTON   HEIDELBERG   LONDON   NEW YORK   OXFORD   PARIS   SAN DIEGO
SAN FRANCISCO   SINGAPORE   SYDNEY   TOKYO

The text of this book as it originally appeared
in *The Architects' Journal* was edited by Susan Dawson, BA, BArch, RIBA

Architectural Press
An imprint of Elsevier
Linacre House, Jordan Hill, Oxford OX2 8DP
200 Wheeler Road, Burlington MA 01803

First published 1975
Second edition 2003

Copyright © 2003, Jolyon Drury and Peter Falconer. All rights reserved

The right of Jolyon Drury and Peter Falconer as the authors of this work has been asserted in accordance with the Copyright, Designs and Patents Act 1988

No part of this publication may be reproduced in any material form (including photocopying or storing in any medium by electronic means and whether or not transiently or incidentally to some other use of this publication) without the written permission of the copyright holder except in accordance with the provisions of the Copyright, Designs and Patents Act 1988 or under the terms of a licence issued by the Copyright Licensing Agency Ltd, 90 Tottenham Court Road, London, England W1T 4LP. Applications for the copyright holder's written permission to reproduce any part of this publication should be addressed to the publisher

Permissions may be sought directly from Elsevier's Science and Technology Rights Departmant in Oxford, UK: phone: (+44) (0) 1865 843830; fax: (+44) (0) 1865 853333; e-mail: permissions@elsevier.co.uk. You may also complete your request on-line via the Elsevier homepage (http://www.elsevier.com), by selecting 'Customer Support' and the 'Obtaining Permissions'.

British Library Cataloguing in Publication Data
A catalogue record for this book is available from the British Library

Library of Congress Cataloging in Publication Data
A catalog record for this book is available from the Library of Congress

ISBN 0 7506 48198

For information on all Architectural Press publications visit our website at www.architecturalpress.com

Typeset and printed and bound in Great Britain

Contents

Disclaimer vi
Preface vii
Foreword ix
Credits x
Definitions xi
Introduction: scope and form of the book xiii
List of technical studies xiv

Technical studies

1 Introduction 1
   Part 1 Introduction 3
   Part 2 Storage and distribution as a total system 7

2 Loading 11
   1 Loading bay design 13

3 External storage 53
   1 Design of container handling areas 55

4 Mechanized storage 73
   1 Storage process 75
   2 Building function 101

5 Automated storage 189
   1 Storage process 191
   2 Building function 213

6 Cold storage 225
   1 Storage process 227
   2 Building function 237

7 Special storage 245
   1 Storage process 247
   2 Building function 255

Bibliography and useful addresses 270
Index 271

Information sheets

1 Vehicle sizes, weights and turning circles 23
2 Loading bay layout and gate entries 33
3 Waste-handling equipment 39
4 Industrial doors 43
5 Loading dock equipment 45
6 Railway layouts 49

1 Containers 61
2 Container-handling plant 65

1 Tote boxes, drawers and storage cabinets 117
2 Shelving 121
3 Racking 125
4 Pallets 135
5 General purpose handling aids 141
6 Pedestrian controlled handling plant 143
7 Forklift family 147
8 Packaging plant 159
9 Battery charging and maintenance areas 161
10 Tractor trains 163
11 Static vertical movement plant 165
12 Fixed-path handling plant 169
13 Towline conveyors 173
14 Conveyors for warehouse use 177

1 Automated-handling plant 211
2 Automated horizontal transport system 223

1 Conveyors for bulk materials 259
2 Bag loading equipment 263
3 Mobile bulk-handling plant 265
4 Intermediate bulk containers 267
5 Mass densities 268

Disclaimer

The purpose of this book is to assist in understanding the mechanics of industrial storage processes. Many of the relationships are of an approximate nature and may be unsuitable for detailed calculations. While reasonable care has been taken, it is possible that errors exist in the material contained and neither the authors nor the publisher can accept responsibility for any results arising from use of information in this book.

Preface

The nature of market forces in the field of distribution and the range of technological processes that have been developed to meet them, make the planning of efficient buildings for storage and distribution vital in the industrial sector. Getting it right, however, is an exacting business – particularly when the designer is under pressure to keep costs down by making the correct initial choice, while at the same time having to remain aware that the building must have sufficient built-in flexibility to allow for the economic or technical changes that will inevitably come along during its lifetime. Thus, while storage buildings are normally designed to outlast a payback period of 25 years, reaching maximum efficiency at the halfway stage, it can now be predicted that a storage and handling system may change three or more times. It was argued at one time that the answer was a 'throw-away' philosophy, with minimum-cost buildings designed to be demolished when the storage system became obsolete. But like some developments in storage itself, this concept has been overtaken by external events. Increasing building costs and greater competition on smaller profit margins mean that manufacturing and distributive industry can no longer afford to shut down or reduce its trading for the lengthy periods that may be involved in alteration and rebuilding.

Changes in the hardware and software of distribution affect storage buildings in a number of ways – the lack of weight-bearing capacity on floor or frame, lack of height and width, shortage of room for further expansion and, above all, insufficient yard space. Planning ahead for considerations of this kind has to be reconciled with often unhelpful and outmoded constraints in the way of legislation and restrictions. There is a worldwide lack of integration – which remains to be overcome – in the way of building codes, fire regulations, the requirements of insurance companies and the rationale of storage designs.

All these are factors which add to building costs. A similar problem facing the designer is the absence of compatible systems in the way goods are handled. Unit load technology has advanced, but not as much as was first predicted. It is easy for designers to become excited by the concept of modular units fitting smoothly together; in fact it will be some time before pallets, freight containers and demountable body units become universally compatible. Certainly as far as the European rail network is concerned, vagaries of tunnels and handling equipment render nearly similar container designs incompatible when it comes to actual practice. Indeed, there is a good argument for resisting a doctrinaire desire for modular conformity because of the variations in the characteristics of goods and the distributive system. Although there are, therefore, still some unresolved areas in the field of storage and distribution, one can distinguish certain broad trends which the designer will have to take into account in planning his or her buildings and discussing them with the client, for whom this book is also intended. Thus, in spite of the slowness of progress towards standardization and the warnings that have to be entered against too inflexible an approach in this respect, there is no doubt that there will be increasing standardization of the size and weight of unit loads, leading to higher stacking, faster handling methods and calling, in turn, for greater headroom, better floors and higher-quality buildings. In line with present trends this means further growth in the development of containers and, in this context, specifically of swop bodies which are really small containers for urban deliveries. Pointers in this direction emerge clearly from planning and environmental pressures which are discouraging heavy transport incursions into towns in favour of container-based 'distribution villages' at the periphery of urban centres and neighbourhoods. The problem here – and it is symptomatic of the range of issues the designer and the client have to face – is that when this is combined with bans against daytime goods traffic movement in towns, there is obviously going to be a good deal of night noise which has to be taken into account when considering location. Recently several operators, subjected to hostile public opinion over this issue, have had to make costly alterations to their loading facilities.

Another important factor is, of course, 'sustainability' including energy conservation, not only in terms of fuel costs but the growing awareness that this raises a question mark over the concept of throw-away packaging. There is a conflict here between the fact that at present it is actually more economic to throw away packs than to use returnable bottles or drums and thus conserve materials. However, as the balance changes, as is happening with metal containers, the distribution industry will have to accept part of the cost of recovery, with all the accompanying problems of transport, storage and baling, and the associated costs of contamination. This really implies 'reverse logistics', a separate distribution system the costs of which are likely to be reflected in prices to the consumer.

Equally, energy conservation will have a major influence on building design. Already the cost of energy in

Preface

the form of heating, cooling and refrigeration forms a high proportion of the overall costs of the storage operation. However, good insulation, and a large volume can achieve near steady-state internal conditions in a temperate climate: high buildings can allow for natural cooling without having to resort to large-scale plant – increasingly costly to run. At the same time, although for most goods cool environmental conditions are required, this may be at odds with working conditions demanded by the labour force. A similar problem occurs over the actual handling of goods. If the systems are manual, the personnel are going to demand certain standards of heat and light – particularly in the case of night work. These have to be weighed against the cost of automated systems which do not require the same environmental standards, but which involve sums of another sort. Ultimately the decision rests on the throughput and the characteristics of the orders handled: for example, in the foreseeable future, the cheapest and quickest way to pick a large number of small orders and discrete items will be by hand, be it with some sophisticated electronic assistance. The task facing the designer of buildings for storage and distribution is, therefore, to balance the need to produce value in terms of immediate cost-cutting efficiency with a longer-term strategy which will provide the flexibility for rapid change in the overall socio-economic situation: also to weigh up simple, low-energy solutions against the performance offered by the immensely wide choice of high technology equipment now available in this field. Making the right choice depends, as one might expect, on both client and designer having access to as much information as is practicable. Thus, we have attempted in this guide to storage building design not only to provide sufficient data about mechanical handling and storage systems as they affect the detailed design of buildings, but also to offer a considerable degree of background information concerning the reasons for the choice of certain systems and an insight into what effect these decisions can have. We hope that in this way we will help designers to balance criteria of pure operational efficiency for an initial price, with others – increasingly important – of the labour market, social conditions and long-term value. These are all factors in the design of industrial storage buildings for such buildings can never be seen in isolation, but as part of a system of distribution in which economic, social and technological elements interact with the development of our community as a whole.

Peter Falconer
Jolyon Drury

Foreword

The universal acceptance over 20 years ago of the container in materials handling made this book, written by two architects in the UK, invaluable for industrial facility managers, materials handling engineers, and architects carrying out industrial projects in the USA, the UK, the EU and virtually all industrialized countries.

As the authors pointed out at the time of their first edition 'The coming of the container has had the effect of unifying materials handling methods worldwide, and inevitably leads to compatibility requirements on pallet sizes, racking, vehicle design, etc., so that storage and handling methods have to be considered on a worldwide basis if the full economy of the container is to benefit mankind'. This is even more true today.

This revised edition presents further evidence that there is increasing in-depth expertise in an ever-widening area of specialized planning and design within the architectural profession. This says that the architect is more than exterior decorator. Increasingly, buildingowners and facility managers can turn to the architect/construction programme manager for the most objective and professional guidance through all phases of their construction programmes. In turn, the architect/programme manager can more and more call on members of the profession for in-depthexpertise in specialized areas.

This is not to say that every architect is a specialist, a manager or even completely competent. Most experienced owners know better. As in any profession, no honest or accurate generalization can be made regarding capabilities or competence. However, increasingly, there are to be found those high levels of competence in special areas of planning and consultation, design and programme management within the architectural profession or within organizations that are outgrowths of architectural firms.

Underlying this thoroughly researched and detailed work of Messrs Falconer and Drury is a basic concern for total cost to the respective industrial organization. The work's primary concern with the operational philosophies behind storage facility needs, as well as the details of what these facilities must accommodate, points out the concern for the 'bottom-line' financial result of such facilities. This concern, then, fits well into the managerial expertise related to total cost (including time as a cost function) that must be further nurtured within the architectural profession.

George T. Heery, AIA
Atlanta, Georgia, USA

Credits

All photos, except those specifically mentioned, are Drury.

Technical study, Introduction 1
1.1 Meigh
1.3 Honeysett
1.4, 1.5 Meigh

Technical study, Introduction 2
1.9, Mechanical Handling
1.10 Power Lifts

Technical study, Loading 1
2.2a/b, 2.8, 2.9 Toomey
2.12 Stockvis
2.14 Matral
2.15 Dexion
2.16 Joloda
2.17, 2.18b Toomey
2.18a Lancer Boss
2.9 British Monorail
2.21 Pengco Ltd

Information sheet, Loading 2
2.31 TRRL

Information sheet, Loading 3
2.43 Shephard Meiller
2.51 Reynolds Boughton

Information sheet, Loading 5
2.55 Hunter
2.56, 2.57, 2.58 Gascoigne, Gush and Dent
2.59b Keyzar Farnworth
2.60, 2.61 GGD
2.62 GGD
2.63 Power lifts
2.64a Stockvis
2.64b Loading Systems
2.65 Newland Conveyors

Information sheet, Loading 6
2.71, 2.72 Shell

Technical study, External storage 1
3.2a/b Abel Systems Ltd
3.3 R. Winterton
3.5 Toomey

Information sheet, External storage 1
Table 3.1i Rubery Owen

Information sheet, External storage 2
3.14 Crane Fruehauf
3.15, 3.16a R. Winterton
3.16b Rubery Owen
3.19a/b, 3.20 Lancer Boss
3.26, 3.27, 3.28, 3.29 Mafi (UK) Ltd
3.30, 3.31 Powell Duifryn
3.32 Braby
3.34, 3.35 Welford Ltd
3.36a/b Canadian National Railway
3.37a SNCF Novotrans

Technical study, Mechanized storage 1

4.4a Toomey
4.6a Mary Kay Cosmetics
4.6b Heery & Heery
4.8 Orenstein & Koppel
4.9, 4.10 Chantrill
4.11 Dexion
4.12 Demag
4.13 John Laing
4.14, 4.15, 4.16 Lansing Bagnall
4.17, 4.18 Dexion
4.20 British Monorail
4.21, 4.24 Toomey
4.26 Lansing Bagnall
4.30 Mechanical Handling
4.31 Cleco
4.32, 4.33 George King
4.36 Post Office
4.37 Pantin
4.41, 4.42, 4.43, 4.44, 4.45, 4.46 Toomey
4.47 Stewart Bale
4.48 Lansing Bagnall

Technical study, Mechanized storage 2
4.50a/c, 4.53 Atcost
4.57 Toomey
4.59 BRE
4.61 Crown Controls Ltd
4.62 Coventry Climax
4.63 Lansing Bagnall
4.64 Pantin
4.66 Lansing Bagnall
4.67 Orenstein & Koppell
4.68 Melford Engineering
4.69 Falconer

Information sheet, Mechanized storage 1
4.72 Welconstruct
4.73 Linvar

Information sheet, Mechanized storage 2
4.80, 4.81, 4.82, 4.83 Dexion

Information sheet, Mechanized storage 3
4.87 Dexion
4.89 Mechanical Handling
Table 4.5 Boltless Systems Ltd
4.92 Bolfiess
4.93 Mechanical Handling
4.94, 4.95, 4.96, 4.98 Boltless Systems Ltd
4.97 Dexion
4.100, 4.103 Mechanical Handling
4.106 Boltless Systems Ltd
4.107a/b Bruynzeel
4.108 Spacemaster
4.110 Dexion
4.112 John S. Bolles

Information sheet, Mechanized storage 4

4.113 Hudawell

Information sheet, Mechanized storage 6
4.121 Ruhery Owen

Information sheet, Mechanized storage 7
4.128, 4.129, 4.130 Mechanical Handling
4.131, 4.132, 4.133, 4.134 Cascade
4.135 Hudswell
4.136, 4.138 Atlet
4.139, 4.140 Climax
4.141 Ameise
4.142 Fleet-Line Manutention

Information sheet, Mechanized storage 8
4.143 Lawson
4.144a Müllers

Information sheet, Mechanized storage 11
4.153 Goss Handling
4.154 Power Lifts

Information sheet, Mechanized storage 12
4.157, 4.158, 4.159 Demag
4.160 British Monorail

Information sheet, Mechanized storage 13
4.163, 4.164, 4.165 MGK Engineering
4.167 Atcost
4.168 MGK Engineering
4.169 A'Court

Information sheet, Mechanized storage 14
4.170, 4.175 Rapistan
4.178, 4.179 Flexiveyor
4.181 Dexion
4.183a Müllers
4.187, 4.188, 4.189, 4.190, 4.191,
4.192 Mechanical Handling
4.198 Dexion

Technical study, Automated storage 1
Frontispiece Dexion
5.2, 5.3 Ohler/Whylen
5.5 Williams
5.6 Demag
5.13 HMSO
5.15, 5.16 Eastern Electricity
5.18 Ohler
5.19 Eastern Electricity
5.21 EB
5.22 Mills K.
5.27 Integrated Handling Ltd
5.28 Eastern Electricity
5.29 SSi
5.31, 5.32 Tranarobot Ltd

5.34 Mills K.

Technical study, Automated storage 2
5.36 Mills K.
5.37, 5.38 Eastern Electricity
5.39 British Steel
5.40 Lansing Bagnall
5.41 SSI
5.43 Mills K.
5.44 Tranarobot Ltd

Information sheet, Automated storage 1
5.46 Demag
5.47 Owen Thorn

Information sheet, Automated storage 2
5.51 EMI

Technical study, Cold storage 1
6.1 Foamglass
6.2 Birds Eye
6.3, 6.5 Crane Fruehauf
6.6 Toomey
6.8 Birds Eye
6.9 Frigoscandia
6.10a/b WCB Clare's
6.11 Birds Eye
6.12 Toomey
6.13, 6.14 Lansing Bagnall

Technical study, Cold storage 2
6.18 Danepak, Thetford
6.19, 6.21 Toomey
6.22 Frigoscandia
6.23 Toomey
6.26 Birds Eye
6.27 Lansing Bagnall
6.28 Eaton Yale

Technical study, Special storage 1
7.1 Bruynzeel
7.2 Crane Fruehauf
7.7 British Mornorail
7.8, 7.9 Cleco

Technical study, Special storage 2
7.15 British Monorail
7.13 Lye Trading
7.14 W. T. Avery
7.16 Lye Trading
7.17 Cleco Electrical Industries
7.18 Matbro

Information sheet, Bulk storage 2
7.25, 7.26, 7.27, 7.28, 7.29, 7.30 Müllers

Information sheet, Bulk storage 4
7.31 Alcoa

x

Definitions

A
AGV Automated guided vehicle. A free path load carrier, usually battery electric, that has fixed path characteristics guided by a buried wire or by infrared beacons: effectively a discontinuous conveyor.
Aisle The corridor for equipment and personnel movement and materials handling between storage shelving and racking.
APR Adjustable pallet racking. The building block of all storage systems.
Articulated vehicle A vehicle comprising a motor unit (tractor) and a load carrying unit (trailer): for greater manoeuvrability the front of the trailer is superimposed onto a bearing plate (fifth wheel) mounted at the rear of the tractor chassis. Thus the vehicle can bend in the middle, i.e. articulate, requiring a much smaller turning circle than a rigid vehicle of a comparable length.

B
B2B Business-to-business.
Bay The storage space between two racking uprights: i.e. pallet bay, which can be several beam levels high.
Beam The metal beam that spans a rack bay, which in pairs support pallets.
Block stacking Unit loads stacked on top of each other.
Bluetooth Personal wireless personal area networking (PAN): connection of handheld data-gathering device to WiFi transmitter.
Bogies More than one axle in tandem.
Bridging plates Detachable metal plates designed to bridge the gap between dock surface and vehicles of different heights.
Buffer An area for goods to accumulate between parts of a system running at different speeds.

C
Cross docking Receiving off one vehicle, sorting the goods and directly loading onto another: no stock-holding.
Curtain-sided vehicle Vehicle fitted with curtain sides to the body for easy side-loading.

D
Dock leveller A hinged bridge between the dock surface and different load bed heights of vehicles. Levellers automatically adjust to different vehicle heights and the rise of vehicle springs as it is unloaded.

F
FATS Factory acceptance tests.
FDS Functional design specification: what equipment has what function and interfaces.
Finger dock A raised loading dock set at an acute angle of 80° plus, so that trucks can be either side-loaded or end-loaded in the conventional manner.
Flat trailer A semi-trailer or drawbar trailer designed as a flatbed, i.e., no sides; some are dual purpose, being fitted with twist locks for container carrying as well. Flat trailers are still favoured in Britain as hauliers consider them more flexible for bulky loads, achieving maximum tonnage without being restricted by cubic capacity of vans. A skeletal trailer is a flat trailer for containers only, with no floor, only twist locks.
Free path A machine not tied to a fixed track.
FS Functional specification: generally the description of the function of a system in a software sense outlining interfaces in controls specification.

G
Gantry crane A form of crane in which the hoist system is suspended between flat beams.
Gross combination weight Weight of vehicle, fully fuelled, plus load, driver and trailer.
Groupage The grouping of small loads (often for export) collected by feeder vans and sorted out into bulk shipment.

H
Hopper A container for granular materials.
Hover-pallet A unit load platform, suspended on a cushion of air.

I
IBC Intermediate bulk container.
Interface Where two elements or conditions meet.
ISO container A container designed to the size, capacity and weight agreed by the International Standards Organization (ISO); suitable for road, rail and sea forwarding.

J
JIT Just-in-time: a term used in manufacturing for deliveries direct to the port of use. A term denoting a taut supply chain.

L
Lpg Liquid petroleum gas.

M
Mezzanine An intermediate floor.
Mobile shelving Shelving on mobile base running on track.

N
Node The point where elements meet.

O
On-line Direct control from a computer
Order picking The selection of a variety of goods to make up mixed orders for delivery.

P
P & D station Position and dispatch station. The end of aisle pallet position for feeding narrow aisle storage.
Pallet A modular-sized load platform that may be of timber, metal, plastics or paper, and which might be disposable.

Definitions

Palletization Generic term for unit load using pallets.
Platten A unit load base designed only for use in a store.
Post pallets Stackable metal framed cages to pallet sizes.

R

Racking the generic term for pallet racking.
Raised dock An area of the floor raised to the truck bed level for easy and fast loading and unloading of goods.
Reach truck A member of the forklift family that carries the load within its wheelbase to reduce its turning circle: a building block of a mechanized storage system.
Reefer A refrigerated container.

S

SATS System acceptance tests: generally assumed to be on site.
Skip Unit load for handling waste. Can be self-compacting.
Stillage A frame with fixed legs on which a load can be placed and moved.
Straddle carrier A container-carrying vehicle that passes over a stack and which can place containers three high.
Swarf Metal shavings.
Swept turning circle Diameter of outer extremity of vehicle at full lock.
Supply chain The generic logistics term describing the organization of the supply of materials between the manufacturer and the user. There are variations of this terminology such as 'value chain' or 'process chain' but they describe the same thing.
Sustainability A term covering a range of environmental objectives: taken in the broadest sense, to reduce the load on planet earth. Typically used in energy saving assessments as widely as a supply chain and distribution system will allow – i.e. right back to 'do we need to do this at all?' Also implies the re-use of facilities to avoid waste, including best practice in energy conservation, transportation planning, community development, increasingly influencing warehouse location.
Swop body A demountable truck body that can stand on its own legs; the truck chassis can then be used again. In many cases similar to an ISO container, but for closed system use, i.e. international rail within the European Union (EU).

T

Tail lift A lifting platform on the rear of vehicles.
TIR Transport International Routier, a term given by Customs and Excise to a vehicle and load sealed at the loading point to permit travel across frontiers without inspection. The vehicle has been constructed to customs-approved standards, and so carries the TIR plate. This is used between EU states and those countries outside.
'Tilt' trailer A semi-trailer or drawbar trailer with a removable 'tilt', i.e. a canvas or plastic sheet covered top, so that customs can examine the goods inside quickly without having to unload them. Also used as a generic term for trailers used in international haulage.
Tote box A container for small items in a closed system.
TOC Train operating company.
Tractor A towing unit of articulated lorry.
Transtainer A gantry crane for container sorting/stacking: can be automated.
Turning circle Diameter to outer wheel at full lock.
Turret truck Free path lifting device for operating at high levels in narrow aisles.

U

ULD Unit load device: used in air cargo for pallets and containers that are modular and of special lightweight construction to fit on aircraft holds.
Unit loads Goods packed onto a modular carriage unit, e.g. pallet, crate, bin, etc., for efficient mechanical handling.

W

WCS Warehouse control system: a term defining the computer control of inventory, replenishment and order assembly and despatch processes.
WiFi Wireless broadband, wireless local area network (WLAN) communications standard that allows data transmission rates of 11 Mbps between equipped devices (i.e. personal data-capture device to host up to 100 m away).

Introduction

Scope and form of the book

Industrial storage can be a very complex operation; its demands are seldom correctly identified, both because management has failed to anticipate developments in the distribution industry, and because of lack of common education and language between user, building designer, equipment manufacturers and specialist consultants. Few parties understand the relationship between a warehouse and transport and distribution system, or the effects that particular solutions will have on other parts of a project.

Other reasons for costly and unnecessary failures can be traced back to an inaccurate brief from the user and questionable assumptions from consultants. Moreover, few architects understand the problems involved, most lack knowledge to check proposals and relate each part to the whole at all stages of the project.

The choice is clear: either the architectural and design professions must educate themselves up to industry's level, or the design of industrial storage facilities will be given to equipment suppliers and turnkey contractors.

This book provides a skeleton on which architects and distribution facilities providers can build up competence. The intention is not to dictate; with such a fast-changing and dynamic industry this would be unrealistic. The information is intended as a guide, to point out where potential failures of interaction can occur, to illustrate the effect of choice of certain types of machinery and equipment on both a particular operation and on the building itself, and to indicate the most suitable consultants to employ for further information.

The architect, systems designer, project manager and project 'champion', whoever is acting as overall co-ordinator, must have sufficient background knowledge to appreciate the actions and problems of specialists.

Therefore, each section of the book which deals with warehouse types – mechanized, automated, etc., discusses the theory behind the operation of the storage process. Architects should not necessarily become physical distribution management or mechanical handling consultants; but they must have sufficient data to check a user's brief, to understand consultants' reports and what lies behind their decisions, and, if necessary, to question both brief and consultants' decisions, as well as how current and future conditions affect the distribution system as a whole.

Layout of the book

The first three chapters – Introduction, Loading and External storage – are applicable to all warehouse building types.

Later chapters deal with specific types of storage buildings, e.g. Mechanized storage, Automated storage and Cold storage. Mechanized storage, the most common type of 'warehouse' includes a summary of master planning and development questions. Each section contains two technical studies: Storage process and Building function (see Contents list., p.v).

Each Technical study, Storage Process starts with an introduction to explain the role of that particular form of storage in the total distribution context. Next, the user specification is set out, what happens in a particular type of warehouse and why, how it is affected by the supply chain, external factors and the distribution system as a whole; what machinery and control methods are involved, and what should be considered in choosing the storage method and the machinery to implement it. In this way, when Technical study, Building function, which deals with the design and elements of the building in detail, is read, a designer should have a basic measure of understanding of the factors contributing to the decisions involved.

Personnel provision and any special requirements for their welfare are also discussed in this study. In each chapter, the list of subheadings in these technical studies remains the same, with the same title and numbering system. For example, Order picking for each storage process will appear under subheading 16, and Security for each type of building will appear under subheading 28. Thus, the book can be read either 'vertically', i.e. conventionally through a chapter such as Mechanized storage, or 'horizontally', so that a designer can gain a broad knowledge of a particular operation across the industry by finding the particular subheading of each storage type. By using these cross-references, designers will be able to gather information quickly, identify potential failures of interaction, and learn of any special conditions that can affect design decisions.

Information sheets

One of the most obvious problems when discussing warehousing with designers, consultants and users has been the lack of basic design data for equipment and mobile plant. Each section is backed up by information sheets, giving data of typical dimensions and performance of mobile and static equipment.

These information sheets are also intended to help designers understand how the wide variety of equipment is used so that if necessary they may question a consultant or client's proposal for a type of pallet racking and handling plant in relation to suitability for the product and the effect on the store in relation to the area available.

List of technical studies

Storage process
1 Introduction
2 Source of goods
3 Form of transport
4 Control of transport
5 Receipt of goods
6 Form of goods
7 Unloading
8 Characteristics of goods
9 Sortation
10 Volume calculations
11 Turnover calculations
12 Variety and flow
13 Type of storage
14 Stock control
15 Stock withdrawal
16 Order picking
17 Picking area
18 Load build-up
19 Order and document check
20 Loading and dispatch
21 Additional data

Building function
22 Structure
23 Floor
24 Building services
25 Special services
26 Building fabric
27 Fire control
28 Security and safety
29 External works
30 Structure-based plant
31 Mobile plant
32 Integration of building and plant
33 Maintenance
34 Management
35 Personnel accommodation
36 Amenity
37 Personnel safety
38 Circulation and parking

Chapter 1
Introduction

TECHNICAL STUDY

Part 1
Introduction

1 The warehouse as part of the distribution system

2 The project team

An introduction to the problems of designing storage buildings, and the role of the project team.

1 The warehouse as part of the distribution system

1.01 Industrial stores are not usually designed to earn profits. Costs incurred are reflected in the production or distribution accounts, and are ultimately passed on to the consumer. Thus as the design of a warehouse affects handling and storage costs, which help to fix commodity prices, the architect or designer bears considerable responsibility to the public. For this reason, a warehouse should be considered as part of the total supply chain and distribution system from the outset. In many warehouses the operator has asked a consultant to develop a brief orientated towards mechanical handling at the expense of the efficiency of the distribution system; several of these are virtually redundant after only a few years' service (Figure 1.1).

Figure 1.1 *In many warehouses the operator has asked a consultant to develop a brief oriented towards mechanical handling at the expense of the distribution system.*

1.02 It is therefore in the client's interest that multidisciplinary expertise should be used in a total system approach; architects, with their inherent knowledge of planning in three dimensions, paired with expert supply chain and materials handling consultants are best placed to evaluate and select storage systems matched to the buildings surrounding them. Consultants should be retained from the outset to examine the economics and flow patterns of the supply chain and distribution system. This responds to the user's manufacturing and marketing potential, working in parallel with, and contributing to, the architect's investigation into the best storage arrangement and building type for the required throughputs: it also considers, in relation to the product's packaging, the potential for mechanical handling and the effects of future change.

Warehouse design

1.03 There are no hard and fast rules for warehouse design; policy decisions depend on type of product, the speed that it will pass through the warehouse, the type of outlet and consumer market being served and the distance of travel involved. For example, there are conflicting opinions about whether storage facilities should be centralized. Two very large household names in the retail trade, one in pharmaceuticals, the other in groceries, have similar outlet patterns but employ different distribution systems. One has a central factory and uses several redistribution centres around the country, operated by contractors. The other employs 13 main bulk storage warehouses, all but three operated by third party contractors, with all 'own label' manufacture and processing outsourced: advanced point of sale-driven computer reordering drives mechanized replenishment and automated sorting for delivery to individual retail outlets.

1.04 Although this decision is usually based on supply chain operations and market research, and is the client's responsibility, the pattern can be seriously affected by other factors. The form and unit size in which the product reaches the store is a prime consideration. This will increasingly be influenced by issues such as 'sustainability', environmental and energy issues, production cost and marketing considerations, without sufficient regard for the storage medium. By understanding the product and its handling properties, design teams can feed back useful data to the client, resulting in a more efficient package, a reduced cost of packaging materials and higher efficiency of storage and handling systems.

1.05 Good examples of this approach are companies which add value to suppliers' contracts and impose detailed packaging specifications, including size, shape and materials, and supply the handling crates: this has enabled them to cut warehousing and handling costs considerably. It is possible to take a supplier to court for breach of contract for unacceptable packaging. Specifications for Internet auctions for major supply contracts include detailed logistics information of this type.

1.06 Equally, transport should be considered as a flexible system, integrated with the warehouse by employing dimensionally co-ordinated unit loads. Even some newly built installations which are considered well planned have cramped loading bays which choke in peak conditions (the company forgot that suppliers' vehicles were larger

Technical Study – introduction

than their own, and only provided very constricted manoeuvring space). In the handbook, data have been included on vehicle types and sizes to aid designers planning for transport.

1.07 The architect's opportunity in this very competitive field should therefore be the co-ordination of these systems, keeping an overall view of the project and its part in the total manufacturing and distribution system. Figure 1.2a/b sets out a typical project sequence for a state of the art retail distribution warehouse including a product sorter, divided into two principal stages: before and after the appointment of the implementation contractor. There are many ways of organizing major capital projects, such as design and build and construction management, the selection of which are outside the scope of this publication. These diagrams illustrate a typical process sequence with the parties, controls and approvals involved at each stage.

2 The project team

2.01 The design of such a complex building as a warehouse, combining building fabric and sophisticated plant, can only be carried out by a team. Many equipment manufacturers offer package deals, especially for complicated installations such as automated high-bay warehouses. Though very knowledgeable in equipment, they are not concerned with other factors outside this sphere. Professional involvement is therefore vital to protect the client. Each specialist member of the team must keep the others constantly aware of the effect which various decisions will have on the project.

Members of the team

2.02 There is no single form for a project team, but the skeleton team outlined here is a useful guide. Size and complexity of a project will obviously govern the content. The part that each member of the team plays in the development of different zones will be discussed more fully in specialist sections of the handbook. The project team should include:

Basic members

Multidisciplinary leader (opportunity for architects)
Representative from client's management:[1] the project 'champion'
Structural engineer
Quantity surveyor/cost consultant
Mechanical services engineer
Electrical engineer
Public health engineer
Accountant/business consultant[1]
Supply chain consultant
Mechanical handling consultant
Mechanical handling engineer
Representative of the insurance company involved.
These naturally group into say six specialist multidisciplined consultants

Team members passing through at various stages

Distribution manager[1]
Existing warehouse manager(s)
Future warehouse manager[1]
Transport manager[1]
Works Council including union shop stewards[1]

[1] Continuing in the team after completion and commissioning of project.

Warehouseman/operatives/drivers selected from the floor[1] (Figure 1.3).
Local authority representatives, i.e. building inspector, factory inspector, fire officer, etc.

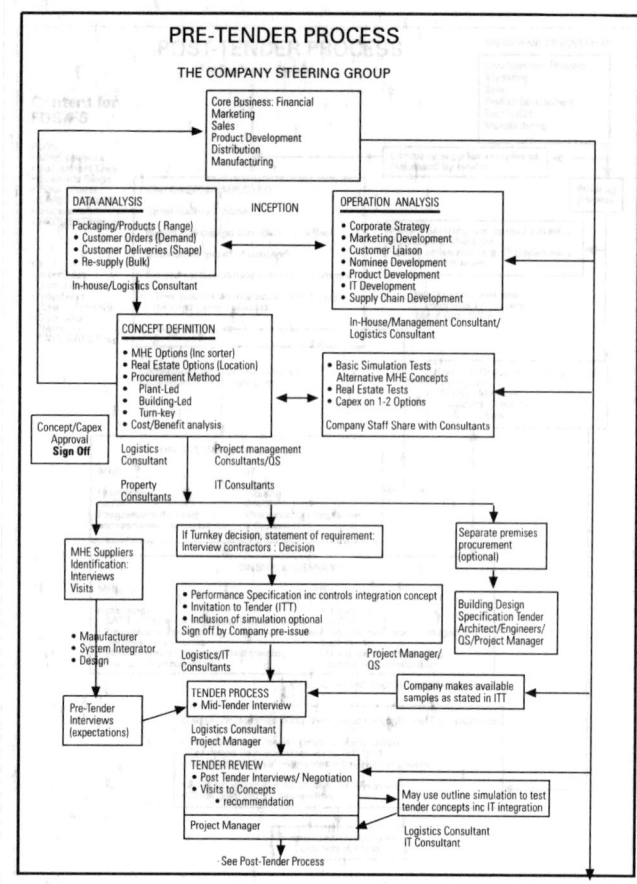

Figure 1.2a *The pre-tender process.*

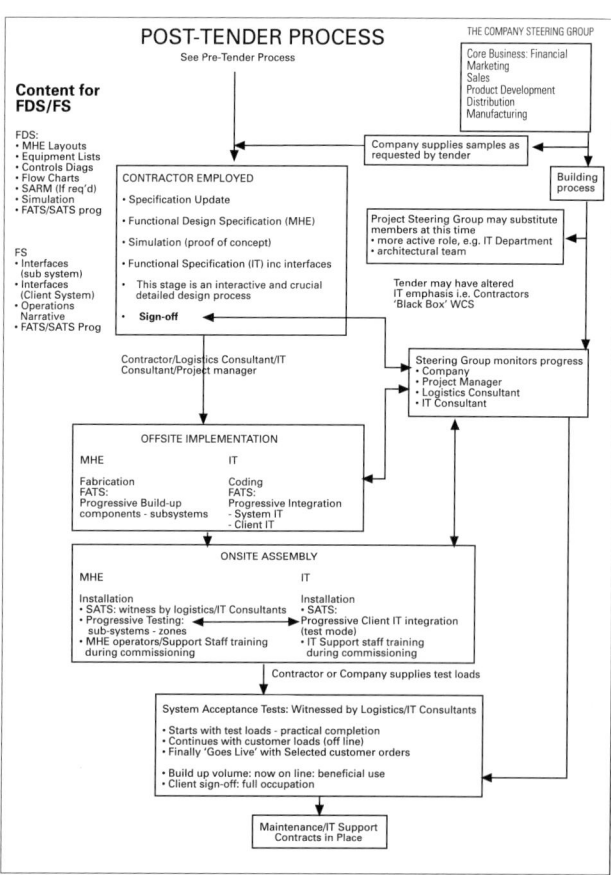

Figure 1.2b *The post-tender process.*

2.03 No project team, however well organized, can operate efficiently without the client's full support. In most cases of industrial storage building schemes, this is the board of the company concerned. The managing director should be kept active and interested throughout all stages of the project. Management lethargy is easily transmitted to the client's representatives within the project team, and will adversely affect the efficiency of the whole operation (Figure 1.4).

For major, innovative projects it is advisable to select a project 'champion' from the management team: projects involving complex information technology (IT) and engineering go through well-documented cycles of success and doubt, and the 'champion' is the guardian of the 'legend'.

Figure 1.3 *The project team should include drivers selected from the floor.*

The brief

2.04 The development of an accurate and far-sighted brief is essential to the success of a storage project (Figure 1.5). To ensure that accurate data are to be collected and analysed, users must be represented on the team. Often, the management of the company concerned is not the real user. One company put the future warehouse manager in charge of the initial project, assuming that if he was to use the installation, he would exert every effort to see that the planning was satisfactory. This worked well, but was a special case as the projected warehouse was of a scale and importance to merit a supervisor of management rank. It is well worthwhile contacting users at all levels, such as plant operation, transport, handling and general maintenance. These members of the team will pass through at different stages so that there is little danger of the team reaching an unmanageable number.

2.05 Labour relations are increasingly entering the sphere of the project team. In the final analysis, all industrial projects involve operatives. The project team should continually inform the labour force of what is happening and how decisions will affect them. Usually, this results in useful information and active co-operation in the commissioning period.

Unions should be kept informed; one installation incorporated some expensive scissor lifts that have never been used, blacked by a union as unsafe. This waste could have been avoided with a little co-operation from each side. However, a shop steward may not be the most expert representative technically, and a balance of union and technically expert personnel should be maintained if possible.

Team action during construction

2.06 The multidisciplinary team should continue to operate at a high level during construction. The architect should define contractual relationships and responsibilities to all the client's members of the team. Members of the team concerned with specific sections of the project, e.g. future section store managers, are often tempted to ask subcontractors to install on-site modifications to the system, without referring this to the general contractor or the architect. Long and expensive claims have resulted. The same applies to informing the client about the effect of changes at the construction stage. Minor variations can be assimilated into a contractor's programme, but major system changes can cause havoc.

2.07 Industrial clients often want to install the warehouse plant as soon as it is possible to gain access,

Figure 1.4 *Management lethargy is easily transmitted to the project team.*

so that initial commissioning can take place while other building operations continue. Unless the timing for this operation is agreed at the design stage, the costing agreed in the initial tender and the client kept aware of his contractual responsibility, the project can run into serious trouble – especially where integral storage plant and building structures are involved. The client must understand what is possible at each stage of construction and be aware of the requirements for special access situations, especially before any new internal route system is complete on an existing site.

For example, one client had planned his distribution cycle so critically close to the project completion date, that when abnormal winter conditions put back the programme and commissioning by over a month, there was trouble in finding alternative accommodation. It was the architect's responsibility to inform the client that bad weather might hold up building, plant installation and thus commissioning.

Technical Study – introduction

Phased developments

2.08 Large projects are often phased developments. The project team in this case has the added responsibility in the design and construction stages of ensuring smooth movements between phases, with as little disruption as possible to the storage process already in operation. Phased development for architects is basically a problem of initial planning. For warehouse operatives, it is one of continuing storage and sorting activities while works continue. The feedback from the initial stages usually results in some modifications to the later phases. Again, contact with the warehouse operatives is essential, both for information and the smooth running of the system as it accelerates to full operating capacity.

Maintenance and costs-in-use

2.09 Even if maintenance and costs-in-use have been considered fully at the design stage as an integral part of the project design, the team should ensure that the correct preventative maintenance procedures are followed. After commissioning, the architect will progressively hand over the responsibility to the management. With complex storage buildings, management should realize the importance of the company core of the team remaining responsible for the continued operation of the project, anyway at first, and that this team is fully aware of the scheme as finally built, with a knowledge of the reasons behind the major decisions.

Figure 1.5 *The development of an accurate and far-sighted brief is essential to the success of a storage project.*

TECHNICAL STUDY

Part 2
Storage and distribution as a total system

1 The warehouse as a means of control

2 The European connection

3 Storage considered as product cost

4 Packaging, the basis of the storage system

5 Transport: an integral part of the storage and distribution system

6 Total system thinking: an example

7 The influence of retail outlet design on the distribution system

Building designers must understand the components that form the total storage and distribution function. The relationship between packaging, method of storage, storage plant and building, and transport and distribution systems are so closely enmeshed that they cannot be considered independently in design.

1 The warehouse as a means of control

1.01 The consumer society has generated a complex manufacturing and distribution network and the warehouse acts as a valve within the system for controlling consumer markets. This is achieved by:
1. balancing machine-orientated mass production with irregular or unpredictable demand, for instance the economic manufacturing quantities for packeted goods
2. balancing irregular and seasonal production with round-the-year demand; e.g. frozen vegetables or raw, perishable ingredients for continuous production
3. building up stocks for seasonal peak demands
4. acting as a redistribution point between the manufacturer and the retail outlet, ensuring that specific items are constantly available.

Economically, it is desirable to manufacture goods in batches. This conflicts with seasonal demand and the consumer's demand to buy any product throughout the year.

1.02 This is especially important in an inflationary situation. Distribution costs form roughly a fifth of the retail price of most consumer goods, and are still rising. The warehouse has become an important economic valve, combining cost benefits of batch production with controlled distribution. To keep prices down, distribution costs must be minimized by efficient storage and transport.

2 The European connection

2.01 The effects of Britain joining the EU are not just of increased areas for sales and distribution, but also of substantially increased competition. Unless storage and distribution systems are considered together, profits will be even harder to come by. Many European companies already run very slick and sophisticated integrated storage and distribution systems, and continental distribution organizations have been buying into British companies. There is a trend towards centralized manufacturing units linked to the storage function on the same site, to reduce costs, especially where a large variety of goods are made. One Swedish cold-store construction company, itself running contract refrigerated warehouses, is planning cold-store 'villages', attached to linked manufacturing units.

2.02 In the European context, efficient storage must play a larger part in stabilizing EU commodity production and distribution.

3 Storage considered as production cost

3.01 As the demands placed on warehousing and distribution operations increase, management should consider warehousing costs in the same terms as production costs, investing in materials handling and storage equipment to increase efficiency, profit margins, and reduce distribution and warehouse costs. The accent should fall on value and running cost rather than initial cost. The present trend towards rationalizing and grouping storage processes (Figure 1.6) is an effort by central organizations to reduce costs and excessive overheads.

3.02 With the high price of industrial land at key locations, modern supply chain techniques can limit the quantity of stock to be held to cope with fluctuations in consumer demand by just-in-time and cross docking practices: success depends on clarity of site and warehouse layout and in maximizing the use of warehouse sorting facilities. High costs result from a lack of co-ordination between transport and storage systems, and between a storage system and its enclosure. This applies not only to manufacturers, but also to specialist companies which provide a contract warehousing and distribution service.

4 Packaging, the basis of the storage system

4.01 The method of packaging goods is a major element in the total system. Packaging is becoming more sophis-

Storage and distribution as a total system

Figure 1.6 *Major centralized distribution warehouse.*

ticated; now it not only protects but can also advertise and act as the basic storage unit. The size and type of package determine the character of a unit load, in turn generating the type of transport to be used, in conjunction with the quantities and distances involved. The form of the packaging and unit load contribute to choice of storage function and its continual operating characteristics and potential efficiency. One example of this is expanded plastic used for packaging; this results in a uniform shape of package which is much easier to handle in bulk, and which suits a mechanized storage system. Another example is polythene film, used to 'shrink-wrap' pallet loads of goods which used to be packed into boxes; this allows better use of the space provided, more stable stacking and easier checking. However, the fire protection problem is increased (this is discussed more fully in Technical study, Mechanized storage 2).

Specification

4.02 Managements hold very different attitudes towards packaging and handling of goods. Some place full responsibility on the carrier and rely on the common sense of the operatives within the store; others spend a great deal of money on packaging the finished product, but accept valuable components packed in old cardboard boxes; the third, and unfortunately rare, category dictates the standards for both incoming and outgoing packaging with a detailed specification for each type of product.(Figure 1.7)

4.03 The specification should include:
1. the best size of the package for storage and distribution of the commodity
2. the number of product units per package, depending on weight, display function, retail requirements
3. the materials in which the product should be packed
4. graphics and codes for transport and storage identification
5. the number of packages per unit load, and the best stacking patterns for stability and volume
6. the type of unit load best suited to transport and storage, e.g. Europallets, air pallets, etc.
7. method of securing packages to unit load, i.e. shrink-wrapping.
8. The disposal and/or reuse at the end of the cycle.

For incoming supplies, this specification should be sent out with the tender documents to the subcontractor. For dispatch, it will save the company a lot of money in the long term. It should be the handling manager's responsibility to dictate these terms to subcontractors and to their own manufacturing departments. One manufacturer finds that a 3 per cent on-cost added to each contract, to ensure correct packaging, is money well spent. The building designer should check that this process is happening, as it is an important aid to the design of the storage system.

5 Transport: an integral part of the storage and distribution system

5.01 In the modern, lean supply chain, the boundaries between transport, storage and mechanical handling are becoming more difficult to distinguish. Containerization has combined storage and transport, ISO containers, swop bodies and semi-trailers being used for short-term storage prior to just-in-time delivery (Figure 1.8). Air cargo literally provides 'jet-fresh' goods, manufactured today on the other side of the world for consumption here tomorrow: global electronics manufacturers have been able to shrink their inventories by a third by the judicious use of air cargo. So the building designer must understand the full implications of modern transport and its potential as a major and integral part of the storage and handling system: as an example, when confronted with a warehouse proposal for a developing economy, the initial sizing may be driven by the need to accommodate strategic stocks of a few commodities due to an immature transport system for a growing number of retail

Figure 1.7 *Well-considered design of basic package – e.g. a range of related interlocking dimensions.*

Figure 1.8 *Containers used as both storage and transport.*

outlets. Later the warehouse may not need to expand, as a mature transport system with an agile supply chain will reduce the need for storage, but will greatly increase the stock lines that will not be in stock for long before delivery to a large number of shops. This will demand a flexible warehouse and storage system.

Road transport and mechanical handling

5.02 Delays in vehicle turnround have been an important and growing cost problem for a long time. Loading bay and marshalling area design will be discussed in Chapter 2. The loading bay is the critical link between the storage system and the transport and distribution systems. Choked space can wreck the successful operation of a

Figure 1.9 *Hydraulic clamp covering whole length of semi-trailer's platform, for handling bricks.*

Figure 1.10 *Portable yard lift.*

warehouse, as slow vehicle turnround causes accumulation in the dock area. By using more mechanized handling facilities on vehicles, the distribution industry can increase productivity of personnel and machinery, reduce operating costs, damages, and ultimately the cost to the consumer (Figures 1.9 and 1.10 give examples of handling aids with vehicles).

5.03 British transport operators have been conservative about mounting mechanical handling aids to their vehicles, compared with European practice. The prevalent attitude is that every extra piece of equipment on a vehicle increases the taxation weight, so decreasing the payload. Superficially, this is true, but many operators have found that their turnround times have been so reduced when handling aids have been employed that productivity has been more than doubled, allowing the numbers of vehicles to be reduced.

5.04 Pressure to modernize with handling aids increases as more shops and factories specify periods when they will not accept deliveries: this, combined with the new drivers' hours regulations and city centre restrictions, is forcing deliveries into shorter periods; this affects not only the peak arrival of vehicles at a warehouse, but also storage, order picking and load assembly functions.

5.05 Typical examples of useful on-vehicle handling aids are the tailboard lift and demountable body units. Tail lifts link transport with the retail outlet: roll pallets can be unloaded fast by the driver, pushing the pallet on to the lift, travelling to pavement level at the press of a button, and pushing the pallet into the shop. Multiple delivery times and traffic obstruction have been greatly reduced by this method.

5.06 Demountable truck bodies have made the haulage vehicle more flexible. One truck chassis can pick up a body pre-loaded at a warehouse, leave it on mounted legs at a supermarket loading bay, pick up the empty unit, return to the warehouse and immediately leave with another laden body (Figure 1.11).

Further, the bodies can be 'trunk hauled', like containers. A European standard has been prepared for swop bodies for use within the EU road and rail systems. (See Technical study, External storage 1.)

6 Total system thinking: an example

6.01 A good example of this can be seen in air cargo and airport catering. Within a very short turnround time, the inventory, stock control, load build-up, transport, delivery and loading into the aircraft is completed. Demountable bodies are mounted on scissor lifts, integral with the lorry, which raise the whole body to aircraft door height. Passenger jets have galleys that break down into unit loads, allowing fast handling and reduced handling staffing (Figure 1.12).

7 The influence of retail outlet design on the distribution system

7.01 As so many factors are mutually dependent for efficiency, a large-scale breakdown or major policy change will disrupt the whole storage and distribution system. An example of this is of a major retail organization acquiring another large chain of shops. These had been modified to fulfil a function that the existing stores did not meet, but were to be supplied from the former central warehouse. Virtually overnight, the capacity of the system was expected to double, which required an expanded computerized stock control function, a larger and reworked transport fleet, a range of new suppliers adding to the already heavy traffic and increased turnover, putting added pressure on loading bays, sorting areas and load assembly zones. Hopefully, major retail expansions are generally better planned: with third party distribution contractors operating out of multiple warehouses, flexibility can be provided within the supply chain.

Storage and distribution as a total system

8 The future

8.01 Warehouse and distribution buildings are likely to be needed well into the future, although it is already possible to see a trend towards a total transportation system, so well controlled that it can act as the storage system itself. This is not pure science fiction: the control systems for 'the agile supply chain' are already available. E-commerce systems exist where the consumer places an order into the computer at home, and the nearest product of that type is directed immediately from within the transport/distribution system, the cost being deducted from their account automatically. 'Fulfilling the promise', the physical distribution, has proved to be the Achilles heel of the e-commerce world. Huge investments have been made in complex handling systems that never fulfilled their promise: it is developments in information technology for order call centres that still require investment.

8.02 In the future, pressure to conserve energy, lifestyle and the environment will influence the supply chain and distribution and storage system design. 'Sustainability' is not just a buzz word but a real social aspiration backed by EU Directives. The 'examination question' must be, 'Why transport and store goods at all?' It is by no means clear that e-commerce (home shopping) reduces vehicle numbers: it may increase them. Similarly, it is no longer proven in terms of 'sustainability' that regional single product plants are preferable in terms of energy, transport or social cost over more local production centres and distribution patterns. But these 'sustainable' environmental benefits may be gained only at the expense of price or taxation increases; for instance, an alternative transport structure, though environmentally preferable, may be far more expensive to run.

Figure 1.11 *This lorry is leaving its swop body on mounted legs at loading bay, and is now ready to receive another.*

Figure 1.12 *Container is lifted to load directly into aircraft deck.*

Chapter 2
Loading

TECHNICAL STUDY

Loading bay design

1 Loading bay position in relation to warehouse perimeter
2 Approach roads, marshalling and buffer areas
3 Detailed problems of bay design
4 Raised dock design
5 Loading ISO containers and demountable body units
6 Bays for refrigerated vehicles
7 Demountable and intermodal body systems
8 Future vehicle sizes

The loading bay is the beginning and end of any production and storage process and must be able to handle peak traffic flows, adaptable to future conditions and operate in all weathers. To achieve this, the warehouse designer must co-ordinate the specialist team of management, system designers, mechanical handling and transport and equipment consultants. If he or she does not, incorrect decisions may be made which are magnified throughout the distribution system. Dimensions of bays, vehicles and equipment are given in Information sheets Loading 1–6. Loading bays are such a key contributor to efficient materials flow in the warehouse that the subject has been separated in this chapter for particular consideration.

1 Loading bay position in relation to warehouse perimeter

1.01 Loading bays are frequently placed at the corner of an industrial building where trucks have room to manoeuvre, catering for both incoming and dispatched goods: for a manufacturing building with a parts store or just-in-time access to a production line and pre-dispatch storage at the end, by flow logic the loading bay should be positioned as close as possible to the beginning and end of the operation. But dedicated warehouses, matched to particular tasks, are essentially materials flow tools. The efficient movement of goods is prerequisite. So as a rule of thumb there can never be enough doors, with high throughput installations demanding yard access on two long sides: some argue that with contemporary sophisticated communications and handling plant, loading bays might be placed at node points around the building.

Advantages and disadvantages of this, compared to a single, long bay are shown in Figure 2.1.

1.02 The designer must plan possible layouts, considering:
1 best flow for vehicles also considering peak conditions, future expansion, and types of vehicle involved
2 the production or storage flow pattern, and possible product packaging and system changes
3 the type of goods involved, considering special features like product incompatibility or fire and corrosion hazards.

User requirements and site constraints usually restrict choices, while planning in co-ordination with the systems designer and plant engineer would eliminate inefficient solutions. Computer models can simulate how the design will affect peak build-ups, stoppages and handling times. These exercises often demonstrate how seemingly insignificant decisions can waste much time and money.

2 Approach roads, marshalling and buffer areas

2.01 Loading bays cannot be designed in isolation, they also require:
1 an approach road within the site area, which is separated from the public road by a supervised gate
2 a marshalling area where trucks accumulate before getting into the loading bay position; this area is vital, as the particular bay may not be ready in time
3 a truck buffer area – a secondary manoeuvring area for large storage buildings where many trucks collect and are sorted for specific loading bays. These areas should be supervised by a traffic office.

Approach roads and marshalling areas

2.02 Where turnround is fast (e.g., a high turnover wholesale warehouse, handling palletized unit loads) the number of loading bays can be reduced by careful marshalling area design. Space savings depend on site and vehicle flow conditions. Cross-manoeuvring should be avoided wherever possible, as shunting vehicles, especially in a counter-clockwise flow requiring blind left-

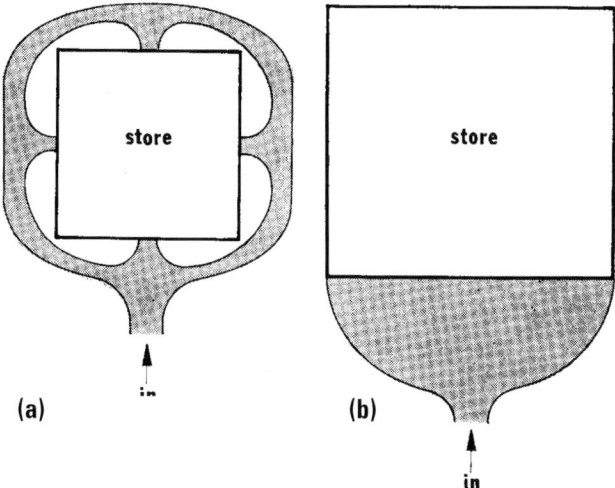

Figure 2.1 *Comparison of loading bay positions*

a	Bays at node points	b	Single long bay
✓	goods are delivered close to process so good mechanical handling;	✓	Allows flexible handling and storage;
✗	not flexible – industrial processes may change;	✓	Fast turnround. large numbers of vehicles operate faster if loading and despatch bays are separated. This is mandatory for customs.
✗	perimeter road needed, with turning space for each bay.	✓ = good point ✗ = bad point	

13

Loading bay design

hand reversing, have been seen to baulk other incoming or outgoing trucks, slowing the whole cycle and considerably reducing the possible work load (Figures 2.3, 2.4 and 2.5)

2.03 To design marshalling areas:
1. establish probable number of types and calculate peaks of different vehicles (in break bulk or mixed long-distance haulage and local delivery situations, arrival peaks vary)
2. examine existing patterns in the area (as vehicle peaks depend on local traffic conditions), the distance that the vehicles have travelled, and the operatives' working day. Future city delivery restrictions will also affect peak distribution. Often a peak of light vans hold up the heavy vehicles, causing jams, so it is best to segregate the flow. With the British rule of the road, a clockwise traffic flow allows articulated vehicles to reverse quickly.

2.04 Dimensions of gate entries, marshalling areas and buffer areas are given in Information sheet, Loading 2.

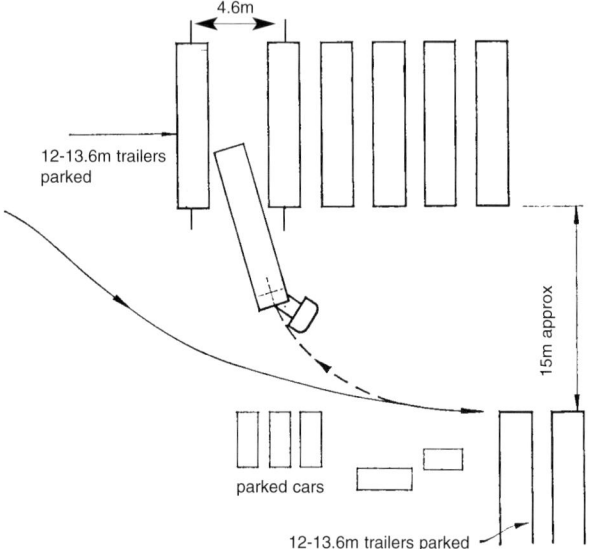

Figure 2.2 *Badly designed layout. A 16.5 m artic can manoeuvre into this space with difficulty in two movements.*

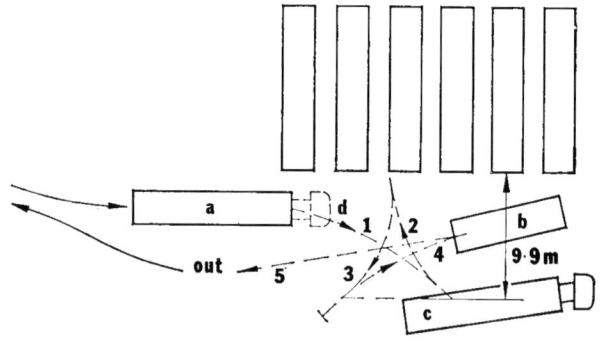

Figure 2.3 *Example of bad layout. Trailer arrived pulled by tractor d. Trailer b was constricting circulation. Tractor d shunted round within 9 m to remove b. Another difficult manoeuvre.*

Buffer or accumulation zones

2.05 Buffer zones should always be provided, even for short waits. It is uneconomic to build the maximum number of loading bays required at peak times, and there is always a chance of a breakdown. A buffer area is also useful for document processing (Figure 2.5a-c). Buffer park size is determined by the estimated turnround time of different vehicle types, against the projected peak flow.

Queueing lanes should be clearly marked with either visual displays or amplified orders for bay allocation. This area should be out of the way of manoeuvring trucks (see Technical studies in Chapter 4, Mechanized storage, and Chapter 5, Automated storage).

3 Detailed problems of bay design

How many bays?

3.01 This is linked to design of marshalling and buffer space. Number depends on:
1. product being handled and speed of handling
2. type of vehicle being loaded
3. predicted traffic flow
4. future growth of goods and traffic
5. financial policy of client.

3.02 Large numbers of bays increase building volume, and thus costs-in-use, and the risks of theft but the marshalling area is smaller and the loading bay buffer is improved. Handling from vehicle into store will be quicker, as the turnround will be fast, and the handling equipment will be working on a wide front.

3.03 Where expansion is anticipated, the marshalling area should be increased and handling speed in the loading bay should be improved. By increasing the marshalling space, there is a saving in building volume and the overall construction cost will be less; turnround speed will be higher for lower plant investment. In this situation the handling system, i.e. forklift trucks, would always operate under pressure, which increases the chance of a breakdown. The designer must co-ordinate with the other consultants in making this decision, as a mistake here can mean the difference between profit and loss for a company.

Straight or angled bays?

3.04 Choice is between 90°, angled or straight-through layout, depending on trade handled and characteristics of the unit load. For instance, if curtain-sided vehicles are loaded from block stacks, ground-level loading with straight-through access is efficient (Figure 2.6). A large soft drinks company finds that this method still allows the quickest turnround. (See also Information sheet, Loading 2 for dock dimensions.)

Figure 2.6 *Hand-stacked load of bulk cartons, loaded over the side from forklift truck. Still used in developing economies.*

Loading bay design

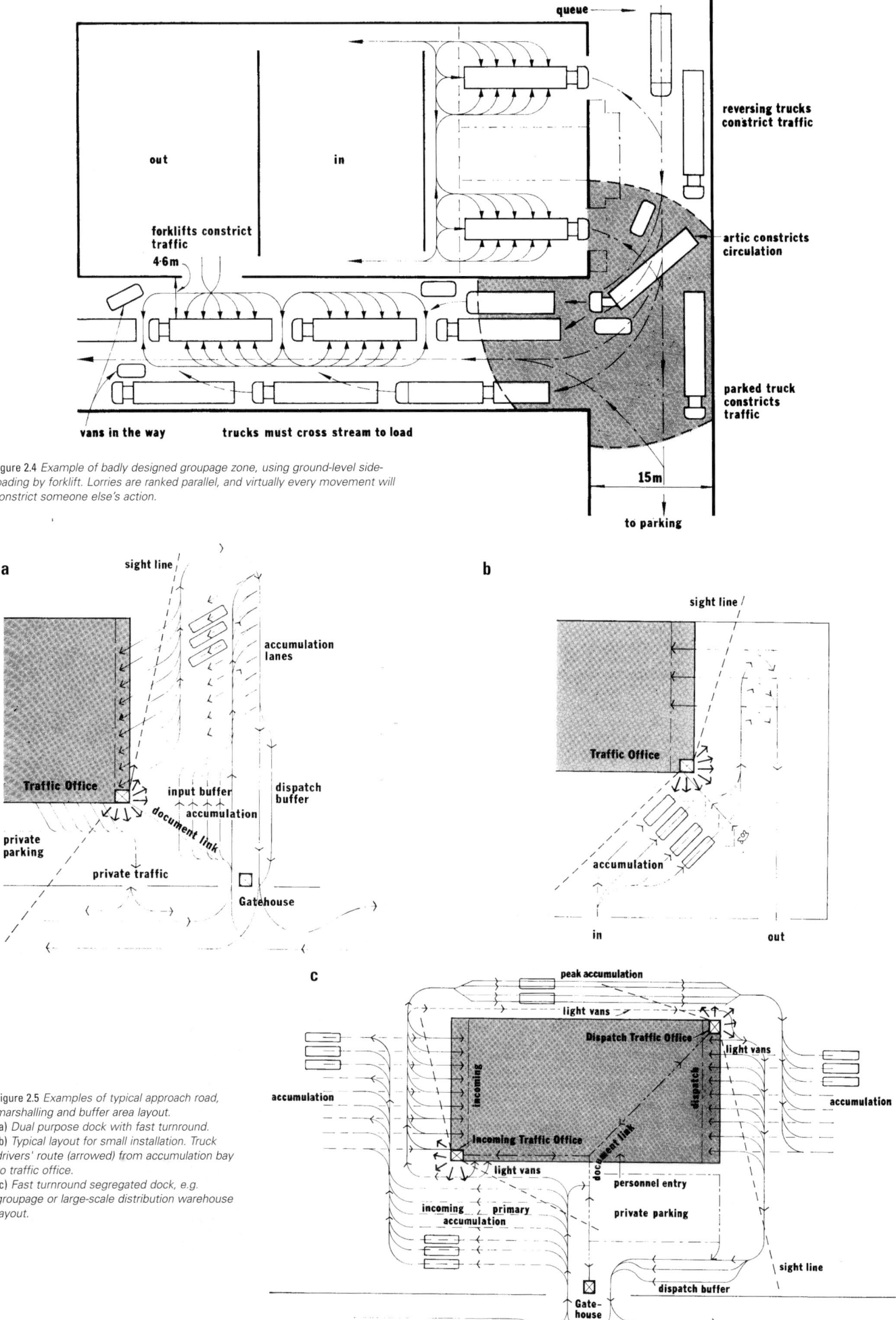

Figure 2.4 *Example of badly designed groupage zone, using ground-level side-loading by forklift. Lorries are ranked parallel, and virtually every movement will constrict someone else's action.*

Figure 2.5 *Examples of typical approach road, marshalling and buffer area layout.*
(a) *Dual purpose dock with fast turnround.*
(b) *Typical layout for small installation. Truck drivers' route (arrowed) from accumulation bay to traffic office.*
(c) *Fast turnround segregated dock, e.g. groupage or large-scale distribution warehouse layout.*

Loading bay design

3.05 But straight-through designs are not suitable for many vehicles and containers, and they hinder future development. They rely on parallel parking, with either ground-level or raised dock loading. It is often slower to position a truck accurately parallel to a dock than to reverse into an end-loading bay.

3.06 There are several arguments in favour of 90° or angled bays. A 90° bay enables a fast turnround, as the driver can easily see to where he is reversing in his mirrors. A 16.5 m articulated vehicle needs 22 m in front for manoeuvring at 90° (i.e. 40 m from the face of the building with a little space for landscaping). If there is not enough length between a 90° dock face and the edge of the site, the saw-tooth arrangement permits manoeuvring. The angle cut out reduces the loading space, but reversing is slightly less difficult with a clockwise circulation. A balance of speed and flow to space available should be decided by the designer when making the decision on the number of bays and size of the marshalling area.

Do not design with too close tolerances

3.07 In many existing bays the tolerances are so tight that turnround times have been hampered, and in some cases it is thought that more money is lost from reduced throughput than the initial savings in reducing area of the building (Figure 2.7). For example, in some bays the driver cannot leave his or her cab due to the narrow high sides of a sunken dock, or other bays are so close fitting for easy side access with forklift trucks, that the reversing manoeuvre has been seriously slowed down. The 'right' solution say for converting an existing building would have been to have specified hinge-down bridging plates and a wider dock. But a minimum dock spacing centre to centre of 4.5 m, preferably 5 m for busy warehouses is a good rule of thumb with 22 m draw forward.

Figure 2.7 Tight loading bay and parking area with many trailers fitted into a small area.

Should the loading bay be enclosed?

3.08 Totally enclosed loading bays are uncommon, due to high building costs and costs-in-use. Their advantages are total independence from the outside environment, and a greater control over theft (Figure 2.8). Other than cost, the major problems are of fume extraction and lighting. Most totally enclosed bays operate straight through with a door at each end, or are for railway wagon loading. See also Chapter 7, Special storage.

3.09 The canopied loading bay is normal. All loading bays should give some weather protection, even if truck dock weather seals are fitted. It is usual to provide 4.5 to 6 m of cover, and a translucent roof covering is advisable to

Figure 2.8 Totally enclosed loading bay. (Note structural clearances, the van at the dock is about 3.6 m high.) Note good light level without glare, clearly marked bay lines, well-painted columns to assist in reversing, extraction grill under stairs and retracted dock leveller. As usual there is a quantity of rubbish and broken pallets, as there is seldom provision in the loading area for its disposal.

achieve adequate illumination on the dock floor. The underside of the structure should not be less than 4.7 m to clear a 2.7 m high container on a skeletal trailer, but higher clearances may be required with special box vans. The canopy should fall towards the building, in order to avoid water flowing onto the vehicles beneath (Figure 2.9).

Raised or ground level docks?

3.10 Loading bays can be equipped with a raised dock or a sunken road, or trucks and containers can be loaded from ground level by forklift trucks or conveyor belts.

3.11 Sunken docks are widely used on flat sites combining the benefits of end loading at trailer floor level with side loading for curtain-sided vehicles at ground level; this allows a constant level factory or warehouse floor and loading bay while servicing two basic groups of trucks. The natural falls of the land on most sites can be used to form a loading bay level change. In sunken docks, gradients should not exceed 10 per cent and should be level for the length of the trailer in front of the face of the dock. If a slope runs up to a dock face, a container or van can easily foul the structure with its roof before the base has reached the dock, and forklift trucks and pallet trucks can 'ground' on the hump produced by the sloping truck bed (Figure 2.10a).

3.12 Where ice and snow are likely, articulated vehicles can skid and jack-knife on slopes, even at low speeds, and can cause extensive and costly damage to the loading area. Wires sunk into the slope keep the surface above freezing point, or an epoxy resin and granite chip non-slip surface (as being used at traffic junctions), can be laid. Slot drains should be provided in sunken docks as mud, slush and water can accumulate under a dock leveller. The decision for a raised or ground-level dock is a function of the duty for the warehouse: a retail order fulfilment centre with bulk deliveries inwards and local deliveries outbound might have a 1200 mm raised dock (or sunken dock) on the goods inwards side, and ground level or 650 mm maximum 'step' on the dispatch side. A distribution centre servicing, say, pallets of bottled drink might have a ground-level reception dock for curtain-sided trailers, but a raised (or sunken) dock for end-loading urban delivery trucks. A parcels hub or transhipment centre might have a raised dock on one side to receive roll cages, and a ground-level dock equipped with extending belts to bulk load trunk trailers on the other. An intermodal transhipment centre or reception dock for a

Loading bay design

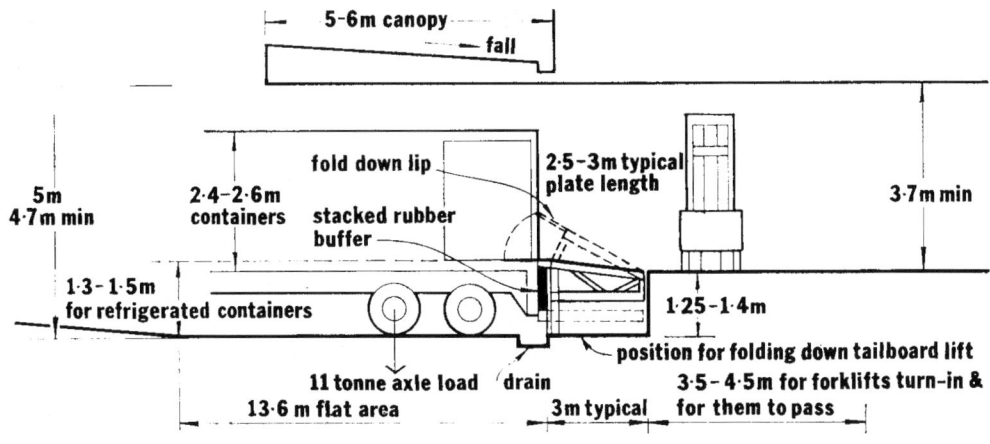

Figure 2.9 *Section through typical loading bay.*

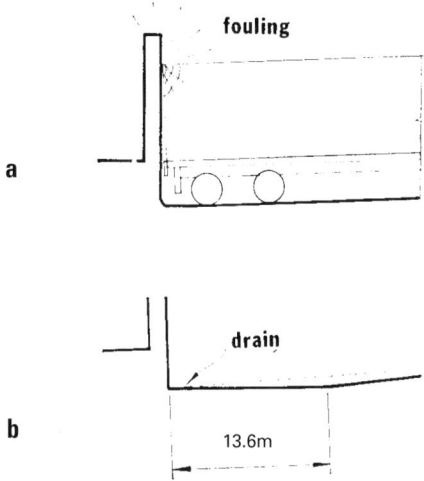

Figure 2.10 *A straight slope (a) can cause a truck to foul. The site should be level (b) where trucks park.*

Figure 2.11(a) *When a truck stops to load it constricts the road. Manoeuvring forklift trucks then block it completely. Externally stacked goods impede loading on both sides.*

Figure 2.11(b) *With two forklifts in operation, the throughway is frequently impassable to heavy vehicles.*

car plant might have raised angled 'finger docks' combining direct trailer floor access for forklifts for side and end handling. Research the goods and vehicle handling demands, and assess these against the topography and climate of the site. (Loading docks so often unwittingly face into the prevailing wind.)

4 Raised dock design

4.01 Raised docks are very efficient for some loading operations and should be used in conjunction with a dock levelling device, as truck bed heights vary from type to type and between unloaded and laden conditions. Some people argue that if nearly all the trucks are of one type, only a few bays need be fitted with leveller plates. Unless the operation is very simple or the future development very clear, this decision is short sighted (Figure 2.11a/b) (for dimensions see Information sheet, Loading 1 and 5).

4.02 Containers on skeletal trailers can have floor heights as high as l.5 m: a 'standard' trailer truck has an average floor height of 1.2 to 1.4 m, although 'super cube' trailers have floors as low as 800 mm; and urban delivery trucks vary from 700 mm to 1.2 m. Forklift or pallet trucks, often run on solid tyres, which may be damaged by continuous level change impacts; a dock levelling device is essential to bridge the gap between the dock and all the above heights, without exceeding the maximum gradient

17

Loading bay design

of 10 per cent (for details of vehicle heights see Information sheet, Loading 1).

4.03 Dock levellers are either hydraulic or counterbalance operated, and should be a minimum of 2.2 m wide, with a non-skid surface, and long enough to ensure that a forklift is nearly horizontal when entering a van or container. Permanent adjustable dock levellers are the most practical and safest way of overcoming the problem. Many trucks for urban deliveries are equipped with tailboard lifts: dock levellers are available that allow the tail lifts to 'tuck' underneath. Designers should be aware that oversteep gradients can drain electric forklift batteries faster and can cause pallet trucks to run away; these should be specified with a brake for loading bay use (Figure 2.12).

Figure 2.12 *Powered pallet truck moving up dock leveller.*

5 Loading ISO containers and demountable body units

5.01 Most common large vehicles today are enclosed trailers (Figure 2.13), ISO containers and demountable body units. International Standards Organization containers and Transport International Routier (TIR) services have had a marked effect on loading bay and marshalling area design. The vehicles that carry ISO containers are large; their loading also requires different handling and packaging, based on special forklift trucks and unit loads.

Forklift trucks and loading bays

5.02 There are conflicting opinions on the best loading bay organization for 'stuffing' and unpacking containers and demountable bodies. By using a raised dock, special forklift trucks can run in and out of the container and transfer the goods directly to and from the storage medium in one operation (Figure 2.14). Small forklifts designed for container stuffing have only a limited use in stacking goods, and a larger truck has to be used as well. This means a buffer space is needed to transfer loads between forklift and reach truck (Figure 2.15). If side loading on a raised dock can be justified, the reach truck or turret truck could be used for loading flat trailers and enclosed units direct; the counter argument is that as most traffic in the future will be containerized, there will have to be a load transfer point between the forklift and reach truck in the store anyway.

5.03 International Standards Organization containers and trailers have conflicting loading requirements. The floors

Figure 2.13 *Typical enclosed trailers.*

of some trailers are not strong enough to accept forklift trucks; so they require either ground-level loading (over the side) or a finger dock – the best compromise for operators required to handle both trailers and containers. A steep, angled, single-sided finger dock (75°–80°), allows either:
1. conventional end loading with a dock leveller or
2. side loading without the forklift having to run on the floor, and
3. ground-level side loading for bulky objects. The steep angle of the dock reduces both on-dock and truck manoeuvring area, and permits fast turn-round cycle.

5.04 Although the detailed stowage of goods in containers is not within the scope of this handbook, the designer should realize the permutations of pallets and the handling plant required, so that the correct space is allocated for the operation. If forklift trucks are used, notice must be taken of the power plants; petrol and diesel are not suitable for container filling, due to rapid fume build-up. Even liquid petroleum gas produces enough toxic fumes to be dangerous in the constricted space of a container, and may contaminate perishables.

Electric traction is best for this work, but then battery-charging provision must be made, with the associated acid problems on the floor (see Information sheet,

Figure 2.14 *Special small forklift truck filling container.*

Mechanized storage 9. Data on forklift truck sizes is in Information sheet, Mechanized storage 7). When designing for container use, wheel loadings of laden forklift trucks or pallet trucks should not exceed 22.7 kN, otherwise the container floor may be damaged. Due to this, designers can choose their loading bay floor surface, knowing that these weights will not be exceeded. A good rule of thumb is that a forklift truck with 2 tonnes lifting capacity is satisfactory, but always check with the mechanical handling consultant.

Pallets and unit loads

5.05 Pallets are the most usual method for loading containers (see Information sheet, Mechanized storage 4: Pallets); note that pallet sizes were standardized before containers. Many companies have standardized pallets suitable for road or rail use, which may not suit optimum packing patterns in containers. If rail wagons are to be loaded as well, a store should be provided to hold both 1200 x 1000 mm road transport pallets, 800 x 1200 mm European rail pallets, and any damaged units. It is good practice to provide an easily accessible store for pallets, as some companies wish to collect theirs, and there are always damaged units that soon clutter a loading area if not disposed of. As an alternative to timber pallets, cardboard or plastic sheet may be used, especially for manual loading, which is economic for 'deep-sea' routes, owing to the need for full volume packing and for stability. Waste collection areas should be provided for this type of packing from incoming containers. Linked with container stuffing is the need to secure the load, as ships can roll 40° and pitch 20°, 50° if the cargo does not completely fill the container, so some form of packing must be inserted to avoid damage. Designers should also provide easily accessible storage for packing, which can be in the form of timber chocks, straps or pneumatic bags. If pneumatic securing bags are used, a flexible airline should be provided.

Load assembly and stuffing

5.06 In order to ensure full and efficient container stuffing, one container or trailer length space (12–13.6 m) should be provided across a 3.5–4.4 m cross-aisle opposite each bay so that loads can be pre-assembled (Figure 2.9). Where space is tight, half the length (i.e. 6.5 m) is considered a minimum.

5.07 Many products cannot be packed together or must be loaded in a special order to avoid uneven weight distribution, poor cargo compatibility or inefficient storage. The pre-assembly area ensures that a cargo is checked and arranged for the best loading and fastest container turnround – this is a further argument for splitting incoming and outgoing loading bays in a large-scale operation.

5.08 With forklift truck loading, manoeuvrability is often more important in the approach to a container than inside it. A straight approach is the best design, and reduces the risk of load shedding when cornering, although most patterns approach the loading bay by a gangway running at 90° to the container; this arrangement demands realistic cornering space, taking into consideration load tolerances, without sacrificing too much floor area. The double handling at the load pre-assembly position can be justified, considering that container stuffing is best carried out in one continuous operation. The load assembly area should be well lit, and clearly marked on the floor, with varying container lengths annotated preferably in a separate colour unique for each. In situations of frequent tightly packed, homogeneous loads, a roll-in system, e.g. Joloda or Berthelat, is very attractive. Forklift trucks or pallet trucks bring the elements of the load to the assembly position, where it is built up on the tracks provided. When the assembly is complete, the whole load is pushed into the container as a unit, liberating the forklift trucks to assemble the next load (Figure 2.16). This is best used with a raised dock, but it can also be used in a different form for loading containers from ground level with forklift trucks, the pallets or goods having normally to be manually handled from the container door to the final

Figure 2.15 *The small forklift exchanges loads with a turret truck at the buffer zone.*

Figure 2.16 *Roll-in system allows container to be loaded in one movement.*

Loading bay design

position. A Joloda track reduces the manual effort considerably, the trucks being removed as the container is filled; however, these demand containers or truck bodies with special grooves in the floor, or the cargo has to be packed on a pallet with sufficient clearance for the retracted track sections to be withdrawn.

5.09 A further ground-based system using forklift trucks is a lifting table, which hoists the forklift so that it can enter the container; these are expensive and can be dangerous if not carefully sited and operated. Vehicle-raising lifts are useful in very constricted situations, although they are an expensive answer to a simple problem (see Information sheet, Loading 11).

5.10 Ramps allow forklifts to stuff containers direct from ground level (Figure 2.17). Available with flat tops so that pallets are horizontal when they enter the container, these ramps need a long run-up zone to the rear; with a maximum gradient of 10 per cent, and container floor heights over l.5 m, plus enough turning area for the stuffing truck before it mounts the ramp; 18 m can quickly be lost. These ramps are not very wide, although sufficient for forklifts, they cannot be used for unloading mobile cargo like cars.

(a)

(b)

Figure 2.18 *Tilt trailer being* (a) *side-loaded,* (b) *end loaded.*

Figure 2.17 *Loading ramp for forklift trucks.*

Side access

5.11 The increasing use of sliding-door and tilt-top trailers and side-door containers have strengthened arguments against using raised dock loading bays. Forklift trucks can load directly into these from both sides and the rear (Figure 2.18). Side door operation in raised docks may be wasteful of building volume, as the full turning width is required throughout the trailer length, unless turret trucks can be used direct. But if high turnover is critical, as in groupage areas, side loading with shuttling fork trucks can be very fast. The truck throughput and easier storage cycles offsets volume loss and can reduce the number of bays required. This has also resulted in a reassessment of the straight-through access loading bay for ground level operation.

5.12 As well as forklift trucks, special telescopic conveyors are available for loading trailers and containers with loose cargo. These are popular with the express mail operators. These can be used with raised docks (roller or belt) or can be mobile and ground based (see Mechanized storage, Information Sheet 14, Specialized Storage Bulk Loading 2, and Info Loading 5). Containers for use over deep-sea routes are often hand stuffed for maximum cube and load stability; if this kind of operation is predicted, designers should provide an area nearby where drop-in conveyor sections can be stored, so as not to inhibit other loading operations. Tilt-top containers and open half-height units for coils, reels and steel work allow overhead loading by gantry cranes (Figures 2.19 and 2.20). Gantry cranes in loading bay situations are only economic if the company specializes in a product requiring special container types or uses a lift-off type of demountable body system for delivery work. For example, the Ford Motor Company parts store at Daventry used gantry cranes throughout the loading bays, as many parts were crated, and most of the vehicles used were flatbeds. Loading bays should adapt quickly to different container types. It is for the designer to check which form is the most likely for the particular product and predicted receipt/dispatch pattern.

5.13 Some trucks may arrive with two 6 m containers on one trailer. In this situation, simply operated hydraulic lifting legs are available, powered by a small motor unit. One or both containers have to be transferred to a stillage or a slave trailer for unloading. Space should be provided near the loading bay for this type of equipment. If there will be frequent container handling, large-scale plant should be provided.

5.14 For a high throughput of trailers, a slave shunt tractor is useful, allowing the trunk units to drop the

Loading bay design

Figure 2.19 *Daventry parts store, loading with overhead gantry-slung stacker cranes.*

incoming trailer in the assembly zone and leave immediately with the outgoing one; all attempts should be made to reduce the number of vehicles 'milling' about.

Lighting

5.15 Unless containers have open tops, there will not be enough light inside to ensure accurate loading, especially in 13.6 m end-loading containers. Mobile or permanent extendible lighting should be provided, with a well lit door zone. Ensure there is no glare to dazzle forklift drivers and cause accidents. Special dock lights are available in tough steel housings on resilient mountings. (See Information sheet, Loading 5.)

Weighbridges

5.16 With the present concern about the overloading of lorries and an increase in spot checks by the Office of the Deputy Prime Minister (ODPM, formerly DTLR), designers may be asked to incorporate some form of weighing equipment in the loading bay area. There are several methods of weighing trucks and containers. A full weighbridge in the assembly area can assess gross weight and axle distribution. Another system is a hand portable set of scales which weighs the truck wheel by wheel; it is disputed whether the total load can be accurately weighed by this method. One development with potential is an automatic axle weighing and computation device in the truck itself, which can also guide the distribution of loading in the container and could eliminate dock weighing. Alternatively, goods can be weighed out of the containers by a device attached to the dock leveller, which weighs the forklift truck and the load as it passes over the top.

Figure 2.20 *Gantry with fork attachment (far side of truck) unloading pallets.*

6 Bays for refrigerated vehicles

6.01 As a rule, the floor of any refrigerated vehicle is 50 to 102 mm higher than its normal counterpart, due to the insulation. Refrigerated containers or 'reefers', are equipped with gas-cooling or integral or clip-on refrigeration machinery. Large-scale reefer operations are discussed in Chapter 6, Cold storage. Some trailer refrigeration units are powered either by a small internal combustion engine that is left running in the dock or by electric compressors which require plug points (sometimes low voltage). The trend now is for cryogenic gases that only require cylinder exchange.

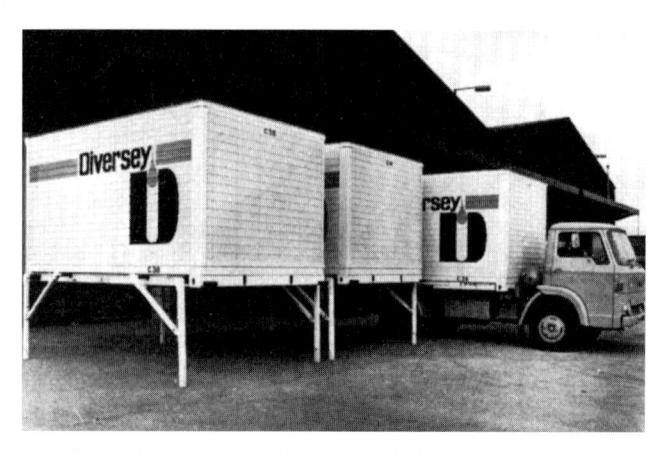

Figure 2.21 *Local delivery vehicle picking up swop body at loading dock.*

7 Demountable and intermodal body systems

7.01 As more companies realize the great potential efficiency of demountable body units for local and long-distance distribution, designers will be asked to integrate these units with loading bays and yards. Demountable truck bodies can be treated as containers fitted with wind-down or hinge-down legs. This is not as simple as articulated vehicle operation, but can be more flexible, especially where access is restricted.

7.02 Demountable bodies can increase the utility of a truck chassis many times because vehicle turnround is as quick as the time taken to change one body for another (Figure 2.21). Some bodies are equipped with ISO-type top corner locks and are built to an ISO standard size for system interchangeability. There are many swop body systems in operation, including demountable skeletal units, so that a container can be left supported on legs for unloading. See Chapter 3, External storage, Information sheet 1. A number of modular-sized bodies are often trunk hauled by articulated vehicles and transferred to small local delivery chassis at strategic points, which either deliver direct to the retail outlet or leave the body there as a unit, taking the empty body back to a marshalling area to be picked up by the returning vehicle. A variation is for the same bodies to be transferred by gantry crane or by reach stacker (a huge forklift), to trains for long-distance operation. Intermodal transportation is a trend towards energy saving.

7.03 A further variation which is proving popular because of its increased flexibility, is to employ a lorry and drawbar trailer with modular 'swop' bodies. This doubles the use of the former as the trailer is dropped in a convenient position in a town, and the lorry is driven on to a further destination, where it in turn leaves its bodies for local delivery vehicles, picks up the empties and then returns to the trailer. The truck then changes its empty bodies for the full ones on the trailer, and starts the delivery process again. Finally, the truck returns to pick up the trailer and returns to base. This has all been achieved by one driver.

7.04 The effect on loading bay design is much the same as for ISO containers in groupage and break-bulk situations. The vehicle entry requirement is similar, as both trunker trucks and local small chassis are liable to use the installation. The buffer area is important, as trunk to local vehicle transfer takes up space. Some demountable bodies are equipped with clip-on or integral tailboard lifts. Often, roll pallets (castered cages) and dollies of stacked plastic crates are used for retail delivery work, and because they are easily handled, they have been used to load at ground level, by pushing the castered cages or dollies onto tailboard lifts of the waiting bodies, powered from a plug. Alternatively, the tailboard lifts can act as a mobile dock leveller by pushing the cages or pallet truck onto the tail lift at dock level, raising the lift to floor height, and rolling them into position. For large warehouses with rapid loading cycles, it is not good practice to dispense with dock levellers: operators tend to forget that suppliers' vehicles are larger than their own. Demountable bodies are often used for short-term storage: the implications of this are covered in Technical study, External storage 1.

8 Future vehicle sizes

8.01 The EU transport executive has fixed the maximum European gross weights for trucks. All EU members have to comply to ensure cross-border access free from different regulations. Articulated vehicles with six axles are limited to 44 tonnes, enabling 12.2 m and 13.6 m containers to be carried, and truck and drawbar trailer outfits similarly at 44 tonnes. Overall sizes are unlikely increase over the present limits, and axle loadings will not exceed 11.5 tonnes, although 13 tonnes is still used within France and gross vehicle weights of 50 tonnes are allowed within the Netherlands. The drawbar combination is popular for light, 'super cube' commodities.

INFORMATION SHEET

Loading 1

Vehicle sizes, weights and turning circles

1 Vehicle dimensions

2 Turning circles

3 Dimensions of US and Australian vehicles

4 Calculations to determine road widths for different types of vehicle

This section gives information on common types of commercial vehicles.

1 Vehicle dimensions

1.01 Table 2.1 illustrates the most common types of commercial vehicles, and gives basic data necessary for design of loading bays. Diagrams of typical vehicles are given to enable designers to spot the specific type used in the storage system they are designing for. The type of vehicle used will depend on type of unit load (see Technical study, Storage process, paras 4 to 6). The precise limits of dimensions in Table 2.1 are shown in key diagrams (Figure 2.22a/b).

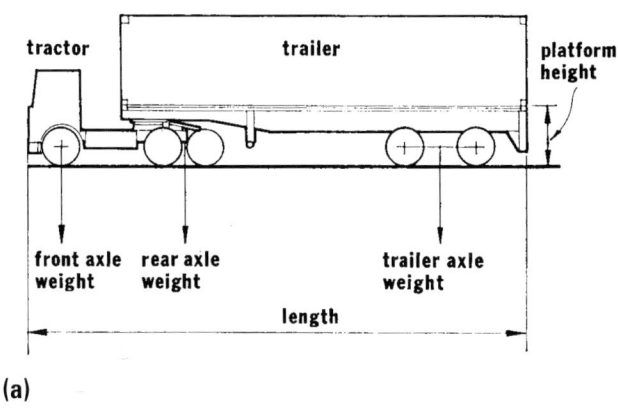

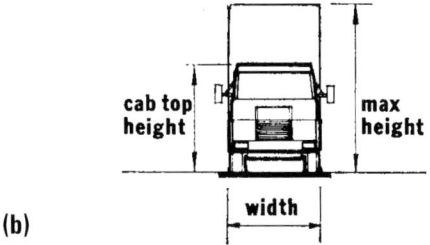

Figure 2.22 *Side view (a) and front view (b) of key tractor and trailer showing limits of dimensions.*

Axle weights

1.02 Table 2.1 shows weights of each axle, and gross combination weight, of typical loaded vehicles.
1.03 Single axle weights are measured through the centre of the wheel. The combined weight of twin axles (or bogies) are measured through the centre point between axles.
1.04 Separate axle weights are provided, as they may sometimes be necessary in design, in calculating loading for existing structures, or in situations where tractor and trailer are separated.

Gross combination weight

The combined weights of tractor, trailer, maximum load and driver equal the gross combination weight.

2 Turning circles

2.01 Table 2.1 shows dimensions for turning circle diameter, and swept turning circle diameter.
2.02 Turning circle diameter is the minimum path of outer front tyre used in calculating kerb clearances.
2.03 Swept turning circle diameter is the minimum path of outer front overhang used in calculating building-to-building clearance.
2.04 Articulated vehicle turning circles are inexact because, when turning with tractor at 90° to trailer, the actual radius depends on relative distance between centre line of kingpin and centre line of trailer bogie, both of which can be varied on some trailers. Therefore, swept turning circles for tractors only (i.e. without trailers) are included.

Drawbar combinations

2.05 Turning circles given are of the rigid truck, but drawbar trailers follow within that circle. All dimensions of turning and swept turning circle diameters are absolute minimum. Both articulated trailers and drawbar trailers pivot on their bogies, causing considerable tyre wear and road surface damage (if frequent). These minimum dimensions should not be used as a planning standard but are for information only. For planning standards, see Information sheet, Loading 2.

Vehicle cut-in

2.06 Swept turning circles give the outer radius. Vehicle cut-in (Figures 2.23 and 2.24) shows clearances within the circle which must be left for body or trailer cut-in. See also gate entry diagrams, Information sheet, Loading 2, which combine clearances for swept turning circles and cut-in.
2.07 Figures 2.23 and 2.24 illustrate typical cut-in and turning dimensions for a 30.4 tonne four axle rigid truck, and a 15 m long 32.5 tonne articulated combination. Although turning circles are given for vehicle types illustrated in Table 2.1, there are occasions where the detailed

Vehicle sizes, weights and turning circles

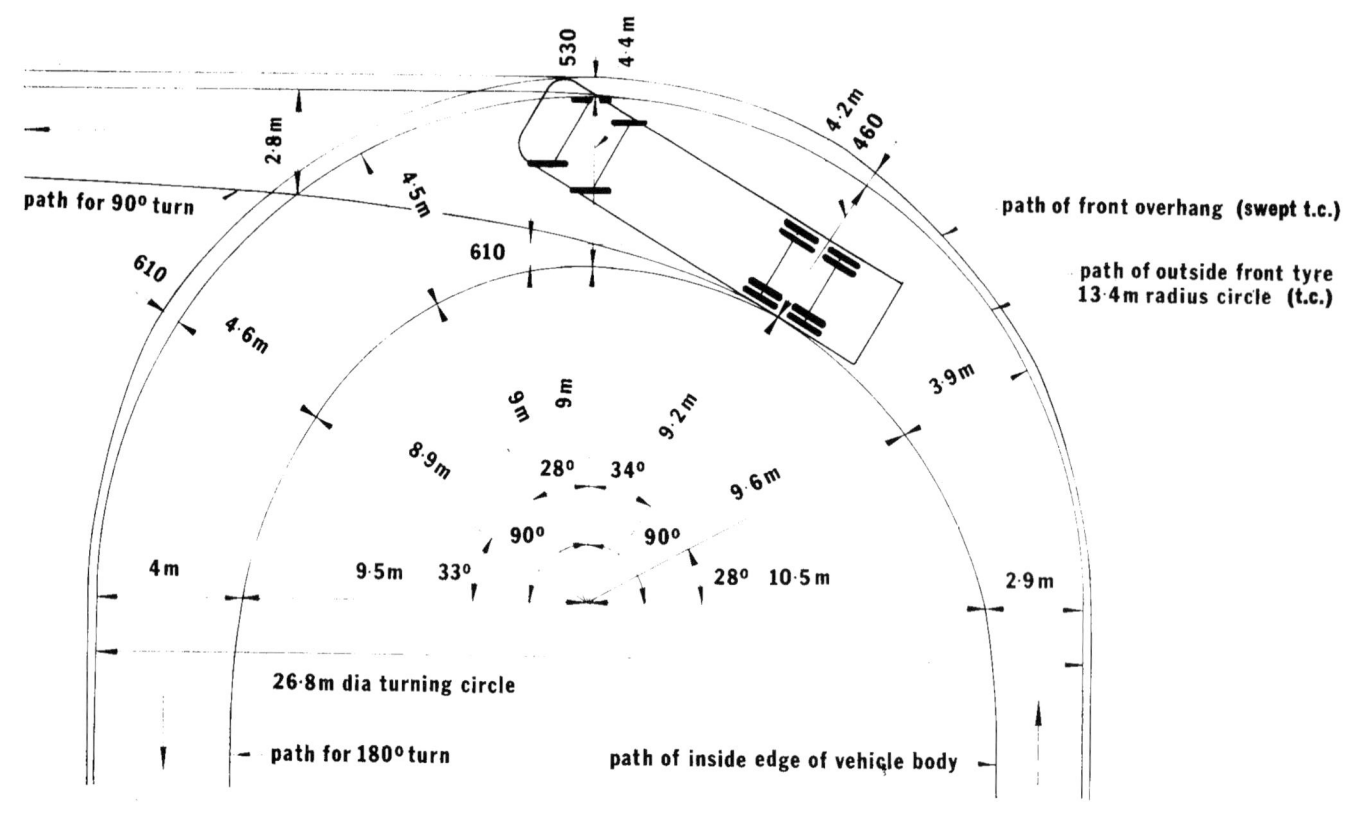

Figure 2.23 *Cut-in dimensions for 30.4 tonnes rigid.*

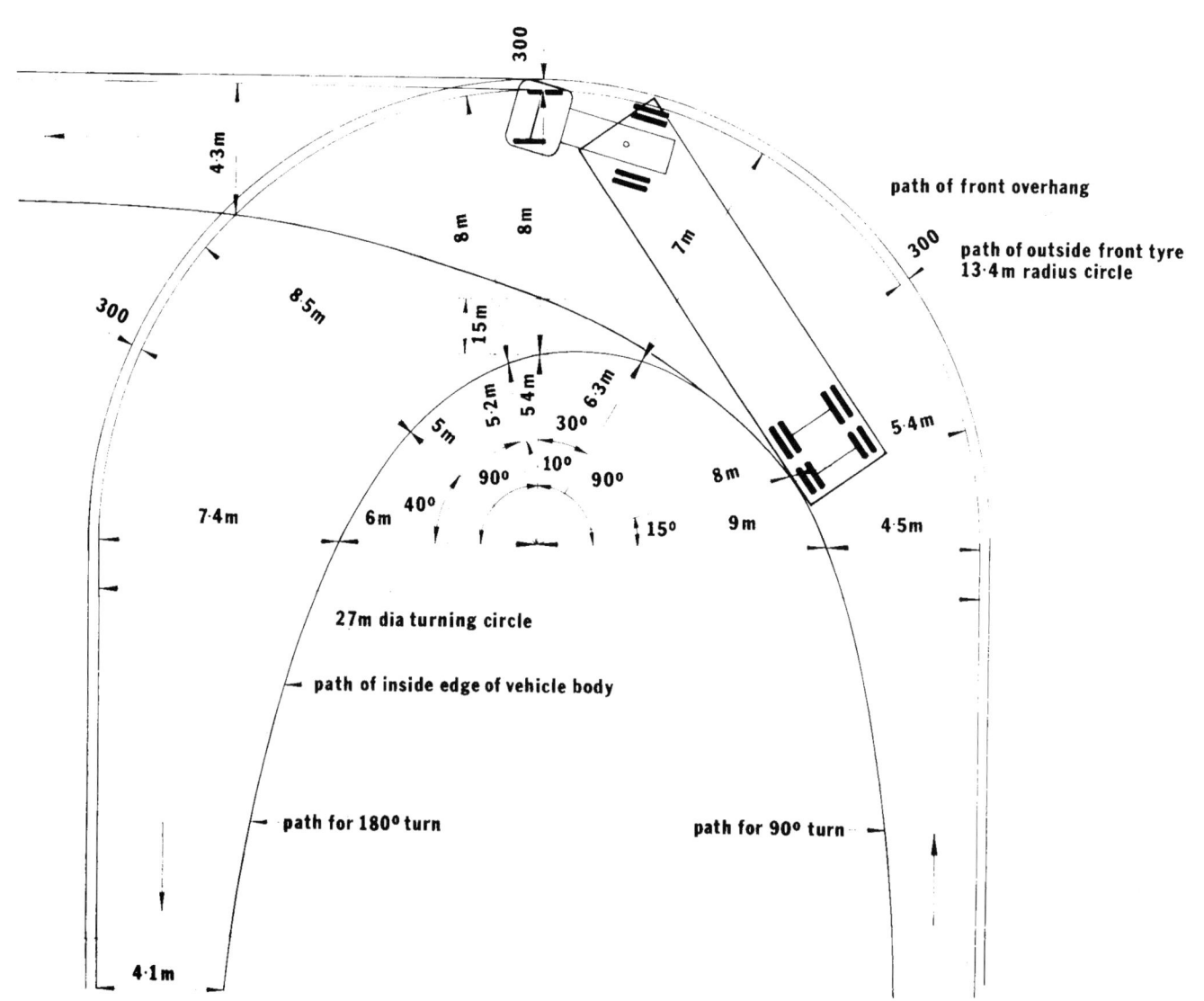

Figure 2.24 *Cut-in dimensions for 32.5 tonnes articulated trailer.*

cut-in dimensions are required for forecourt and loading bay planning for vehicles not similar to the diagrams in Figures 2.23 and 2.24. The following diagrams and formulae enable accurate turning diagrams to be built up for any commercial vehicle types: this can be particularly useful when faced with constricted space for manoeuvring and where a calculation based on a predominance of a particular vehicle type is acceptable.

3 Dimensions of US and Australian vehicles

3.01 The typical vehicle dimensions and weights illustrated by vehicle types in Table 2.1 refer mostly to European standards and regulations. The permitted sizes and axle weights are more complicated in the USA and Australia, however, as in both these federations vehicle legislation is state controlled. In some US states two or three trailers are allowed to be towed on interstate or specially designated highways: called 'double bottoms' or 'triple bottoms' – an articulated truck towing one or two additional trailers. These vehicles are becoming increasingly popular in the USA, and in some parts of Australia ('road trains'). Designers will increasingly work on projects including interchange stations, where 'road trains' are broken down for conventional haulage. Figures 2.25 and 2.26 illustrate how a 'short double bottom' cuts in less on a bend than a 15 m articulated truck.

4 Calculations to determine road widths for different types of vehicle

4.01 Computer-aided design (CAD) programs such as AutoTrack are now widely used as a 'drawing board' CAD tool for checking turning and manoevring dimensions (see Figures 2.27, 2.28 and 2.29). A wide library of vehicle types is available; but as in all computer applications there are words of warning. If in doubt on a tight site, still arrange a real test in a car park; it can be less expensive! For practical purposes the maximum amount of cut in and maximum turning width may be calculated using the following.

4.02 A rigid vehicle:
$A = a - b$ and $B = a - b + d$
where $b = \sqrt{a^2 - c^2}$
Symbols used to define the maximum cut in and turning width for a rigid vehicle:
a = Outside turning radius of first axle
b = Outside turning radius of rear axle
c = Wheel base
d = Vehicle width
A = Cut in
B = Turning width

4.03 An articulated vehicle:
$A = a - g$ and $B = a - g + j$
where $g = \sqrt{e^2 - h^2} + \frac{1}{2}j$
Symbols used to define the maximum cut in and turning width for an articulated vehicle:
a = Outside turning radius of first axle
b = Outside turning radius of rear tractor axle
   = $\sqrt{a^2 - c^2}$ (if a tandem axle bogie, through the centre line between the axles)
c = Wheelbase of tractor
d = Vehicle tractor width
e = Turning radius of kingpin = $\sqrt{(b - \frac{1}{2}d)^2 + f^2}$
f = Distance of kingpin in front of tractor rear axle
g = Outside turning radius of trailer rear axle
   (if a tandem axle bogie, this is through the centre line between the axles, or if a tri-axle bogie, this is through the centre line of the centre axle)
h = Wheelbase of trailer
j = Width of trailer A = Cut in B = Turning width

4.04 A drawbar trailer combination:
$A = a - g$ and $B = a - g + j$
where $g \sqrt{K^2 - h^2} + \frac{1}{2}j$
Symbols used to define the maximum cut in and turning width for a drawbar trailer combination:
a = Outside turning radius of first axle
b = Outside turning radius of rear tractor axle
   = $\sqrt{a^2 - c^2}$ (see note in Figure 2.28)
c = Wheelbase of tractor
d = Tractor width
e = Turning radius of coupling = $\sqrt{(b - \frac{1}{2}d)^2 + f^2}$
f = Distance from rear tractor axle to coupling
g = Outside turning radius of trailer rear axle
   (see note in Figure 2.28)
h = Trailer wheelbase
i = Trailer length
j = Trailer width
k = Turning radius of trailer steering axle = $\sqrt{e^2 - l^2}$
l = Drawbar length
A = Cut in
B = Turning width

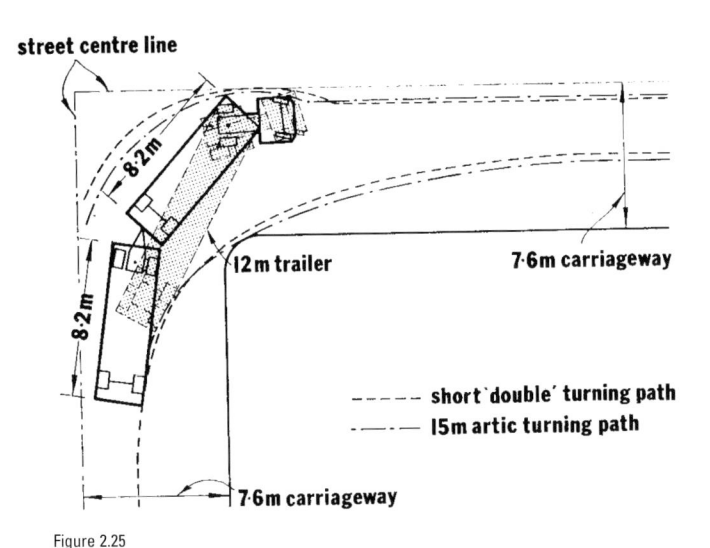

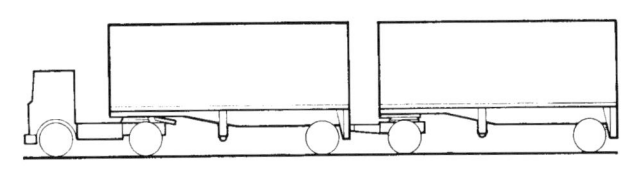

Figure 2.25

Figure 2.26

Vehicle sizes, weights and turning circles

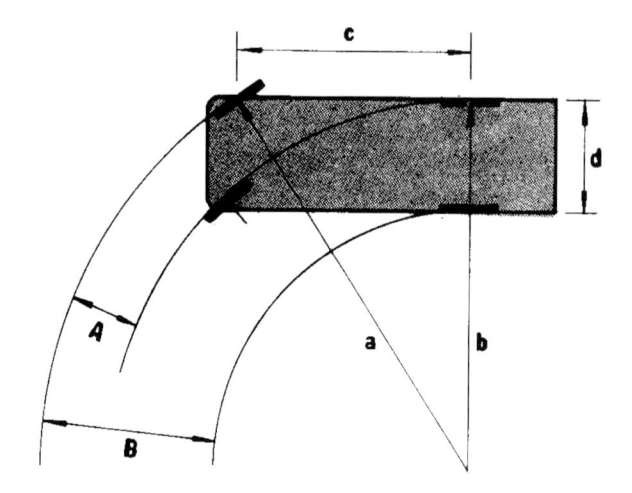

Figure 2.27 *A rigid vehicle.*

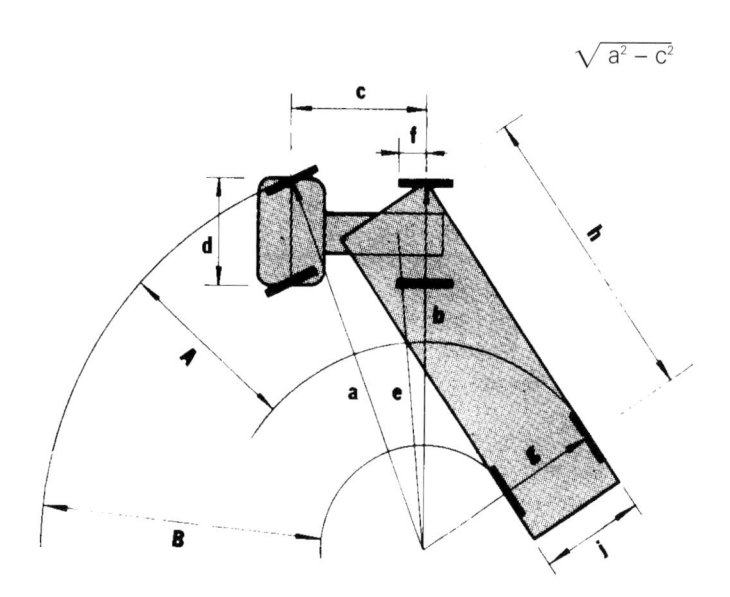

Figure 2.28 *An articulated vehicle.*

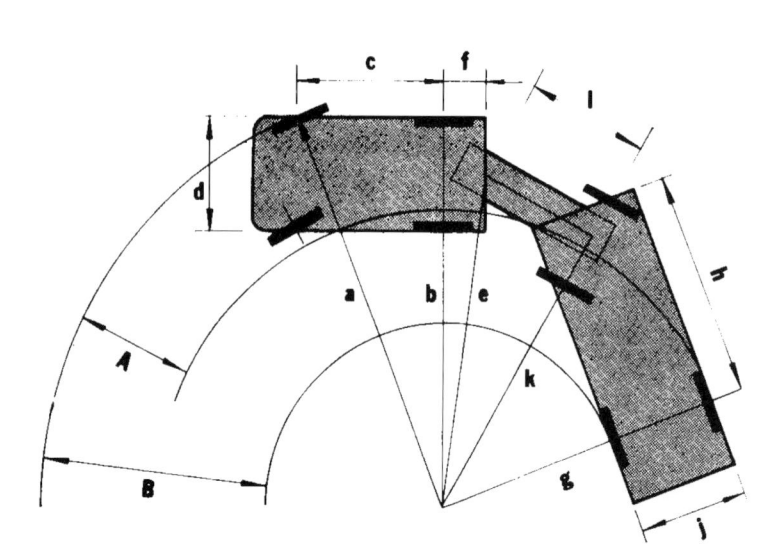

Figure 2.29 *A drawbar trailer combination.*

Table 2.1 Sizes, weights and turning circles of road transport vehicles

	Length (m)	Width[1] (m)	Cab top height[1] (m)	Maximum height[2] (m)	Platform height (m)	Front axle weight (tonnes)	Rear tractor axle or bogie weight (tonnes)	Trailer axle or bogie weight (tonnes)	Gross combination weight (tonnes)	Turning circle diameter (m)	Swept turning circle diameter[2] (m)
Five-axle articulated with refrigerated body	16.5	2.55	2.74	4.00	1.32*	5.5	10.1	16.9	44.0	24–30	(15–54)
Four-axle articulated with wide spread trailer axles	15	2.5	2.74	4.22	1.32*	5.5	10.1	16.9	32.5	24–30	(15–54)
Tractor with twin steer front bogie	16.5	2.5	2.48	4.04	1.37*	8.2 (bogie)	9.7	24.6	38.0	24–30	(16.5)
Three-axle tractor Second steering axle as part of rear bogie. With three trailer axles, this is suitable for unevenly laden containers	16.5	2.5	2.74	4.22	1.32*	3.7/3.9	10.1	24.8	44.0	24–30	(14.0)
Three-axle tractor. Typical TIR outfit	16.5	2.5	2.92	4.12	1.40	3.7	12.6	16.2	44.0	24–30	(15.54)
						(6.5)	(15.5)	(16)	(38)		

(Figures in brackets show European weights; generally the UK is in line with EU axle and gross vehicle weights. 6 axle articulated trucks can be 44 tonnes.)

Vehicle sizes, weights and turning circles

Table 2.1 Sizes, weights and turning circles of road transport vehicles – continued

	Length (m)	Width[1] (m)	Cab top height[1] (m)	Maximum height[2] (m)	Platform height (m)	Front axle weight (tonnes)	Rear tractor axle or bogie weight (tonnes)	Trailer axle or bogie weight (tonnes)	Gross combination weight (tonnes)	Turning circle diameter (m)	Swept turning circle diameter[3] (m)
Articulated pantechnicon van *High volume for light goods.*	14	2.5	2.54	4.4	0.46	4.5	9.9	9.9	24.3	24–30	(14.0)
Articulated tanker *Holds 28640 litres.*	16.5	2.5	2.74	3.81	1.37	5.4	10.1	17	36(44.0)	24–30	(15.9)
High capacity tipper *For coal, ash etc. Sand tippers are shallower. Maximum raised height 9.2 m.*	14	2.5	2.74	3.96	–	5.7	10.1	16.7	32.5 (36.0)	24–30	(13.1)
Powder tanker *Bottom discharge is type shown. Pneumatic discharge and tippers also available.*	15.5	2.5	2.74	3.96	1.37	5.7	10.1	16.7	36(44)	24–30	(15.9)
Three-axle truck, two-axle trailer (drawbar trailer) *Most types in UK have only two axles each. This is typical European vehicle. (Figures in brackets show European weights)*	18.5	2.5	2.92	4.12	1.40*	6.1 (6)	16.3 (18)	4/6.1 (8.8)	44.0 (38)	20.7	21.1

28

Table 2.1 Sizes, weights and turning circles of road transport vehicles – continued

	Length (m)	Width[1] (m)	Cab top height[1] (m)	Maximum height[2] (m)	Platform height (m)	Front axle weight (tonnes)	Rear tractor axle or bogie weight (tonnes)	Trailer axle or bogie weight (tonnes)	Gross combination weight (tonnes)	Turning circle diameter (m)	Swept turning circle diameter[3] (m)
Two-axle truck, three-axle trailer (drawbar trailer) *Typical European vehicle.*	18.5	2.5	2.92	4.12	1.40	7.5 (6)	11.5 (10)	8.1/8.1 (6.75/15.25)	44.0 (38)	16.5	17.7
Four-axle rigid *These types can now gross 32 tonnes; usually tankers or tippers.*	9.75	2.5	2.64	3.51	1.37	11.9 (bogie)	18.5	–	30.4	25.6	26.5
Three-axle articulated tanker *Holds 18180 litres. Useful in restricted forecourts.*	12	2.5	2.43	3.20	1.32	4.8	9.4	10.1	24.3	24–30	(13.4)
Three-axle rigid *Includes tippers, tankers, mixers.*	8	2.5	2.64	3.05	1.63	6.1	18.2	–	24.3	23.2	24.4
Three-axle rigid tipper or skip lorry *If under 5.64 m outer axle spread, 20.2 tonnes on road (see IS Loading 3).*	7	2.5	–	3.35	–	6	18	–	24	17.4	18.9

Vehicle sizes, weights and turning circles

Table 2.1 Sizes, weights and turning circles of road transport vehicles – *continued*

	Length (m)	Width[1] (m)	Cab top height[1] (m)	Maximum height[2] (m)	Platform height (m)	Front axle weight (tonnes)	Rear tractor axle or bogie weight (tonnes)	Trailer axle or bogie weight (tonnes)	Gross combination weight (tonnes)	Turning circle diameter (m)	Swept turning circle diameter[3] (m)
Pantechnicon *For large light goods.*	10.5–11	2.5	–	4.23	0.46	6.1	10.1	–	16.2	20.1	21.3
18 tonne rigid *Popular type.*	8.5	2.5	2.43	3.58	1.16	7.5	11.5	–	18	21	22
Tipper *Same size for two-axle skip lorries, truck mixers. (Maximum raised height 4.81m.)*	6.3	2.5	–	2.64	1.22	7.5	11.5	–	18	18.3	18.9
Van (1 tonne) *Smaller vans as for cars (see AJ Metric Handbook).*	4.4	1.78	1.93	–	0.43	1	1.5	–	2.5	12.2	12.8
Van (2 tonne) *Long wheelbase shown, as for bread delivery, laundry etc.*	6	2.24	2.82	–	0.76	1.6	3.2	–	4.8	13.1	14

30

Vehicle sizes, weights and turning circles

Table 2.1 Sizes, weights and turning circles of road transport vehicles – *continued*

	Length (m)	Width (m)	Cab top height[1] (m)	Maximum height[2] (m)	Platform height (tonnes)	Front axle weight (tonnes)	Rear tractor axle or bogie weight (tonnes)	Trailer axle or bogie weight (tonnes)	Gross combination weight (m)	Turning circle diameter (m)	Swept turning circle diameter[3]
Brewer's dray	6.5	2.29	2.29	–	0.92	3.5	8.6	–	12.1	14.3
15.2											

Three-axle, 400 mm wheels for low height loading. Swop body

| **Fire appliance (medium size)** | 8 | 2.29 | 3.4 | 3.4 | – | 3.5 | 4.8 | – | 8.3 | 15.2 | 16.2 |

For larger types, use 16 tonne rigid dimensions.

| **Dustcart (medium capacity)** | 7.4 | 2.29 | 3.20 | 4.0 | 0.46 | 4 | 6.8 | – | 10.8 | 14 | 15.2 |

For larger capacity, use 4 axle rigid.

| **Articulated van** | 12.5 | 2.5 | 2.74 | 4.0 | 1.32 | 4.8 | 9.4 | 10.1 | 26 | 24.30 | (13.4) |

Typical van serving supermarkets. Fitted with cooler and tail lift, this unit would carry roll pallets.

[1] Not including mirrors, which can increase width to 3.1 m max.
[2] Includes 2.44 m container or fixed body. Varies with springs, wheel and frame depth.
[3] Swept turning circle diameter column, figures in brackets refer to the swept turning circle of tractor unit only (without trailer).
*These trailers can carry containers; add 150 mm for height of container floor.

INFORMATION SHEET

Loading 2

Loading bay layout and gate entries

1 Loading bay layouts

2 Gate entries

This section indicates typical dimensions of loading bay layouts and gate entries.

1 Loading bay layouts

1.01 Figures 2.32 to 2.37 illustrate normal operating conditions in loading bays. Each diagram has a broken line representing absolute minimum clearances (where shunting is likely) and an unbroken line representing preferred dimensions which allow easy manoeuvring and prevent jams. A dotted line shows space for fast turnround. Scales are shown in metres.

1.02 For general requirements of the immediate loading bay zone and marshalling areas, refer to Technical study, Loading 1. For internal store spatial requirements and their influence on bay spacings (e.g. width required for the pre-assembly of roll pallets in food distribution warehouses) refer to Technical studies, Storage Process, paras 4 and 5. For detailed dimensions see Figures 2.30 and 2.31a/b.

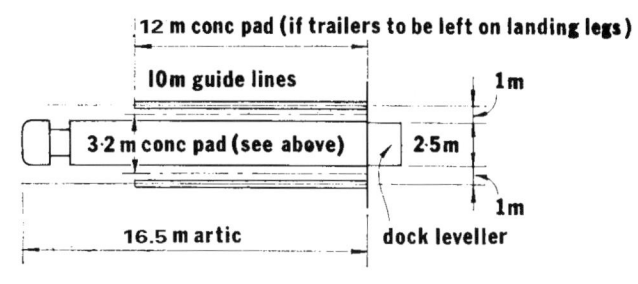

Figure 2.30 *Plan of loading bay.*

1.03 Figure 2.32 (left) 90° dock with a 3.5 m bay opening. For end-loading vehicles, where lateral space is at a premium, loads are carried away from the dock to another zone, as all dock space is required for forklift manoeuvring. (The Freight Transport Association suggests a 3.3 m minimum bay width, which is considered tight with the swing-out demanded by 16.5 m articulated vehicles – 'artics'.) On principle, narrower bays mean that the truck driver needs more depth in front of the bay to move out before he can swing round. For example, in the 3.5 m bay (left) an articulated container truck is turning out as sharply as it can for the clearances. If the bays were 3.3 m, only 1 m would be saved longitudinally over five bays, but the draw forward area must be nearly 5 m greater to provide swing-out clearance; this can hinder the next vehicle manoeuvring to use the bay.

1.04 Figure 2.32 (centre) 90° dock, 4.0 m bay spacing. For bays with busy cross-dock forklift circulation, e.g. cold stores. Where fast turnround is also required, a minimum of 4.5 m bays are recommended with a 5 m spacing preferable.

1.05 Figure 2.32 (right) 90° dock, 5 m bay spacing. For pre-loading accumulation of roll pallets in distribution warehouses. Actual dimension will depend on needs of the accumulation area behind the dock. Thirty-five metres from dock face is the absolute minimum (33.4 m is possible, as some operators will state, but allows no clearance for error and is not recommended). Continuous line at 40 m shows that a small increase in depth of marshalling area can accelerate manoeuvring, by allowing artics to pass (42 m plus is preferable for manoeuvring drawbar trailers).

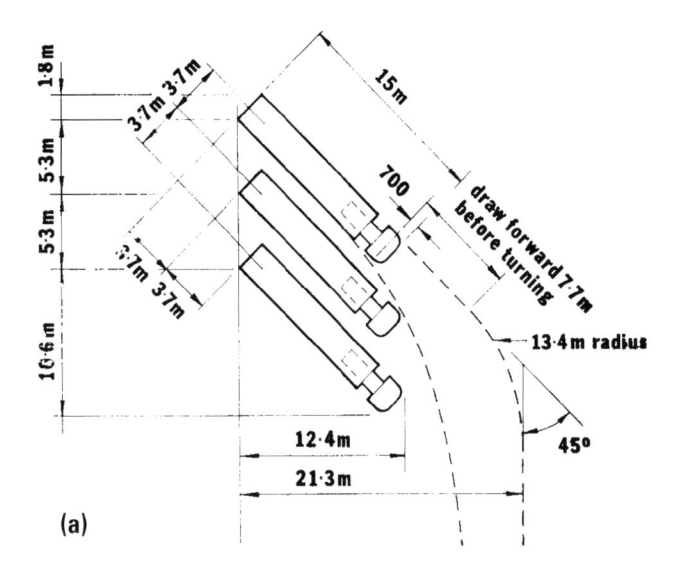

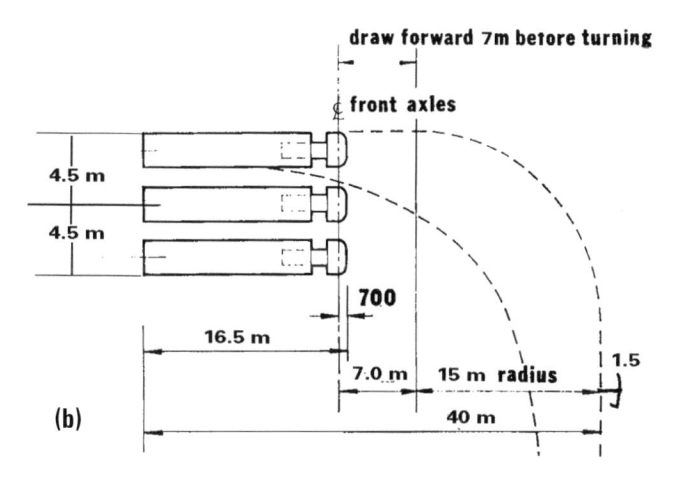

Figure 2.31(a) *Parking at 45° (3.7 m typical centres).*
(b) *Parking at 90° (4.5 m typical centres).*

Loading bay layout and gate entries

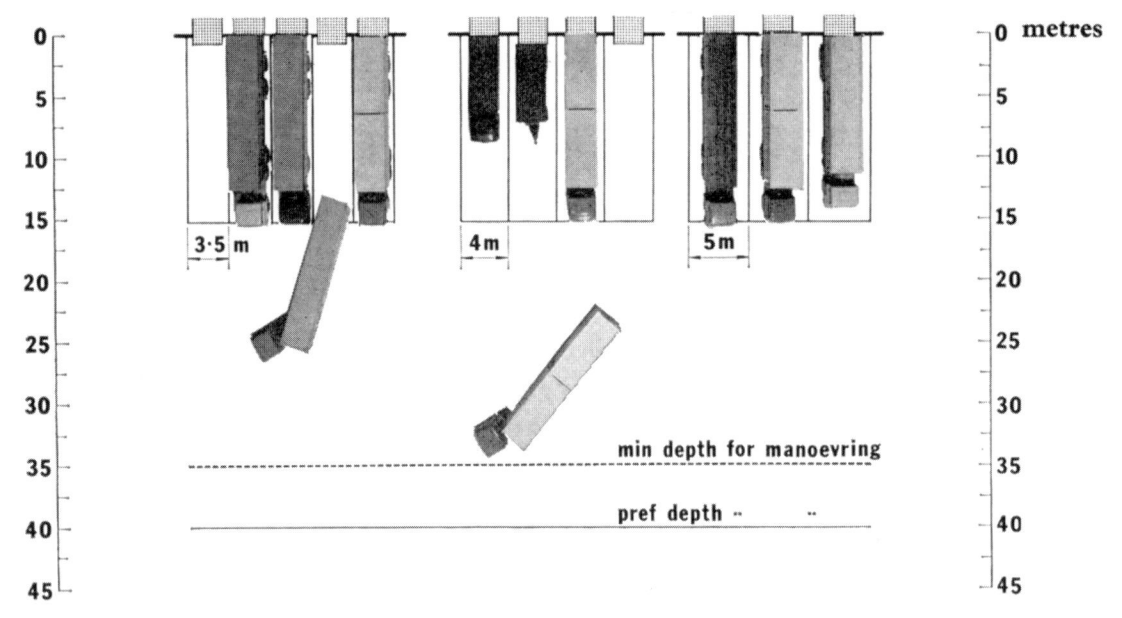

Figure 2.32 *(Left) 90° dock 3.5 m bay spacing; (centre) 90° dock spacing; (right) 90° dock, 5 m bay spacing.*

1.06 Side loading bays. A 7 m clearance is minimum for two forklifts to load a vehicle from each side. This is typical of a groupage centre, where most traffic is tilt-topped trailers for TIR work (Figure 2.33). The bays show rear forklift clearance, and space required for 16.5m and 18 m long vehicles. In the loading bay, the dotted line is minimum length for artics, the continuous line is minimum length for trucks with drawbar trailers. On the left, a truck with trailer is positioning to drop the trailer, so that the truck can turn round and 'nose' the trailer into the bay (as the centre vehicle is doing). If bays are segregated by pillars and door piers, the trucks need to draw further forward before turning to clear the structure.

1.07 Angled docks will change the pattern of movement on the dock. They allow a narrower forklift manoeuvring cross-route, but forklifts serving long rows of vehicles can cause heavy on-dock traffic with a linear distribution, rather than forklifts shuttling within the confines of a vehicle's width as with 90° bays.

1.08 Note the clockwise direction of flow in Figure 2.34 (45° dock: min 3.5 m bay spacing). This is ideal for British trucks; the driver can quickly reverse on his 'view' side.

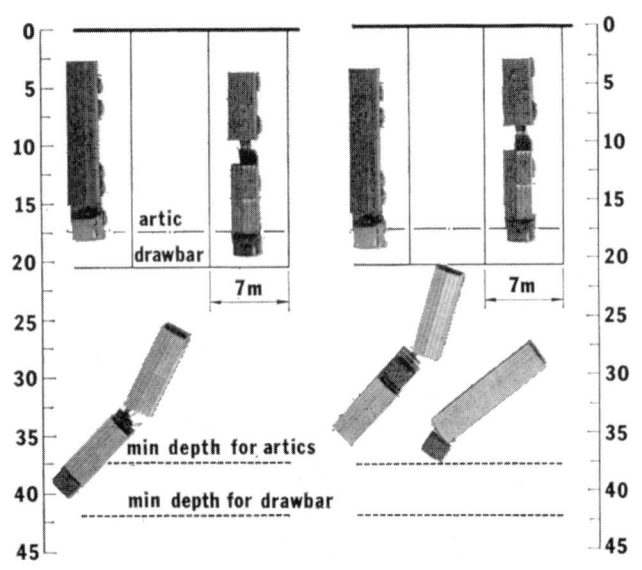

Figure 2.33 *Bays for internal loading from each side from floor level.*

(Inevitably, continental vehicles have to reverse on their blind side.) Figure 2.34 shows the sort of mixture of articulated units, drawbar combinations and container trucks that is liable to be found at a general purpose warehouse. The 3.5 m bay width is an absolute minimum; it is less than with 90° bays, as the swing-out clearance is not so critical. Wider bays are preferable, especially where drawbar units are expected, which are more difficult to reverse. Figure 2.34 also shows an articulated vehicle turning out as steeply as the trailer clearance allows.

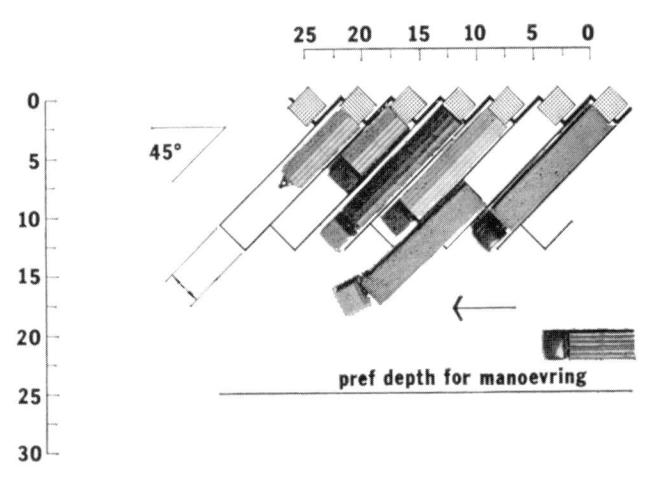

Figure 2.34 *45° dock, 3.5 m bay spacing.*

1.09 Side and end loading tanker bays. Figure 2.35 (left) shows a conventional 90° bay, with additional clearance to allow personnel to remove hoses laid along tank side. Rear clearance allows connection to valve points without the operator fouling tanker or valve assembly. Figure 2.35 (left) shows a 0.7 m clearance on nearside of tankers for valve connection, and 2.5 m on offside for pipe sections stored on the side of the tank. Some tankers allow connection from either side. Thirteen-metre tankers are shown. Bay lengths are 15 m for artics, and 18 m for drawbar tankers, popular in Europe (2 m allowed at back of bay for valve clearance). Often straight-through bays are used for tankers; allow preferred clearance on each side of bay.

Loading bay layout and gate entries

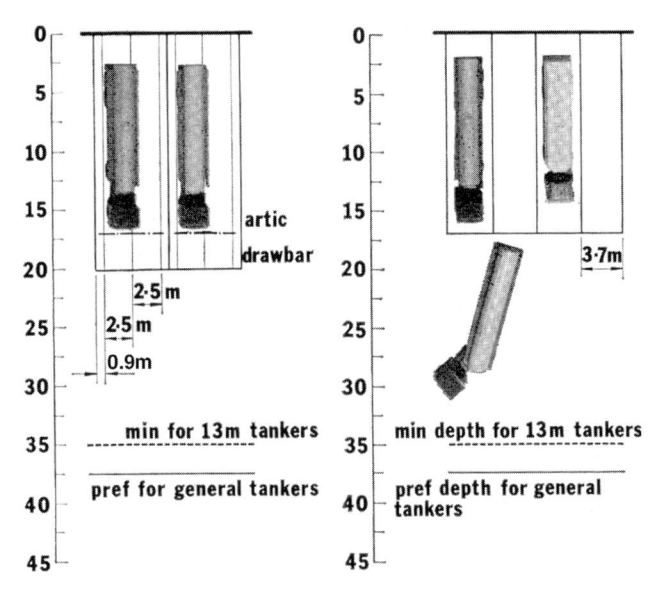

Figure 2.35 *(left) side-loading tanker bays; (Right) 3.7 m end-loading tanker bays.*

1.10 Mixed traffic bays: e.g. parcels operation. Figure 2.36a, vans are manoeuvring into accumulation bays, and reversing into 3.2 m wide loading bays for manual handling. This allows driver access and gives sufficient width for load accumulation behind the van doors. To the left are the trunk vehicle bays with a raised dock; 5 m bays allow rolls of roll pallets or special cages to accumulate. On the left, a drawbar outfit has dropped its trailer, turning round to nose it into the bay. In Figure 2.36b, ideal manoeuvring depth is measured from 5 m behind the van loading bays to allow for heaps of goods behind the vans. In both Figures 2.36a and b, the heavy trucks have to pass through the light van manoeuvring area, which can lead to peak congestion. Figure 2.36c shows the top arrowed entry for light vehicles only, and the bottom for segregated heavy trucks; the van turning area can be smaller, as it is not catering for heavy vehicle movement. In restricted sites, the access could be cut to the depth of the thick line up to the heavy vehicle manoeuvring area; an articulated unit is shown which has just turned in its own length to reverse into the free bay, and a further one is waiting positioned to begin the same manoeuvre. The drawbar outfit in the bay will find the area tight; these conflicting requirements dictate a compromise solution, depending on site characteristics and the sizes and types of vehicles expected.

1.11 Figure 2.37 shows an example of a straight-through docking area for single-sided side loading. This is often used for steel stock and other lengthy goods. Loading is on the offside for accurate vehicle positioning) and to allow the driver to descend away from the traffic. Seven metre clearance is for forklift manoeuvring. Six metre road width is adequate for passing and drawing out. See Chapter 7, Special storage.

2 Gate entries

2.01 The width of the gate and its depth from the back of the pavement line depends on the type of road, its width and frequency of use. The further back the gate from the roadway, the narrower it can be. This can now be set up in CAD to suit any plot/roadway relationship: if in doubt contact your transportation/traffic engineers. The paths shown are just a 'ready reckoner' for outline and sketch proposals for gate feasibility: always check by CAD and Autotrack.

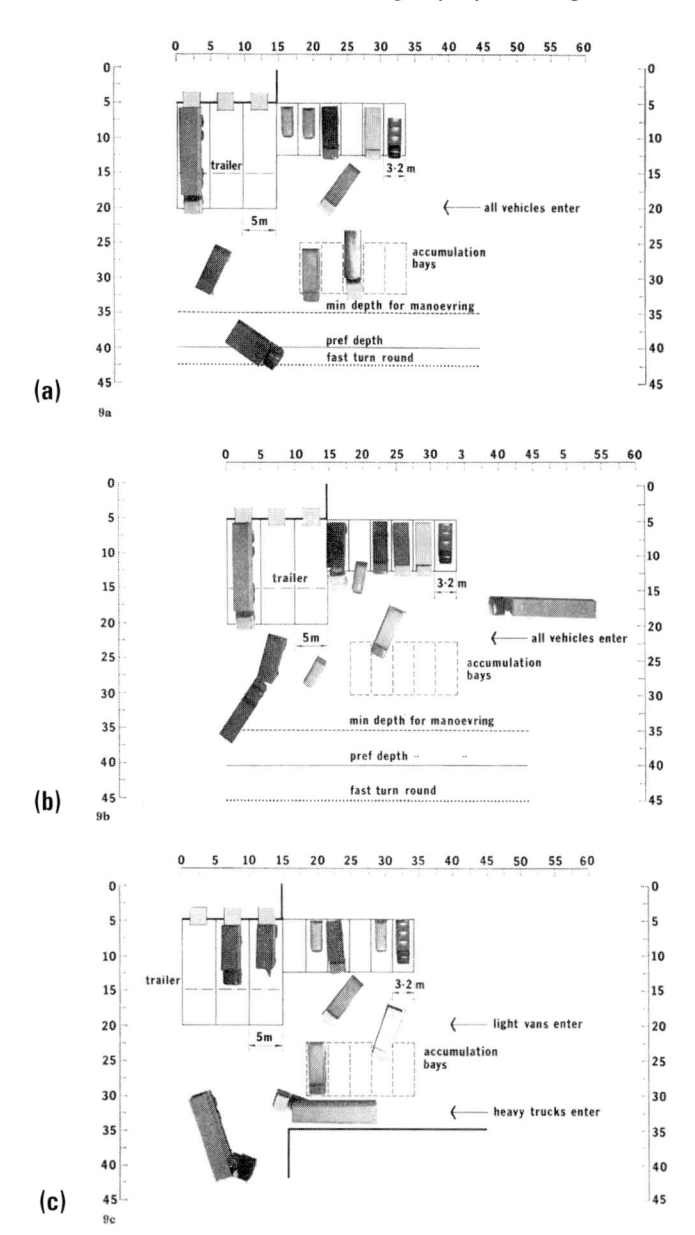

Figure 2.36 *Problems of mixed light and heavy traffic.*

2.02 Figures 2.38 to 2.41 show conventional road widths of 9.1 m, 6.1 m and 3.5 m. The narrowest is not suitable even for private one-way approach roads if a 90° turn is to be made, unless a substantial manoeuvring area is provided in front of the gate entry.

2.03 The shaded areas in Figures 2.38–2.41 represent a typical 16.5 m artic vehicle path. Information to calculate other vehicle paths is given in Information sheet, Loading 1. In all cases, the most realistic solution has been taken, with the truck swinging out into the oncoming lane to achieve the required turning circle. If this is unacceptable due to the speed and weight of traffic coming the other way, the effect will be as for the narrowest road shown, greatly increasing the width of the cross-over and the depth of the gate back from the road.

2.04 Figure 2.38 shows a one-way street. This is a typical town warehouse entry. Use can be made of the width of the carriageway for swing out to gain the required turning clearance. Figure 2.39 shows a two-way street, with vehicles entering and leaving from both directions. To allow the gate to be as near to the pavement line as possible, the trucks have to swing across the oncoming traffic when turning left. This is common practice. If unacceptable, the gate has to be further back

Loading bay layout and gate entries

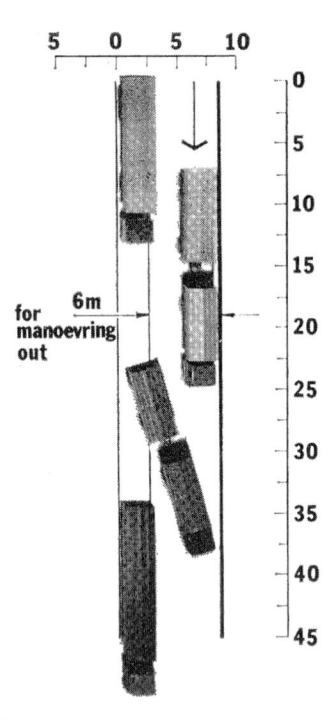

Figure 2.37 *Straight-through dock for single-sided side loading.*

and the cross-over wider; i.e. the truck will use the narrower road widths.

2.05 If two-way traffic is of sufficient frequency to merit a wide entry gate (Figure 2.40), this allows simultaneous movement. A typical situation is shown where complete clearance at all cut-in points between the two vehicles would be wasteful. This is a typical situation of a warehouse at the end of a service road.

2.06 Figure 2.41 is suitable for busy two-way traffic approaching from both directions. In some cases, such as entries to container ports and groupage centres, the traffic volume is sufficient to merit clearance for simultaneous movement for entry and exit in both directions. A typical situation has been illustrated, where the clearances are sufficient for movement but not enough for vehicles to pass when actually making the 90° turn. This would increase the width of the entry by over 50 per cent and would also demand that the gate position intrude further into the site. The diagrams are considered acceptable for slow speed work, where there is good visibility. For this reason, boundaries should be in the form of wire-mesh fencing, rather than walls, to allow for long-distance sight lines; incoming vehicle drivers can see outgoing vehicles before they enter the gate zone and this prevents vehicles being caught when swinging across oncoming traffic. If high-speed cornering and full passing on the bend are required, this should be considered as highway engineering and is not a gate entry situation. Contact the local authority.

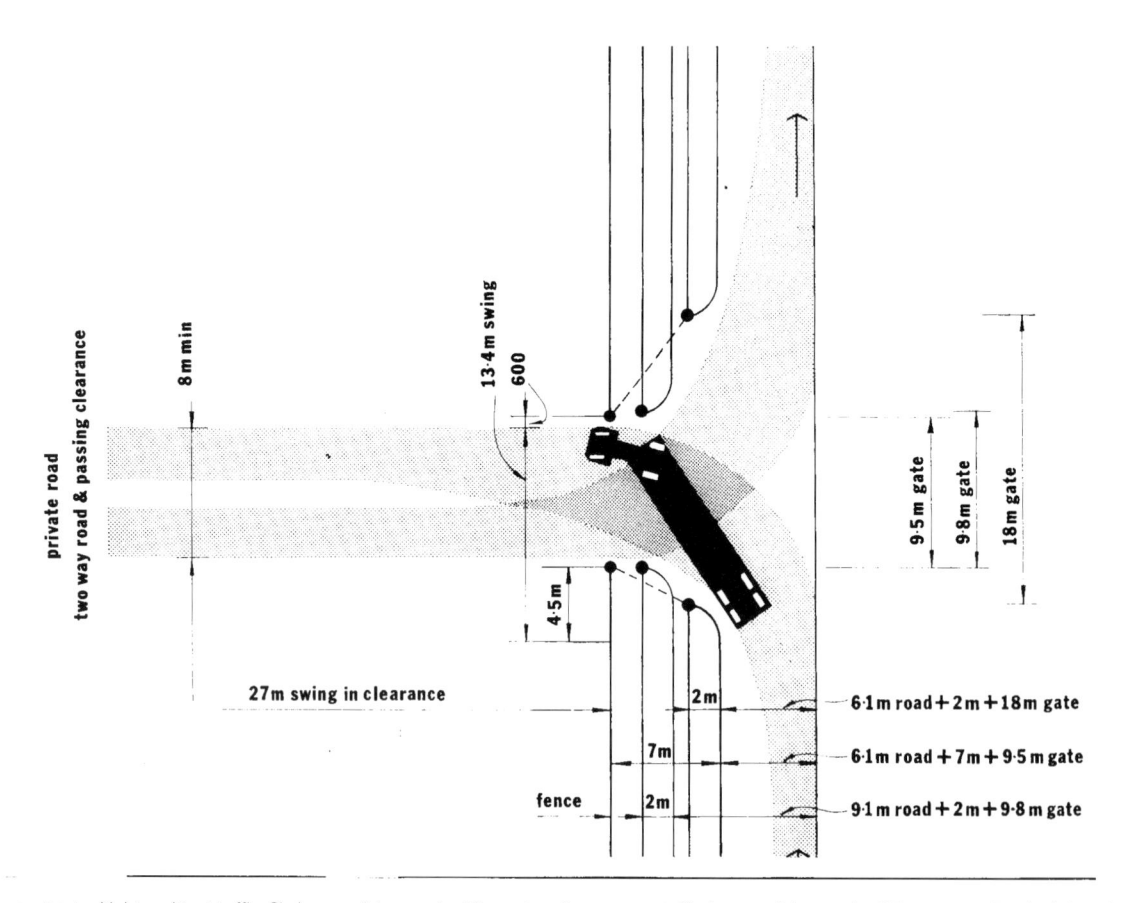

Figure 2.38 *One-way street with intermittent traffic. Choice one: 6.1 m road + 18 m gate + 2 m pavement. Choice two: 6.1 m road + 9.5 m gate set 7 m back from front edge of pavement. Choice three: 9.1 m road + 9.8 m gate set 2 m back from front edge of pavement.*

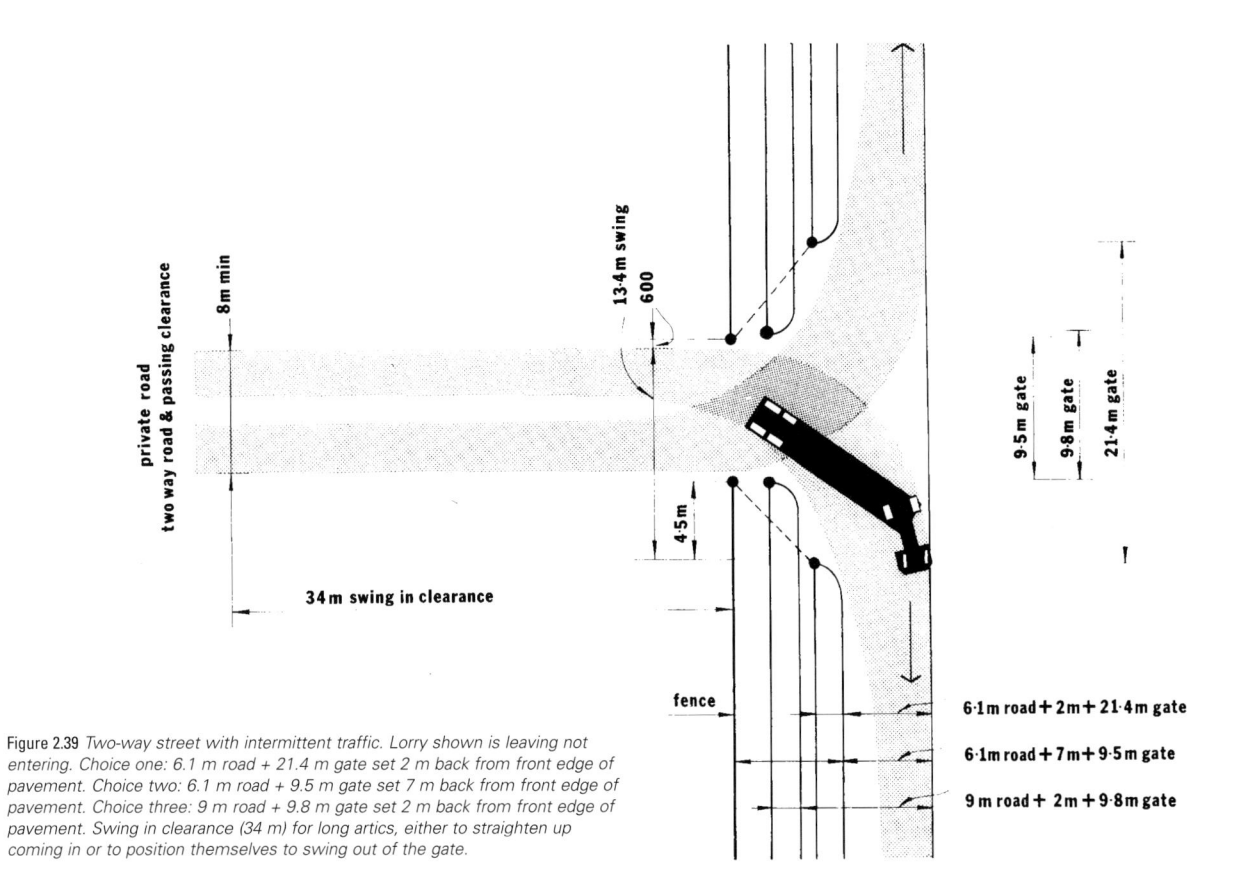

Loading bay layout and gate entries

Figure 2.39 *Two-way street with intermittent traffic. Lorry shown is leaving not entering. Choice one: 6.1 m road + 21.4 m gate set 2 m back from front edge of pavement. Choice two: 6.1 m road + 9.5 m gate set 7 m back from front edge of pavement. Choice three: 9 m road + 9.8 m gate set 2 m back from front edge of pavement. Swing in clearance (34 m) for long artics, either to straighten up coming in or to position themselves to swing out of the gate.*

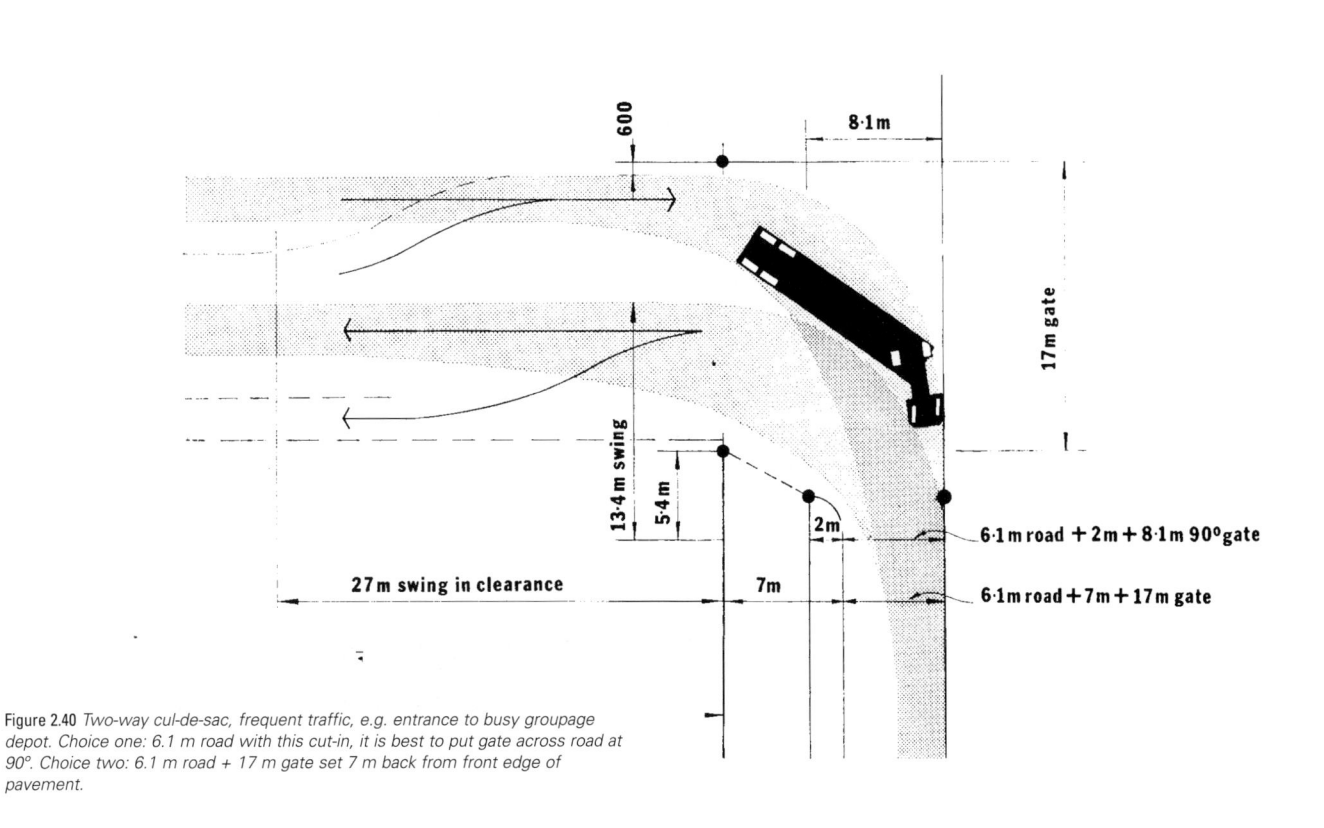

Figure 2.40 *Two-way cul-de-sac, frequent traffic, e.g. entrance to busy groupage depot. Choice one: 6.1 m road with this cut-in, it is best to put gate across road at 90°. Choice two: 6.1 m road + 17 m gate set 7 m back from front edge of pavement.*

37

Loading bay layout and gate entries

Figure 2.41 *Frequent two-way traffic. This is designed to allow two drivers to pass in typical working situation. Choice one: 6.1 m road + 28 m gate set 2 m back from front edge of pavement [en] this is uneconomic, and only used if building is very close to boundary. Choice two: 6.1 m road width + 17 m gate set 7 m back from front edge of pavement. Choice three: 9.1 m road + 20 m gate set 2 m back from front edge of pavement. Choice four: 9.1 m road + 17 m gate set 4.2 m back from front edge of pavement.*

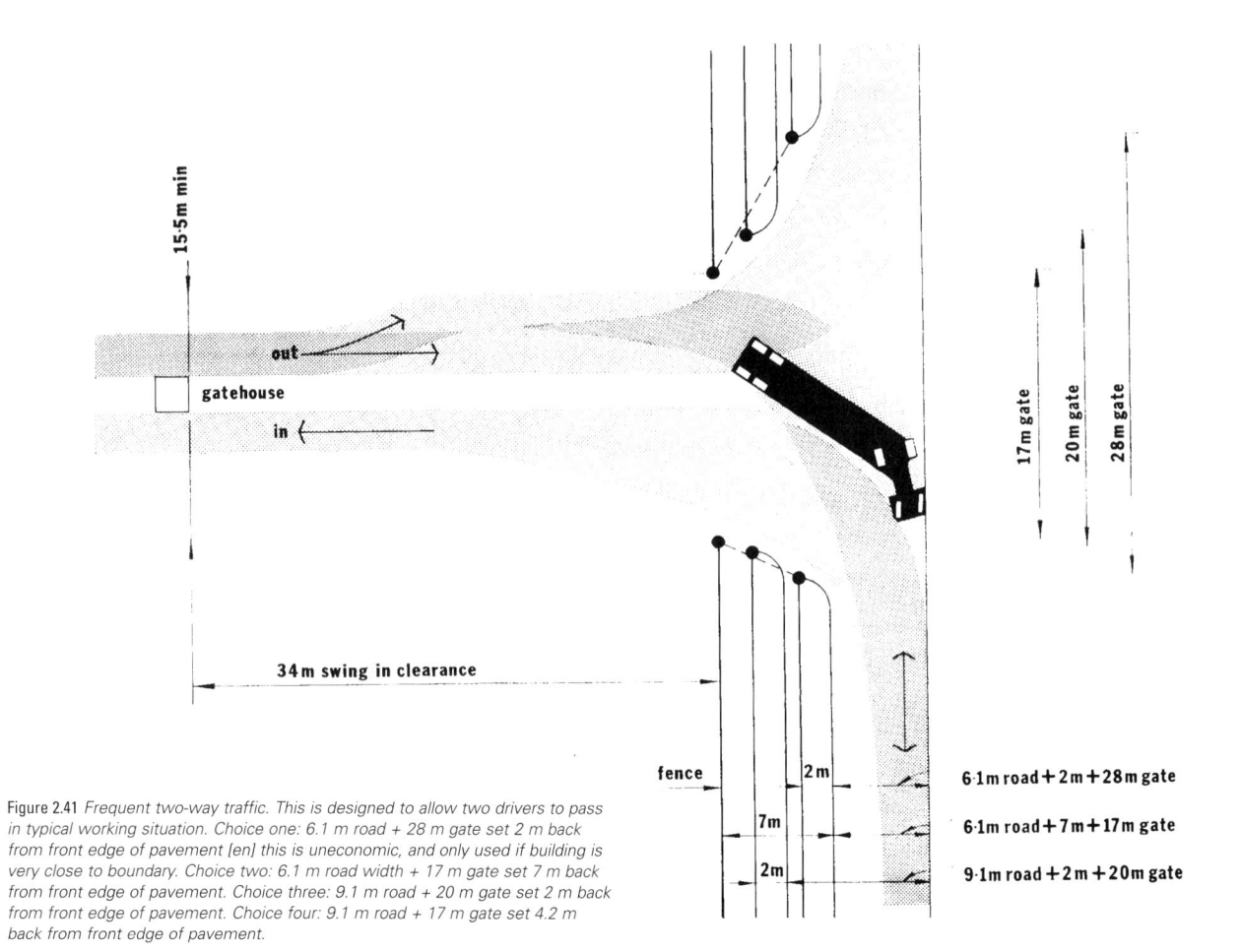

Figure 2.42 *Herringbone loading dock: note how lateral dimension of vehicle manoeuvring area is reduced. This clock is now more than 30 years old and still works.*

38

INFORMATION SHEET

Loading 3

Waste handling equipment

1 Introduction

2 Waste handling equipment

This section gives information on types and dimensions of waste handling equipment.

1 Introduction

1.01 As a result of the EU Waste Directive expressing the view that 'the polluter pays', industry and authorities have become committed to waste segregation and recovery, and more aware of the dangers from pollution by industrial waste products. Legislation prohibits dumping of toxic, corrosive and dangerous products into drainage systems, onto waste land or into rivers. Specialist companies are now available with national container hire and collection services for waste products, which take on the responsibility for segregating and processing the waste for eventual disposal. Much research has been done on the recycling of waste products, to reduce the drain on natural resources, and into the possibility of generating power from products that have to be destroyed.

1.02 This information sheet illustrates the type of equipment available for waste handling, and the planning requirements for its inclusion in buildings. It is not only concerned with industrial by-products, but with refuse collected in warehouses and supermarkets, generated by the increasing use of disposable packaging. It could also apply to residential areas, which may soon have centrally placed compaction plant feeding containers, reducing the large amount of open space devoted to turning areas for refuse vehicles, and as a result of the diminishing labour resources for refuse collection.

2 Waste handling equipment

Compaction machinery

2.01 Waste packaging materials from de-trashing product in storage and order-picking operations should be segregated and baled or if there is sufficient (say 30 cu m/day uncompacted), compacted into a skip, which is carted away by a specialist service provider. Before it is dumped into the skip, waste may be reduced in bulk by a compactor. Compactors are either built in, or, for smaller installations, are mobile and can be carried like a skip from building to building as required. Skips used with compactors are always enclosed skips, unlike the familiar open skips used in the construction industry.

2.02 Static compactors are available in a large range of capacities. The most common type, as used in hospitals, warehouses and housing areas, is not space consuming, and loads at compaction densities of 550 kg/m^3 into 8 to 30 m^3 skips (Figure 2.43). Accessories are marketed to suit special requirements, such as hydraulic tipping mechanisms for large, wheeled bins, 'Eurocarts' (Figure 2.44),

Figure 2.43 *Static compactor with 20 cubic metre skip placed on dedicated raised dock.*

Figure 2.44 *Device for tipping 1100 litre bins into compactor.*

Waste handling equipment

and chutes and hoppers for hand loading. Compaction is operated by hydraulic power, activated by an electric pump, on normal three-phase supply.

Figure 2.45 *Static compactor and skip placed outside the building and fed by chute from the first floor.*

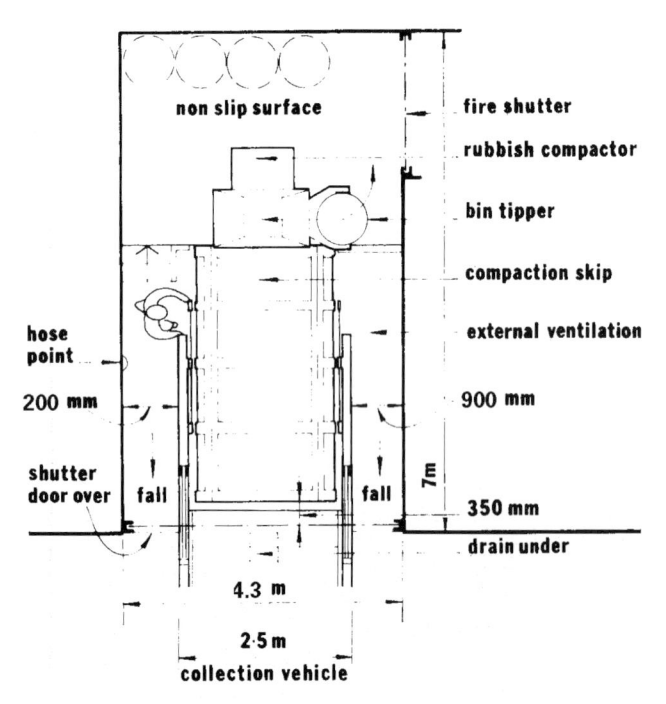

Figure 2.46 *Dimensions of waste handling area with compaction skip. The collection vehicle is a lift-on type. Seven metres typical for small containers and normal handling space (manual)*

Figure 2.47 *30 m skip in loading bay attached to clock-mounted static compactor.*

2.03 Compactors can be placed either in or outside the building (Figure 2.45). If internally mounted, the machine can be sealed against smells and vermin; a typical unit will fit in a space 7.7 m long (including the 10 m^3 skip), 5.2 m wide, allowing for space for the operator (see Figure 2.46). Planning depends on the waste collection system used, for instance whether mechanical sweepers will be dumping from the base of their collection hoppers into a compactor set in a pit, or whether wheeled bins are tipped hydraulically into the compactor, set at floor level. The collection skip position must be at the same level as the compactor's outlet, and it is often the collection vehicle's access and the provision for the skip that finally decides the planning for the compactor space. If the collection system for the compactor is not sealed, the input position should be clearly marked, well guarded and fitted with easily seen safety cut-out points; space should be left round the compactor, for collecting spillage. Design of waste disposal areas is shown in Figures 2.46 and 2.47).

2.04 Approaches at both input and skip positions should be clearly lit. Skips designed for pressure packing are sized according to the application and the capacity of the compactor, and, although of similar appearance, vary in detail according to the collection method for the vehicle. Contact the user about preferences, and expansion potential.

Skip collection vehicles

2.05 These employ two basic methods – winch or drag-on, and lift-on. Lift systems are the conventional skips used in the building industry, with hydraulic side arms which swing over the skip and lift it up onto the flat bed of the vehicle (Figure 2.48b). The disadvantage here is in internal positions, where a typical 4.3 m ceiling clearance is required (but up to 5 m to satisfy some city authorities).

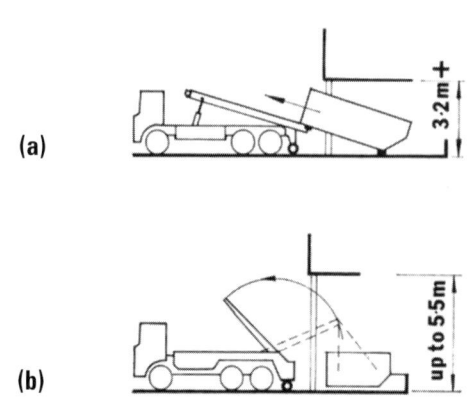

Figure 2.48 *Headroom dimensions of (a) drag-on skip and (b) lift-on skip.*

Refuse areas have been seen which require the skip collection vehicle to drag the skip out to gain lifting clearance, and to push the empty unit into position. This wrecks the floor surface quickly, and can damage the skip, the compactor and the vehicle.

2.06 The drag-on system is less suitable for confined situations. The skip is either dragged on with a hydraulic arm, or winched up guides on the vehicle's chassis requiring a minimum of 5.5 m head clearance. In some cases the truck can remain outside the skip chamber (Figure 2.48a), and can position the empty unit accurately onto the compactor, under full control (Figure 2.49). The skip is usually fitted with a roller at the rear end for partial support as it is dragged towards the vehicle, the front having been lifted clear; some trucks are also fitted with a roller that is lowered as a stabilizer during the lifting operation. Check that the weight transmitted through this will not crack the floor. Vehicles for 10–12 cu m skips are normally in the 17 tonne gross class, with two axles. The larger skips, up to 30 m3 capacity, are collected by 32 tonne four-axle rigids, depending on the weight of compacted material. Should the larger compaction skip transfer be inside the building, allow 5.5 m clear height. Typical turning circles are:

 16.2 tonne two-axle rigid; 3.8 m wheelbase; 18.28 m
 24.3 tonne three-axle rigid; 18.28 m
 30.4 tonne four-axle rigid; 21.34 m

For a centralized, large scale compactor, e.g. for a major industrial complex, articulated vehicles are beginning to be used in conjunction with large capacity drag-on skips.

(a)

(b)

Figure 2.49 (a) *30 cu m skips outside the building attached to static compactors in this printing works;* (b) *30 m³ skip with static compactor located at the raised dock of this warehouse.*

Special purpose skips and tanks

2.07 Because of increasing public concern about dangerous liquids, tank units have been produced for handling by skip-carrying vehicles. Both basic skip systems can be used for this; the tanks tend to be specifically designed for the liquid concerned. Contact the factory inspector, fire officer, petroleum officer, the user's insurers and the disposal contractor about special connection points and emergency provision. In case of accidental spillage, tank areas should have wash down facilities and interceptor gulleys. Special purpose skips are used for materials like hot solids and swarf. Swarf handling is now more sophisticated, with oil recovery and compression into bales being increasingly used.

2.08 Skip areas for should have provision for washing down, and a non-slip surface. Hydraulic Eurocart tippers are available, although some operators prefer to build a ramp to tip in the refuse. One system employs bins that are handled by a forklift truck, which lifts the bin and tips it over the skip.

2.09 One form of skip collection by a compactor vehicle very popular in the USA, the Dumpster, has arms that allow the vehicle to be nosed up to the container, pick it up in full view of the driver and then reverse to a position with sufficient headroom for the arms to raise the skip over the top of its compactor for discharge (Figure 2.50).

2.10 The truck then replaces the skip in position. Note: the term 'Dumpster' is used as a generic for all skips in the USA. The Lo-skip can carry ordinary or compaction skips in low headroom and confined areas, and can operate under 2.1 m minimum clearances. This could be useful in applications such as the collection of waste from old premises with low-slung pipes (Figure 2.51).

2.11 When designing for skips with side connection points, design the space with sufficient width to allow the driver to fix the chains, with the skip off centre.

Figure 2.50 *Front-loading bin collection vehicle: the front lift-arms empty the bin over the cab.*

Figure 2.51 *Skip collection vehicle for areas with low headroom, 3.6 m.*

Loading 4
Industrial doors

INFORMATION SHEET

1 Use

This section gives information on types of doors for internal and external use.

1 Use

1.01 While doors to industrial storage buildings are primarily for access, they also have to provide security, weather protection and thermal insulation. The ways the doors will be used depends on the type of storage; some remain open all day, some, e.g. in cold stores, continuously open and close, while others seldom open, e.g. for waste collection skip bays. There is a wide range of door types and sizes, with specifications tailored to particular applications. Table 2.2 gives typical door types in general use, with their principal applications. Figures 2.52 and 2.53 illustrate some typical doors in use.

External doors
1.02 The three generic types are doors enclosing a ground level loading area, through which vehicles pass for over-the-side loading, doors attached to loading banks and rapid rise doors out to yard areas.
1.03 Ground-level doors for wide openings can be sliding, sliding-folding (the most usual) and vertical roller or telescopic shutter types. Sliding and sliding-folding doors can be powered, but require guide rails at the base that are liable to become filled with dirt, and present a drainage problem.
1.04 Horizontally sliding doors are useful where handling plant will pass through frequently. Sliding/folding or horizontally sliding/shutter doors only need open to the width of vehicle passing through, so the minimum area is open to elements. Vertical nesting doors or roller shutters need to open to the full width and height of the vehicle, resulting in greater heat loss, more dust and rain intrusion. 'Fast' doors have been introduced to solve this problem in busy access areas; these are also called 'rapid roll' doors, opening and closing in 3–4 seconds, triggered by inductive loops in the floor or *photo eyes*. If a panel of a sliding-folding door is damaged, it is usually still openable, whereas if a nesting door is damaged, e.g. by forklift mast, the whole door jams. Ground-level doors should have an external canopy for weather protection extending at least 5 m forward of the opening and 3 m on either side (see Technical Study Loading bay design, Figure 2.9). The canopy will reduce the amount of water brought into the warehouse by delivery vehicles, helping to keep the floor dry (forklift trucks can skid on damp, smooth floor surfaces). A drain channel with a grill pattern to squeeze moisture out of tyres fitted outside the door rail has been used successfully.

Rapid rise doors
1.05 Doors large enough to accept ISO containers on skeletal trailers and big box vans are available with power assistance; they are made of a stretched fabric, with rapid rise drums opening and closing in 3–4 seconds. The acti-

Figure 2.52 *Sectional overhead doors.*

Figure 2.53 *Fast door between a load assembly area and external loading bay; here it is rising as the forklift approaches it.*

Industrial doors

Table 2.2 Typical doors and applications

Type	Material, Width x height (m) St / Tm / Al	Electric hydraulic or pneumatic	Special requirements	Ideal applications	Suitability for fire doors	Resistance to damage	Insulated doors
Sliding shutter	30 x 6	Yes	Track in floor is vulnerable to damage	Wide openings where vehicles manoeuvre; where security is important	Poor on large doors	Good	No
Up-and-over	9.1 x 6 / 6 x 6 / 0.9 x 6	Yes	Not ideal above 9.1 m width between jambs	Garages and loading banks; good security	Average	Good	Good
Roller shutters	9.1x6 / 7.6x6 / 9.1x6	Yes	Not ideal above 9.1 m in width between jambs	Garages, loading banks; fair security	Poor (Good if in pairs)	Average	No
Sliding doors	No limit	Yes	Room to slide into when open. Bottom guide required on wider openings	For economy or where clear opening is not required; fair security	Good	Good	Good
Hinged doors	9.1x9 / 6x6 / 7.6x7.6	Not ideal	Strong jambs, level floors and space outside building for when door is open	Where a cheap, small, secure door is required; good security	Fair	Average	Fair
Collapsible gates	15.2x6 / Not suitable / 9.1x6	Yes	Guide in threshold required	Where security and vision are required	Impossible	Poor	No
Flexible doors	3x4.5 made of rubber or plastic in steel frame	-	Firm side fixing. Limited air pressure	For internal use where a draught stopper is required for busy openings; also as secondary closers to external door openings which can be left open during working hours yet allow fork trucks to push through	Not suitable	Good	No

St = Steel; Tm = timber; Al = aluminium.

vation is by proximity sensors generally set in the floor. Be careful about applications facing the prevailing wind, as they are constructed like a sail and can blow out of the side guides. Check that there is manual provision in case of power cuts; in some cases this is difficult.

Doors for raised dock loading bays

1.06 Raised dock loading bays are discussed in Technical study, Loading 1, and in Storage process, paras 6 and 7.

1.07 There are two types of external doors for raised docks: door incorporated into a dock shelter, or similar construction surrounding each dock leveller. The vehicle reverses into position within the dock shelter, itself forming a weather seal. A roller shutter door is then wound up, and the dock leveller adjusted to the truck's floor level. This door is often used in cold stores, incorporating insulated door panels. With insulation, it is impractical to use roller shutters, so the door usually follows guides parallel with the dock ceiling; this requires low-output heaters to prevent the mechanism icing in cold stores.

Internal doors

1.08 These must allow forklift trucks and similar plant to move through; transparent rapid rise doors are often now used. They are often opened by pressure pads or photoelectric cells. Impact doors are also useful; these are manufactured from a flexible material, usually reinforced rubber. These are used where draught stopping and vehicle movement are more important than speed. Rapid rise doors can keep out draughts between zones and between a loading dock and the store, and are sometimes fitted behind sliding or shutter doors, left open during normal operation, but shut for security at night. If used on a two-way flow circulation route, they should be fitted with see-through panels and pads activating a warning siren. Doors to isolate fire zones are normally roller shutter or sliding on an inclined track, activated by fusible links.

Security

1.09 While all doors can be made secure against intruders, the cost of providing security locks, thief-proof hinges and a strengthened door can be very high; check the requirements of the user's insurer. Large doors have been pulled from their mountings by determined thieves who attach chains and haul them out with a lorry. There are sophisticated alarm systems for use with large doors, but some are troublesome, such as light beams which are activated by any bird that is caught inside the warehouse.

1.10 For cold store door requirements, see Chapter 6, Cold storage.

1.11 There is no substitute for a properly constructed personnel door alongside a vehicle entrance. Machinery and personnel should be segregated where possible, and although there are ingenious solutions of wicket doors in the main door structure, a separate door gives more security and can have full fire escape rating, with easy operation and no risk of fouling.

INFORMATION SHEET

Loading 5

Loading dock equipment

1 **Dock levellers**
2 **Bumper pads**
3 **Dock shelters**
4 **Dock lights**

This section gives information on types and makes of equipment used in the loading dock.

1 Dock levellers

1.01 Dock levellers are not a luxury. Only by the correct choice and application of equipment can a loading bay reach its full potential (Figure 2.54). Always consider dock leveller investment in terms of long-term costs to the user, of the potential increase in numbers of vehicles handled, of pallet truck and forklift truck battery life and tyre bills. Steep gradients, short leveller plates and tight turns on chequer plate ramps to save space are not an economy.

Figure 2.54 *Typical loading bay. Dock levellers are spaced apart to allow loads to accumulate behind vans, as there is limited rear space.*

1.02 There are several types of dock leveller, designed to suit specific requirements.

Conventional dock levellers

1.03 The gradient should never exceed 1 in 10. Length of dock leveller plate is a function of height differential between the vehicle and the dock surface. Container floors can be 1.55 m above the ground, and vehicles can rise 150 mm as they are unloaded.

1.04 There are three types of leveller operation: Counter-balanced, mechanical and hydraulic. Counter-balanced levellers tend to be considered old-fashioned, and can suffer from bounce under load conditions. They require deep pits to accept weights. Mechanical dock levellers (Figure 2.55) are the most popular in Britain. They work on a spring-loading principle. Pits can be very shallow (430 mm from one manufacturer). These are well-tried units and are virtually maintenance free after initial spring adjustment. Hydraulic levellers (Figure 2.56) are the norm

Figure 2.55 *Mechanical dock leveller in raised position, showing connections and depth of pit required.*

Figure 2.56 *Hydraulic dock leveller. These are for light vans and so are nearer the ground than usual.*

in Europe. They are more expensive than mechanical types, and are particularly suited to heavy-duty operation. Because they are quiet in operation, they can be used in urban areas, where the 'clang' of a mechanical leveller hitting the truck deck during night loading would be unacceptable to local residents. Hydraulic levellers usually employ individual pump units: new standards in reliability in hydraulics allow the use of centralized pumps for a range of levellers without fear of total breakdown. Consider cost of hydraulic pipe work against individual small pumps: the latter has proved to be cheaper in the past.

Loading dock equipment

Builder's work

1.05 Few dock leveller manufacturers include for builder's work in their quotations, either for forming the pit, or for drilling and grouting fixing points. Leveller pits can be costly. Check the leveller's tolerances from the manufacturer; usually pits have to be very accurate. Installation problems seldom occur when manufacturers can supply a sub-frame for building in. Top plates can also be manufactured without excessive side clearances (up to 40 mm).

Free-standing levellers

1.06 If enough space is available, consider free-standing dock levellers (Figure 2.57). These are standard levellers mounted in a steel sub-frame with integral legs, standing in front of the raised dock. In some cases, this has been cheaper than forming pits, especially in existing buildings. Free-standing levellers cost more than the basic unit.

Figure 2.57 *Dock levellers added to existing tobacco warehouses to allow rear loading of containers or side loading of flat trailers.*

1.07 Where existing premises need a higher dock to suit the high container floors, a very long leveller plate is often required to meet the maximum 1 in 10 gradient. This is often uneconomic: a successful solution could be to build a free-standing gradient of chequer plate out from the dock face, equipped with a standard free-standing leveller. This can be angled to suit vehicle reversing lines in constricted premises.

1.08 Most levellers are available in 1.8 m and 2.1 m widths. Dock levellers are mostly equipped with spring-loaded lip plates (Figure 2.58). These fold back on impact to form a bumper surface, and a flush finish when not in operation. They spring up and out, directly the leveller plate is lifted to meet a vehicle. It is worth specifying these for security, as when the leveller is not in use, and the lip is folded flush with the dock, a roller shutter door can be located into a pocket in the leveller surface and a strong, intruder-proof barrier is formed.

1.09 Specify dock levellers that can tilt, for trucks also tilt on their springs as they are unloaded. If the leveller cannot tilt, the loading equipment's tyres will be damaged and the loads may topple over.

Flush folding dock levellers

1.10 The folding dock leveller (Figure 2.59a/b) is useful where no pit can be formed or where most vehicles suit the height of the dock and the cost of a full leveller installation would not be justified. These units can be face mounted directly into the concrete, equipped with big buffer pads so that trucks can reverse right up to the dock face. The leveller plate is spring loaded, and is lifted vertically by an operative as the truck backs onto the pads. It then hinges down to form a bridging plate (usually 1.8 m wide). These are basically folding dock-to-vehicle bridge plates and should not be used where any great variation between vehicle floor heights is anticipated. When the vehicle leaves, the leveller folds back vertically flush with dock face.

Figure 2.58 *Typical dock leveller showing lip plate in retracted position and bumper pads.*

Figure 2.59 (a) *Folding dock leveller for use in constricted space.* (b) *Dock board takes up small variations in height.*

Mobile dock levellers

1.11 In areas with constricted manoeuvring space, quick turn round is often more important than the simultaneous unloading of several vehicles. A mobile dock leveller (Figure 2.60) is available, which is basically a hydraulic dock leveller running on a carriage mounted on rails, bolted to the dock face. Its advantage is that valuable time need not be wasted by big trucks struggling to manoeuvre accurately in a tight space. Another successful application is in bays used mostly by light vans, where

Loading dock equipment

Figure 2.60 Mobile dock leveller can slide along rails bolted to dock face. Useful for old buildings where trucks have difficulty in positioning accurately.

time would be wasted shunting vans to make way for a large vehicle. The truck can position wherever there is room and the leveller can be slid along to its rear door position (Figure 2.61). When not in use, the plate can be lifted nearly vertical, and the unit pushed to an unobtrusive corner. These are useful for rail-side operation, allowing flexibility in positioning.

Figure 2.61 Mobile dock leveller.

Elevating docks and lift tables

1.12 These are small scissor lifts, and are available as mobile units. They are especially useful when converting existing premises. Typical uses include:
1. where the warehouse floor is at ground level, and there is no room for a ramp, or no money for a raised dock to be built.
2. where the existing dock is too low for modern vehicles and there is neither room for a long leveller plate, nor for a free-standing dock extension with a leveller (Figure 2.62). The elevating dock can be positioned at the best angle to suit the reversing line, and can be fitted with shaped side plates to meet the angle of the existing dock when lowered. Full-sized units to lift up forklift trucks are available. Elevating stop bars prevent pallet trucks rolling off during lifting: they can be controlled from the ground or by a man riding up with the table.
3. when building a raised loading dock in a ground level warehouse. The elevating dock bridges the gap between warehouse floor and dock surface, saving space and adding flexibility over a ramp.

1.13 Mobile versions (Figure 2.63) are useful in urban areas, for handling numbers of roll pallets at shop or school premises. They are in direct competition with vehicles equipped with tailboard lifts. Not all suppliers' vehicles have tail lifts, and they are often out of action due to bent guide rails caused by drivers backing too hard into docks. Power is usually from an integral electric motor/hydraulic pump unit, from mains supply or battery. Ten-second operating cycles are possible: maintenance is low.

Figure 2.62 Elevating dock used where the old dock (left) is too low, and a dock leveller would reach too steep a gradient in the space available. Note raising lip to prevent wheeled dolleys rolling off platform.

Figure 2.63 Mobile dock leveller loading roll pallets.

2 Bumper pads

2.01 Vehicles can impose high-impact loadings to docks, even at low speeds. To prevent damage, stacked rubber composition bumper pads should be fitted to the dock. This is not a luxury, a 177 kN kg trailer travelling at 2 kph will cause an impact of about 667 kN kg. Twenty-five millimetres of cushioning will reduce this to 78 kN. Reinforced concrete docks have disintegrated under constant impact. Check with the leveller manufacturer about the correct height and pitch for fixing (see Figure 2.58).

47

Loading dock equipment

3 Dock shelters

3.01 A typical dock shelter (Figure 2.64) consists of a flexible material, e.g. reinforced polythene sheet, bonded to a steel frame, standing proud of the building face, with a truck-side face of rubber pads or a pneumatic seal. This is placed over a dock leveller position to form a hermetic seal between an enclosed loading dock and a box trailer or container. This is necessary for cold storage areas and in handling perishable foodstuffs and electronic equipment. There is no need for a canopy. Advantages are weather protection, security and dust protection. Management often considers them a luxury for our temperate climate and cost. Check unit cost against that of a canopy. Extending shelters are also available for rail-side use.

Figure 2.64 *(left) Enclosed loading bay with dock shelter: retracted leveller with shutter door locked into leveller plate. (below) Flexible sheet type dock shelter.*

4 Dock lights

4.01 Containers and vans are too long for effective light penetration. Accidents and damage have occurred due to lack of light and glare caused by the difference between internal and external light levels. Integral container lights are frequently broken. Spring-loaded dock lights are useful. They are available with one to three joints, and with extended lengths of up to 2.3 m.

5 Loading ramps

5.01 These are useful for loading vehicles by forklift truck or powered pallet truck from ground level. They are usually made of steel in one or two sections, mounted on a mobile frame with securing jacks that screw down to the ground. Because the gradient must not exceed 1 in 10, they are space-consuming in operation and when stored. They are too narrow (1.8 m) for unloading cars from containers (see Technical study, Loading 1, Figure 2.17).

6 Extending conveyors

6.01 These are for stuffing containers and trucks manually to achieve maximum volume (Figure 2.65). The conveyors can be dock or ground mounted. They can move vertically, turn on their axis, and extend to the end of a container, retracting as the vehicle is loaded. Especially useful in groupage depots, where deep-sea services require maximum volume loading. They are used extensively in Europe for loading rail wagons with goods like sacks. (See Technical study, Bulk storage, and Information sheet, Mechanized storage 8 and 9.)

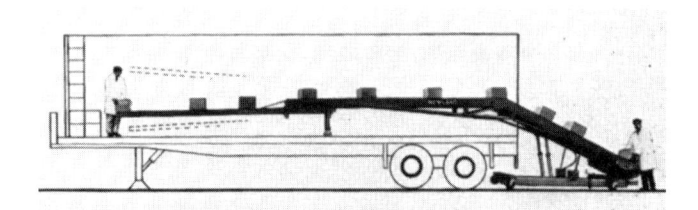

Figure 2.65 *Extendible conveyor loading a container to maximum possible volume.*

INFORMATION SHEET

Loading 6

Railway layouts

1 Dimensions of rail wagons and track

This section gives design data on layouts of railway wagon track. It is to be used for general guidance only, as Network Rail should be consulted about any detailed plans for linking storage with railway tracks.

1 Dimensions of rail wagons and track

1.01 This information sheet is not intended to act as a basis of design for rail-track alignment, curve radii or points design. Network Rail should always be contacted concerning any advance plans to link a warehouse to nearby railway tracks. Each 'territory', which replaces the old rail region, has a civil engineering depot, and there is also a civil engineering department for each division now often managed by a third party contractor.

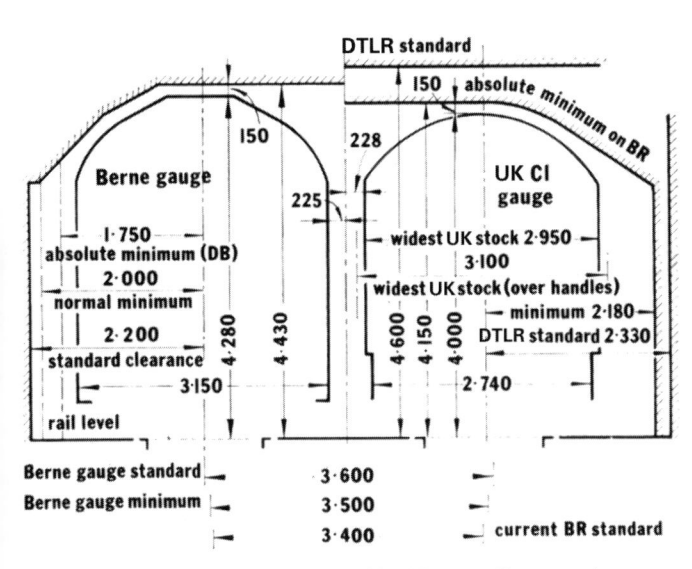

Figure 2.66 *Cross-section comparing typical UK and European (Berne gauge) standards for rolling stock giving controlling dimensions for use in railway planning: design elements (bridges, platforms, etc.) must be clear of these profiles.*

1.02 A guide to designing spaces surrounding rail wagons is shown in Figure 2.66. Walls, foot and pipe bridges, and platforms (if straight), must be clear of these controlling dimensions. It is safer to plan track foundations for the maximum axle loadings of a typical wagon in use of 25.4 tonnes. Figure 2.67a/b shows lengths and overhangs in relation to the wheel base; this data is useful in calculating cut-in and swing-out on curves, so that adequate clearance is allowed for personnel or plant between the trucks and a wall. Some railway lines and sidings have restrictions on loading: check this with Railtrack before proceeding with design. Remember if planning unloading on a curved siding, that the camber of the track is liable to lower the base of door runners on box vans by several millimetres; make sure that this will not foul platform edges on the cut-in.

1.03 If using dry goods, the type of wagon most likely to be received are high-speed, two-axle, side-loading vans, designed especially for forklift access with palletized dry goods. These have a maximum load and truck weight of 35.5 tonnes, and long, sliding doors. The container-carrying flat trucks are approximately 19 m long, and are bogey units with 17.7 tonne axle loads. A bridge plate is needed for forklift access to wagon mounted side door containers; the 2.4 m container width is approximately 300 mm less than a normal wagon.

(a)

axle load tonnes	min overhang m	min wheelbase m	min dimensions adj wagons m
17.7	1.06	3.65	2.13
25.4	1.52	4.5	3.04

(b)

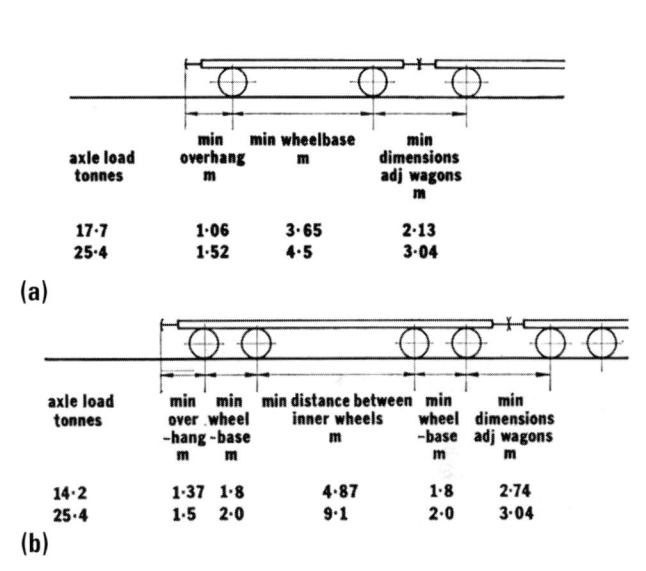

axle load tonnes	min over-hang m	min wheel-base m	min distance between inner wheels m	min wheel-base m	min dimensions adj wagons m
14.2	1.37	1.8	4.87	1.8	2.74
25.4	1.5	2.0	9.1	2.0	3.04

Figure 2.67 (a) *Two-axle wagon dimensions.* (b) *Bogie wagon dimensions.*

Truck and platform height

1.04 There may be a problem of relating levels of the new 'Lowliner' container flat trucks (Figure 2.68). These are designed to carry 2.59 m high containers within the loading gauge. Conventional container flat trucks and Freightliner trucks have a rail-to-bed height of a nominal 965.2 mm, but this can vary 50 mm between wagon types whereas the 'Lowliner' is only 836.6 mm. One hundred millimetres average depth of container floor should be added to these dimensions for forklift access. Side loading allows little tolerance for floor height variation if forklifts are to be used freely. If different types of trucks are delivered, an operator will be faced with unloading one of the truck types manually. The alternatives are:

1 Remove all containers from rail trucks before loading.
2 Run forklifts at ground level; this requires some manual intervention to push pallets to the container door, which is likely anyway, especially if full volume stuffing is required for deep-sea services.

Railway layouts

3 Install the dock to 'Lowliner' height, and have a raised section, using a scissor lift for example. Often container wagons come in units of three, with a total length of approximately 59.3 m, buffer to buffer, so this would be expensive.

1.05 Solution 2 seems the most flexible, but negates the use of the new two-axle trucks designed for pallet handling from a raised dock. Designers should therefore carefully examine the type of traffic to be handled before they make a decision on the platform height.

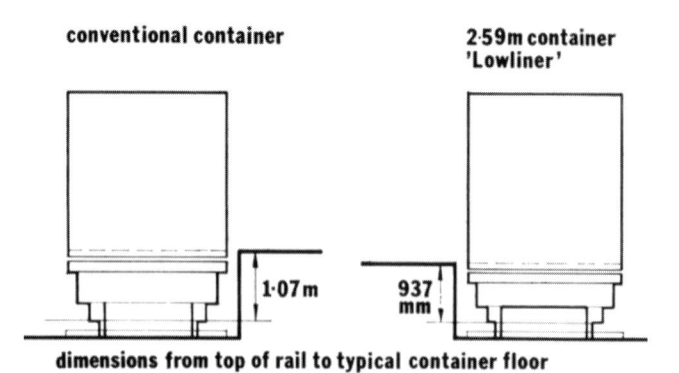

Figure 2.68 *Container wagon floors have different heights, and may also vary up to 100 mm in laden and unladen condition. To run with 2.59 m (8'6") high containers within the UK W6A gauge some international wagon sets are now 825 mm above rail level: for even taller containers and future cross Channel 'piggy back' trailer services drop well 'pocket' wagon sets are already in service with beds only 475 mm above the rails, requiring containers to be lifted out for discharge.*

1.06 Shunting methods include road–rail tractors (Figure 2.73). Winch systems are also available. A small machine like a motorized wheelbarrow is useful for individual truck handling. There is a Network Rail code for wagon handling, so check any shunting ideas for private use with the TOC.

1.07 Intermodal transfer operations will require wider clearances (Figure 2.69): see Chapter 3.

Figure 2.69 *Intermodal freight sprinter.*

Fuel tankers

1.08 Possibly the most frequent type of railway access met by designers today is for fuel tankers. There are large numbers of privately owned tank wagons in operation carrying oil fuel, oil and chemical products, and bulk powders. With the trouble experienced with road tanker crashes involving acid and caustic product spillage, more of this traffic will return to the railway, both in bulk tankers and in tank containers on skeletal wagons.

1.09 For oil fuels the design of reception areas for tank wagons is comparatively simple (Figures 2.69 and 2.70). The oil companies have consultancy departments to advise customers in planning their reception areas. As long as there is continuity at rail joints, wagons are earthed to the tracks through their wheels and need no further earthing points for pumping heavy fuel or spirit.

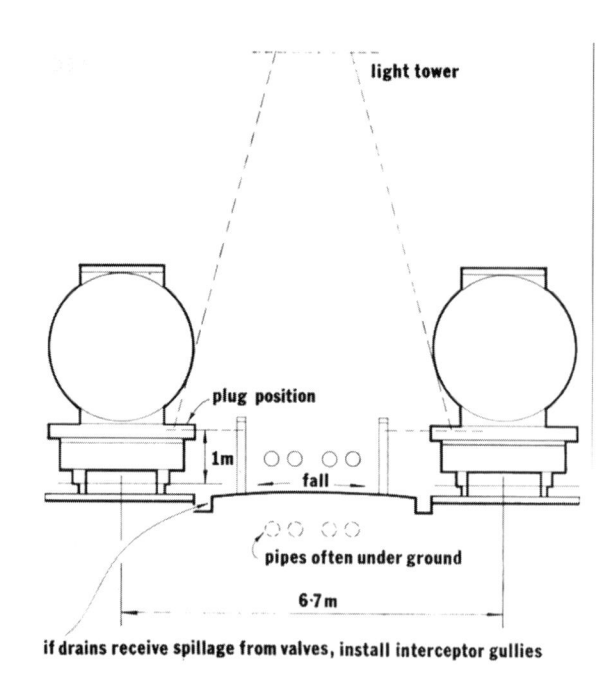

Figure 2.70 *Section through tanker reception point, showing minimum centres for double-sided unloading.*

Heavy fuel oil tankers are insulated, but not heated; the refinery or distribution tank depot calculates the journey length and unloading period and loads the oil sufficiently hot to remain pumpable on arrival. It is also unusual to supply any heating to valves, pipe work or pumps at the reception point, and the pipes are emptied by positive displacement pumps; any residue is cleared by the next load. Pumps operate in the open with meter points, so that the customer can check wagon capacity against loading tickets from the refinery (Figure 2.71). It is not advisable to provide access to wagon hatches, as is done for road tankers. Rail wagons are self-venting, and the fuel tankers do not need cleaning on customers' premises. These checks are performed at the refinery.

Figure 2.71 *Double-sided discharge area with underground pipes and drain channels.*

1.10 The design of modern joint valves and pipe fittings precludes most spillage; usually, a little sand laid on the ballast is sufficient for spillage collection.

Lighting

1.11 Adequate lighting must be provided for night deliveries. One oil company tried lighting on gantries, which were found to be too high and cast a shadow on connection points. Plug-height lights proved to be a glare source. One solution is to place light towers between the connection plug positions (Figure 2.70).

Plug positions

1.12 Railtrack's minimum for considering a number of wagons as a separate train is five to six units. Tankers are unloaded simultaneously from multiple plug positions (Figures 2.71 and 2.72); fuel oil tankers have been designed so that the connection points are at constant centres, i.e., if a large bogey truck is used, it would fit onto the same plugs as two rigid chassis units.

Figure 2.72 *Detail of plug point.*

Fire

1.13 There is little fire problem with fuel oil but all electric equipment must be flameproof. If low-flash products are to be handled, contact the factory inspector, petroleum officer and the local fire officer. This also applies to areas for handling caustic, corrosive or explosive powder products.

Powder tankers

1.14 Powder tankers either discharge by gravity, or are vacuum assisted. These units tend to be owned by the manufacturers, who will supply any data required for designing the handling equipment most suitable for their product (Figure 2.73).

Figure 2.73 *A Unimog road/rail tractor used in local depot shunting.*

Local wagon movement

1.15 Where there is mainline electric traction from overhead cables for safety and cost, this often stops at the entry siding. For local yard movement, traction owned and operated by the site is required (Figure 2.73).

Chapter 3
External storage

TECHNICAL STUDY

Design of container handling areas

1 The potential of containers and demountable bodies

2 Design

3 Demountable bodies as storage

4 Security

5 Personnel accommodation

6 Check list

External storage, in the context of this handbook, means the short-term storage of ISO containers and demountable truck bodies. The planning of this important type of storage is described in detail, as mistakes can be very costly in wasted plant, effort and area. This chapter does not cover external storage on the ground of non-containerized loads, such as building materials. Planning of such simple storage areas is described in the Mechanized storage chapter.

1 The potential of containers and demountable bodies

1.01 The ISO container has revolutionized the transport, storage and packaging industries. The potential of a standard range of box sizes for most commodities is enormous. It means that intermodal trans-shipment is cut to a minimum, costs are reduced and turnround is speeded up because modular units and advanced mechanical handling techniques are used (Figure 3.1). Size standards are laid down by the International Standards Organization. For instance, it was widely predicted that 20 ft x 8 ft x 8 ft (6.1 m x 2.4 m x 2.4 m) containers would become the standard unit, but now the most popular is the 40 ft (12.2 m) unit, with a marked preference for 8 ft 6 in and 9 ft 6 in (2.6 m and 2.75 m) height.

Figure 3.1 *Different heights of ISO containers makes stacking difficult.*

This extra height over the original standard, sponsored by the deep sea shipping industry, allows greater cubic capacity and potential extra payload important on long voyages; the 45 ft (13.6 m) container is also now popular, though maintaining the locking points at 12.2 m as before. Although the larger sizes caused some initial problems on sea (due to the rigid cellular nature of ships) and rail (due to lower European rail loading gauges) maritime, road and rail equipment rapidly adapted to accept new generations of containers. The 4 m height limit for lorries in EU countries, 8 ft 6 in and 9 ft 6 in high containers require special drop frame trailers and rail wagons. A further complication in Europe has been the introduction of 2.6 m x 2.6 m section containers, designed specifically for the German rail system. Outwardly similar to ISO containers, they have caused confusion at ports as they did not conform with the stacking tolerances of first generation container ships: this has been resolved with later shipping generations.

1.02 In spite of these development issues, the ISO container is the most adaptable unit of goods transport available. Within the basic frame, tanks, bins, tipping bodies, hoppers, pressure vessels and many special forms can be built (see Information sheet, External storage 1). Containers can be stacked three or four high when full, and six high when empty, reducing the ground area previously needed for storage by semi-trailers. However, the heavy plant required to handle containers needs manoeuvring space and savings may not be as great as anticipated, due to bad planning.

1.03 The potential of the container as a total system still needs careful exploitation. There has been much investment in land-based plant, skeletal trailers, cranes, straddle carriers and in the numbers of containers themselves. The automated container ports in Hong Kong, Japan and at Europort in Rotterdam demonstrate how very fast turnround of third generation container ships and dynamic handling on the dock maximize the use of huge, but still very restricted for their throughput, port areas. The planning layout of such facilities is a specialized business.

Technical study – design of container handling areas

1.04 Mobile, plug-in refrigeration units enable perishable goods to be stored for some time before breaking-bulk or trucking out to the consumer. Industry was quick to realize that their own stores could be greatly reduced if goods could be left in other operators' containers. Where ISO containers are efficient for intercontinental operations, they are bulky for local delivery work and impose a heavy weight penalty.

Demountable bodies

1.05 International Standards Organization containers are an open system of heavy construction, for 'deep-sea' use and for stacking three or four high when loaded. Demountable bodies (BS EN 284) are on the same principle, but are a closed system (i.e. an EU range of standard sizes) and of lighter construction (so cannot generally be stacked when full).

1.06 The standard sizes adopted by the EU multimodal road/rail system and the current most popular sizes, 7.15, 7.45, 7.82 x 2.5 m wide x 2.67 m high, the first two of which fit conventional drawbar combinations 18.5 m long, and 13.6 m for articulated trailers. General trends for closed top inter–urban distribution are towards 13 ft (3.9 m) lengths, so that three can fit on a 40 ft (12.2 m) trailer (Figure 3.2a), and 10 ft (3 m) lengths, so that two can fit on the lorry and two on the trailer of a drawbar outfit.

1.07 Demountable body units enable a truck chassis to be used continuously, with turnround times as fast as it takes to drop one body and pick up another, not necessarily of the same type. Modular demountable truck bodies offer a very high efficiency trucking system, and it is easy and cheap to store them on integral legs (Figure 3.2b).

Future conditions

1.08 Designers should plan with future vehicle weights and configurations in mind. The EU transport commission has fixed European gross vehicle weights for articulated vehicles limited to 44 tonnes, allowing a full 40 ft (12 m) container to be carried; and truck and drawbar trailer combinations are also rated at 44 tonnes allowing two full 20 ft (6 m) containers to be carried. Designers should note that overall sizes are likely to increase: these are minor increases driven by special applications and the gradual acceptance of joint US/EU standards For example, former 15.5 m articulated trucks are now generally 16.5 m long accounting for 13.6 m long trailers and swap body/containers. Drawbar combinations have been allowed to grow from 18 m to 18.5 m length with special retracting drawbars to handle 2 x 7.82 m bodies to maximize cubic performance with swap bodies. Chilled vehicle widths have grown from 2.5 m to 2.55 m to allow for more efficient insulation. In Sweden, for long-haul internal use, much longer vehicles are permitted, including 'road trains' of at least two trailers: this is similar to Australian practice. In the Netherlands, gross vehicle weights of 50 tonnes are accepted for internal transport. Both are EU members, and their influence may be felt in future size increases.

2 Design

Approach roads

2.01 At terminal points in the system – factory, store, or marshalling area – allowance should be made for heavy trucks to arrive in peak conditions. To ensure smooth traffic flow, a computer model to simulate the surrounding roads and daily traffic flow conditions can now be made. Analysis of differing traffic flows would show where peak build-ups and stoppages will occur, and thus where road improvements should be. In several cases, a container-handling area has been re-sited due to the great cost of local road improvements required to handle future peak traffic conditions. Peaks are generated by ship or train arrivals and departures: these may be at any time throughout the day or night. It is important for maritime and intermodal container areas not to be constrained by traffic curfews.

Figure 3.2 (a) *Three swop bodies on one trailer.* (b) *Swop body is parked on legs, while truck moves out from beneath.*

Figure 3.3 *Container stacks overturned by wind.*

Buffer areas

2.02 Buffer parking and assembly space should be provided for peak build-up and emergency holding for incoming and outgoing traffic. Areas should be provided, especially in groupage depots, for pooled container and skeletal trailer facilities. 'Tilt' trailers and containers on skeletal trailers can choke the loading bank area, unless planned from the outset. For demountable bodies, space should be left for parked chassis and unused body units. Designer or consultant should analyse flow at an early stage and compare cost/efficiency of layouts not only in terms of vehicle turnround, but in handling plant efficiency in the buffer area. If a buffer zone is not provided and a truck breaks down in peak conditions, major blockages always occur in the assembly position and soon affect major transport links.

2.03 Buffer areas are also important for documentation. Designers sometimes forget that containers have to be checked so that they can be routed to the correct stack area. At present, container codes are checked manually, but scanner readers are being developed that can read numbers on the side and ends of the container, and this, linked with a self-checking computerized bill of lading, would simplify present documentation. The manual system requires a physical check; either the container moves past a fixed point, or a mobile checkpoint moves round the assembly area, often linked with closed-circuit television. The automated system requires containers to pass a scanner beam, and should be carefully positioned so that the traffic flow is not impaired and the buffer space can operate efficiently. Clearly marked lanes, stopping points and a clear visual display instruction system for drivers can help a great deal. Avoid tight turns and route-crossing points hidden by container stacks. Serious accidents have occurred by fast-moving handling plant colliding with a turning vehicle, partially hidden behind a block of containers. Essentially routing should be one way with clearly marked priorities. A clockwise periphery route is the most effective in Britain as drivers are always in a position to see what is happening in the container stacks. If automated handling plant (e.g. wire-guided straddle carriers) is used, road vehicles and especially personnel should not enter the stack areas, moving only to peripheral assembly zones.

Down draughts

2.04 High stacks of empty containers can become unstable in buffet and eddy conditions, and the funnel effect of stacks can produce high velocity down draughts (Figure 3.3). Injury has resulted by personnel being pushed against containers, and the accuracy of the plant in placing can be impaired.

Parking

2.05 Parking surfaces in container areas should be well drained, so that water does not build up in container stacks, caught between falls and container bases. Falls and cambers can impair the speed of alignment of side-loaders and straddle carriers. Containers should not rest on an apex, as there is risk of serious structural damage to the bottom container in the stack. Areas for container stacking should be designed for loadings of not less than 100 kN/m2, with aisles for special wheeled plant, weighing about 100 tonnes with a fully laden 40 ft (12 m) container. On corners or when braking, where skidding with plant would be disastrous, a non-slip surface should be laid. The type of epoxy-based granite chip surface now being used for junctions in London is not cheap, but is money well spent. Dimensions of parking areas are decided by the type of handling plant, and are illustrated in Information sheet, External storage 2.

'Reefer' parking

2.06 Parking areas for 'reefer' (i.e. refrigerated) containers require special conditions. Several plug-in systems are available. One accepts stacked containers attached to a central spine, others rely on ground connection points. When left on skeletal trailers, electric power or cooling gas points are usually provided at strategic positions for a group of four containers back to back. These areas should be well lit and carefully marked out, leaving a walkway for personnel to connect the plugs safely. Plug positions should be well marked, preferably in high reflective paint, and well protected from impact (Figures 3.4 and 3.5). (This subject will be handled in more detail in Chapter 6, Cold storage.)

Figure 3.4 *Detail of a refrigerated vehicle plug point. These allow the trucks to act as external storage without running their engines or using up their batteries. Note drain, protective kerb and spring loaded cable reels.*

Personnel

2.07 Some personnel will always be required to work in container areas. Future installations will be more likely to have 'white collar' workers for operating automated systems. Well-designed personnel facilities have led to cost benefits, due to a good management/personnel relationships and improved standards of operation. Large-scale container areas are not conducive to human occupation, and lack of forethought can lead to costly industrial disputes.

Inland container areas

2.08 These are of three types: the inland intermodal container port and groupage area, the large industry marshalling zone, and the conventional small-factory or warehouse yard. All three share the basic problems, but with a difference in scale. Inland container groupage areas, such as the Daventry Intermodal Rail Freight Terminal have similar conditions to a seaport, with the added problem of transferring units to various types of transport, i.e. truck to train, truck to truck. This terminal is

Technical study – design of container handling areas

Figure 3.5 *Well-planned truck park for refrigeration lorries, with plug-in positions for integral refrigeration units, clearly identified bays, and raised area to protect the plug points and allow safe personnel movement.*

typical in having provided the 'pump primer' for the development of extensive surrounding warehouse and freight processing areas that attract agents' and importers' break-bulk facilities, so generating more traffic and security controls. The change in type of transport means peak conditions for both rail and road movement; these do not often coincide, as container trains are scheduled out of passenger peaks, and especially in break-bulk situations, local delivery vehicle peaks occur right at the start of the working day.

Figure 3.6 *Swop body interchange park. Note truck and drawbar trailer for maximum cubic capacity.*

2.09 In urban situations, overcrowding can prove very costly (for instance, where the best container stack organization constricts the operation of the break-bulk zone and vice versa). Although this often does not seem important, as the groupage and break-bulk area is probably handling a small percentage of the total traffic by value, a constriction in the approach or buffer to this zone can generate long vehicle hold-ups, the smaller vehicles baulking the large container trucks, so putting a brake on the whole system.

2.10 There are no hard and fast rules for organizing groupage and break-bulk areas, but the following points are important:

1 Free-flowing traffic is critical.
2 Manoeuvring space must be provided for the largest trucks.
3 Areas should be provided for parked trailers and containers on skeletals, continental drivers to rest in their cabs and unsheeting 'tilt' trailers and containers (Figure 3.6). If a side access bay is to be used, space should be provided for dropping the sides of the trailer, for Customs to check seals before leaving the site and for a segregated area to contain light feeder vans.

2.11 The sites that tend to be allocated are often 'leftovers' or old railway yards, by nature a triangle or bent rectangle. These sites do not lend easily to the grid distribution generated by containers and their handling plant.

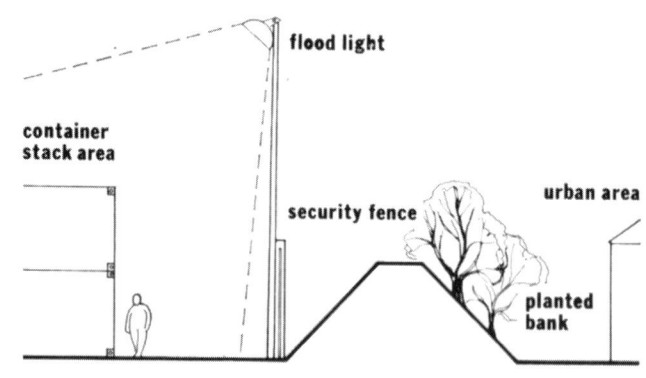

Figure 3.7 *Screening of containers in urban areas.*

Environmental problems

2.12 There are environmental side issues in urban areas that often become lost in the design of the handling system. For instance, stacks of empty containers act like drums in heavy rain, their shape amplifying the noise in the immediate neighbourhood and producing discomfort for local residents. Wind can also be an annoyance. Security is a serious problem, not only because of theft but also because of personal safety. Children like to play

Technical study – design of container handling areas

Figure 3.8 *Robust barrier in parking area.*

near big machines, and container stacks and handling plant are very tempting. The expenditure on a carefully designed perimeter barrier is a definite cost benefit, compared with the costs granted against a maimed child. Reduced insurance premiums are offered for well-designed security systems; this must not be treated as an afterthought. Perimeter barriers can also be used for noise attenuation and visual relief in urban situations (Figures 3.7 and 3.8).

3 Demountable bodies as storage

3.01 Demountable truck bodies are often used as cheap, short-term storage: the stockless warehouse.

Most types of swop-body systems are automatically dropped by the truck and have integral hinge or wind-down legs (Figure 3.9). One type requires a gantry for removal from the prime mover, and another a system of rails. The storage potential of these units is very valuable and saves expensive warehousing, eliminates double handling and takes the goods to the exact position where they will be required. The bodies cannot be stacked like ISO containers, but they can be block-parked very close indeed; there is no need for straddle, carrier or crane access, but only for the truck chassis to reverse under the body. A buffer zone should also be provided, with manoeuvring space for both truck and local delivery vehicles. Several swop bodies can be trunk-hauled by only one vehicle, to an urban marshalling point for transfer to small delivery vehicles carrying one body each. Trunk vehicles are either articulated or (as is becoming more popular, due to their potentially greater cubic capacity) truck and drawbar trailer outfits. Swop bodies are often block-parked in urban marshalling

(a)

(b)

Figure 3.10 *Intermodal depots need to be secure.* (a) *Note 2.7-m tall steel paling fence with outward sloping pointed tips.* (b) *Gatehouse for busy intermodal yard. Note sliding gate, traffic lights, 5 m high canopy, secure accommodation, exit barrier.*

Figure 3.9 *Two types of landing legs: the swop body's landing legs are folded up; the trailer's hydraulic legs are extended.*

areas, for short-term storage, and local delivery vans pick them up as required on a first-in, first-out principle, much as pallets can be handled in a warehouse. This method has particular potential again when planning e-commerce fulfilment systems. (See Technical study, Mechanized storage 1.)

4 Security

4.01 Great care should be taken over the security of external storage areas, as it is easy for an intruder to be missed amid and underneath the tightly parked body units. Efforts should also be made to prevent children from gaining access and playing in these areas, as serious accidents have occurred due to drivers' vision being restricted. A well-designed fence and a high level of gantry lighting help. The lighting is not wasted, as with the increase of daytime city delivery restrictions, there will probably be many more night movements (Figures 3.10a and 3.11). For employees' safety, and the fast coupling and deposit of bodies, clear markings should be placed on the ground, ensuring a predetermined parking pattern. Traffic flow should be one-way and clearly marked out (Figure 3.10b).

5 Personnel accommodation

5.01 In swop-body parks, as in container-handling areas, some form of personnel accommodation is likely to be required; this is liable to be in the form of an office, toilets and washing facilities. At major interchange points, with numbers of long-distance vehicles passing through, rest and vending facilities should be provided for the drivers. This is no luxury; it gives an incentive for drivers not to waste time in café's on the road, which in turn reduces the risk of theft. Some form of covered provision should also be made for basic truck and body maintenance, even if it is of a 'driver-does-it-him/herself' nature. The securing locks and lifting systems on demountable body trucks can break down, and bodies become damaged in tight urban areas. An under-ceiling clearance of 6 m is required,

Figure 3.11 Large light tower: note also large areas required for container handling. Behind are two container cranes.

allowing access to a chassis with a lifted body. A roof-mounted chain hoist is useful for removing jammed bodies. Electrical points, water and an airline should be provided, with a store for basic equipment like jacks and portable hydraulic pumps.

6 Checklist

	Whom to contact
Can the local roads support the future goods traffic?	Local authority, Department for Transport, Local Government and the Regions (DTLR), transport consultant, management
What type of traffic is expected?	Shippers, management
What quantity of future traffic? Growth?	Business consultant
What peaks will be generated by the local and long-haul traffic patterns?	
Growth?	
Will break-bulk facilities be required?	Management
Should vehicle types be split?	System designer
Position of buffer/assembly area	System designer
Road/rail peaks	British Transport Police, Network Rail – local authority, shippers, transport consultant
Type of container stack and area required:	Mechanical-handling consultants, shippers
600 40 ft (12 m) containers plus processing = 4.45 hectares	
3000 40 ft (12 m) containers plus processing = 20 to 25 hectares	
Optimum circulation. Clear markings	System designer
Vehicle/plant segregation in rail sidings	Mechanical-handling consultants, shippers
Security, road surface, aisle distribution, personnel, pilferage, entry control	Police, management, system designer
Prevailing wind, local weather	Meteorological office
Surrounding environment, urban areas: visual, aural environment	Local authority, management
Personnel accommodation	Management
Maintenance facility, plant parking	Plant manager, plant manufacturer

INFORMATION SHEET

External storage 1
Containers

1 Sizes

2 Types

3 Method of moving

4 Capacities

5 Identification

This information sheet describes the range of sizes of ISO containers, types available and typical uses.

1 Sizes

1.01 As explained in Technical study, External storage 1, container sizes are to remain in imperial, due to pressure from the US trucking industry. Sizes are therefore given in imperial, with rounded-up metric equivalents in brackets.

2 Types

2.01 Types of containers, with sizes, materials and uses are shown in Table 3.1.

3 Method of moving

3.01 Containers are lifted, secured and stacked by 'twist locks' on the corner castings (Figure 3.12). Containers can be stacked six high when empty, three or four high when laden, depending on weight and lifting equipment. Some are fitted with 350 mm wide by 100 mm deep forklift pockets at the base (positioned at 900 mm centres equidistant from centre line of container) (Figure 3.13). (See Information sheet, External storage 2.)

4 Capacities

4.01 Maximum capacity for 20 ft (6 m) container = 20 tonnes. Maximum capacity for 40 ft (12 m) container = 30 tonnes. It is unusual for 20 ft (6 m) units to gross more than 12 to 15 tonnes, or for 40 ft (12 m) units to rise over 20 tonnes. Only full cube packed commodities (e.g. tinned fruit juice) result in 20 tonnes, 20 ft (6 m) containers. Most container-handling machinery is not designed for continual handling of maximum loads.

5 Identification

5.01 Coding and identification is marked in standard positions on end doors and sides. They give type of container, its owner, its size and capacity, and its unique serial number. New developments include radio data tags buried in the structure of the container for real time identification in transit and in stacks: there is also potential for these tags to contain electronic inventory (the way bill) of the contents.

Figure 3.12(a/b) *40 ft (12 m) container being lifted by reach stacker. Twist locks can be seen at corners.*

External storage – containers

Figure 3.13 *Containers can be stacked four high, three deep, by a reach stacker, by loading progressively from the rear.*

Table 3.1 Types, sizes and uses of ISO containers

End door and side and end door container

Ft	in	(m)	ft	in	(m)	ft	in	(m)
20		(6.09)	8		(2.43)	8		(2.43)
30		(9.14)	8	6	(2.59)			
40		(12.19)						

L   W   H

Materials and construction

Steel, aluminium, plastics-faced ply with steel frame

Use

General dry goods. Side and end door containers are useful where loading areas are constricted for large trucks or for railway use.

Tilt top container

Ft	in	(m)	ft	in	(m)	ft	in	(m)
20		(6.09)	8		(2.43)	8		(2.43)
30		(9.14)				8	6	(2.59)
40		(12.19)						
44		(13.6)						

L   W   H

Materials and construction

Steel with open top, covered with composite plastics 'tilt' with end doors

Use

For loading long steel or paper reels with an overhead crane, and for outsize loads for deck cargo.

External storage – containers

Tilt container

Ft	L in	(m)	ft	W in	(m)	ft	H in	(m)
20		(6.09)	8		(2.43)	8		(2.43)
30		(9.14)						
40		(12.19)						

Materials and construction

Steel frames with low sides, 'tilt' frames and complete 'tilt' covering in composite plastics. Skeletal end doors and detachable corner posts. Some have fold-down end-panels for standing when empty (four fit within one normal container size)

Use

For bulky goods more suited to side loading, or with special unloading and handling circumstances (e.g. vehicle tyres, metal coil). Also aids customs examination.
Tilt is top container illustrated.

Half-height container

Ft	L in	(m)	ft	W in	(m)	ft	H in	(m)
20		(6.09)	8		(2.43)	4		(1.21)
40		(12.19)						

Materials and construction

Steel or aluminium with 'tilt' top and end doors. Some skeletal, i.e. above with post and rail sides for carrying steel

Use

For open top or with tilt for steel bars, high weight goods (e.g. chemical drums).

Bulk containers

Ft	L in	(m)	ft	W in	(m)	ft	H in	(m)
20		(6.09)	8		(2.43)	8		(2.43)
30		(9.14)						
40		(12.19)						

Materials and construction

Steel or aluminium container with strong end doors. Some have metal sheet roofs with hatches, some with 'tilt' tops. Some end doors have hatches for powder handling. Can be mounted on tippers (as in illustration) or fitted with pneumatic discharge equipment. Also available with plastic liners thrown away after discharge

Use

For increasing trade in bulk materials.

External storage – containers

Tank container

Ft	L in	(m)	ft	W in	(m)	ft	H in	(m)
20		(6.09)	8		(2.43)	8		(2.43)
30		(9.14)						
40		(12.19)						

Materials and construction

Steel or aluminium tanks mounted on ISO sub-frames

Use

For bulk liquids and powders. Some tanks are pressurized, heated, or insulated.

Insulated container

Ft	L in	(m)	ft	W in	(m)	ft	H in	(m)
20		(6.09)	8		(2.43)	8		(2.43)
30		(9.14)						
40		(12.19)						

Materials and construction

Steel, aluminium or plastic faced ply with insulation. End door and side and end door types

Use

For goods needing temperature controlled environment during transit
(Similar in appearance to standard container).

Reefer 'refrigerated' container

Ft	L in	(m)	ft	W in	(m)	ft	H in	(m)
20		(6.09)	8		(2.43)	8		(2.43)
30		(9.14)				8	6	(2.59)
40		(12.19)						

Materials and construction

Two types: 1, Autonomous, i.e. fitted with own refrigeration source on front bulkhead. These are plugged into power sources on ship and vehicle. One type carries cooling cylinder with structure; 2, non-autonomous, i.e. container is plugged into central refrigeration source while on ship or in park, and container insulation maintains temperature during delivery. More popular type.

Use

For refrigerated goods.

Multimodal containers/swop bodies

Ft	L in	(m)	ft	W in	(m)	ft	H in	(m)
23		(7.15)	8	2½	(2.5)	8/9		(2.67.2.75)
24		(7.45)	8	2½	(2.5)	8/9		(2.67/2.75)
25		(7.82)	8	2½	(2.5)	8/9		(2.67/2.75)
40		(12.2)	8	2½	(2.5)	9		(2.77)
44		(13.6)	8	2½	(2.5)	9		(2.77)

Below 26 ft (8 m) length, gross weight 35273 lbs (16000 kg); above 40 ft (12.2 m), gross weight 74956 (34000 kg).

Materials and construction

End and side door steel box construction with folding support legs, forklift pockets, straddle lift
gripper lugs. Also skeletal floor pan constructed as above so that curtain sided bodies can be fitted on top with or without end doors.

Use

Intermodal road/rail traffic within EU: specially designed and certified for secure transborder operations. EN 284: 1992. Special models within this standard for transporting cars, steel coils, etc.

INFORMATION SHEET

External storage 2

Container-handling plant

1 Types of container handling plant

2 Which system makes the most of site potential?

3 Maintenance

4 Simple container handling systems

5 On-vehicle handling aids

6 'Piggy back' and 'Kangaroo' systems

1 Types of container-handling plant

1.01 Container-handling systems range from gantry and 'Transtainer' cranes to straddle carriers and forklift trucks. As ISO containers are large, their handling plant must be large as well. The designer should be able to anticipate how areas are used, and so design for the plant from the outset. The choice of a particular handling method is related to type of traffic (e.g. ship to shore, train to truck or truck to ground), number of containers handled per hour, and the distance of travel which depends on the size and shape of the site, and the potential for expansion.

Figure 3.14 *Gantry crane.*

Gantry cranes

1.02 Gantry cranes are mostly used for unloading containers from ships, and at a smaller scale, for high density rail interchanges. Specially designed for container traffic, they are capable of substantial cantilever lifting, with spreaders mounted on rotating tables, so that the containers can be aligned straight into a stack or onto a vehicle (Figure 3.14). These are expensive pieces of plant, and generate linear planning. Designers must be careful not to plan cross routes where a stoppage might interfere with crane movement.

Mobile gantry cranes

1.03 This type is basically a gantry crane on rubber tyres, combining the mobility of straddle carriers, although slower, with the wide spans and height of a gantry crane (Figure 3.15). These, too, tend to generate linear planning, although they can steer out of track and 'crab' if required. Mobile gantries also have a spreader on a revolving table, as it is thought that the operator can realign a container quicker than the time taken to shunt a large vehicle to an accurate position. One advantage of mobile gantries over gantry cranes and straddle carriers is their ability to unload railway wagons and transfer the container directly to the stack or to another mode of transport, while being capable of quick movement to another task at a different part of the site (see Figure 3.21). If cross-movement is anticipated, the designer should plan the container area with some form of grid so that a wheel width is left at all times. These gantries, often under the generic trade name 'Transtainer' can be fully automated if remaining in their wheel track zone.

Straddle carriers

1.04 Straddle carriers are efficient in linear stacking situations up to three containers high (Figure 3.16). Developed from smaller types originally designed for the timber trade, the container-carrying straddle carriers are fast and manoeuvrable, but are expensive to buy and operate. The industry is worried by the high maintenance costs and 'down' time of sophisticated machines, but on the whole they are versatile. They work on the principle of driving over the top of a container, and positioning a spreader beam onto the top casting. This spreader is usually adjustable for 20, 30 and 40 ft (6, 9 and 12 m) containers. Although manually operated at present, wire-guided automated models have been developed which with scanner code readers and transducers backed by GPS positioning devices eliminate the present criticism of high operator positions causing slow alignment.

Forklift trucks

1.05 Forklift trucks can be used for container handling, but not all containers have fork tunnels. Most operators equip their forklifts with high level spreader beams as well (Figure 3.17). The development of 'piggyback' trailer trains and, in the USA, double stack height container wagons has resulted in a new family of 'front lift'

External storage – container handling plant

Figure 3.15 *Mobile gantry.*

Figure 3.16(a) *Two parked straddle carriers. Container crane in the background.*
(b) *Straddle carrier stacking containers three high.*

machines based on big forklifts called reach stackers: as the name implies, using their extending booms they can position a trailer or container onto a train on the track beyond the immediate track next to the machine. While versatile, they are very heavy, with 80 tonne axle loads requiring serious pavement design (Figure 3.17a/b).

When using 'conventional' big forklift machines, the forks must be 2.4 m long or be fitted with 2.4 m sleeves, ensuring evenly distributed support, otherwise serious damage to a container floor can result. When using 2.4 m forks or sleeves, care should be taken that the rated capacity at the 1.2 m load centres is not exceeded. Special types of forklift trucks with raised cabs can be used for empty container handling and stacking up to six high (Figure 3.18). For laden units, a special heavy-duty truck is required. A useful development for empty container handling is the slewing mast truck, that can place the container at 90° to the direction of travel, load like a normal fork truck, and travel in aisles like a side loader (see Information sheet, Mechanized storage 1).

Figure 3.17(a) *Forty-five tonne reach stacker. Note 15 metre width of aisle.*
(b) *Reach stacker can load containers three high, three deep.*

Sideloaders

1.06 The sideloader is very useful in container areas where throughput does not justify straddle carriers: like forklift trucks, there are special models designed for container handling (Figure 3.19a). These machines lift a container from the ground, or from a truck, or stack, traverse the mast, and so place it on to the wide platform for stability (Figure 3.19b). They are capable of fast travel in aisles no wider than themselves (Figure 3.20). Models are available with small turning circles, enabling them to fit into very tight stacks (see Information sheet, Mechanized storage 1). Reach stackers are beginning to replace sideloaders.

External storage – container handling plant

Figure 3.18 *Note raised cab for driver vision.*

Figure 3.20 *Sideloader stacking containers in parallel.*

(a)

(b)

Figure 3.19(a/b) *Sideloader placing container onto vehicle trailer.*

2 Which system makes the most of site potential?

2.01 To reach an optimum solution, evaluate each particular situation carefully, eliminating systems that are unsuitable (Figures 3.21 and 3.22). Some operators claim that straddle carriers are not as efficient as mobile gantries; straddle carriers demand large turning aisles and wheel width spaces, whereas a mobile gantry can span over 10 container stacks in block (Figure 3.23). The straddle carrier is faster, but wastes space; the mobile gantry has to be fed by tractor train, forklift truck or side loader. Aisles between container stacks are useful for visual number checks, where block stacking can lead to confusion. All container stacks should be organized into high-, medium- and low-speed lines to increase efficiency, with these areas clearly marked out. Some argue that an aisle system built up by a mobile gantry is most efficient, while those using reach stackers or sideloaders claim greater speed and efficiency than straddle carriers (reach stackers can stack three or four high and double stack, requiring an aisle of their own width (15 m) only every fourth row). Sideloaders can also block stack containers for one destination, for gantry crane removal (Figures 3.24 and 3.25). For slower work cycles and short distance travel from rail or road wagon to stack, a reach stacker or forklift truck is efficient especially if it can be used for other jobs.

2.02 Other sections of the industry, particularly stevedores, prefer the stillage trailer system (Figures 3.26–3.28) – this can be used with break-bulk flat trucks and stillages as well as articulated straddle lifters. These units are popular in inland container terminals, and for feeding 'Transtainer' cranes and now carry containers two high (Figure 3.29). Side transfer machinery is useful in a stack to rail/road or road/rail situation. Container lifting side transfer plant is usually based on a semi-trailer, which will carry the container from the pick-up position to the stack like a normal lorry. The best systems are a good combination of these machines, each performing a specific function, and working to a calculated cycle for

External storage – container handling plant

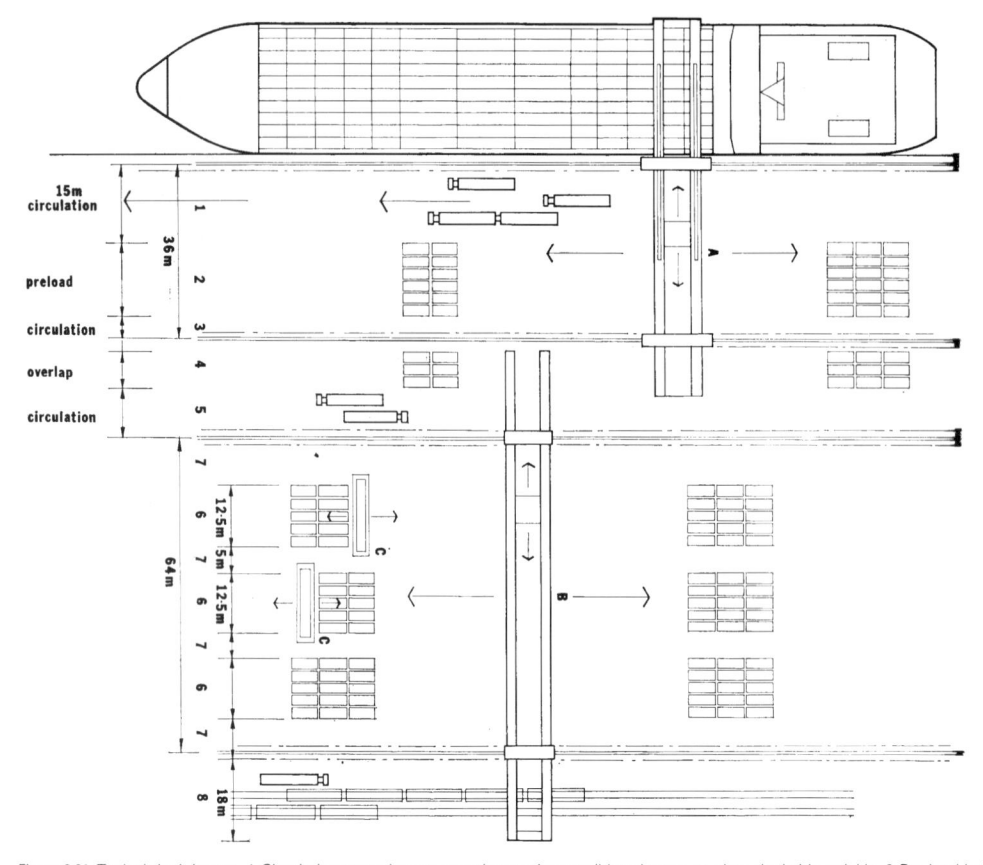

Figure 3.21 *Typical dock layout. 1 Circulation zone: import containers taken to ribbon layout, to clear dockside quickly. 2 Pre-load holding zone: built up before ship arrival in crane 5 slack periods. 3 Circulation zone: (one way) 3.5 m. 4 Overlap zone (7.5 m) between container crane A and gantry crane B. B sorts the next shipload and transfers containers to zone 4. 5 Circulation zone (8.5 m). Truck route to feed express containers direct to export loading stacks and crane A. 6 Export block stack. 7 Circulation zone: for crane C (rubber-tyred travel lift type crane for feeding crane B). 8 Transport interchange for export containers. Accessible by crane B or C.*

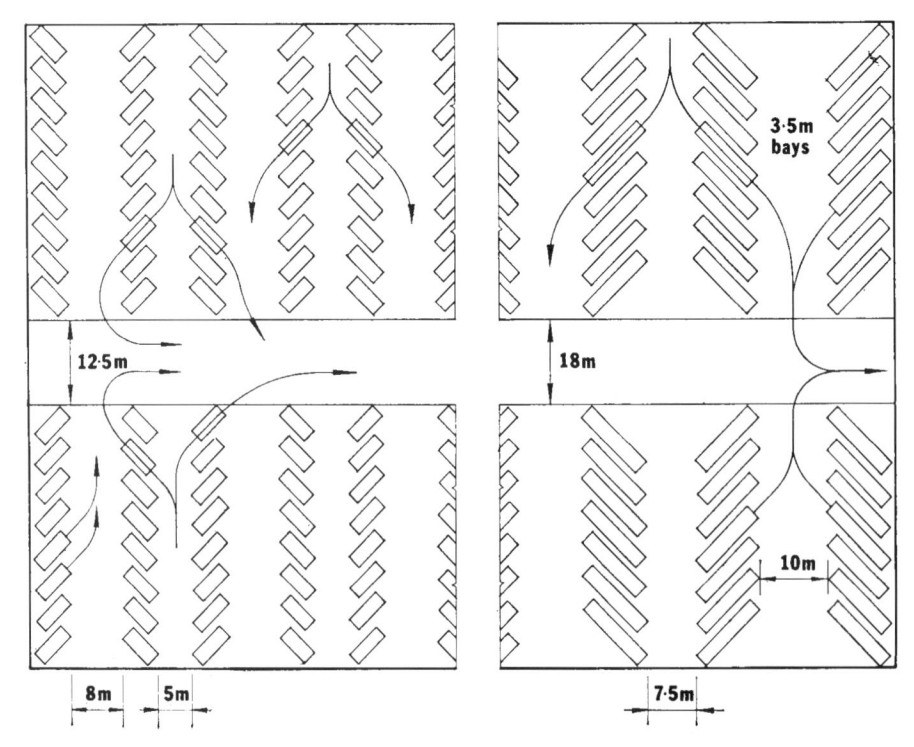

Figure 3.22 *Typical layout for 20 ft (left) and 40 ft (right) containers on stillage trailers. These can be parked very close together.*

External storage – container handling plant

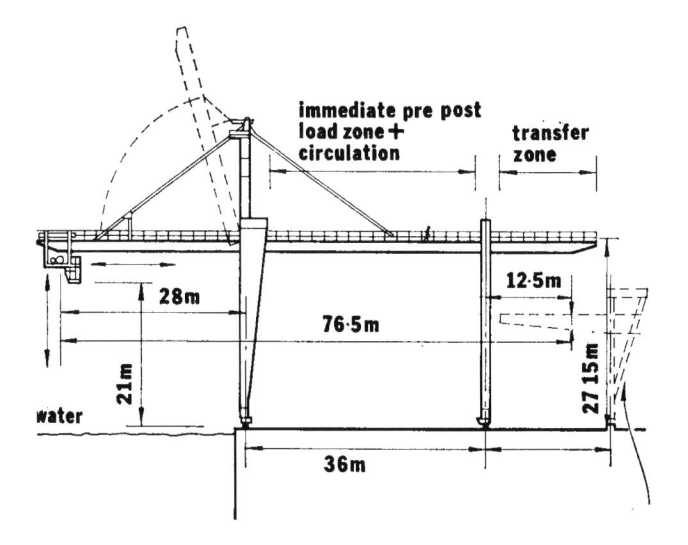

Figure 3.23(a) *Shiploading container crane (portainer).* (b) *Gantry crane (transtainer) for sorting containers and feeding shiploading crane.*

maximum utility. The designer must be aware of each system's potential, yet plan a flexible system so that change can quickly be accommodated.

3 Maintenance

3.01 All this sophisticated plant requires parking and maintenance areas close to the activity. Once the handling system has been decided, the designer should contact the plant manufacturer and ascertain any special maintenance requirements. If straddle carriers are brought into buildings, the door should be at least 10 m high. Maintaining these units often demands hydraulic platforms and gantry cranes within the building.

4 Simple container-handling systems

4.01 Many factories or warehouses only handle containers in small numbers and at infrequent intervals. Unless the plant can be used for other purposes, expensive container-carrying forklift trucks or sideloaders are uneconomic. There are several cheap and simple systems for the small operator. The best method is not to remove the container from the skeletal trailer at all (see Technical study, Loading 1). If two 20 ft (6 m) containers arrive on one 12 m trailer, however, one will have to be removed for unloading. If there is a mobile crane on site of sufficient capacity, this can be used with a special lifting frame, or spreader. There are simple mobile gantries on the market, that lift ISO containers from their top or bottom corner castings, and will place the unit on a slave trailer or onto the ground. Most of these do not move when lifting a container, the vehicle backing underneath (Figures 3.30 and 3.31). Some gantries are designed for 20 ft (6 m) containers, and are used in tandem for 40 ft (12 m) units, and others are capable of handling all sizes, with adjustable spreader beams (Figure 3.32). Also popular are portable hydraulic lifting legs, which can be handled by one man and are usually powered by a small portable hydraulic pump/motor unit. These legs are clipped onto the corner

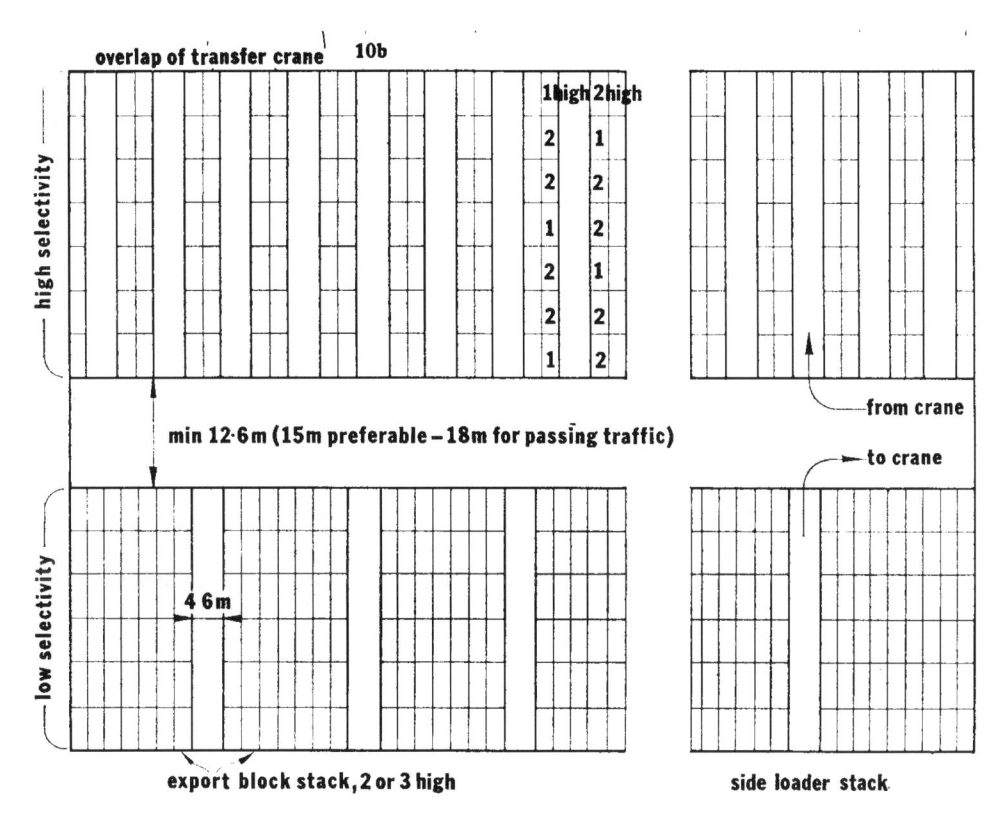

Figure 3.24 *Typical inland container area. Twenty-foot (6 m) containers are shown. Sideloaders can load truck and rail wagons direct, as well as stack. Top left, ribbon layout is for fast selection, i.e. imports. Top right, block layout where high individual selectivity is not important.*

External storage – container handling plant

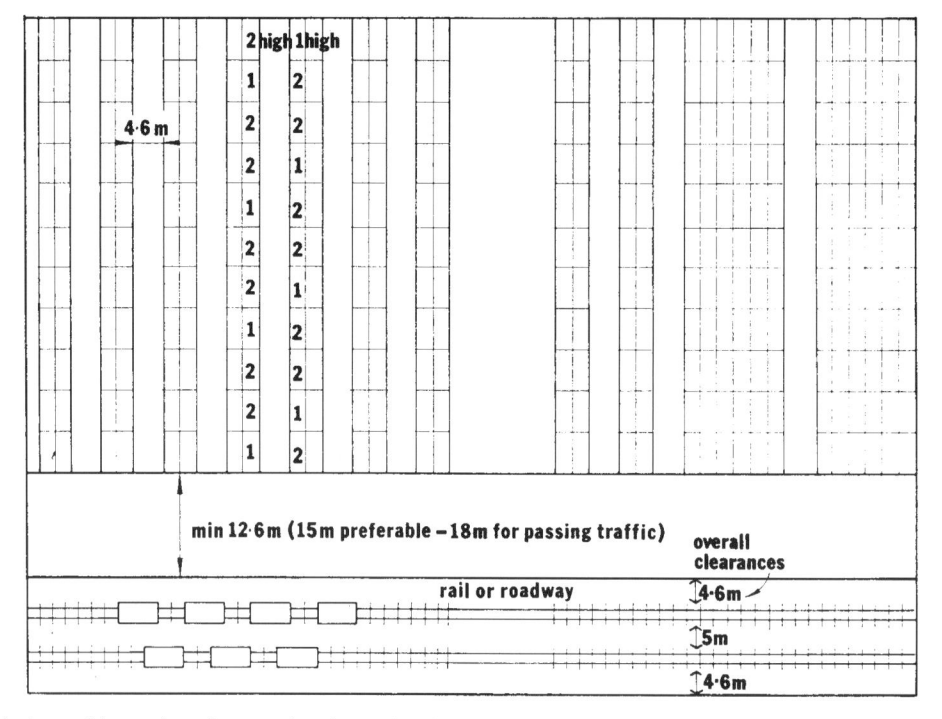

Figure 3.25 (a) *Typical layout for import ribbon stack or where containers have to be selected quickly. They are stacked alternately one and two high, so that only one container need be moved to reach another. Bottom left, lower selectivity ribbon layout. Sideloaders can operate on bad surfaces. An alternative now popular is to use reach stackers: these can stack four high, four deep but need 15 m aisles. But in the same area occupied by 231 12.2 m containers in the top left of (b) 528 containers can be staged, though requiring a greater level of control for identification in the deeper stacks.*

Figure 3.26 *Tug towing stillage trailer with ISO container (see Figure 3.22).*

Figure 3.28 *Close-up of tug with elevated fifth wheel coupling.*

Figure 3.27 *Heavy-duty forklifts can be adapted to handle stillage trailers (roll-on/roll-off load).*

Figure 3.29 *Stillage trailer with ISO 'flat' for loads unsuitable for containers for roll-on/roll-off use.*

External storage – container handling plant

castings, and then lift the container off the truck and onto the ground. Castors to clip onto container castings are also available (Figure 3.33).

4.02 For short-distance horizontal transport in small installations, forklift trucks of 3 to 5 tonnes capacity can be equipped with special roller bottom forks to push the container sideways, or a special low level trolley can be attached to the forks. Alternatively, if break-bulk and loose-load operation is normal, a special low-level trailer can be attached to stillage trailer tugs or tractors, which can also carry normal palletized goods (see 2.02).

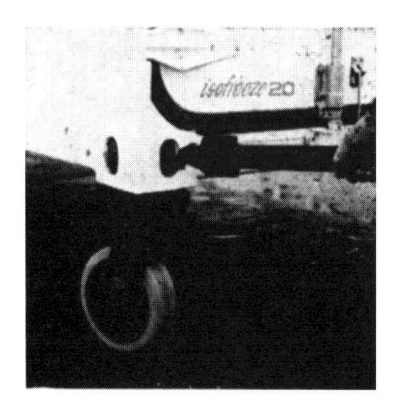

Figure 3.33 *Detail of container wheel.*

Figure 3.30 *Hydraulic mobile gantry.*

Figure 3.31 *'Four-poster' mobile manual gantry.*

Figure 3.32 *Adjustable spreader beam.*

Figure 3.34 *Artic tractor with self-loading crane.*

Figure 3.35 *Typical sliding trailer loading crane. Useful for many general purpose goods.*

External storage – container handling plant

(a)

(b)

Figure 3.36(a) *Canadian 'piggyback' system drives the trailer directly onto railway wagon.* (b) *transcontinental train of 'piggybacks'.*

Figure 3.37 *Kangaroo tractor loading trailer onto rail wagon.*

Figure 3.38 *Trailer being lifted by reach stacker. Note clearly marked lanes for load transfer.*

5 On-vehicle handling aids

5.01 Certain types of externally stored goods, especially goods for the building industry are more suitable for flatbed trailers. Vehicles equipped with integral cranes and forklifts allow autonomous handling at both storage and delivery premises (Figures 3.32-3.35).

6 'Piggyback' and 'kangaroo' systems

6.01 The 'piggyback' system, extensively used in the USA and increasingly in the EU, employs either gantry cranes or a special wheeled lifting machine, the reach stacker in Europe, the sideporter or piggybacker in the USA, which places the semi-trailer directly onto the rail wagon. These machines can quickly be adapted to handle ISO containers. Also in the USA there is a system of transferring box vans, 'flexivans', from trucks to trains. The rear of the trailer rests on a turntable on the flat car, the trailer's running gear is removed, and a special tractor swings the body through 90°.

6.02 'Kangaroo' is a European rail-based system, similar to 'piggyback' except that due to the lower loading gauge, the wheels of the trailer are in deeper wells. A special loading tractor drives the trailers up ramps and over the flat trucks until the correct position, when the well is lowered, and the trailer secured. If a 'kangaroo' terminal is incorporated in the container area, as is possible in inland situations, a large marshalling zone should be provided at the end of the sidings, clearly marked in lanes for the parking of incoming and outgoing trailers (Figures 3.36 and 3.37).

6.03 Various side-loading devices are available for road/rail interchange, where the truck is driven next to the rail wagon, and there is direct transfer. As these systems are usually integral with the carrying vehicle and as they run parallel to the rail tracks, there are few problems for designers, except ensuring that the hard-standing next to the rail track is capable of taking hydraulic stabilizer point loads during transfer. These systems are used extensively for the road/rail transfer of waste containers (Figure 3.38).

Chapter 4
Mechanized storage 1

TECHNICAL STUDY

Mechanized storage 1

Storage process

1 Introduction
2 Source of goods
3 Form of transport
4 Control of transport
5 Receipt of goods
6 Form of goods
7 Unloading
8 Characteristics of goods
9 Sorting
10 Volume calculations
11 Turnover calculations
12 Variety and flow
13 Type of storage
14 Stock control
15 Stock withdrawal
16 Order picking
17 Picking area
18 Load build-up and assembly
19 Order and document check
20 Loading and dispatch
21 Additional data

Mechanized storage ranges from simple manual handling and forklift truck operation to complex integrated handling systems. Although it is becoming more difficult to distinguish between mechanization and automation, some highly sophisticated mechanized-handling plant is still best controlled by an operator, with their actions planned by a computer. (Chapter 6, Automated storage, covers full automation.) Small-scale industrial storage systems for work in progress and supplies tend to be incorporated in-plant or within other retail or commercial facilities: it is in this type of storage that architects and designers are often involved. Larger storage systems, increasingly to do with processing orders generated through computers require clear, process-driven planning integrated with the building: architects and designers have an important role in understanding the process and providing operationally efficient and flexible premises.

1 Introduction

1.01 The users' aim is that goods should be stored, sorted and dispatched in the most efficient manner, for the lowest cost. To fulfil this brief, the mobile handling equipment should be treated as an integrated concept. Product and packaging affects the form of transport, the mechanical handling and storage medium to be employed. Mobile plant has a major effect on planning storage areas, type of storage and the ultimate cubic efficiency of the racking. The requirement for maximum cubic storage is a reflection of the initial product and its packaging. The issues are value rather than cost – long-term low operating cost and flexibility – not elemental savings in isolation (the 'tick in the box') that can cost dearly later on. The objective is 'agility' – rapidly implementable flexibility to accept changes in stock, operating climate and customer demand patterns. Supply chain economies – 'transparency' of stock between manufacturer, stockist and consumer, are still evolving. The supply chain target of zero stock, zero fault, maximum access and order fulfilment rely heavily on the logistics systems supporting them: someone has to keep and process some stock – speed and accuracy are still key ingredients.

1.02 In manual storage, human dimensions determined the scale of the operation; in mechanized storage, the determining factors are, using the maximum cubic capacity of the building and placing, locating and picking goods correctly in the shortest possible time. The initial design decisions will be determined by the economic policy of the user, for instance, if he or she requires a quick return through rental, or if the store is part of a production process. There are many factors vital to the success of a mechanized storage installation outside the building designers' range of knowledge. Architects and designers should not necessarily become mechanical-handling engineers, but should appreciate these problems and should know why certain decisions are made, if all the other parties are to be successfully co-ordinated.

Master planning

1.03 The basic warehouse proposition is driven by a number of key questions equally relevant whether the client will be the operator or a third party contractor. This is a basic checklist explained in depth in the following text:

1. What type of warehouse? See User specification in para 1.04.
2. Where should it be? It is assumed that site location selection has been made by others, but that the selection criteria for the selection of 'the best buy site' is an iterative process with the selection and 'fit' of the warehouse type and size.

3 How big? A function of days storage required to be held by pallet number and variety: a supply chain and business decision. As a rough guide: many speculative warehouse units vary from 4500 to 15000 sq m. Regional distribution centres tend to range from 30000 to 50000 sq m.
4 How tall? A function of the required capacity related to the site available, funding rules, technology options (i.e. capital versus operating cost). A rule of thumb (to be tested for each case): 12 m to haunch up to 4500 sq m; 15 m clear above this area for storage system flexibility. This is not a major cost implication. (See also Chapter 5, Automated storage, where the footprint can be dramatically reduced for stockholding if 30 m high.)
5 What shape? Selecting the proportion most operationally effective for the access demands, the storage function and what is fundable and most economically fits the site: a balancing act. A ratio of 1:2.5 to 1:3 for conventional stockholding warehouses: if dedicated to 'cross-docking' trans-shipment as parcels sorting and e-commerce stockless order fulfilment centres, 1:4 or more.
6 What is the target plot ratio? Considering an area for truck and staff parking and single or double-sided yard functions, at best 45 per cent, but often for major facilities with a perimeter roadway servicing truck-washing plant, trailer buffer parking, suppliers' vehicle waiting area (see Chapter 2, Loading), at best 40 per cent or even down to 35 per cent. This is what forces buildings and therefore storage technology higher on constrained sites.
7 What proportion of loading docks/doors related to floor area? There can never be enough doors! 1:1000 sq m for stockholding warehouses, but 1:500 sq m for cross-dock trans-shipment operations. One parcels hub (with a footprint ratio of 1:5) required 1:150 sq m (docks with doors in every bay on both long faces of the building.
8 Should raised or ground-level loading be provided? This is a function of topography, site shape and the type of storage operation: see Chapter 2, Loading. For an order fulfilment centre, raised docks on one face for 'trunk' deliveries, low dock or ground level on the opposite elevation for urban deliveries.
9 How big should the office area be? Attached to or within the warehouse envelope: proportion typically 5 per cent for warehouse operations, but up to 10 per cent if major administration is on the site.
10 What is the long-term development strategy? Expansion of the building envelope, or internally by changing the storage and handling technology. This in turn informs and is informed by site selection.

With adequate parking for delivery vehicles and work people, 40–45 per cent site cover for a warehouse is a rule of thumb. This tends to be true whether for terraces of speculative units with car parking consolidated to a separate area of site or a large regional distribution centre with extensive truck buffer parking on two sides of the building. The stockholding volume and turnover calculations should determine the shape and characteristics of the warehouse: for example, as an order fulfilment centre with large trucks delivering bulk loads requiring a complete elevation of raised truck docks on one side of the building with a similar elevation on the opposite side with ground-level loading for the light vans delivering individual orders. With a plan proportion typically 2.5–3:1 there is an opportunity to exploit any natural falls of the site to achieve the façade of raised docks avoiding expensive excavation. Similarly for a parcels sorting centre, where truck loads of parcels arrive, are sorted for various destinations by a sorting machine that tends to be linear, and leave again, the building proportion length to depth can be 5 or even 6:1. Location on the site will be driven by the size and shape of the building, both façades needing raised loading docks, and the areas of truck (or rail wagon) parking required.

The operational demands of the types of warehouses set out in paragraphs 1.07–1.10 inform these decisions.

User specification

1.04 The term 'mechanized warehouse' is generic for a range of storage types and users. Basically it consists of four types of storage:
1 stockholding warehouse
2 transit warehouse
3 accumulation warehouse
4 repository.

In fact, most mechanized warehouses are a compromise between several of these functions, so the characteristics of the company's trade should be carefully examined before any design decisions are made. Often, a company's present trading pattern is a result of an existing storage and distribution system; a user specification based on this situation may be obsolete before a new building is commissioned. Organization during the initial planning stage is based on the users' desire to make use of the maximum cubic capacity, the fastest method of handling goods, for the lowest cost. The economics of using handling-plant are inevitably entwined with the warehouse building, and the system is ultimately a compromise between the building designer and the mechanical-handling engineer.

1.05 To decide which system is best suited to the client's requirements, the speed, capital and operating costs of moving unit loads through the various types of warehouses should be compared. One of the major decisions that affect basic design is to what level the warehouse will be mechanized. Mechanization has advantages of accuracy, reduced personnel and the possibility of future developments towards automation, balanced against maintenance requirements and potential breakdown. Cost and efficiency of control systems should be equally considered, and the overall flexibility of the scheme in terms of pattern of trade, handling methods and the characteristics and potential of the site.

Types of mechanized warehouse

1.06 A warehouse that is not designed for change can quickly alter from being a cost benefit to a liability. The designer should be able to assess the factors for and against the types of storage available (Figures 4.1a–c).

Stockholding warehouse

1.07 A stockholding warehouse provides surge capacity to match consumer demand and peak requirements – typically a national distribution centre (NDC). Function is usually split between bulk and active stock sections. Order picking is from active stock, and is usually planned round unit loads. The bulk stock is used to replenish the active stock or to supply full unit loads. The reason for this type of store is logistic. It is usually impossible to supply a customer direct from a factory in the time available, or economically to gear the line to this type of production. With just-in-time deliveries and taut supply chains, this warehouse type may be a dying breed.

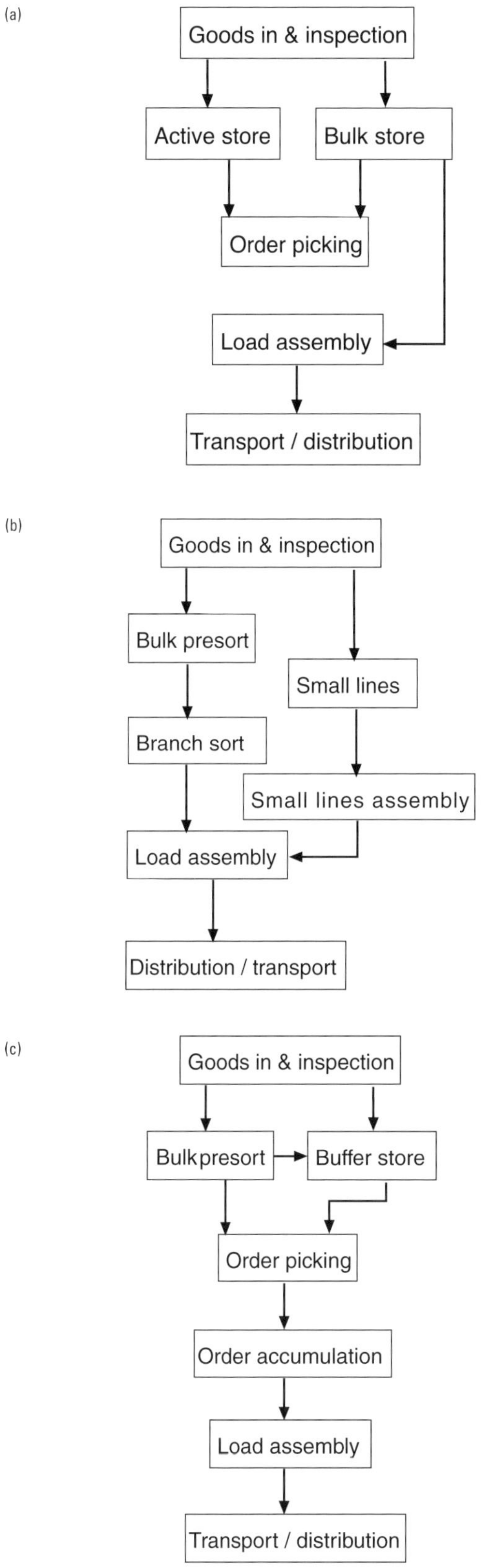

Mechanized storage – storage process

necessity in saving transport and distribution costs. The cost of 'trunk' hauling goods is less than half that of delivery. A variation is the order fulfilment centre, delivering the e-commerce 'promise', where picking orders to very tight schedules is an operational requirement: these can be major local employers, running to three shifts of pickers. They may be virtually stockless at the end of each cycle.

Accumulation warehouse

1.09 The Accumulation warehouse collects components required for a particular operation, e.g. a pre-production parts store for a batch production line. All items should be immediately available when the manufacturing operation requires, and double handling and order picking should be avoided. The sortation process tends to be earlier, often with a primary sortation as the goods enter the store, with storage separated into fast-moving bulk lines, and slower parts that are racked in their own areas of movement speed. 'Buffer' storage is often used to provide the exact order requirements for the production process: surge capacity is needed, as some parts are liable to be rejected, and others may build up a surplus. A high level of stock control is required in these stores. These are typically the 'Just-in-case' stores – the feeders for the just-in-time systems to avoid penalties from late deliveries.

Repository

1.10 A repository provides storage space, often for hire for long periods, for spare materials and equipment. The main difference between this and the three other categories is that the amount of usable space is more important than the speed of handling. A typical example is a furniture repository and strategic food stocks.

2 Source of goods

2.01 Typical businesses which are satisfactorily served by manually oriented storage processes are order fulfilment centres for e-commerce, cash-and-carry stores serving the smaller retailer, spares depots, small component stores for specialist production, furniture depositories, interprocess storage and handling in small factories. The goods originate from a large number of private and industrial sources or, in the case of spares depots, from the production side of the company concerned. Only in the latter case can the package size and material be controlled.

2.02 Due to the varied range of storage functions, goods will be received from many sources. For example, an RDC for a retail organization will receive goods from local sources within Britain, from the EU and worldwide, by road, rail and air freight. A warehouse for pre-process storage (in manufacturing) will receive goods from another factory of the company, another department of the same factory or, as with the motor industry, from a wide range of outside suppliers.

2.03 All goods, except those produced on the spot, will arrive by road, rail or air packed in some form of intermodal container. Goods produced within the site pose a different set of conditions. Special storage applications such as steel stockholding impose different constraints and will be discussed in Chapter 7, Special storage. The Internet allows companies to tender worldwide for suppliers: tightening the control of the supply chain with just-in-time deliveries on 'draw-down' from far away sources (i.e. the vendor keeps the stock), is reducing the

Figure 4.1 (a) *Stockholding warehouse.* (b) *Transit warehouse.* (c) *Accumulation warehouse.*

Transit warehouse

1.08 The transit warehouse is usually a stage in the distribution system of an operation involving bulk purchase and distribution to a number of outlets. Typically a regional distribution centre (RDC) is a warehouse serving a chain of retail outlets, located in an optimum position for the sales area. The sortation function is similar to a stockholding warehouse, but more stock tends to be picked direct from the bulk store. Transit depots are an economic

Mechanized storage – storage process

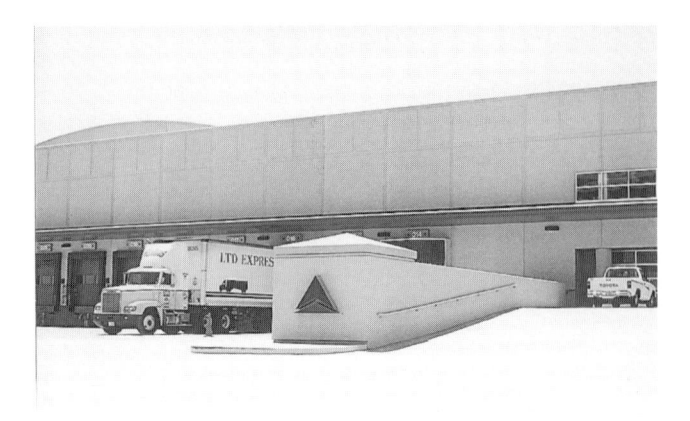

Figure 4.2 *Raised loading bays with dock shelters: note ramp to warehouse floor level for small vehicles to the right.*

size of warehouses, but at some risk of stock-out if there are breaks in the transport system. The balance between minimizing inventory and risk of failing customers remains a key supply chain logistics issue.

3 Form of transport

3.01 Depending on where the goods originate and the method used to package them, a wide range of transport can be expected. Whether for a small, essentially manually handled warehouse or a store big enough to justify substantial mechanization, many different types of heavy lorries should be planned for. Most goods from 'deep-sea' sources will arrive in ISO containers or occasionally air cargo unit load devices (ULDs). From the EU, ISO containers, articulated and drawbar trailer combinations, the latter often with demountable bodies, should be expected (Figure 4.2). With a manufacturing industry, for a pre-production store, it is easier to predict the type of transport, as the number of suppliers is often less than for the retail trade. If large regular numbers of parts are involved and the site has suitable access, bulk consignments by rail can be economic. Intermodal trains are a trend, driven by environmental necessity; with demountable road/rail truck bodies or piggyback trailers this is also a satisfactory and flexible solution. Intermodal distribution parks will continue to be a trend.

3.02 Light vans and trucks will also be involved, especially where small-scale suppliers are used. Each industry generates a particular transport pattern, based on type of supplier, characteristics of the goods, distances involved and the distribution system for the company. The transport manager should be contacted at an early stage if possible to ascertain if there is an existing pattern. Suppliers may not continue the same mode of transport; they will use whatever suits their economics best at the time.

4 Control of transport

4.01 In this type of storage operation, most vehicles will be of the largest sizes. To avoid providing large buffer areas for vehicle arrival, or risking a queue tailing back to the public road, every effort should be made to spread delivery and dispatch peaks throughout the day. The 'integrators', the express parcels carriers such as Federal Express, are winning an increasing market share in distribution by their superior control of the process and track and trace ability: their delivery patterns are less easy to control. Often management does not realize the effects of vehicle peaks on the whole storage operation.

Installations have been seen where, to clear a backlog of trucks, handling plant has been diverted from inside the store. This blocks the line further up, as the remaining plant cannot handle the greater influx of goods; soon all buffer space is full, goods waiting to be stored constrict the loading bay area and the whole storage cycle gets out of phase.

Delivery times

4.02 With the satellite tracking of vehicles and 'transparency' in inventory and ordering processes via the Internet, management is increasingly able to dictate delivery times to suppliers: accurate timing for long-distance trucking is becoming realistic although still difficult in the congested urban environment. Booking systems are now commonplace: receiving 'slots' should be allocated by the 'dock master' on the availability of loading bays and the handling systems to distribute the stock in the warehouse. The designer should point out how useful land is wasted if occupied only during peak periods, the overall effect on the handling and storage system, how extra handling plant is likely to stand idle for much of the day, the added intangible factors of considerable peak strain on the facilities, and the greater chance of stealing and accidents. Management should be consulted about daily and seasonal peaks.

Vehicle flow

4.03 The control of transport on the site is important in the efficient use of the warehouse. Vehicle flow should be one way round the site wherever possible, with routes, accumulation and parking zones clearly marked. An audiovisual communications system to call vehicles forward from a position well out of the manoeuvring and loading bay area prevents accumulating vehicles constricting circulation (see Technical study, Loading 1). Light vehicles, if numerous, should be segregated from heavy traffic. They have a faster throughput, and constrict heavier vehicles.

4.04 Vehicle control is bound up with documentation, security and the type of loading dock best suited to the application. Plan vehicle routes in a clockwise direction for 'right-hand drive' countries such as Britain and Japan and anti-clockwise for 'left-hand drive' nations, to keep the drivers' side in view of the docks – a speed, control and safety issue. For large-scale operation, a control box at the gate with a document-handling system to the traffic office is an advantage (see Technical study, Loading 1,

Figure 4.3 *Forklift trucks with extending fork carriage discharging pallets from side loading curtain-sided trailer.*

Figure 2.5a–c). The office will then be a step ahead of incoming traffic, and can plan movement to the most efficient bay for the part of the store involved. They can also control the vehicles more accurately by anticipating trucks' arrival and doing any 'shuffling' necessary before a jam occurs. For dispatch vehicles, a gatehouse linked with the traffic office helps security, and clears the dock area more quickly in that the drivers will collect their documents as they leave the site without blocking circulation in the loading area (see Technical study, Mechanized storage 2, para. 38.01). Remember that at least one large vehicle buffer space is needed close to the gatehouse on both the receiving and the dispatch sides, as document delivery is sometimes slow or the documents are inaccurate, requiring confirmation.

Traffic office siting

4.05 The traffic office should be in a commanding position, able to view accumulation and loading bay areas. A segregated dock system may have two traffic offices. In a segregated dock, two accumulation areas are also needed, and free circulation must be possible at all times to and past these areas. In the smaller-scale operations, drivers will bring their documents to the traffic office, and the route from the vehicle parking area should not cross the stream of circulating traffic. Serious accidents have occurred by pedestrians' vision being obscured by high-sided vehicles.

4.06 The type of storage operation also affects the control of transport. For example, if the store is for components for machine production mainly arriving in cages and post pallets, for block stacking, side loading is often the quickest way to turn the vehicles round. As the vehicles need at least 5 m between them for forklift trucks (Figure 4.3), it would be wasteful of space to place the accumulation area next to the loading zone. In a warehouse for the retail trade, the dock is mainly handling pre-grouped loads of roll pallets for rear loading; then the vehicles need to use a bay as near their next load as possible, and accumulation opposite the bay ensures a fast turnround.

4.07 In some large-scale mechanized installations, the designer has to integrate road haulage circulation with tractor trains or forklift trucks from another part of the works. Clearly marked priority signs and warnings should be provided where routes cross truck ways. Crossings after blind corners or areas of parked trucks should be avoided; this may sound obvious but it is often neglected. If hidden access is unavoidable, a mirror can be useful, but beware of glare and of high vehicles fouling it, as their roofs swing several inches off vertical on cambers or when turning.

4.08 'Sustainable' transport policies will place more emphasis on rail-based deliveries for large-scale installations. 'Sustainability' is a much wider issue than transport, involving total energy use calculations for the supply chain, but in distribution transport and load planning are major components.

4.09 Rail wagon arrival depends on timetabling. Intermodal trains are generally 'split' off-site in a siding into more easily handled 'rakes' of wagons. If wagons have to be shunted across major vehicle routes, these tracks should be carefully marked and a visual and audible warning installed. There is no point in planning fast circulation and efficient vehicle accumulation if they will be baulked for long periods at a rail crossing. Check with management and the rail service provider that the peaks will not conflict.

5 Receipt of goods

5.01 Buffer space is required after unloading. Goods have to be checked against documents; in some cases shrink-wraps removed prior to sorting out for storage. Unless the form of packaging is specified in a supplier's contract, goods can arrive in old cartons, unsuitable for the storage process in operation and must be unpacked and re-palletized. It is better to provide space to repack than risk a protracted stoppage in the warehouse or injury to operatives. The same applies to damaged pallets (Figure 4.4) and stillages of an unsuitable size for the storage plant or medium. Care should be taken to segregate incoming and pre-assembled goods for dispatch in single loading bay zones, and space should also be provided for pallet trucks and weighing gear. A strip of at least 6 m should be allowed inside the cross circulation zone for this buffer area. As a rule of thumb, provide sufficient area to receive at least one complete vehicle load: in high throughput warehouses turning trailers round every 20 minutes, space for at least half a vehicle load behind every dock will be required to keep the dock free. (See also 20.1, Loading and dispatch.)

Figure 4.4(a) *Space should be provided in the unloading area for the disposal of load strapping and packing material. Added tyre sections act as buffers, and chocks on chains prevent the truck from moving forward.* (b) *Clear lanes for laying out the incoming load for check-in behind the loading dock.*

6 Form of goods

6.01 Most goods received in mechanized storage installations are unit loads, in the form of pallets, roll pallets, crate dollies and stillages; packed into ISO containers, trailers, box vans or flat vehicles. As a rule, except in groupage operations and some cases of specialist component supply, large numbers of loose-packed small packages should not be expected. The exceptions to this are containers arriving from 'deep-sea' routes that have been hand-stuffed for maximum use of volume. Tighter supply chain management and environmental controls results in suppliers delivering goods 'de-trashed' to the distribution customer in their preferred unit load for direct merchandising and display, such as 400 mm x 600 mm plastic crates. These tend to be transported stacked on dollies (a slave frame on casters) of plan base about 600 mm x 800 mm. There are pallet and crate 'pools' to service industry with unit load devices of common sizes and types.

7 Unloading

7.01 The type of unloading organization depends on mode of transport, product and the type of storage operation. If all goods are palletized and arrive in tilt or flat trailers or side-door containers and a high throughput is needed, then a finger dock is the most effective. Finger docks use more space but have faster handling speed, but with a normal 90° dock more vehicles can be handled at once in the same space, so turnround is nearly as fast, with less chance of a troublesome load constricting the whole system (see Information sheet, Loading 1). The designer should assess the relative merits carefully with the transport manager, considering possible future trading patterns and vehicle types. Some companies receiving numerous small loads unload at random into wheeled cages which are then removed at once to a sorting area, and taken in rotation. This clears the dock quickly. Other methods for frequent small deliveries include light mobile belt units taking individual parcels directly out of the loading area, or fixed belts for larger handling operation. Mobile conveyors are quickly removable by one operative.

7.02 The unloading of pallets in mechanized warehouses is normally achieved with forklift trucks. In raised docks, if light vans with loose loads are anticipated, it is worth providing a special bay with a ramp so that a powered pallet truck can be used for unloading. Difficulty has been found in some cases with suppliers arriving at a store with a small van, with goods loaded on pallets placed at their premises by a forklift truck operating at ground level. The ramp could also be used for a forklift truck in this case, but ought not to exceed 1 in 12. If there is not the space, a scissor-lift table can be provided for lowering the forklift or raising the van or specify an elevating dock leveller. (See Information sheet, Loading 5.)

7.03 Space should be provided in the unloading area for storing or the disposal of load strapping and packing material for recovery (Figure 4.4), especially if involved with 'deep-sea' ISO containers. (See also Loading Information Sheet 3, Figure 24b.)

7.04 In a warehouse for the retail trade there is a particular problem as, unless a segregated bay layout is planned, vehicles arrive with empty pallets and roll pallets from their delivery rounds. In several installations, peaks of returning vehicles restricted movement in loading area. In one dock, vehicles from the first delivery round to the nearer supermarkets arrive at approximately 9.30 to 10 a.m. meeting the second phase being loaded. Large numbers of empty roll pallets accumulate in the dock area, although there is a towline system to remove them as fast as possible (Figure 4.5a–c). Some roll pallets are inevitably damaged during retail distribution, and these are liable to accumulate, as they have to be sorted for

(a)

(b)

(c)

Figure 4.5 (a) *Numbers of empty roll pallets have accumulated, and heaps of broken units have developed round the edge. Pallets are also awaiting sorting to the rear. At peak times, these would overflow into the loading area.* (b) *Damaged roll pallets have collected in a corner, and are beginning to encroach on circulation space.* (c) *Damaged roll pallets have encroached from the left towards the towline track; reach trucks have to wait until the tow cart has passed to get by. The roll pallets on the right are waiting for sorting.*

damaged units. Once removed from the loading area, these roll pallets usually end up in a corner of the yard, or an empty loading bay. Space should be provided for this. However much space that can be spared in a loading bay area for pallets, it will never seem enough.

Unloading rail wagons

7.05 Unloading rail trucks is an over-the-side operation, and sliding door wagons and side access containers allow normal fork truck access. If the train carries ISO containers, standard pallet heights are applicable, but if normal wagons are used, clearances are lower. Travel distances are greater; economically, a train can be counted as a long picking face (see Information sheet, Loading 6).

8 Characteristics of goods

8.01 It is worth considering whether the goods concerned have any special characteristics, for example, are they easily damaged? It is at this point before they are sorted and mechanically handled into the store that any extra protection can be added.

9 Sorting

9.01 Prior to storage, the goods are generally 'scanned-in', i.e. recorded and labelled or coded for data feedback to the stock control section. Once recorded, goods can be either allocated a rack, or randomly stored and the driver records where they were placed (see Stock control, para 14). In smaller low-height installations, most of this area can be dispensed with, as the same forklift usually stores direct from unloading into the racking. This is only possible if the turnover is relatively slow, as the road vehicle turnround will be hindered due to the forklifts being away in the racks. For faster operation, the unloading unit meets the plant serving the racking at a point in the sorting area. This point can be a forklift-to-forklift or a forklift-to-reach truck interface, but in all cases these positions should be clearly marked. (See Technical study, Loading 1, Figure 2.15.) Note:

1. If a high lift machine is used in the racking, take care that there is sufficient clearance at the interface point. Some turret trucks that lift to 10 m plus are 3.9 m tall when operating at low level. Often there is a firewall and this is convenient for use as a run for pipes and cables. Ideally the unloading forklift should just intrude into the rack zone, but some managements prefer all unsorted goods to be kept 'truckside'.
2. Container stuffing forklifts, although capable of being equipped with three-stage masts, are not very efficient in rack areas.

9.02 Goods in this area are sorted for high-, medium- and low-user stock. If the number of stock lines is small and the throughput is high enough for a block stack, the sorting area is purely for recording case numbers as the forklift truck passes through. The same applies in pre-production storage, where large loads of high-user parts in post pallets can be block-stacked.

9.03 With mechanized parts storage, the sorting process can be more complex. Bulk loads may require splitting down into tote boxes prior to storage, and this is space consuming. It is likely that with industry's greater packaging awareness this process will disappear, and modular 'ready-to-use' packs have been introduced that can be stored on pallets in the normal way and withdrawn from bulk to access storage as required.

10 Volume calculations

10.01 This is the key to successful warehouse planning. Initial calculations should be made in a feasibility study at sketch design stage. Volume calculation is dependent on the storage system proposed, the characteristics of the commodity and the speed of throughput predicted. Different storage methods produce various volume char-

Table 4.1 Volume characteristics of types of storage

Type of storage	Cubic space utilization (%)	Effective use of medium (%)
Bulk stacking	100	75
Post pallets	90	75
Drive-in racking	65	75
Pallet racking (APR)	30–50	100
Gravity live storage	80	70
Powered mobile racks	80	100

acteristics. Unless the designer is particularly skilled in accurately assessing warehouse volume, a mechanical-handling consultant should be included into the design team.

10.02 Store throughputs and build-up patterns can be simulated quickly and accurately with computer aid, and various aisle widths and handling-plant work cycles compared against initial and long-term costs and the expected throughput and return. The designer's responsibility is to understand the implications of any form of storage suggested. Table 4.1 gives a rough estimate of the volume characteristics as a check. Adjustable pallet racking (APR) is the most widely used storage medium offering a compromise between individual pallet selection and efficient space use: any of the other methods listed in Table 4.1 have to be carefully considered as often they have hidden inefficiencies or operational issues: the selection criteria are set out later in this section.

10.03 At this point, site characteristics have an influence, with type of storage required, and the money and erection time available. For example, the site might be small when the area required for vehicle circulation has been subtracted and, thus, demand a high rack installation in order to achieve the required capacity. This has to be balanced with the increased cost of high lift narrow aisle trucks, of a double reinforced super-flat floor, and for stronger foundations.

11 Turnover calculations

11.01 Turnover calculations are based on the demands of the distribution or production systems. This will determine whether block or rack storage will be required, what mix of these and what scale of mechanization will be required. This should also be considered at the sketch design stage. For example, in a warehouse serving the retail outlets of a region, planned demand from supermarkets and predicted seasonal peaks and growth of certain products, linked with the most economic distribution pattern, will dictate the throughput of the store. Further detailed examination of the delivery and dispatch patterns will determine the exact requirements day to day, with the addition of a built-in overload ('headroom') and expansion capacity. The warehouse can be functionally divided into three basic zones: goods reception and dispatch, stockholding, and order picking. The effect of increasingly tight supply chains through order and stock 'transparency' between companies' computer systems is to minimize stock holding and increase turnover. This means that many order fulfilment centres merely break down bulk loads from suppliers into customer orders: there is no stock at the end of the day. The throughput

Mechanized storage – storage process

(a)

(b)

Figure 4.6 (a) *Mobile racking;* (b) *roll through (live) pallet. Storage reduces forklift traffic.*

can be further increased and the sorting cycle times reduced by the suppliers pre-sorting the customer's distribution such that the only task required is to reorganize unit loads of product between trunk haulage vehicles and smaller local delivery vans: this is 'cross-docking'. Many distribution warehouses now need to combine these instant, rapid and traditional turnover characteristics on one site, and the proportions of these turnover 'bands' can change within the life of the building. The proportion of reception and dispatch area to stockholding, i.e. low height predominantly vehicle driven as opposed to high-bay volume driven can only be determined by analysis.

11.02 The storage volume and turnover demand, i.e. the variety of stock, the time it needs to dwell in the warehouse and the speed of access required when the stock is needed is also decided by analysis. The shape of the stockholding area, i.e. long and thin or nearly square, is a function of the storage system selected and the speed of access and handling required. The selection criteria for storage systems are discussed later in this chapter. Data are available from manufacturers on forklift, reach truck and turret truck cycle times, although beware of these figures being optimum performances in ideal conditions. The possibility of meeting optimum throughput cycles should be balanced against the availability of volume and area, and the cost of the operation. The same applies for a pre- or inter-process store, but calculation is easier as production cycles can be accurately gauged.

12 Variety and flow

12.01 The wide variety of goods to be stored affects the level of mechanization required. If the stock is a large number of different lines, the warehouse organization will have to be based on the relative speed of movement of goods so that mobile plant can work economically. If the flow of several commodities is very fast compared with a general medium level over the bulk of the stock, but not enough to justify block stacking (Figure 4.6a), it is worth considering a live system on a first-in, first-out basis rather than keeping a forklift truck shuttling in and out of the racking (see 11.1 and 4.6b). If, as in many retail and pre-production warehouses, there is a large variety of stock to be dispatched in small lots, the main store really backs up the primary function of order picking and dispatch. A hybrid solution will probably result.

12.02 Analyse the characteristics of the storage processes in terms of throughput per item. The typical product quantity curve is shown in Figure 4.7a. One of the 'facts of life' is the Pareto curve: 80 per cent of the throughput originates from 20 per cent of stock variety. This Pareto is determined by a stock turnover analysis, often refered to as the A, B, C analysis or 'runners, repeaters and dwellers'. For very product focused stores this can increase to 90/10. But the converse is also true: 20 per cent of the throughput originates from 80 per cent of the stock lines, the medium and slow movers. It is the very slow throughput items, the 'tail' that has to be maintained to satisfy customers' expectations, that is space consuming. Stores can be classified into categories requiring different treatment (Figure 4.7b–d).

- High throughput, low variety. This requires block stacking, drive-in racking, or live racking.
- Medium throughput, medium variety. This requires a mixture of bulk storage racking and active storage.
- Low throughput, high variety. This is basically an access store; pallet racking and order picking divided

by speed of throughput. This type will have more personnel involved.

13 Type of storage

13.01 The type of storage and handling system to be adopted should be determined by the requirements of the logistics of the situation rather than being driven by a preconception of the type or shape of the building. Ultimately site constraints may drive an iterative design process between the optimum storage system and the building footprint but the operation should have priority; that is where the long term money lies. The selection of a storage system is therefore based on the most efficient and safe method of putting away, accessing and order picking the goods. In brief, the parameters which affect the choice of the system are:

Stock characteristics
1. The variety of items in stock.
2. Size, shape and weight of individual items.
3. Item dispatch rate and difference between items.
4. Ratio of stocks held to throughput.
5. Change in volume of goods in storage to volume of goods assembled for customer delivery.
6. The requirements to dispatch in quantities smaller than manufacturers' unit packs.

Customer order characteristics
1. Number of customers' orders to be picked per session/shift.
2. Number of items per customer order.
3. Volume or weight of orders both individually and in an hour/shift.
4. Time required between receipt of order and dispatch of goods.

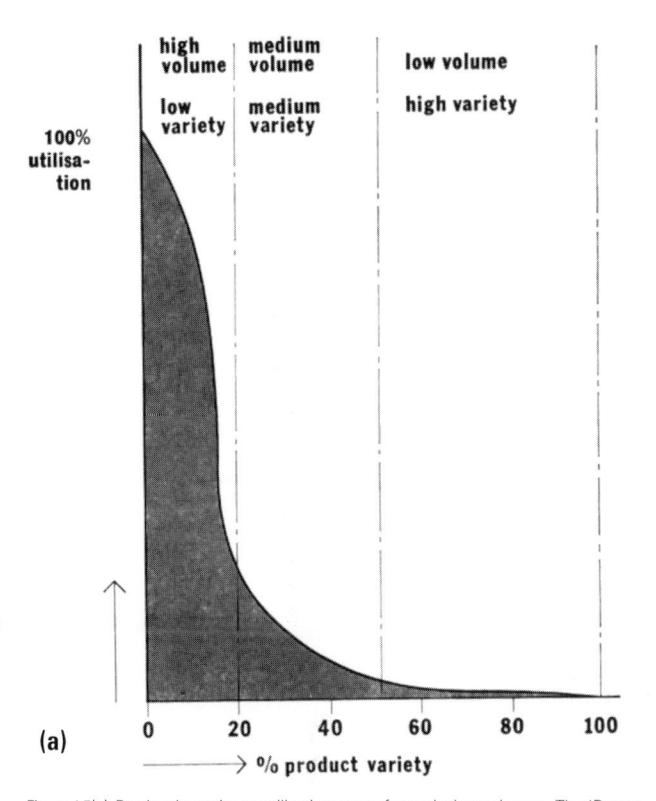

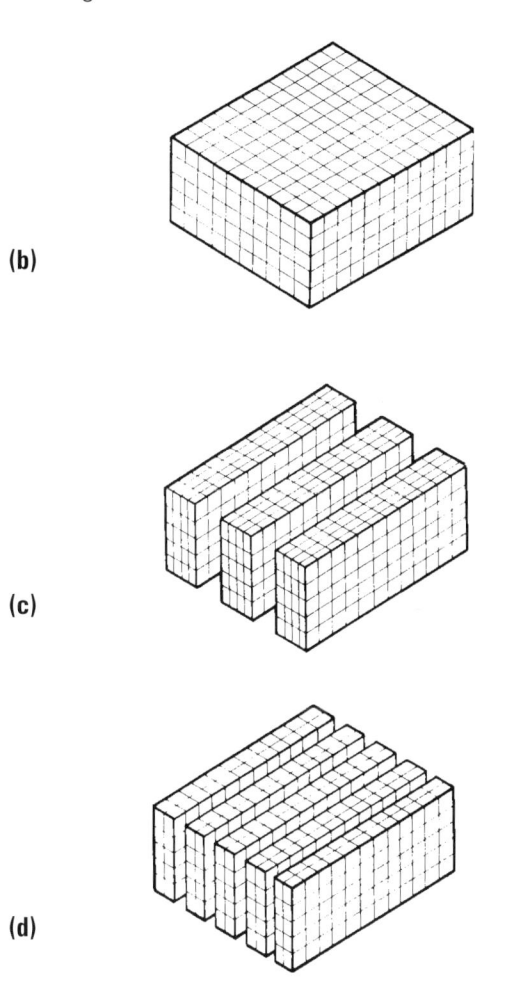

Figure 4.7(a) Product/quantity or utilization curve for typical warehouse. The 'Pareto curve': 80 per cent of the throughput originates from 20 per cent of stock variety; conversely 100 per cent variety means that utilization is extremely low. (b, c, d) Utilization versus selectivity. Volume utilization falls off steeply as product variety exceeds 20 per cent. (b) 100% utilization (low) selectivity; (c) 50% utilization, 30% selectivity; (d) 35-50% utilization, 100% selectivity.

5 Frequency of customer dispatches.
6 Significance of any 'special' order requirements, i.e. fragility, security, perishable.

13.02 Having examined the demand for order-picking and assembly, and for the storage method most economic in terms of space and flow, next examine the type of handling required: essentially manual, mechanized or both with manual order picking.

Manually operated facilities

13.03 Successful planning of a manual storage building or zone depends on dimensional control based on human measurements, a good working environment, and understanding of how a person is used as 'handling plant'. Designers tend to consider humankind only in terms of intellectual and environmental needs, not as a hardworking industrial machine. Compared with lifting and carrying mechanical plant people are inefficient, as they have low power-to-weight ratio and variable performance. This inefficiency is balanced by a person's ability to do two or more things at once.

13.04 An average warehouse operative can, simultaneously, carry an awkwardly shaped, damaged parcel up a flight of twisting stairs, compensate for the shape of the parcel in relation to clearance in the stairwell, keep a hand over the damaged section to prevent further spillage and think of the paperwork and the next process. This versatility is at the same time a person's great advantage over a machine. He or she can handle a wide range of aids, and is limited only by the weight and size of the object to be handled. The human hand has 22 possible separate movements, coupled with a very flexible, cushioned yet strong outer skin, enabling a wide variety of shapes to be easily and carefully handled. A machine needs clamps and other complex attachments. In order picking, for instance, a person is still the most effective tool available, in that he or she can simultaneously carry out a clerical function with manual selection and visual distinction.

13.05 The EU Handling Directive is proscriptive in how often and how much men and women should lift, both continuously and occasionally. Similar regulation exists in most industrialized countries: through the OSSHA in the USA for example. Although under subsidiarity, EU member states (i.e. the UK) can make their own detailed rules such as training standards, the practical lifting and continuous handling limits are very similar (Figure 4.8).

13.06 Although computers can produce detailed picking sequences and can check the pickers' accuracy, a person can still pick small goods more efficiently than a machine. This is especially true in the case of small loads, less than pallet size, for which the high cost of automated selection mechanism is often unjustified.

13.07 In consistency of performance, a person compares badly with a machine. He or she can be thoughtless and irresponsible and also cause malicious damage. Inconsistency is usually caused by fatigue; ideally the work should spread a person's output evenly over a shift rather than exhaust him or her in one huge effort. Unlike machines, a person's efficiency decreases after 'recharging' (i.e. taking a meal) and his or her overall effectiveness decreases steeply over the period of the shift. This becomes important when considering system manufacturers' productivity claims: these tend to extrapolate the peak performance over an entire shift.

13.08 Because a person is limited to carrying comparatively small loads, unit cost per ton of cargo handled is high compared with a machine. A person's first cost involves only a pair of overalls, gloves and the cost of an advertisement, but running costs can prove very expensive; redundant machines can be sold but personnel have to be paid redundancy money. An old or outmoded machine can be scrapped; a person often has to be paid a pension.

13.09 Boredom can be a special hazard for anyone engaged on repetitive work. Order picking with stock lists introduces a measure of interest, and some companies introduce a productivity bonus as a further incentive. The designer of manual systems has the responsibility of designing for a human being not only as a machine, with specific motions to perform, but also as an individual. Bad working conditions are often at the root of industrial unrest.

13.10 Manually operated storage usually combines bulk stock and order picking. In operations such as cash-and-carry, a pedestrian-controlled reach truck places pallets of goods on three-level racking. The top two levels are replenishment stock for the base section, used for direct picking. Another system (often used on the Continent) is a bulk rack area backing up a live storage picking face, where packages are unpacked from the 'outer' and placed in gravity flow lanes, so that customers can pick the commodities required in an environment more like a large supermarket than a warehouse. Spares and components are often stored in tote bins, cartons or cages, for direct picking and replenishment from bulk stock, often block stacked in the same area. Drawers and mobile shelf units are also used. (See Information sheet, Mechanized storage 1). These methods allow many small parts to be stored in a confined space, and yet be equally accessible. Racks should be carefully positioned for personnel to stack and pick stock without overreaching or twisting under load to cause themselves injury. Racks should be spaced far enough apart for those working in the rack area to move freely without colliding with passing barrows. This dimension will be governed by the type of barrow and the operation, i.e. if drawers are involved, the

Figure 4.8 *This stack is just within EU handling guidelines!*

operative will intrude further into the aisle (for dimensions see Information sheet, Mechanized storage 1). Mezzanines can double volume where usable height is limited by human dimensions. This involves goods lifts and inter-floor belts. (See Technical study, Mechanized storage 11.)

Mechanized facilities: Block stacking

13.11 This is the stacking of unit loads one above the other in blocks several loads wide and deep (see Figure 4.6a). Blocks are separated by a grid of aisles which provide access for each block. The advantages are that no special storage equipment is needed except for pallets. This is the cheapest form of storage as far as capital investment in equipment is concerned. If loads are crush-sensitive, use post pallets or drive-in racking (drive-in racking is really a type of block stacking). With post pallets in Britain, shoe-type legs are traditionally used, which wastes space. In the USA for example, 1100 × 1200 mm stacking containers can accommodate 40 per cent more material by eliminating the stacking shoe. Typical cost savings in a large-scale American operation are 20 per cent on in-plant handling, 14 per cent transport and 13 per cent storage (using pallets nested with a conical peg and recessed cone). (See Information sheet, Mechanized storage 4.)

13.12 Area required per pallet position for various block widths and stacking heights is shown in Figures 4.9 and 4.13, the latter showing comparative areas for pallet racking. Up to four pallets high, the floor area require-

Figure 4.10 *Drive-in racking. Forklifts arrive right into the racking, placing pallets in front of each other on projecting rails.*

ments for block stacking are much lower. Figure 4.9 also shows that little advantage can be gained from having blocks larger than 20 pallets square. One consultant calculated that where material is block stacked two or three stacks deep from the aisle and the store is bounded by normal factory service aisles, 34 per cent can be added to the actual pallet area to allow for internal aisles. If the block stack is isolated and requires its own main aisles and marshalling area, a further allowance should be made to increase the basic pallet area to 180 per cent. A designer or materials-handling engineer should, of course, develop his or her own factors according to the peculiarities of the goods and unit loads.

13.13 Disadvantages of block stacking include the difficulty of obtaining direct access to the block, except for top loads at edges of aisles, and overall poor selectivity. This is a drawback if several varieties of items are to be held in stock, and in this case drive-in racking might be a better solution (Figure 4.11).

13.14 The dispensing of part pallet loads is difficult unless post pallets or drive-in racking are used. The need for stability and prevention of load crushing limits most block stacks to two to three pallets high. Again drive-in

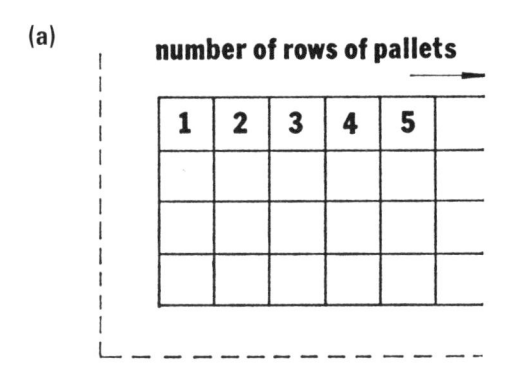

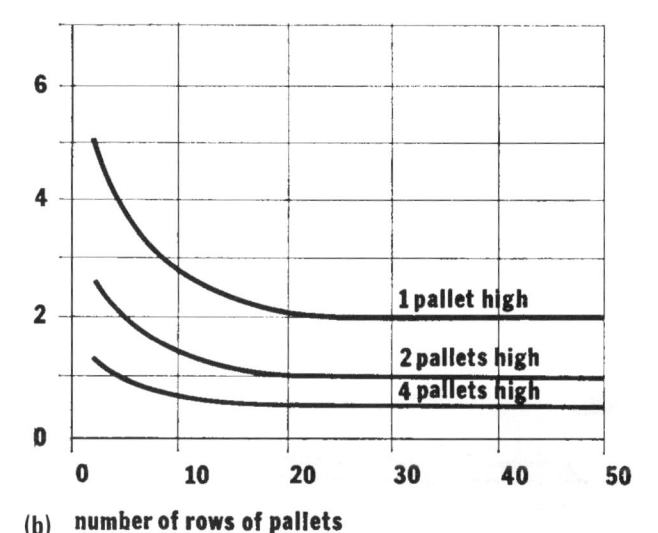

Figure 4.9 *Rough calculations for feasibility studies. To find the area per pallet position for block stacking a given number of 1200 × 1100 mm pallets: (1) divide the number of pallets by four (i.e. assume they are stacked in rows four deep and count the rows in (a). Ignore aisle spaces (dotted). These are included in the graph calculation; (2) Decide how many pallets high the block stack will be. Using (b), by reading the number of rows of pallets along the bottom line, and the number of pallets high along the right hand vertical, area in m² can be found. For example, 200 pallets at four rows deep = 50 rows. Stacked two high, area required = 1 m² per pallet position.*

Figure 4.11 *Block-stacked kegs.*

Mechanized storage – storage process

racking is the answer to load crushing. Drive-in racking, with the pallets' edges resting on rails and without cross members, allows up to 65 per cent cube utilization, as loads can be nearly up to the base of the unit above (Figure 4.12). Some products in large post pallets or stacking crates allow heights of up to 10 m block-stacked by an overhead stacker crane.

13.15 The poor selectivity afforded by block stacking will probably bias the type of storage against a random block system, and a system of allocated storage will probably have to be employed, i.e. areas in a warehouse set aside for particular items. Block stacking is best suited for the storage of palletized goods and inherent unit loads such as bales or drums, in buildings where available headroom limits storage height, and where variety is low and throughput is high (Figure 4.11). Block stacking can be ideal where goods are stored in complete loads prior to removal to the active area for order picking, and in load marshalling areas before dispatch where random storage is acceptable because no order picking is involved.

Pallet racking

13.16 The limits of racking height are determined only by the height of the building and by the capability of the device used for placing and removing the unit loads. Advantages include: direct access to every single item held in the store; a great advantage in order picking when a large variety of items is involved. Direct access also gives 100 per cent selectivity, allowing the use of random storage with considerable savings in floor area requirements. Because racking supports pallets or unit loads, stability and crushing resistance are not important. Stacking heights of seven loads high are now possible with high lift reach trucks and narrow aisle trucks: reach trucks lifting to 10 m high, and narrow aisle (turret) trucks to 14 m plus. The 100 per cent selectivity means that there can be a first-in, first-out system where necessary. High capital cost is the principal disadvantage. Pallet racking is most suitable for storage of palletized goods and other unit loads where there is a wide variety of lines in stock. It is particularly suitable as an active store for order picking.

The curve in Figure 4.13 – gross area per pallet stored – is a ready floor area reckoner for concept planning with racked storage: the curve contains assumptions of aisle width, the space required at rack ends for changing aisles, and the level of technology selected. From right to left; counter-balanced forklift truck lifting to three high racking working in a 3.5 m aisle, 1.33 sq m/pallet stored: reach truck in a 2.7 m aisle lifting to four pallets high, 0.95 sq m/pallet; reach truck in a 2.9 m aisle lifting to nine high, 0.43 sq m/pallet stored, a popular solution in modern distribution centres; narrow aisle turret truck in a 1.8 m aisle lifting to 11th level, 0.3 sq m/pp, also popular replenishing multilevel order picking (see Figure 4.22); and finally a very narrow aisle free or fixed-path system lifting to 15 pallet positions high, 0.2 sq m/pp. (See also Chapter 5, Automated storage.) Note, that this concept area calculation applies to the racked area only: it does not account for goods-inwards, order sorting or dispatch assembly areas (see also para 13.12).

(a) *Forklift trucks.*
Aisle width = 3.4 m
Stacking height = 6 m
Box pallets over width of building = 18
Total number of pallets = 396
Utilization = 100 per cent

(b) *Normal stacker.*
Aisle width = 3.4 m
Stacking height = 10 m
Box pallets over width of building = 30
Total number of pallets = 660
Utilization = 166 per cent

(c) *Stacker with grapple.*
Aisle width = 780 m
Stacking height = 8 m (10 m)
Box pallets over width of building = 880 (1000)
Utilization = 220 per cent
(250 per cent with large boxes)

(d) *All-purpose building with universal stacker crane.*
Utilization = 35 to 50 per cent

(e) *Warehouse with pallet rack and order-picking machines.*
Utilization = 65 per cent

(f) *Pallet warehouse rack structure also serving as roof support.*
(see Automated storage)

Figure 4.12 *Block stacking: (a – c) Comparison of type of block stacking. Warehouse dimensions: width 20.4 m; height 11.7 m; length 46 m. Box pallets 1600 × 1600 × 2000 mm, weighing 1200 kg. (Pallet racking: d – f) Comparison of pallet racking and stacker cranes. Utilization refers to pallet places available, not that achieved in a store turning over stock, which will vary according to stock and operatives.*

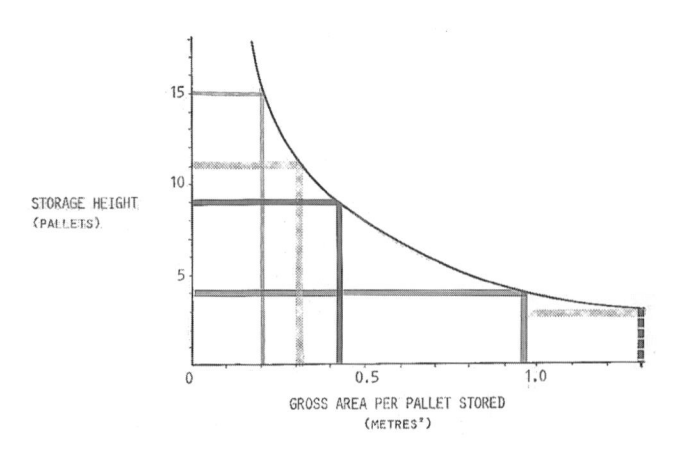

Figure 4.13 *To find the floor area per pallet position for pallet racks for a given number of 1200 × 1100 mm pallets. Right to left: forklift truck/reach/bendi-truck; high lift reach truck; narrow aisle turret truck; very narrow aisle system. Read typical area per pallet stored on the bottom scale.*

Mechanized storage – storage process

Figure 4.14 *Typical reach truck retracting its mast within its wheelbase.*

Choice of racking and handling plant

13.17 Racking and handling plant should always be considered as one integrated system. Up to heights of about 6 m, normal forklift trucks can be used, but aisles need to be as wide as their swept turning circle and the tolerance of the swinging load. If floor area is at a premium, aisles can be narrowed by using reach trucks, whose turning circles are more compact by retracting their masts during travel within their wheelbase (Figure 4.14). If more volume capacity is required and a 50 per cent reduction in selectivity is acceptable, storage can be two loads deep in the racks (Figure 4.15). (This is different from drive-in racking; the racks are normal pallet racking, and the reach truck has a pantograph action on the fork head so that the rear pallet can be placed without fouling the cross members.) If the area-to-volume ratio needs to be increased, keeping 100 per cent individual pallet selectivity, narrow aisle trucks can be specified, where the aisles need only be marginally wider than the widest pallet (Figure 4.16). There are several forms of these trucks available, with lifts of 6 to 7.5 m. Usually these do not turn in the aisle, but are either side loaders with a mast that

Figure 4.15 *Pantograph attachments allow forklift to stack loads two deep from one aisle.*

Figure 4.16 *Narrow aisle reach truck.*

Figure 4.17 *Transfer position between turret truck and forklift from loading bay known as a P&D station.*

moves across the chassis on a carriage to push the pallet into the rack, or can rotate at the base of the mast to allow double-sided access without having to leave the aisle. Other forms have a conventional mast facing the direction of travel and a fork system that will extend either side. A third method uses a conventional forklift with a special three-way attachment, but this has to be aligned correctly before entering the racks. All these types are 'free path', in that they can also be used in the warehouse for general purposes.

13.18 For a higher cubic capacity with the minimum of floor area, free-standing racking can be built to over 18 m high. For 12 m work, free-path turret trucks are available that can also be used for general duties (Figure 4.17). Several models allow the operator to rise with the load and so can use this as an order picker as well. (All dimensions of forklift trucks are in Information sheet,

87

Mechanized storage – storage process

Mechanized storage 7.) These machines require aisles only a little wider than the pallet length. Fitted with side guide wheels running in channels at the rack base or wire guidance for greater accuracy, these machines can lift to over 14 m. Obviously the amount of vertical rack divisions and lift height are governed by the average height and weight of the pallets handled, and the capacity of the turret trucks.

13.19 Most racking manufacturers offer adjustable systems that can be quickly altered to suit the maximum cubic potential with various pallet heights throughout the store (see Information sheet, Mechanized storage 3). As a rule, beam pallet racking has a 35–50 per cent cubic space utilization, and the height from the ground to the top of the highest load should not exceed six times the depth of the rack. Thus with back-to-back racking, the unrestrained height potential is greater; if exceeding the 1:6 rule, some form of restraint is needed, such as bolting to the floor. (See Information sheet, Racking.) For higher cube utilization, live storage and powered mobile racking can be used. Both these share a cube efficiency of approximately 80 per cent.

Live racking

13.20 Live racking means a number of sloped racks, into one end of which the pallets are inserted and through which they either flow under power or gravity to the other end for dispersal: first-in, first-out – FIFO (Figure 4.18). Gravity flow is not usually to be recommended with standard pallets, as jamming can occur and impacts can be substantial. Some gravity systems employ pallet carrier frames, themselves wheeled trolleys to eliminate pallet quality issues. If this is required, a 1 in 36 gradient is adequate. Live racks which allow a mixture of gravity rollers and power accumulation brakes are more usual. It is most effective to use pallets in these racks, though drums are often stored free. Advantages include high space utilization, as only one aisle is needed at each end. However, much space can be lost in the racking if pallets are not loaded to full height. The system is compatible with mechanized sortation systems, such as automatic dispensing of cartons. First-in, first-out is automatic, and selectivity is good as long as each rack division is devoted to one product. Random storage is not feasible except in load marshalling. Effective applications include mechanized warehouses with low variety and high throughput where first-in and first-out operation is important, such as semi-perishable foodstuffs. Any items of regular shape, cartons, tote boxes, as well as pallets, are suitable, where throughputs are fast and varieties are low.

Figure 4.18 *'Live racking' at the picking end. Note pallets on 'plattens' for smooth running on the incline.*

Figure 4.19 *Mobile racking.*

13.21 Powered mobile racking has proved successful for dense, varied stock with a medium selectivity rating such as frozen carcasses or dairy products in cold stores where full cubic use is important. It is expensive and slow to install. A reach truck driver can operate the movement controls until the correct aisle opens (Figure 4.19). Although dense stock is possible, only one aisle can operate at a time.

High-bay mechanized warehouses

13.22 Above 10 m, installations begin to be classed structurally as high bay. (Heights above 7.5 m gain an extra hazard fire rating – see Fire control, para. 27). Although most fall into Chapter 6, Automated storage, some high-bay warehouses are mechanized. These consist of stacker cranes with full driver control. The majority of these run on tracks at the base, stabilized at the top. One crane is offered as a more stable unit with additional support two-thirds of the way up the rack. A further system, popular in stores for heavy stillages like engines in vehicle production, has a mast suspended from the roof structure or top of the racking, allowing free travel within the rack and a rotating fork head (Figure 4.20).

Figure 4.20 *Gantry slung stacker/order picker. Allows narrow aisles but only one crane per gantry.*

Structural racking

13.23 Once racking becomes semi-structural or structural costs rise considerably. Careful economic studies should be carried out to examine whether the increased cube and throughput benefits increase with the saving in site area, or are eliminated against the extra cost of structural racking, specialist fixed-path handling plant, stronger foundations and building structure. See also Chapter 5, Automated storage.

Overhead cranes

13.24 Overhead cranes feature in special storage applications such as steel stockholding (see Chapter 7, Special storage), and can be used for such commodities as rolls of newsprint. Overhead stacker cranes are limited in flexibility by the track and gantry, and are expensive to install. All these systems discussed have been used to great effect in some installations. It should be remembered that the successful choice is a result of many integrated factors; alternatives should be carefully assessed and costed.

14 Stock control

14.01 Stock control and distribution systems in mechanized storage buildings are so complex and need such fast and accurate stock appraisals that computers are now generally used for this purpose. The rack organization has a bearing on how this is achieved and how successful the result will be. With a small, comparatively unsophisticated computer, (it can be a laptop), stock can be randomly stored within the user-rated sections of the store, and its position recorded for data processing. Random storage should be specially programmed to prevent the rack spaces closest to entry and discharge points of the aisles gradually becoming filled up with slow-moving items, while fast-moving items have to travel further within the warehouse. This gradually reduces the utilization of the handling plant.

14.02 A computer, if used, will work out the best picking pattern for the reach truck wherever the goods are stored: there are several proprietary systems that transmit these data to screens on the trucks. Some installations that continue the order-picking function within the bulk rack dictate a planned storage facility with allocated spaces for particular commodities (see Chapter 5, Automated storage, for fuller descriptions of computer-aided stock control).

15 Stock withdrawal

15.01 In mechanized storage, withdrawal follows a similar pattern to stacking except that often now the retrieval path for optimum handling plant travel is calculated by a computer. For easy identification from a moving reach truck, graphics for rack location should not be less than 75 mm high x 13 mm thick (Figure 4.21). For bulk withdrawal with a set pattern, as in warehouses serving the retail trade, all rack spaces should be coded with a similar code in each aisle. Corresponding numbers help stacker truck drivers to remember where high user locations are, and the position of other frequently picked commodities.

16 Order picking

16.01 A wide range of order-picking methods achieves the required speed and volume in a mechanized warehouse (for basic considerations see para. 13). If handling more than 500 orders a day with more than two items per order, bulk order picking can prove more economic than sequential picking. Bulk order picking involves progressive movement, picking several orders at a time. The items are then sorted for individual orders. Bulk picking can save personnel time; the picking operation is more efficient due to less travel per order and the increase in number picked at one time. If later order sortation is mechanized, there can be substantial savings in cost.

16.02 Sequential order picking involves progressive movement through the storage area, selecting the commodities to complete an individual order such that one circuit is travelled for each order.

16.03 In most warehouses, conventional methods of order picking involve excessive personnel movement or, if

Figure 4.21 *This shows the main rack code, ZA, and the pallet position code ZA2/194. The rack behind is numbered ZA1/194; i.e. transverse aisle pallets are numbered .../194 for identification. Also illustrates adjustable pallet racking.*

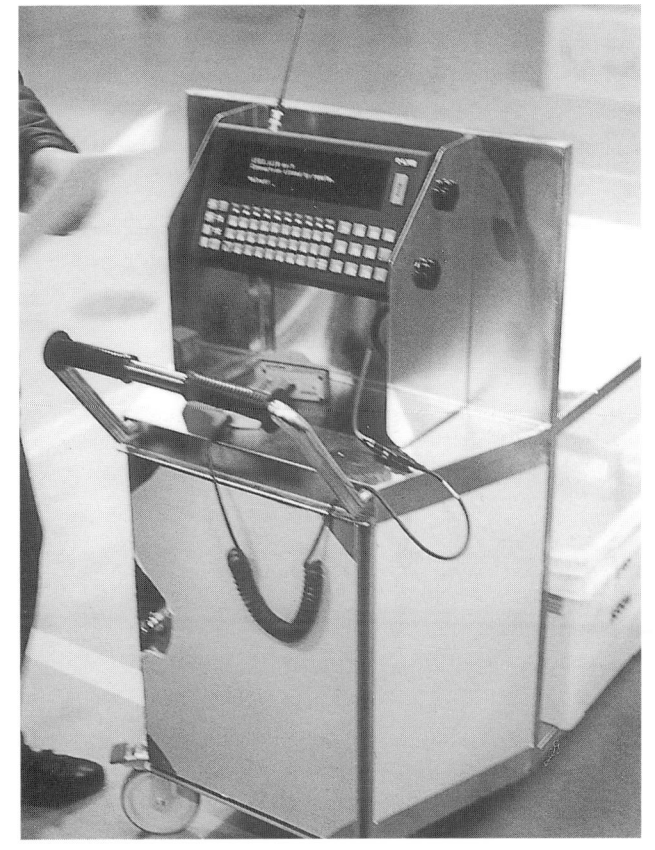

Figure 4.22 *Radio data terminal mounted on picking cart: note screen giving location and description and bar code wand for proof of pick.*

Mechanized storage – storage process

Section

Plan

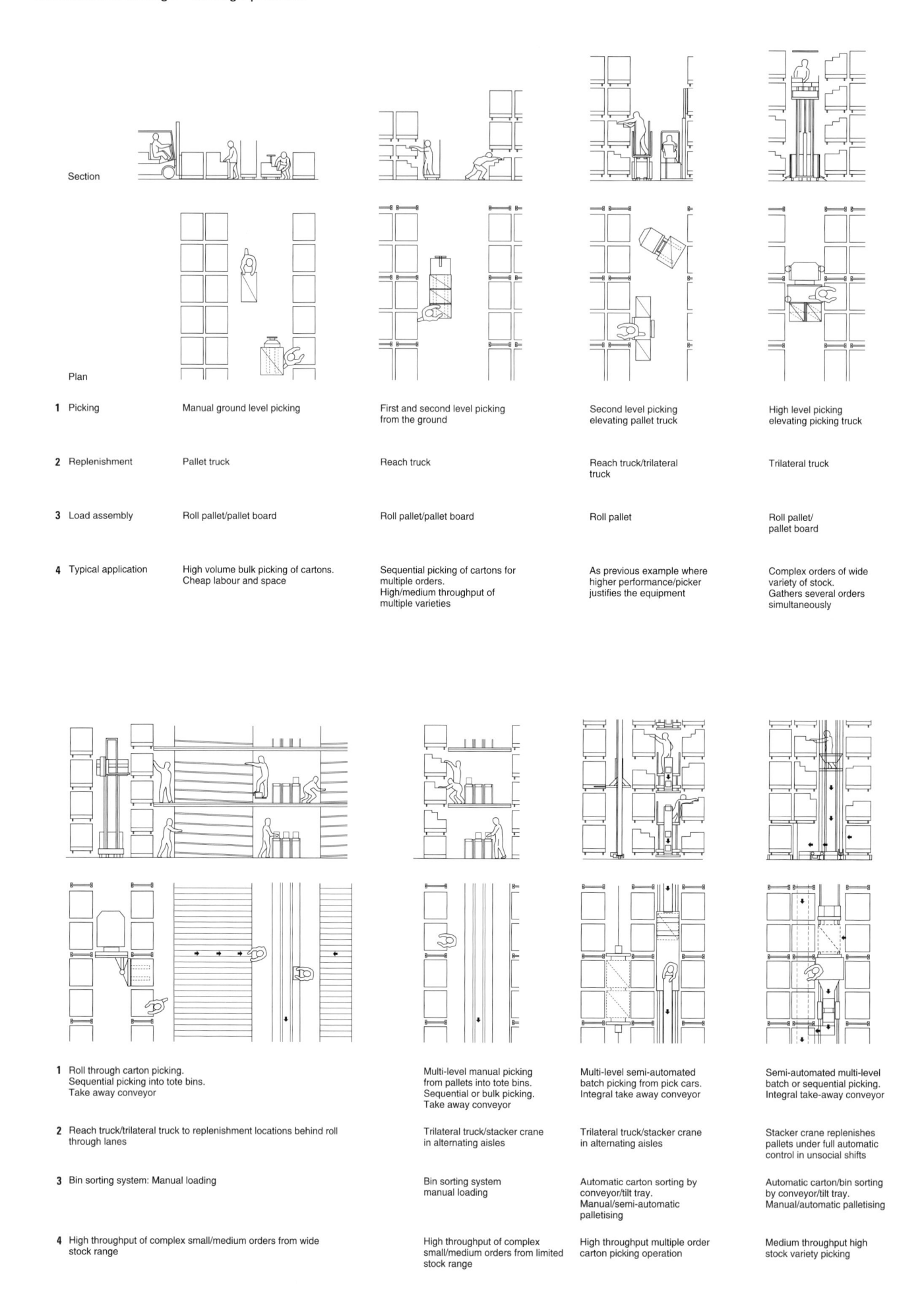

1	Picking	Manual ground level picking	First and second level picking from the ground	Second level picking elevating pallet truck	High level picking elevating picking truck
2	Replenishment	Pallet truck	Reach truck	Reach truck/trilateral truck	Trilateral truck
3	Load assembly	Roll pallet/pallet board	Roll pallet/pallet board	Roll pallet	Roll pallet/pallet board
4	Typical application	High volume bulk picking of cartons. Cheap labour and space	Sequential picking of cartons for multiple orders. High/medium throughput of multiple varieties	As previous example where higher performance/picker justifies the equipment	Complex orders of wide variety of stock. Gathers several orders simultaneously

1		Roll through carton picking. Sequential picking into tote bins. Take away conveyor	Multi-level manual picking from pallets into tote bins. Sequential or bulk picking. Take away conveyor	Multi-level semi-automated batch picking from pick cars. Integral take away conveyor	Semi-automated multi-level batch or sequential picking. Integral take-away conveyor
2		Reach truck/trilateral truck to replenishment locations behind roll through lanes	Trilateral truck/stacker crane in alternating aisles	Trilateral truck/stacker crane in alternating aisles	Stacker crane replenishes pallets under full automatic control in unsocial shifts
3		Bin sorting system: Manual loading	Bin sorting system manual loading	Automatic carton sorting by conveyor/tilt tray. Manual/semi-automatic palletising	Automatic carton/bin sorting by conveyor/tilt tray. Manual/automatic palletising
4		High throughput of complex small/medium orders from wide stock range	High throughput of complex small/medium orders from limited stock range	High throughput multiple order carton picking operation	Medium throughput high stock variety picking

Figure 4.23 *Order picking techniques.*

Mechanized storage – storage process

order separately, several orders can be picked simultaneously, wastage is reduced. When the storage pattern is assessed at stock control stage into bulk, general, and small use lines, it is then more efficient for each class of goods to be held in a unique position and employ the method of order picking best suited to the scale of operation. Figure 4.23 summarizes order-picking techniques and the duties to which these are suited: these are further explained in the following techniques. This figure and the text concerning space planning for the various order-picking techniques (see paras 16.01–16.15) should also be checked against the order picking performance values included as Additional Data in para. 21.1. Note that the performance values are provided as a guide for planning purposes only and should not be used as benchmarks.

16.04 There is still no machine that can match human versatility of selection and single unit picking, but there are considerable aids to help the picker reach this position and inform him or her of the correct number of items to be picked. Most order-picking systems are linked to a stock control computer; for complex picking operations, e.g. small components for batch production or multiple orders for 'home shopping', the computer can 'launder' the orders to group picking, handling and dispatch characteristics, and will calculate the shortest and easiest picking path (Figure 4.22). If the storage has allocated positions, based on order picking accessibility, personnel soon learn the principal sections of the warehouse and, with the aid of numbered aisles and rack positions, quickly identify the loads required. Pickers can be further assisted by electronic identification of the stock to be picked: 'pick to light' systems indicate to the picker where the next pick is located and how many items are required by illuminating an LED display at that location. To prove to the stock control system that the correct pick has been made, essential if additional down-stream checking processes are to be eliminated, the picker can 'scan' each item handled (slow), wear a specially equipped scanning gauntlet (faster but can be cumbersome) or can pick onto a trolley equipped with a 'field' scanner much like a checkout (faster still). Computer controlled manual small item picking techniques will continue to evolve (see Figure 4.22).

16.05 The simplest method of order picking generally employed in picking for supermarkets where a wide variety of cased products are handled, is along the bulk racks at floor level (Figure 2.24a), this may not present a large enough picking face for the collection speeds mechanized, repeated movement of the mechanical plant. The greater the area, the more walking has to be done by the staff: measurement has shown that often 70 per cent of a picker's time is walking, with only 30 per cent selecting and picking. If instead of handling each

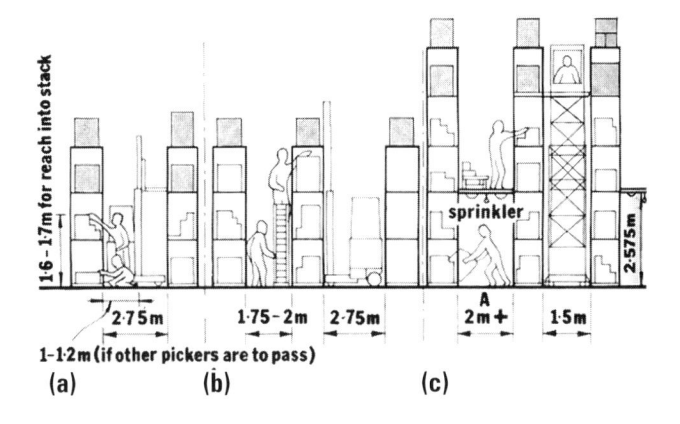

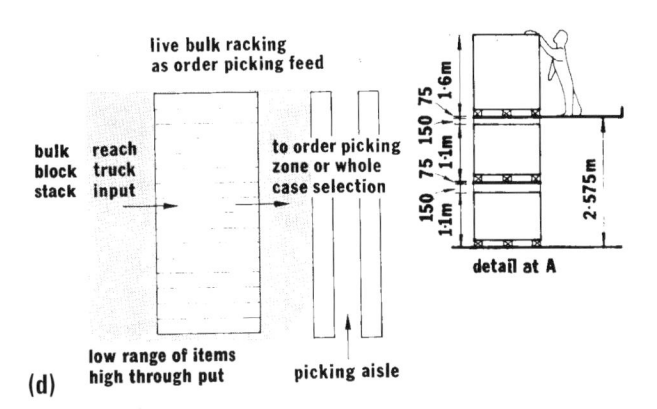

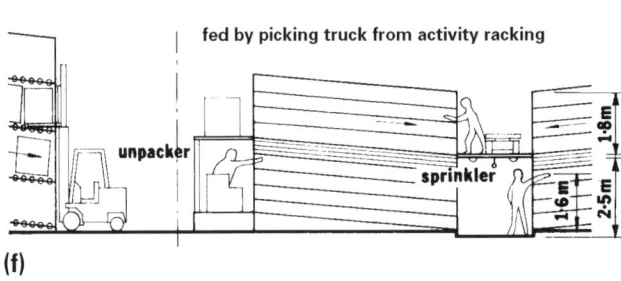

Figure 4.24(a) *Picking aisle (2.75 m) at floor level. Back-up stock (shaded) at high level is lowered to picking face by reach truck in same aisle.* (b) *Picking aisle at floor level. This time reach truck is in separate aisle (2.75 m) so picking aisle can be narrower (1.75 to 2 m).* (c) *Picking aisle (2 m plus) floor and mezzanine level, with turret truck in separate (1.8 m) aisle.* In (d), *goods pass from bulk block stack (left) to live bulk racking (centre) to picking aisle (right). Multi-line live racking. Goods are picked onto the belt (e, f) right, which takes them to the lower level for assembly into roll pallet loads. This type of racking is hand-loaded and demands a large area behind the input face to accommodate pallet loads of goods to replenish the flow lines. The pallets are raised to the mezzanine level by a forklift truck.*

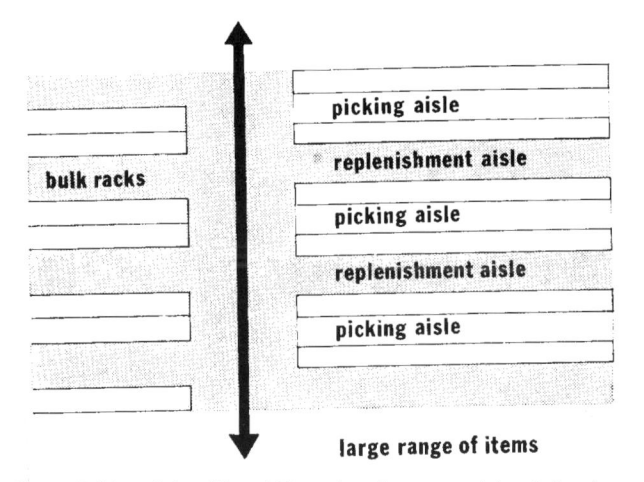

Figure 4.25 *Enlarged plan of* Figure 4.24b: *reach trucks move stock from bulk racks (left) to replenishment aisles (right), allowing plant-free picking aisles. Shaded area is reach truck path.*

Figure 4.26 *Stacking and order picking aisles arranged alternately at a warehouse in Holland, with turret truck and pallet transporter working in combination. Note how flat trusses allow maximum cube stacking, and the racking on a plinth which guides the turret truck's wheels.*

required in a mechanized warehouse, and it is preferable to have personnel grouped in a dedicated picking zone out of the way of mobile handling plant. As a rule, in medium-sized operations, the picking area is replenished from bulk stock; whenever the pallet from which the goods are being picked is nearly empty it is replaced by a full pallet from reserve stock (often stored above the picking positions). For larger and faster picking cycles, bulk stock is often moved to an active reserve stock area, and then is withdrawn by a machine allocated to feed the picking positions. This generates a section of racking backing up the picking face. If the number of lines to be picked is small, live storage can be effective and is efficient in volume; this can be designed to handle goods in full pallet form (Figure 4.24d), or the unit loads can be unpacked at the upper end and the live racking used as a carton dispenser (Figure 4.24e/f). The latter enables more lines to be picked, but involves additional labour. A development of this to double the effective picking area is to install a mezzanine in the aisle (Figure 24c), but it should be remembered that this needs intermediate sprinkling and lighting, and a method has to be found to carry the goods to the sorting area: lifts or conveyors.

16.06 Many fast-picking operations are achieved by an alternate aisle system. Pickers work from two faces on as many levels as can be reached safely in an aisle unique to the picking operation generally picking into trays or tote bins onto conveyors. The aisles on the other side are used for replenishment and the upper levels of racking used for reserve stock (Figures 4.24b and 25). Although this only reaches 50–65 per cent volume utilization, it does allow for fast replenishment and uninterrupted picking, without plant interference (Figure 4.26).

16.07 Mobile racking can also be used for order picking on a two-tier system (Figure 4.27). Bulk stock is carried at the lower levels, and picking takes place at the upper one, arranged in such a way that pickers do not get crushed. This system combines a high volume of bulk storage and medium selectivity with multi-face order picking. There are differing views whether the pickers should operate at ground or high level. At ground level, pickers can build orders direct into roll pallets for removal by pallet trucks or be towed in trains by forklift.

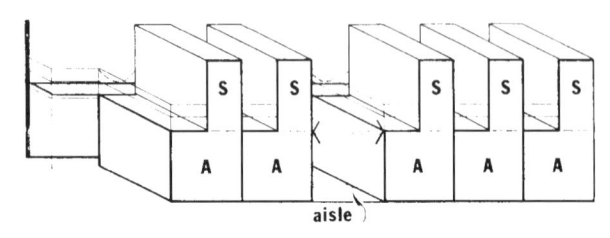

Figure 4.27 *Mobile racking, with pallet racking A below, shelving S above.*

16.08 Another effective method in large installations is for picking to be done into towline trucks (Figure 4.28). Goods can either be picked into roll pallets that are then placed in a towline frame, directly onto trolleys, or the roll pallets themselves can be converted for towline operation. A major advantage of a towline system is that orders can be dispatched at the end of a picking aisle and automatically routed to the load accumulation position. Empty trolleys or containers can be handled in this way and returned to the picking zone and stored automatically in a siding until required.

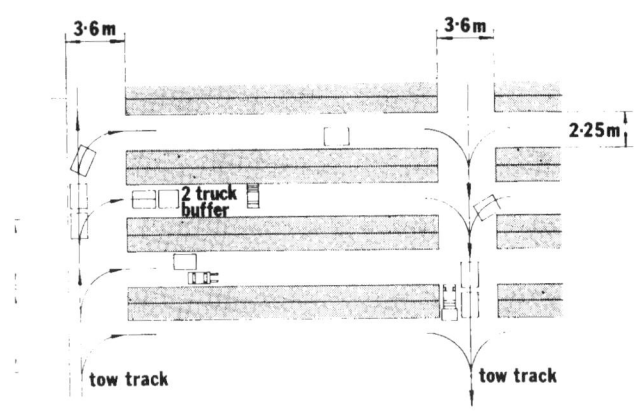

Figure 4.28 *Order picking with tow trucks.*

16.09 In larger-scale operations requiring the build-up of a lot of small loads, e.g. retail pharmaceuticals, business-to-business (B2B) stationery and 'home shopping', conveyors are useful for prioritizing, routing while transporting the trays or crates in which the picked goods are placed to a load assembly position. In bulk order picking areas, operatives work in special picking aisles; goods can be picked into tote bins sized to suit the average order, which are then coded and placed on the conveyor, positioned at the end of the rack or running down the aisle. In most cases, multilevel conveyor lines alternate with replenishment aisles (Figure 4.29).

16.10 In some installations, a more efficient and cheaper picking operation could have resulted from reassessing

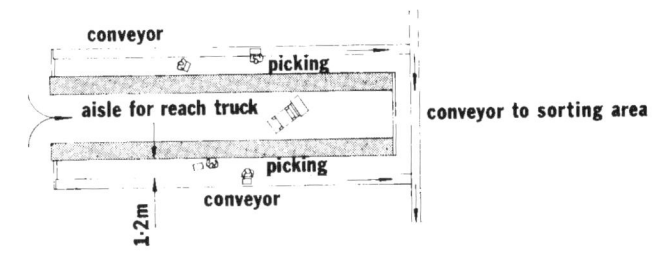

Figure 4.29 *Picking into tote boxes, sent by conveyor. Reach truck aisle feeds racks (shaded).*

the speed of product movement and racking planning rather than accelerating movement between the picking and load accumulation area. The efficiency of the whole warehouse is most important, and the installation of special in-store transport systems can have side effects by creating constrictions at certain points and impairing the operation of other sections.

Fixed-path and free-path order pickers

16.11 Fixed-path order pickers and guided free-path 'pick cars' can optimally route the picker round the storage locations, allowing the picker to handle typically up to six orders at a time (Figures 4.30 and 4.31) (Automated versions are discussed in Chapter 5.)

16.12 Operating in the horizontal and vertical planes simultaneously the driver can always work at eye level. The volume utility is about 60 per cent. Fixed-path order pickers combine pallet storage with order picking, useful for medium throughput operations or where the majority of withdrawals are full pallet loads. They are restricted by having to return to the end of an aisle to leave or collect each load, but can place the pallet on to a mezzanine for further picking or sortation. One of the advantages of using a free-path special purpose turret truck is that they can stock the racks with pallets like a narrow aisle reach truck, the operator can rise with full load to the maximum height, pick full pallets or order pick in safety, and then carry the load directly to the assembly zone without double handling. They also enable a greater amount of flexibility in allocating machinery to racks. One type of machine has an additional useful feature for order picking, where the elevating cab works independently from the fork carriage, so that when a load is being built up, the operator can lower the forks a little at a time to keep the working surface conveniently at hand level.

16.13 Special purpose pickers can also be used to collect multiple orders at one time on the principle of 'gather and dispense'. One large pharmaceutical bulk warehouse used to work on this principle. Picking towers ('panelveyors') were used for general goods picking; these are really rack-height mobile frames of shelves with an operator's cage that can be raised or lowered on either side (Figure 4.30). The operators served about 230 stock lines each (there were 2300), and pick from a summary prepared by the stock control computer. The operators collected the goods from their section for each shop served, and place the goods on one of the shelves. When an order is complete, the goods were placed into a tray and these are placed onto a takeaway conveyor to the load assembly area. While this installation was eventually replaced by outsourcing the entire operation, the technique was sound and has considerable potential for large, high

Figure 4.31 *Free path order picker picking from tote boxes.*

Figure 4.30 *Mobile picking towers used in pharmaceutical warehouse.*

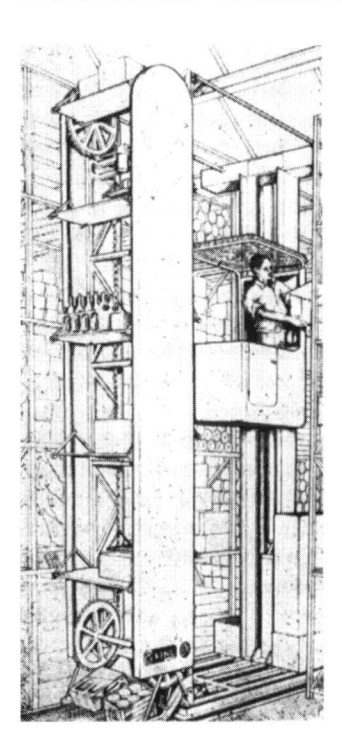

Figure 4.32 *Highly mechanised order-picking system, consisting of mobile picking tower and lowerator, picking from pallets.*

throughput picking operations with multiple stock lines. (More complex computer-controlled operations are discussed in Chapter 5.)

16.14 An intensive mechanical order picking system involves a high-speed belt running at the base of the racking to the load assembly area (Figure 4.32). The operator works in a mobile picking tower with an elevating platform. He or she picks goods into a tray from a computer written manifest. When a tray is full, it is placed with a coded destination onto a circulating lowerator, which places the tray on to the removal belt, so that the operator can immediately start a new cycle. This machine can travel horizontally at 61 m/min and the lowerator moves at 18 m/min; full pallets are stacked conventionally from the opposite side of the picking face.

16.15 The planning of any order picking system depends on the type of goods stored, the speed of picking required, and the most economic compromise between picking plant, personnel and rack height. Consider several alternatives at the sketch design stage, discuss these with the client, and plan for future flexibility; if the installation involves fixed-path picking plant, future alteration can be very costly and time-consuming.

17 Picking area

17.01 In mechanized installations safety is of prime importance on the operator-rack, conveyor or high rack machine interface. Noise and vibration can be designed-out of pick-to-belt installations. The ergonomics of order picking has received a great deal of attention: the main pick-to-light suppliers can provide assistance based on their particular systems. Discomfort whether through lifting and reaching, or through eye strain from screen technologies reduces efficiency and accuracy. Warehouse environment characteristics that affect order picking are:

1. space available for order picking related to the required throughput. Planners often neglect space to buffer replenishment stock
2. the predicted picking activity per metre run of order picking face
3. available headroom (several consultants have found that productivity rises in high, airy spaces)
4. special environmental requirements (chilled foodstuffs need gloves that tend to make item picking difficult)
5. the ratio of order picking work effort involved in selecting quantities of one item for one order to the effort required in selecting quantities of one item for a group of orders.

A high level of lighting and ventilation helps efficiency. Remember on multilevel mezzanine schemes, alternative means of escape have to be planned to cross conveyor lines.

18 Load build-up and assembly

18.01 Warehouses with bulk order picking require an area for orders to be consolidated into unit loads. Even small, simple operations, picking full pallet loads, cannot dispense with this, as a buffer and sorting area is useful for incoming as well as outgoing goods. City delivery drivers should load their own vehicles, as they know the local area and delivery cycle. Group loads well in advance of the vehicles' arrival and segregate this area from incoming sorting. Clearly marked lanes (related to numbered areas) for each van bay are useful when assembling loads. The most personnel can do is pick the correct goods and assemble trolleys so that they can be either wheeled to the vehicle for direct loading or taken to a belt end after unloading is completed. Provide space for empty trolleys; if large deliveries are anticipated, roll pallets will be used and will collect in this area for transfer. Security is important (see Security and safety, Technical Study 1, para. 28). Documents will be checked during load build-up in small-scale operations. Provide room for the checker to walk round assembled goods, and to examine random packages without snagging racking or trolleys.

Conveyors

18.02 The sorting area in a mechanized warehouse can be complex, and space-consuming if not carefully handled. As described in para. 16, bulk order picking at over 500 orders per day is likely to mean that goods will arrive from the picking zone by conveyor, partly sorted or unsorted for consolidation into unit loads for distribution; if sequentially picked, goods just have to be grouped. Areas with conveyor lines have to be carefully planned as not only the layout of the conveyors themselves has to be considered, but also wheeled traffic circulation and future flexibility. In all but the smallest operations, the conveyor lines from the order picking area are split into accumulation lanes for mechanical sorting. More goods 'snarl-ups' can occur at positions of changing conveyor lanes than anywhere else (see Information sheet, Mechanized storage 14). The greater the diversity of package types in relation to the diverting method, the more complex will be the decision about what type and surface of conveyor will be chosen.

Choice of type of conveyor

18.03 Some order picking areas, where tote bins or small wire baskets are used, employ overhead conveyors to the sorting area. These systems are extensively used in the fashion clothing industry, can queue and be directed round various circuits (Figure 4.33). They impose extension problems for reach trucks and there are especial clearance difficulties with turret trucks that can be approximately 4 m high when at their lowest position. Overhead tracks routed round the structure and building services may impair access and maintenance. The overhead conveyor can be used with its queuing ability as a multi-track accumulator, and can take the load right to the loading bay if no further sortation is required; in one large warehouse the return loop removes all empty distribution containers from the loading bay, pushing them out of the way above head level, the circuit acting as an empties store, passing an inspection area to remove any broken containers.

Figure 4.33 *Lightweight overhead track conveyor used in book store.*

Mechanized storage – storage process

Tilt tray conveyors

18.04 Tilt tray sorting conveyors, 'sorters', are an instance of part automation in a mechanized warehouse. The tilt tray sorter is an expensive and space-consuming item, particularly useful in high-volume, high-variety situations, as it combines the sorting and transport function. These units consist of closely spaced trays mounted between axially disposed pivots, on carriages that travel round a fixed track at between 1.2 and 1.8 m/sec. Because the sorter generally relies on gravity for the accumulation of goods after tilting, tilt tray sorters are usually elevated at about 3 m, requiring 5.5 m clear height space. The tray is tilted by a pneumatic roller or electric trip when it reaches the correct sortation point. These conveyors can be used in two ways; with the 'gather and dispense' principle of picking several orders together (Figure 4.34), if a computer guides the picking personnel, and they are picking a small range of products for a series of similar orders, the computer can automatically sort the goods into the correct lanes (see Chapter 5, Automated storage). With a more mixed situation, the pickers can stick on a bar-coded label printed with the picking list; the pack or tray will pass a scanner on its way to the sortation area triggering the sortation order. At its simplest, the tilt tray conveyor can have a simple mini-computer memory unit, programmed by the operator to divert all packages of a certain code to the correct destination. Operators can handle 80 packages per minute in this way. With a slightly more sophisticated peripheral computer linked to the stock control unit, the picker sticks on a photosensitive label which will activate the tilt diverter when it coincides with the correct photo-electric cell. This performs the same function as an operator, but much faster. At the destination, the tray tips the goods down a chute. Length of package is unimportant as long as the receiving conveyor can handle it, as the machine can be programmed to link rows of trays together for tipping and directing long and bulky objects (in some cases with sensitive light beams, this can be done automatically). A sorting process involving tipping means that goods can experience intense local shocks. Before deciding on a tilt tray, look at the fragility of the goods and the strength of their packaging.

Figure 4.34 *Tilt tray sorter.*

Belt and roller conveyors

18.05 Belt and roller conveyors are also suitable for dispatch sorting; they can have powered or unpowered rollers, and belts with a wide variety of surface textures for different applications (see Information sheet, Mechanized storage 14). These types are floor based, and sterilize an area on either side of them, the amount of

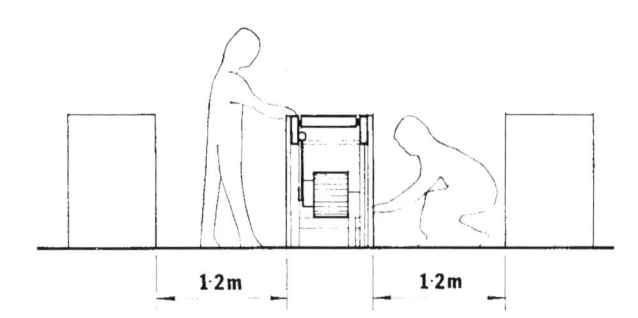

Figure 4.35 *Clearances required for accumulation conveyor.*

space lost depending on their height above the ground, any turns, joints and inclines (Figure 4.35). With high throughputs, the main supply conveyor will be high speed. This reduces the time available for control and recognition, so a deceleration and spacing mechanism is needed on the conveyor line, with high-speed diverters and multiple lanes. This is costly, and the deceleration and spacing controlled accumulation belts use up valuable floor space. Conveyors cannot be considered in isolation; there must be space for maintenance, and for work to diverters, which have pneumatic or electric operation, and room for personnel to clear blockages safely.

18.06 When planning these areas, conveyor manufacturers should be contacted from the outset, and all accessories – diverters, tilters and accumulators – should be designed into the initial scheme. Back-up facilities and maintenance planning is of prime importance, especially in high throughput areas. Consider at the initial planning stage:

1. How suitable are the goods for handling in this way?
2. How effectively can they be coded for identification during sorting, manually or mechanically?

18.07 The way some goods behave during conveying is crucial to sorting efficiency, and is influenced by shape, rigidity and the interface of the conveyor's surface and the base of the package. Blockages can affect the operation of the whole warehouse system. Friction levels between some conveyor materials and packages and the effects of uneven weight distribution and humidity can all lead to diverters mistiming and, so, damaging goods and causing blockages. If there are a large variety of goods and fast sorting speeds it can be cheaper and simpler for coding and handling to unitize items into a standard box, if this can be made compatible with the order-picking system.

18.08 Less space-consuming than flat accumulation conveyors are tiltable versions, with chute accumulation. Belt conveyors can run at an angle, and the doors open automatically to the correct channel, controlled in the same way as the tilt tray conveyor (Figure 4.36). Various commodities and package types limit turning radii and

Figure 4.36 *Tilted band conveyor used for Post Office sorting.*

Mechanized storage – storage process

acceptable slopes; tilt conveyor makers should be made aware of any space or height restrictions due to structure or other plant at an early stage.

Packaging equipment

18.09 More plant can be expected in dispatch sortation areas, especially in post-manufacture storage. The development of unit loads and the rising cost of transport and handling have brought many improvements in packaging. Manufacturers and retail organizations expect goods to reach their customers in as good condition as they left the warehouse. Many loads are still manually assembled. An experienced team can assemble pallet loads from conveyors very fast, judging size and shape, rejecting unsuitable or damaged packages. But to reduce personnel, and with increasingly standard packaging, palletizing machines are being specified for sorting areas (Figures 4.37 and 4.38). Some will shuffle various sizes of goods into the most efficient pattern to be placed on the chosen pallet size. Many accumulation lines feeding different products to one machine can be accommodated by an integral accumulation conveyor. As each lane assembles the load, the information can be fed to a mini-computer attached to the palletizer. When the appropriate goods are released, sensors tell the 'brain' to choose the correct pattern. Up to 20 different patterns are a normal capacity for a palletizer. There are various types including totally mechanical, variations with vacuum heads, simplified machines for small operators and developed pick and place robots. These palletizing machines normally require 220 volt or 414 volt three-phase power sources, and a compressed air supply (see Information sheet, Mechanized storage 8). Palletizers will form a constriction at the end of a number of load accumulation lines, and generate their own traffic in the form of an empty pallet supply to their magazine, and a further conveyor sortation system or a pallet truck route to the load assembly area. Work cycles can be very fast, depending on the variable factors of package size, pallet size and the number of layers. These machines are space consuming; a typical high capacity palletizer requires an area 9.4 m x 3.35 m x 3.65 m high, requiring this area again surrounding it (Figure 4.38).

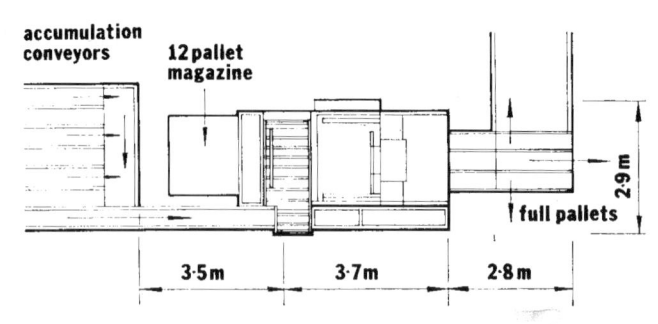

Figure 4.38 *Plan of typical palletizing machine. Top right is buffer track required for slower shrink wrapper.*

Shrink-wrapping

18.10 The development of shrink-wrapping pallet loads resulted in more stable pallet units that are sealed against accidental exposure to the weather, and which dispense with the cardboard outer. This helps visual selection during order picking, but can lead to easier theft. Stretch film wrapping has generally superseded shrink-wrapping as being faster and more energy efficient. For bulk dispatch, shrink-wrap tunnels or stretch-wrap pads taking full pallet loads should be positioned at the end of the accumulation lines or at the output side of a palletizer (Figure 4.39).

18.11 A number of small goods-in-travel shrink-wrappers are now available. Especially useful in storage operations that include a certain amount of load breakdown and repackaging, motor spares for example, these small machines operate fast on the conveyor line, but usually dictate primary sortation (special narrow lightweight conveyors are available for packaging machine supplies). If a groupage production line for special packs is anticipated, this should be planned from the outset as it can affect the space allocation to the order picking zone, and can constrict the flow to the sorting and assembly area.

Figure 4.37 *Gantry robot for palletizing crates of meat.*

Figure 4.39 *Shrink-wrapped palletized load emerging from shrink-wrap tunnel.*

Table 4.2 How to calculate approximate number of roll pallets in dispatch assembly area

	Load platform size Length (m)	Width (m)	Number of roll pallets	Weight of load and vehicle (tonnes)
Rigid vehicles	5.1	2.3	18	11
	6	2.3	21	13
	6.9	2.3	24 (28)	14 (30 gtw)
	7.5	2.3	27 (31)	15 (32 gtw)
Artic vehicles	10.2	2.3	36	21–23
	11	2.3	39	23–24
	11.75	2.3	42	29–32
	12.6	2.3	45	32–36

Note 1: Figures in brackets are roll pallets for drawbar trailers, and gross weight of vehicle with drawbar trailer.
Note 2: These 720 x 800 mm roll pallets are placed three abreast in the trucks. Other types are larger, and are packed two units across: adjust the numbers accordingly.

Re-packing operations should be removed by a spur conveyor away from the picking zone, so that personnel have a more pleasant environment, and a breakage will not affect the whole picking operation. This arrangement is also required in warehouses for supermarkets, where bulk cheese is cut up and repackaged.

Banding machines

18.12 In some ways in competition with shrink or stretch wrapping machines and in others complementary to them are banding machines. These can also be placed at the output side of a palletizer, and operate at the same speed (depending on the amount of bands that need to be applied, and whether the pallet requires turning for double direction banding (Figure 4.40). A banding machine mechanically wraps a pallet load with retaining plastic bands, cuts the band and heat-seals the ends together. A binding machine does the same with wire or twine; this is intended for smaller unit loads like soft cartons that could still move within a shrink-wrap. Both make necessarily accurate loading operations, as for 'deep-sea' container services, much easier to plan and operate. Horizontal and vertical banders are marketed, and if the load is fragile an operator is required for placing paperboard angles to prevent corner crushing. Banders can be fully automatic; a 400 lux light level is suggested for this area.

19 Order and document check

19.01 In storage systems using full pallets, checking is often carried out before vehicle loading, in the load assembly area. However, with small goods accumulation and palletizing into orders, a check is often required prior to the pallets or roll pallets being sent forward to the dispatch accumulation area (Table 4.2). If palletizing, shrink-wrapping or banding machines are used, the documentation check can be made immediately after this, using the inherent circulation constriction to the best advantage and allowing a check on the routeing of goods to the correct dispatch bay. A duplicate copy of the printout for the accumulation conveyor operator can be used for this, or special lists can be drawn up. Many loads are still hand assembled, and then checking is simultaneous.

19.02 The traffic control office is often used to issue checking and drivers' documents; check the distance involved to the sorting area, and whether any possibly dangerous routes have to be crossed; delay in the transit time for documents can delay checking. If the traffic office is too far away, some form of printout or visual display terminal will be needed at the checking point. (On-line visual displays are discussed in Chapter 5, Automated storage.) A buffer area should be provided for some pallets that will be returned to the accumulation area as incomplete or incorrect; one to two pallet spaces per checking line, for example. A minimum light level of 400 lux is suggested for this area also.

20 Loading and dispatch

20.01 In its most simple form, this is an area where roll pallets or normal pallets are assembled prior to loading, and where document checking can take place (Figure 4.41). Layout depends on the organization of the loading bay and lorry assembly area (see Technical study, Loading 1). If there are few bays and fast turnround the accumulation space should be large enough to pre-group a complete load before a vehicle's arrival (Figure 4.42),

Figure 4.40 *Vertical banding machine.*

Mechanized storage – storage process

Figure 4.41 *Load assembly area of large food distribution warehouse. Congestion occurs when incoming roll pallets meet full units seen here awaiting dispatch.*

Figure 4.42 *Roll pallets are being accumulated into vehicle loads, in anticipation of being called forward to the loading bay: lanes are clearly marked.*

Figure 4.43 *Partly loaded trucks with a line of roll pallets behind their doors.*

swop bodies for easy trunk haulage-delivery cycle interchange (see Technical study, External storage 1). Whether this space is to be provided in-line or transversely in several lanes depends on the shape of the building, the routing of the fork trucks, and the position of the loading bay relative to the racking. The planning of the assembly area is made easier if the load pattern is similar day by day. For instance, in a large warehouse serving supermarkets, the detailed content of loads will differ, but basic load characteristics will be the same, whether deliveries are several times daily, daily or weekly. With stock control computers linked to retail ordering systems, a prediction pattern can quickly be calculated. In these situations, a daily order-picking schedule can be fixed, based on predicted vehicle arrival patterns. Loading bays combining incoming and dispatch are possible here, sharing an incoming and outgoing sortation area. However, in peak situations, when the system is under pressure, the incoming empty roll pallets quickly constrict the operation of the load assembly area. In theory, even with closely spaced van bays at 90° to the dock (Figure 4.44), there is usually room for both activities (i.e. about 6 m buffer space before load assembly where empty pallets can be quickly handled to one side). What happens in practice is that vehicle arrival is staggered, so some trucks are being loaded when others arrive (Figure 4.45), this means that the partly loaded trucks have a line of roll pallets behind their doors. The path for empty roll pallets is therefore already constricted and soon the buffer space becomes jammed with full pallets, empty ones, and broken units to be sorted out for repair. If a dual-purpose bay must be used, designers should plan the

Figure 4.44 *Truck in position, filled with empty roll pallets. Note that the roll pallets are full of packaging materials being returned to the distribution centre for consolidated recycling.*

and to be well into assembling the next one during the loading operation (Figure 4.43). Small goods delivery rounds in cities are complicated by small consignments, and heavy daily and seasonal peaks. These peaks will necessitate fast moving between unloading and loading for the next round. The evening peak may be inward only; the morning peak can be in both directions and occurs when the first returning vehicles coincide with the next batch for midday deliveries. Loading bays quickly become choked with vans and heaps of pallets and empty cages. A flow system with clearly defined and marked areas should be designed, to integrate with the load build-up zone. The space required should be sufficient for a load and a half of the most common size of vehicle anticipated. Vehicle sizes are still growing, with

Mechanized storage – storage process

Figure 4.45 *Even at non-peak hours, incoming empty roll pallets are already clogging up dispatch assembly areas: provide recycling drop-off on the "circuit".*

(a)

(b)

Figure 4.46(a) *Suppliers' vehicles are often larger than the users', and may require a different unloading technique. Note tarpaulin on the dock, and broken roll pallet carrying a waste bin. No real provision has been made for debris disposal. This also applies (b) to external areas.*

dispatch load assembly area so that there is always room to clear empties and broken pallets, and insist that a substantial buffer space is essential to keep flow running smoothly. Suppliers' vehicles will use the single bay, and these goods will have to be checked in (Figure 4.46). If there is room, it is preferable to remove the cross route out of the immediate loading bay zone, and clearly mark lanes for each direction on the floor, preferably in different colours. If incoming roll pallet tracks are marked 'No waiting' on the floor, there is a good chance of operation without blockage. If roll pallets are used during the order-picking process, empty units should be stored as near to the order-picking area as possible; some large installations have conveyors just to handle the empties, but one major user has found that even this is not fast enough to stop the jams, and changed to straddle trucks that can move eight nested stacks of roll pallets at a time at a greater speed.

21 Additional data

21.01 Sustainability

Whereas the true implications of 'sustainability' questions whether the supply chain requires stock holding at all (i.e. needs to exist) and the right to manufacture 'economically' by centralizing both manufacturing and distribution locations to benefit from economies of scale (assessed against the actual, energy and social cost of transport), at a local 'shallower' level the emphasis on sustainability has, prompted by the ODPM, refocused planners on the potential for using 'brownfield' sites to construct warehouses and distribution centres. This is commendable on sites such as Hams Hall, a rail equipped old power station with good road access on the perimeter of the West Midlands conurbation. It may be less easy to handle if planning controls force distribution and order fulfilment centres towards inner city sites: consumer home delivery services may benefit, but regional distribution may incur higher operating costs from restricted operating hours (urban neighbours), restricted and peaky re-stocking due to curfews for heavy goods vehicles, sites that are less than ideal shape for modern warehouses with compromised access, and planning restrictions on building height.

Out of hours deliveries to town centres works well on the EU mainland, but with efficient distribution locations and premises. Similarly, in conurbations in the US, in New York for example, retail and consumer deliveries have polarized towards dedicated internet-driven personal deliveries (often two-wheeled) and rationalized deliveries to inner city retailers where suppliers have delivered to out-of-town third party operated 'staging': these are multi-customer cross-docking and stockholding facilities that pick, assemble and 'detrash' retail replenishment items, much of it delivered on a Just-in-Time basis by Fedex, UPS or another 'integrator'.

Maintaining a high level of efficiency, whilst blending essential delivery logistics with urban regeneration without imposing high additional costs, will become a serious challenge for the 'urban partnerships' in the UK. Whether the European or US delivery models are adopted, resolving social and inner-city planning conflicts will prove demanding for the design, planning and logistics professionals involved. Whatever the pressures, it is important not to compromise the key design and operating principles set out in this chapter.

21.02 Picking performance and system selection guide

Method	Typical units picked/hour	Cost index (items or packs)	Performance index
A Man to part			
1 Picking from pallets on the floor (powered pallet truck and roll cage)	150–180	1	2
2 Manual from shelving	150–180 (with data transmission)	2	3
3 Manual from carton roll-through (with take-away belt)	300–500 (with data transmission)	5	4/5
4 Second level picking/low level narrow aisle shelving (mid-level picking truck)	150–200	2/3	2
5 Multi-level pallet/shelf picking (narrow aisle high level picker)	150–250 (with data and multiple picks)	4/6	4
6 Pick cars (automatic location and take-away belt)	300–500 (with data and multiple picks)	7	7
B Part to man			
7 Vertical carousels	300+ (plc operated)	6	6
8 Horizontal carousels (can have independent rotation on each level)	500+ (automatic location and data to picker)	7	7
9 Miniload ASRS (one aisle or more with conveyor carousel to picker)	250+	5	5/6

NB: Performances are industry averages/man/hour of peak performance. Cost and performance indices are out of 10. Both such performance and cost indices are highly debatable and are for guidance only.

Figure 4.47 *The roof structure of a warehouse can cause a pallet position to be lost throughout the length of a whole aisle at each turn position.*

Figure 4.48 *A big box structure allows both freedom in positioning racking and full height stacking.*

TECHNICAL STUDY

Mechanized storage 2
Building function

22 Structure
23 Floor
24 Building services
25 Special services
26 Building fabric
27 Fire control
28 Security and safety
29 External works
30 Structure-based plant

31 Mobile plant
32 Integration of building and plant
33 Maintenance
34 Management
35 Personnel accommodation
36 Amenities
37 Personnel safety
38 Circulation and parking

22 Structure

22.01 Mechanized storage buildings house sophisticated plant and large quantities of valuable goods. Maximum cubic capacity for the expenditure is important, and by using high lift, narrow aisle reach trucks and turret trucks, storage can be right up to roof level.

22.02 The structure and fabric of a mechanized warehouse is not only an enclosing shell, but also a frame to which mechanical handling plant is attached, e.g. conveyor lines and order-picking machinery. At the same time, the structure should provide as large column-free spaces as are economically possible, considering movement characteristics of handling plant, dimensions and tolerances dictated by rack spacing and future flexibility and bearing capacity of ground. Ideally, a mechanized warehouse should allow a clear span with no column intrusion into the storage space; 30 m wide bays are regularly built economically from steel. Although vertical expansion is cheaper than lateral, vertical travel speeds on handling plant can be considerably slower; the cost balance of this should be carefully studied before any decisions are made. Generally, 12 m clear height structures are institutionally fundable; these heights allow reach trucks to operate to six to nine pallets high: for warehouses larger than 15000 sq m there is an argument for 15 m height to structural haunch (also fundable) for additional stacking flexibility, accommodating chilled store linings without sacrificing stacking height and providing the volume for three mezzanine picking levels (Figures 4.47 and 4.48).

22.03 With the requirement to store high, and for the frame to carry sprinkler lines, lighting, heating and ventilation services, the steeply pitched roof, portal-framed warehouse can no longer be realistically considered as an economic solution in the long-term, except for bulk storage and small manually operated installations (see Technical studies, Mechanized storage). What is required is a well-insulated big box. The steep pitch of a portal frame interferes with stacking space and, even if the racking is erected to maximum height at the apex of the pitch, there is considerable danger of forklifts fouling the structure, services or sheeting (Figures 4.49 and 4.50). Recent developments in shallow pitched portals and curved rolled steel roof frames allow very wide spans without the expense and loss of cubic storage capacity of trussed designs, both economically and with sufficient suspended load capacity for the suspension of basic environmental services. Column spacing is also very important and can hamper storage efficiency. With such frames, a favourite for distribution centres is alternating 8 m and 7 m column spacing, allowing 15 m between any internal columns.

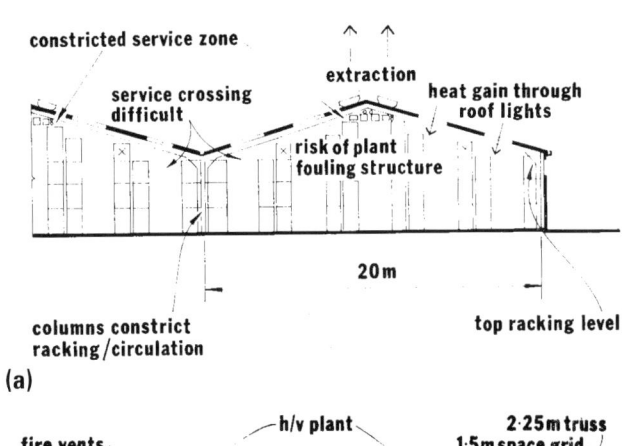

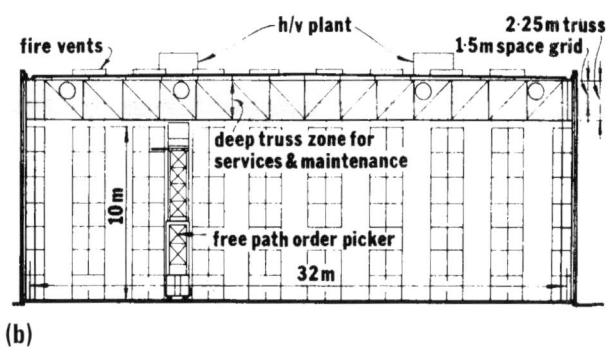

Figure 4.49 *Comparison between (a) portal frame and (b) 'big box' structure.*

101

Mechanized storage - building function

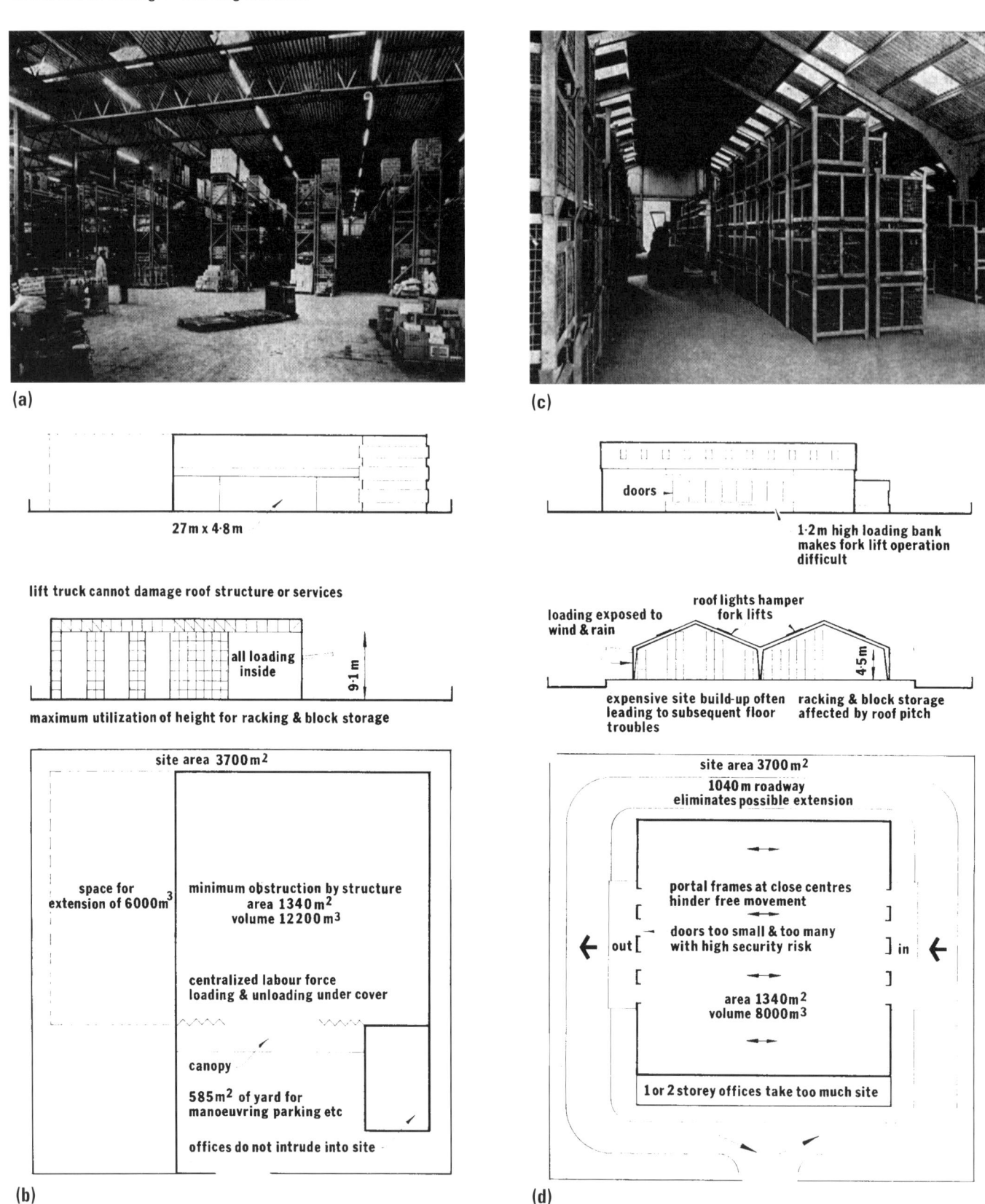

Figure 4.50 *Detailed comparison between different types of structure (a b big box, and c d portal frame structure). Good b and bad d layouts are also compared.*

Materials

22.04 The relative performances of cladding and insulating materials are discussed in the AJ Handbook of Building Structure, DETR, *The Building Regulations*, London, 1994, See also *Building Construction Handbook*, 2001, R. Greeno and R. Chudley, Architectural Press, and *Building Regulations in Brief*, R. Tricker, in press. Initial expense on an efficiently insulated sheet material can save considerable expenditure on heating and ventilation plant in a large warehouse.

22.05 A big, insulated, wide span box with a deep, flat truss roof structure allows stacking as near to the roof sheeting as load and mast tolerances allow and enables building services to be run in the roof void, unhindered by racking and possible damage by plant. For example, roof water can be routed through the truss without intruding into the floor zone. A straightforward big box is remarkably cheap; the cost has fallen in real terms over the last decade remaining at around £250/sq m with simple services. The extra cost of 10 m clear headroom against

6.0 m on a building area of more than 10000 m² is about 7 per cent. If the extra volume can be used effectively, the initial area could possibly be smaller.

22.06 A wide span cambered frame allows marginally greater volume utilization, but clearance has still to be left for suspended services (Figure 4.51).

22.07 The advantages of a wide span structure are:

1. range of planning possibilities for general enclosed warehouse spaces is greatly increased by reduction of number of columns intruding into the storage area
2. potential use of the volume is improved
3. a greater degree of servicing adaptability and quicker installation can be achieved; pitched-roof design has led to difficult cross-routes for pipes and awkward changes of level
4. prefabrication as a small number of large elements with fewer columns and bases makes for fast erection (often as a key requirement; see para 34)
5. free floor has great potential for adaptability of racking and choice of handling plant.

22.08 If a rack structure over 10 m high is used, large areas of unrelieved wall face the weather. Consider the effects of wind buffet and heat changes on the cladding. Both have been known to affect the tight tolerances required between stacker cranes, turret trucks, order pickers and racking. If there is continuity between the handling plant and racking and the roof or wall structure, extra bracing is often needed to combat potential movement. Fixed-path order pickers and stackers may put stress on the structure by running against their buffer stops. A 15-tonne machine with a 1-tonne pallet decelerating sharply from 140 m/min plus impact, can make solid-looking structures move alarmingly. The factory inspectorate can expect that fixed-path plant be tested to run against these stops, to prove that the structure will not be permanently deformed. These are a worse problem with high-bay automated stores (see Technical study, Automated storage 2).

Figure 4.51 *Typical big box structure.*

23 Floor

23.01 The floor finish should be designed as carefully as the mechanical-handling equipment that operates over it. Both designers and management tend to believe that a hardened granolithic screed is the most suitable for all purposes because it is cheap and requires no special treatment, but this can be a false economy, as it is quickly damaged by fats and oils as, for example, in a cheese-cutting and packing line. 'Superflat' floors are no longer at a premium: high lift equipment elevating loads to 10 m and above requires a Class 1 floor, 3 mm in 3 m variance in flatness. General storage to say 6 m can work with a Class 2 floor, 3 mm in 6 m variance in flatness.

Floor loadings

23.02 The rule for flooring in a mechanized warehouse is to have a well-prepared base calculated to accept the wheel loadings of plant such as turret trucks and narrow aisle order pickers. As a guide, the ISO recommends that container floors shall withstand a wheel load of not less than 26.7 kN per wheel, assuming width of not less than 180 mm and centres of 760 mm. However, some forklift trucks and turret trucks exceed these loadings; e.g. a 12m lift narrow aisle stacker/order picker imposes a 36 kN front wheel load on the loadside when the pallet positioning attachment is extended laden. Check with the equipment manufacturer. However good the floor surface, it can only be as good as its base. As a rule of thumb, for busy high lift warehouses with goods handled to at least 10 m (five or six pallet locations high), provide for a Class 1 floor finish with a 75 kN UDL and a 100 kN point loading.

Important factors in floor design

23.03

- *Wheel loadings.* Forklifts have been known to break up floors very fast, not from insufficient reinforcement but because it was in the wrong position. 'Jointless' floors, with the concrete laid in continuous bays with inserted crack inducers, are available and reduce the risk of expansion and construction joints breaking up with wheel abrasion.
- *Rack weights.* Will special bases or double reinforcement be required for high racking? Turret trucks work to close tolerances in high racking; there is no room for settlement. Consider also the chance for future rack repositioning. Rack combinations with a height/depth ratio of more than 6:1 need either roof restraint or floor bolting. Bolt positions, if not specifically planned and reinforced from the outset, may lead to radial cracking and local surface failure.
- *Point and impact loads.* For example, post pallet feet, stacked post pallets and stillages and heavy set-downs.
- *Product characteristics.* What is the effect of accidental spillage?
- *Tyre scrub.* High-speed turns and rapid deceleration by forklifts and tugs on major forklift or tow train routes can quickly bring up a faulty floor surface, especially if there is spillage as well.
- *Mobile plant.* Straddle trucks and pallet trucks with small front rollers can be made dangerously unstable by bumping on expansion joints. A poor floor can dramatically increase tyre and castor bills

Types of floor specification

23.04

- *Granite screed.* For general purpose, high-use warehouses, a screed of granite chippings 12 mm thick, set in a mixture of cold bituminous mastic and Portland cement has proved effective and durable.
- *Concrete.* Another well-tried method is to lay the whole floor with 250 mm-thick road mix concrete with a road-paving machine, finishing with a 12 mm hardened granolithic screed. This method is fast and the paver can work to tight tolerances. The lack of expansion joints is a great advantage.

Mechanized storage – building function

- *Jointed floors*. Although as efficient between the joints as jointless flooring, these may break up along the joint lines, where handling plant with polyurethane wheels and roll pallets with metal castors abrade the edges.
- *Epoxy jointless floor*. An accurate and long-lasting finish is the epoxy-based jointless type. This is hard-wearing and can be laid to tight tolerances. Some can be laid with a non-skid finish at route crossing points, and are resilient enough to stand continuous heavy impacts from metal objects. It can handle heavy block stacks, and its jointless character makes it ideal for food processing areas or where oil or chemical spills may be expected (see Technical studies, Cold storage 2, para. 2). The extra cost should be offset against the maintenance costs of conventional granolithic screed, replacement costs for forklift tyres, castors for pallet trucks and roll pallets, and stoppages due to joint break-up.

Always use a specialist flooring contractor who guarantees not to sublet any of the work; the method of laying and care over curing is critical to success.

24 Building services

24.01 In this type of warehouse building services are usually 10–30 per cent of the total warehouse cost. Using a 'big box' and a well-insulated outer skin, large warehouses may show only small variation in temperature and other environmental conditions. Two or three air changes are sufficient per day except in order-picking areas, where more ventilation is needed. (This figure is for handling-plant powered by electric traction; if any internal combustion machinery is used, localized extraction is required.) For order-picking areas, air changes can be minimized by ensuring a constant circulation; air movement gives a feeling of freshness. With big box buildings, summer heat build-up can be dissipated at night by pumping cool air in from high level (Figure 4.52). This sustainable solution should ensure a normal summer variation of less than 5°C. A light-coloured roof surface will combat insolation.

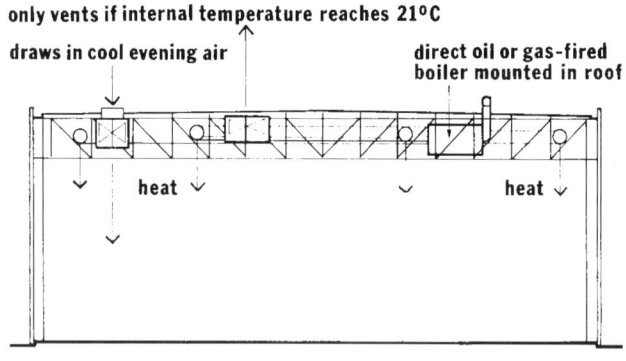

Figure 4.52 *Services in 'big box'.*

Heating and ventilation

24.02 The Factory Act 1961, still in place at the time of revision, stipulates 'that reasonable working temperatures be maintained'. Designers should plan for temperatures of 19°C in light duty areas, i.e. load assembly and order picking, and 15°C in heavy lifting areas or parts of the store intermittently used. Both blown air and radiant heat have proved effective in manual storage installations. Lightweight buildings are susceptible to excessive heat gains caused by insolation, which can normally be controlled only by ventilation.

24.03 Usually one to two air changes per hour are acceptable in warehouses, but in areas of intensive manual work the aim should be for air movement between 0.16 and 0.51 rn/sec. It is air movement which gives a feeling of comfort rather than replacement of extracted air. Adequate ventilation and heating will also eliminate condensation from the structure – drips can seriously damage stored goods in cartons. Properly insulated roof and wall cladding will reduce this possibility and allow operatives to work efficiently in comfort. Fumes must be extracted from the loading bay area, especially if it is also used for assembling loads.

24.04 For winter heating, blown hot air is effective; the volume and insulation characteristics of the building and the added heat gain from lighting and handling plant keep the building at a comfortable temperature. With a deep truss flat roof or a space grid, combined heater and ventilation units can be mounted either within the truss depth, or on top of the roof surface, so as not to intrude on the storage space. The external road/loading bay interface may prove to be troublesome in winter, but dock shelters and air curtains help combat this (see Technical study, Loading 1) (Figure 4.53). Shrink-wrapping plant in the load assembly area can add to the heat, especially if there are several units; this should be considered when planning summer ventilation. If shrink-wrappers are close to the order-picking area, extra extraction should be provided, as they give off an unpleasant smell of hot polythene film. (Some machines have built-in extraction equipment.)

Figure 4.53 *Structure continued over totally enclosed loading bay.*

24.05 The heat requirement of a warehouse can be diminished by heavy insulation in roof and walls and exclusion of draughts from the main doors by the use of internal walls and small self-closing or air barrier doorways. Where there is a manufacturing process the process heat may be put through a heat exchanger, such as a Munters wheel, through which the warehouse air may be re-circulated or the warehouse topped up with warm air.

24.06 There are many possible heat sources, such as the cooling side of the refrigeration system, the heat from electrical transformers, lighting systems, and where goods are warm from the manufacturing process, early storage within the warehouse will provide extra heat when required. Because warehouses often need no deliberate air changes and when full of goods have their own in-built heat balance, it is possible to provide some of the heat by solar radiation, just as it is possible to keep warehouses cool by the use of the cool night air drawn from some feet above the ground. With the emphasis on sustainable power and heat sources, it may be common practice within the next 10 years to heat warehouses entirely by drawing their heat from process or extract systems, cooling systems, effluent, rubbish disposal and sewage systems. Heat pumps can be used to draw the heat from all these sources but are more costly to operate because of the electrical power required.

Natural versus artificial lighting

24.07 In big box warehouses, the use of natural lighting is questionable, especially for perishables. Structures 10 m high with full racks and narrow aisles usually require permanent, supplementary artificial lighting to 200 lux minimum level. Natural light from roof lights increases heat variation adding to the cost of ventilation and heating plant, and may produce glare within the racking by intense light and shade contrasts. Infrared and ultraviolet rays can also damage packaging and fade printed labels and cartons. Successful naturally lit installations have been built, and it is suggested that model studies be made to investigate the effects of sunlight on the orientation of the building arid the racks within it. Glare can be dangerous with forklift trucks, resulting in racking damage and possible injury by misplacing pallets on upper levels. Generally high lift warehouses are more effective operationally with artificial light: multilevel order-picking mezzanines require high, even lighting levels for clear label identification (300 lux at least) that is only complicated by the changes in natural light.

Lighting

24.08 Temperature control is closely linked with lighting. Even light levels are essential for accurate picking and eliminating fatigue (caused by glare from light sources reflected by racking and loads). Sloping roof lights exposed to direct sun require four times the ventilation needed by north-facing roof lights with the same roof insulation. The Chartered Institute of Building Services Engineers (CIBSE) Code suggests a minimum lighting level of 150 lux for the loading area, 100 lux in racking for large item storage, 200 lux for medium sized items, the norm for palletized stock, and 300 lux for small goods racks and sorting and dispatch functions: 500 lux is suggested for self-service racking areas and issue counters as in do-it-yourself (DIY) outlets, usually achieved with low-level supplementary lights. Order picking of small parts from tote boxes or drawers also requires 400–500 lux depending on the type of item. In manual sorting where loading bays are likely as a check point and in primary sorting areas, 200 lux should be the design objective.

24.09 Psychologically, where order picking takes place, some communication to the outside world is important, as it has been found that operatives are more contented if they can see what the weather is like outside.

Special problems of lighting mechanized storage buildings

24.10 *Vertical lighting.* In mechanized storage buildings, unlike most other buildings, light is required primarily on vertical surfaces, i.e. racks. No light sources should be obstructed by stores or their racking. This may be particularly difficult where the layout is changed in accordance with the stock position. When racking is moved often and a lower intensity of lighting is acceptable, continuous fluorescent tubes at right angles to the aisles are effective.

24.11 *Glare.* Lighting into deep bins or racks from a relatively narrow access space may cause shadows of the tops of the bins or shelving (Figure 4.54). If the equipment is lowered to give maximum penetration to the bins, it

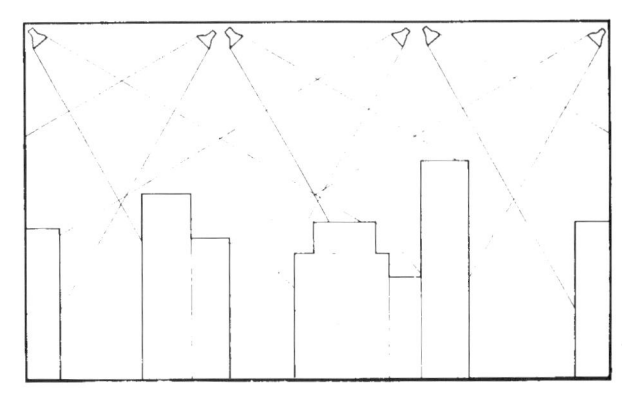

Figure 4.54 *Lighting into narrow aisles causes shadows.*

becomes an obstruction. In multilevel spaces, it is extremely difficult to prevent glare from all angles of view. The problem is accentuated if the operators are on mechanically operated platforms (e.g. free-path order pickers) which can move up and down. In high-bay storage, glare from ceiling lights may prevent easy identification of goods. Some storage buildings are fitted with overhead travelling cranes, which complicate the lighting problem, since the crane driver must have a good view of the floor and his vision must at no time be impaired by glare. Specialist advice should always be sought. The recommended reflection factors for the ceiling, walls and floor are 0.60, 0.40 and 0.20, respectively. Racking usually provides reflectance of 0.20.

Methods of lighting

24.12 Some methods applicable to particular cases are now described. In all cases a well-maintained white ceiling and walls improves distribution of lighting.

24.13 Lighting from gangways only. Where the building is laid out so that positions of gangways are well defined and unlikely to change, lighting can be concentrated over the gangways and directed outwards and downwards. Where the ceiling and walls are of high reflectance (and likely to remain so during the life of the building), diffusers may be sufficient. The effectiveness of this method depends on the gangways being long in relation to the width of the building, and on the horizontal distribution of lighting being relatively unobstructed. Bare tubes are preferable, and louvres should not be used.

24.14 Lighting in racked areas. It is usually satisfactory to provide a single or twin line of fluorescent tubes along the centre of the gangway (Figure 4.55a). When using high drive-in racking, combining even background lighting in the aisle, with vertical fluorescents in the racking, is very efficient (Figure 4.55b).

24.15 Lighting from side walls only. Where the building is relatively narrow in relation to its length, fittings mounted in the angle between the wall and the roof can sometimes cover the whole area. But drivers will tend to have the light facing them when they are moving among objects stored, so that the nearside of what they wish to see may be in shadow (Figure 4.56).

24.16 Overhead trunking. Where goods are stored in racks, it is usually desirable to ensure that the lines of lighting coincide with the gangways between racks, but where racks may be moved about this is impossible. There are many lighting trunking systems which can be suspended over the rack areas, and permit the layout of fittings to be changed as the racks are moved.

24.17 Lighting on mobile plant. Lights on fork trucks operated by the driver are best for detailed operation, although a lighting scheme is still required for personnel, stocktaking, etc.

Mechanized storage – building function

(a)

(b)

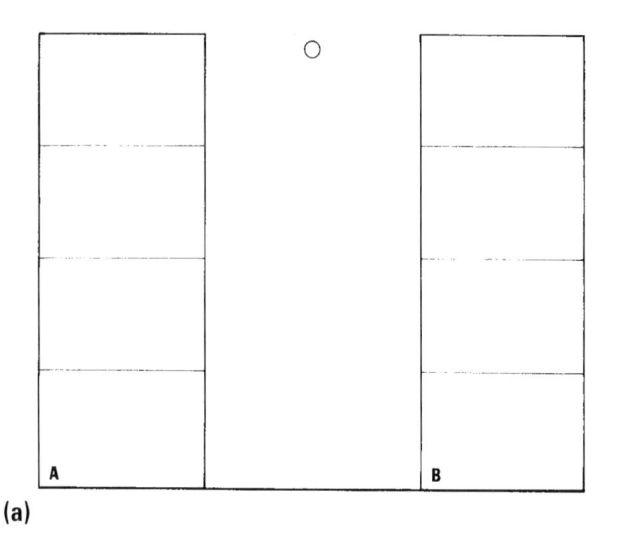

Figure 4.55 *In drive-in racking vertically mounted fluorescent lamps provide clear vision within discharge lamp background illumination.*

Figure 4.56 *Nearside of object onto which driver is loading may be in shadow.*

Lighting sources

24.18 Two broad categories can be distinguished. Where linear sources are required, up to 15 m ceiling height fluorescent tubes are the obvious choice, and in most cases the high efficiency types such as white and warm white are good enough. High frequency fluorescent installations provide an extra energy saving (about 20 per cent) and can be operated via lighting control systems.

24.19 In high-bay storage structures, general diffusing fittings will waste too much light on the upper walls and the most economical solution is likely to be a limited number of high power sources giving narrow beams of light downwards. In these cases, high intensity discharge lamps such as mercury discharge lamps or other point sources with an integral reflector (corresponding to the incandescent reflector spotlight) have been used successfully (but drivers looking up to see 10 m above themselves may find point sources troublesome, if not carefully diffused).

24.20 High-pressure mercury lamps give a very bluish light, but they can be obtained with fluorescent envelopes which give a better colour. All the reflector types are colour-corrected in this way. Alternatively, mixed fittings are available in which a mercury discharge lamp and an incandescent lamp are enclosed in one housing: another alternative is the tungsten halogen tubular lamp. High-pressure sodium lamps may also be useful, especially in high racks. Precise guidance as to which of these alternatives is likely to be the best in any given circumstances should be sought from a specialist. 'Kolorarc' and 'Kolorsun' give a much higher lumen output for the same rating and very good colour rendering. They usually save on installation and running costs.

Service routeing

24.21 The path of building services should not affect handling plant and inhibit the use of racking. One architect was taken to court for installing rainwater down pipes on the 'wrong' side of the stanchions through a misunderstanding, making work more difficult for forklifts and reducing the store capacity by a complete rack space at each column position. In another case, a sprinkler main was positioned so that the whole top length of a rack was useless for normal loads, as the tolerance was too tight for the reach truck to lift the pallet in. Service routeing is critical round doors or breaks in the structure. Beware of conflicts with overhead conveyor lines and overhead tracks for stacker cranes, order pickers and where mobile racking is used.

25 Special services

25.01 Fixed-path stacker cranes and order pickers require an electric source, either on a reeled cable or on a busbar system. Machines such as palletizers, shrink-wrappers and diverters for conveyors require compressed air services. Loading bay equipment, e.g. banders, binders and nail guns also operate on compressed air. A vacuum source may be needed for certain types of palletizer, and for vacuum tube document carriage systems. Special service routeing should be flexible, as machines are moved to suit changes of the storage pattern.

26 Building fabric

26.01 The increased use of forklift trucks has reduced in-store product damage by five times; the damage to static storage plant, racking and the building fabric has risen accordingly. Where there are many forklift trucks, crash barriers should be installed to lessen serious damage to the structure and cladding. If a forklift route runs round the perimeter the fabric may be damaged by impact and abrasion. Most damage occurs when forklifts turn out of aisles with their loads in travel position, and when the truck is lifting its load as it places itself to enter the racks. Ground-level damage can be reduced if enough clearance is provided in the aisles (using 'swept' turning circle data), and by a hard composition-rubber bumper strip up to 1.5 m high running along susceptible wall surfaces, painted in bright alternating stripes. Columns, door openings and rack ends should also be guarded in this way on movement routes. A sheet cladding material easy to remove and replace will also save later expense. Deeply scored and cracked brickwork produces dust and may let the weather in (Figure 4.57).

Damage to racking

26.02 Racking is damaged both by impact and abrasion. Most is easy to replace in sections. Vertical and horizontal members are painted in contrasting colours to help drivers to identify and position accurately. Adjustable member-retaining clips prevent horizontal members from being lifted out of place by accident from underneath. (See Information sheet, Mechanized storage 1).

26.03 High racks over 10 m in mechanized warehouses offer very large faces to the weather. Consider the effects of differential heating of the south face of the building on structure and plant. Roof-hung stacker cranes or order pickers, or racking with links to roof or wall structure have been known to jam where one face exposed to direct sunlight has expanded, and this has been reflected through movement in the structure. (See also High-bay problems in Technical study, Automated storage 2, para. 26.)

27 Fire control

27.01 Fire control in mechanized warehouses is an increasing problem. Plastics packaging materials and shrink-wrapping, although flame-proofed, have added to the danger to personnel by producing noxious fumes when hot, by spreading the fire, by dripping onto such combustible material as cardboard cases, and by diverting water from sprinklers. Immediate detection is therefore of prime importance. (Fire control in high-bay warehouses will be discussed at length in Chapter 5, Automated storage.)

27.02 The use of sprinklers in warehouses is set out in the Loss Prevention Council (LPC) Rules 1990, which superseded the Fire Officers Committee (FOC) twenty-ninth edition, 1973. The construction and code of practice for sprinklers is set out in BS 5306 Part 2 1990, and BS 5878 1988 Fire detection in buildings, Parts 1–5. It is also likely that insurance companies will insist on sprinklers and break-glass fire alarms in all warehouses, and multi-level sprinklers in buildings over 7.5 m high. It is very important to consult the client's insurers at the sketch design stage, as some large-store owners have been forced to pay 35 per cent premiums because corners were cut on fire control.

27.03 The principal aim of a detection system in a warehouse is to catch the fire before it can spread. The fire should be detected quickly, and checked and extinguished in the cell or rack space of origin. The system should be capable of operating those sprinklers needed to achieve this, and the rate of water delivery from the sprinklers must be high enough to ensure success. Install hose reels and hydrant points as well. The system should be robust, simple and easy to reset after a fire. This approach necessitates a separate detection system for each rack bay, capable of operating selected zoned sprinklers. An effective method, developed by the Joint Fire Research Organization, uses a line detector (Figure 4.58). This should cost little more than a standard system, owing to reduced water storage and pumping requirements, and possibly lower insurance premiums.

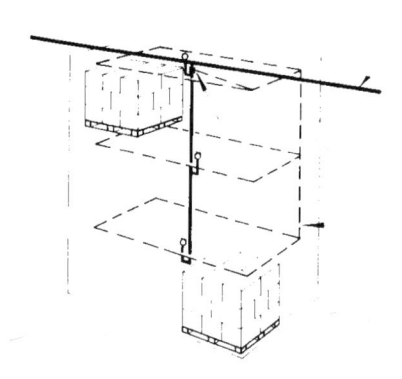

Figure 4.58 *Line detector.*

27.04 Full-scale fire tests have confirmed that solid masses of stock burn with greater intensity as the amount of horizontal channel ways is increased, and as stacks become higher, simulating vertical flues. The speed of fire-spread can be exceptionally fast in high racks. This is serious in pallet racking, since the pallets are exposed to air on all sides (Figure 4.59). The necessary density of discharge to extinguish the fire is in direct relation to both the stack height and the degree of combustibility of the stock. Smoke is a further problem. Smoke in a food warehouse may taint a large amount of stock; some materials smoulder without activating sprinklers – coffee beans, for example. There are arguments for and against smoke vents in high rack arrangements. One argument against is that it spreads the fire more quickly up the rack. However, it is generally thought preferable to burn out one insured rack and prevent the

Figure 4.57 *The scuffmarks at high level occur where forklifts have scraped by with their forks high to clear the drivers' vision. Note also the new plates covering badly scored brickwork, marked even before they could be painted.*

Figure 4.59 *Fire test on high rack storage.*

fire jumping from rack to rack across the underside of the roof owing to great stack pressure and no venting; immediate large-area venting clears the smoke and makes fire-fighting easier. Vents operated by fusible links should operate at 71°C.

27.05 From the user's angle of cubic capacity, intermediate sprinkling is a waste of space. The sprinkler mains are difficult to handle in adjustable racking, virtually reducing adaptability to nil. Some do not like the idea of wet system sprinklers overhead at all, as stock damage from leakage is possible. (This can be insured against.) For these reasons, foams and gases have been considered. It is thought that gas is not effective in a large volume warehouse for long-term extinction. Carbon dioxide (CO_2) has often been mentioned, but this is dangerous to personnel. Carbon dioxide is fatal with 10 per cent in the atmosphere; 28 per cent is often quoted as the level required to extinguish a rack fire. Bromochlorodifluoromethane (BCF) and bromotrifluoromethane (BTM) gases are considered to be the most effective for closed-cell storage.

27.06 The arguments about the use of high-expansion foam continue; experiments with foam have shown that foam generation stirs up the air and so causes better combustion, the foam level chasing the fire up the racking and the flames spreading more quickly than normal from the increased turbulence. A foam installation can be designed to fill 1 million cubic feet volume in one minute. However, there can still be stock damage through overall dampness, and to ensure extinction, foam has to be topped up every half-hour. Unlike water, foam has to be left for some time to ensure that smouldering has been extinguished. Some tests illustrated that directly the foam deteriorated, some smouldering pallets started to flame again. (See also Automated storage.) It should be remembered that if the warehouse is artificially lit, emergency lighting off batteries or separate generation will have to be installed. Pedestrian escape routes, often tortuous in warehouses at the best of times, should be especially well indicated and lit.

27.07 The efficiency of ordinary-hazard sprinkler systems may diminish with rack heights over 7.5 m in the three lowest categories of combustible stock, and 4.4 m in the fourth and most hazardous category, unless intermediate sprinkling is provided. The limit for ceiling-based sprinklers is 7.5 m. Installing intermediate sprinkling is well advised as it may contain a fire that would otherwise run very fast up the stack. Almost inevitably, it will be necessary to have pump supplies – few town mains can produce 2.3 m³/min at a pressure necessary to maintain the density of discharge at the highest and most remote part of the warehouse. Insurers require two pump sets, one of which must be diesel driven, and two separate reservoirs. On the basis of a 45-minute discharge, the minimum capacity of a reservoir is liable to be 11,300 litres (112.5 m²). It is suggested that warehouses should be sufficiently heated to ensure that a constantly charged sprinkler system can be used without any risk of freezing. If there is any doubt about this, the sprinklers should be installed on a wet-and-dry pipe system. However, there is a problem of time lag; when a system is charged with compressed air, there is bound to be a time lag of as much as three minutes. Remember that where sprinkler protection is provided only at ceiling or roof level, the requirement is for the design area of sprinkler operation to be increased by 25 per cent, requiring also larger-capacity pumps and reservoirs. The basic fact to remember is that the extra cost of intermediate sprinkling over 4.5 m can be considered well spent in the light of insurance premiums. The insurer and local fire officer should also be contacted early in the design process concerning fire stop walls and zone segregation. The maximum volume without segregation allowed is normally 1080 m³. These can fundamentally alter a warehouse's operation if they have to be installed as an afterthought. Problems have been experienced with providing openings through firewalls large enough for handling plant, for instance between a sortation area and the loading bay. These rules are recommendations; they are negotiable with the insurers and the fire officer.

27.08 Intermediate sprinkling requires a minimum of 150 mm clearance for the sprinkler head above the highest unit load to be effective, but must also be clear to avoid damage from handling plant. This affects volume utilization. Room must also be allowed for sprinkler down pipes in the racking. For intermediate systems, sprinkler heads 3.5 m apart in alternate rack positions are considered sufficient for ordinary hazards. The heads should alternate, as fire spreads sideways first, and then rapidly upwards.

27.09 Live storage racking is a major problem, owing to the density of stock. Sprinklers can also be staggered effectively up to six pallets deep, but for greater runs, full individual sprinkling for each channel is required. Drive-in racking has the same problem, but standard intermediate sprinkling, mounted between the cantilever rails, is possible. Mobile racking is difficult for intermediate sprinkling, but top mounted piped services with swivel joints located clear of lift truck movement envelopes work effectively.

28 Security and safety

28.01 There are two types of security in mechanized warehouses:
1 safety for people from machinery; an issue for the planning supervisor and the Health and Safety Executive
2 security of goods from theft.

Safety for people

28.02 The safety aspect of mobile handling plant is largely one of common sense and circulation planning. To conform with the EU Handling Directive and health and safety legislation a risk register must be prepared during the design stage. Some basic guidelines to prevent accidents:
1. Avoid blind corners, or give adequate warning.
2. Design carefully against glare.
3. Ensure that mobile racking and fixed-path handling plant has a fail-safe pedestrian cut-out.
4. Guard ramps against accidental misalignment.
5. Guard all sorting and palletizing plant.
6. Ensure that pedestrian routes, particularly means of escape, are clearly marked both on the floor and at eye level. Most safety aspects are covered by the Factory Inspectorate and EU publications (see Bibliography).

Security of goods

28.03 Security from theft is an ever-present problem. In large-scale warehouses, especially where multiple shifts of order picking staff are employed, losses can be considerable. Many warehouses holding consumer goods can lose between 1 and 5 per cent of their stock annually in this way. Shrink-wrapping, unit packaging techniques and computer controls have not helped. On the whole, a deterrent is more effective than prosecution after the act. Designers can help by placing control points (e.g. documentation issue offices) in order-picking areas and traffic offices in load-assembly and incoming check areas, in positions that dominate these zones. Amenity areas and lavatory and wash zones must not be a 'through' route between inside and outside without a measure of supervision. If a policy of spot searches is instigated, which has been proved to work without alienating labour, the search rooms should be carefully designed to give a sense of security so that operatives do not feel harassed. Closed-circuit television is useful for store security, safety and for keeping track of handling plant in extensive rack areas. Television is only as vigilant as the security officer watching the battery of screens. Also, care is needed to place cameras where they cannot be damaged by passing handling plant.

External security

28.04 Ensure that forklift and truck parking areas cannot be used as a convenient step-ladder for intruders. A strong boundary fence helps; also, avoid placing rainwater down pipes near possible entry positions, running up past flat roofs with roof lights. If an intruder is really determined, it has been shown that he or she will gain access somehow, and, remember, that it is thought that the majority of warehouse robberies are 'inside' jobs.

29 External works

29.01 For detailed planning of external areas including the siting of loading docks and yards, see Technical studies, Loading 1 and External storage 1. Mechanized storage installations, especially those handling pre-production parts, often require extensive external storage. Many goods are not worth using up valuable space in a building, e.g. post pallets of rough castings, and empty stillages. Areas for these should be marked out for block stacking, and should be well lit for winter, and well drained; with castings and stillages from a production line, oil interceptors may be required on the drains. NetworkRail should be contacted for any external works with railway tracks.

30 Structure-based plant

30.01 This includes goods lifts, paternosters, pallet elevators and lowerators, stacker cranes and order-picking machinery (Figures 4.60 and 4.61).

30.02 Goods lifts, paternoster lifts and pallet elevators. These were widely used in old multi-storey warehouses, but are now used for mezzanine handling, for example, when an order-picking area is mounted on a number of mezzanine levels. Goods lifts can be made flame-proof with electro-hydraulic and pneumatic controls for dangerous areas, e.g. where there are chemicals or paints. Some goods lifts, for use where headroom is at a premium, have a fully hydraulic motion from a ram at the side of the platform, effectively a static forklift mast.

Figure 4.60 *Manually operated vacuum palletizer.*

Figure 4.61 *Free-path order picker. Note operative has safety harness fixed to the truck.*

Mechanized storage – building function

Scissor lifts can be effective for single-stage lifts and need no shaft or counter weights. Some can lift a maximum weight vehicle; large scissor lifts are often used for difficult level changes between new and existing buildings, where a ramp would be too space consuming. Such scissor lifts require enclosed cars under EU safety legislation and should have a safety 'skirt' and guarded sides.

30.03 Pallet elevators. These have continuous action and integrate well with accumulation conveyors. They work on the paternoster principle, but return to the thickness of a belt on the return side. A typical use is from a mezzanine order-picking area, with pallets being moved automatically down the lowerator, through a shrink-wrap tunnel, and then on to the load assembly position to be palletized. (A lift or elevating device will cause a circulation constriction here.)

Mobile structure-based plant

30.04 Fixed-path, manually controlled stacker cranes and order pickers. These are floor, rack or roof supported, depending on type of machinery or rack chosen. The effects of acceleration and deceleration on structure, floor and racking should be considered. Double reinforcement of the slab is sometimes necessary against 'rippling', especially where heavy stackers impose 'hunting' loads. Fixed-path plant must be removed for major repairs, either along cross tracks to the maintenance bay or by a conventional gantry crane. A gantry crane in the sorting area is also useful for handling parts of shrink-wrap machines, palletizers, etc.; a one-ton lift is normally enough for general purposes, but before lifting out stacker cranes, check with the manufacturers first.

31 Mobile plant

31.01 This includes plant for lifting and plant for horizontal travel. All mobile plant should be considered as an integral part of the storage system, as the turning and lifting characteristics affect the positioning and height of the racking.

Lifting plant

31.02 Typical sizes, turning circles, weights and applications of forklift trucks (Figure 4.62) are given in Information sheet, Mechanized storage 7. Reach trucks are basically the same as forklifts, but designed specifically for narrow aisle operation (Figure 4.63). Whereas forklifts are designed for both inside and outside, on a variety of surfaces, reach trucks are designed for operation in racks on flat floors. There is a wide range of accessories and fittings (see Information sheet, Mechanized storage 7). To save stacker and reach truck

Figure 4.62 *4500 kg capacity forklift working in assembly plant buffer store.*

Figure 4.63 *Reach truck.*

drivers from spending time reversing, several manufacturers have placed the operator at 90° to the direction of travel. The logical development from reach trucks, for higher, narrower aisles was the turret truck. In some makes, the operator still has to sit at ground level and crane his or her neck but is aided by push-button rack height selection. Other makes allow the operator to rise with the fork carriage.

Horizontal travel plant

31.03 Horizontal-movement vehicles include tractor-drawn trains, overhead and ground-based conveyors and towline trucks. Forklift trucks are not considered economic for horizontal transport over distances of 70 to 80 m; they are designed primarily as stacking machinery. If goods are small and unpalletized (such as crates used in order assembly), conveyors are useful: if unit loads are to be handled, towline trucks or tractor trains are effective.

31.04 Conveyors have been described in Technical study, Mechanized storage 1, para. 18. There are many speeds, and special surface textures for slopes and accumulation. If roller conveyors are involved, check that roller pitch is correct for the product handled, especially on bends (Figures 4.64 and 4.65). Linear induction, motor-powered conveyors with very low maintenance costs and trouble-free, high speeds (see Information sheet, Mechanized storage 14) are being developed. Plate conveyors perform a similar function to tow trains. Capable of running flush with the floor surface, and of tight loops and turns, these conveyors are useful in sorting and dispatch accumulation areas, for instance, in parcel grouping. Plate conveyors are slow, but can be strong enough to be crossed by forklifts. Plate conveyors can be routed round any number of loops and picking positions, but their length is limited by the required speed of the package.

31.05 Towline truck systems are similar in theory of operation to plate conveyors, with the added benefit of

Mechanized storage – building function

Figure 4.64 *Accumulation conveyor.*

Figure 4.65 *Manual packaging with overhead conveyor.*

automatic routeing, queueing, and sidings for temporary holding. These trucks can be drawn from a drag chain in the floor (or a cable), or from an overhead conveyor system. The same barrows can be used for order picking, transport to the packing area, or returning goods and empty pallets to the storage area. Direction is gained by simple pin codes on the trollies. Parked barrows may block loading bay and goods assembly areas if these are not carefully planned keeping in mind other plant and that as the barrows are dragged by a pin at the front, they cut in on corners. Clearance should be left for personnel to pass safely, especially where there is cut-in near stanchions or in two-way tracks. However, a towline may act as a useful buffer during meal-breaks, and can accumulate empty barrows and carry them round until required. (See Information sheet, Mechanized storage 13.)

31.06 Tractor trailer trains are most economic for long distances, e.g. between pre-production parts store and production line in a large factory (Figures 4.66 and 4.67). Electric and internal combustion tractors are available,

Figure 4.66 *Tow tractor pulling roll pallets to sorting area.*

Figure 4.67 *Heavy-duty tow tractor*

which are capable of towing trains of up to 10 tonnes at speeds of 24 kph Above this weight, special industrial tractors can take gradients of 1 in 10, and some versions can be used externally or in fire-proof areas. Tractor trains are much faster than towlines. The former tend to steer on a close radius with little cut-in, owing to the castor action or steering on the trailers. Greater clearance is needed with two-way operation, as trailers have been known to 'hunt' at speed. If any internal combustion tractors are used in store, this must be taken into account when planning extraction.

32 Integration of building and plant

32.01 See building fabric, structure-based plant and mobile sections. Integration of building and plant is considered in detail in Technical study, Automated storage, para. 32. Warehouses must be built for change; planned life spans continue to get shorter.

33 Maintenance

33.01 Building maintenance in mechanized warehouses should be kept to a minimum. Low-maintenance materials help, but maintenance is also required for the impact, abrasion and vibration caused by handing plant. There is a direct correlation between structural damage by mobile handling machinery and the productivity bonus incentives offered to operatives. For example, in one large warehouse, operatives carry roll pallets two at a time on a rider pallet truck to the assembly area. To get a higher bonus, they all manage to secure a third roll pallet with one hand and a knee, and occasionally a fourth one. Not surprisingly, racking and roll pallets are often damaged. The designers must mount bumper bars and guards on the structure and rack ends, and ensure that main circulation routes do not coincide with unprotected columns or cladding. The sight of deeply gouged and cracked brickwork and scratched forklift trucks is common. At what point does maintenance cost outweigh gain from increased productivity?

33.02 In a 'big box' type of warehouse, roof-slung heating and ventilation plant, lighting and sprinkler lines all

Mechanized storage – building function

Figure 4.68 *Mobile sweeper. Note the hoppers of these sweepers can lift to tip into a compaction skip: just tipping onto the ground is not acceptable!*

need access for maintenance. Deep roof trusses allow catwalks, which, if positioned near the tops of the racks, can also be used for lighting and sprinkler repairs. Free-path order picking plant can be used for general maintenance as long as the correct guards and fail-safe devices are fitted. To keep a warehouse running smoothly, good housekeeping is important. Mobile ride-on sweepers and floor cleaners should be provided. These run on batteries similar to a forklift or are powered by liquified propane gas (LPG) (Figure 4.68). A rubbish compactor can be very useful in the loading bay area where baled waste is put into a skip. (See Information sheet, Loading 3.) With the use of integrally coloured cladding internally, a waiver can be obtained against the frequent repainting often required by the local authority.

33.03 The external appearance of large warehouses may act as beneficial publicity for their operators, but can also have the reverse effect if unsuitably treated. Sheet steel insulated panels are not only easily replaceable after impact damage, but can be integrally faced with a coloured plastic or stove enamelled finish.

Lighting maintenance

33.04 For maintenance, access from above by walkway or from below by mobile platform is essential. Turret trucks and free-path order pickers can sometimes be used for this function, but consult the Factory Inspectorate, as there are regulations concerning special guards and fail-safe devices. Every effort should be made to encourage the maintenance of good reflecting surfaces.

33.05 Where access for lamp replacement is difficult, ordinary incandescent lamps are unlikely to be economical, despite their small size and low initial cost. This is because their life at 1000 hours is much less than that of the other sources available. Discharge lamps, including fluorescent tubes, have lives from 2500 hours to 7500 hours.

34 Management

34.01 Speed is now so important in the construction and fitting-out of distribution buildings that any project that is not 'fast track' appears to be dead slow. There are good operational reasons for this urgency: fulfilment centres are the 'concrete' form within the supply chain, whether as cross-docking and sortation or stockholding facilities. The building is a static envelope for a highly dynamic process: and that decision to construct will have been as a result of an equally fast-track and dynamic consultancy and cost evaluation process with the objective of cutting process and operating costs whilst improving customer service

levels. In other words, once the decision has been made to proceed, time is money and adherence to the program essential in achieving the valuable competitive edge.

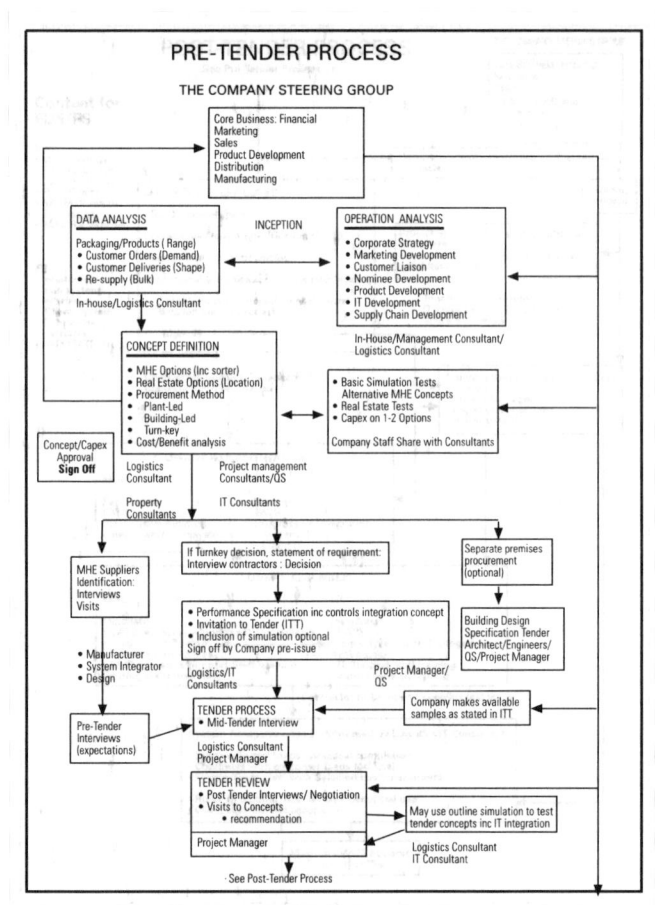

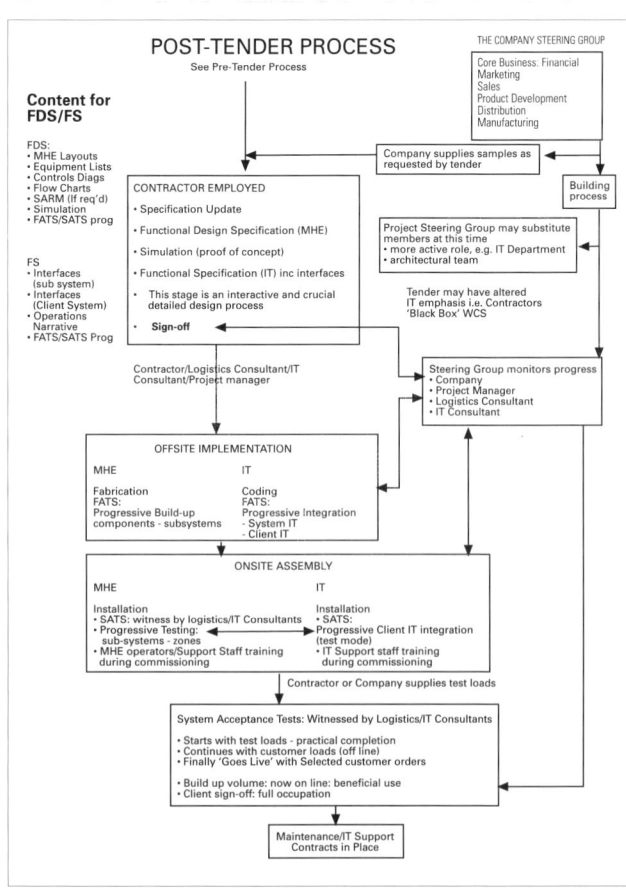

34.02 The Pre- and Post-Tender warehouse project flowcharts included in Chapter 1 are reproduced here to demonstrate the essential linkages that have to be monitored continuously right through the design and construction process to ensure that commissioning and hand-over target dates are achieved. This model was based on a typical major regional distribution warehouse using mechanized materials-handling with advanced electronic order picking and assembly information, including manual discrete item order picking from pallets and roll-through carton dispensers to conveyors in turn feeding a high speed sorter for order assembly: it is a fairly typical high turnover order fulfillment centre for electronically-generated orders. The example was assembled from a number of similar projects within the last five years, combining fast track construction with parallel handling and control systems development.

34.03 The Concept Definition stage is key to the fast-track process, setting out the project time scale and researching whether it will be more valuable (in all business senses) to locate and fit out a user-ready or pre-owned building, or construct a new one. Of course, the user-ready decision generally avoids the time spent in obtaining development and statutory approvals unless a Change of Use is required, the down side often being sub-optimal location and premises risking the degradation of the supply chain process or an above average rental. As the Concept Definition stage leading to the first major Board approval often over runs (necessary with an iterative process that it is better to get right at the beginning: projects have foundered due to later knee jerk changes), building and handling process design and procurement often start late and are wanted 'yesterday'. Maintaining design and implementation process control are key. These Pre- and Post-Tender project management process diagrams may not be exhaustive, but are typical of what needs to be achieved in a very short space of time: specialists including 'professionals' and trade contractors must communicate and not take 'positions' for such a project to succeed.

34.04 Major projects like this can be achieved within 15–18 months depending on their size and level of complexity, including the essential client systems–warehouse system integration commissioning trials, often 8–12 weeks, which are ignored at the user's peril: it is no longer the basic substructure, structure, cladding and services that take the time, but the mechanical handling fit-out with its mezzanines, conveyors, miles of site wiring and computer integration. But the envelope has to be in place, weather tight and dust-free for the fit-out to begin. For instance, 33 000 square metres of wide span, high bay distribution space was recently put in place in just 13 weeks (be it on a pre-prepared site), thereby allowing 10–13 weeks basic fit-out (racking, mezzanines and conveyor and sorter chasses), 6–8 weeks running gear and site wiring installation with parallel internal activities such as cold chamber installation, and external equipment and controls Factory Acceptance Tests (FATS): then 8 weeks beginning to run-up mechanical systems with parallel finishing activities (and the trades have to be mobilized and scheduled with military precision), followed by 10–12 weeks Site Acceptance Tests (SATS), testing and commissioning both static and mobile elements with systems integraiton. That is a year to practical completion from a standing start. It is only then that serious customer systems integration can commence, hence a 15-month program. The importance of this last stage, Systems Acceptance Tests, is often misunderstood or just plain neglected (especially if a project is running late), and can lead to expensive litigation.

34.05 The project manager, whether architect, other design professional, construction management professional or handling consultant (this selection as stated in Chapter 1 depending on the lead characteristics of the project) does need to be encyclopedic: they must maintain an overview of the entire project including how the Client's development team are performing. The essential skill is understanding the project matrix and keeping it up to date, such that whenever the Steering Committee demands the status of any part of the project the manager can truthfully say 'I know who has this in hand'.

35 Personnel accommodation

35.01 The number of personnel in a mechanized warehouse is generally falling except for order fulfilment centres; order picking requires more personnel. Most members of the staff of a mechanized warehouse are highly skilled, either as order pickers or turret truck drivers. The environment of tall racks is exacting, and some form of amenity accommodation should be provided. Companies with order-picking staff have found that order-picking productivity has been improved by high airy spaces and by the inclusion of occasional clear storey windows in one of the walls. This is for visual relief from the picking face and so that weather conditions can be seen; industrial psychologists say that this is a basic psychological need.

Office accommodation

35.02 With computer-operated stock control, documentation is reducing slowly: the paperless warehouse is still aspirational. But office accommodation is not likely to grow as fast as storage; check carefully the number of clerical personnel needed and what documentation systems imply, considering future expansion, a change towards automation, and a different distribution pattern. The rule of thumb of providing for 10 per cent of the storage area as office accommodation should be tested, but is proven (Figure 4.69). One of the present drawbacks with computer operation is the growth of white-collar staff to process the software. As offices tend to be placed on a perimeter so as not to encroach on valuable storage volume, the office should be insulated against noise, vibration, fumes and dirt from heavy traffic passing nearby on its way to and from loading bay and assembly areas. Other offices required are the traffic manager's, which should have optimum visual range, and those for non-management staff such as shop supervisors, shift supervisors, shop stewards and security staff. These offices are best located where supervisors have most contact with the staff they supervise, but, in large installations, should be equipped with a document link to the main office.

Figure 4.69 *'Big box' warehouse showing adjoining office accommodation.*

Mechanized storage – building function

36 Amenities

36.01 Heated locker and changing rooms should be provided for operatives. They should be able to dry wet clothes and store personal effects securely. Many large warehouses that operate smoothly have strategically placed beverage machines so that forklift truck drivers can stop for a quick drink when they like as long as they achieve their quota of work. This usually operates with a bonus scheme. If management prefer set tea-break periods, then an amenity area away from the racks should be provided, which can also be used by the order-picking and loading bay staff. In this case, parking for mobile handling machinery is necessary. The Factories Act demands a room for operatives' meals segregated from the storage zone. Smoking is obviously forbidden in the warehouse, so the amenity room is useful for this also.

36.02 Lavatory and washing accommodation should be separately provided for warehouse staff and lorry drivers, as joint access can lead to valuable stock 'walking out'. If order-picking staff are involved, accommodation for women and clerical staff should also be provided and some managements insist on segregating clerical staff washrooms from those for general personnel.

37 Personnel safety

37.01 Personnel safety precautions are very important. There is a great deal of fast-moving machinery and heavy weights are being raised and lowered. Unit loads are often unstable when delivered, so space should be allocated in the incoming check area for re-packing; this is also useful for changing broken or non-standard pallets before storing.

37.02 Accidents are inevitable. A first-aid room with equipment for handling broken bones, fractures, electrocution and crush injuries should be provided in the amenity zone. If possible, the first-aid room should be near to a loading bay that can take an ambulance. This room should be equipped with 600 lux lighting, hot and cold running water, and a high level of ventilation; in one installation, air inlets were positioned over lorry-parking areas and sucked in diesel fumes.

37.03 All ramps, catwalks and pedestrian routes shared with mobile plant should have a strong dividing rail in a bright colour, and floor markings. If blind corners are inevitable, a carefully placed mirror can be useful, but beware of glare, and consider load tolerances and fork lift mast heights, as they tend to lift on the move.

37.04 Security against theft has been discussed in para. 28. For bonded goods, such as spirits, highly sophisticated security systems are available. (See *Building Services Handbook*, 2001, R. Greeno and F. E. Hall, Butterworth–Heinemann.)

38 Circulation and parking

38.01 There are several traffic systems to be considered, some of which conflict:

1 External heavy vehicles.
2 External light goods traffic.
3 External passenger traffic.
4 External pedestrian circulation.
5 External inter-store transport.
6 Internal main storage traffic; input.
7 Internal main traffic; output.
8 Internal sub-systems.
9 Internal pedestrian routes.

All these have to work together to be successful, but safety must not be sacrificed for expediency. Points 1 and 2 have been discussed in Technical study, Mechanized storage 1, para. 4. External passenger traffic is directly related to office and warehouse staff numbers, and ideally should be segregated from heavy traffic. Some visitors' parking should also be provided since maintenance staff and suppliers often require access to the premises. If a shift system is operated, extra space as a parking buffer is required. Warehouse personnel parking should not be in a position where staff can shift goods into their vehicles unseen. Also consider office and warehouse expansion.

38.02 External pedestrian routeing should be segregated from heavy traffic, since heavy lorries have blind spots in rearward vision, and pedestrians can be hidden until too late by parked vans. If pedestrians have to use the same gate, a heavy-duty crush barrier, painted in 'dayglow', should be erected between the routes.

38.03 Internal routes depend on the type of plant and the store arrangement. For block stacking, the theoretically ideal route is a 'cartwheel' (Figure 4.70). Routes should therefore be as direct as possible. With racking, the installation may be large enough to require primary and distributor routes before reaching the aisles. Treat this circulation as a normal road system with priorities and passing clearances. If towline trucks or conveyors are used, the cross routes with other plant must be carefully planned. Towcarts are slow-moving, and if the circuit is busy it is often difficult for a forklift to get across; an interruptor can be fitted, so that a forkiift driver can make his own gap. Pedestrian escape routes must be especially carefully handled, as unrestricted egress is essential. These routes should be clearly identifiable with illuminat-

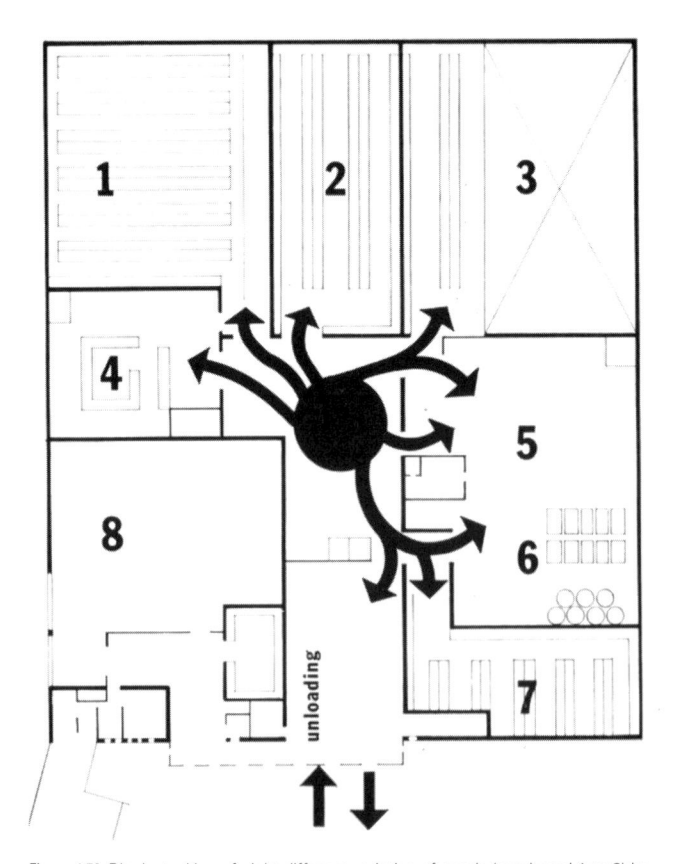

Figure 4.70 *Block stacking of eight different varieties of goods (numbered 1 to 8) by 'cartwheel' method. All goods are unloaded into central area; forklifts can then move radially, taking the shortest possible distance from centre to each block stack.*

Mechanized storage – building function

ed wall signs and floor markings. Zebra crossings should be marked where escape routes cross principal, internal circulation routes.

38.04 If vehicle routes are needed to an external area, rapid rise doors with 3-second opening/closing cycles are effective in reducing draughts and providing weather protection. Some operators prefer a more expensive type of door that slides under pneumatic control, activated from compression pads (Figure 4.71). If there is two-way traffic through the doors, it is advisable to fit a warning system, and separate pedestrian access should be provided. Compression pads that give adequate warning by light and siren to any approaching vehicles or personnel can be placed at an adequate distance calculated from the average operating speed. If there is frequent use, a hot air curtain may be required to prevent intense local heat loss; check the orientation of the door to the area's prevailing wind. A drain grating to squeeze water from forklift tyres is advantageous, saving on floor wear and lessening chance of skidding. Where a large number of order-picking staff are involved, the personnel should be segregated from the main plant routes. If their routes to the amenity and lavatory areas have to pass through the active zone, the path should be clearly marked and protected where possible.

Figure 4.71 *Door zone for high throughput. Plan (a) and section (b) show major forklift or tractor train route out. If impact doors are used, omit opening pads.*

Dimension (a) time lag required to operate doors x speed of plant in m/sec.

Dimension (b) number of seconds warning x average speed of plant in m/sec. Rapid rise doors can open/close in 3 seconds.

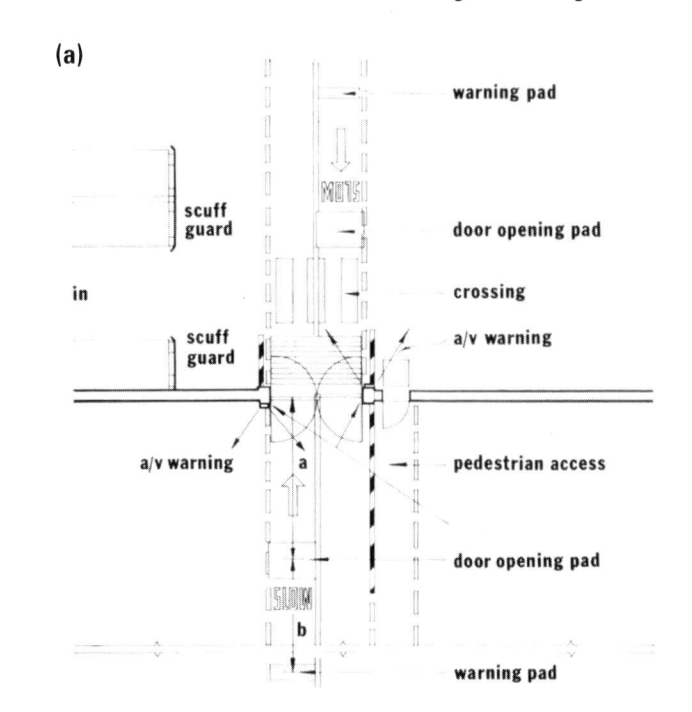

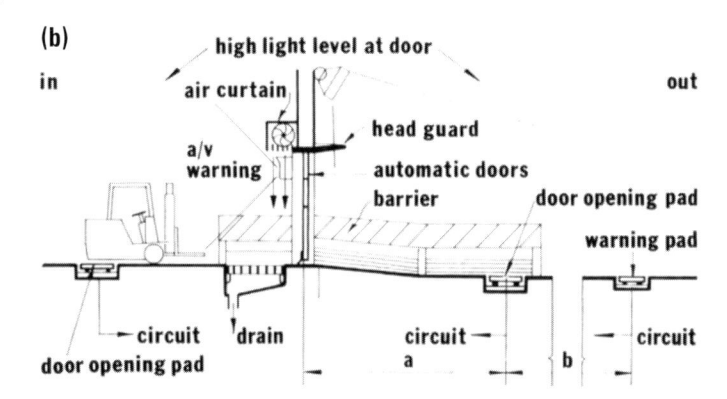

INFORMATION SHEET

Mechanized storage 1

Tote boxes, drawers and storage cabinets

1 **Tote boxes**

2 **Drawers**

3 **Small goods handling**

4 **Designers' checklist**

The importance of efficient storage and handling of small goods and parts is often underestimated by designers, and can cost companies a great deal of money.

1 Tote boxes

1.01 A tote box is an intermodal container specifically designed for small parts storage and fast manual order picking. It is replacing the drawer or shelf unit for some applications, as it provides the additional flexibility of being able to be used as the transport and storage medium on the shop floor.

Materials

1.02 The standard type of tote box is made of metal, plastics or board and can be straight-sided or semi-open at the front for easy access. Steel tote boxes (or tote bins) are strong, durable and easy to stack, and do not deform under load (Figure 4.72). They do however, corrode in

Figure 4.73 *Plastic tote boxes, attached to metal louvre panels, can be used in several different ways.*

certain conditions and impose much weight on racking and shelving. Aluminium is lighter, but expensive. Plastics boxes are increasingly popular, being corrosion resistant, and can be moulded with an integral colour to any shape and size required. Colour coding is possible and has been used, both in the store and on the shop floor, by many companies. Plastics bins with small loads can be clipped on to louvred metal panels, thus eliminating shelving altogether (Figure 4.73). Mobile louvre panel frames are increasingly used in such industries as electronics manufacture, where an operative's whole day's supply of parts is accommodated in tote boxes sized for the part and colour-coded for the manufacturing stage (Figure 4.74). Some paper products tote boxes are still available, but they are not very strong and are a considerable fire hazard. They are usually assembled at the store from printed sheets.

Size

1.03 Sizes vary from 76 mm x 100 mm x 50 mm, to 1.5 m/750 mm x 500 mm. Bins with a large cubic capacity do not necessarily mean reduced costs in this type of storage. Large-capacity boxes, infrequently replenished, waste volume and may be overloaded, making them difficult to handle. For space requirements see Figure 4.78.

Figure 4.72 *Stacked metal tote boxes.*

117

Mechanized storage – tote boxes, drawers and storage cabinets

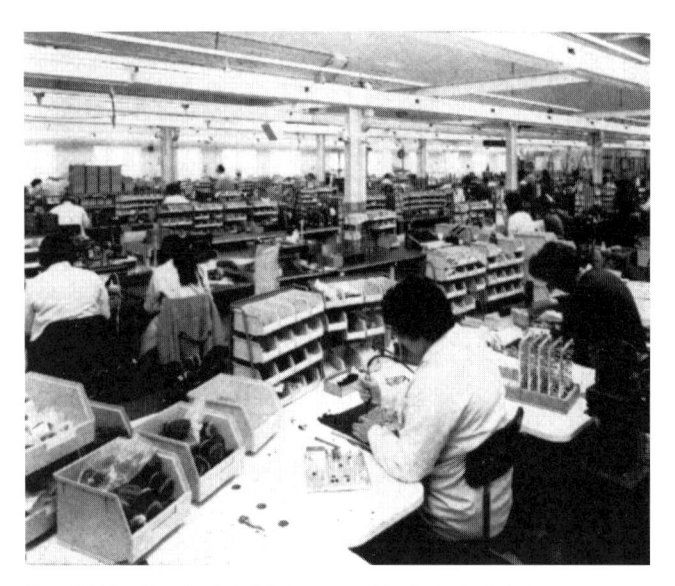

Figure 4.74 *Supplies of parts in tote boxes, used in electronics industry.*

Shape

1.04 Tote boxes can be divided to suit the product. Special moulded plastic inserts are available for fragile goods. Considerable volume wastage is caused by the tolerance that has to be left above and between tote boxes for easy picking and placing. A simple method of increasing volume efficiency is to use mobile racking (see Information sheet, Mechanical storage 2). In some cases, it has been found more economic to use the manufacturers' returnable special boxes and trays, which have been designed specifically to suit the product.

Method of storage

1.05 Most plastic tote boxes and several of the steel systems nest, and in certain circumstances dispense with shelving altogether. Louvre panels are suitable, and each 300 mm x 450 mm section of the panel can support 73 kg weight, with average end frame capacities of up to 408 kg (Figure 4.75). Heavy-duty panels with loads up to 1907 kg are available. As well as tote boxes, shelves, clips, hooks and tool holders can be clipped to louvre panels, giving additional flexibility for shop floor and spares depot. Cantilever shelving is also used for metal and paper tote boxes which cannot be clipped to louvre panels. This shelving is mounted on slotted angle uprights so that the shelves can be adjusted for bin height. Other systems for heavier steel tote bins include frames mounted in post pallets, so that the pallets nest to form a storage rack, and act as a dispense unit on the shop floor.

Shelving for tote boxes

1.06 Shelving for tote boxes is usually steel. Uniformly sized boxes can be stored on cantilever brackets with continuous shelving above, saving up to 25 per cent of normal shelf space, but this is best used for relatively slow-moving goods (Figure 4.76). Most shelf systems adjust to suit bins, tote boxes and special rack components such as cable reels and tyre spindles. In small-goods operations, storage capacity can be increased by over 50 per cent by a two- or three-level mezzanine system (Figure 4.77) (but this may mean expensive multi-level sprinkler installations.

Packing and stock control

1.07 Tote boxes are ideal for spare parts storage, where the access problem is not so vital. Colour-coded boxes guide the picking personnel quickly and accurately. Open-ended boxes, with a set number of units stored in each, enable the picker to tell at a glance when stock needs replenishing. When goods are withdrawn, a pre-printed stock control card on the box can be altered to show how much stock remains. Stacking or nesting boxes using the cut-away front pattern avoid the need for shelving. The principal disadvantage of this is that if the base units have not been calculated to hold slow-moving or reserve stock, all the boxes above have to be removed to allow replenishment.

Potential

1.08 Tote boxes have generated an industry of their own and manufacturers should be contacted to find out their

Figure 4.75 *Louvre panels used in high-density storage.*

Figure 4.76 *Simple steel shelving for metal tote boxes.*

Figure 4.77 *Mezzanine system.*

Mechanized storage – tote boxes, drawers and storage cabinets

full flexibility. Very intensive tote box storage has been successfully operated in high-rack, narrow aisle layouts, using fixed-path order-picking machinery.

1.09 A sophisticated tote box development is a fully automated highly intensive store called Conserve-a-trieve, of American origin, now available in the UK. The machine, a scaled-down stacker crane, was originally designed for document handling; it works in a very narrow aisle with tote boxes in racking. Control is by personal computer. The system of tote boxes ten high and ten deep on each side of the aisle has an 11-second average retrieval time.

2 Drawers

2.01 These are still used for small components such as tool heads. Drawer units are generally slow to operate, requiring the extra movements of opening and stepping back before identifying the goods, which can also inhibit aisle movement (Figure 4.78). Special tray drawers often swing open on a pivot system and are less space-consuming (Figure 4.79). Tote boxes have largely replaced drawers throughout the greater part of industry.

Pigeon holes and small drawer units

2.02 These use the same type of steel sheet construction as long span shelving. A wide variety of pigeon hole and drawer sizes are available from several manufacturers, with various weight ratings. Drawers are space-consuming in comparison with tote boxes but are still useful for high-security small goods and valuable spares. An example of this is drill bits, where semiprecious stones are often used as the cutting head. For very small goods, such as nails and screws in bulk, metal drawers are obtainable with adjustable division plates; these are still used effectively in small-scale operations. The development of the multi-sized plastic tote box and ironmongery products being shrink-wrapped in preset quantities will make this type of drawer less popular.

Special cabinets and heavy tool drawers

2.03 For tools and drill heads, which can be very heavy, these drawers are available in swing-out pivot form, allowing narrower aisles, as the picker stands parallel to the drawer instead of behind it (Figure 4.79).

Mechanized small parts and tool cabinets

2.04 For tools, drill heads, spares, etc. there are mechanized systems based on the vertical conveyor principle as used in document filing. The goods are stored in bins or on shelves at an output point. They circulate vertically on an endless chain. This type of installation is not cheap but provides dense, secure storage and quick access to a wide range of components.

3 Small goods handling

3.01 The handling of small goods in high-speed, high-density systems is a complex problem. There is a definite point where so many parts are handled so fast that drawers, mechanical cabinets and even tote boxes become redundant. In manufacturing units like the automobile industry, fast-moving parts in cage pallets, bins and stillages are block-stacked. Small parts needed in large quantities can be used directly from the storage cage without the need for decanting into tote boxes. The need for replenishment can easily be seen, a reach truck brings a full stillage to floor level, removing the empty unit. This should not be confused with tote box operation, as too often boxes are seen piled on floors, constricting circulation. In some factories, where management is concerned about machine operators running out of parts, a pile of full and empty tote boxes accumulate round their plant, which quickly conflicts with the operation. This is unnecessary if the supply system has been correctly programmed from the outset of the store design.

Reducing multiple handling

3.02 Although a neat way of storing small parts, tote box systems involve multiple handling. Normally, goods arrive loose or on a pallet at the warehouse; they are off-loaded, checked and sorted into tote boxes and stored; the original packaging material has to be collected and batched for disposal. It is likely that there will have been five or six movements by the time the goods are initially stored, before any selection or delivery process is operated. In this context, the use of drawers or tote boxes is questionable. A universal package should be developed, for transport, storage, picking and shop floor use. The designer should feed back data from pre-design studies to establish the best size of package for stacking on pallets, and order picking, or for direct transit and use as a container in the production zone. One computer-manufacturing company already works on this policy, and expects to start phasing out tote boxes soon for vendor packs.

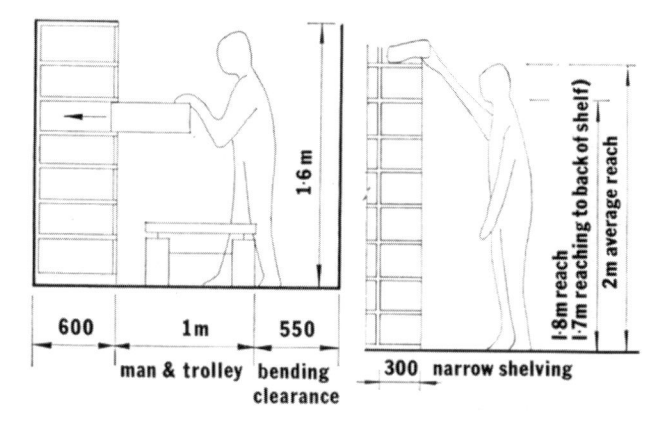

Figure 4.78 *Space requirements for ordinary pull-out drawers. Tote box space requirements are similar, less 600 mm drawer depth.*

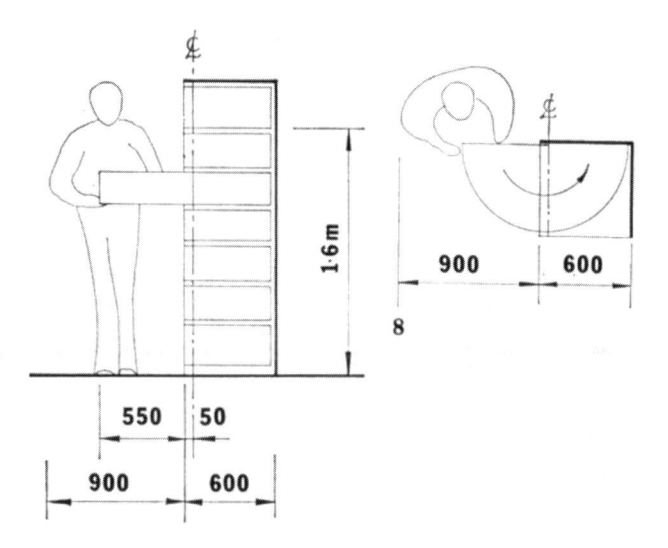

Figure 4.79(a/b) *Space requirements for swing-out drawers (operative picks at right angles to the drawer (b) rather than opposite as in Figure 4.78.*

4 Designer's checklist

4.01 The demands of stores for small goods for production or spare parts should be understood by the designer. Movements that do not seem particularly significant initially can have long-term, costly repercussions throughout the system. It is helpful to follow this pattern:

1 Predict daily/hourly throughput and flow per day for each outlet.
2 With this data, assess the optimum flow pattern for the goods, ensuring that critical supply routes do not converge at constrictions.
3 Calculate the best picking and replenishment pattern in the store, sorting the parts or goods into high-, medium- and low-use sections, allowing the most-used units priority access.
4 Design in flexibility so that a product or commodity change can be reflected quickly and cheaply within the store. This type of trade is changing increasingly quickly.

Design process

4.02 The handling and transport managers should be contacted throughout this design process, and the following questions checked:

- Has the product demand pattern been thoroughly studied? The intention is to minimize journeys from the store to production or load assembly areas, optimize the storage mode and minimize labour, time and cost.
- If there is a small-goods or parts store, is it operating at its highest potential? Is the new system to be a continuation of the old, and is the previous system suitable?
- How much space is under-utilized? Some is inevitable, but is it a minimum?
- Are personnel being used efficiently? Will picking staff follow carefully routed patterns?
- Why are tote boxes or drawers being used? Could a single package be used throughout the system instead?
- If it has been decided that tote boxes are the most effective storage medium, these units should be selected in the size, material and properties best suited to the product. It is the responsibility of production control personnel to decide whether one part has a unique box delivered frequently, or whether a group of parts are packed into a bigger box and delivered twice a day. These decisions are fundamental to a storage building and handling system design.
- Where should tote bins be grouped? Does the character of the parts change after the intermediate process and are they still suitable for tote box handling? Whatever happens, avoid situations that can generate heaps on the store or factory floor.

INFORMATION SHEET

Mechanized storage 2
Shelving

1 Slotted angle shelving
2 Boltless shelving
3 Light duty cantilever shelving
4 Long span adjustable shelving
5 Multi-tier slotted angle and lightweight clip-on shelving
6 Mezzanine floors
7 Typical mezzanine installation
8 Live racking
9 Mobile shelving
10 Special lightweight racks, shelves
11 Timber frame shelving

This sheet describes types of simple shelving.

1 Slotted angle shelving

1.01 Several manufacturers produce lightweight racking from slotted angle (Figure 4.80). This is useful for small parts and spares stored on shelves. Adjustable shelving is important as spares operations change frequently and it can be expected that tote boxes will be changed to suit the product in that particular store location. This type of shelving is easy to adapt, with cross members quickly unbolted or unclipped; shelves can be adjusted to any level within 19 mm. Units can either be assembled from slotted angle lengths by the user, or purchased purpose made. A very wide range of shelf sizes and types is available; this includes open back shelving, closed back, long span with steel or chipboard shelving and with steel sides, back, and shelves with adjustable steel vertical dividers.

Typical evenly distributed load per shelf:

914 mm long: 457 mm wide: 158 kg
1828 mm long: 451 mm wide: 317 kg (18 mm chipboard)
914 mm long: 610 mm wide: open back: 294 kg (with diagonal braces).

2 Boltless shelving

2.01 Performing an intermediate function between slotted angle and pallet racking, this is a steel clip-on system. Shelves are supported at the corners with adjuster clips which slot into uprights; alternatively, long spans can be achieved with horizontal beams with an added clip-on steel surface. This shelving is used for heavier parts, such as high-density boxes of screws and fittings, and in open shelf form for storing comparatively heavy packs, of paper for example. Installations up to 6.1 m high have been used, but 2.1 m heights meet most hand-loaded shelf requirements. Frame loads exceeding 2034 kg can be met:

Open back: 914 mm long 451 wide: 294 kg (using beams);
braced back in place of beams 294 kg.

3 Light duty cantilever shelving

3.01 This gives more storage space than conventional shelving and added product flexibility by presenting undivided lengths of shelving (Figure 4.81). Shelving is supported on steel cantilever arms which pass through central steel uprights. Shelf levels are adjustable within 76 mm spacing in one system. They are useful for lightweight goods where most of the goods require manual-handling and are similarly packaged with a fast stock rotation, the clear shelves allowing stock to be slid along to replace packages that have been removed. Usual

Figure 4.80 *Simple slotted angle shelving using chipboard shelves.*

4.81 *Light duty cantilever shelving.*

Mechanized storage – shelving

Figure 4.82 Long span adjustable shelving.

height, 2.12 m with four shelves. Shelves up to 7.3 m long in 914 mm increments: typical maximum shelf loads: 5.5 m long, 457 mm wide shelving, 141 kg.

4 Long span adjustable shelving

4.01 Designed to meet span requirements exceeding 914 mm and loads up to 544 kg per shelf. Construction is a range of steel beams and panels, mounted on slotted steel vertical frames (Figure 4.82). Steel panels are usually supported by integral ledges on the beams. A heavy-duty version, with 3.04 m beam lengths is available; this is very useful for bulky light goods, where inspection is required on the shelving; maximum loading is 9070 kg per frame. A typical installation uses long span shelving for storing typewriters for inspection prior to dispatch.

5 Multi-tier slotted angle and lightweight clip-on shelving

5.01 When handling large numbers of small parts manually, the volumetric efficiency of the storage is low; this limitation can be overcome with multi-tier shelving (Figure 4.83). This should not be compared with mezzanines; the upper tiers of shelving and the floor are an integral part of the slotted angle frame.

6 Mezzanine floors

6.01 For heavier manual operation; these can be in the form of a flat deck mounted on heavier duty shelf and drawer units, or as complete purpose-made structural steel frame, with one or two levels. The latter case can accept a floor loading with 15 mm plywood flooring of 688 kg/m² giving internal column loadings of 10.67 tonnes, versions with additional steel floor support beams can accept up to 1952 kg/m². These systems, offered by several manufacturers, are complete with handrails, stairs and, if required, steel framed and panelled offices.

7 Typical mezzanine installation

7.01 Drawer units at ground and first floor, and palletized goods too big for shelving on the top deck, supplied by a forklift truck running in an aisle at one end of the racking.

Figure 4.83 Three types of storage for different types of product.

Mezzanine storage must be designed with reference to demands by statutory authorities and the firm's insurance company. Note also the Health and Safety at Work Act regarding open mesh flooring and guard rails.

8 Live racking

8.01 For high throughput picking, such as cash-and-carry operations (Figure 4.84). The goods flow by gravity on inclined roller conveyor tracks to the picking face. These store-and-dispense units are often used where the public is allowed to pick the goods, as they can be made to look like large display cabinets.

8.02 Live storage provides the best possible stock rotation by achieving a first-in, first-out cycle. This system is mainly suitable for applications involving comparatively few stock lines. Cartons or product packaging need to be of a high standard to avoid crushing.

9 Mobile shelving

9.01 Useful where there is limited space available and permanent 100 per cent stock accessibility is not required. Mobile shelving can give up to 60 per cent more storage space than conventional shelving (Figure 4.85). Construction is similar to clip-on steel shelving or slotted angle shelving, mounted on a mobile base. Some manufacturers offer their timber frame shelving on a mobile base. Typical loads are 3 tonnes on two tracks or 4 tonnes on three tracks. Mobile frames are suitable for drawers, shelves or tote boxes. Manual, electric, pneumatic, hydraulic and cable operation are available. The power system should be chosen on the potential damage to the product being stored. Some power systems have proved unpredictable. A problem has been personnel who, becoming impatient with the slow operation of mobile racking, have tried to help by pushing, causing units to come off their tracks and jam. One system employs horizontal guide wheels as well, to prevent this contingency. If a power system is used, personnel safety is provided by a press bar at foot level that immediately cuts the power on impact.

Mechanized storage – shelving

Figure 4.84 *'Live' shelving in a pharmaceutical warehouse. Note inclined track with barcode labels and 'pick car'.*

9.02 There are two possible arrangements; the conventional method is lateral movement, with the shelves resting face to face (Figure 4.86b). One manufacturer offers a longitudinal movement, arranged up to four racks deep (Figure 4.86a). The latter allows a larger picking face to be exposed at any time, although marginally losing volume capacity over lateral moving units. A person can push four mobile units with adjustable shelving in steel or timber.

Fire risk

9.03 There is some controversy about the fire risk involved with mobile shelving. One manufacturer considers that there is less fire risk with timber construction, as any fire would be localized; steel shelving would transmit heat, causing spontaneous combustion, and could buckle the rack stopping movement, so eliminating the possibility of fire officers reaching the seat of the fire in time to gain control. Intermediate level sprinkling is possible in mobile shelving and racks, using a jointed supply main.

10 Special lightweight racks, shelves

10.01 Single- and double-sided cantilever racking for light metal sections and bars. Distributed loads of up to 10 tonnes are possible, double-sided. Sheet metal racks for vertical or horizontal use can also carry 10 tonnes. Typical size for a horizontal sheet rack 2.5 m × 1.3 m × 1.2 m high.

Figure 4.85 *Lateral mobile shelving in use.*

Other special racks include tyre racking, multi-rail open frames for clothing and many other types produced to special order.

11 Timber frame shelving

11.01 Similar to the steel systems, but with timber slotted frames. A high level of fire performance is claimed, with an improved storage environment. Shelves rest on steel clips, located into slots in the timber. Loads of up to 400 kg per shelf are permitted.

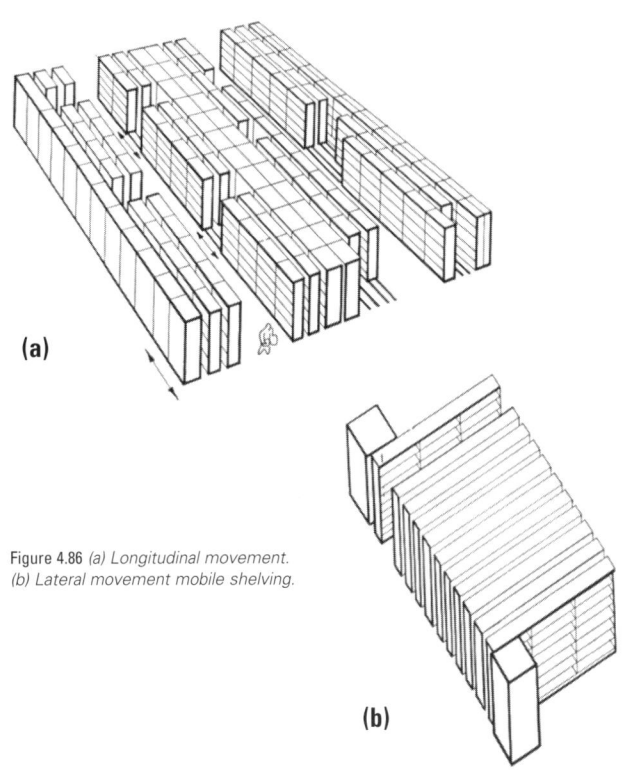

Figure 4.86 *(a) Longitudinal movement. (b) Lateral movement mobile shelving.*

123

INFORMATION SHEET

Mechanized storage 3
Racking

1 Introduction

2 Standard adjustable racking or shelving

3 Pallet racking

4 Special racking

5 Live racking

6 Mobile racking

Racking is the most important storage element in a warehouse. This sheet describes types of free-standing racking- adjustable, static, live and mobile. Structural racking is discussed in Chapter 5, Automated storage.

1 Introduction

1.01 Racking can be structural or free-standing. Structural racking is an engineering problem, and because it forms a rigid chassis for the building fabric and handling equipment, it cannot be adaptable. (See Chapter 5, Automated storage).

Free-standing racking

1.02 Before choosing the type of racking, consider:
- the crushability of the goods. If live racking is required, will bracing be needed?
- whether goods will be palletized or cartons loaded directly onto shelves (see Tables 4.3 and 4.4)
- the loadings involved
- the required rate of stock rotation; if the goods are crushable, and a rotation more suited to block-stacking is predicted, drive-in racking should be installed
- degree of accessibility required
- volume of building available to the volume of goods
- the amount of order picking; certain types of racking are better suited for this
- is racking needed at all? Could post pallets be block-stacked to achieve the same throughout for less cost? For example, if the goods must be highly accessible and have a high turnover, live racking may be required. Or, a large volume of goods stored in a tight area, which must also be highly accessible, may require mobile racking. (See Technical study, Mechanized storage 1, paras 13 and 16.)

1.03 Tables 4.5 and 4.6 compare different types of racking.

Shelving

1.04 Static or adjustable (Figure 4.87). Available with steel aluminium or timber frames. (See Information sheet, Mechanized storage 2.)

Table 4.3 Load mounting

Load mounting	Heavy unstable load	Flat cards/sheets	Sacked/bagged loads	Small unit loads	Drum reels/barrels	Coils	Casks	Bales	Textile raw materials
Special cradle with/without pallet	*								
Standard pallet	*	*	*	*	*	*	*	*	
Flat board pallet + decking supports		*	*		*		*		
Direct mounting on timber panels		*	*	*		*	*	*	*
Drum supports					*				
Post pallets – cage/bin		*	*		*	*		*	
Coil supports				*	*				
Skips/skeps with skids									*

Mechanized storage – racking

Table 4.4 Classification of materials for handling and storage as unit loads

Description	Examples	Storage method	Description	Examples	Storage method
Materials not strong enough to withstand crushing – not suitable for unit loads	Automobile components, made-up textiles, electrical appliance components, manufacturing chemists' sundries, light engineering products, glassware	On pallet in rack	Large irregular loose materials	Moulded plastics; sheet metal pressings	On post pallets and stacked
			Small irregular loose materials	Machined and moulded parts, pressings, forgings	In case pallets and stacked
Materials strong enough to withstand crushing – suitable for unit loads	Casks and drums, sawn and machined timber, sheet materials	On pallet, or self-palletized and block stowed	Materials hot from production processes	Castings and forgings	On post pallets and stacked
			Materials too long to be handled other than by side loader or boom	Steel sections, tubes, timber	Horizontally in tube or bar racks
Irregular shaped materials, strong in themselves suitably packed into unit loads	Goods in cases, crates or cartons	On post pallets and stacked, on pallets in rack or self-palletized	Materials strong enough to withstand crushing but subject to damage	Partly machined automotive parts, painted finished materials, books	Steel box pallets with special partitions
Bagged materials which form a flat surface under load	Grain, powder, and similar	On pallet and block stowed	Perishable goods	Frozen meat, vegetables, drink	Cartons, soft packs pallets, box pallets, etc.
Bagged materials which do not form a flat surface under load or will not take pressure	Forgings, moulded or machined parts, nuts and bolts	On pallet in rack			

Table 4.5 Mechanical handling

	Block stacking	Post pallets	Drive-in racking	Beam pallet racking	Gravity live storage	Powered mobile racking
Cubic space utilization %	100	90	65	35–50	80	80
Effective use of installation capacity %	75	75	75	100	70	100
Accessibility of unit load %	10	10	30	100	30	100
Order picking %	1	30	30	100	30	100
Speed of throughput	Fastest	Good	Poor	Good	Good	Quite good
Load crushing	Bad	Nil	Nil	Nil	Some	Nil
Stability of load	Poor	Fair	Good	Good	Fair	Good

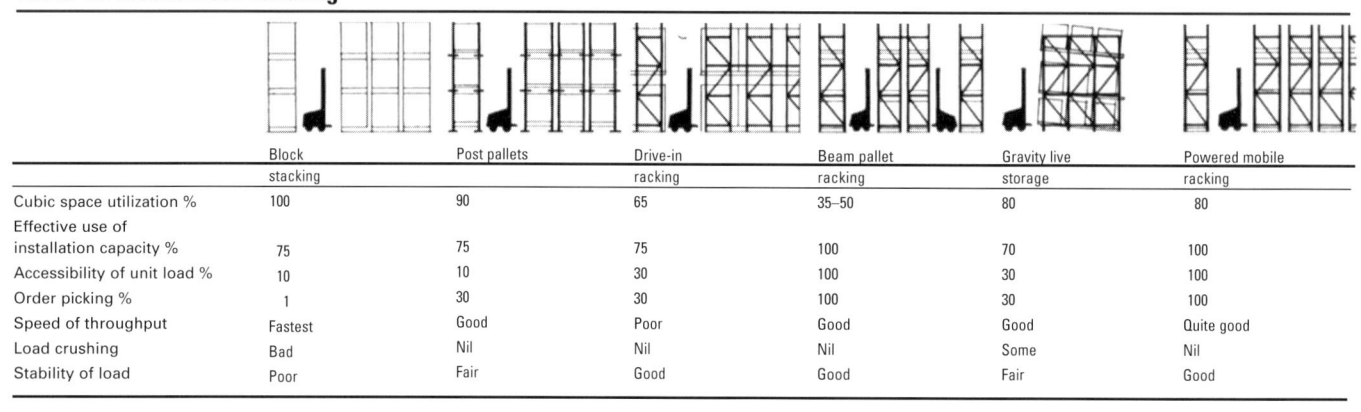

Table 4.6 Manual handling

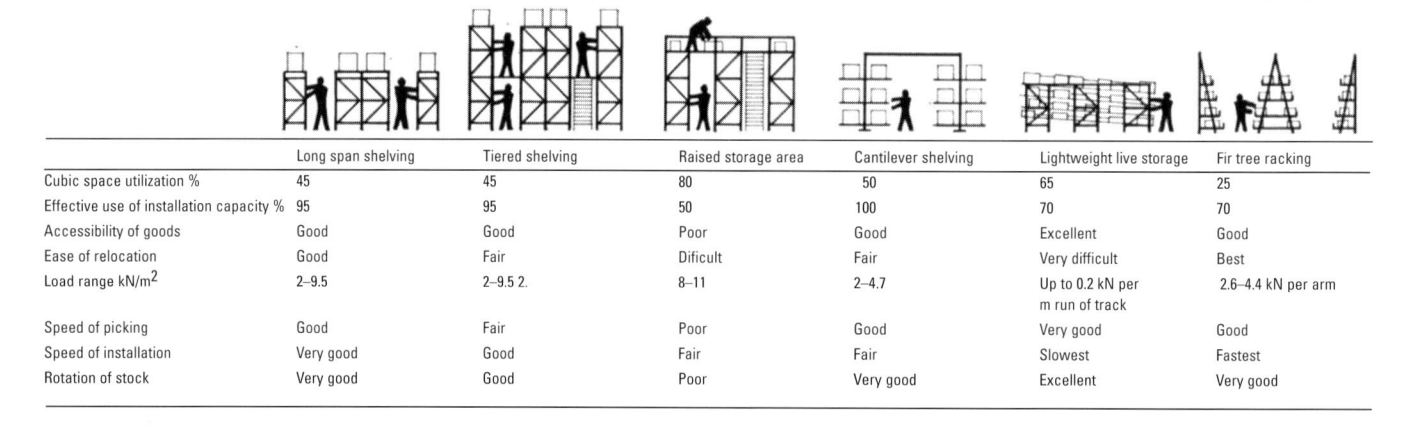

	Long span shelving	Tiered shelving	Raised storage area	Cantilever shelving	Lightweight live storage	Fir tree racking
Cubic space utilization %	45	45	80	50	65	25
Effective use of installation capacity %	95	95	50	100	70	70
Accessibility of goods	Good	Good	Poor	Good	Excellent	Good
Ease of relocation	Good	Fair	Dificult	Fair	Very difficult	Best
Load range kN/m^2	2–9.5	2–9.5 2.	8–11	2–4.7	Up to 0.2 kN per m run of track	2.6–4.4 kN per arm
Speed of picking	Good	Fair	Poor	Good	Very good	Good
Speed of installation	Very good	Good	Fair	Fair	Slowest	Fastest
Rotation of stock	Very good	Good	Poor	Very good	Excellent	Very good

2 Standard adjustable racking or shelving

Shelving

2.01 This is suitable for light and medium duty work. Mostly used as shelving, adjustable units can be assembled rapidly and adapted to change and expansion. Each shelf can be adjusted independently; used efficiently, this allows the storage space to be used to the full. Most adjustable shelving can be altered without tools. Many companies buy adjustable racking and never use this potential; the additional investment must be justified.

Slotted angle

2.02 This is popular in smaller installations and in factory stores. Built from rolled steel angle, with slots cut into it (Figure 4.88), any rack size or shape can be quickly bolted together. This Meccano-like system is very adaptable and inexpensive.

3 Pallet racking

Tubular racking

3.01 Early installations often employed tubing with 19 to 51 mm bores. These were adjustable along rack lengths but not for individual positions. The basic construction is much like scaffolding (Figure 4.89).

Boltless, adjustable pallet racking (APR)

3.02 The most widely used form of racking today (Figures 4.90 and 4.91). The choice of the racking is closely linked with the choice of pallet, or chance of pallet

Mechanized storage – racking

Figure 4.87 *Simple shelving.*

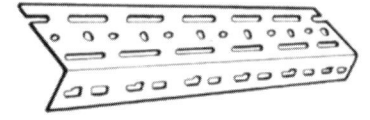

Figure 4.88 *Slotted angle.*

size being sent in by suppliers, as shown in Table 4.3. The size and weight of pallet or stillage determines whether double pallet spacing can be allowed. (See Information sheet, Mechanized storage 4.) In the UK the Storage Equipment Manufacturers Association (SEMA) provides useful guidelines for racking selection and planning installation.

Tolerances and clearances

3.03 Two-way entry pallets require 75 mm minimum overhang at the front and rear of the rack. Four-way entry pallets such as typical industrial 'pool' pallets require 50 mm minimum overhang; with non-reversible four-way

Figure 4.89 *Tubular racking.*

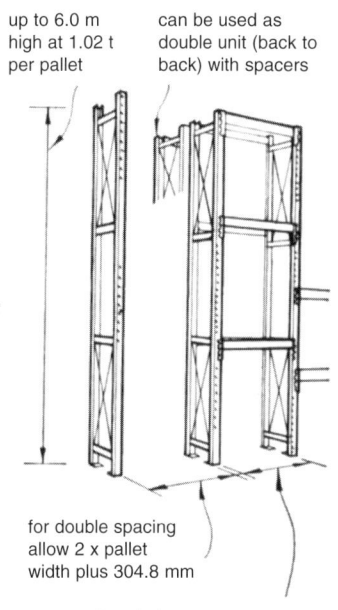

up to 6.0 m high at 1.02 t per pallet

can be used as double unit (back to back) with spacers

for double spacing allow 2 x pallet width plus 304.8 mm

pallet width plus 100-160 mm

Figure 4.90 *Adjustable pallet racking.*

pallets, the corner blocks must be positioned directly over the supporting beams, otherwise the pallets may be damaged. With this type, corner blocks are often too small to ensure safe pallet location. If post/skid pallets are used, the support legs should be directly over supporting beams. Cartons or skips should also overhang 75 mm front and rear.

3.04 The following clearances are required to permit easy location and retrieval of pallets (Figure 4.92):
1. Lateral spacing. Allow 75 mm between adjacent pallets and between outermost pallets and vertical members up to 6 m stacking height, and 100 mm for stacking to 12 m.
2. Vertical clearance. Allow a minimum of 75 mm measured from top of load to underside of support beam at next level up to 3 m stack height, thereafter 125 mm to 9 m and 150 mm to 12 m lift height. The increase in spacing is due to driver paralax and the flex/camber of the forklift mast.

3.05 When the full lift height of a forklift truck is to be used, ensure that the true required height of lift is calculated (Figure 4.93). The required height for the topmost row of pallets is from floor level to loaded pallet platform, when the pallet is raised sufficiently to permit easy withdrawal, accounting for the depth of pallet stringers and

Figure 4.91 *Adjustable pallet racking in use. Note clear labelling and protection bollards.*

127

Mechanized storage – racking

Figure 4.94 Anatomy of pallet racking.

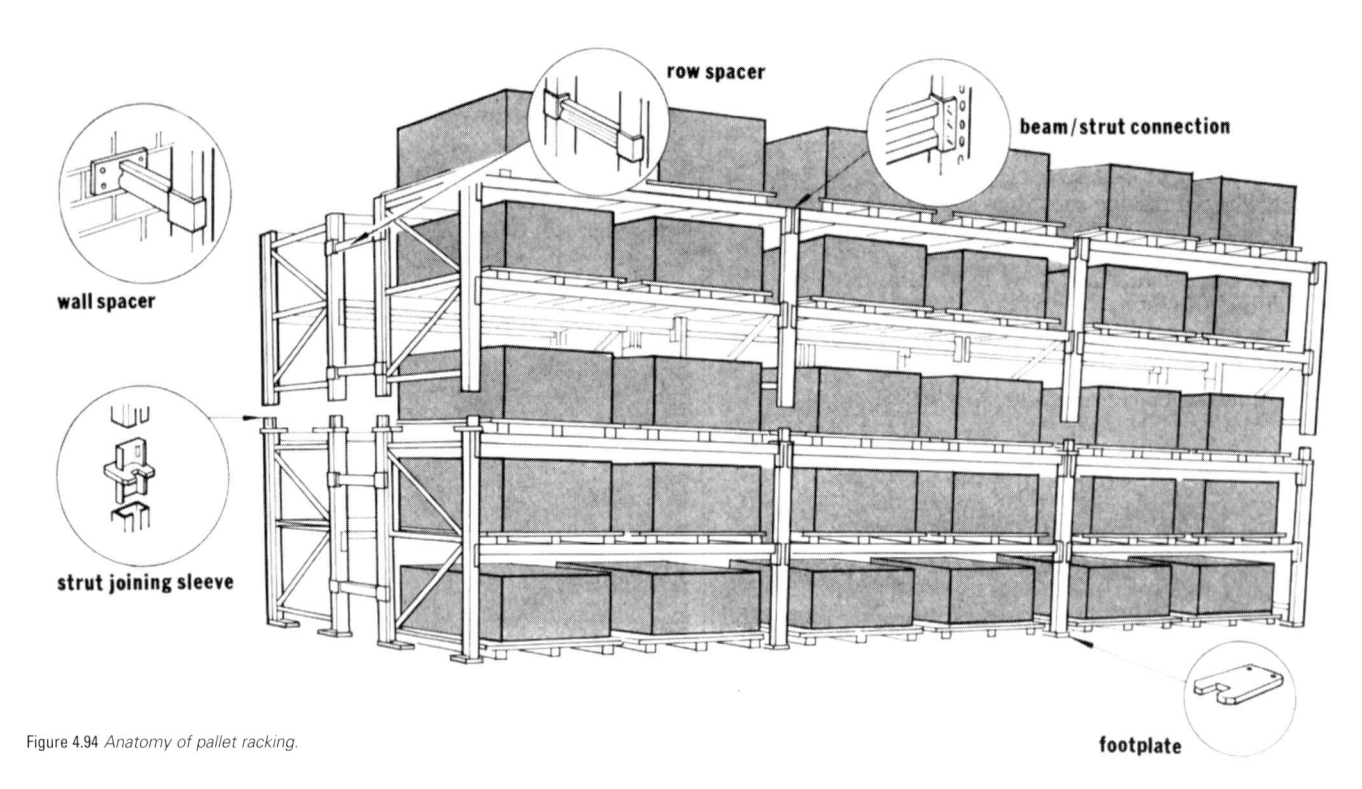

clearance. This may well be 150 to 180 mm above the level of the topmost beam. (See Information sheet, Mechanized storage 7, concerning free lift masts.)

3.06 Several racking manufacturers paint vertical and horizontal members in contrasting colours to help forklift drivers locate levels accurately; this should reduce racking damage. With high lift racking using turret trucks, guides are placed at the base to keep trucks in line.

3.07 Modern modular adaptable racking systems can be tailored precisely to the varying load conditions within a structure and are able to extend in the vertical and horizontal planes (Figure 4.94). Economically, modular racking is best, as the base unit takes the most weight; savings can be achieved by using different steel section for the frames to take the weight of various components. The frame looks the same throughout its height, but the steel is of different sections. One example, Boltless Systems frames, are self-stacking and can be joined in heights up to 18.23 m. Several strengths of frame are employed for each frame size, so that the structural level can be maintained to the corresponding load requirement, ensuring the right size of component for the job. Bearer beams are supplied in a range of lengths and capacities to suit the load. Typical fixing is a pair of connectors that lock positively into vertical members, with a lock to prevent accidental lifting out by forklift trucks (Figure 4.95a/b).

3.08 Pallet racking has become a standard product. Many similar systems provide a racking system that is easy to erect and adaptable (see Table 4.7). At present standard data is not produced by the racking manufacturers, so designers find it difficult to compare safety, strength and adaptability. The Storage and Equipment Manufacturers Association is the guardian of standards for these specifications.

3.09 The vertical spacing of the beams affects the loading capacity of the end-frames. The wider the spacing, the lower the frame-loading capacity. When calculating load potential, consider the distribution of the load over the whole racking structure. There should be a uniform load distribution throughout the rack. Always consult the racking manufacturers about working stresses (Figure 4.96).

3.10 The choice of method of clipping horizontal bearers to vertical frames is important. Accidental displacement by handling plant must be prevented while retaining adaptability. Various interlocks are offered by the racking manufacturers. There is controversy about whether frames should be bolted or welded. Manufacturers who still use bolted construction do so to simplify transport and make replacement easier. It is claimed that bolting is as safe as welding.

3.11 The important design parameters are the yield strength of the members and their ultimate tensile strength. Beam-loading figures incorporate a 2:1 safety factor, based on collapse or deflection, whichever is the greater. With hot-rolled steel frames, a safety factor of 1.65:1 is used. With cold-rolled frames, the safe load is calculated on 0.2 per cent of the proof stress. Some manufacturers quote a 3:1 ultimate safety factor; this does not hold to the point where the racks begin to deteriorate.

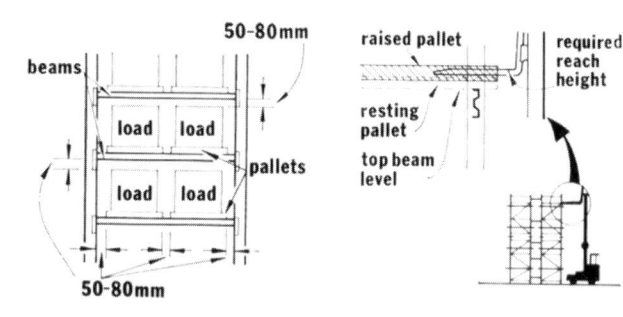

Figure 4.92 Pallet clearances.

Figure 4.93 Forklift position in top rack.

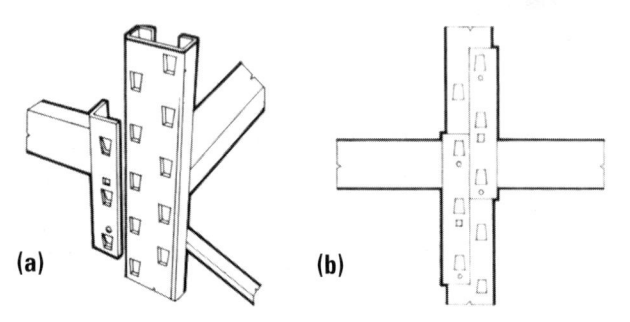

Figure 4.95 Locking clips.

Mechanized storage – racking

Table 4.7 Types of standard pallet racking

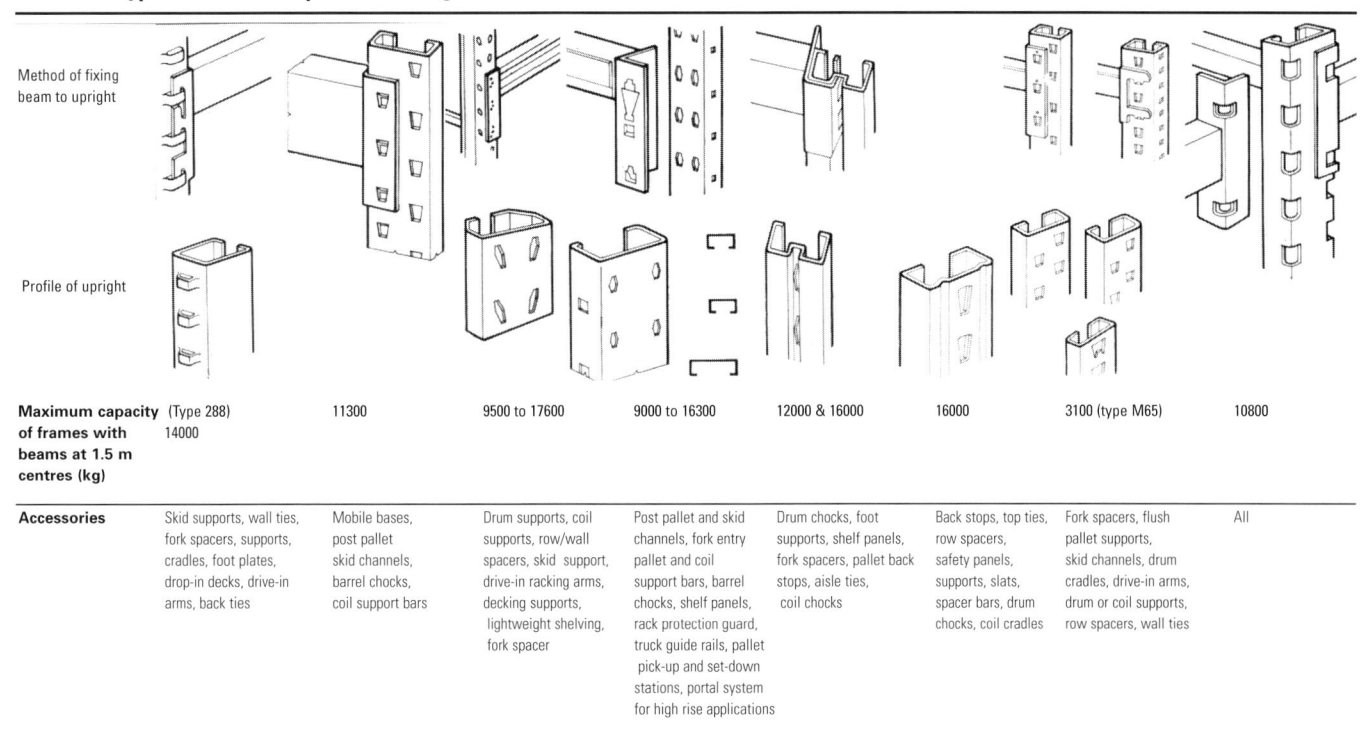

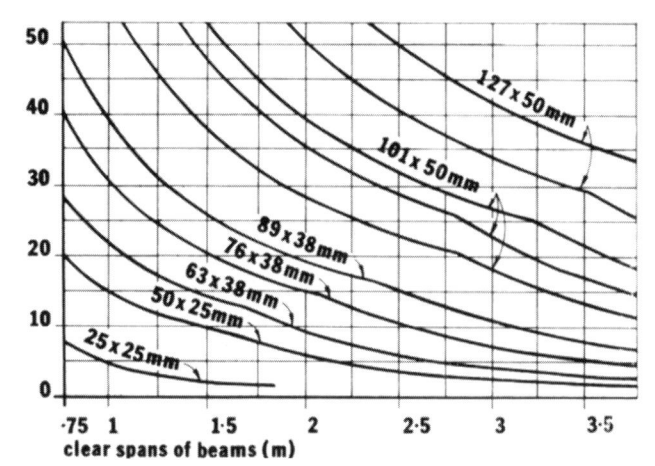

Method of fixing beam to upright								
Profile of upright								
Maximum capacity of frames with beams at 1.5 m centres (kg)	(Type 288) 14000	11300	9500 to 17600	9000 to 16300	12000 & 16000	16000	3100 (type M65)	10800
Accessories	Skid supports, wall ties, fork spacers, supports, cradles, foot plates, drop-in decks, drive-in arms, back ties	Mobile bases, post pallet skid channels, barrel chocks, coil support bars	Drum supports, coil supports, row/wall spacers, skid support, drive-in racking arms, decking supports, lightweight shelving, fork spacer	Post pallet and skid channels, fork entry pallet and coil support bars, barrel chocks, shelf panels, rack protection guard, truck guide rails, pallet pick-up and set-down stations, portal system for high rise applications	Drum chocks, foot supports, shelf panels, fork spacers, pallet back stops, aisle ties, coil chocks	Back stops, top ties, row spacers, safety panels, supports, slats, spacer bars, drum chocks, coil cradles	Fork spacers, flush pallet supports, skid channels, drum cradles, drive-in arms, drum or coil supports, row spacers, wall ties	All

Figure 4.96 *Shelf beam loading graph (per pair of beams).*

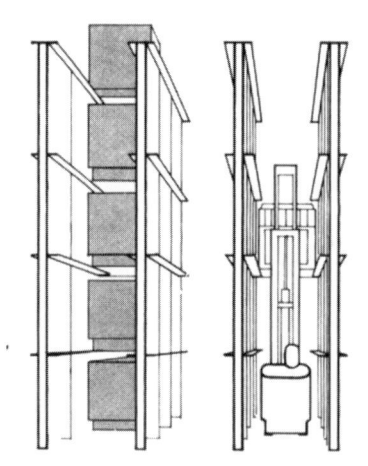

Figure 4.98 *Drive-in racking.*

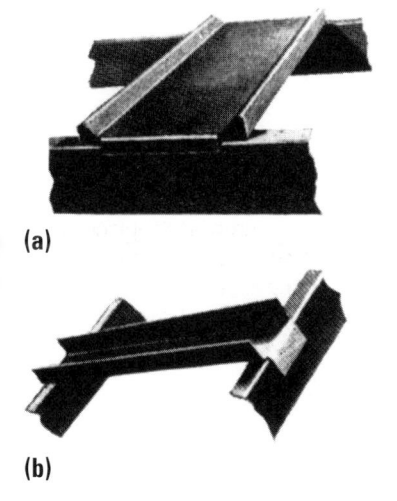

Figure 4.97 *Drum cradle (a) and skid support (b) are special bearer beams.*

Figure 4.99 *Special rack for glass.*

129

Mechanized storage – racking

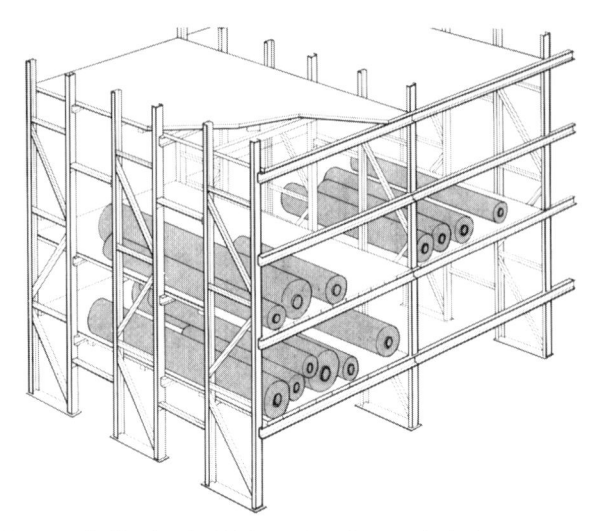

Figure 4.100 Racking for rolled fabrics made up from standard units.

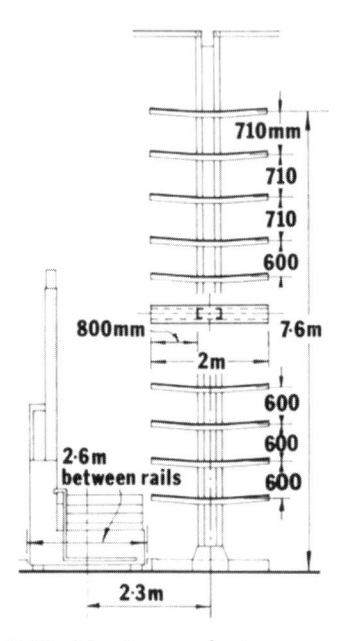

Figure 4.101 Typical fir tree racking for high lift narrow aisle sideloader.

Figure 4.102 Fir tree racking is suitable for long narrow objects.

3.12 Most manufacturers recommend a height/depth ratio of 6:1 for free-standing racking; over this height, racking should be bolted to the floor. If they are bolted, the floor finish need not be so precisely laid. Point loads from the vertical members must be within the limits of the floor.

3.13 Special purpose bearer beams for drums, coils or skid-mounted cartons can be supplied (Figure 4.97). Drive-in racking has double-sided cross frames, with stronger central bracing and skid plates welded or bolted to the frames instead of the conventional bearers (Figure 4.98). The pallet rests on its edge on the skid; this enables pallets to be stacked several deep. Pallet racks are available for two-deep pallet storage; the forklift is equipped with pantograph fork carriage. (See Information sheet, Mechanized storage 7.)

4 Special racking

4.01 This includes fir tree racks for steel coils, racks for plate glass (Figure 4.99), long racks for rolled fabrics and carpets (Figure 4.100), and drum racking or cantilever bearers for tubes or sheet materials. Special racking should be matched to the characteristics of the product to be stored (Figures 4.101 and 4.102). Most of these applications are one-off jobs, tailored to a particular product. Careful studies should be made of how the handling plant, also requiring special attachments, will interact with the racking. One installation handling steel coils employs a gantry slung stacker crane, incorporating 360° rotation for the coil bearer. At the tip of the crane's bearer is a closed-circuit television camera, so that the operator can position accurately and quickly. The racking here is interesting too, as to gain maximum use of volume the bearers for the coils are staggered. (See Chapter 7, Special storage, Steel stockholding.)

5 Live racking

5.01 See also Information Sheet, Mechanized storage 2, storage 1, paras 8.01, 8.02.

Gravity live racking

5.02 The lateral and vertical tolerances apply as in adjustable pallet racking. Wheels are used for light loads, and rollers for the heavier units (Figures 4.103 and 4.104). A fall of 1 in 75 has been found to operate effectively for gravity storage but trial and error is often the best way to achieve the correct gradient. Drums simply roll down guides. The high capital and maintenance costs can be justified with high stock throughput and first-in, first-out applications. For pallet loads, braking should be specified; the shock of each pallet moving down the tracks may cause instability and a fouled pallet load is difficult and time-consuming to extricate. Braking should be specified for weights above 50 kg; lightweight centrifugal brakes are available (Figure 4.105). For full pallet loads, use powered live storage, so that heavy loads can be completely controlled. Greater speeds of throughput are possible if the load is completely stable.

5.03 Powered live racking uses roller chains, with location dogs, widely spaced slats to coincide with pallet dimensions, and powered rollers to carry goods. Transporter systems (moles) can also be used in this way. (See Technical study, Automated storage 2, para. 31 and Information sheet, Automated storage 2.)

Mechanized storage – racking

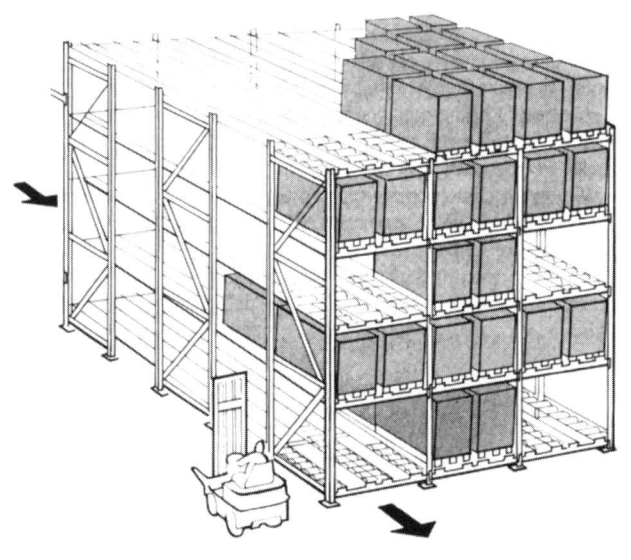

Figure 4.103 *Gravity live racking for full pallets.*

Figure 4.104 *Manual picking from live racking.*

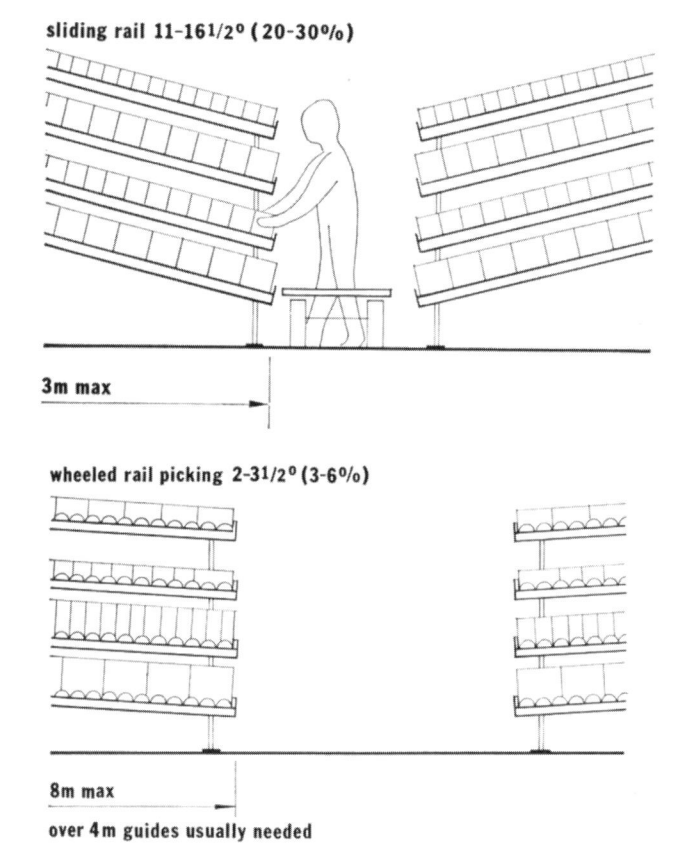

Figure 4.105 *Foot-operated brake release on manual carton dispenser.*

Figure 4.106 *Standard tracks for live racking.*

Figure 4.107 *Manual mobile shelving.*

Figure 4.108 *In many cases, nearly as much space can be gained by using narrow aisles and high lift machines as by more expensive mobile racking and general purpose reach trucks. Compare with Figure 4.110.*

6 Mobile racking

Manual mobile racking

6.01 Manually operated mobile shelving and racking has long been popular in spares stores, libraries, and stores for a wide range of cartoned stock requiring 100 per cent selectivity (Figures 4.106 and 4.107).

6.02 Two systems are available; the most popular moves face-to-face and parallel (Figure 4.107a/b); the other slides laterally, offering more picking faces simultaneously. A person can push four units loaded with 900kg without difficulty. Some manufacturers offer adjustable shelving in steel or timber, mounted on a mobile carriage; others

131

Mechanized storage – racking

Table 4.8 Comparison of powered mobile racking with other systems

	Block stacking	Post pallets	Drive-in racking	Beam pallet racking	Gravity live storage	Mobile racking
Cubic space utilization*	100%	90%	65%	35-50%	80%	80%
Effective use of installation	75%	75%	75%	00%	70%	100%
Accessibility of load	10%	10%	30%	100%	30%	100%
Order picking	1%	30%	300	100%	30%	100%
Load crushing	Bad	Nil	Nil	Nil	Some	Nil
Stability of load	Poor	Fair	Good	Good	Fair	Good
Ease of store relocation	n/a	n/a	Fair	Good	Difficult	Difficult
Speed of installation	n/a	n/a	Good	Fastest	Fair	Slowest

*Access gangway area is not included, but working gangways are.

manufacture integrally based shelving, specially designed for mobile use.

6.03 There is some controversy about the fire risk of mobile shelving. One manufacturer considers that there is less fire risk with timber construction, as fire would be localized; steel shelving would transmit heat, causing spontaneous combustion, and could buckle, stopping rack movement and so preventing fire officers reaching the seat of the fire in time to gain control. Intermediate-level sprinkling is possible in mobile shelving and racks, using a jointed supply main.

Power-operated racking

6.04 Manual racking is limited by a maximum 6–8 tonne loading. Power-operated racking overcomes this and ensures that the racks move together. Lighter manually operated racking caused operators to become impatient, and to push eccentrically, moving the racks off their tracks and jamming them. Mobile racking is basically adjustable pallet racking on a powered base (see Table 4.8), and the same tolerances and pallet clearances apply (see paras 3.03 to 3.05). These racks allow compact storage and 100 per cent selectivity, once the aisle is opened (Figure 4.108). The controls can be place at a height for operation by forklift drivers (approximately 1.6 m). Racks are moved by motor over chain or direct drive; when a lever is pressed, the rack on which it is mounted and all those behind it moves, opening a space for the forklift to enter (Figure 4.109). Typical horsepower requirements to

Figure 4.109 *Note density of storage with mobile racking: here 1600 m² handles 10,000 products.*

Figure 4.110 *Manually-operated rack opening mechanism.*

Figure 4.111 *Rack opening mechanism has been operated, causing racks to open.*

overcome initial inertia are 1/8 hp for 8 to 10 tonne loads and 10 hp for 1000 tonne loads.

6.05 Safety devices are usually in the form of kick bars, at floor or breast height, that immediately cut all power when depressed. Photoelectric sensors and interlocks are used for heavier installations. In case of power cuts, even heavy racks can be manually handled without much effort.

6.06 Check that foundation and floor finish are suitable for mobile racking. The stresses are different, as some racks are loaded more heavily than others. Floor dusting has occurred adjacent to rails and channels. The surface finish should accept vibration. Epoxy finishes are sufficiently flexible for this.

Mechanized storage – racking

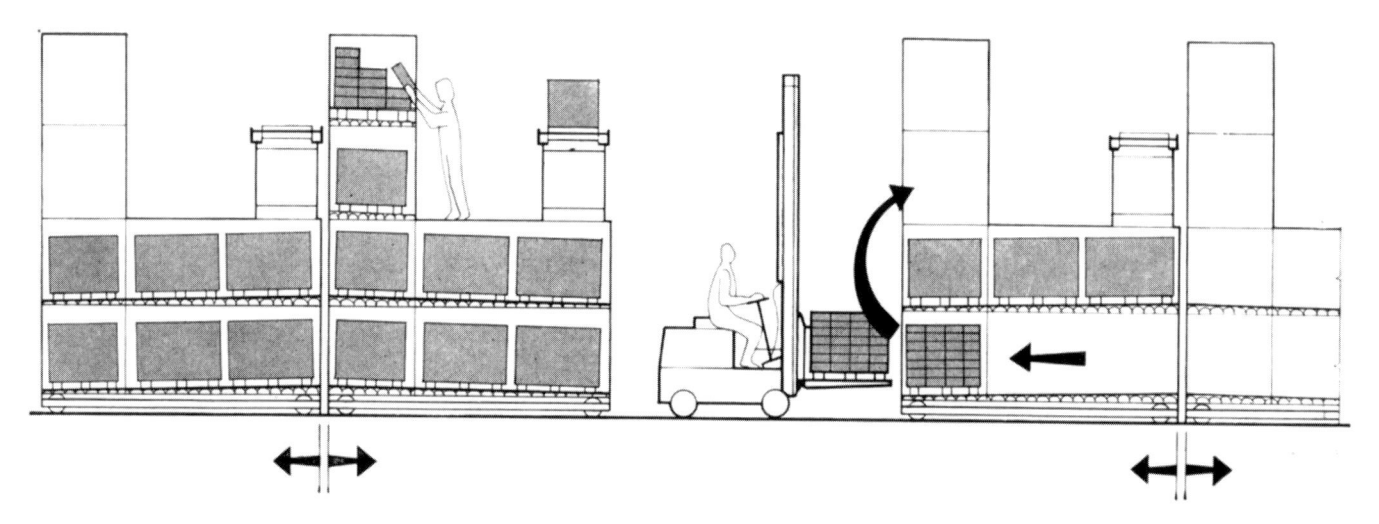

Figure 4.112 *Back-up stock is placed below, and order picking above on mezzanine. Forklifts either transfer loads between levels, or replenish loads in adjacent racks.*

6.07 A typical operating time cycle is a rack-opening speed of 76.2 mm/sec with stacking aisle width of 2.743 m to accept a 1800 kg capacity forklift truck, plus load; it would therefore take 36 seconds to open the aisle fully, although the machine could start to move before (Figures 4.110 and 4.111). Radio control can decrease this time lag; a central controller opens the appropriate aisle and directs the forklift driver to the rack bay, so aisles are always open by the time the forklift arrives. A possible future development, providing high-volume utility and automated storage, would be the use of a wire-guided free-path stacker working in 12 m-high mobile racking. This could also operate with a gantry-slung stacker crane.

6.08 Combined storage and order picking on an upper level of mobile racking has been operated successfully in a warehouse handling light fittings (Figure 4.112). Order picking from free-path, elevating cab machines is also possible with mobile racking; one installation uses custom-built machines with elevating cabs, and rotating masts to pick from either side. This last feature reduces rack movement and could be calculated for maximum picker efficiency by the stock control computer.

INFORMATION SHEET

Mechanized storage 4
Pallets

1 **Pallet types**

2 **Size standards**

3 **Materials**

The pallet is universally recognized as the basis for unit loads. This sheet gives dimensions, types, materials of pallets, and pallet converters, post and roll pallets.

1 Pallet types

1.01 A pallet is a portable platform, with or without superstructure, for assembling a quantity of goods to form a unit load for handling and storage by mechanical appliances (Figure 4.113). It consists of a deck on bearers constructed for transport and stacking and with the overall height reduced to a minimum, which can be handled by forklift and pallet trucks. It was thought that unit loads would dispense with pallets, especially with shrink-wrap and banding techniques, but this has not happened, as the pallet gives stability, and is quicker to handle than 'squashy' cardboard wraps; indeed, the number of pallets is constantly rising.

1.02 The two basic types of pallet are the two-way entry and four-way entry timber pallets (Figure 4.114a/b). In both, decks can be single or double sided, i.e. reversible. Low-profile versions popular in the USA are available in both, with heights of $2\frac{5}{8}$ in (66.7 mm) or 3 in (76.2 mm) depending on whether single or double ply top boards are used (Figure 4.115a). With six-high stacking 1 ft^3 (0.03 m^3) is claimed to be saved for every ft^2 (0.09 m^2) of floor area.

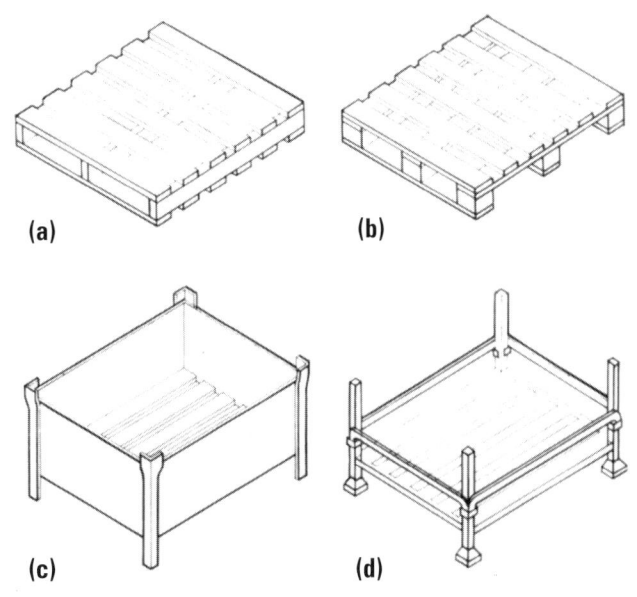

Figure 4.114 *(a) Two way entry pallet. (b) Four-way entry pallet. (c) Steel box pallet. (d) Steel post pallet.*

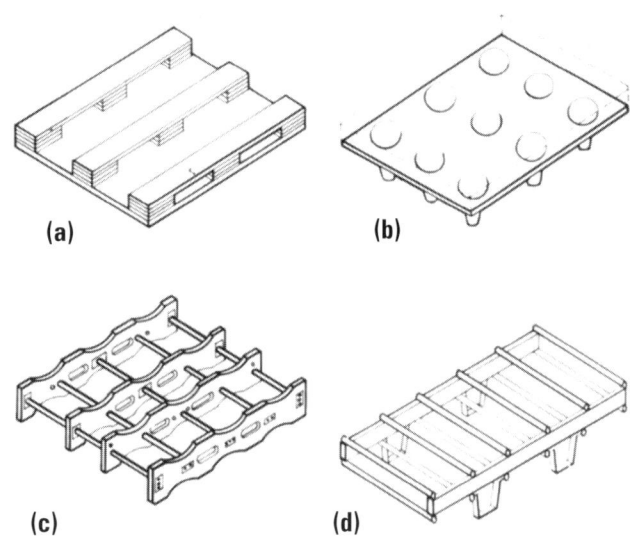

Figure 4.115 *(a) Low profile pallet. (b) Disposable corrugated board pallet with cone legs. (c) Key spacer pallet. (d) Special drum pallet (see Figure 4.120).*

Figure 4.113 *Bins to modular pallet dimensions loaded into container by forklift.*

Mechanized storage – pallets

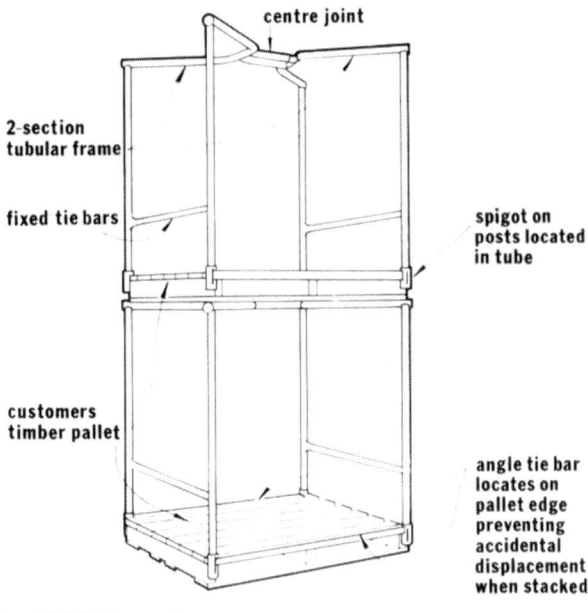

Figure 4.116 *Pallet converter.*

But handling low-profile pallets calls for greater driver accuracy, and can lead to slower work cycles. These pallets are more expensive than the standard types, but would be cheaper if there was a greater demand.

Pallet converters

1.03 A pallet converter (Figure 4.116) is a device attached to a timber pallet to secure the load and to provide a method of stacking unit loads without conventional racking. Recently pallet converters have begun to be increasingly used, especially in the retail trade. Previously, they had been used principally in cold stores for hanging meat, and as a stacking method. However, pallet converters can greatly increase the utility of a pallet in block stacking; a converter overcomes the problem of loads that are too weak to be block stacked normally unless equipped with post pallets or drive-in racking. This is particularly attractive to the small operator, and where a temporary stack is required without recourse to racking, but the load is not suitable for stacking. As a racking system, converters are not economic, as they are more expensive per position than racking, but they can be used as such in certain situations up to six pallets high, with loads limited normally to 1 tonne per pallet, although one manufacturer offers stacking six-high with 2 tonne loads.

1.04 There are two types of converter: one uses the structure of the converter to withstand the weight of the pallets above, and the other ultimately lets the bottom pallet take all the weight (not a disadvantage as the load is transmitted through the strongest part of the pallet, the corners). Pallet converter structure is normally tubular steel or angle. Some converters are simply four corner posts and a bridging structure across the top. More sophisticated units can be equipped with side panels, turning a timber pallet into a box pallet. Some converters can be totally dismantled, so that when not in use they have a dissembled stacking ratio of 10:1.

Pallet collars

1.05 These work on the principle of converters, in that they adapt a normal pallet to an instant bin (Figure 4.117d). They can be in timber or steel mesh, and are largely self-locating. They can be block stacked. Pallet collars are useful for small part order picking, as they can be removed layer by layer for convenience as the load is picked.

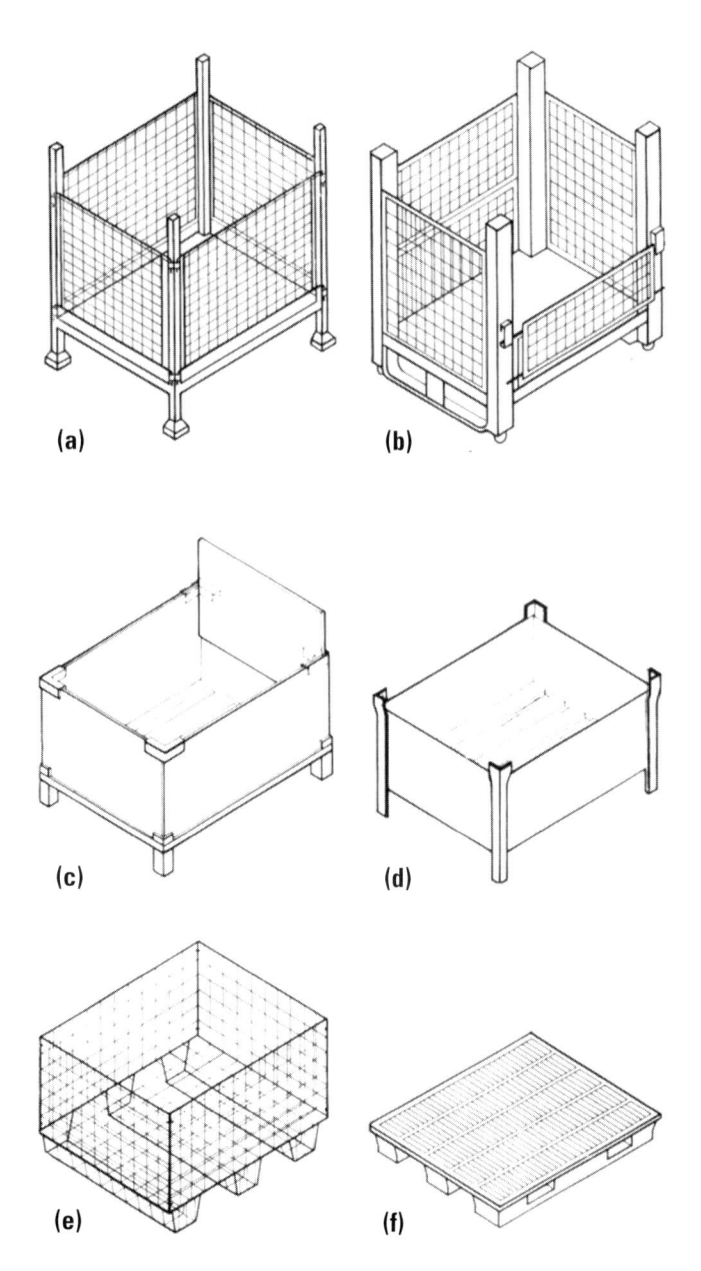

Figure 4.117 *(a) Standard post pallet with feet (waste volume) (used in Figure 4.118). (b) Post pallet with canes (greater capacity possible than a); (c) Pallet with detachable side. (d) Collapsible timber pallet with collar converters. (e) Collapsible wire mesh box. Direct order picking to retail distributors. (f) High-quality plastic pallet.*

Post pallets

1.06 Post pallets are used for components, spare parts and materials more suitable for bins. Most post pallets, cage pallets, box pallets and demountable side pallets are made from steel. These can be block stacked 10 m high; UK post pallets tend to use a shoe-type leg (Figures 4.117a and 4.118), but they tend to waste volume. Increasingly a rail and conical peg stacking system is used, saving a considerable amount of space (possibly 13 per cent volume saving (Figure 4.117b). Most post pallets are 40 x 48 in (1016 x 1219 mm), but some use metric sizes for containers. 1016 x 2200 mm units have been used for body panels in a vehicle factory and component store. Some post and cage pallets can be folded, so that up to seven can be returned empty in one pallet. Post pallets with hinged fronts are useful for order picking, as goods can be seen (Figure 4.117c).

Mechanized storage – pallets

Figure 4.118 *Contrast between palletized and non-palletized goods.*

Figure 4.119 *Roll pallet or roll cage: the workhorse of the distribution industry.*

Figure 4.120 *Special pallet for radioactive material.*

Roll pallets

1.07 A roll pallet is a castered container, used as a link between a warehouse and a distributor (Figure 4.119); loading and turnround times are claimed to be cut by up to 80 per cent. Many sizes and types are available; most can be dismantled and nest for storage (e.g. two roll pallets can hold ten dismantled units, one all the bases, the other the sides). A typical size popular in the UK is 800 x 700 x 1500 mm, with a working load of 508 kg. In Germany, two sizes are used, 720 x 800 x 1500 mm and 640 x 800 x 1500 mm. Many types of sides are available for various products, e.g. packaged foods, textiles, sides of bacon. Casters are usually 102 mm, in nylon or other plastics, and usually only two wheels steer, for towing ability in warehouses and stability in vans. Special versions can be specified for chilled use or high security.

Stillage

1.08 A stillage is a load board which may be very similar to some forms of pallet, but stillages are not normally intended for stacking.

Platten

1.09 A platten is a special pallet for 'captive' use, i.e. in-store only. They are often specifically designed to work with an automated stacker crane system, where tolerances are critical and differences in pallet size or shape could be disastrous (Figure 4.120).

2 Size standards

2.01 Although the advantages of palletization are very clear (Figure 4.118), as yet it has been impossible to achieve a final set of dimensional standards. There are three basic groups.

ISO container module

2.02 The first group, sea-based operators, argue that the 8 ft (2.4 m) ISO container is here to stay, and that investment in equipment is so great that it would be unrealistic to change. 1100 mm width pallets with lengths of 800 mm, 900 mm, 1100 mm and 1400 mm can be used in ISO containers; 1100 mm x 1100 mm pallets are the most economic for maximum volume utilization (so important for 'deep-sea' containers), allow more variety of carton dimensions than any other pallet, are ideal for carrying drums on road vehicles and offer greatest flexibility between transport modes. These pallets tend to be restricted to 'deep-sea' operations and are often sacrificial.

Packaging module

2.03 The second group base the pallet dimension on the packages to be stacked on them. It has been suggested that an international packaging module should be based on 400 mm x 600 mm (recognized as the standard ISO TC 122). This is compatible both with the 800 mm x 1200 mm European standard pool pallet, sized for railway interchangeability, and with the 1200 mm x 1000mm 'industrial' pallet. There are between 60 and 70 million European pool pallets in use and 30 million 1000 mm x 1200 mm pallets. This group argues that these sizes are already standard in many countries, and that equally high investment has been made in automated warehouses and other storage areas based on this size as on ISO container areas. To base a standard on a module of a container size ignores the vast number of products that never travel in containers and need the best pallet size for general use. Also, although 2 x 1100 mm pallets will fit across a standard ISO container, there may not be sufficient clearance in an insulated unit. 800 mm x 1200 mm is uneconomic for container use, but the 400 mm x 600 mm package size would suit both European pallets; it has been suggested that the 1100 x 1200 mm pallet would be the most economic for all methods of transport. The largest pallet pool offers both sizes, and will return interchange types within the price of the operation.

Mechanized storage – pallets

Table 4.9 Pallet sizes

Imperial (inches)	Metric (exact values (mm))	Metric (ISO/BSI rounded up* (mm))
Pallets for materials handling*		
32 x 48	812.8 x 1219.2	800 x 1200
40 x 48	1016 x 1219.2	1000 x 1200
48 x 48	1219.2 x 1219.2	1200 x 1200
48 x 72	1219.2 x 1828.8	1200 x 1800
Pallets suitable for ISO containers[†]		
		1100 x 800
		1100 x 900
		1100 x 1100
		1100 x 1400
40 x 48	1016 x 1219.2	1000 x 1200
ISO Types R198 and R329		
32 x 48	812.8 x 1219.2	800 x 1200
32 x 40	812.8 x 1016	800 x 1000
40 x 48	1016 x 1219.2	1000 x 1200
48 x 64	1219.2 x 1625.6	1200 x 1600
48 x 72	1219.2 x 1828.8	1200 x 1800
		1100 x 800
Insulated ISO container internal sizes		
	2235 (ACT Line)	
	2235 (OCL Line)	
	2254 (BEN Line: refrigerated)	
	2178 (Insulated)	
Pallet heights (ground to underside of deck)		
5	127 (max)	
5½ (USA[‡])	140 (1200 x 1600, 1200 x 1800 pallets and International average)	
2⅝ (USA[‡])	(66.7)	
3 (USA[‡])	(76.2)	

*BS 2629: 1960 Part I, Pallets for materials handling
[†]BS 2629: Part II: 1960.
[‡]New type of low profile pallet developed in the USA; there are 2⅝ in high for single deck, and 3 in for a multiple deck. These offer considerable volume savings with high racks, e.g. a saving of 362 mm in a typical six-high block stack 0.45 m³ approx.

2.04 A third group states that any standard is unrealistic, with such a wide variety of goods. Pallets should always be chosen for the greatest economy, for the particular transport and storage mode, and product characteristics. So much investment has been tied up on both sides that it is unrealistic to standardize on one particular size, or base a pallet size on a package dimension, which is sized for display and ease of distribution, i.e. one product with several different sized packs. The standards should be a minimum number of sizes, but flexible and not a rigid single one.

2.05 The basic differences are between nations with land-based and maritime economies, between road and rail traffic and the 'deep-sea' container trade. Now there is no agreement between nations, and little within countries. Standards committees have tried to fix a majority view, but large multinational companies are unlikely to accept standards that conflict with their economic interests. So warehouse and distribution system designers are left with metric and imperial pallet types, which look similar in operation, until, for example, it is found that sufficient tolerance has not been left in the racking for the larger unit. For this reason, it is inevitable that some waste of storage volume will occur, as installations are planned to accept the larger sizes of pallets used by a particular industry, unless substantial re-packing is accepted.

Actual sizes

2.06 The pallet size for which the storage is being designed must be fixed at the initial sketch design stage; this is vital to racking and handling plant alike. Table 4.9 gives the range of actual sizes.

3 Materials

3.01 Pallets are traditionally made of timber or steel, but recently of plastic, and expendable paper plastics have been developed (see Figures 4.114, 4.115 and 4.117). Timber pallets are still virtually the cheapest and strongest type available (see Figure 4.114a/b). Plastics as yet share only a very small sector of the total market (see Figure 4.117f). But timber pallet prices are likely to increase by between 10 and 15 per cent, while plastic pallet prices will probably stay static. Tests have shown that a life of six to eight years can be expected with plastic, but operators are waiting for a guarantee of this before making large-scale changes.

Plastics compared to timber

3.02 The advantages of plastic over timber are:
- weight: plastic is only half the weight of timber
- cleanliness: they are being adopted by the food industries. The more complex plastic pallets need mechanical cleaning, as they have dust-catching crevices
- colour coding: operator's name can be moulded in for return
- durability: plastic withstands impact damage better.

3.03 Disadvantages of plastic pallets are: they are more costly; they can deform under load, making fork entry difficult and, when wet, can slide off forks. At present plastics pallets' applications tend to be specialized, and timber is likely to continue to be popular for some time.

Disposable pallets

3.04 These create a rubbish problem, and like 'prefabs' are used long after they should have been replaced, often resulting in the need for repackaging before entering the storage system. Because of expendability, prices need to be very low; for this reason one-piece mouldings from plastic, foams and vacuum-moulded polyethylene, have been produced, as well as cardboard and plastic composites. These pallets tend to suffer from lack of strength and resilience in use. Cardboard sheet pallets supported on nine plastic 'cups' have been used effectively and are

Figure 4.121 A special trolley for conveying stacked cages so that they can be transported as a roll pallet. Injection moulded plastic dolly for transporting stacks of crates for direct merchandising, replacing the roll pallet in some sectors.

cheap, but stacking is a problem, as the cup legs are not strong enough for block stacking (see Figure 4.115b).

3.05 Cellular material pallets. These are made from cardboard sheets filled with a cardboard honeycomb. These are very rigid and strong for their light weight; the cardboard call be impregnated with a flame-retardant compound. This pallet type is mostly seen as the base to a fall cube pack, as for a computer component.

Cages

3.06 Developments in supply chain logistics coupled with the growth of hypermarkets and superstores has introduced the cage pallet and the plastic crate into distribution. This combines order picking, transport and retail display into one unit, eliminating a complete handling stage. Cages have four feet of open wire construction: although some fold flat when empty, cages are bulky to store, and produce poor volume utilization, especially in transport (Figure 4.121). Having been developed in France, there are still no firm dimensional standards, although two sizes are most likely:

Length	Width	Height
1150 mm	850 mm	1000 mm
600 mm	850 mm	670 mm

Crates will still stack, even when they are of different sizes, i.e. 600 x 800, 600 x 400, 400 x 300 (Figure 4.122).

Reference

BS 2629:1960, Pallets for materials handling. HMSO (Aa8).

Figure 4.122 *Crate dollies (600 mm x 800 mm) for stacking Eurocrates.*

INFORMATION SHEET

Mechanized storage 5

General purpose handling aids

1 Hoists and lifting devices

2 Pedestrian trucks and trolleys

This sheet describes low technology, i.e. non-specialized equipment, which can handle all types of goods.

1 Hoists and lifting devices

Uses
1.01 In manually operated stores, loading bays, repair workshops. Can easily be carried about on vehicles.

Capacity
1.02 Up to 500 kg.

Space requirements
1.03 Will turn in their own length. Space depends on whether used as stacker or hoist.

Equipment design
1.04 Can be converted to stacker or hoist. Very simple strong components. Some fold flat for storage in small space (Figures 4.123, 4.124 and 4.125).

Building needs
1.05 Flat or smooth floors. Stowage space.

Figure 4.123 *Small hoist, which can be converted to a hand stacker. Size 740 x 840 mm x 2.3 m max height.*

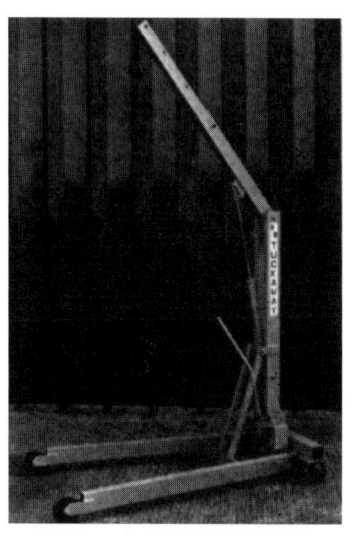

Figure 4.124 *Floor crane; can be folded and stored flat.*

2 Pedestrian trucks and trolleys

Uses
2.01 Order build-up. Transfer within manually operated warehouse.

Sizes and shape
2.02 No standard size and shape, and can be made specially to order. 460 mm is minimum width for picking in narrow aisles. If used as dispatch cages, size should be commensurate with internal body dimensions of carriers' vehicles; this also applies to tail-lift sizes. One man can move 2.02 tonnes on steel wheels and 0.76 tonnes on soft rubber tyres.

Space requirements
2.03 Should be capable of turning in their own length, allow space for empty trolleys and damaged units.

Equipment design
2.04 A very wide variety of designs, within an equally wide range of weights. Choice depends on particular application. Most types of hand truck are available off the peg.

Building needs
2.05 Level floors.
2.06 Typical pedestrian trucks and trolleys are shown in Figures 4.126 and 4.127. (See also Information sheet, Mechanized storage 6.)

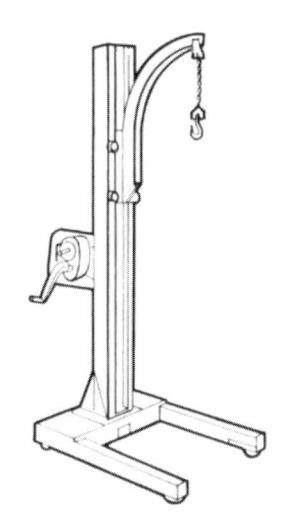

Figure 4.125 *Combined trolley and lift.*

Mechanized storage – general purpose handling aids

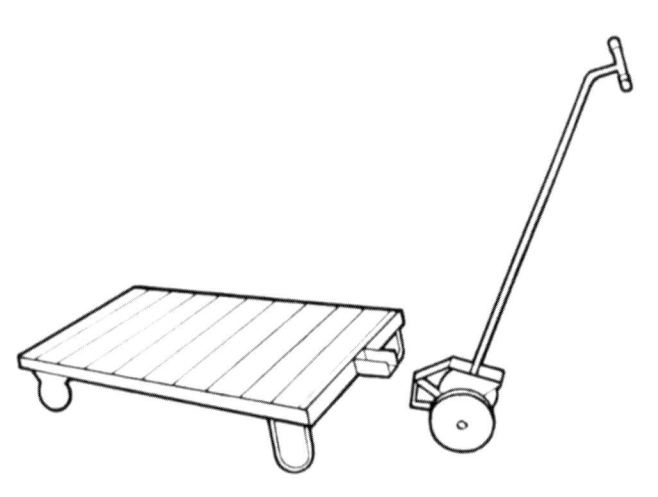

Figure 4.126 *All-purpose tug/lift unit comprising platform and handle. Length 1.15 m x 760 mm wide.*

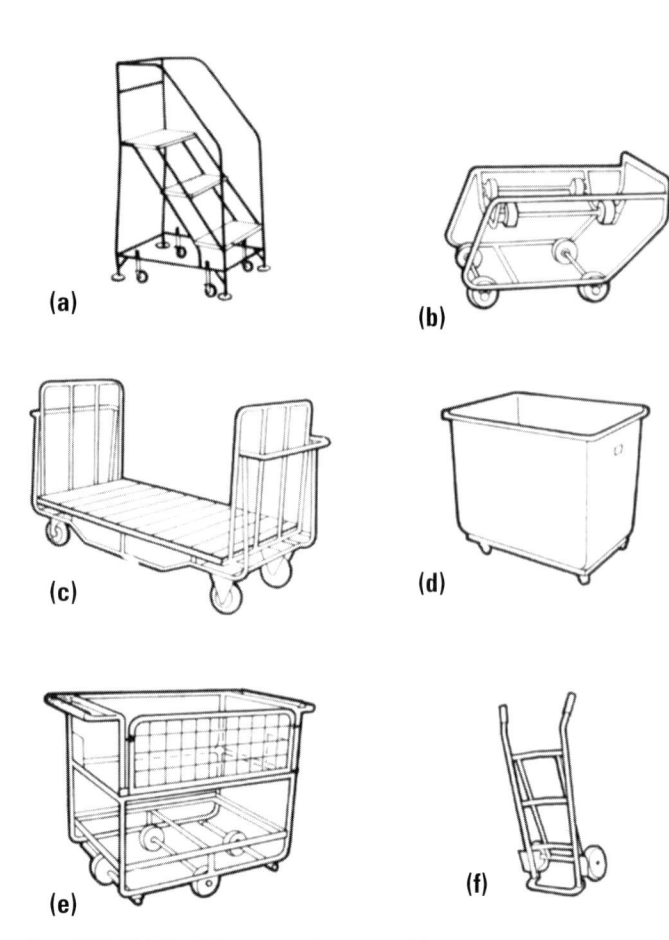

Figure **4.127**(a) *Mobile picking steps; when mounted the sprung castors retract, leaving a firm base. (b) General-purpose warehouse truck, 1.5 m long x 840 mm wide. (c) Parcels trolley, 1.2 m long x 700 mm x 940 mm high. (d) Drum Trolley. Upper wheels allow drum to roll for discharge, 900 mm x 500 mm x 380 mm high. (e) Mobile polythene bin, 940 mm x 630 mm x 1.2 m high. (f) Sack truck, 400 mm x 150 mm x 1.2 m high.*

INFORMATION SHEET

Mechanized storage 6

Pedestrian controlled handling plant

This sheet gives information on types of pedestrian controlled plant used in storage buildings (Table 4.10).

Table 4.10 Typical pedestrian controlled handling plant

Powered pallet truck

Uses and limitations
Internal transfer, loading vehicles on docks, order build-up, transporting roll pallets to load assembly position. For use with all types of pallet and cages. Some with long forks carry three roll pallets at once.

Sizes and capacity
1800 to 3000 kg capacity. Fork lengths 750 mm to 1.8 m. Speeds up to 3.6 km/h running light. Widths up to 850 mm, usually 760 mm.

Space requirements
Turns in its own length, but needs additional clearance for overhangs. Some have 200 degree turn on the single power steering wheel. Aisle width depends on fork length. **a** (90 stacking aisle) 1840 mm (truck + 1000 mm pallet) **b** (intersecting aisle) = 1570 mm Turning circle 1.78 m radius with 960 mm long forks.

Equipment design
Can be fitted with special forks. Some of the large capacity units can also be ridden on, and can tow other non-powered pallet trucks behind if long distances are involved.

Building needs
Level floors. Single- or three-phase charging point. Can handle ramps to 1 in 10.

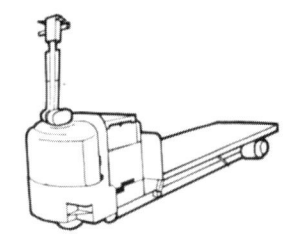

Platform truck

Sizes and capacity
Similar in design and capacity to powered pallet trucks. 1500–3000 kg. Overall length 1.7 m with 914 mm platform; 2.7 m with 1.829 m platform. Longer platform lengths are available to special order, with 787 mm width. Travel speed 4.8 km/h unladen 3.2 km/h laden.

Space requirements
Turning radius, machine only, 1.37 m; with platform 914 mm; with 1.8 m platform 2.4 m.

Equipment design
Similar to a powered pallet truck, this raises load platform about 100 mm for travel. Some pedestrian platform trucks have a small folding platform at the rear with a short arm so that the machine can be ridden.

Building needs
Level floors. Single or three-phase recharging supply. Typical wheel loading (unladen) 726 kg on drive wheels, 199 kg on trailing wheels.

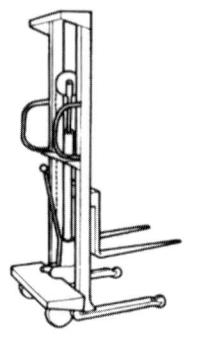

Mechanized storage – pedestrian controlled handling equipment

Manual stacker truck

Uses and limitations
Internal lifting. Best used as secondary lifting device in loading area. Ideal as portable unit travelling on delivery vehicle. Pallet and stillage handling. Lift is restricted and slow. Heavy loads can tire operator. Can be fitted with numerous small attachments for lifting drums, rolls, sacks, etc.

Size and capacity
Very varied with loads from 0.2 to 0.76 tonnes lifting up to 1.8 m. Width 763 mm on standard straddle. Check that lifting centres are suitable for pallet handling.

Space requirements
Will turn in its own length and with 914 mm x 762 mm pallet could be operated in 1.5 m aisle.

Building needs
Level floors.

Usually manually powered for travel and lift using hydraulic hand-pump for lift, so is restricted in lifting ability in height and weight. Power and manual control.

Pedestrian-controlled forklift truck

Uses and limitations
Internal lifting under localized conditions with relatively light loads up to 3.6 m. Pallet handling. Can be fitted with most attachments.

Sizes and capacity
Lift height up to 3.6 m. Load up to 0.9 tonne. Straddle width from 889 mm to 1.3 m. (Not less than 1.2 m for maximum lift.)

Space requirements
Will turn in its own length and with 914 mm x 762 mm pallet would work in 1.8 m to 1.9 m aisle. (Needs more space for manoeuvring than manual lift truck with power lift.) Capacity – 0.56 tonne load at 457 mm centres to 3.6 m in 1.8 aisle.

Building needs
Level floors. Charging point either single or three phase.

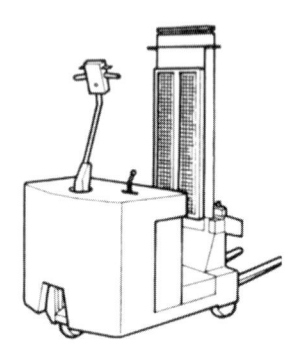

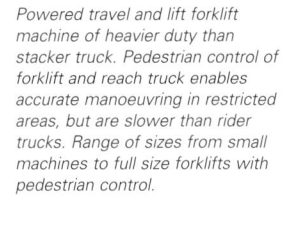

Powered travel and lift forklift machine of heavier duty than stacker truck. Pedestrian control of forklift and reach truck enables accurate manoeuvring in restricted areas, but are slower than rider trucks. Range of sizes from small machines to full size forklifts with pedestrian control.

Powered and manual stillage truck

Uses and limitations
Internal transfer of long loads on special stillages. Cannot be used for pallet handling.

Size and capacity
Length overall 1.68 m (depending on type of stillage used); width 0.8 m; height lowered 152 mm to 203 mm; height lift 76 mm; maximum width of load 0.6 m; capacity 2.03 tonnes.

Space requirements
Will turn in its own length but can carry a 3.6 long load for which overhang must be allowed.

Equipment design
Wheel material should be cast iron but can be used with polyurethane or rubber wheels for lighter loads.

Building needs
Level floors.

Powered or manually propelled for carrying stillage (See Information sheet, Mechanized storage). Often special machines for special purpose stillages, e.g. pipes. Some can swing stillage 90° manually to stack in narrow aisles.

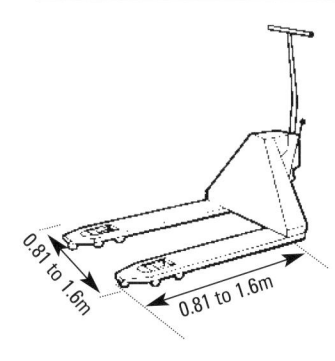

Mechanized storage – pedestrian controlled handling equipment

Manual pallet truck

Uses and limitations

Internal transfer within warehouse for order build-up, loading vehicles on raised docks general pallet handling; with tail-lift vehicles. Increasingly used in retail premises for handling bulk goods, can be used as a stillage truck with adapter fitted. Where loading ramps are used pallet trucks with brakes should be supplied.

Sizes and capacity

If over 1500 kg capacity and long distance travel is required, a powered truck is better, as operatives soon tire when pushing heavy loads. Fork lengths available from 0.81 m to 1.62 m. Widths also vary from 460 mm to 680 mm. Where gangways are very narrow and stability is important, a heavy truck should be used with as much width between forks as possible. Height lowered 83 mm; height raised 203 mm. Pallet width should be 152 mm over fork (typical length is 1.06 m for a 1.21 m pallet).

Space requirements

Will turn in its own length. Additional clearance for overhangs.

Equipment design

Large wheels in nylon or with solid rubber tyres are required on uneven floors or for heavy loads; steel wheels are also available but are less popular nowadays.

Building needs

Level floors, articulating axles available for trucks to be used in old buildings, but a good chance of unstable loads. Shaped or angled fingers for drum, paper roll handling. Skid adaptor for stillages.

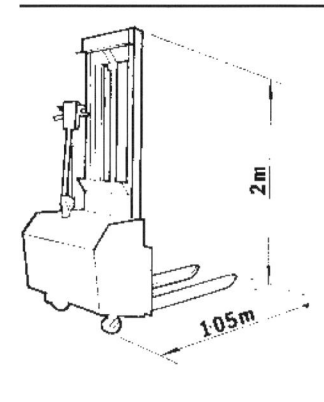

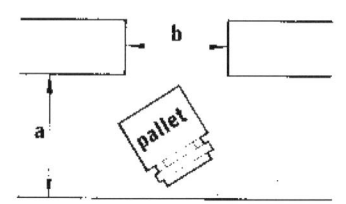

Power travel and lift pedestrian-controlled stacker truck.

Uses and limitations

Internal lifting under localized conditions with relatively light loads up to 3.6 m. Pallet handling. Not suitable for horizontal movement over anything but shortest distances. Would work well with pallet truck. Can be supplied with attachments.

Size and capacity

Capacities to 1500 kg at 600 mm centres. Straddle with 864 mm to 1.3 m. Now available in more compact form. Travel speeds to 4.8 kpm laden.

Space requirements

Will turn with full load in 2.2 m aisle. Tyres tend to be polyurethane. Lift height to 3.8 m (triple extension mast). **a** = 1300 mm (800 + 1200 mm pallet) 1500 mm (1000 + 1200 mm pallet) **b** = width of largest load + 100 mm increase of b means a can be reduced.

Equipment design

Can be fitted with scissors mechanism to make it into a reach truck. Batteries will now work full shift without recharging.

Building needs

Level floors; single or three-phase supply.

When travelling, the pallet rests on the stacker frame, which has travel wheels; power lifting is independent of the travel frame, and is directly into the rack. Only suitable for short travel distances

INFORMATION SHEET

Mechanized storage 7
The forklift family

1 **Counter-balanced forklift trucks**

2 **Rider controlled reach trucks**

3 **Free-path order pickers/stackers and turret trucks**

4 **Side loaders**

The family includes forklift trucks, reach trucks, turret trucks, side loaders and free-path order pickers. The principles of their use have been described in Technical study, Mechanized storage 1. This information sheet gives most common sizes, capacities and types of mobile lifting equipment based on forklift technology, so that performances, aisle widths, clearances and turning requirements can be roughly assessed at sketch design stage. At no time should these typical dimensions be used for a final design scheme. The manufacturer of the plant to be used should be contacted at the earliest possible stage.

1 Counter-balanced forklift trucks

1.01 Maids-of-all-work in a warehouse. They can lift all warehouse loads and are available from 1200 kg capacity to 5000 kg for normal use. Much larger trucks are available for handling stillages and ISO containers. Forklifts take up more space in stacking areas than reach trucks or turret trucks (Figure 4.128a–c).

1.02 Developments include more accurate control for electric trucks, hydrostatic steering and automatic height selection for high lift machines. A well-tried development, especially for turret trucks and order pickers, is wire guides in aisles, freeing operators to pick goods, or allowing full automation for stacking yet keeping free-path characteristics. The ranges of forklift types have polarized into two groups within each capacity; internal use compact machines with solid tyres and electric power, and internal combustion (i/c) engined trucks for general purpose and external use, of more rigid construction, oscillating rear axles and pneumatic tyres. Table 4.11 illustrates dimensional implications of internal and external forklift trucks of similar capacity.

1.03 Forklifts can be fitted with electric traction from batteries, or diesel, petrol or liquid petroleum gas (lpg[2]) i/c engines. Care should be taken in designing installations when using internal combustion-powered trucks, as fumes may build up. At present 60 per cent of the UK market is for electric trucks, but this is likely to drop to 55 per cent if the present trend towards internal combustion power for certain applications continues. The largest growth area is in the distribution field and now many operators are hiring or leasing their forklifts. It has been estimated that 8200 trucks are available for hire in the UK, which helps small operators with little working capital. Designers should plan racking clearances to allow for different leased plant to be used with flexibility of plant operation in mind.

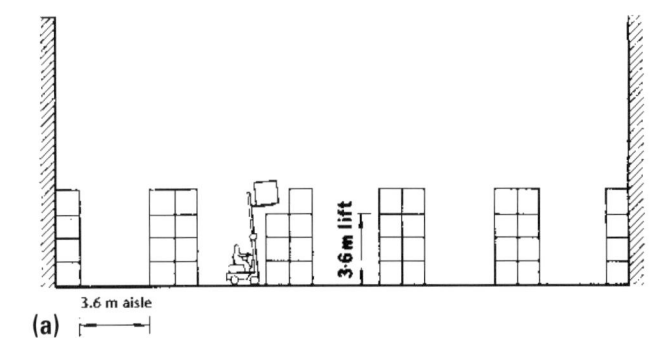

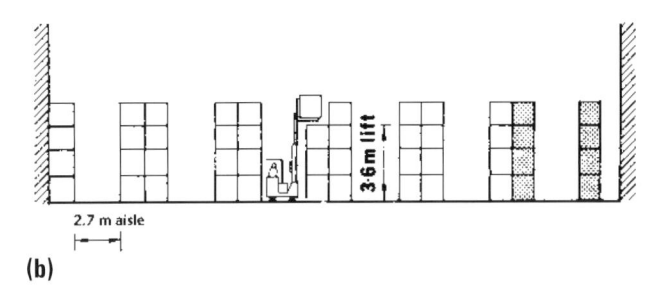

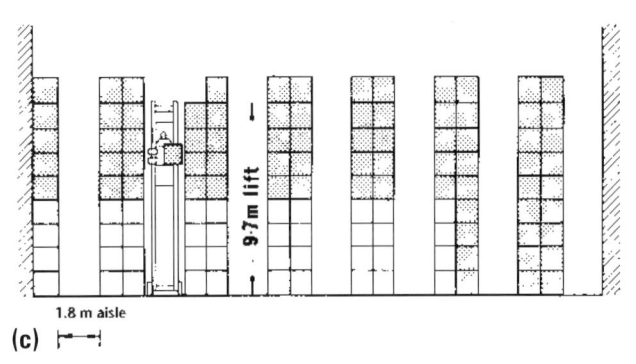

Figure 4.128 *(a) Aisle and storage layout using 1 tonne capacity forklift with 1200 x 1000 mm pallets. (b) Layout using 1 tonne reach truck increases storage capacity by more than 20 per cent over (a). (c) Layout using a narrow aisle stacker/order picker with increased lift height increases storage capacity by a factor of 2 over (a).*

Table 4.11 Sizes, weights and turning circles of forklift trucks and reach trucks
(Diagrams show limits of dimensions contained in the table)

Capacity (kg)	Total length plus forks (m)	Weight (unladen) (kg)	Maximum stacking lift (m)	Tilt (f = forward; b = back) (degree)	Extended mast height (m)	Lowered mast height (m)	Width (m)	Turning circle (inner) (m)	Turning circle (outer) (m)	Aisle clearance a (m)	b (m)
45 000 kg This class of forklift is mainly designed for laden container handling but can also be used in heavy industry and steelworks	9.78	49 900	8.5	6°f 12°b	9.78	6.12	3.5	0.760	7.6	8.2 11.2 14.5 6.8	6.7 (including 6 m container) 10 (including 9.1 m container) 13.4 (including 12.1 m container) 4.3 (machine alone)
Reach stacker	15.000	80 000	12.0		(telescopic boom)		4.4			18	16 (including 13.6 m container)
23 000 kg Suitable for container handling; also used for heavy lifting industry, e.g. steel coils	7.95	28 750	6.4	6°f 12°b	8.4	5.2	3.1	0.685	5.7	(as above)	
Raised cots for empty containers		(14.8)									

148

Capacity (kg)	Total length plus forks (m)	Weight (unladen) (kg)	Maximum stacking lift (m)	Tilt (f = forward; b = back) (degree)	Extended mast height (m)	Lowered mast height (m)	Width (m)	Turning circle (inner) (m)	Turning circle (outer) (m)	Aisle clearance a (m)	b (m)
9000 kg Popular large capacity forklift in industry for heavy loads, e.g. steel work and cable drums	5.29	12 065	4.6	6°f 12°b	5.69	3.4	2.49	0.430	4.06	6.3*	3.7*
5450 kg Developed specially for handling empty containers and stacking them up to 3 high	4.85	15 440	8.3	6°f 12°b	9.6	5.05	2.4 3.6 (spreader)	0.635	4.6	10.9 12.6 14.3	6.7 (including 6m container) 10 (including 9.1 m container) 13.4 (including 12.1 m container)
5450 kg Useful general purpose forklift for external use for 5–6 tonne unit loads	4.5	7530	3.65	6°f 12°b	4.6	2.6	1.8	0.121	3.03	5.1	2.9
2700 kg Popular size of heavier standard forklift. Integral combustion engined truck with pneumatic tyres for mainly external use.	3.9	5307	4.3	3°f 10°b	5.03	2.6	1.66	0.09	2.3	4.06	2.17
Cushion-tyred electric truck for internal use	3.5	4990	4.3	3°f 10°b	5.04	2.6	1.12	0.127	2.1	3.7	2.06
1300 to 2200 kg A popular category seen in many warehouses and factories. Internal combustion engine (diesel, petrol/lpg) and pneumatic tyres.	3.6	2630	4.27	5°f 10°b	4.85	2.62	1.14	0.127	2.1	3.86	2.05
Electric unit with solid tyres. Dimensions within each i/c engined and electric range do not alter significantly.	2.7	2680	3.66	2°f 10°b	4.2	2.3	0.96	0.127	2.1	3.5	2.05
900–1300 kg Popular size for the smaller operator or for light pallets	2.79	2132	3.66	2°f 10°b	4.2	2.26	0.91	0.05	1.7	3.15	1.7

Capacity (kg)	Total length plus forks (m)	Weight (unladen) (kg)	Maximum stacking lift (m)	Tilt (f = forward; b = back) (degree)	Extended mast height (m)	Lowered mast height (m)	Width (m)	Turning circle (inner) (m)	Turning circle (outer) (m)	Aisle clearance a (m)	Aisle clearance b (m)
Under 900 kg Small rider forklift useful for unloading and light duty work in confined spaces, e.g. on factory floor	2.65	2730	3.5	3°f 8°b	4.04	2.3	0.92	Inner wheel reverses on full lock	1.34	3.05* (including 200 mm operating clearance)	1.78
Three-wheeled stacker truck (2600 kg) Intermediate model between forklifts and reach trucks. Exploits narrow aisle capabilities, but has fixed mast and conventional fork attachment. For over 3.5 m lift, hydraulic extension stabilizers are often fitted, that retract to allow the narrow width for tight turning.	2.01	3050	6	-	6.8	2.5	0.87 (1.01 with stabilizers)	Not applicable	1.64	2.55	1.78
Scissor or pantograph reach truck (2040 kg)	1.97	2490	5.5	3°f 5°b	6.39	3.4	1.24	Not applicable	1.6	2.34	1.72
Gallows or moving mast reach truck (2040 kg)	1.92	-	8.3	2°f 5°b	9.05	2.1	1.01	Not applicable	1.77	2.85	1.7
Four-way reach truck (2040 kg) Combination of reach truck and sideloader. Uses the scissor principle as a reach truck. Steering turns through 180° to allow instant 90° changes of direction. The frame can take extensions for handling long bars and tubes. Aisles need only be a few mm wider than reach truck in sideways travel position plus load.	1.85	2980	6.03	-	6.9	3.7	1.96	Four-way steering		2.26	2.0

*Aisle clearance for truck only (i.e. without 1200 x 1100 pallet).

Mechanized storage – the forklift family

Mast types

1.04 Many attachments and several mast types are available for varied lift heights and performances: All trucks derate as lift increases; e.g. a 3.2 tonnes lift derates to approximately 0.9 tonne at 8.5 m. The following mast types are available as standard:
- Non-telescopic single-stage. Usually found only on the simplest low-cost stacking machines.
- Two stage mast without free lift. An outer upright and an inner upright, to the top of which is mounted the hoist cylinder. As the hoist cylinder moves up, this pulls chains over a block, lifting the fork carriage. In practice, a few inches of free lift are usually possible (Figure 4.129a). (Duplex mast.) Two stage mast with free lift. These can be with partial free lift giving free travel, or full free fork lift at any mast position. The latter is the most common and should be capable of stacking goods in any position within the lifting range (Figure 4.129b). Hydraulic rams and lift chains tend to be complicated.
- Three stage mast. Permits high stacking without suffering the penalty of height when the mast is retracted. Capable of low-headroom operation, e.g. inside ISO containers. Hydraulics and chain routeing become complex. Because of the extra components on three stage masts, some loss of load centre has been experienced, and these cost 30–50 per cent more than two stage types. Full free lift is possible (Figure 4.129c) (Triplex mast).
- Four stage mast. The main advantage is low collapsed height. Used for exceptionally high stacking, sometimes on reach trucks. Even more complex chains and hydraulics cause further loss of load centre and increases in cost.

Exhaust emissions

1.05 These are especially important in food storage, as they may contaminate it. Liquid petroleum gas engines produce carbon monoxide emissions as high as petrol units (Figure 4.130). Some operators in very confined spaces such as ships' holds, where recharging is impracticable, use exhaust 'scrubbers'. Carbon monoxide (CO) output of a new lpg unit should be half that of a petrol engine, but it increases with engine wear and poor engine tuning.

1.06 There are no regulations governing exhaust emissions in enclosed spaces in the UK to date; in the USA, it is suggested that the level should not exceed 50 ppm CO, 0.005 per cent exposure on the basis of an eight-hour shift, five days per week. Design extraction facilities on this basis. For nitrogen oxides, 5 ppm is reasonable. (Note that catalytic converters only convert CO to CO_2, and nitrogen oxides are still emitted.) Electric trucks are still really the only answer in cold stores and the food-processing industry.

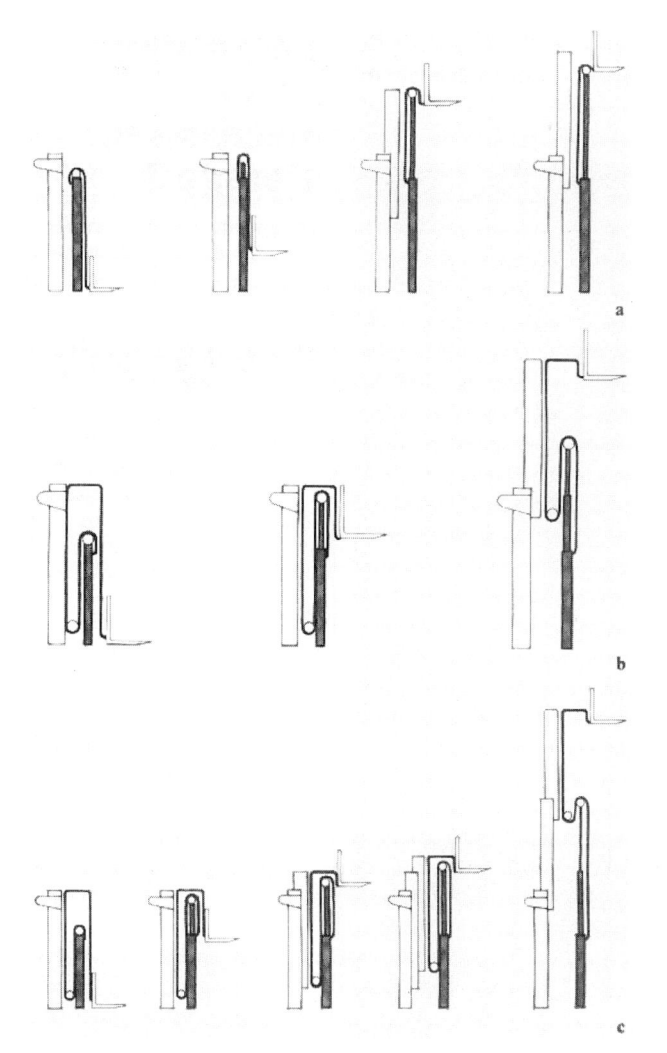

Figure 4.129 *Types of mast (rising from left to right). Outlines of basic mast on left, inner upright (shaded) on right, on top of which hoist cylinder (shaded) rises. (a) Two-stage mast with little free lift. (b) Two-stage mast with full free lift. (c) Three-stage mast.*

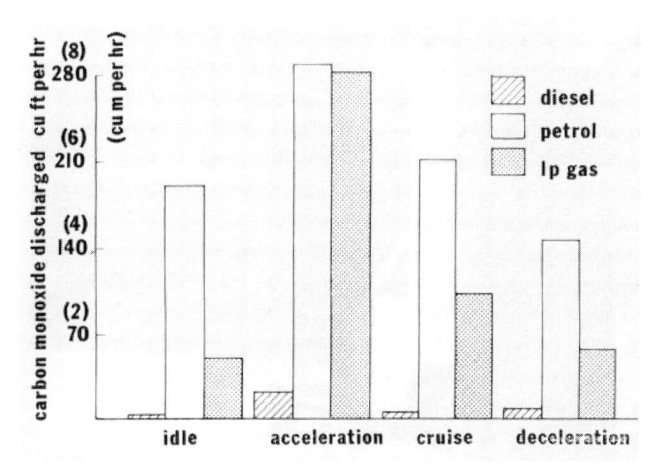

Figure 4.130 *Histogram showing emission of carbon dioxide from diesel, petrol and liquid petroleum gas vehicle engines in good tune.*

Building needs

1.07 Level floors and ramps not to exceed 1:12 for intermittent working. Charging points are required for electric trucks, either in the loading bay or special maintenance area. (See Information sheet, Mechanized storage 9.) Table 4.11 shows typical sizes and properties.

Forklift attachments

1.08 There are many attachments available to enable forklifts to handle various shapes and sizes (Figures 4.131–4.136). Some may need increased hydraulics. The maintenance area should be able to cater for hydraulic repairs (see Information sheet, Mechanized storage 9).

2 Rider controlled reach trucks

2.01 Suitable for narrow aisles of 2.7–3 m depending on pallet type and height of lift: lift heights are now available to 10.5m beam height. Reach trucks are the general indoor workhorse of the distribution industry. Some models can be driven from the elevating fork carriage, giving them an order-picking facility. If travel distances of

Mechanized storage – the forklift family

Figure 4.131 *Turning fork attachment with arms set in palletized load carrying position.*

Figure 4.132 *Turning fork attachment with arms set in load clamping position.*

Figure 4.133 *Push/pull attachment in extended position with load on slip sheet about to be withdrawn onto platen arms.*

Figure 4.134 *Rotating paper reel clamp with short and swinging arms.*

Figure 4.135 *Forklift with high mast and clamps for paper reels.*

over 45 m are expected to be frequent, check battery capacity, as some reach trucks have smaller storage capacity than forklifts of the same size. Flat floors are required. There are two basic types:
- Gallows type: the most popular where the mast moves forward with the fork carriage.
- Scissors type: the mast stays in-board, and the fork carriage moves forward with pantograph action. Slightly more stable with heavy loads. Typical applications have been discussed in Technical study, Mechanized storage 1. Table 4.11 shows sizes and properties of typical reach trucks.

3 Free-path order pickers/stackers and turret trucks

3.01 For use in very narrow aisles and high racking. See Technical study, Mechanized storage 1 for applications. Turret truck operators do not usually rise with the fork carriage. These machines are very versatile, being able to operate in aisles between 25 mm and 150 mm wider than the widest load, with side-guidance wheels, and can be used for general warehouse and loading work as well (Figure 4.137). Developments include wire guidance and fully automated on-line control. (See Technical study, Automated storage 1.) Table 4.12 shows sizes and properties of free-path order pickers (Figure 4.138), stackers and turret trucks.

Mechanized storage – the forklift family

Figure 4.136 *Stacker truck with spindle for lifting carpets.*

Figure 4.138 *Free-path order picker truck with operator at picking level.*

4 Side loaders

4.01 There are two types: single side loaders and dual side loaders.

Single side loaders

4.02 A very useful type for general use in lifting long and awkward loads such as steel sections and textiles into racking. Can be fitted with many special fork attachments, such as outrigger forks for springy loads. They are able to work in aisles 150 mm greater than their width, or only 25 mm wider with in-rack guide wheels. Some models are fitted with four-wheel steering to alleviate cut-in on tight turns. They can have adjustable ground clearance of 125 mm. They are available in a wide range of capacities, up to the container handling giants illustrated in Technical study, External storage 1.

Dual side loaders

4.03 For very narrow aisle work, allowing double-sided access without having to leave the rack to reposition. Some can be used as order pickers with an elevating operator's cabin.

4.04 Always check with manufacturers for turning and clearance dimensions. Side loaders for use in racks should not need to be jacked when lifting. Flat floors are required. Table 4.13 shows sizes and properties of side loaders.

Figure 4.137 *Free path narrow aisle order picker. Note side guides and P and D stations to the left at the end of the aisle.*

153

Mechanized storage – the forklift family

Table 4.12 Free-path handling equipment

Free-path, narrow aisle stacker/order picker

Elevation

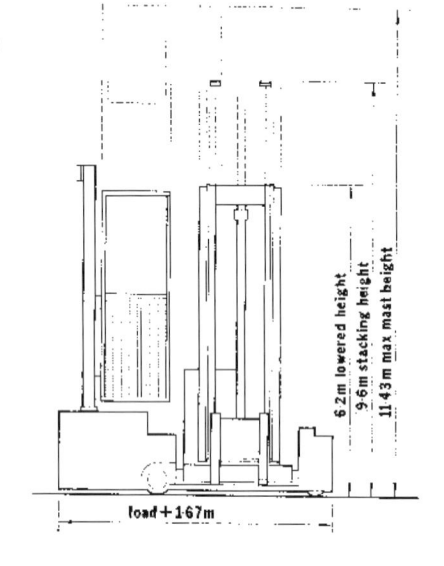

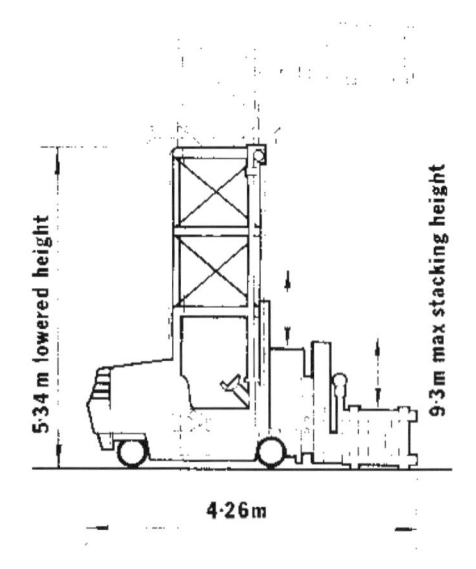

(6.2 m lowered height; 9.6 m stacking height; 11.43 m max mast height; load + 1.67 m)

Plan

forks swing from side to side

working aisle load + 610 mm (+1200 pallet = 1.81 m)

transfer aisle 3.65 m

Free-path stacker/order picker with elevating cab, fixed mast and rotating fork

(5.34 m lowered height; 9.3 m max stacking height; 4.26 m)

1.7 – 1.85

working aisle 1.85 with 1200 pallet

transfer aisle 4.26 m min (4.53 m with 1200 pallet)

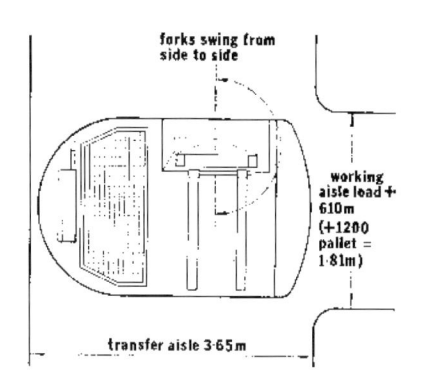

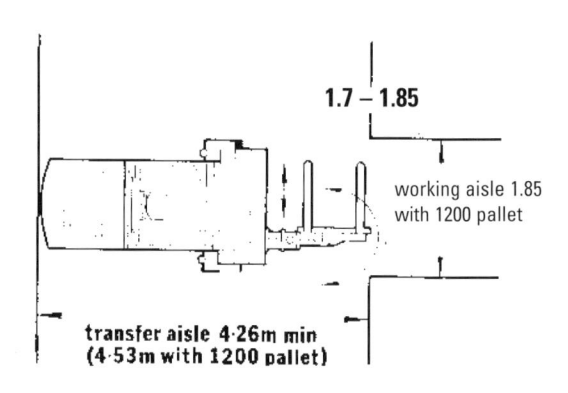

Description: This model is custom-built. It incorporates a separate order picking cabin and fork attachment mounted on independent masts. The advantage of this is that as the pallet load of goods is picked the relationship between the pickers' hand level and the top of the accumulating load can be adjusted to save operator fatigue.

Capacity 1 to 3 tonnes

The four-post mast gives extra stability. This type can be used out of the aisle as a forklift truck. The free lift on the fork carriage also allows differential movement between the pallet and the picking platform. Maximum mast height: 10.03 m.

1520 kg

Table 4.12 (Continued)

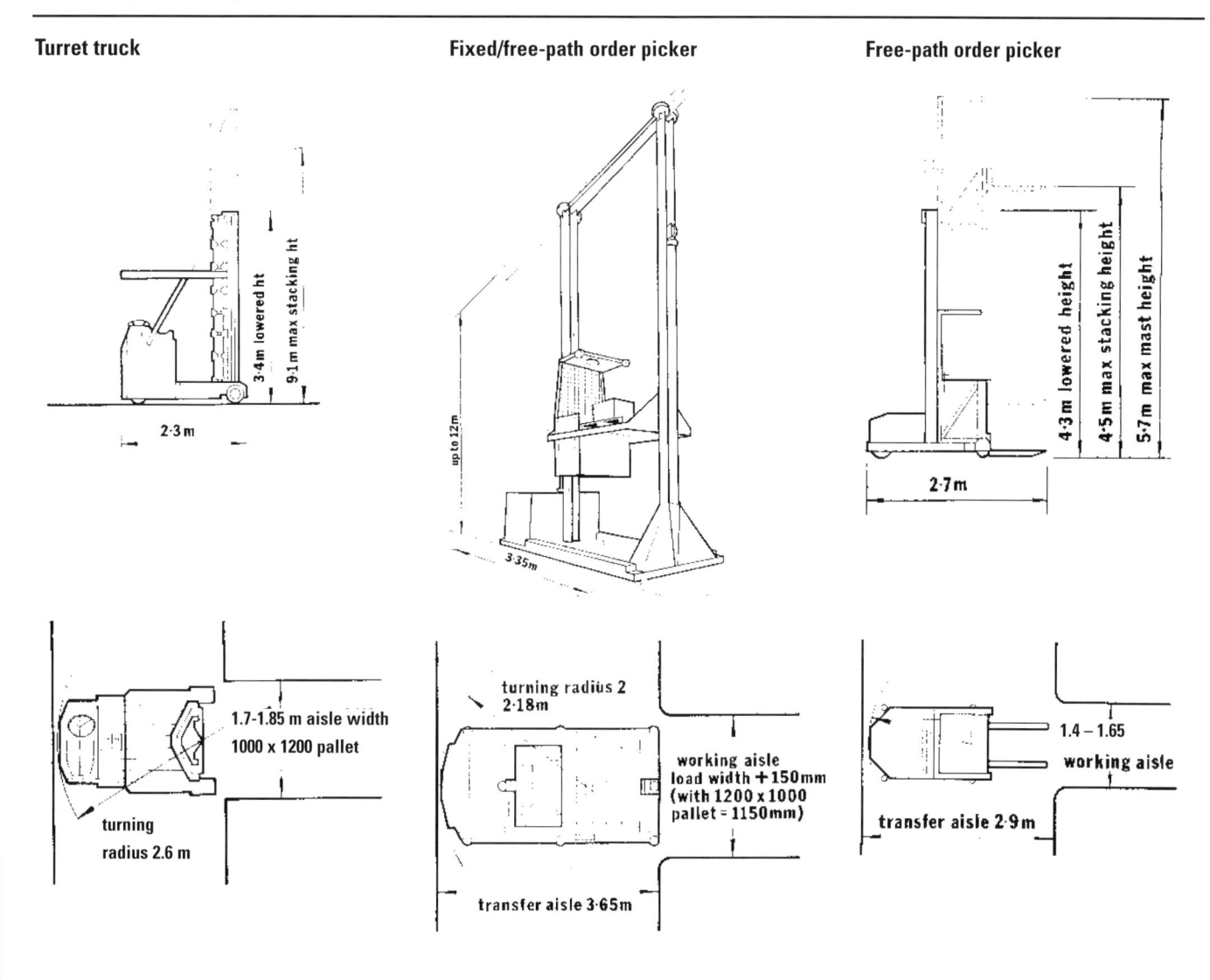

Turret truck	**Fixed/free-path order picker**	**Free-path order picker**

Turret truck dimensions: 2·3 m width; 3·4 m lowered ht; 9·1 m max stacking ht. Plan view: 1.7–1.85 m aisle width, 1000 × 1200 pallet; turning radius 2.6 m.

Fixed/free-path order picker dimensions: 3·35 m, up to 12 m. Plan view: turning radius 2·18 m; working aisle load width +150 mm (with 1200 × 1000 pallet = 1150 mm); transfer aisle 3·65 m.

Free-path order picker dimensions: 2·7 m; 4·3 m lowered height; 4·5 m max stacking height; 5·7 m max mast height. Plan view: 1.4–1.65 working aisle; transfer aisle 2·9 m.

Turret truck operators do not rise with the fork carriage. In high racks they work to close tolerances, so level floors are required. Revolving and sliding fork carriages allow access to racks on each side without the need to turn the

1100 to 2200 kg

When in the picking aisle the machine is guided by rails at base of racking and is further stabilized by a rail over the aisle centre. this type can be higher than others, and when travelling between aisles it can be driven like a manual free path machine.

1100 to 2200 kg

This type is a simpler machine than the others. The pallet onto which the goods will be picked rests on the fixed forks in front of the operator's cabin. Some machines incorporate a small amount of lift for the forks to relieve the picker of stooping and reaching. These are increasingly popular for the smaller warehouse operator.

500 to 1000 kg

Mechanized storage – the forklift family

Figure 4.139 Turret truck entering aisles. Note guide rails at base of racking, and use of post pallets in racking.

Figure 4.140 Reach truck, illustrating narrow aisle, and how load is carried within wheelbase. Mast moves forward to place load.

Figure 4.141 Narrow aisle stacker truck: a forklift with no reach action, relying on mast angle and short dimensions to reduce aisle space; often used in smaller stores.

Figure 4.142 A narrow aisle adaptation of a conventional forklift: note tilting forks and sliding central pivot.

Table 4.13 Sizes, weights and properties of sideloaders

Capacity and type	Total length (m)	Weight (unladen) (kg)	Maximum stacking lift (m)	Extended height (m)	Lowered mast height (m)	Width (m)	Turning circle a (inner) (m)	Turning circle b (outer) (m)	Aisle width (working) (m)	90° turn-in (m)
In-store sideloaders single side Used in warehouse for handling large loads such as pipes, steelwork or coils. A wide range of sizes and capacities. Some very large versions can carry coils in steelworks (see Special storage, Chapter 7) and some use one or two operators' platforms rising with the forks to act as order pickers for large loads as well. Capacity: 4000 to 5000 kg		6000	Custom built so variable			1.8	0.914	3.6	2.2	3.2
In-store dual sideloaders/order picker Useful for stacking and picking on both sides of an aisle without having to turn around. The mast rotates and traverses from side to side. Both these types are usually solid tyred and are sometimes fitted with small horizontal guide wheels to run in rails at the base of racking.	3.65	6–10,000	5.4	6.4	3.74	1.9	0.914	3.6	2.2	3.3
General-purpose sideloaders A large family of general-purpose machines of varying capacities. These have proven to be very useful in industry and to timber yards and builders' merchants. More stable for external use than forklifts and combine narrow aisle stacking with fast stable travel.	4.3	6500	5.4	6.5	3.8	2.06	0.41	4.1	2.8	4.3

	3.2	5.8	3.4	1.8	0.152	2.67	2.1	3.6

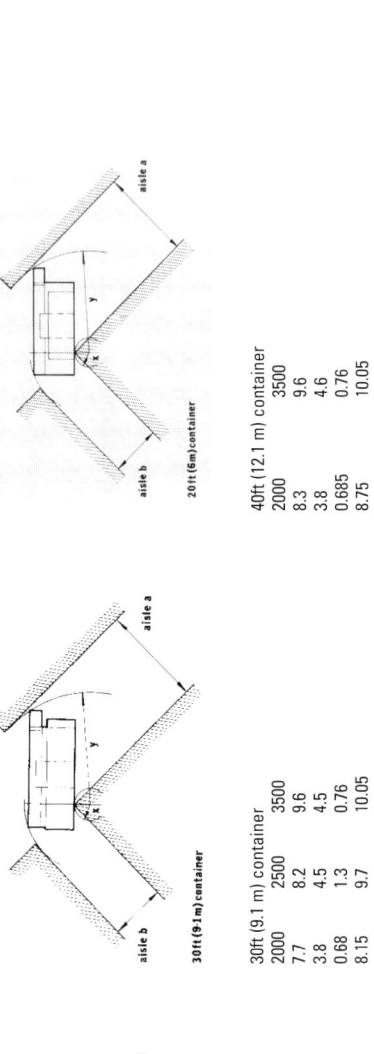

4-way sideloaders
A variation of sideloader for special industrial conditions and restricted conditions. These machines have wheels that all turn through 180° allowing instant 90° direction changes and 'crabbing'. The machine can thus act as a reach truck side-on. Machines of this type have been used successfully in glass works for handling large sheets of plate glass.

	5450	4.8						
	5.54	7.57	4.5	2.6	0.84	5.4	3.2	5.6
	12,610	6.1						

Heavy-duty sideloaders have been used in industry for some time. They are scaled-up general-purpose models; they usually use integral hydraulic stabilizers for heavy lifts; steel fabriciators, handling whole trees in saw mills, coil carrying (see Chapter 7, Special storage).

	9.5	7.7	4.7	3.7	0.76	9.1	(see below)
	47,000	5.5					

Container handling and heavy lift sideloaders
A special type of sideloader developed as the container trade grew. Various ratings are available, for 20ft (6.1 m) and 40ft (12.1 m) containers. These are big machines designed for rugged use, fast work cycles and rapid travel fully laden (see Chapter 3, External storage).

Aisle widths of container-carrying sideloaders

Lancer Boss model five

	20ft (6 m) container			30ft (9.1 m) container			40ft (12.1 m) container		
Capacity (kg)	2000	2500	3500	2000	2500	3500	2000	2500	3500
aisle a (m)	7.7	8.2	9.6	7.7	8.2	9.6	8.3		9.6
aisle b (m)	3.9	4.5	4.5	3.8	4.5	4.5	3.8		4.6
radius x	0.68	1.3	0.76	0.68	1.3	0.76	0.685		0.76
radius y	8.15	9.67	10.05	8.15	9.7	10.05	8.75		10.05

INFORMATION SHEET

Mechanized storage 8

Packaging plant

1 Use

This sheet gives information on properties of plant used for packaging.

1 Use

1.01 Use of plant is discussed in Technical study, Mechanized storage 1, paras 18.11 to 18.14. Packaging plant includes palletizers, depalletizers, shrink-wrappers, banders and pneumatic nail guns.

Palletizers

1.02 Mechanical or vacuum-mechanical operation, depending on size. Up to 50 pallets per hour can be palletized by a high capacity unit, with regularly shaped cases. Normally, where the machine must arrange combinations of packages, it averages 30–40 pallets per hour (Figures 4.143a/b and 4.144). Transistorized controls form the 'brain' that holds the range of stacking patterns for the product. Twin-headed versions are available.

(a)

(b)

Figure 4.143 (a) *Automatic palletizer, showing palletized load emerging on a conveyor;* (b) *gantry robot palletizer which rotates to stack or nest crates.*

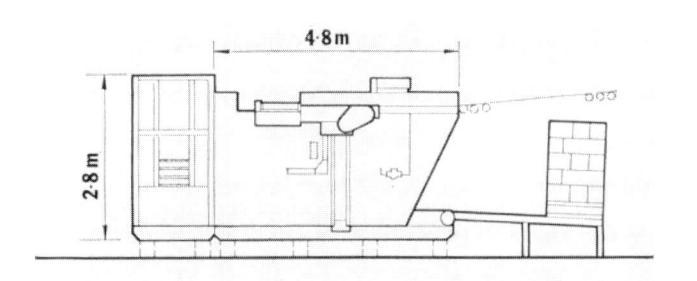

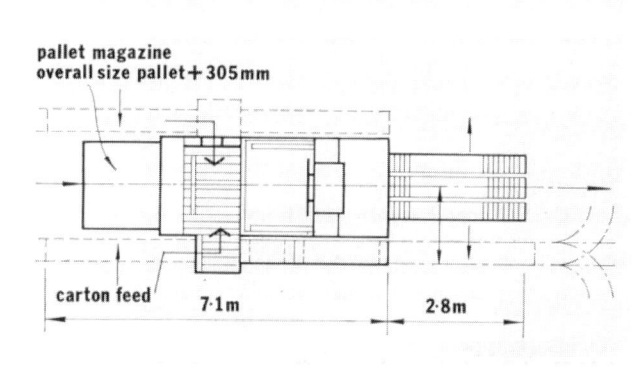

Figure 4.144 *Dimensions of typical automatic palletizer. (a) Elevation. (b) Plan (alternative carton feed positions are dotted).*

Depalletizers

1.03 Used to unpack regular loads from pallets. A typical use is unloading empty bottles or crates for filling and repacking. Typical machines unload 400–600 bottles per minute. Mechanical and vacuum versions are available (Figure 4.145).

Shrink-wrappers

1.04 Used for placing polythene film over pallet loads of goods, and heat-sealing the film and shrinking it by passing it through an oven (Figure 4.146a). Capacities vary, depending on size of pallet, thickness of film, and whether a straight-through or single entry is used. Units weigh about 1000 to 2000 kg, depending on size and performance. Shrink-wrap tunnels can be linked, so that large objects such as machine components can be wrapped in one operation. In order to shrink the film tightly, air is extracted, and this is the main source of heat build-up in the surrounding area. The machine casings are usually well insulated.

Stretch-wrappers

1.05 Now more popular than shrink wrap units, using rotary wrapping techniques with thinner fill and no heat (Figure 4.146b). Either the reel of wrapping is rotated round the static pallet (more readily built into conveyor systems), or the pallet is rotated on a table with a static reel: this tends to be in smaller installations fed by fork trucks.

Mechanized storage – packaging plant

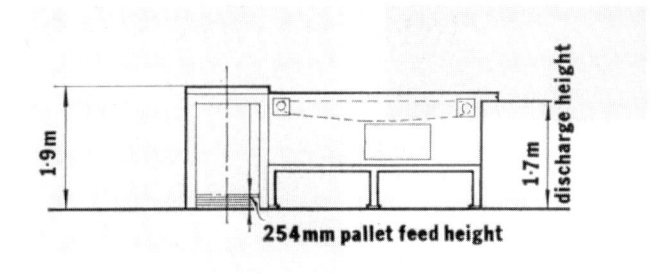

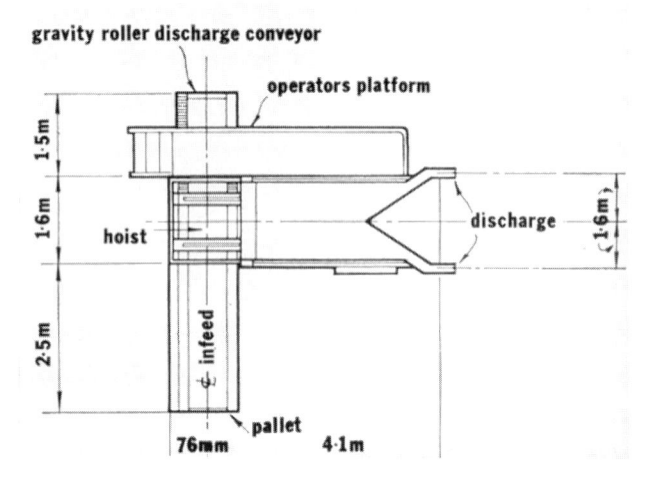

Figure 4.145 *Dimensions of typical depalletizer. (a) Section. (b) Plan.*

Banding machines

1.06 To stabilize unit loads. These may be used after shrink-wrapping with very difficult loads, or in place of shrink-wrapping where a seal is not required. Available in vertical or horizontal form, these machines can handle strapping automatically or may be manually controlled. Horizontal banding load cycles tend to be in the region of 10 seconds each for one band, 25 for two bands and 40 seconds for three bands; operation can be activated by a pre-programmed banding pattern and sensors on the approach conveyor. Vertical banding cycles are faster, strapping up to 400 cartons per hour (Figure 4.147).

Pneumatic nailer/stapler

1.07 A wide variety of these machines are marketed. They are used for making and sealing crates in the packaging area, and for assembling abnormal size cartons. Hand tools are mostly used, so only an airline is needed.

Figure 4.146 *Views of shrink-wrapper. (a) Exterior. (b) Rotary automated stretch-wrapper. Heat-seal heads are incorporated into the winding mechanism.*

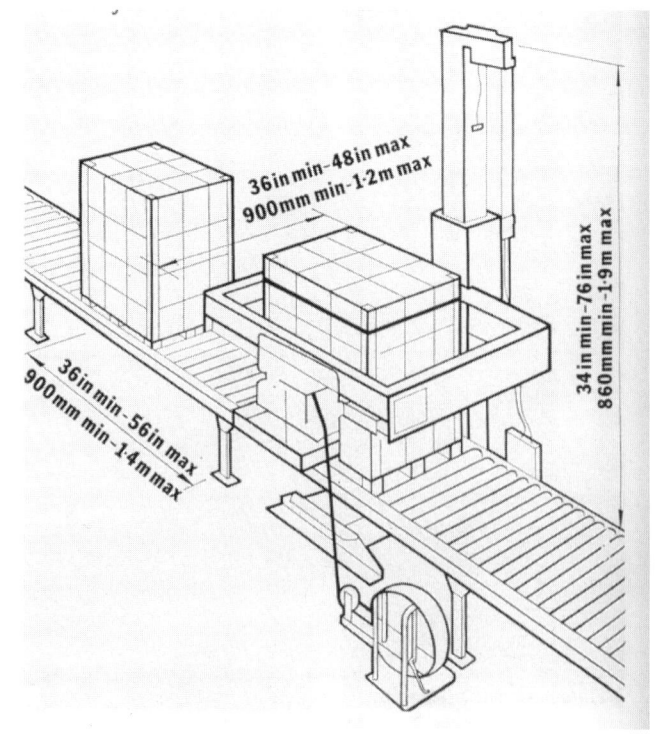

Figure 4.147 *Dimensions of horizontal bander.*

INFORMATION SHEET

Mechanized storage 9

Battery charging and maintenance areas

1 **Battery charging areas**

2 **Maintenance areas**

3 **The use of internal combustion engine powered forklifts and tractors**

4 **Services required in forklift charging and maintenance areas**

This sheet gives information required for designing charging and maintenance areas.

1 Battery charging areas

1.01 Free-path mobile mechanical handling plant which is electrically powered requires an area for battery charging. Traction is still by lead acid battery. Batteries are designed to give a high discharge rate over periods up to eight hours. Common practice is to charge lead acid batteries over an 8- to 12-hour period, but shorter charges are possible with new types of equipment. Battery-powered forklift trucks are either plugged into a charger direct (Figure 4.148), or (for continuous truck use), batteries are slid or lifted out and replaced by fully charged units. Traction batteries are heavy; some operators slide the batteries out on to trolleys fitted with roller beds. A 2-tonne capacity chain hoist is useful in these areas, as counterweights sometimes require removal for battery access. If a spare battery pattern is used, a container is required to hold batteries over the charging process, to protect them from damage from other plant.

Types of charge

1.02 It is common to charge batteries for eight hours, but some large organizations use boost charging to put 65–75 per cent of the charge into the batteries in about an hour. Charging systems are available that will charge batteries fully in five hours. Boost charging is the application of high currents to batteries discharged to about 10 per cent and lifting them to about 80 per cent of full charge in very short periods. It is popular, but is not recommended by battery manufacturers. A widely used charger is the taper charger, so named due to the manner in which the current is applied. There are two types; the single stage taper charger is mainly for slow charges and battery balancing over 10 to 12 hours. The double stage charger is for higher ratings, charging in eight hours.

1.03 Whether batteries are charged in situ, or away from their vehicles, a special area should be provided. It should be well ventilated, and forced circulation is often required in areas of high ambient temperatures; batteries give off heat when charging. Fire protection is also important, and there should be provision for neutralizing any spilt electrolyte. With large installations, equipment for dispensing distilled water can be installed, converting mains water.

Figure 4.148 *Battery charging and changing area. Note quick change trolleys.*

Floor

1.04 The floor of a charging area can be damaged by spills, and wheel abrasion. Ideally, a strip of heavy-duty epoxy-based jointless finish should be laid, which is impervious to acids, alkalis and which can withstand heavy impacts from batteries without permanent deformation or cracking. The area of special floor should extend further than the actual charging zone, as acids can be transferred by tyres; constant truck movement could indent a conventional floor finish, if softened by long-term acid exposure.

1.05 All charging plant, distilled water tanks, and spare batteries should be guarded against accidental impact damage.

1.06 Battery chargers are sometimes supplied as a package with the forklift trucks, but usually are produced by special manufacturers; contact the charger manufacturer of the client's choice early in the design process, as some installations require special conditions and safety features.

Typical sequence of activities of battery charging and maintenance areas

1.07
- Every day. Inspection of battery cells and topping up.
- Every 40 hours of forklift operation. (As truck maintenance is staggered, most of these functions will take place at the same time.) Check electrolyte levels in batteries. Check speed controller timings. General maintenance on tyres, brakes, power steering and hydraulic pumps will also be required.
- Every 160 hours of operation. Give batteries an equalizing charge, clean pump motor, blow carbon dust out of motors. Grease all round truck, checking hydraulic hoses and connections, and electrical connections.
- Longer term maintenance involves the 'taking down' of traction motors, and general dismantling for repair. Substantial oil spillage can occur during maintenance, and certain hydraulic oils are very corrosive to normal concrete flooring.

2 Maintenance areas

2.01 The long-term maintenance zone should be part of the charging area, but should be separated to prevent interference to normal charging movement by components and 'dead' trucks. The maintenance area should also have 2 tonne hoist provision; this could be shared with charging activities if the installation is small. A hydraulic lift and a pit are often specified, and should be well guarded.

2.02 Lighting levels of 400 lux minimum are suggested for these areas. There should be space for spares storage; plastic tote bins mounted on an expanded metal sheet are useful for small parts, and larger parts, e.g. wheels and tyres, can be placed in racks. Space should also be planned for keeping jacks, grease guns, and all the dirty paraphernalia that maintenance bays generate. A lorry-loading access door is an advantage, with the chain hoist able to extend over the truck bed. Forklift trucks tend to be delivered two or three at a time on special articulated low loaders; plan external access for a 15 m articulated vehicle.

3 The use of internal combustion engine powered forklifts and tractors

3.01 In place of battery charging, a fuel dispensing area is required; check from the outset with the fire officer, insurance company and officer responsible for petroleum regulations about any special measures that might be required. These can be especially stringent with lpg replenishment; removable gas bottles are usually used, and the bottles filled from a bulk tank outside the building or by a special contractor. Diesel filling areas are dirty, and solid and cushion tyres can transfer the fuel over a wide area of floor if a special surface is not provided in the maintenance zone. Diesel can quickly corrode a concrete floor, increase wear on tyres and cause dangerously slippery areas. These activities should be in a separate part of the warehouse building, as far from stock as possible. If any i/c engine test facilities are included, these should extract directly to the outside, with a high level of ventilation. Take care not to extract fumes near other higher intakes.

4 Services required in forklift charging and maintenance areas

4.01
- Compressed air for tyre inflation, cleaning.
- Cold water. Hose and tap (for floor swilling, hand cleaning).
- Hot water. Pressure hose cleaning, hand washing.
- Distilled water. Battery areas only.
- Grease. Centralized pressure greasing in large installations.
- Hydraulic oil. Centralized hydraulic oil reservoir in large installations.
- Power. Special three-phase supply for battery chargers. Check with charger manufacturer.
- Mains power for power tools used in maintenance area.
- Drills, grinders, power for pump for hydraulic lift.
- Steam. Special for diesel trucks, especially if operating often externally. Steam cleaning is effective for degreasing, and is cleaner than water jets. N.B. This can now be supplied in a proprietary mobile unit, such as by Karchër.

INFORMATION SHEET

Mechanized storage 10

Tractor trains

1 Use
This sheet gives dimensions of typical tractor trains.

1 Use

1.01 Tractor trains are useful for long inter-store runs requiring faster speeds and more flexibility than tow carts. The lighter types of tractor, for towing up to two tonnes, are usually battery powered, and cannot keep travelling up ramps without recharging. Heavier tugs for between 7 and 20 tonne train loads may be electric, petrol, diesel or lpg powered. Speeds of electric vehicles decrease considerably with heavy loads, and frequent gradients can drain the battery. Some tractors have load platforms of their own. They require a recharging bay. Table 4.14 gives properties and dimensions.

Table 4.14 Sizes, weights and capacities for tractor trains

Key diagrams

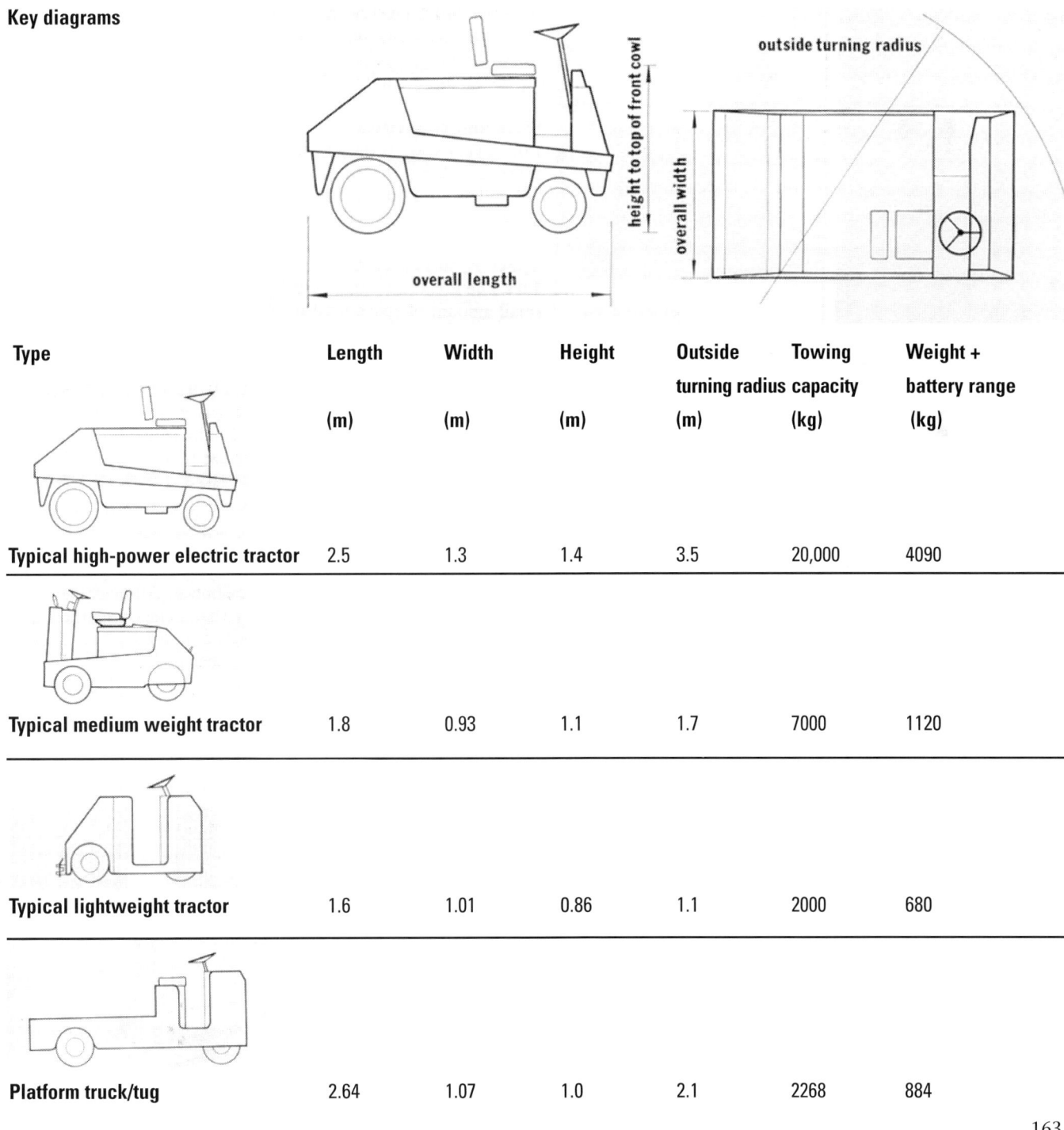

Type	Length (m)	Width (m)	Height (m)	Outside turning radius (m)	Towing capacity (kg)	Weight + battery range (kg)
Typical high-power electric tractor	2.5	1.3	1.4	3.5	20,000	4090
Typical medium weight tractor	1.8	0.93	1.1	1.7	7000	1120
Typical lightweight tractor	1.6	1.01	0.86	1.1	2000	680
Platform truck/tug	2.64	1.07	1.0	2.1	2268	884

INFORMATION SHEET

Mechanized storage 11
Static vertical movement plant

1 Properties

2 Lifts

3 Continuous pallet elevators and lowerators

4 Spiral conveyors

5 Vertical belt conveyors

6 Scissor lifts

This sheet gives information about lifts, elevators and lowerators, spiral conveyors, vertical belt conveyors and scissor lifts.

1 Properties

Uses and limitations

1.01 Used where mezzanine sorting is necessary, where lack of space eliminates ramps or normal conveyors, and for over-rack order picking. Also useful in joining new buildings to old units at different levels, where space is restricted. These methods are slower than belt conveyors, more expensive and complicated, but can carry large unit loads.

Sizes and capacities

1.02 A very wide variety of sizes is available, from carrying individual cans to a packaging area, to elevators for full pallets, and rack and pinion or scissor lifts capable of lifting a full 44 tonne truck.

Space requirements

1.03 The great attraction of this type of equipment is the small amount of space used in comparison with other plant for inter-floor movement. Space should be allowed for queueing on either side, and for maintenance access.

Equipment design

1.04 Most plant can be automatically fed and discharged, with accumulation conveyors and spacer stops. Special types of lift with pneumatic/electro-hydraulic control instead of exposed electrics are available for use in areas of high fire risk.

Building needs

1.05 Lifts of this type usually have their own independent shafts, thus requiring only a foundation. Some pallet elevators require a pit for belt clearance. All machines should be well guarded, and any shafts clearly marked and protected. Most of this equipment can suffer considerable abuse unless safety interlocks are specified.

2 Lifts

2.01 Available as four-post or single-post, cable or hydraulically operated units, or can work on the scissor lift principle (Figures 4.149 and 4.150). Other types are available with combinations of these features (e.g. for explosive atmospheres, a lift elevated with rams pulling chains on the forklift principle).
- Cable lifts need overhead clearance for motors, and space for counter weights.
- Hydraulic lifts work in confined headrooms, but require a pit for the retracted lifting gear. With hydraulic lifts, the motor/pump units can be isolated up to 30 m away, useful in confined areas.

3 Continuous pallet elevators and lowerators

3.01 A modification of the paternoster. The load platforms are made of slats that are rigid with load in the horizontal position, but which bend over rollers to return flat to save space (Figure 4.151). Normal operating speed: 0.5m/sec 15–20 pallets per minute, depending on the pallet size and weight. Most modern elevators are automatically fed. Various protective devices are available. Variations of load platform are available for pallets, barrels, casks and paper rolls. The units have integral supporting frames, incorporating motors and pulleys and can discharge at several floors. Paternosters are also used: whereas continuous elevators are exactly as described, paternosters combine transport and storage, useful for space efficient buffer holdings.

4 Spiral conveyors

4.01 These range from the vibration type, used for light, small packages to single bottle or can units employing a screw conveyor in a vertical configuration (Figure 4.152), and to larger spirals of powered rollers for large cartons. Useful for the fast transport between levels of small, regularly sized products. Speeds of between 600 and 1200 units/minute are possible. Working with a filling line and palletizer, very fast cycles can be achieved.

5 Vertical belt conveyors

5.01 Not a new method, originally designed for mailbags and baggage in airports. Basically, they sandwich a package between a drag belt and another flexible belt (Figure 4.153a), partly supported on an airbag, so that the

Mechanized storage – static vertical movement plant

(a)

(b)

Figure 4.149 (a) *Electro-hydraulic lift. (b) Free-standing lift.*

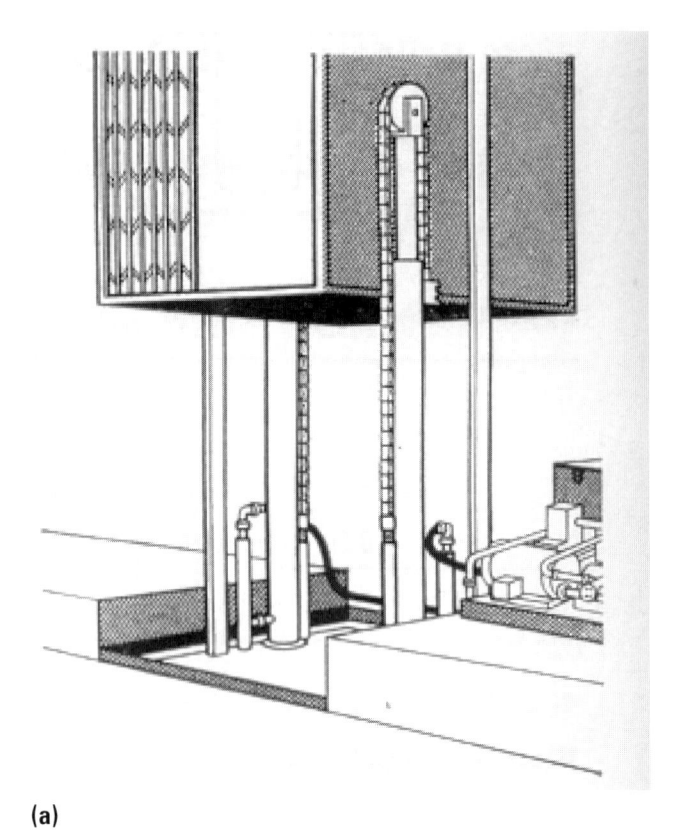

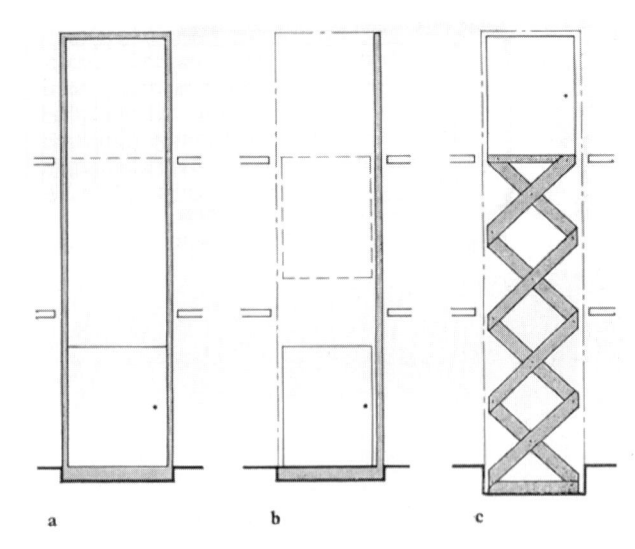

Figure 4.150 (a) *Four post lift. (b) Single mast lift. (c) Multiple scissor lift.*

(a)

(b)

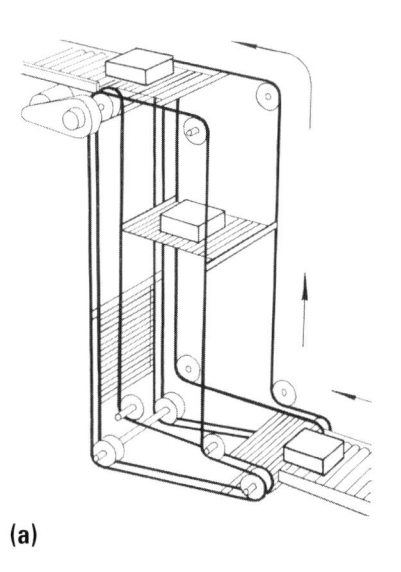

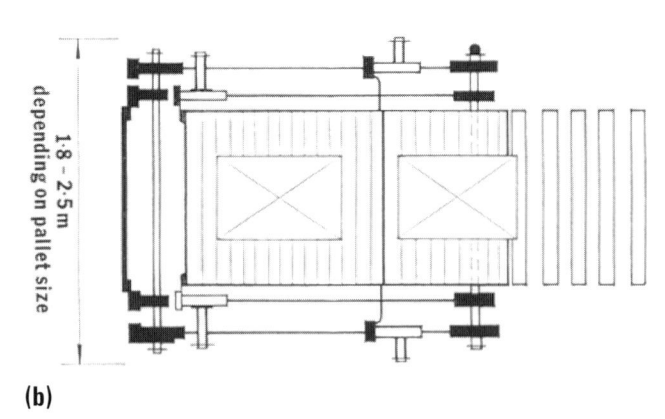

Figure 4.151 *Pallet elevator/lowerator (a) in action (b) plan.*

belts deform to the shape of the package. This form of vertical conveyor offers fast handling of individual packages of very varied sizes. They are only used for elevation; down travel is provided by a spiral chute (Figure 4.153b). Sizes can be supplied to suit the range of commodities handled.

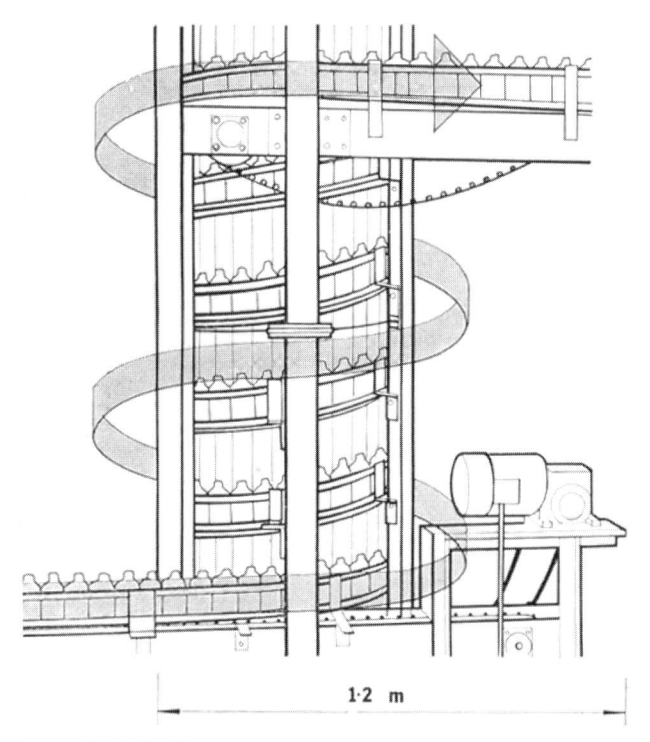

Mechanized storage – static vertical movement plant

Figure 4.152 *Vertical spiral screw conveyor for small products.*

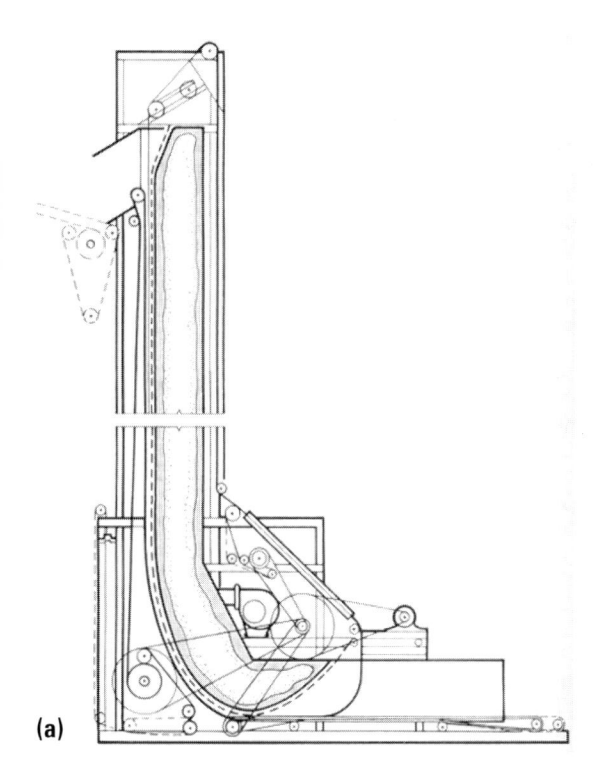

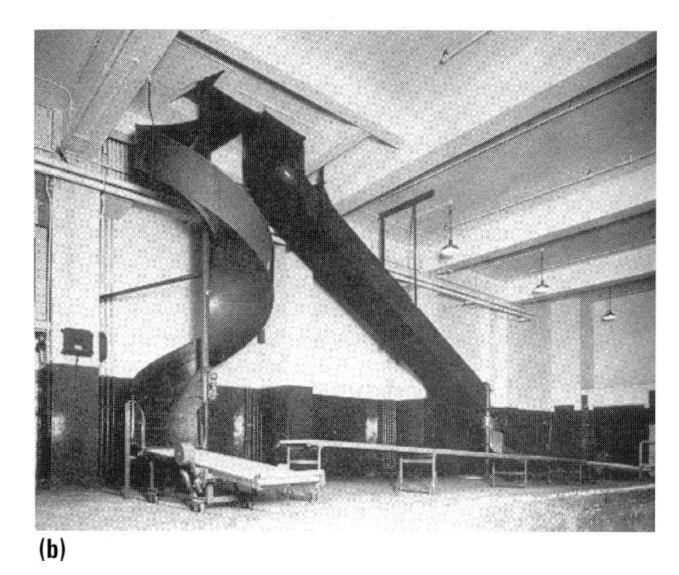

(a) (b)

Figure 4.153 *Vertical belt conveyor (a) for upward movement. This is designed for soft packages and lifts them against an inflated air bag in the centre. It can be made to any height to order, and (b) spiral chute for downward movement.*

6 Scissor lifts

6.01 A well-tried and simple method of raising a variety of unit loads (Figure 4.154). The lift tables can be equipped with rollers, so that pallets can be automatically accumulated on a roller conveyor, and released in single or multiple units on to the lift to suit its work cycle. Scissor lifts can be single- or multi-stage; as a rule no special foundations are needed, all the spread being in the lifts' own structure. Most types are supplied with full guards and safety features. This form of lift is comparatively slow, and is especially useful for lifting in infrequent situations, such as a forklift truck and load between a new warehouse and an old factory, where a 1 in 10 ramp would not be accommodated.

Figure 4.154 *Scissor lift on ship handles cargo between decks. This is similar to truck lifts used for basement loading bays for large inner city retail outlets.*

INFORMATION SHEET

Mechanized storage 12

Fixed-path handling plant

1 Uses

2 Systems

3 Stacker cranes

4 Order pickers

5 Gantry cranes

These include manually controlled stacker cranes, gantry cranes and order pickers. Versions which are automated are described in Chapter 5, Automated storage. This sheet gives designers typical dimensions and performances of equipment, for use at sketch design stage only. Manufacturers should always be consulted.

1 Uses

1.01 Fixed-path manually controlled plant is useful for block-stacking and in high racks above 12 m. Below 12 m, new types of free-path stacker/order pickers are more flexible. Fixed-path equipment uses very narrow aisles and roof suspension, does not need aisles for block stacks, and can place loads not acceptable to forklifts on to lorries (Figure 4.155).

2 Systems

2.01 Various systems are available for medium-rise warehouses where the manufacturer supplies both racking and stacker cranes. Stacker cranes work to tight tolerances within racks. Accurate construction is important.

2.02 There are many varieties of fixed-path handling plant particularly for specialized uses like steel stockholding, and sheet board stores. Both the machine and the supporting structure are costly and they lack flexibility. Within racks, stacker cranes are generally limited to one machine per aisle, or a transfer carriage is necessary; this can be extremely complicated as rails have to be correctly aligned, and need electrically operated locks and side-travel device (see Figure 4.162). Operators of fixed-path order pickers and stackers experience discomfort in high, narrow aisles, with fast acceleration rates, and substantial deceleration stresses are imposed on structure and racking.

3 Stacker cranes

Uses and limitations

3.01 Lifts and carries pallets or long loads in narrow aisles and stacks up to 30 m plus with twin masts (Figure 4.156a shows typical single mast). Mechanical faults have caused difficulties, but latest units are more reliable. Lacks flexibility and restricts change of use. Types of stacker crane are shown in Figures 4.155, 4.156a and 4.157.

Sizes

3.02 To order.

Space requirements

3.03 Aisles 1.37 m to 1.67 m. For roof-mounted units, clear height is required over racking for carriage. 1 m is usually enough, but sprinkler clearance is also required.

Equipment design

3.04 Racking, if integrally structured, must be strong enough to support crane. If floor mounted, it must have close tolerance finish or self-levelling jacks; if roof mounted, it needs rigid support, taking into account tolerances and summer expansion.

Figure 4.155 *Gantry slung stacker crane – effectively an upside-down forklift.*

Mechanized storage – fixed path handling plant

Figure 4.157 *Gantry hung stacker crane.*

Building needs

3.05 Three-phase power. Bus bar or winding cable.

Prices

3.06 Generally expensive.

4 Order pickers

Uses and limitations

4.01 Very useful for high density stocks of small parts and components, or bulk picking. Dimensions are similar to stacker crane. The fixed path is an advantage in this case, as accuracy is important, and the machine will be continuously used; it can also deliver loads to mezzanine sorting areas.

4.02 Fixed-path order pickers are becoming more popular; several ranges are offered with standard components and performance limits (Figures 4.156b, 4.158 and 4.159).

Sizes

4.03 To order.

Space requirements

4.04 Aisles 1.37 m to 1.67 m. For roof-mounted units, clear height is required over racking for carriage. 1 m is usually enough, but sprinkler clearance is also required.

Equipment design

4.05 Racking, if integrally structured, must be strong enough to support crane. If floor mounted, it must have close tolerance finish or self-levelling jacks; if roof mounted, it needs rigid support, taking into account tolerances and summer expansion.

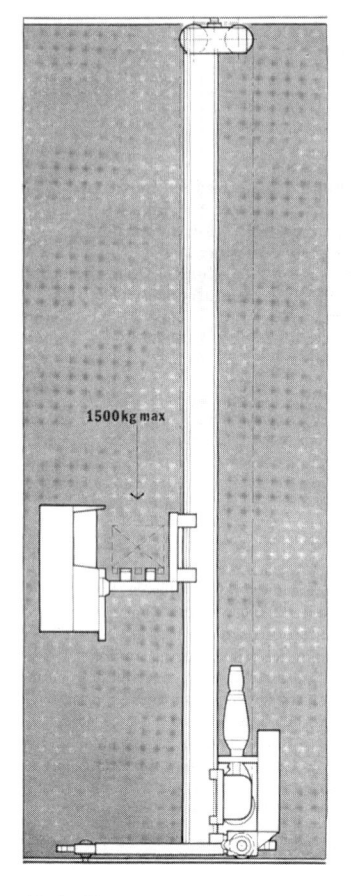

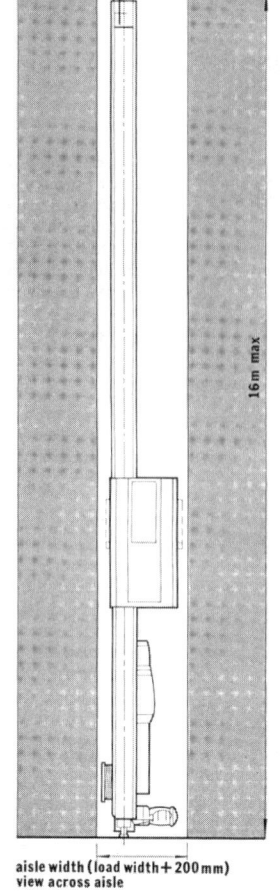

Building needs

4.06 Three-phase power. Bus bar or Festoon cable.

Prices

4.07 Generally expensive.

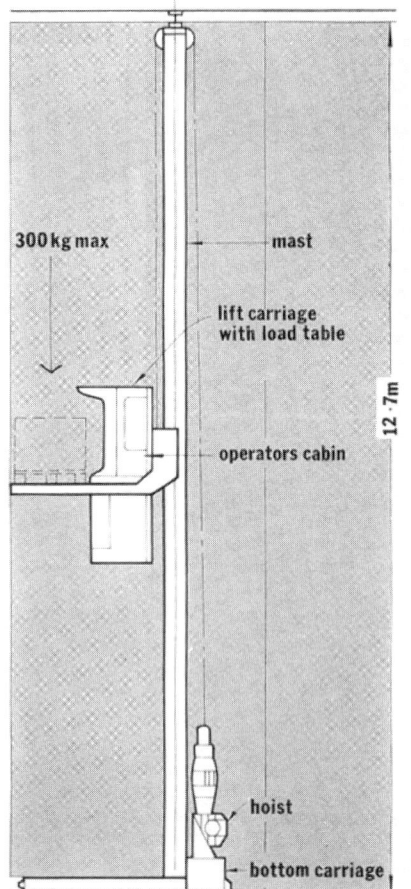

Figure 4.156 *(a) Typical single mast stacker crane viewed (left) parallel to aisle and (right) across aisle (racks shaded). (b) Order picker viewed parallel to aisle.*

Mechanized storage – fixed-path handling equipment

Figure 4.158 *Fixed-path order picker in 950 mm wide aisle used here with tote boxes.*

Figure 4.159 *Fixed-path order pickers used for a spares storage picking system.*

5 Gantry cranes

Uses and limitations

5.01 Lifting and carrying of non-palletized loads or containers (Figures 4.160–4.162). Allows dense use of floor space. Lacks flexibility; cannot pass or store in racks without transfer carriage. Can be remote-controlled, or controlled by cable, as well as from integral cab. Can be used for pallets with special fork attachment but is not as effective as a forklift. This is a useful piece of plant in a large loading bay, especially if there are non-standard loads, such as large crates too big for standard fork trucks.

Figure 4.160 *Gantry crane using special stillages for storing pipes on for tree racking.*

Size and capacity

5.02 Depending on application. Small, low-cost versions are available for loading and maintenance bays.

Space requirements

5.03 Clear height required over stacking height for beam and lift carriage and hoist machinery. Types are offered with over- or under-slung hoist and carriage equipment.

Building needs

5.04 Three-phase supply. Support is needed from building structure.

Prices

5.05 Vary considerably, based on size and capacity. Typical 15 m span/2 tonne with pendant control would cost £10 000 plus.

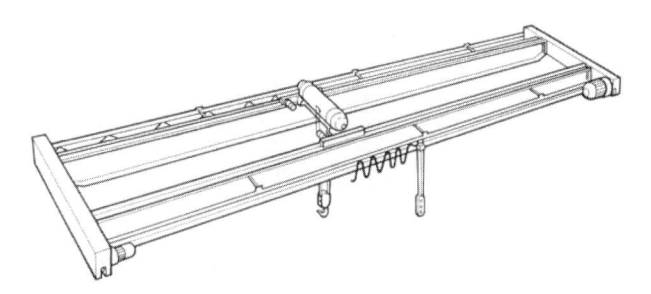

Figure 4.161 *Double girder overhead gantry crane.*

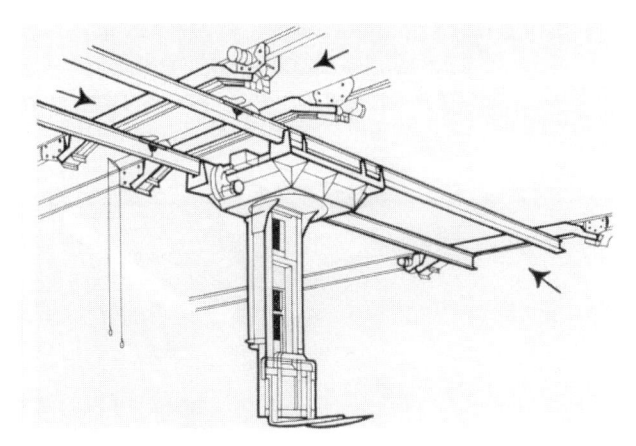

Figure 4.162 *Gantry-slung stacker crane showing transfer mechanism and rotating stacker carriage with forks.*

171

Information sheet

Mechanized storage 13

Towline conveyors

1 Use

2 Components

This sheet describes components of towline conveyors.

1 Use

1.01 Conveyors are described in Technical study, Mechanized storage 1, paras 18.02 to 18.10.

Definition

1.02 A towline conveyor is an endless chain running in an overhead track or channel in the floor with means for towing floor supported trucks, dollies or carts. These units can provide both a transport and linear sorting function.

1.03 Towline carts are ideal for large groupage depots and parcels sorting. A new use is 'U'-framed tow carts which each carry up to four roll-pallets between racking and load-accumulation zone. They also carry nested empty roll pallets out of the loading bay area.

Figure 4.163 Simple pushing cart.

Figure 4.164 Cart fitted with accumulation bumper, and selective route control (shown ABCD).

2 Components

Towline carts

2.01 There are three main types:
- Pushing cart. Most frequently used, non-powered spurs, i.e. sidings, rigid steel bumpers (Figure 4.163).
- Cart fitted with accumulation bumpers. When pressed, the bumper raises the pin, releasing it from the chain (Figure 4.164).
- Carts with dual push and accumulation bumpers. This is the most sophisticated form. Sliding bumpers lock a dog on the chain so that other carts cannot approach (Figure 4.165).

Carts should have a minimum length-to-width ratio of 1.25:1, preferably 1.5:1 for stability when being pushed off into spurs. 203 x 51 mm castors in a low friction material are best for towline operation.

2.02 Carts are seldom used for loads of more than 1400 kg, but 3000 kg are possible. Speeds of over 24 m/min are seldom required. With tow chains, fast speeds lead to accelerated wear and increased maintenance. A typical high speed, heavyweight cart system, 2700 kg carts moving at 36 m/min at 3.6 m centres, requires substantial deceleration cushioning (2700 kg at 36 m/min generates 230 kg kinetic energy).

Conveyor chain

2.03 The most common chain is the low profile type, with a forged chain sliding in steel trough section (Figure 4.165). Drive chains work on the caterpillar principle; special chains are used for contaminated and very dirty areas.

Straight track

2.04 The most common type has a track in the floor which is usually 75 mm deep formed from mild steel channel (Figure 4.166). There are several installation procedures; the general contractor can leave an open trench in the floor surface, the specialist installation subcontractor fixes the channels, and the contractor then grouts round. Tracks are usually fixed at 1.5 m centres. Care must be taken with floor finishes, as break-up round joints is possible. A possibly more acceptable method is to have a base slab laid by the general contractor, and the channels then aligned and fixed with shot bolts. The final 90 to 115 mm finish can thus be laid monolithically, but care should be taken over vibration. For installation in previously jointless floor finishes, the trench can be saw-cut and the channels fixed by epoxy-cement two-part glue. This applies only to straight track, and is useful in not disturbing previously laid jointless finishes. Overhead tracks are vulnerable to forklift damage, and trucks are less

Mechanized storage – towline conveyors

Figure 4.165 *Section through floor showing cart attached to chain.*

stable than with floor chains. Drag method is by chain sling and rigid hook, tow ring, or two-piece nylon strap and adapter; the most sophisticated method is a rigid mast fixed to the towing shoe, with a shock absorbing bumper/stop. If products are likely to be damaged by falling lubricating oil, a guard should be fitted.

Drive units

2.05 Separate drives for loops are preferred, because if there is a jam on a spur it only stalls one small motor, not the whole system. For big chains, 11 kW is a typical motor size. Motors should be positioned at least 6 m away from bends; on multiple drive systems, motors should be located so that they will share identical loads if possible, unless deliberately of different powers, for example owing to a space constriction for the motor size. Motors can be positioned plus or minus 30 m from each other, as the chain helps to equalize the power. Drives should be placed at the base of ramps, minimizing chain pull, and lengthening chain life. A powered spur drive should be placed at the end of a spur. A transfer drive is always located at the merge end of the conveyor. For power calculations, add up the working load; 25 per cent is chain friction, 2 per cent is cart rolling resistance. Divide the total load by the working load to find the number of drive units.

Horizontal turns

2.06 Direction is changed by running the chain over rollers; the rollers, with ball bearings top and bottom, can be sealed for life. A 1.8 m radius is usual, but 1.5 m is possible in certain situations.

Vertical turns

2.07 30.4 m radius bends are the maximum for normal chain operation.

Chain removal and cleaning section

2.08 These should be placed approximately 6 m beyond each main line drive unit. Maximum intervals should be at 90 to 150 m throughout the system, also at the top and bottom of ramps.

Track expansion joints

2.09 These should only be run at 90° to the direction of the floor expansion joint. If not at 90°, there is a chance of chain pinching.

Non-powered spurs

2.10 Load speed is critical. Unpowered spurs should not generally exceed five carts deep with 450 kg loads; larger spurs are possible if speeds are 18 m/min or slower, or if carts are empty. With gravity spurs, involving gentle slopes, a good standard of concreting is essential. In warehousing, carts are generally pulled off these spurs for order picking (Figure 4.167). Non-powered spur intersections should not be positioned less than a cart length plus a cart width apart, in order that one cart will not push two others into two spurs at once. After a bend, a spur should not start less than four cart lengths beyond the tangent line of 90° bend, or 4 1/2 times after 180° bend.

Powered spurs

2.11 Carts should never be planned to accumulate on powered spurs. Powered spurs are generally used with accumulator carts, where shunt shocks cannot be tolerated. 30 m/min should not be exceeded for powered spurs.

Ramps

2.12 All ramps involve custom engineering; rises should be a maximum of 17.6 per cent, preferably 10 per cent. Vertical bends have removable cover plates, where flat runs have welded plates. Great care should be exercised with towline ramps, as a runaway cart can do a great deal of damage, and injure personnel; warning signs should be placed at top and bottom. At the top of 'down' ramps, a pushed-cart detector is required with a limit switch at about 10 m from the start of the ramp, based on speed and gap between carts. If a cart shunts another on the slope, the fault will show on a panel, and the circuit will shut down.

Automatic accumulation stops

2.13 Blocks rise out of the floor to catch the cart's bumper and so slip the pin from the drag dog. These can be automatically controlled, or by a switch operated by a forklift driver, for example, who wants to cross a busy track. When a spur is full, the leading cart will trip a switch, protecting the entrance to the spur, diverting

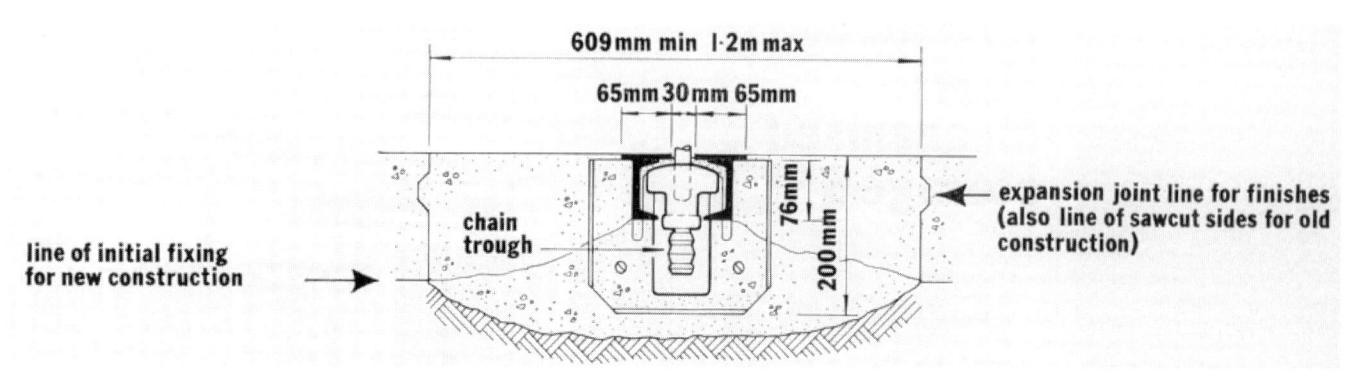

Figure 4.166 *Typical construction for installation of towline track.*

Mechanized storage – towline conveyors

other carts away. There are four ways to accumulate carts. The tow pin can be moved up or sideways, or the tow chain can be moved across or down with overhead drag units, pin withdrawal or trip is effective. Carts can congest if planned to accumulate on bends of more than 10°.

Direction controls

2.14 Pins with simple 10-unit selection, which meets a tab in the floor, releasing the drag pin, or also dropping an auxiliary pin into a spur slot (see Figures 4.164, 4.165 and 4.168). Sensing fingers that are activated by the cart's draw pin, coinciding with sensing pins on the cart that operate a power switch or slip the dog, resetting when the cart has passed. Carts can be electrically diverted, by photo-electric sensors reading a bar code, or radio control. Towlines can also work with automatic car lifts.

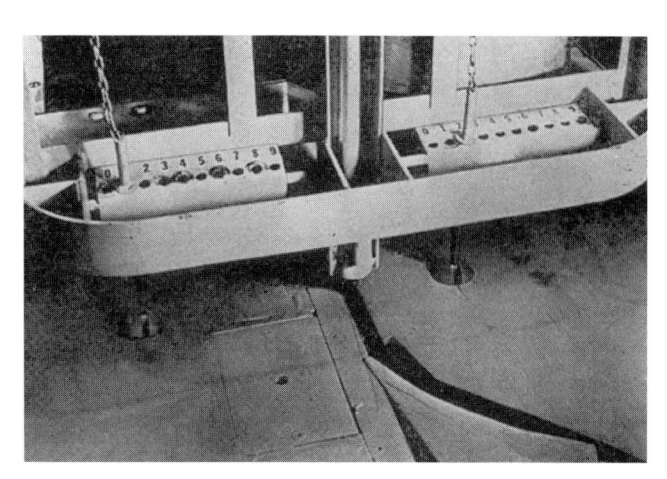

Figure 4.168 *Close-up of typical junction.*

(a)

(b)

Figure 4.167 *(a) Switchcart loops feeding reach truck (left) another switchcart is waiting to be unloaded in loop. (b) 90° spur (right) joining a main route.*

INFORMATION SHEET

Mechanized storage 14

Conveyors for warehouse use

1 Use

2 Roller conveyors

3 Belt conveyors

4 Plate and slat conveyos

5 Pneumatic conveyors

6 Overhead conveyors

7 Sorting conveyors

8 Pallet conveyors

These include roller, belt, plate, overhead, pneumatic and sorting conveyors.

1 Use

1.01 Conveyors are ideal for transport and sorting of many goods. They are not cheap, but in overall cost for order picking, inter-zone transport and sorting, load assembly and packing, they are economic for heavier and faster duties. Small, low-cost, portable conveyors are very useful in loading bays, especially for groupage operations. (See Technical study, Mechanized storage 1).

Limitations

1.02 All conveyors form a barrier to other movement, although they can be routed over obstructions and combined with elevator/lowerators for major level changes.

1.03 Conveyors can also feed palletizing plant, shrink-wrap tunnels and banding machines. The possibility of automatic accumulation, diversion and sorting makes a conveyor system more attractive than several forklifts shuttling at high speed, or towline trains which load and unload mechanically. However, the scale, speed and flexibility of the operation should be carefully assessed before deciding to fit a large conveyor system. In some installations, a great deal of money has been spent on complex conveyor sorting and transport systems which are working to only a third of their capacity even in peak periods. £350 per metre run is a high price to pay for idle plant.

2 Roller conveyors

2.01 Roller conveyors are the most widely used for warehouse duties. Powered (Figure 4.170) or gravity operated, they are the cheapest form of conveyor, and can be obtained in a wide range of configurations to suit the type of goods being handled, from full pallets to small cartons.

2.02 Before deciding on a roller type, the characteristics of the package should be examined. Rollers are not suitable for goods that deform easily. Roller pitch should be calculated to support the package smoothly at all times, without risk of snagging and continuous vibration.

Figure 4.170 *Powered roller conveyor.*

BS 2567 provides useful guidelines for non-powered roller conveyors. It suggests that under any rigid, flat-based object there should be a minimum of three-roller contact. Flexible loads, such as thin cardboard cartons, may need reduced roller pitch, or require a wheeled conveyor to prevent sagging. Rigid, flat-based loads can be carried on rollers narrower than the load, but flexible packages require rollers to be wider than the load. The possible distortion of loads on bends often determines the minimum roller width. The minimum pitch on straight track depends on the diameter of the roller used; six pitches are suggested by BS 2567: 38, 50, 75, 100, 150 and 200 mm. Pitch may be reduced at loading points to accommodate shock loads. Curved track is available in multiples of 30°, 45°, 60° and 90°. The radius of the curve is measured to the inside face of the inner frame rail, and Table 4.15 shows roller diameters and curves for parallel rollers.

2.03 Special sections (see Figure 4.171) include switch sections, butterfly junctions, turnovers and turntables, hinged gates and transfer cars. Some accessories require manual assistance or a mechanical diverter.

Size and capacity

2.04 Roller conveyors are usually formed in standard 2.43 m sections, with a range of widths including 304,

Mechanized storage – conveyors for warehouse use

308, 460, 700, 760, 970, 1120 and 1270 mm (the last three suitable for pallets). Allow 75 mm minimum over dimension of rollers for total width (more if powered) (Figure 4.172).

2.05 The following data should be considered when choosing roller type, surface and bearings:
1 Maximum and minimum size of load.
2 Maximum and minimum weights.
3 Particulars of package surface if not rigid or flat.
4 Special operating conditions, e.g. from chilled storage.
5 Whether fixed or adjustable supports are required.
6 Maximum accumulating load per 2.5 or 3 m run.
7 Conditions of loading: batching or single units.
8 Whether there will be impact shocks (locally or continuously).
9 Clearance heights and design restrictions.

Table 4.15 Roller diameters and curves for parallel rollers

Roller diameter (mm)	Radius of curve (mm)
25.4	630/800
38.0	630/800
51.0	800/1000
63.5	800/1000
76.1	800/1000
88.9	1250

Equipment design

2.06 Rollers can be steel or plastic, depending on required performance. Surface textures can be used for slopes with powered rollers. The frames are normally of angle or channel sections (Figure 4.173) supported at centres to suit conveyor weight and load, and the floor surface. Roller bearings are normally semi-precision ballraces or nylon bushes. Flexible supports can increase the slope of gravity rollers or alter the height of a flat section to help manual picking. Wheeled supports with retracting conveyor sections are useful in loading bays. Flexible versions that can follow a variable, curved path round obstacles are also marketed.

2.07 For non-powered rollers, gradients of 2–5 per cent are normal, but can be as low as $\frac{1}{2}$ per cent depending on load, roller surface and bearing, and length of travel. Powered rollers can move goods up gradients and allow selective accumulation. Sometimes this is cheaper with short sections of belt conveyor (which can also boost long unpowered roller sections). In most large warehouses, powered rollers achieve a measure of individual section control (only possible with belts by using over-belt equipment, whereas with roller systems, diverter gear and accumulation sensors can be mounted within the pitch).

2.08 Rollers are driven by a flat belt, or a vee belt running beneath the rollers and tensioned to press against them; this method is considered best for long runs (Figure 4.174a). More expensive are chain and shaft drives, which (linked with dog clutches and sensors) allow accumulation and sorting (Figure 4.174b). Special chain and shaft drives are used for powered curves. Other variations include roller sections with power brakes with progressive deceleration for fragile loads.

2.09 There are two types of accumulator roller conveyors:
1 A combination of chain and roller conveyor (Figures 4.175 and 4.176). A continuous set of rollers are chain

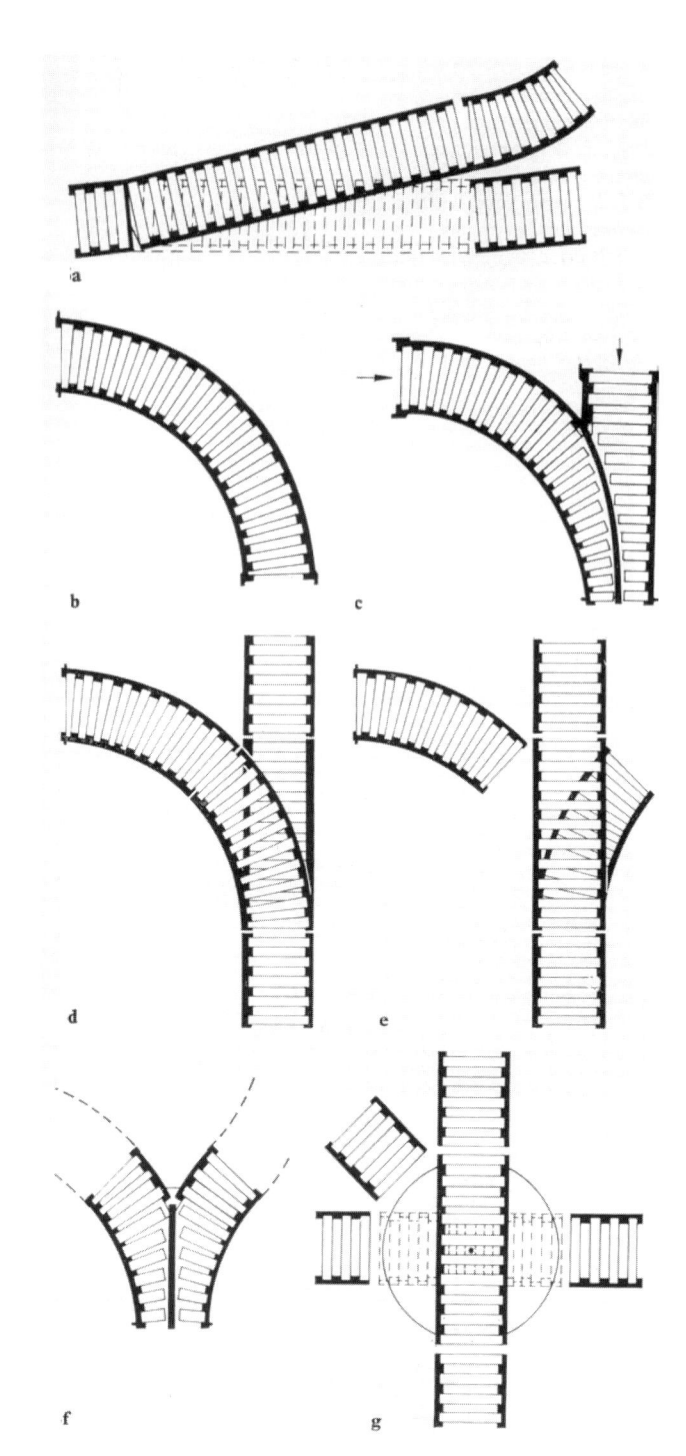

Figure 4.171 *Flow patterns. (a) Switch section. (b) 90° degree bend. (c) Turn out junction. (d) Turnover junction. (e) Butterfly junction. (f) Turntable.*

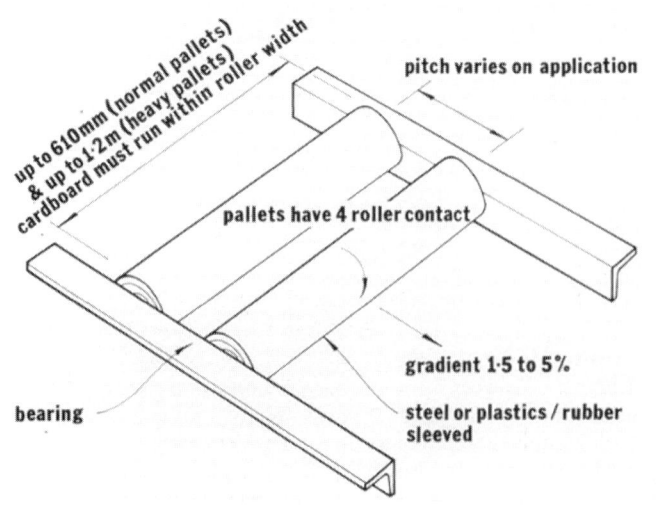

Figure 4.172 *Anatomy of roller conveyor.*

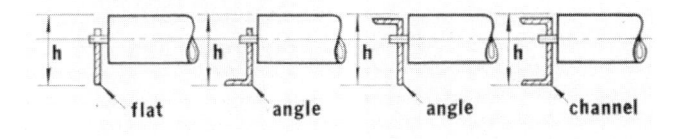

Mechanized storage – conveyors for warehouse use

Figure 4.173 *Typical arrangements of frame members.*

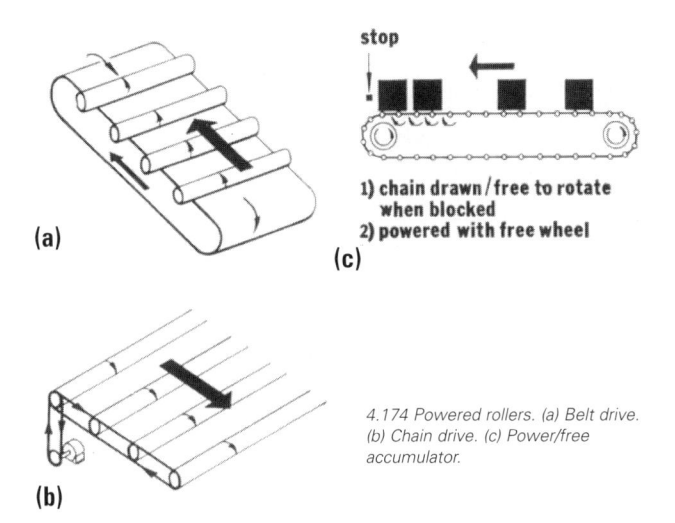

4.174 *Powered rollers. (a) Belt drive. (b) Chain drive. (c) Power/free accumulator.*

drawn, yet are free to rotate under a load when it comes up against a spacer bar (Figure 4.174c).

2 Powered rollers with sensor devices that automatically remove the drive from the rollers. A typical system drops the roller that tensions the belt under the carriage rollers pneumatically, and this can be arranged for as many pallet lengths as the accumulation requires. This is the most usual type of accumulator.

2.10 Combinations of powered and free rollers, with spurs and cambered curves, down-grade brakes and accumulation sections are a versatile method of high-speed sorting and bulk transport in warehouses and groupage areas handling large quantities of cartons. Curve and accumulator speeds of up to 30 m/min are normal, with the ability to move at 60 m/min on long, straight sections.

Wheel conveyors

2.11 These are a variation of roller conveyors, with overlapping wheels to support packages with soft or irregular bases. They can be curved, powered, and are often used as diverters, being pushed up between the pitch of rollers when the package activates a sensor. Free caster or fixed angle diverter actions are available.

2.12 Combinations of roller and belt conveyors are also available (Figures 4.177 and 4.178). Extendible portable conveyors are useful for stuffing containers (Figure 4.178 and 4.179).

3 Belt conveyors

3.01 See also Information sheet, Bulk storage 1, on belt and slat conveyors, and Technical study, Mechanized storage 1, para. 16.

Uses and limitations

3.02 Belt conveyors are normally used in warehouses, for long straight inclines and flat sections (Figure 4.180a–d), where roller accumulation is not required, and where layout requires movement by power rather than gravity. Suitable for high throughputs, belt conveyors are often part of a larger conveyor system of rollers and accumulation equipment (Figures 4.177 and 4.181). Belt

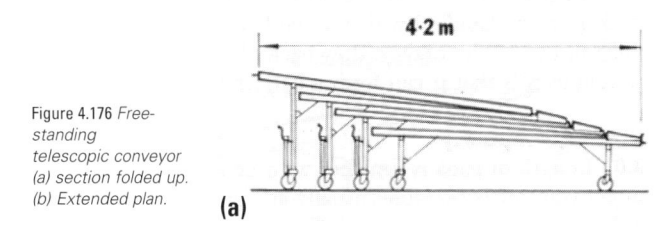

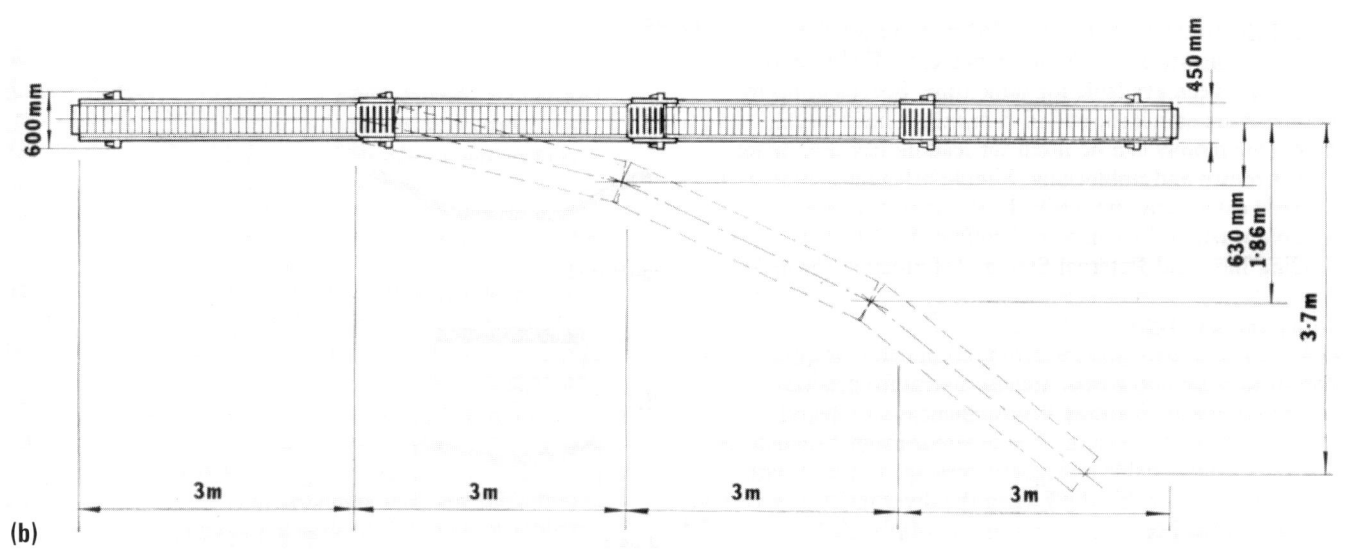

Figure 4.175 *Combinations of powered and free conveyors in factory.*

Figure 4.176 *Free-standing telescopic conveyor (a) section folded up. (b) Extended plan.*

Mechanized storage – conveyors for warehouse use

conveyors are particularly suited for use with small packages, and for loads with uneven or soft bases. Belts are capable of close radius bends at a wide range of angles (Figure 4.180e), and are efficient for incline work for general goods. A wide range of covers are available including plastic, e.g. neoprene for food stuffs, polytetrafluoroethylene (ptfe) for easy tilt sorting, and rough surfaces for steep inclines. Check the friction characteristics of goods to be carried before choosing the incline surface, as some covers are ideally suited to certain loads. On normal belts, inclines are limited to 18°, but this can be increased to 35° by using a cleated belt, to 40° with rough rubber or a chevron pattern, and for certain products up to 70° with integral cross-bars. Check whether the type of package to be handled will stay stable on certain slopes and not roll back. The biggest drawback of any conveyor in warehouses is that it can form a barrier for other movement.

Figure 4.177 *Combination of belt and roller conveyor.*

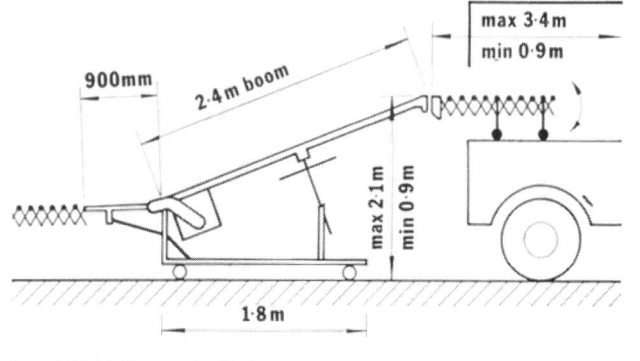

Figure 4.178 *Mobile motorized belt.*

Figure 4.179 *Extendible roller conveyor 'stuffing' truck.*

Size and capacity

3.03 Length of runs is limitless with booster motors, and direct transfer is possible (usually at right angles) to another belt. Selective sorting can be effected by tilt or inclined belts. Belt widths of 30, 750, 900 mm and 1 m are usually available from stock, in 75 mm increments. Fully metric belting has been available for some time. Speeds of up to 60 m/min are standard, but 30 m/min is more usual. Reversible motors can be fitted for loading bay use, or for sorting return and unblocking. Simple belt units, some with powered extensions, are available at low cost, as are portable versions for container 'stuffing' (Figures 4.178 and 4.182). (See Loading and External storage information sheets.)

Equipment design

3.04 Steel band conveyors, widely used in cold store and food processing operations, are also useful for general warehouse duties. A recent development is an integral system of magnetic sorting. The inherent magnetic qualities of steel banding enable a magnetic message, which is rubbed off when the diverting mechanism has been activated, to travel with the goods.

3.05 Slat conveyors operate on the belt principle, and are normally used for heavy duty work. Some accept wheeled plant over them; slat inclines are limited to 15–18° angles, unless back rest plates are fitted. Slat conveyors can carry full pallets, where their advantages of rigidity and of a solid surface between idler and power rollers and the load is best used (Figure 4.183b).

3.06 Plate link belting is increasingly used for the approach lines to packaging and small-scale shrink wrap machines. They are also used for example, in re-packaging after order picking to place the goods in a different 'outer', and in shrink wrapping small parts into more convenient retail units. Available in plastic or metal, plate link belting can be obtained in most sizes, from 25 mm for pharmaceuticals, to 1250 mm for full pallets.

Building needs

3.07 Overall belt widths are normally 102 mm to 150 mm greater than the moving surface itself. Motors are usually placed underneath, running on a standard three-phase power supply. Space should be provided for motor access. At least 1.2 m should be left between parallel belt runs. On some models designed for manual picking, the supporting legs are adjustable for operators' convenience. Prices: these vary considerably, depending on duty, size, belt materials, frame and motors.

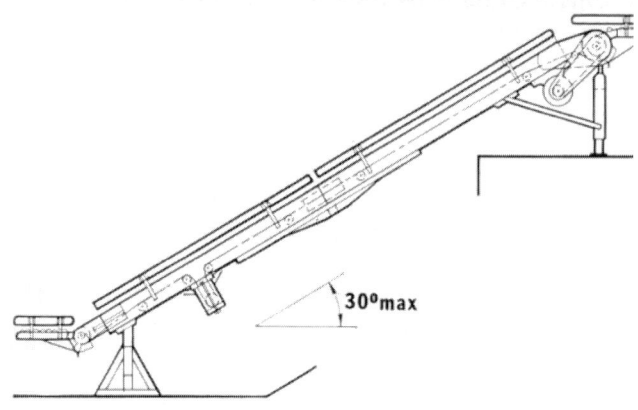

Mechanized storage – conveyors for warehouse use

Figure 4.181 *Typical inclined belt conveyors as used from order picking mezzanine levels to feed a sorter.*

4 Plate and slat conveyors

Uses and limitations

4.01 These are for heavy-duty use, often flush with the floor. They could be considered as a combination of conveyor belt and tow carts, being made of continuous overlapping plates, but are mounted on a track with rails and roller guides. Plate conveyors are less limiting to circulation than normal conveyors, and can be driven over by wheeled plant (check with the manufacturer what wheel loadings are acceptable). Plate conveyors need not be set in the floor (Figure 4.184), but can be mounted in the conventional manner. Normal uses include parcels and baggage sorting (Figures 4.185 and 4.186), but they are also used for heavy-duty goods such as paper reels and steel coils.

Sizes and capacity

4.02 Typical widths range from 400, 500, 600, 800, 1000 to 1200 mm. For standard use, loads of up to 14 kN/m run are acceptable, but heavier duty versions are available for casks, barrels and heavy components. Maximum speeds are up to 100 m/min, although for use flush with the floor they tend to be slower.

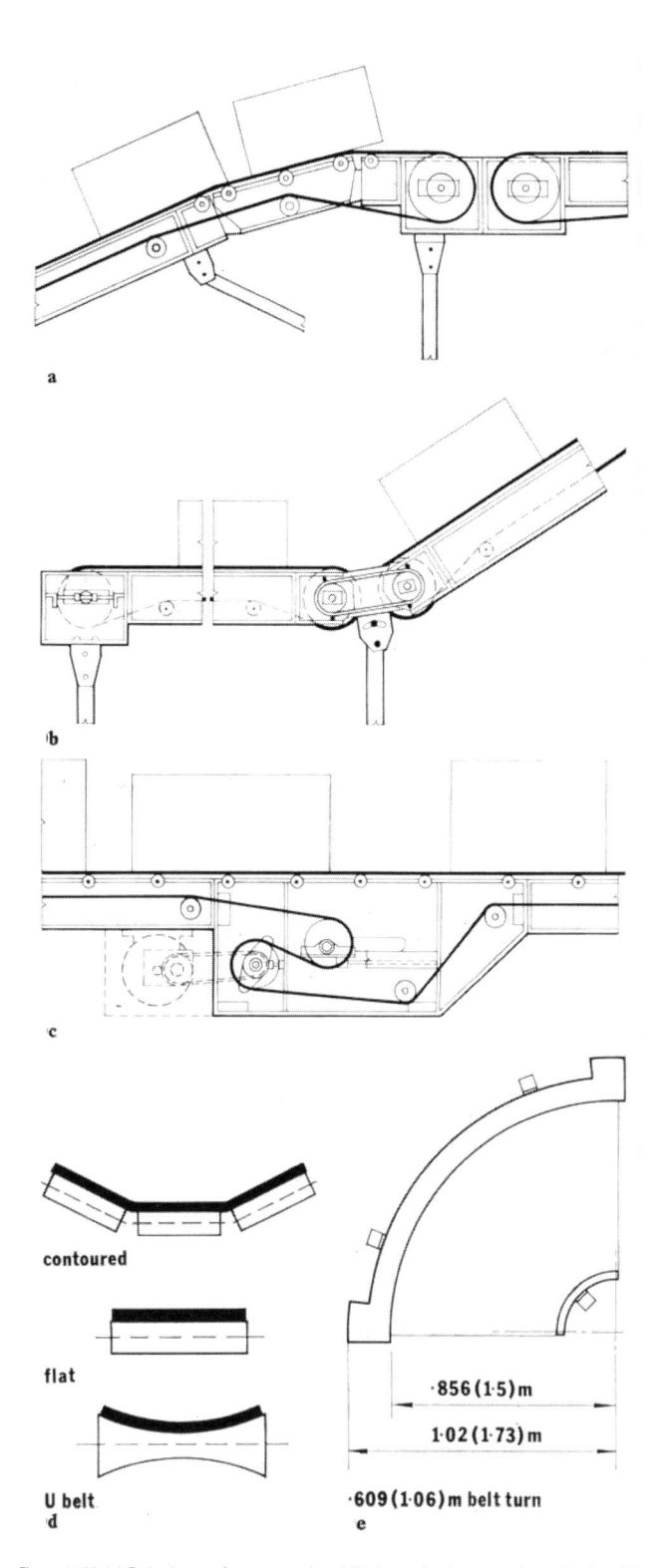

Figure 4.180 *(a) Belt change from upper level. Link section lessens abrupt incline. (b) Belt change from flat to inclined run (adjustable). (c) Belt drive and tension units. (d) Types of belt cross-section. (e) Belt powered bend dimensions for 609 mm wide belt (bracketed figures for 1.06 m wide belt).*

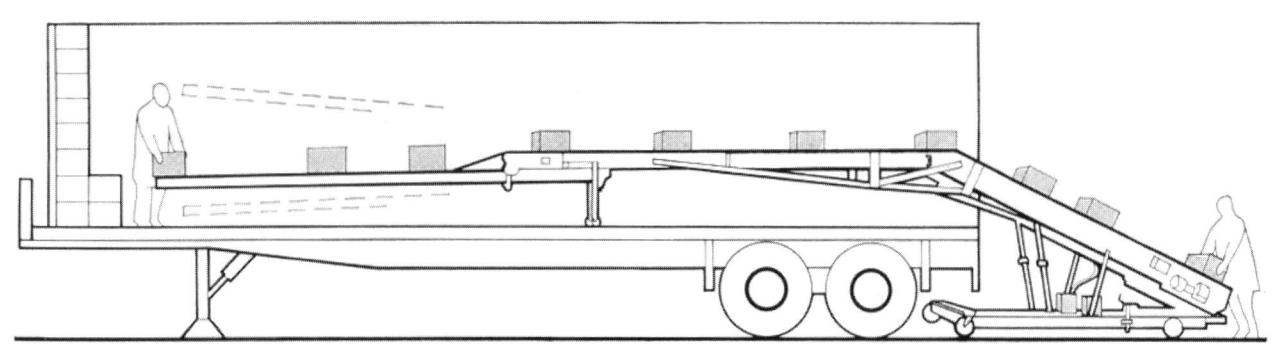

Figure 4.182 *Extendible portable belt unit loading a container conveyor (carousel) as used in airports.*

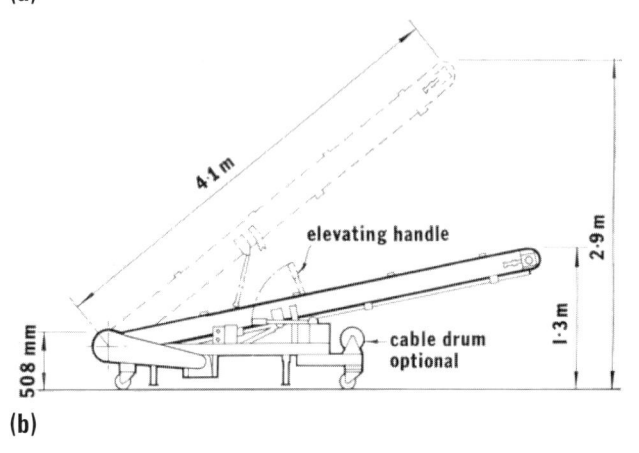

Mechanized storage – conveyors for warehouse use

Figure 4.183 (a) Dock belt conveyor, which extends, rotates and elevates for loading sacks. (b) Mobile slat conveyor.

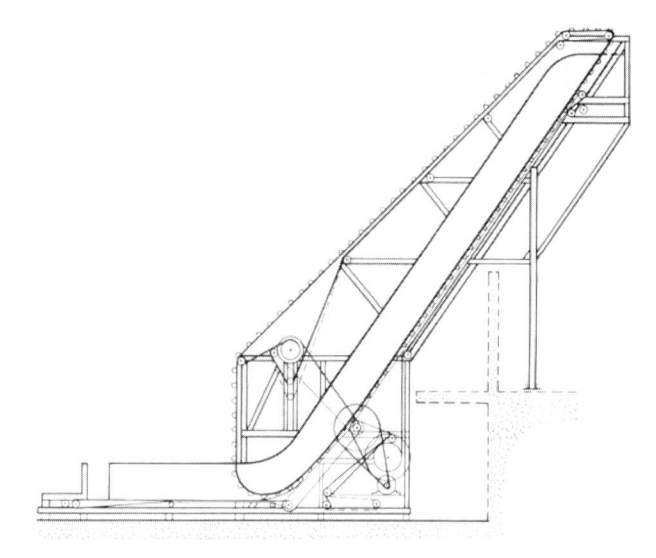

Figure 4.184 Steep incline conveyor Packages are sandwiched between lower and upper corrugated and weighted belt.

Equipment design

4.03 Plate or slat conveyors are powered by a drag chain, with metal or plastic rollers set in a channel. A typical chain is 5 mm thick, with links at 203 mm pitch. One system employs guide wheels on all four faces of the chain for reduced wear and increased stability. Some are now powered by linear induction drives, reducing noise and wear. Horizontal bends are available at 5°, 10°, 20°, 30°, 45°, 60°, 90° and 180°, with standard radii of 750 and 1200 mm. Vertical ramp bends are available at 5°, 10°, 15°, 20°, 30°, 45°, with 750 mm and 1200 mm radii. The plates or scales are bolted to the drag chain, overlapping each other. Plate material is steel, plastic or rubber, depending on the duty required, and can be supplied with a non-skid surface for inclines and plant crossings. Motors are underneath the belt for raised operation, or in pits as with towline conveyors, when a sunken unit is installed. Some plate conveyors can be supplied with tipping plates, so that they can act as a tilt-tray sorting unit as well, or can be tilted en masse, as in tilt belt operation.

Building needs

4.04 If set in the floor, a special pit must be cast with the floor to accept conveyor and motors. Steel edge plates are cast in, and concrete must be laid to fine tolerances. Over the floor, standard supports are used. Typical chain and track weigh about 18.5 kg/m run, although heavier-duty models weigh more and require a heavier support structure. Check with the manufacturer what the point loads on the floor are likely to be. Power is by a three-phase electrical supply. This machine can be very flexible, being able to change direction quickly through its track and carriage design in either the horizontal or vertical planes. If set in the floor, this becomes less easy.

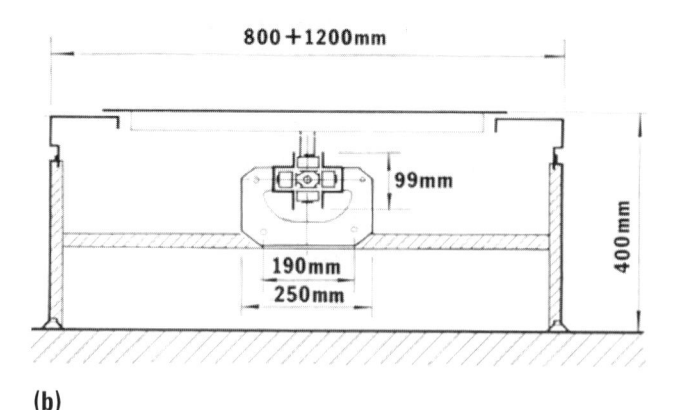

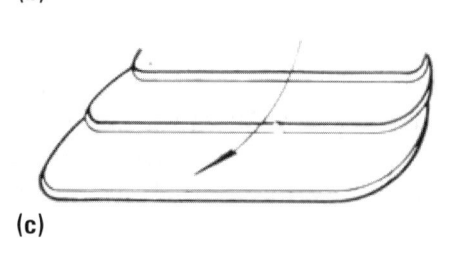

Figure 4.185 (a) Plate conveyor turns into tilt tray sorter: here with simple mechanical induction device; (b) section; (c) overlapping scales.

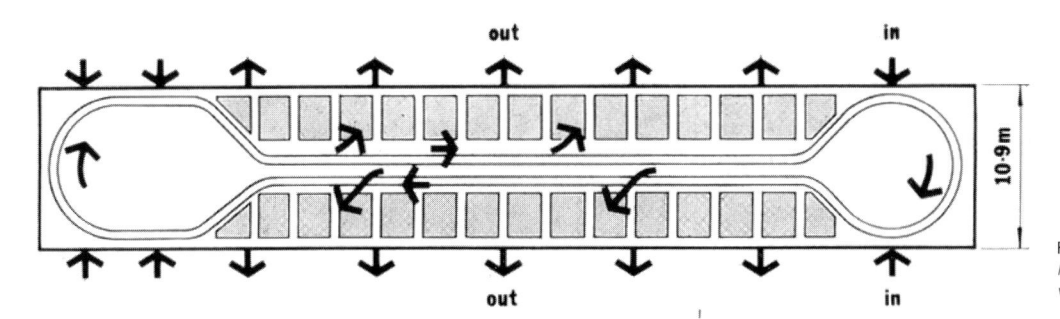

Figure 4.186 *Plate conveyor circuit in loading bay, sorting parcels from trunk vehicles to local delivery vehicles.*

5 Pneumatic conveyors

Uses and limitations

5.01 Airfilm conveyors are a specialized form of warehouse transport, but may increasingly be used in the future. The hovercraft principle is used in reverse, in that the package rides on the air blast, and the conveyor itself has no moving parts. Present airfilm conveyors are mainly for light, small packages, where there are straight runs, and comparatively narrow tracks. They are basically long air tables, with surface openings that give direction as well as lift (Figure 4.187 and 4.188). Large numbers of packages can move fast and easily, but air wastage is a serious limitation.

5.02 One system (Figure 4.189) has been suggested which incorporates an air conveyor and plastic ptfe ball valves with a very low coefficient of friction, which contain the air until the pallet depresses the ball valve, liberating a directional air jet supplying lift, and sufficient forward motion to overcome any friction from the valves. Pallets used in the system must have flat, single piece floors or base boards (plastic pallets would work well).

5.03 Air-supported tracked conveyors are based on articulated hollow plates with air fed vertically and horizontally through shaped outlets (Figure 4.190 and 4.191). With nozzles of the correct shape, efficiencies of 80 per cent are possible. Friction is negligible, and speed control is by adjusting air pressure. The only moving parts on the conveyor bed are idler wheels at the turn points. Air pallets work on similar principles (Figure 4.192). A great deal of work has been done on air cushion handling technology recently, and full-scale commercial systems will soon be available.

Building needs

5.04 These are limited to the air compressor requirements and a standard conveyor base.

5.05 Helical conveyors are used to transport containers such as bottles and aerosols at high speeds with stability. Triple helical worms can handle such inherently unstable units as plastic containers and are very useful for supplying palletizers. The worms are often machined from plastic, matched exactly to the shape of the containers to be handled.

6 Overhead conveyors

Uses and limitations

6.01 These conveyors keep goods off the floor, clearing it for the use of wheeled plant. But overhead tracks can constrict forklift trucks. Overhead conveyors cannot be altered or moved easily if requirements change. Where headroom is limited, this conveyor will obstruct wheeled plant and personnel unless the chain speed is slow. With their ability to queue, rise vertically as lifts, and be routed

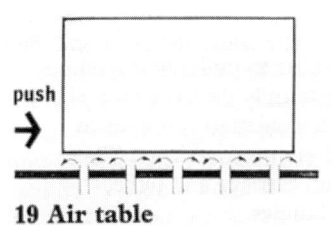

19 Air table

Figure 4.187 *Air table. The package moves over the surface of a hollow chamber full of compressed air. Air escapes through holes in surface. Goods can be moved with 1/1000th of power required to lift them. Can take several hundred kgs distributed weight.*

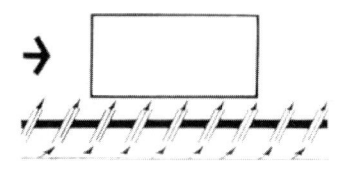

Figure 4.188 *Air conveyor. Basically a long and narrow air table. Angled airflow mean that goods are propelled as well as lifted. Used to transport high volume/low weight goods at high speeds. Very suitable for packages on the way to palletizer from order picker.*

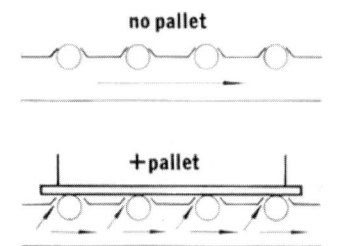

Figure 4.189 *Air in the floor. Same as 'air table' except that holes in surface equipped with ballcheck valves, so that air only escapes when load is over area. Load also partly supported on balls. The system is more economical for large surface areas and heavy loads.*

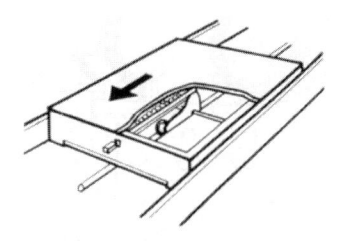

Figure 4.190 *Air cushion. For use in live storage racking or buffer storage. Seal increases directional air supply to pallet if load increased, and is cut off when pallet stops. Speed controlled by degrees of pressure of wheel on seal.*

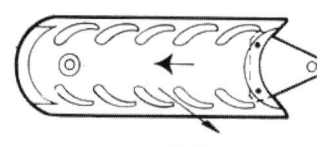

Figure 4.191 *Air supported/tracked conveyor. Plan view of undersurface of one link. Articulated hollow units linked together at each end, with air fed vertically and horizontally into the linked units to give lift and direction. Shape of escape outlets gives extra thrust.*

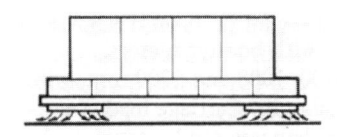

Figure 4.192 *Air pallet. Must have flat floor. Pallet rests on hollow pad with perforated membrane escapes through membrane perforations, round the circumference of disc and supplies lift. Air supply is either flexible line or integral blower.*

Mechanized storage – conveyors for warehouse use

Figure 4.193 *Monorail conveyor used between automated warehouse and order picking area: each carrier is individually powered and can run at 1.8 m per second.*

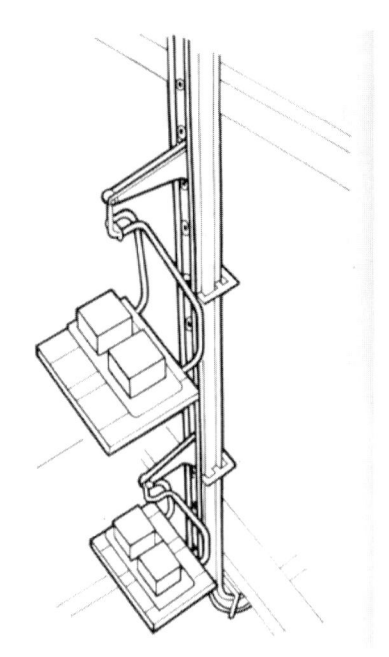

Figure 4.195 *Chain conveyor used as vertical lift.*

(a)

(b)

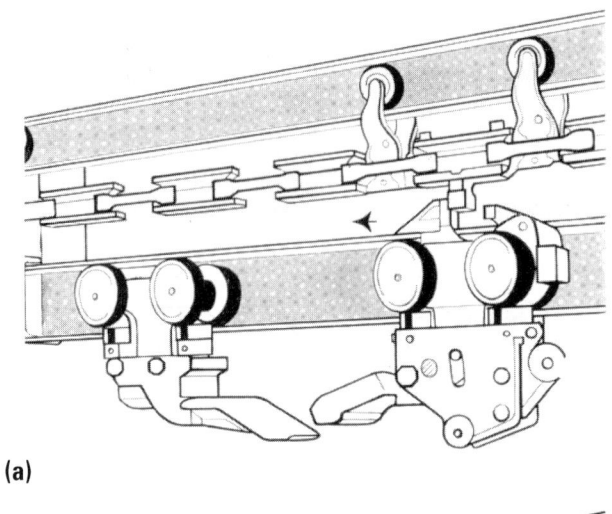

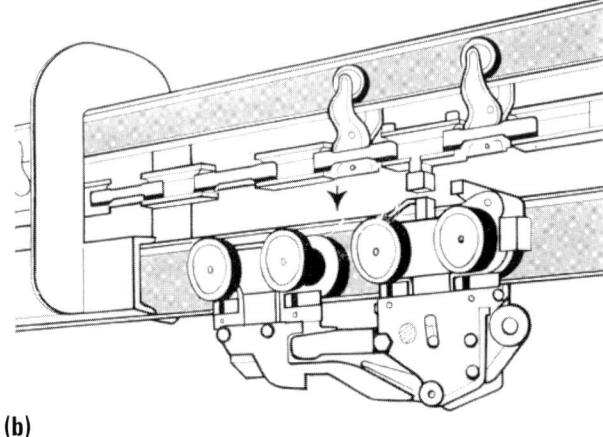

Figure 4.194 *(a) Overhead support carriage approaching already accumulated carriage. (b) The lug of the support carriage locks into the accumulated carriage ramp, releasing the pin from the chain.*

around structural obstructions, these conveyors can be used very successfully in warehouse operations.

Sizes and capacities

6.02 Chain lengths are limitless, with booster motors. Standard bends are usually 700, 1000 and 1700 mm, with the capability of 900 mm vertical radii. Carriage loads vary from 150 to 1000 kg per hanger; hangers can be connected for heavier loads. Speeds range to 0.45 m/sec. With individually powered monorail carriers there are no chain drives: speeds can be up to 1.8 m per second (Figure 4.193).

Space requirements

6.03 This depends on the width of the carrier, but overhead conveyors sterilize an area at a fixed height above the floor. The system can be elevated locally to cross aisles and door positions. In some installations, an overhead conveyor is used for order picking; the gangway should be 1.5 m–1.8 m plus the width of the carrier to leave adequate clearance for the swing-in.

Equipment design

6.04 Overhead conveyors are similar to underfloor towlines in operation. They can be mechanically directed by a pin system (Figure 4.194) and be used as an accumulation conveyor or moving buffer store for full and empty containers. There are many variations of drag head, carriage and table, designed for specific speeds and duties.

6.05 Extra equipment includes automatic chain switching, controlling carriers in and out of the main line, vertical hoists that convert the track and carriage into a lift (Figure 4.195), full queueing ability, free track turntables, and it can be adapted to full on-line computer control.

Building needs

6.06 Provision is needed for track suspension from the roof, or floor. Allow for the load in structural calculations. The system should be integrated with services and sprinkler lines. Power is usually three phased, to several motor points. If an overhead system is planned, the manufacturers should supply the dead and operating weights to the structural engineer at the earliest instance.

7 Sorting conveyors

7.01 These include drive-off and push-off/plough diverters, slide-slat and tilt-tray sorters and tilt-belt conveyors, and are extensively used in item picking and sorting operations as in chilled stores and in e-commerce fulfilment centres.

Drive-off and push-off diverters

7.02 Drive-off diverters are faster than push/plough-off methods. Many are designed for high speed sorting, and are costly as they have to be engineered as part of the conveyor.

7.03 Deflectors are the least expensive type of diverting mechanism. There are two types. Fixed position or stationary arms are the least expensive, physically brushing the goods off to one side. Pivoting arms, powered by air cylinders, motors or solenoids move back and forth across the conveyor surface. Other movable arms do not swing, but move across for the package to touch, the momentum pushing it off the conveyor surface. Both types can be powered by adding a short belt to boost the deflected item, and prevent any jams at the turn point. Pop-up deflectors can only be used with roller conveyors, either gravity rollers or powered rollers and wheels.

7.04 Drive-off diverters protrude slightly above roller or wheel conveyor beds to engage the bottom of the package and carry it off the conveyor. Belts can be used if short drive-off sections are inserted between belt runs. Both push-off and drive-off diverters may be blocked by damaged packages. As a rule, speed is usually responsible for blockage. If high speed sorting of small goods is anticipated, an inclined belt is less prone to jam. The belt is laterally inclined and, as parcels move along the lower face of the conveyor, flaps open, releasing the package onto the accumulation line. Control can be manual or 'on-line'.

Slide slat conveyors or shoe sorters

7.05 These slide physically to divert packages to the correct channel. Typical speeds are 5500 packets per hour if 300 mm long, and 2000 per hour if 1.2 m long. Slide slat sections can easily be integrated with belt or slat conveyors. Typical slide slats move at 49 m/minute (Figure 4.196). Shoe sorters are similar but plastic lugs engage the load and progressively slide across the conveyor in the slots between the rollers. Speeds up to 1m/sec are possible.

Tilt tray sorters

7.06 A combination of sorter and conveyor (Figure 4.197). Unlike other systems, the carriage unit actually does the sorting at the required point on the circuit. Mechanically a tilt tray is a series of closely spaced trays, mounted between axially disposed pivots on carriages that travel around a fixed track. Each tray is held in the horizontal position by a cam plate, which locates onto a peg mounted on the carriage. The cam plate is lifted clear of the peg for tilting. Controlled either manually (with a limited memory unit) or automatically (by package codes and sensors) the movement carriage tilts at the discharge point by pneumatic or hydraulic activation. Loads of up to 70 kg can be carried, with trays at 300 mm, 460 mm, 600 mm or 900 mm centres depending on load size. If longer loads are handled, the trays can be programmed to tilt in series. Speeds of up to 2m/sec are possible although 1.5 m/sec is more stable for tip-off. Most modern tilt tray sorters are linear induction powered: no chain drive, so quiet with progressive start-up. One is powered by 'caterpillar' belts and can go up inclines with the plates horizontal. If still a drag chain,

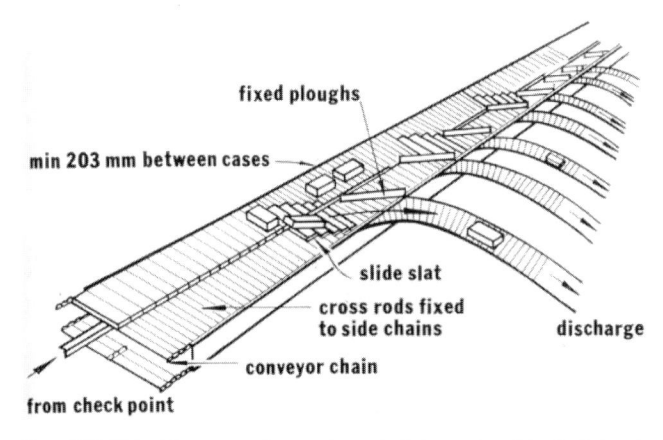

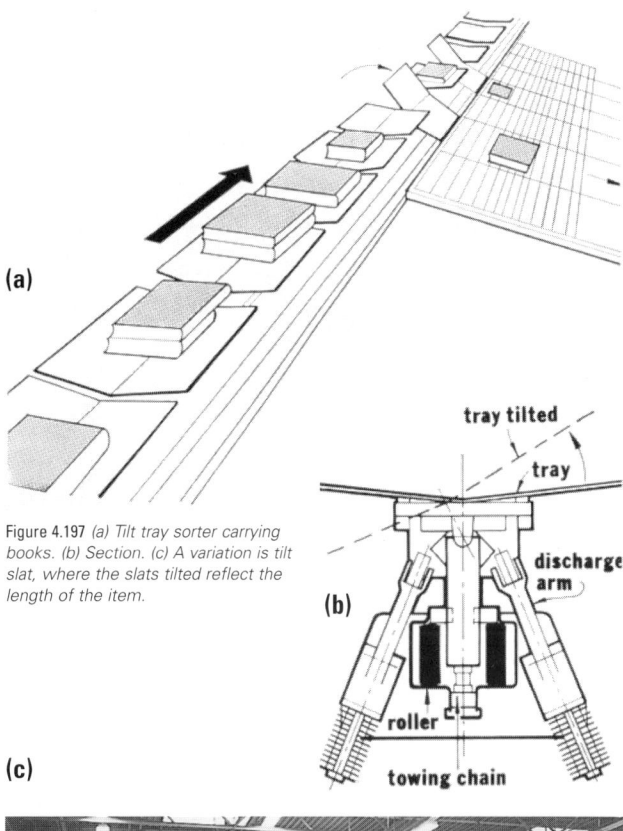

Figure 4.197 (a) Tilt tray sorter carrying books. (b) Section. (c) A variation is tilt slat, where the slats tilted reflect the length of the item.

Figure 4.196 Slide slat conveyor. A computer controlled console unit is situated next to the conveyor infeed and recognizes the number of carrying slats, and remembers their destination. As each case approaches destination, slats slide automatically to fixed plough. Slats 760 mm wide. Unit 1.5 m wide. Up to 91 m long. Minimum floor to top height plus 760 mm.

Mechanized storage – conveyors for warehouse use

Figure 4.198 A conveyor system serving a three level mezzanine storage system leading to the dispatch sorting area.

that pulls the carriages around the track is powered by a three-phase motor, from a 3.66 m diameter combined sprocket/tensioner. Motors are from 2.2–22 kW to suit the application.

7.07 Although the number of discharge stations is only limited in theory by the length of the conveyor, costs rise steeply over 125 sorting positions. Tilt trays are very efficient for high-speed sorting in warehouses involved in bulk order picking. Bulk orders can be withdrawn from live racking direct onto the tilt tray conveyor, either under manual control or fully 'on line'.

Tilt belt conveyors

7.08 These are flat belts, where the supporting rollers are mounted on a hinged axle. When a package is to be diverted, the section usually drops sharply on one side. Control and throughput tend to be similar to tilt tray units. Operation is usually single–sided as roller tilting is complex if double-sided discharge was installed. These diverters rely on regular-based packages, and a combination of belt and package material that allows immediate sliding: if friction is not quickly overcome, package and belt damage can occur (Figure 4.198).

Pallet conveyors

8.01 Pallet conveyor systems have become 'an art' in themselves. Although their use as integral feed, despatch and buffer mechanisms within automated warehouses is discussed in Chapter 5, as they can also be usefully employed within mechanized warehouses, for completeness the technical features are included in this section.

8.02 Pallet conveyors combine roller conveyors and chain conveyors, both directly supporting the timber boards of the pallet. Euro Pallets (see Mechanized Storage Information Sheet 4) have three No. 1200 mm long bottom boards (runners) in the long dimension only and so can only run on rollers in this direction. Industrial pallets, although with perimeter bottom boards all round, run better on rollers in the long (1200 mm) dimension: both pallets handle better with their shorter dimensions (800 mm and 1000 mm, respectively) across a chain conveyor (i.e. at 90° to the direction of travel) (Figure 4.199).

8.03 *Size and capacity.* Pallet conveyors have to be very robust: pallet weights of up to 2000 kg are supported, but 1500 kg is the 'normal' specification to allow for differential and out of balance loading. There is 'a kit of parts' supplied by several specialist manufacturers, which include pallet entry and transfer sections from forklifts, in-travel weighing and dimension checking, load straightening, accumulating roller and chain sections, right angle bends (either chains pop up between the rollers, or rollers lift the pallet off the chains), and transfer sections interfacing with stacker cranes or shuttle cars.

8.04 Pallet conveyors are not fast: for load stability they generally run at 0.5 m/sec. They combine electric roller and chain drives with pneumatic lifting devices for actuating direction changes. Generally mounted on frames 400–600 mm above the floor (for maintenance access), they provide a definite 'grain' across a warehouse. This is discussed in the next chapter.

8.05 *Equipment design.* The mechanical engineering of pallet conveyors, though differing in detail and quality of engineering between manufacturers (you get what you pay for) is now so well proven that it is the furniture of the workplace. Thicker roller walls, generous section side frames, readily accessible tensioning of chain drives, 'daisy chain' plc-driven motor controls that allow changing a drive without losing the logic, all contribute to resilience. The real skill is in the controls and sequencing: p.c. controlled, generally arranged as a number of sub-systems integrated within the overall warehouse management system, simulation at the design stage is essential to prove that the proposed layout can meet the required throughput. (See Technical Study 2, para 34).

Figure 4.199 A 90° direction change. Note rollers sink to deposit pallet onto chains running in opposite direction.

Figure 4.200 Manually propelled system that both transports and acts as inter-process storage medium. By depressing a foot pedal units can change direction of travel from one set of rails to another at 90°. Stacks of crates on accumulation conveyors (left) are transferred by a special handling unit to the take-away chain conveyor (right).

8.06 Similar, but down-sized systems are employed for handling stacks of crates, either on dollies, platens or just as crate stacks in the prepared food, dairy and meat industries (Figure 4.200).

8.07 To avoid the constraint on movement for other handling plant at ground level, pallet conveyors can be mounted at high level (suspended from the roof or on a mezzanine,) or can be robust versions of monorail overhead conveyors, (paras 6.01–6.06). These monorails, used extensively in automotive assembly, are nowadays also 'a kit of parts': effectively inverted track-mounted automated guided vehicles running on roof-slung railways, with points, accumulation spurs, integral lifts and transfer stations. As stated in 8.05, the art is in the controls and either integration with the warehouse management system. (See Chapter 5.)

Chapter 5
Automated storage

Technical study

Automated storage 1

Storage process

1 Introduction
2 Source of goods
3 Form of transport
4 Control of transport
5 Receipt of goods
6 Form of goods
7 Unloading
8 Characteristics of goods
9 Sorting inbound unit load
10 Volume calculations
11 Turnover calculations
12 Variety and flow
13 Type of storage
14 Stock control
15 Stock withdrawal
16 Order picking
17 picking area
18 Load assembly
19 Order and documentation check
20 Dispatch collection and loading
21 Additional data

Automated storage, in which plant is planned and controlled by computer and automation, is the most sophisticated storage type.

---

1 Introduction

1.01 Automated warehouses for predictable unit loads, i.e. pallets, tote bins, etc., are now virtually a standard product from many manufacturers. The furniture of the workplace, these pallet silos are proprietary machines with clear planning and operational rules. However, it is the processes that precede and follow the actual storage and retrieval operations that require careful planning and specification. Automated storage offers fast and accurate mechanical handling and stock management, controlled by a computer. In practice, this can still be exacting to achieve. In spite of improved handling and control methodology, companies have found that lifetime costs overtake predicted savings. What has been lacking is a broad-based approach to design, and a full understanding in designers of the impact and implications of automation on the total supply chain and distribution system.

1.02 Computer-manipulated stock control is now standard practice to decrease lead times, 'if I want it tomorrow I'll ask for it tomorrow', and to provide inventory 'transparency' to reduce stock levels and calculate the positions in the racking best suited for moving stock quickly.

The development of automated warehouses
(a bit of history is always worthwhile)

1.03 The first automated warehouses were quite different from the commoditized products now on the market: they drove development of some very innovative building types to be able to accept the optimum heights offered by this type of storage, then in excess of 20 m, now often 30 m. What subsequently happened was the racking manufacturers developed their products for a 'standard' rack-supported structure, and the stacker cranes and feed conveyors became modular elements in the system. The development of the mini-computer for overall control, in turn driving Programmable Logic Controllers (PLCs) managing individual zones or pieces of equipment also revolutionized automation into a less expert field. The first automated warehouse to attract widespread attention was that of the Brunswig Drug Company in Los Angeles. It was built in 1960 but, although successful in technical operation, was put out of action by a company policy change (an example of the importance of forward planning). The next major development was for the kitchens of Sara Lee, Chicago, whose cakes are now in virtually every supermarket freezer, a warehouse whose complexity and sophistication of control systems and handling plant blazed the trail for development all over the world. It was a cooled store for perishable cakes, handling over 100 product types 'on-line'.

1.04 In Europe, development started in countries with limited land and expensive labour, such as Sweden and Switzerland. By the mid-1960s, several high-bay automated warehouses had been built for the retail and pharmaceutical trades and for parts storage for the manufacturing industry (e.g. Oehler's warehouses for Suchard Chocolate in France (Figure 5.1), West Germany and Switzerland, for the Dr Maag pharmaceutical company in Dielsdorf, and the warehouse in Lausanne for the Baumgartner Papiers, SA). The Dr Maag warehouse (Figure 5.2) was constructed with vertical pre-cast

Automated storage – storage process

Figure 5.1 *Automated warehouse for Suchard Chocolate. Note high-level order picking.*

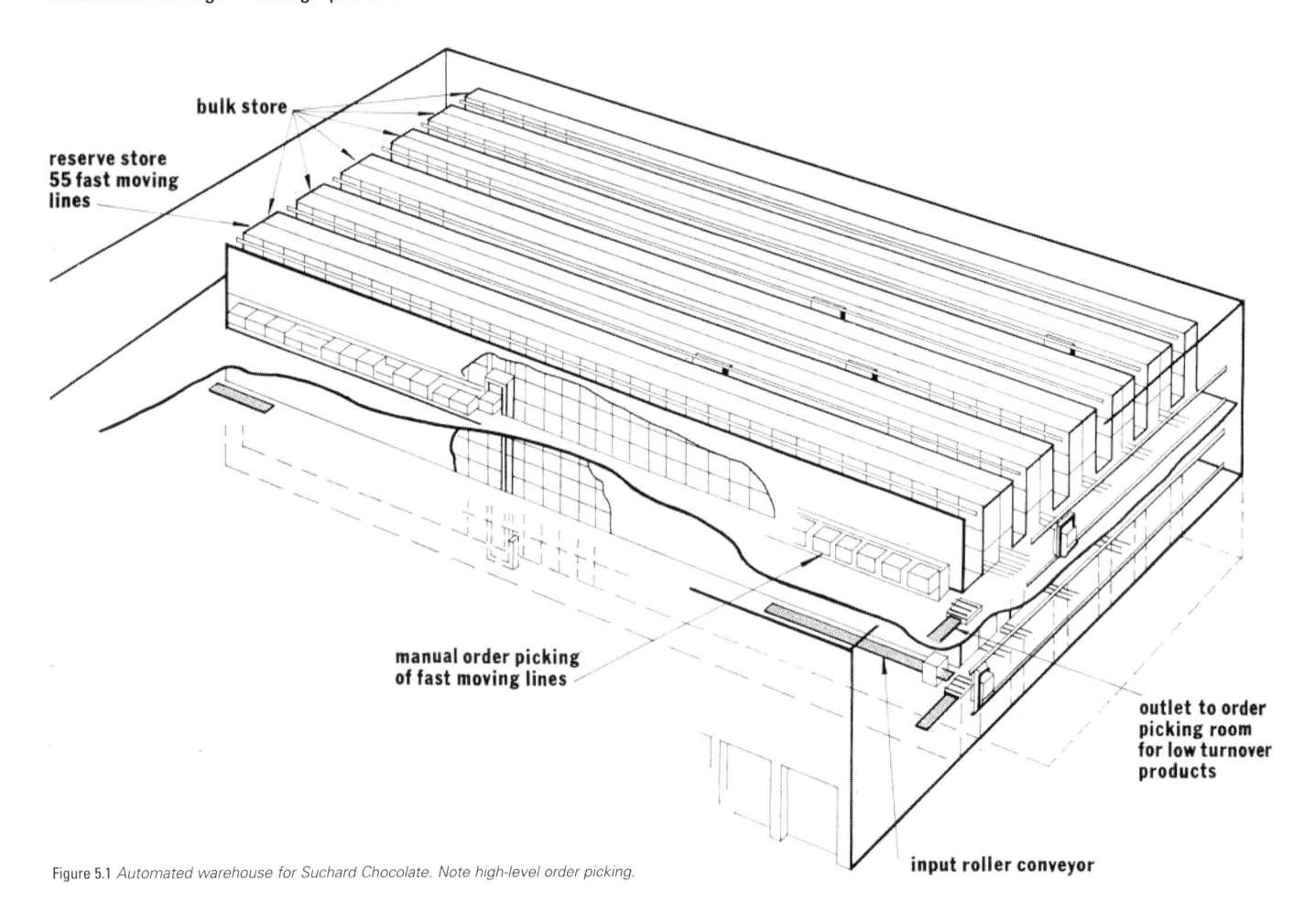

Figure 5.2 *Dr Maag pharmaceutical warehouse, built from pre-cast concrete 'T' members.*

Figure 5.3 *Erection of structural racking for the Baumgartner Papier warehouse, Lausanne.*

concrete rack elements, and in the paper warehouse the steel racks were an integral part of the building structure (Figure 5.3). These installations were 'on-line' controlled.

1.05 The Volvo Company in Sweden had built an automated store for parts and spares that used standard pallets as the storage medium, and their competitor Saab-Scania also built a high-bay store at that time. In Lucerne, Mannesmann Demag built Viscose Suisse (Figure 5.4), a 29 m-high warehouse of slip-formed concrete, but with pallet supports made of steel and bolted to the cross walls.

1.06 In the US, automated stores developed quickly, but fewer were high bay as there was less pressure on industrial land. Installations with live storage and automated cranes were developed, such as the Ford Motor Company's parts store at Plymouth, Michigan, which was only 12 m high. Complex horizontally oriented systems, i.e. not high bay, were designed, as at the US Navy's Oakland warehouse, handling over 15,000 lines. This relatively simple warehouse broke even in under three years. Most automated warehouses in the USA were for goods with very high flow rates with small or large variety of product lines (Figure 5.5).

1.07 In the UK, the CWS warehouse at Birtley, County Durham incorporated many novel features, including 'on-line' control, structural racking and an order-picking system that brought the goods to the pickers, called 'carousels'. Unfortunately, this installation suffered from a protracted and complicated commissioning period, such that although providing a useful case study never met its

Automated storage – storage process

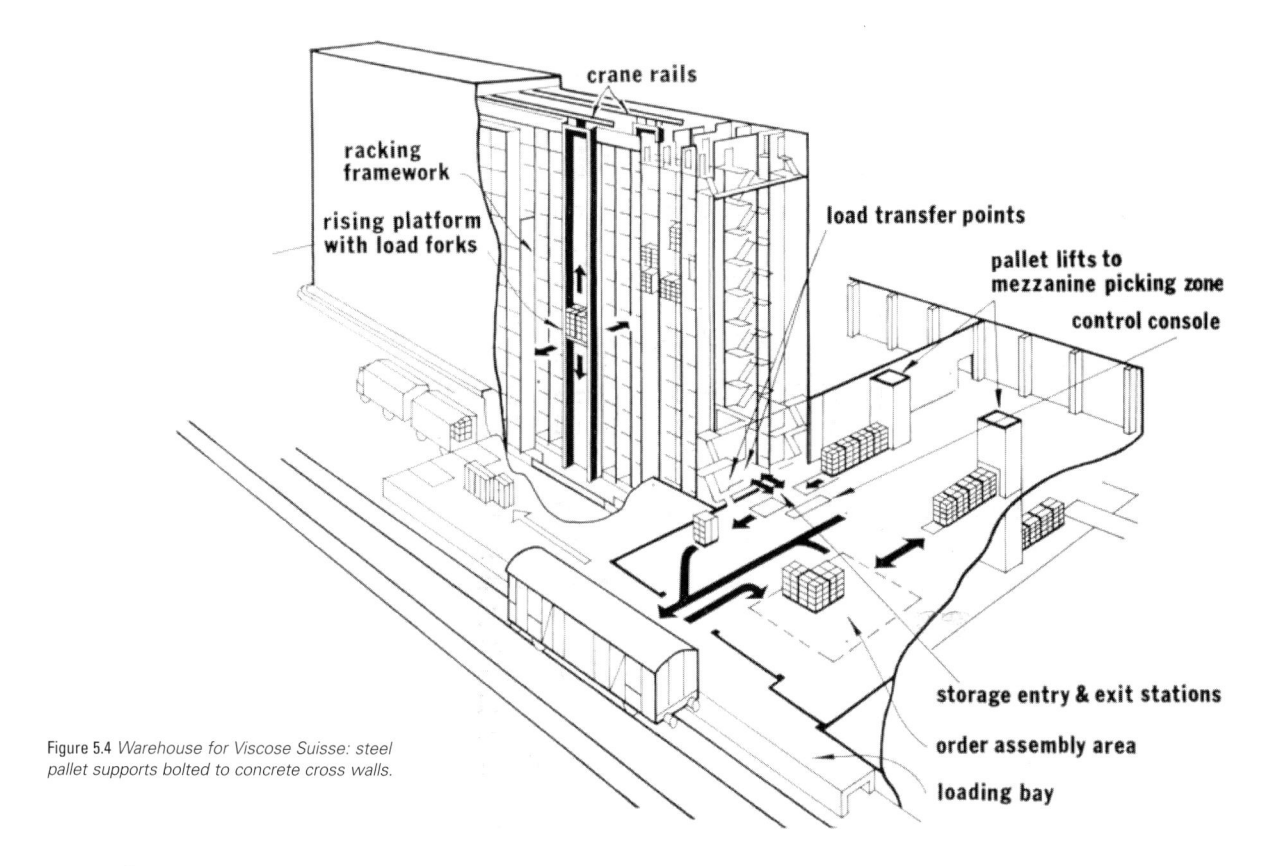

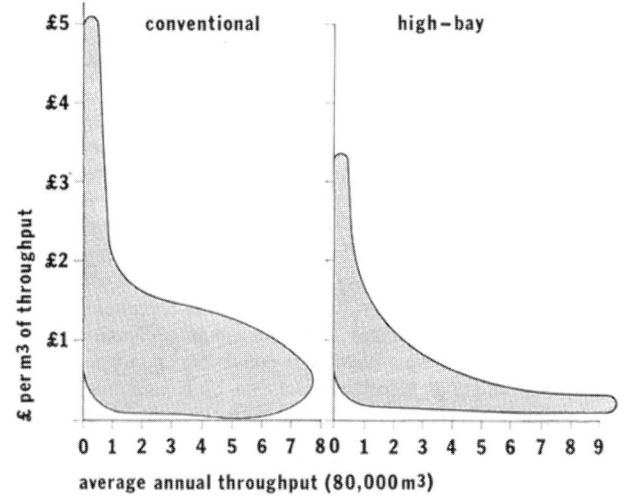

Figure 5.4 *Warehouse for Viscose Suisse: steel pallet supports bolted to concrete cross walls.*

Figure 5.5 *Economies of scale in conventional and high-bay warehouses.*

potential: it set back automated development in the UK by at least two years.

1.08 Other British automated warehouses of the late 1960s included Boots at Nottingham (Figure 5.6) (which used a peripheral mini-computer for real-time control and a central computer for process documentation) and the stores for Perkins Engines at Peterborough and for car bodies at Pressed Steel Fisher (PSF), West Bromwich. The former store was controlled by consoles at the end of each aisle, the latter by punched cards. The PSF warehouse incorporated air-conditioning with humidity-control in 20 m-high aisles so that unpainted car bodies did not have to be treated before storage. Of these four, three used stacker cranes and one used a transporter system; only one was fully operational at the time.

1.09 In Japan, the automated warehouse was developed as a 'standard' product for work in progress and parts storage in factories rather than for retail distribution

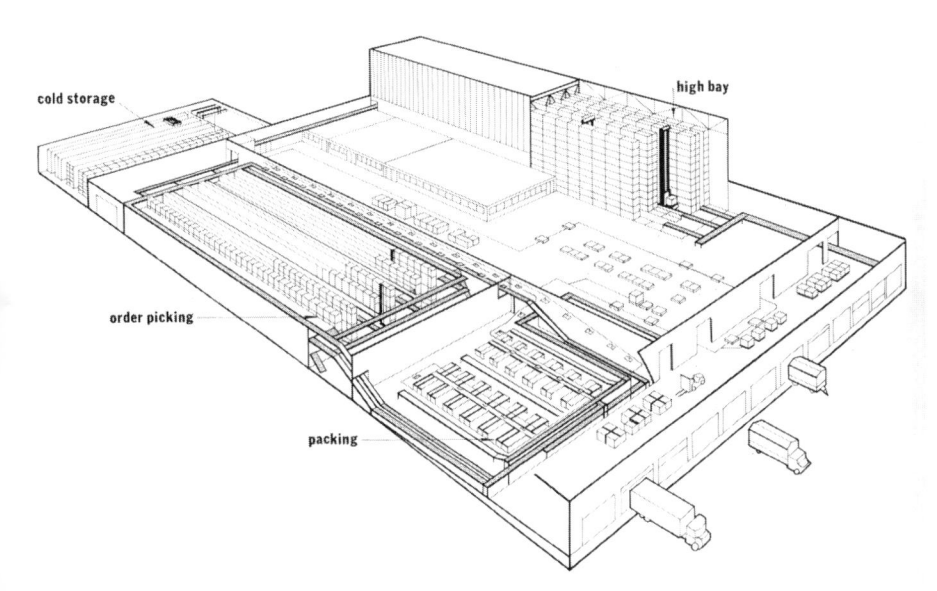

Figure 5.6 *A typical retail distribution warehouse: note the small area occupied by the automated warehouse in comparison with the order picking, packing and load accumulation zones.*

systems. Many Japanese manufacturers improved and exploited manufacturing licences from European and US originators: they then launched their own products onto the Western market and very good they were too for 'standard' applications: but the 'art' of automated warehouses is to use technology to reduce costs for specific (i.e. bespoke) operations.

1.10 European automated warehouses tend to have generally been more successful than UK ones. Sometimes a highly mechanized, and not automated warehouse, would have been the solution. There has been some seriously costly litigation as a result of the client body not understanding how automation will inevitably affect the client's corporate culture.

1.11 Even when having taken care not to automate redundant functions, the result is that automated warehouses are still not the 'standard' solutions in the UK that they often are elsewhere.

1.12 Reasons for the success of UK automated warehouses included one or more of the following:
1. The company was a step behind its competitors and wanted to be two steps ahead at one leap. Tilda Rice at Raynham in Essex is a good example, where the automated warehouse combined with new milling technology enabled a new branded product strategy.
2. The company had already a highly developed stock control system: it was logical to exploit the full potential of flexible manufacturing by integrating an automated parts warehouse into multi-storey manufacturing.
3. Rationalization of a diversity of interests, possibly of merged companies, by streamlining every stage of the distribution system drove an automated warehouse as the central inventory control mechanism.

Planning

1.13 Planning an automated warehouse should be entirely system driven. This cannot be achieved without a clear process flow chart. The diagram (see chapter 4, section 34) sets out the logical stages and design team content for the planning and design process. The key to successful automation is eliminating any exceptions: standard product characteristics, predictable input and output rates. In planning an automated warehouse, the fundamental issues have to be identified from the outset. Techniques often alien to designers and operators in the warehousing field are needed to predict throughput and future trade. (See Chapter 4, Section 34.) If high peaks are a clear demand, either high levels of redundancy have to be built into the design (expensive) or alternative operations in the peaks are required: for example, in some Japanese breweries the peaks are handled by manned teams with automation being used for off-peak stock build-up and pre-sorting for the next peak.

The team

1.14 More than in any other section of the storage industry it is important that designers fully understand the potential and operation of all the systems involved. The project leader chosen should have the expertise and the skill to integrate the diversity of parts and systems that compose an automated warehouse. It should be the co-ordinating designer's responsibility to inform the client of the suitability of the brief (which is often inaccurate). Adaptation of an automated system after construction affects every element, and is both difficult and expensive.

Total system approach

1.15 When automation has been selected as a realistic and economic concept, the control system should be developed in parallel with the handling system and building design.

Consultants

1.16 A consultant should be appointed at the inception of the project. The consultancy organization or systems integrator must be able to appraise production and distribution plans, assess throughput requirements, develop or at least select the most appropriate 'software' and integrate computer control with machinery. Some of the larger equipment manufacturers, especially the European ones, offer integrated consultancy services (which, unless run as a totally separate professional organization, will inevitably be partisan).

Client/designer relationships

1.17 Packaged deals, 'Green field to hand shake', by consortia of equipment manufacturers and control specialists may be the most effective method for particular projects: but the consultant/architect team should remain in place to validate the design and to ensure conformance with demand and planning conditions. (See the pre- and post-tender organizational diagrams in Figure 1.2a/b, Industrial Storage 1, Technical Study 1.)

Implications of automation

1.18 In assessing the brief, the designer should consider the following:
1. Is the need to reduce distribution costs best achieved in this case by automation? Are there strategic supply chain issues that render automation redundant? For example, can the control of the supply chain allow just-in-time distribution for cross docking that eliminates the need for long-term stock holding at all. There are also 'hidden' costs such as the creation of 'software', the increase in data-processing staff and possible losses due to system breakdown.
2. Does improvement of customer service depend on improved warehouse function or is it the transport and distribution system that is at fault? There have been some very expensive failures when the design of the automated system has ignored some of the basic assumptions of customer service.

1.19 Automation means replacing an operative by a machine, with advantages of accuracy, reduced personnel and standardization of equipment and control systems.

How much automation?

1.20 The following questions should be asked:
1. Are all functions still relevant? Briefs tend to be based on client's existing operations and it is wasteful to automate redundant functions. Always establish the expectations of the customers as a result of the improvements: there must be consultation.
2. Is there an existing data-processing system that could be used more effectively?
3. Will the cost of mechanizing some particular functions limit the capital resources for the rest of the warehouse system, so that other areas cannot be brought up to a commensurate standard? If so, the overall potential will be restricted.
4. Should on- or off-line control be used? The present trend is towards both on- and off-line mini-computers, as slaves to a central master control.

5 Automation is also advancing in order picking and sortation: home shopping and B2B consumables and parts supply have been exploiting automated solutions for consistent accuracy rather than sheer speed: but individual item picking is still best achieved by the dexterity of people.

1.21 The biggest problem with automation is that people have to play a new role.

1.22 With the application of sophisticated data-processing techniques, and the use of more reliable handling plant, there can be substantial overall reduction in the cost of distribution, but much of this is through the reduction of inventory, tighter supply chains and rationalized manufacturing.

Summary

1.23 In automated warehouse projects (see Section 1.2):
1. overall project control by one person, the 'champion' or team is essential
2. users do not always know accurately what is required; they may be under pressure from several sources, and be trying to tighten up the wrong part of the system – a full reappraisal during product definition – should be made
3. it is important to choose a consultant and supplier suitable for the type of warehouse involved
4. if computer-controlled systems are to be used, the 'software' should be designed in parallel with the handling and building systems from the outset
5. a total-system approach to design is necessary; the control system must be developed and tested in parallel with the 'hard', i.e. the storage and construction, products.

User requirement specification (URS) Project definition

1.24 Definition: an automated high-bay warehouse is a pallet silo, equipped with high racking to cover a minimum site area, capable of fast turnover and automated materials handling, with simultaneous stock control. Key areas for review are:
- Consistency of incoming goods: will the goods already be de-trashed, placed in warehouse-compatible unit loads and coded for picking and sorting by the suppliers? Will this need to be done in advance? This can save space, time and labour.
- Does the order selection and picking system match the customer's requirements: consultation is essential.

1.25 Before the user finally decides on an automated warehouse he or she must accept a three to five year commitment for the following:
1. The maximum weight of the unit load for dispatch. This will affect the transport and distribution system and possibly the type of goods acceptable by the warehouse.
2. The size and type of pallet. The pallet best suited to the system may prove too dear or unsuitable to leave the warehouse. Although checking equipment is available, one broken pallet can jam an automated system; so is the use of standard road pallets justified? Will the acceptance of a narrow range of sizes conform to the metric pallets used throughout the EU, or will the size conflict with pallets arriving from suppliers or for dispatch in ISO containers? (See Information sheet, Mechanized storage 4, Pallets.) The user should decide the strategy to be followed. An automated warehouse for contemporary market conditions should be capable of adaptability and expansion.

1.26 Users who want to reduce distribution costs per unit (as distinct from having low-capital cost distribution facilities) may find automated distribution an economic necessity. Machine-intensive distribution systems will become more attractive as labour costs increase faster than those of mechanical plant. The need for more accurate dispatch to save expense on vehicle journeys and wasted sorting will also make automation attractive, as the reduction of dispatch error saves on total distribution cost.

1.27 Performance specifications have been used as user specifications for automated warehouse design, especially by packaged deal consortia. This is a dangerous practice unless there is a user requirement specification in place, prepared by the materials handling consultant. The elements of automated operation need to be precisely stated and to cover all possible development patterns that the client may take during the period for which he or she is committed. By describing the parts in detail, and relating these to the whole, a detailed skeleton should emerge as a base which the project team can work from and which can be reassessed at various stages in the design process to ensure that the original strategy will not be lost during operational planning.

2 Source of goods

2.01 Sources of goods for automated storage are the same as for mechanized storage warehouses and are described in Technical study, Mechanized storage 1, para. 2.

3 Form of transport

3.01 This is also the same as for mechanized storage warehouses and is described in Technical study, Mechanized storage 1, para. 3.

4 Control of transport

4.01 See also Technical study, Mechanized storage 1, para. 4.

4.02 Automated storage systems are uneconomic if calculated to accept large throughputs of goods for only a short period of the working day. Some peaks are inevitable due to delivery demands and drivers' hours limits, the distance of travel and local road conditions; seasonal peaks should be taken into account when calculating storage capacity (see para. 9). Automation is now embodied in total supply chain solutions, with suppliers' just-in-time manufacturing systems 'transparent' to the warehouse operator: with the ability to delay or call forward stock at short notice to fulfil production delivery demands. Stacker crane movement patterns require incoming and outgoing pallets to be handled from the same end of the aisle, which means a single loading bay and sorting area (Figure 5.7). Automated-handling systems offer fast load build-up, so that truck turnround times can be reduced. The collection documents must be received early enough, ideally on-line, for crane cycles to be calculated by the computer (Figure 5.8).

4.03 The use of satellite navigation (GPS) techniques to locate, track and identify incoming loads allows the stock management system to plan storage, order picking and sorting regimes. The integration of customer order demands with availability of stock while maintaining minimum inventories is one of the serious control challenges in 'delivering the promise' in e-commerce. It

Automated storage – storage process

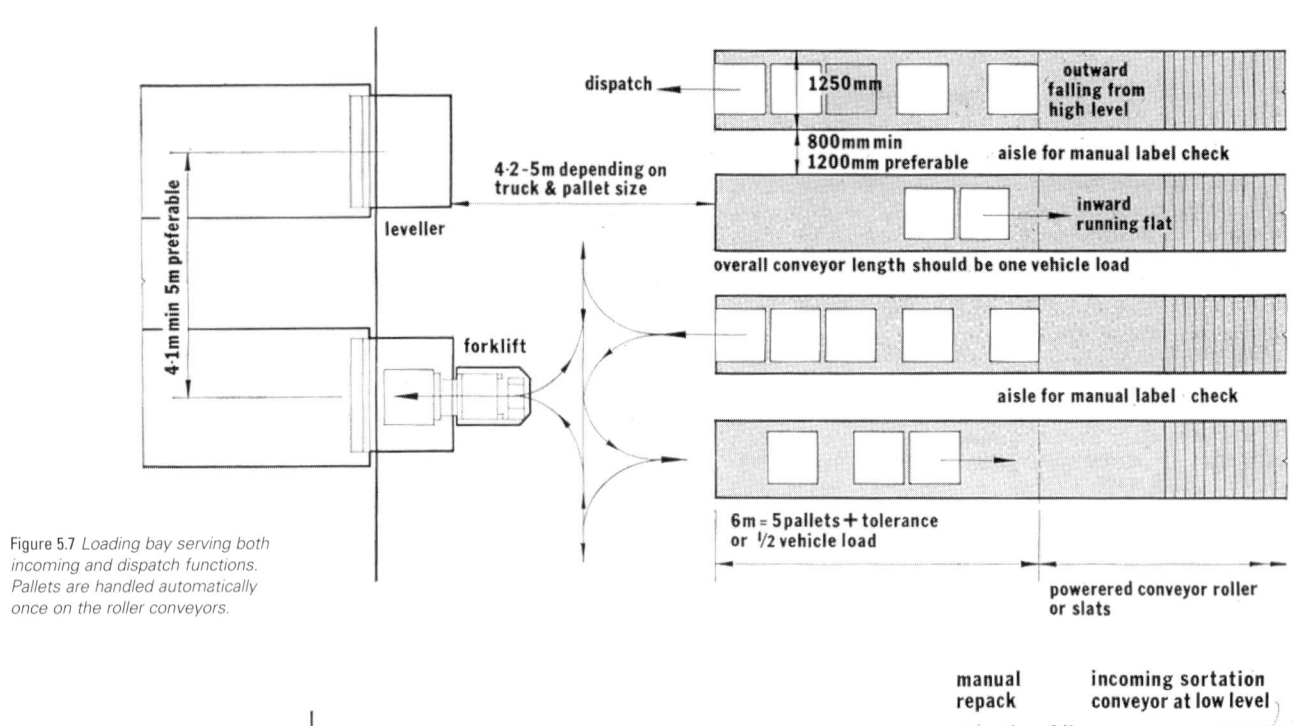

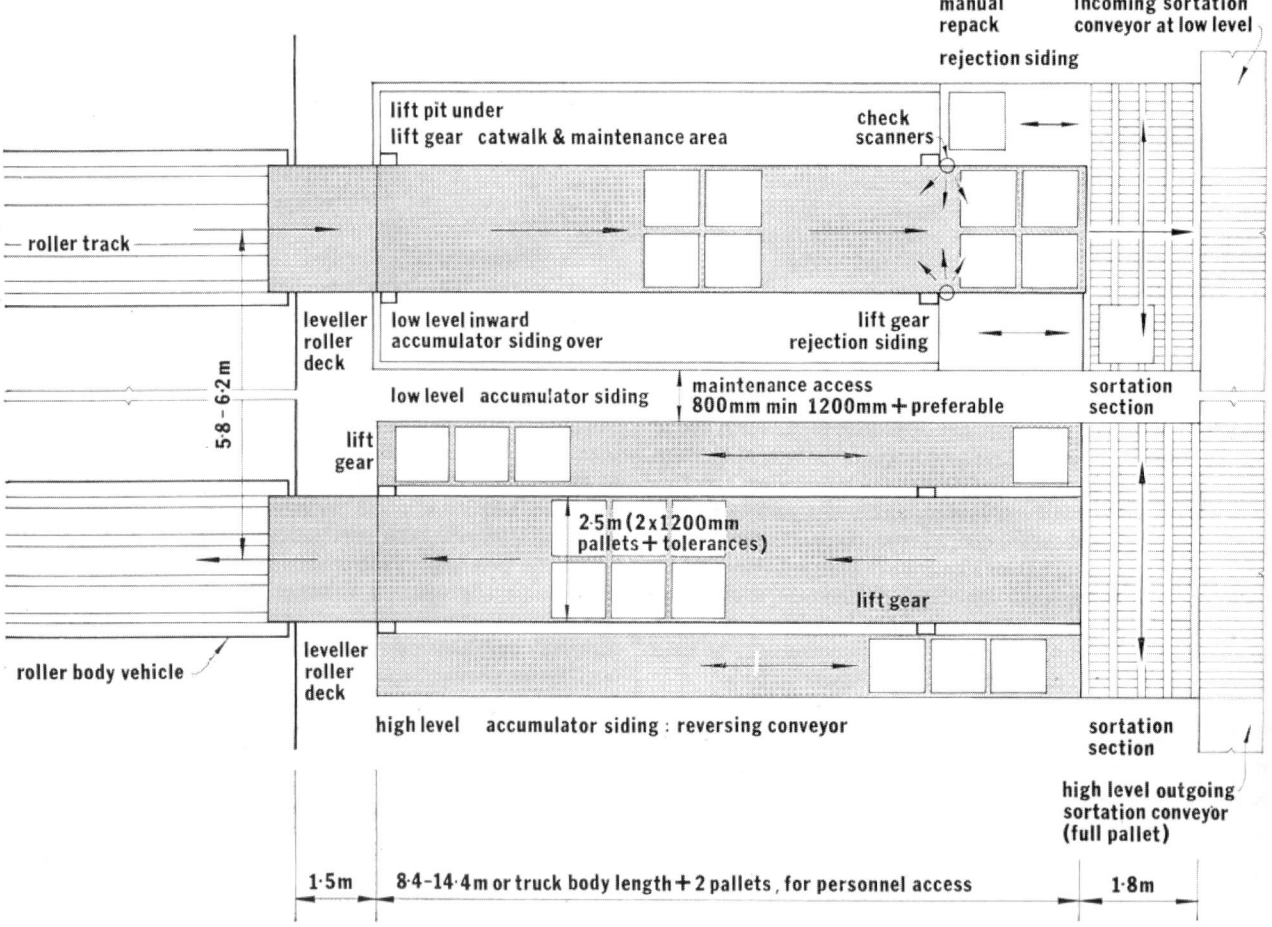

Figure 5.7 *Loading bay serving both incoming and dispatch functions. Pallets are handled automatically once on the roller conveyors.*

Figure 5.8 *For fast vehicle handling the conveyors are double decked, mounted as lifts. Driver documents at gatehouse inform the computer of the incoming load, starting preparation of the dispatch. The truck enters the bay allocated while the dispatch load is accumulating on the upper level. The incoming load fills the conveyor at truck level, which then drops a level, allowing the conveyor above to lower to the truck bed and load the dispatch goods. Label check is completed simultaneously.*

reduces the peak build-up of vehicles, and system-imposed queueing allows the stock control computer to plan the best stacking and picking patterns to avoid goods accumulating and jamming the sorting area. A block-allocated delivery policy for principal suppliers also reduces vehicle peaks, and the set pattern allows the computer to clear any backlog before predicted arrivals.

The use of optical scanners and radio data tags (RFI)

4.04 Traffic control automation can be taken a stage further by eliminating the traffic office and the document function of the gatehouse (leaving the latter as a security check). Optical scanners are now available can read clearly typed documents. The technology is available for the identification tag on a trailer or freight container to contain the details of the entire contents, such that it can be matched with the data already sent to the computer. The truck can then be allocated a loading bay with the goods also identified by radio data tags scanned-in and checked-in against the electronic manifest. The computer selects an accumulation lane opposite the loading bay and indicates this on a gantry-hung visual display screen on the approach road. The process can be very fast; order picking operates as before, the return load accumulating as the previous vehicle is being handled. When the vehicle has been loaded, either the loading forklift driver activates the traffic control periphery, or the leaving vehicle can activate a sensor. The control periphery would call forward the waiting truck by visual display or pre-recorded voice message. This is not a complicated program, and it is likely that this type of automated traffic control will be used increasingly in high throughput installations such as with air cargo and perishable goods.

5 Receipt of goods

5.01 After trucks have been automatically called forward, the operation is as for mechanized storage (see Technical study, Mechanized storage 1, para. 5).

6 Form of goods

6.01 Goods for handling in automated warehouses should be in uniform unit loads (i.e. pallets): consistency of all dimensions is a prerequisite. Some pallets are unsuitable for the automated storage system (see Information sheet, Mechanized storage 1, para. 1.01). The user is committing him or herself to a pallet type when he invests in an automated system. A certain amount of tolerance can be allowed economically, e.g. the difference between 1100 and 1200 mm wide pallets. The size chosen should be the one most likely to arrive according to the trade involved. There is still an issue in the EU about pallet sizes, between 'industrial' pallets 1200 mm x 1000 mm, and 'Europallets', 1200 mm x 800 mm, and with 'Imperial' pallets as used by the USA, 4 ft x 4ft, 4 ft x 3 ft, (1220 mm x 914 mm). Automated warehouses can be designed to handle all these sizes, but it is at the expense of storage efficiency and mechanical complexity. One way of avoiding the complexity and concerns about pallet quality, but at the expense of cubic capacity, is to place all incoming pallets onto slaves or plattens, internal pallets matched to the handling system. Shrink-wrapping and banding help load stability, important in maintaining the load profile (no leaning or overhangs), required by the in-feed systems for automated warehouses. Some users like to remove the plastic film at the loading bay to lessen the fire risk, however, and others puncture it to avoid condensation.

7 Unloading

7.01 An intermediate unloading method is required between the transport and the automated system. If conventional loads are involved, a forklift system is usually operated. Fully automated discharge of unit loads is available for handling frequent loads from few suppliers. Roller bed trailers are extensively employed in air cargo and in some major breweries and soft drinks manufacturers where load quality and consistency is guaranteed: this requires long-term transport contracts to justify the investment (Figure 5.9a/b). With forklifts in the loading bay of an automated warehouse, the stuffer truck usually shuttles between the vehicle and a check-in area. The same loading bay and buffer zone dimensions apply as in Technical study, Mechanized storage 1, para. 6; a load and a half, with space for segregation and personnel access bay should be provided for both incoming and dispatch loads. Incoming

(a)

(b)

(c)

(d)

Figure 5.9 (a) *Truck reverses on to special dock, and* (b) *locks in place: then discharge is automatic.* (c/d) *Automated trailer discharge onto slat conveyors feeding automated warehouse.*

Automated storage – storage process

pallets still have to be checked in automated stores and code labels added for correct routing.

8 Characteristics of goods

8.01 Any goods are suitable for automated storage, as long as they are properly packaged (Figure 5.9c/d). The characteristics of the goods and their packaging should be carefully examined during the design of the system. Package strength is important, as packages have to accept acceleration and deceleration stresses with automated sorting systems. Some space has to be allocated in the loading bay area for re-palletizing; the de-palletizing/re-palletizing unit (Figure 5.10) is another machine which may break down. Goods should be assessed for maximum cube potential of the pallet loads. It is worth dictating to suppliers the maximum and minimum pallet-stacking heights, as well as the pallet type itself, and the lateral loading tolerances acceptable by the load centring and checking devices, which are necessary before acceptance into automated storage areas. Goods for de-palletizing and automated sorting also need to be regular and consistent: high-speed conveyors and sorters require stiff bases and shapes that prevent tipping or rolling.

9 Sorting inbound unit load

9.01 The choice of sorting method depends on the stock control system used, the level of automation, the type of supplier and the method of unloading. Some buffer space for manual checking is always required in case of system breakdown or for random system checks. Automated sorting relies on the code attached to the pallet load. With regular suppliers (e.g. parts for machine production) the code labels can be fixed at the suppliers' premises; sorting can be automatic from the immediate unloading position and any unlabelled goods can be ejected into a buffer line. The sorting space allowed should ideally be two truck loads for each goods inwards bay: one laid out for checking and dispatch into the warehouse, one ready for the next discharge operation.

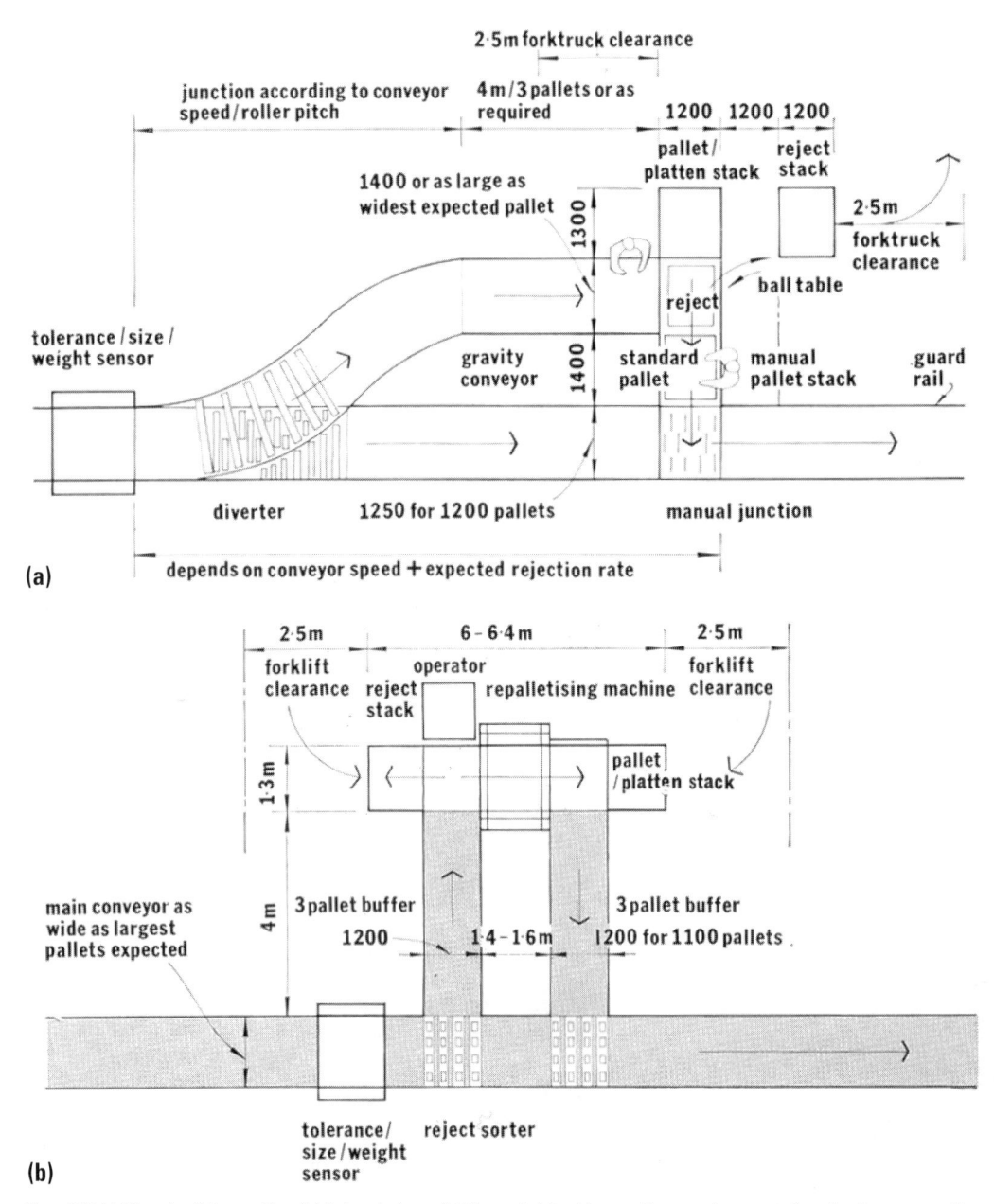

Figure 5.10 (a) Manual pallet re-packing. (b) Automated re-palletizing and plattenizing machines are important, if road pallets are used in an automated warehouse, to avoid broken pallets passing to jam the automated equipment in the racking zone.

Automated storage – storage process

9.02 If conveyors run directly into the loading bay, space should be allocated for manual loading and code check. This can be done by cut-out sections on the powered roller conveyor, as in an accumulation unit. Some systems weigh pallets in motion, check their size and load tolerances, check their codes and, if unsuitable, reject them into a siding (Figure 5.13). Sensors, switches and stop-start devices are required for this automatic operation, adding to the chance of breakdown; loading bays and buffer areas serving both inward and dispatch goods must be kept clear and operational. Load check gauges are advisable for any loads where long-distance transport has been involved that can destabilize them.

Coding methods

9.03 These include optical mark reading, bar codes and radio data tags. Some scanners can also read normal clear type, optical character recognition (OCR), a useful function for use in manual override situations. Magnetic codes on special cards are also used. Optical scanners can read codes as the pallet passes (Figure 5.11), and one form, spray scanners, can read labels out of true, so the pallets need not be straight (Figure 5.12).

9.04 With multiple suppliers, as at a grocery warehouse, automated sorting is more complicated; the diversity of goods handled and the different speeds of throughput require a buffer area for pallets to wait while the stock control computer clears any backlog in the user sections. If the incoming goods data has been processed while the truck is waiting for the loading bay to be freed, the buffer area can be minimized.

9.05 With many suppliers, goods are checked off against a recorded manifest, so that when passed as correct, the central data-processing computer can draw up the suppliers' accounts. But in some operators' experience, many suppliers cannot be guaranteed to label pallets correctly and the diversity of pallets requires a careful check anyway. Some operators prefer to code all incoming pallets themselves, so that they have full control in case of system breakdown.

Pallets and platens

9.06 Automated systems are difficult to recover when loads jam: it is important to control the quality of the pallets to be handled on the conveyors, and to make allowance to accept some overhang and off-centre (Figure 5.13). Pallet quality is down to specification and quality control at the suppliers (a contractual issue), and in the system-wide tolerances (Figure 5.14). Beware that automation suppliers do not minimize load tolerances to suit their 'catalogue' designs (Figure 5.15).

Feeding the storage area

9.07 Powered roller and chain conveyors are used for transport to the storage area, as they offer greater scope

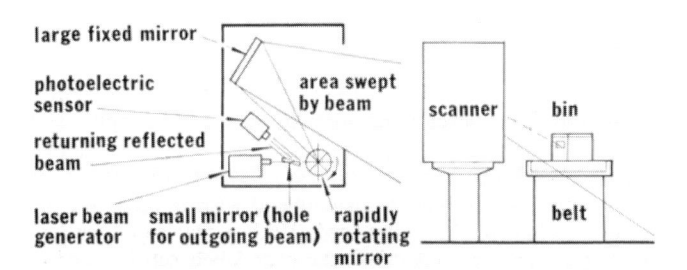

Figure 5.11 *Spray beam scanner.*

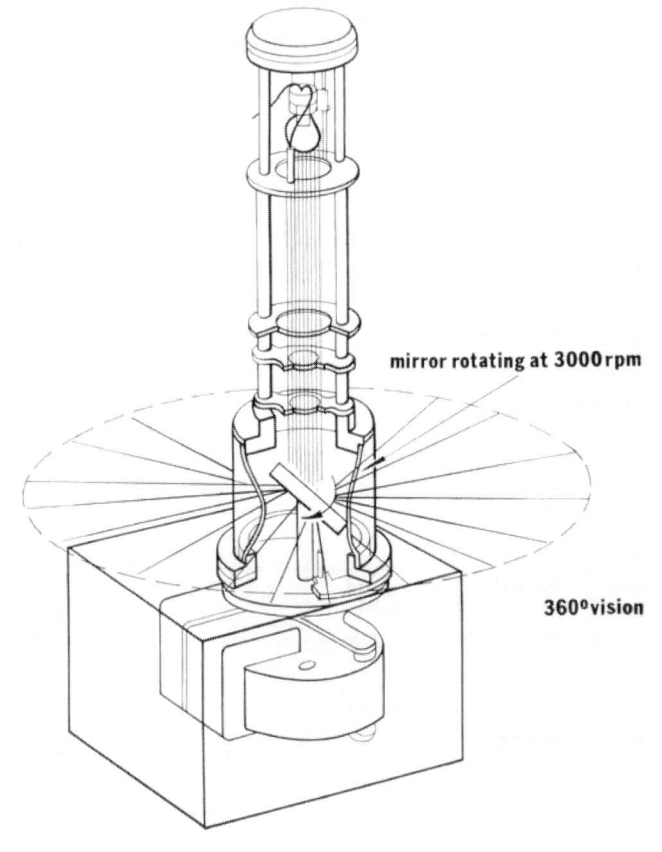

Figure 5.12 *Detail of spray scanner with 360° vision.*

Figure 5.13 *Automated pallet in-feed; pallet passing through dimension check gauge.*

Figure 5.14 *This pallet has a broken corner. Timber resin leaves a deposit on the rollers that may drop off and affect the mechanical equipment.*

Automated storage – storage process

Figure 5.15 *A platten being transferred into a stacker crane.*

Figure 5.16 *Modern SCADA control system: shows dynamic movement of AGVs and cranes.*

for automated sorting. Overhead systems have also been used successfully and, if transporter systems are used for the storage medium, these can run under line control to the loading bay and sorting area. Towline carts and shuttle cars have also been used, with roller platforms for automatic loading and discharging at the transfer positions.

Automated guided vehicles (AGVS) are another well-tried method, operating fully on line by dead reckoning with location buttons in the floor or ceiling, or by following a wire buried in the floor surface. A variation of this is a wire-guided train of pallet trucks, but these have to be unhooked and discharged manually. Automated guided vehicles are not as fast as conveyors for transport or sorting, but leave floor areas clear, and do not require substructures, special services or the considerable maintenance required by conveyor lines.

10 Volume calculations

10.01 These will determine whether the store has to be 'high bay' and to what level it should be automated, if at all. A consultant is of great importance, as volume and turnover calculations are linked with software development and the type of plant. However, the designer should be able to understand the processes that led the consultant to his conclusions. Computer techniques can be of great benefit here, as peak and system breakdown situations can be simulated for various flow and turnover speeds, and the most likely constriction points and the resulting need for buffer zones, quickly observed (Figure 5.16). This can be programmed to print out graphically for easy interpretation by the designer.

10.02 Daily, weekly and seasonal peaks should be calculated to decide to what peak level the store should be designed. Seasonal and daily peaks can quickly push an automated storage system out of sequence. In some installations, stacker cranes cannot keep up with increased input, even when the store is part empty. If the decision is incorrect, the warehouse will be either mostly empty, or rapidly choked in loading bay and checking zones. Searching questions should be asked of the equipment and control systems' suppliers and sales people about peak capacities and expansion potential.

10.03 One way to avoid the daily peak situation is to allocate block delivery times to suppliers. Otherwise, trucks have to be ranked to keep pace with the store, or buffer space should be provided between the loading bay and the racking, with the stacker cranes programmed on a priority basis. This tends to be clumsy; as a rule, pallets should be kept 'off the floor'.

10.04 Although racking is now normally organized into notional divisions of goods with similar stock delay times, the most important area to invest for lost effectiveness remains the load assembly zone. Other parameters to consider include the likelihood of unpredicted peaks caused by new ranges of product or multi-shift operation, for instance the increasing chance of night deliveries to city shops. Flexibility can carry a heavy cost penalty.

11 Turnover calculations

11.01 These are inseparable from volume calculations and variety and flow demands. See also Chapter 4, Technical Study 1, paras 10 to 13.

11.02 Two examples: for a component parts or B2B order fulfilment centre the choice of picking to individual order or 'bulk' picking will be critical. The former may demand pallets being constantly withdrawn and replaced in the automated warehouse, driving up crane cycles and placing heavy loads on the in-feed and output conveyors: or the latter which withdraws complete pallets to a designated picking zone. This last is more space consuming but operationally safer.

11.03 Many large-scale systems combine three turnover sectors based on an ABC or Pareto analysis: (1) pallets only for the fast throughput class (the Pareto analysis should indicate that 80 per cent of the demand is for 20 per cent of stock variety), either to be dispatched as whole pallets or as part pallets with no residue by layer picking or de-palletizing; (2) part pallets, the medium movers where 60 per cent of stock variety may provide 15 per cent of stock handled, is the sector which often causes operational problems and results in inefficient space use; and (3) the slow movers, where 20 per cent of stock handled represents 80 per cent of stock held.

12 Variety and flow

12.01 This depends on the type of trade that the warehouse is to serve, i.e. whether it is performing a stockholding or transit function (see Technical study, Mechanized storage 1, para. 1). This affects the stock control system and the method chosen for order picking (see paras. 14 and 16).

13 Type of storage

13.01 This complex decision should be based on a systematic evaluation of data. Many variables are involved:
1. Should the handling plant be controlled by a computer on- or off-line (i.e. should the warehouse be treated as a 'black box')?
2. How high should the store be?
3. Should a stacker crane or transporter type system or wire-guided, free-path machines be used?
4. Should the building be integral with the racking?
5. Should the associated sortation and handling activities be fully automated?

All these questions are closely related to the volume and turnover requirements (para. 10), and to how much the user is prepared to spend on the plant and the control system in relation to the potential of his future business.

Control

13.02 There is a clear advantage in treating the warehouse control system (WCS) as a 'black box'; the central computer is then free to multitask, batching orders for passing down to the warehouse for processing. The WCS can itself have 'intelligence' to progress dispatch order patterns and to rearrange stock to suit the order demand, to optimize equipment cycles and picking operations.

13.03 Real-time working with mini-computers has most in-built flexibility. 'Real time' is data handling of a function that is actually happening, not prediction or retrospective stock evaluation work. Process control units (or mini-computers) can be used singly or in groups, they are easily programmed and adapted, and can be linked on-line to the main data-processing unit to receive work cycle instructions and pass back updated stock information. Mini-computers are safer in shutdowns, i.e. if one unit fails, the whole system does not suffer as with full on-line working. Quite sophisticated machines can cost as little as £5000.

13.04 There is a master–slave relationship between a central data processing unit which is often off site, and the peripheral mini-computers driving the WCS. Mini-computers are integrated into the central data-processing unit to receive orders and feedback information on a real time or batch basis.

Choice of storage system

13.05 The height of the store will be decided by the volume of stock to be held in relation to the site area available, including space for truck assembly and loading bays, and the possibility of expansion. Whether the structure should be integral with the racks depends on the height of racking required, the type of handling plant to be used, and the requirement for later adaptability. One manufacturer claims that, if over 20 m high, integral racking can save over 30 per cent of the building cost over a comparable conventional building (see para. 22). Having chosen control methods, and store height, the storage plant should be chosen. It could be:

1. the stacker crane type of in-aisle, fixed path machine
2. free-path, wire-guided machinery
3. rail-mounted multi-aisle access stacker cranes with either curve-going tracks or transfer carriers between aisles
4. integral 'mole' or shuttle car in rack storage systems. Both transporter and live rack storage systems can be very dense, and tend to be selected for chilled storage, where first in, first out operations are required.

13.06 In many cases it is site constraints (i.e. lack of area, rock or ground requiring piling) that has forced up the warehouse height and therefore suggested an automated solution. Equally, if the majority of available ground is required for order-picking, sortation and assembly the bulk storage area will benefit from the smallest footprint: remember that about 45 per cent site cover is the maximum achievable with parking, marshalling and landscaping taken into account.

Stacker cranes

13.07 The most commonly used storage and retrieval method in high-bay automated stores is the stacker crane (Figure 5.17). They are generally floor supported with a guide rail supported from the top of the racking. They can be distributed one to an aisle, or equipped with a transfer carriage to serve the low user aisles. If the racking is not integral, the stacker can be mounted on a gantry carriage for multi-aisle operation.

13.08 Stacker cranes move slower vertically than horizontally, so that the optimum length to height ratio can be gained from typical operating speeds and work cycles. All stacker cranes should be able to be manually controlled in case of system failure and so include a form of cabin. For

Figure 5.17 *Stacker crane – note structural racking with air cargo containers resting on 'top hat' sections.*

the handling of tote bins rather than pallets (for parts or documents), where the height is generally limited by the smaller loads, very fast cranes are available, one being driven by a toothed belt. Whereas 25–30 double cycles (pallets in and out) for the larger crane systems, at least 40 double cycles per hour are available from the 'mini-load' systems. Some of these systems can store up to 10 bins inwards and outbound alongside the crane's mast or combine a takeaway conveyor within the crane and racking to reduce shuttling.

13.09 Stacker crane operations need load transfer and buffer positions at the end of the aisles (P and D stations). Because of the economics of stacker work cycles (unless separate cranes are used for input and dispatch) cranes always return to one end of the aisle. The transfer position therefore handles both inward and dispatch goods. Transfer positions are normally the ends of powered roller conveyors, or tables for forklifts to place the pallets. (With the throughputs required to justify stacker cranes, forklift operation has to be intense and tends to be clumsy.) Conveyors are often at two levels; incoming pallets pass through a centring device (Figure 5.18) to ensure that the pallets are not too big, and are stable and evenly stacked. (It is essential to eliminate damaged pallets in the racking.) If the loads have been platenized, centring is still necessary to line up the load with the crane's forks. Often several checking and centring machines are used between the loading bay/sorting area for immediate rejection, others for in-travel stability checks if transfer distances are long, and a final check before the stacker pick-up position (Figure 5.19).

13.10 Stacker cranes work on a wave pattern for economy of movement, they pick up the load from the lower position, store it, retrieve the outgoing unit and return this to the upper level. Conveyors, with right-angle transfer devices and centring machinery are well proven and safeguard the system with accurate pallet location and presentation (Figure 5.20). If each aisle has notional high, medium and low user sections, sorting conveyors are required at the input point. The central data-processing unit or mini-computer will calculate the optimum movement cycle for the crane, considering the priority of the goods involved; and will pass over slow-moving goods until there is a free cycle to store them. This arrangement needs two conveyors in parallel with right angle transfer. It is usually simpler for the cranes to store the pallets in the order that they arrive, providing a buffer for three waiting units. If high peaks are anticipated, buffer capacity should be provided between the sorting area and the transfer points, to avoid choking in the loading bay area; this can be

Figure 5.19 *Height sensor relays data to the computer so that pallet location can be sized as near the load height as possible. This increases warehouse volume efficiency with varied height loads.*

Figure 5.20 *Input roller conveyor sorts pallets to crane input tracks: note the sensors and limit switches to right.*

simulated on a computer. In high-throughput operations with a limited number of varieties of stock, stacker cranes can handle two pallets at a time, and store them two deep in the racking or into a first in, first out roll through or 'mole' system (see Figure 5.22).

Free-path automated plant

13.11 The stacker crane is likely to remain the basic pallet handling unit in large stores, and will continue to grow in height. Free-path automated machines (Figure 5.21), may be more suitable for the smaller operator with medium height warehouses, generally about 12 m stacking height, although 18 m is possible. Developments in accuracy of wire guidance, and free-path stacker-order pickers, means that these machines can be used as general handling aids out of the aisles and wire-guided in racking with free positioning. Such plant is not as fast as fixed-path stacker cranes, but resolves the issue of warehouses funded by

Figure 5.18 *Centring device to line pallet up for stacker crane's forks.*

Figure 5.21 *Free-path, narrow aisle stacker.*

financial institutions where there can be more concern about future resale than current planned operation. Hybrid trucks, rail guided in the aisles for speed with direct power and data pick-up and free path location between aisles are successfully operated.

Transporter systems

13.12 Transporter systems (Figure 5.22) sophisticated mini-railways, are suitable for lower throughputs than stacker cranes. They do not offer 100 per cent immediate selectivity, but can be flexible in operation. The system consists of principal distribution tracks at many levels, which move vertically by using elevators and a special transporter carriage. This supplies subsidiary storage tracks at 90° to the distributor. These operate much like a childen's puzzle. Withdrawal of goods tends to require a certain amount of shuffling, but this can be controlled by the computer. Transporters are suitable for a limited number of lines of stock, requiring medium speed throughput. Benefits are simplicity of control and mechanics and high use of volume. Transporters can also act as conveyors and sorters between loading bay and racking, and can build up complete despatch loads.

Live storage

13.13 Automated live storage is used successfully by operators with high throughputs and a limited number of lines such as soft drinks or dairy products. It is suitable for full pallet and carton loads, and for supplying order-picking stations. A stacker crane or transporter carries the incoming goods to the input position of that product line's particular channel. The goods then flow on a first-in, first-out principle. With loaded pallets, live storage should be powered, or at least power braked, as local shocks can be intense with gravity operation. At the output position, the pallets are picked by a stacker crane or transporter for dispatch, or transfer to an order-picking station. The crane can be used as a bridge between the live racks and a sorting conveyor, with on or off-line control.

14 Stock control

14.01 There is now great understanding of stock control in industry: it goes far deeper into the running of the supply chain than the warehouse. The automated warehouse, or a necklace of them at key transport interchanges can operate as dynamic supply chain controllers (the entire supply chain can be totally 'transparent'); there is really no excuse for warehouse operators and their customers not to know where anything is at any time. The hierarchy in the stock control system in turn orders/receives feed back from the WCS, and then zone controllers.

14.02 The control system chosen for an automated warehouse will decide how the handling plant moves within the racks. This depends on the type of goods being stored, the throughput and volume characteristics, and the order-picking requirements. The consultant should examine warehouse control at an early stage, as it is fundamental to the choice of control system, the complexity of software and the height and length ratio of the aisles.

14.03 Zone control is a method of solving the supply and demand problem within a storage system, such as:
1 how long commodity lines should be stored
2 how long incoming goods take to be processed and what happens to them when they enter the storage zone
3 how long it takes to locate the goods, and pass them for sorting and dispatch assembly
4 where the various parts of the storage offer the highest and slowest speed potential
5. load build-up for dispatch.

14.04 Computerized stock control allows random storage, as the computer 'thinks' so fast, that goods can be stored in the best position for stacker crane efficiency. The computer (by on- or off-line control) informs the crane of any free slots in the sections relevant to the goods' movement speed.

14.05 If there is a high throughput and a wide range of goods with varying flow speeds, it is often economic to divide each rack into three or more sections (Figure 5.23) so that the fastest movers are at the input/delivery end. Such positions are flexible, and can be altered for seasonal variations by reprogramming the computer. With high throughput and a smaller range of goods, and clearly defined limits between product speeds (e.g. some stock frequently moved to an order-picking area, and other goods that might not move for months), the user speed differentiation can be by rack,

Figure 5.22 *Transporter: this runs to an elevator at the end of each aisle.*

Automated storage – storage process

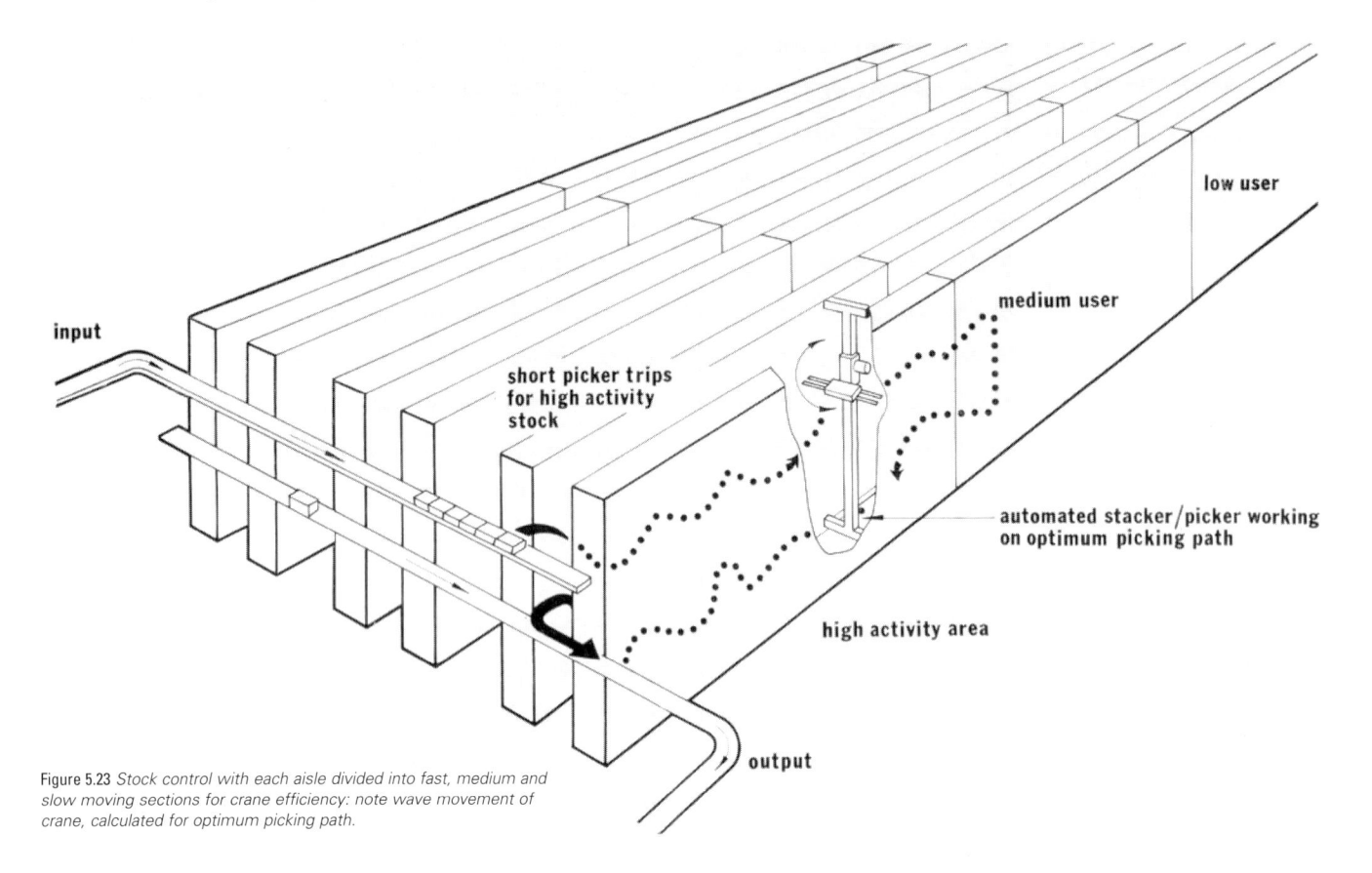

Figure 5.23 Stock control with each aisle divided into fast, medium and slow moving sections for crane efficiency: note wave movement of crane, calculated for optimum picking path.

using stacker cranes in the high and medium user areas, with a transfer carriage to place the stacker crane in the low user aisles when required. Some installations have complete high user aisles (Figure 5.24), so that the stacker cranes can feed the order picking face by cross-aisle transfer. These control decisions can have a major effect on the distribution of the building on the site.

14.06 Stock control is affected by transport operations, seasonal peaks, the development of trade (automated warehouses tend to develop their own), and by the policy of the company concerned, i.e. whether the warehouse is one of several regional distribution centres, or the main centralized post-production store. Flexibility should be built into the stock control system, as company policies change, and a profitable building can soon become an expensive liability. Care should also be taken concerning expansion, predicted or not, as mergers and a change of policy to absorb other unprofitable warehouses often cannot be foreseen.

15 Stock withdrawal

15.01 With stacker cranes this is the same as for input, but when transporter systems are used the operation is more difficult; some shuffling usually occurs, requiring spaces to be left free on either side of the aisle.

16 Order picking

16.01 One function can still not be economically automated: the final picking of discrete articles generally has to be done manually. Everything else can be automated to the point of taking the picker by computer-controlled stacker crane or pick car to the picking position (Figure 5.25), informing the operator by visual display of what to pick, checking by a scanner on the takeaway conveyor that the right type and number of articles has been selected, with the control system not permitting the device to progress and reprocessing the order if incorrect (Figure 5.26). This degree of automation has been used successfully in order fulfilment centres for the pharmaceutical and components industries. Several stacker crane manufacturers offer machines with order picking cabins, with on- or off-line control to the bay. Various arrangements of integrated takeaway conveyors have been suggested, but in-aisle sequential systems usually involve filling a number of crates or bins for particular orders and taking them to an output position at the end of the aisle.

16.02 Large-scale order-picking functions in order fulfilment centres can now be automated to up the actual

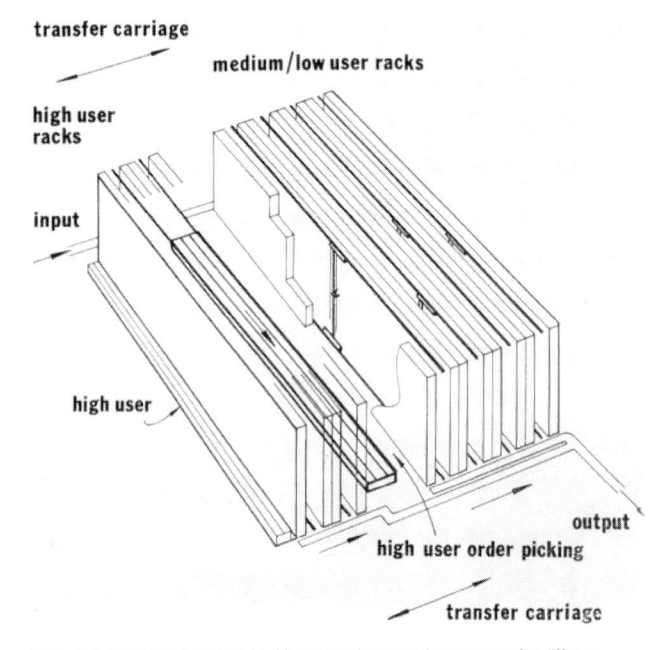

Figure 5.24 Stock control organized into complete warehouse areas for different speeds of goods movement. This allows all stacker cranes to work in the fast section: a transfer carriage takes a stacker crane to an aisle in the slow area when required. This system is suitable for seasonal goods with predictable popularity peaks.

Automated storage – storage process

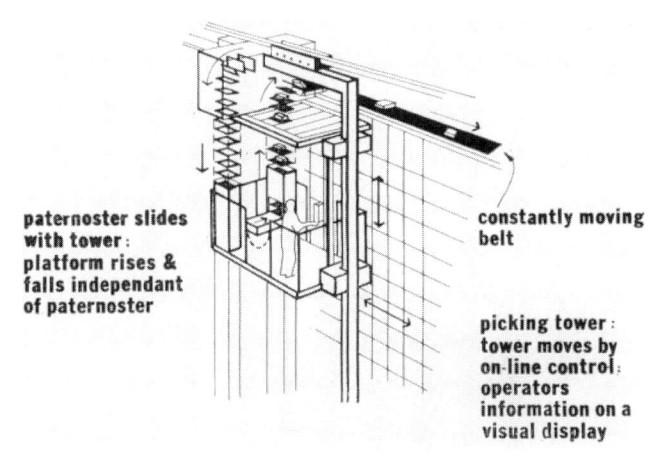

Figure 5.25 *Order-picking tower for continuous discrete item picking: tower movement is automated.*

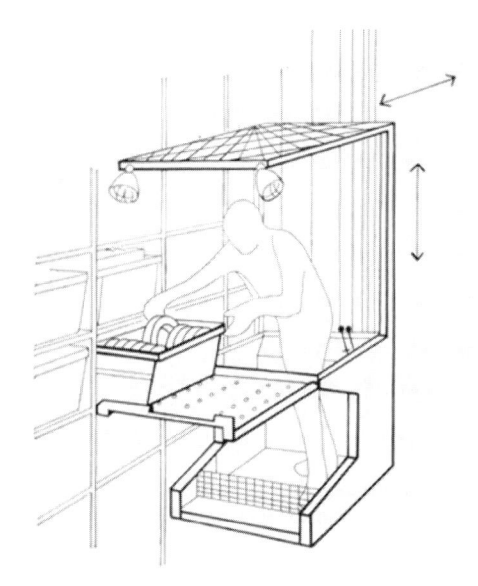

Figure 5.26 *Order-picking from tote bins: the crane has located the picker automatically.*

point of pick, which for discrete item picking still tend to be manual. Several automated warehouses operate multilevel mezzanine alternating aisle picking systems, fed by automated cranes, with manual item picking guided by illuminated data displays into crates coded for individual customers and routed round the system under computer control. The order-picking process is labour intensive; there are two basic methods:
1 Taking the operator to the goods.
2 Bringing the goods to the picker.

Free-path plant for order picking

16.03 There is scope for free path plant, with the possibility of wire guidance in and between aisles in medium-sized installations. The pick car allows multiple orders to be assembled simultaneously in crates (generally up to six at a time), with the unit guided automatically between locations (Figure 5.27). The operator is informed about what products to pick and from which side of the aisle to pick from by a light code and/or from a screen on the car. These systems are widely used in the pharmaceutical industry. Fully automated free-path picking is also used by this industry, picking small pill bottles and sachets.

Fixed-path plant for order picking

16.04 Fixed path order pickers give quick aisle-to-aisle transfer (45-second cycles are possible) (Figure 5.28).

Figure 5.27 *Free path machines like this are now being automated by wire guidance or light beams.*

Consider also the picking personnel's environment of continuous vertical and lateral acceleration and deceleration forces in fixed-path machines, especially if they are to be automatically guided to the picking position. Entry into the EU implies that British equipment is now subject to the stringent Federation Européenne de la Manutention (FEM)

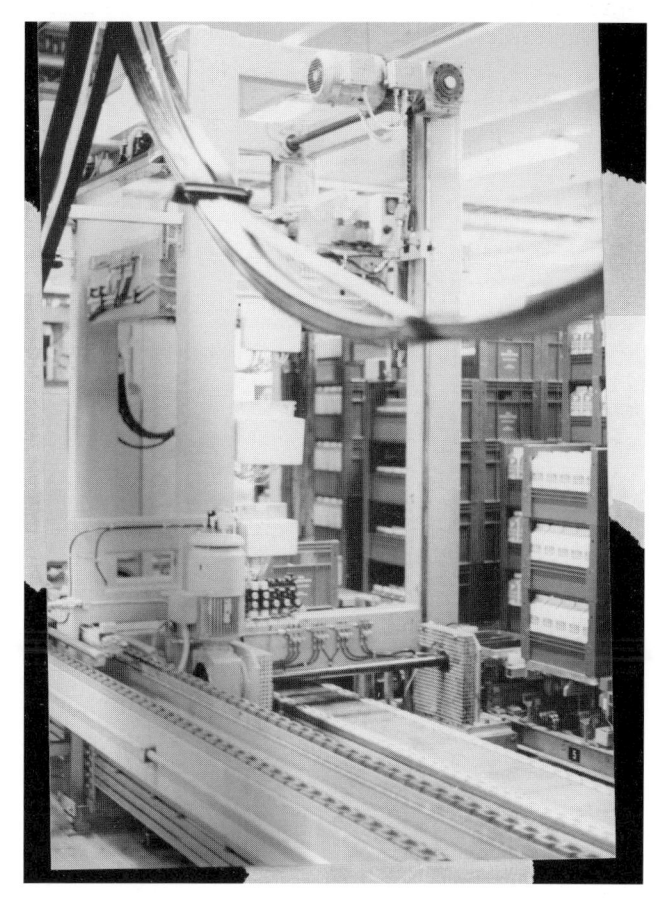

Figure 5.28 *Crate picker-stacker builds stacks of mixed crates and dispatches them across chain conveyor.*

205

Automated storage – storage process

regulations concerning operator conditions with mechanical handling plant.

16.05 As automated warehouses involve high throughput operations, fast order picking of discrete items and less than full pallet loads can prove a problem. Space can be used more effectively for intensive storage if the pickers are kept out of the racks and the goods are brought to them. Pickers operate faster if movement and walking distances are minimized. Line produced picking lists linked with a gather and dispense principle (bulk picking) can enable high speeds and accuracy to be achieved. The planning of gather and dispense cycles involves the programming of sorting machinery. The consultant should consider this at an early stage. (See Mechanized Storage 1, Order picking.)

Transporter systems

16.06 Transporter systems can be used for order picking, bringing the goods to the picker and automatically returning part loads to the racking. The 90° direction changes possible with one of these systems (Figure 5.29) could save space in the picking zone. Queueing and accumulation characteristics can be built into the programme (Figures 5.30 and 5.31), and priorities can be arranged so that if a picking zone is full, transporters can circulate a buffer track to keep the junctions clear.

Carousels

16.07 Carousels are rotating powered racking or shelving systems bringing the load to the static picking location, usually covering the ends of several racks (Figure 5.32).

Rotation can be horizontal or vertical. Vertical carousels are more popular, are free standing, can extend through several floors and although computer controlled for stock presentation generally rely on manual picking. Horizontal carousels can be very fast machines linked to automatic picking heads: used extensively with tote bins, they can have independent rotation direction at each storage level,

Figure 5.29 *Cartrac transporters being used as both transport and as order-picking carousel.*

Figure 5.30 *A low-rise automated storage building in France where van bodies are stored before final assembly. Note the 'mole' storage machine on the bottom track, and a similar unit carrying a van body overhead.*

Figure 5.31 *Not all automated warehouses involve pallet racking and lifting to great heights: this installation in France uses an automated transporter system as controlled roll-through storage for pallets of drums. Note the smoothness of movement implied by a stack of two pallets being handled together.*

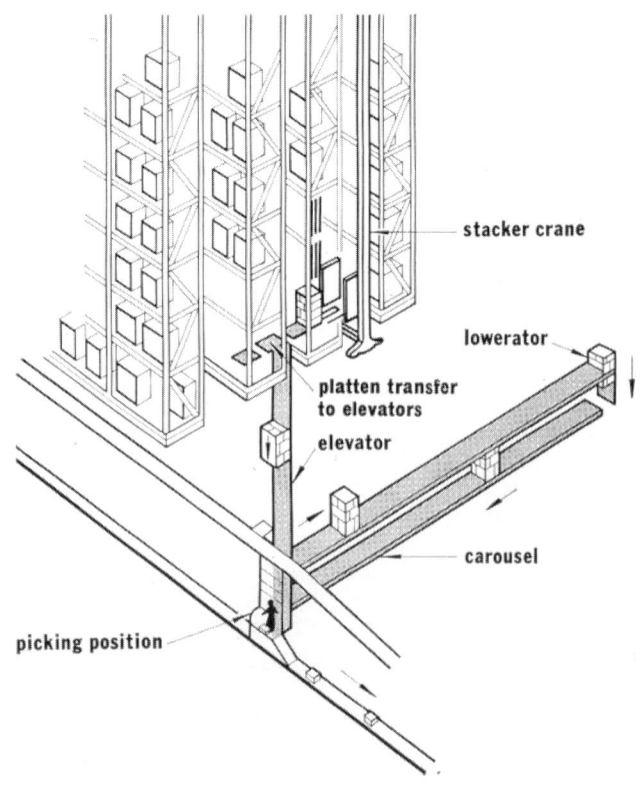

Figure 5.32 *High user carousel brings pallets to the order-picker at CWS warehouse, Birtley.*

such that the next pick is always taking the shortest route to the picking head while the last pick is in hand. In excess of 400 picking operations per head often serving two carousel ends are possible. These systems are expensive but accurate and space efficient: but they need similarly intensive replenishment 'campaigns' and considerable back-up infrastructure (conveyors) to achieve their full potential.

16.08 Completely automated picking can also be implemented with a limited number of lines in live/roll through racking. Such systems stock cartons on inclined tracks, releasing them in order sequence onto an adjacent belt: such systems can be multilevel, and can either pick sequential orders, or pick batches of orders to feed a subsidiary sorter. Systems like 'Ordermatic and 'Itematic' have been used in chilled and frozen storage which is inhospitable for staffing for over 20 years now. A variation of this system for small items, pharmaceuticals, cigarettes, confectionery is the 'A' frame, where the storage tracks are steep, feeding by gravity dispenser onto takeaway belts: here orders tend to be released sequentially into tote bins at the ends of the belts. The bins themselves can be automatically routed around 'A' frames.

16.09 If pallets, tote bins or plattens are used in the picking zone, an empty return conveyor is required, feeding a magazine at the input side of the store. Care should be taken that this does not conflict with other conveyor feeds. Some installations pile pallets at the end of the stacker crane aisle, so that groups can be treated as dispatch freight when the crane has a free cycle; the pallets are sorted automatically into a storage area.

17 Picking area

17.01 Picking areas should be treated as for Technical study, Mechanized storage 1, para. 17, with a minimum level of 400 lux light, and sufficient ventilation to provide comfort conditions for the pickers. If a picking tower is used in racks, it should be made as comfortable as possible; comfort and safety go hand in hand. Lighting can be integral with the tower.

17.02 Picking from transporter systems can be isolated from the plant, as the transporter will stop at the correct bay and remain until the correct number of packages have been recorded by a sensor on a takeaway conveyor. The picker can be protected from all moving parts by a screen. Noise can be a problem with so much machinery, but various silencing methods are available; contact the equipment manufacturers.

18 Load assembly

18.01 In automated systems, load assembly requires tilt tray, tilt belt, slide slat or various combinations of belt or roller conveyors. These have been discussed in Technical study, Mechanized storage, para. 17, and Information sheet, Mechanized storage 10.

18.02 The basic difference is in the control system. The greater the number of orders being assembled at one time, and the number of lines involved, the more complicated will be the software. Automation enables much higher sorting speeds, compared with manual operation. Some installations have got out of phase between the picking and sorting operations, and it has taken considerable time to restore the situation. The problem is again that computers work very fast, and machinery comparatively slowly. There is no substitute for simulation during the design stage to test batch picking and assembly principles, and against whose results physical commissioning can be measured.

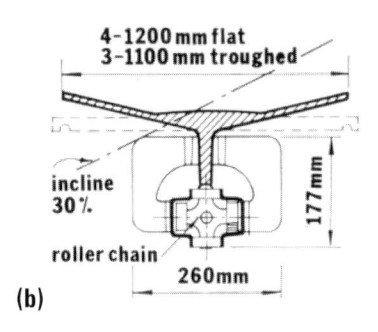

Figure 5.33 (a) Tilt tray or tilt slatsorter, up to 12,000 items per hour. (b) Detailed section.

18.03 Some automated sorting systems involve tipping goods down chutes. Check that the packaging is sufficient for the shock environment that is experienced; impacts of 140 g have been recorded on steel chutes on the first bounce, and 200 g on the second; test packages have shown that shocks are greater if the angle is steep enough to force packages to bounce on their apices.

18.04 Automated dispatch sorting areas are space-consuming. Tilt tray and tilt belt chute accumulators are linear, they can be looped to save space, but this may affect the intermediate transport between sorting and the loading bay (linear systems are often most economic in the long run) (Figure 5.33). Accumulation conveyors are a parallel function, fed from a high-speed supply and sorting cross conveyor.

18.05 One of the benefits of a transporter system is that it can be used for sorting full pallet loads direct to the loading bay, and accumulate the goods, without further handling (Figure 5.34).

18.06 Palletizers, banders and shrink wrappers, if under fully automated control, require buffer conveyors at input (especially if goods are shrink-wrapped after palletizing, as the latter machines operate faster). If high-peak throughput is necessary, more shrink-wrappers should be provided than palletizing machines, with a sorting mechanism between them, and at the shrink wrap tunnel output to redirect the pallet to the correct loading bay. This can all be on-line, but the software can be complex. Buffer space and diverting mechanisms should be provided in case of breakdowns; this too can be simulated at the design stage (Figure 5.35).

18.07 Clearance should be left for the maintenance of the large number of switches and sensors used in automated accumulation and sorting conveyors. One of the major problems experienced with this type of operation has been access for quick repair in case of breakdown.

Automated storage – storage process

Figure 5.34 *Shuttle car serving load-accumulation conveyors: note elevator to racking at the end of the aisle.*

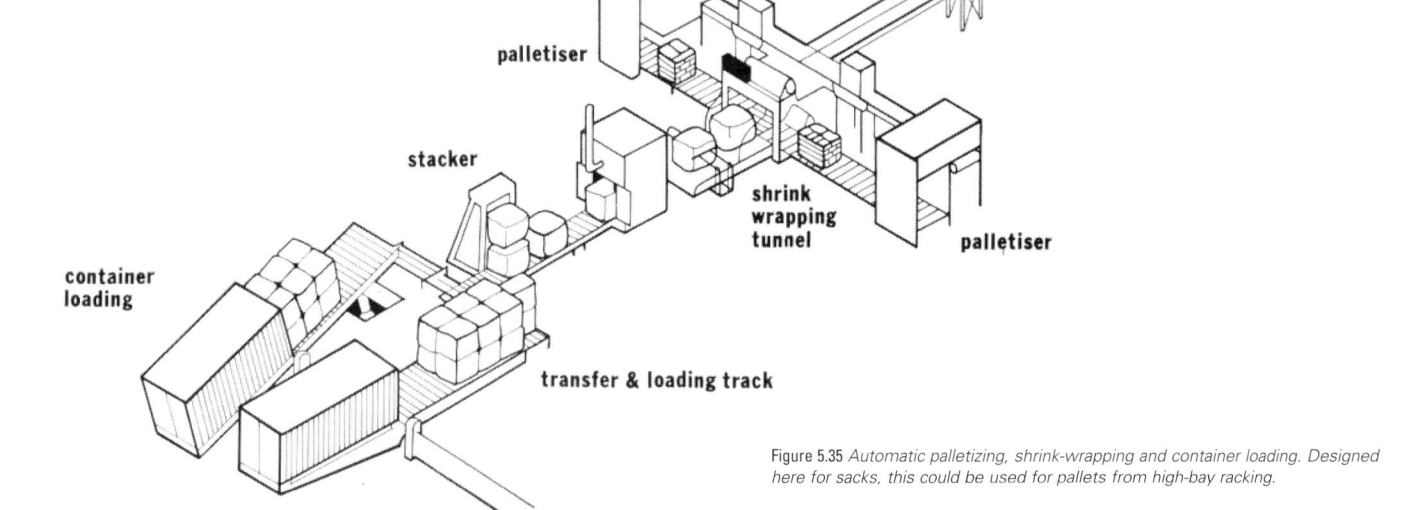

Figure 5.35 *Automatic palletizing, shrink-wrapping and container loading. Designed here for sacks, this could be used for pallets from high-bay racking.*

19 Order and documentation check

19.01 An automated system performs this check prior to sorting for palletizing. Once palletized, the correct routing to the load accumulation point can be checked manually or automatically. Manual checking is a question of pallets moving past an operator in a console, who checks them off a printout or on a visual display. This can be automated by a code label being printed-out and applied at the palletizer, the pallets then passing an optical code scanner. It is at this point that full pallet loads selected from the store join those that have been built up by order picking. Buffer track is needed for the rejection of incorrectly coded pallets, and mistakes in routing.

20 Dispatch collection and loading

20.01 Load assembly is a fast-moving function in an automated warehouse. Pre-assembly can operate with the computer always working one load ahead, described in para. 4, by scanning collection documents before the incoming trucks have entered the accumulation lanes; a suitable loading bay can be allocated, and the return load assembled. If only full pallet loads are involved, this can be achieved as fast as it takes the previous truck to load, clear the bay, and the incoming vehicle to unload, i.e. 8–10 minutes.

20.02 Load accumulation is affected by the distribution of goods in the racks. If the required pallets are high user goods in several aisles, the picking will be fast, but if mostly low user material in few racks, and other orders are being assembled simultaneously, the operation will be slower. As shown in Technical study, Mechanized storage 1, many load assemblies can be predicted day by day, and small goods order picking and pallet build-up can be instigated by the computer daily to be ready for the truck to arrive.

20.03 Accurate vehicle arrival can never be a foregone conclusion, due to traffic conditions or breakdown. 'Sidings' should be provided so that pallets can be re-routed to allow the load to be accumulated without disrupting the picking cycle or the operation of the loading bay. This can also act as a peak buffer, when several vehicles are accumulating for each bay, and fast turnround is critical.

20.04 In peak conditions, the computer may have to operate different picking and storage cycles from normal speed working. Pressure can be taken off the loading zone by routing easily fulfilled orders involving full pallets to one area of loading bays for fast turnround. More complicated orders should be allocated a larger number of bays for slower turnround cycles. If the collection documents have been processed when the vehicle enters the site, the trucks can be assembled randomly, and the central computer left to allocate bays based on updated data on loading bay and order assembly progress.

20.05 Both software and sorting plant can be complicated, as several loads will be accumulated at a time; in case of failure manual override is necessary. An elevating double-deck conveyor would segregate incoming and outgoing goods, and allow immediate loading after discharge for vehicles with tracked floors. Catwalks should be installed with this system, to provide access to the conveyor surface in case of blockage.

20.06 The amount of automation involved in dispatch sorting depends on the throughput, and how critical peak service is to the user. Lower-key operations are used with combinations of on and off-line control, with forklift trucks and towline trains for accumulation, which although slower, are less prone to breakdown.

20.07 An integrated system for automatically palletizing goods and loading ISO containers has recently been proposed; this could be useful in high turnover operations, especially those involved in exports such as groupage warehouses (Figure 5.35).

21 Additional data

21.01 *Trends in radio communication.* Developments in mobile telephone technology are spinning-off into the distribution workplace. WiFi is the broadband wireless local area network communications standard (WLAN) that allows data transmission rates of 11 Mbps (fast by 2003 standards) between a base station (say in an order picking zone) and a data processing hub (the warehouse control system) up to 100 metres away. This base station will catch the communications from order picking staff using 'ring scanners' with Bluetooth technology, literally barcode or radio data tag scanners that are on the picker's finger with no encumbering wires. As the operative picks or packs, the item's label is scanned, the proof of pick being transmitted through personal wireless personal area networking (PAN), to a transmitter attached to their belt, to be forwarded through the 802.11 wireless communications protocol to the base station. The same technology in reverse can provide picking data onto a monocle over one of the picker's eyes. The ring technology is already in place for parcels delivery and collection with a leading 'integrator', the others rapidly following suit. The implication is much more freedom of movement for materials handling and delivery staff combining increased productivity with greater accuracy (right first time) and security, in turn driving real time replenishment and re-ordering reducing inventory (but maybe not risk).

Information sheet

Automated storage 1

Automated-handling plant

1 Order pickers

2 Stacker cranes

The operation of automated-handling plant has been described in Technical study, Automated storage 1; para. 13 describes stacker cranes, and para. 16 describes order pickers. This sheet gives properties of a typical stacker crane and order picker, for use at sketch design stage, but plant is usually custom-built, and manufacturers should be contacted.

1 Order pickers

1.01 Order picking for discrete items is still generally a manual operation. In automated storage systems, mechanical control is limited to transporting the human picker automatically to the appropriate rack position (Figure 5.45), and showing on display system how many of which product are to be picked (Figure 5.46a).

1.02 Multi-person picking towers are partially computer controlled; they take the pickers to the correct bay, and the pickers then bulk pick from a printout or from a visual display.

1.03 The tier picker is the nearest approach to a fully automatic carton layer order picker to date (Figure 5.47). A vacuum head picks a whole layer of cartons from a pallet and lowers it on to the carriage pallet. There are wire guided fully automated pickers for pharmaceuticals made by PEEM/Knapp, employed in Germany. These can be used for kitting small components as in electronics assembly, or for spares.

2 Stacker cranes

2.01 Stacker cranes automatically lift and position pallets in narrow aisles generally up to 30 m high (Figure 5.46b). Cab is included, but only for emergency and breakdown use. Bottom rail supported cranes, rather than top hung, are becoming more popular. Typical speeds are 180 m/min horizontally and 120 m/min vertically. Movement motors are equipped with special controls for inching and final positioning (Figure 5.48). Electric pick-up can be from bus-bars at high or low level, or by a festoon cable. Aisle clearance is 200 mm plus width of widest pallet plus overhang.

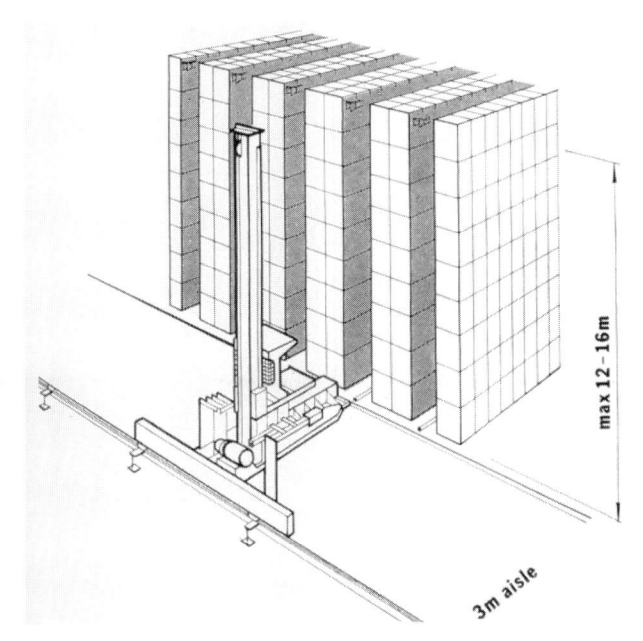

Figure 5.45 *Stacker cranes and order pickers can move from one aisle to another with a transfer carriage.*

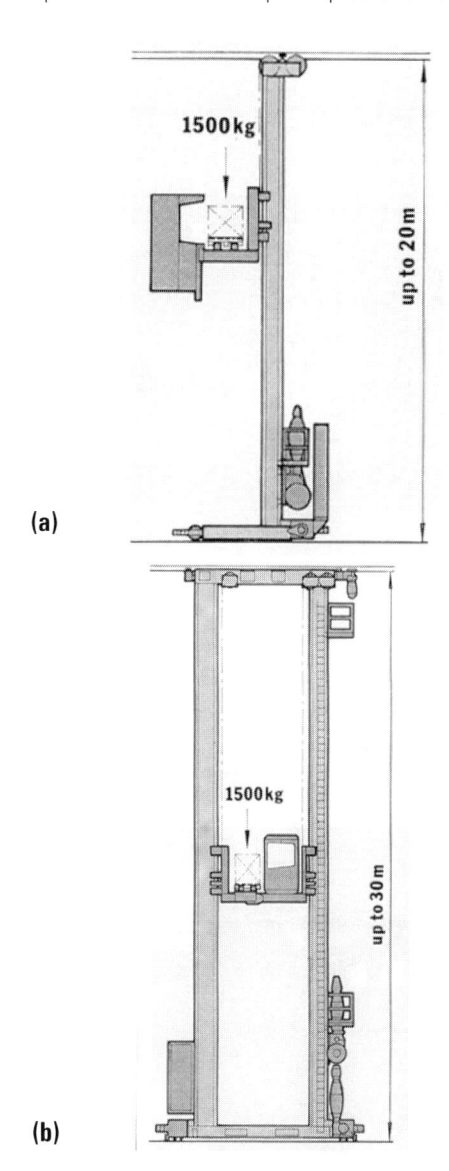

Figure 5.46 *Dimensions of (a) order picker, (b) stacker crane.*

Automated storage – automated handling plant

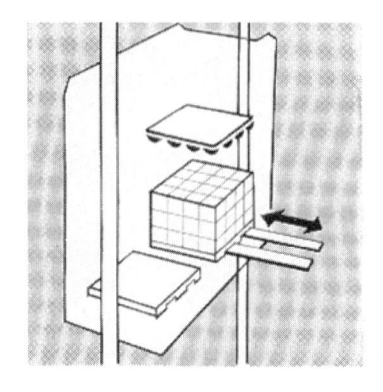

a) Forks extend from carriage.

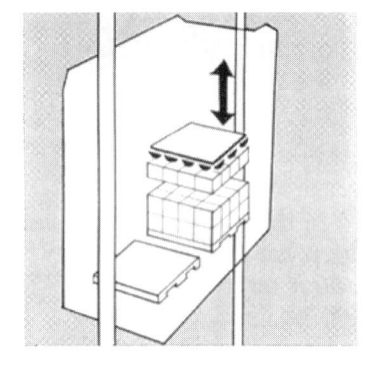

b) Vacuum head is lowered onto top tier of boxes.

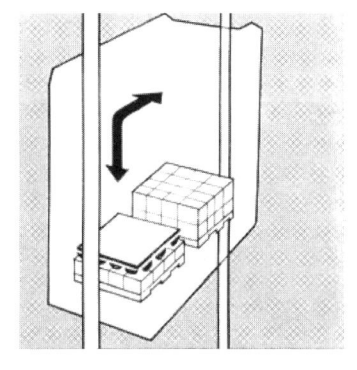

c) Head lifts tier and lowers it on to pallet.

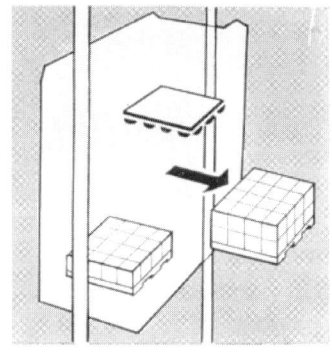

d) Forks return rack pallet.

Figure 5.47 *Automated tier picker.*

Figure 5.49 *Shuttle car with festoon cable in low profile chain.*

Figure 5.48 *(a) In this automated warehouse there are three access levels: this is the top one, showing the stacker cranes and the pick-up point. (b) Here the AGVs integrate directly with the stacker cranes, with no P & D station. (c) The cross-aisle for curve going stacker cranes; note 'points' system in the foreground.*

Technical study

Automated storage 2
Building function

22	Structure	31	Mobile plant
23	Floor	32	Integration of building and plant
24	Building services	33	Maintenance
25	Special services	34	Management
26	Building fabric	35	Personnel accommodation
27	Fre control	36	Amenity
28	Security	37	Security and safety
29	External works	38	Circulation and parking
30	Structure-based plant		

Technical study 1 (paras 1 to 21) dealt with automated storage; this second study (paras 22 to 38) covers the design of the building.

22 Structure

22.01 Automated warehouses need not be high bay, but high land prices in Europe have encouraged them to be so. Over 30 m is now possible, and even higher buildings are planned. They impose special structural conditions and the basic question is whether to choose a structure integral with the racking or to have racking separate for flexibility. A factor here is whether fixed- or free-path automated-handling plant is to be used, and if fixed path, how will it be supported and guided. In using structural racking the intention is to exploit the racking's potential stiffness, thus minimizing the peripheral support structure and eliminating wasteful columns. One manufacturer claims that cost savings of over 30 per cent are possible with integral structures over 15 m (Figure 5.36). High racking has to be stiff to accept pallet loads on the upper levels, and it is therefore logical to hang cladding on the exterior of the racks and just stiffen the building across aisles which have already been made quite stiff by crane rail supports.

22.02 Although integrally structured high-bay warehouses have operated successfully, there have been problems. High automated stacker cranes work in racking to tight tolerances, which must be achieved in their manufacture and erection. Allow for this in the design of structure and control systems. One Swedish company experienced considerable commissioning trouble with their high-bay store. The stacker cranes were not stopping in a precise enough position for immediate engagement of the forks, causing them to retract in a way that did not retrieve the pallet cleanly. To ensure the correct alignment of crane forks, often based on an optical reflective system which can account for structural tolerance, it has been found necessary to use separate fine positioning systems. Accurate site welding becomes increasingly difficult at heights over 30 m. Inaccuracies in the support rails will make a stacker crane operate out of the vertical. The cranes themselves are subject to manufacturing tolerances; the problem arises where these crane and rack tolerances interact. There is a set of FEM standards that set out acceptable high-bay racking and stacker crane construction tolerances.

22.03 Care should be taken over structural design: several loaded stacker cranes decelerating simultaneously in parallel aisles have made one installation sway alarmingly. Another user found that somehow a transfer carriage had allowed two cranes to operate in one aisle. Factory inspectors now tend to insist on 'running cranes against their stops' during commissioning to check that no permanent deformation occurs. Torsional forces can also be generated in stacker cranes when the loaded forks retract from a rack bay to the centre of the carriage.

Figure 5.36 Erection of structural racking under construction – note how the roof and cladding 'chase' the racking.

Automated storage – building function

21.04 Buffeting by wind in high-bay warehouses has proved troublesome, especially where steel cladding has been hung directly from racking (Figure 5.37). High buildings with large wall areas are subject to high wind loadings and, if the buffeting coincides with the vibration wavelength of the racking, considerable movement can occur; a crane may cause serious damage to rails and motors. One warehouse was designed with a special space frame between cladding and racks to absorb the buffet. Expansion of racks caused by insolation can also affect operation of stacker cranes. Long high walls catching direct sunlight tend to act as radiant heaters but this is less of a problem with insulated sandwich steel sheet. Concrete cladding transferring heat to racking has caused cranes to jam in at least one European warehouse – the tolerances between plant and racking must have been very tight.

Figure 5.37 *Cladding hung directly onto racking.*

22.05 The type of roof decking is important; steel sheet is often bolted or welded to a sub-frame sprung from rack heads, and is either welded and laid to falls, or covered with a lightweight foamed screed. Dark surfaces such as asphalt with chippings soak up heat and cause a cumulative effect down a rack range; end frames bow outwards at the ceiling position, complicating accurate control of cranes. A reflective finish or insulated roof decking can minimize the effect of insolation.

22.06 Automated warehouses generate large areas of peripheral equipment housed in buildings of conventional height. It is therefore important to detail the joint between high and low bay carefully to accept different expansions and to dispose of run-off from the large area of cladding above (Figure 5.38).

22.07 Care should also be taken in integrating services with structure, ensuring that movement of racks will not break pipe or cable mountings, and that services will not encroach on tolerances already reduced by structural movement.

22.08 If free-path machinery is to be increasingly used for medium-sized installations (see Mechanized storage), there will be a requirement for adaptable racking, quite independent of the 'big box' building enclosing it.

22.09 A further question is whether high-bay integral rack structures should be steel, concrete, or composite. For fire control, concrete is an attractive proposition (see para. 27), but it is not easy to adapt and is initially expensive. However, the 17 m high Dr Maag warehouse in Dielsdorf was easily erected from cruciform pre-cast concrete sections from which metal pallet rails are can-

Figure 5.38 *Low-rise peripheral building round high-bay pallet silo.*

tilevered. Outer racks are T-shaped, providing an integral cladding function also. Stacker cranes run on top rails, fixed to crossbeams that stiffen the concrete sections laterally, and on base rails cast into the floor.

22.10 Foundations for automated warehouses are complicated, since racking and vertical members can impose high point loads, and deceleration of heavy stacker cranes produces high forces. Structural consultants should be involved from the outset, as the condition of the land might preclude economic high-bay development. With the tight tolerances required, only minimum settlement can be accepted. Manufacturers of equipment can handle this problem, but if the warehouse has been in use for some while, adjustment can be expensive both in lost time and in reprogramming and commissioning the plant for accurate final positioning. Some international warehouse construction companies offer a complete structural service with their warehouse and control package, backed by considerable operating experience in countries such as Switzerland where seasonal temperature variations can make ground conditions difficult. Conversely, the decision to go high bay may be driven by foundation concerns; in one example, an intermediate height (12 m) mechanized warehouse to be built near a river was going to need a piled slab: analysis proved that the 'additional' capital cost of a 22 m narrow aisle automated warehouse was cheaper through a much smaller footprint saving piling costs, with the added benefit from automation giving labour savings and 24-hour operation.

Summary: integrated structures

22.11

Steel – advantages:

Adjustable to varied loadings.
Short preparation period for fabrication.
Little problem with transport and assembly.
Easily adaptable.

Steel – disadvantages:

Danger of distortion or collapse in case of fire.
Relatively high maintenance costs (these have been reduced in some modern finishes).

Danger of corrosion if aggressive materials are stored.
High elasticity for critical tolerances; in certain conditions this can be advantageous.

Concrete – advantages:

Fire resistant.
Cheaper maintenance.
High inherent stability and little deformation.
Corrosion resistant.
Large dimensions are economic.

Concrete – disadvantages:

High investment in building.
High investment in site equipment.
Lengthy preparation of site, unless pre-cast is used.
Can cause transport and assembly problems.
Not easily adaptable.

Up to 18 m racking can be constructed from cold rolled steel section, but above that height hot rolled is required, which increases the price by about 25 per cent. Pre-cast concrete tends to cost 15 per cent to 20 per cent more than steel up to 30 m high, and 40 per cent to 50 per cent more over that height (Figure 5.39).

Figure 5.39 *Structural racking in an automated high-bay warehouse made of welded hollow section tube.*

23 Floor

23.01 The floor of a high-bay warehouse can be critical to the tolerance of racking and stacker cranes. Stacker cranes are subject to oscillation caused by acceleration and deceleration in the aisle and irregularities in the floor rail. Slight irregularities in a running rail, which can be magnified by crane running systems, produce additional oscillations in the mast. These can be of approximately the same magnitude as the stresses caused by acceleration and deceleration and when in phase can cause high oscillation peaks. A damper may have to be fitted at the top of the mast, often in the form of additional sprung side guide rollers to the upper rail.

23.02 The floor of an automated warehouse does not have the same function as that of a mechanized unit, where adjustable racking rests on the floor surface, and free-path plant relies on the overall floor finish for the tightness of tolerance in high stacking (Figure 5.40). Free-path machinery becomes uneconomic compared with fixed-path stacker cranes at about 12 m; although manufacturers claim up to 18 m heights are possible with top guide rollers.

Figure 5.40 *Free-path, high-rise machine (here semi-automatic). Floors have to be constructed to very tight tolerances (Class 1).*

23.03 In high-bay automated units with fixed-path stacker cranes the floor is an integral part of the foundation and a base for crane rails, that are shimmed and grouted accurately into place. Racks tend to be bolted through to the slab, bolt mountings having been accurately cast with the final finish. Manufacturer's installation specification should be checked at an early stage in the project for consistency with floor tolerances: unforeseen shimming can be time-consuming and lead to a substantial claim.

24 Building services

24.01 Environment should be carefully tailored to the requirements of the stored products. The large cubic capacity of automated high-bay warehouses and their insulation to prevent rack expansion caused by insolation, mean that the buildings can have virtually steady-state thermal characteristics. As stacker cranes accelerate and brake rapidly, there is heat gain from the motors. Some background heating may be needed in winter – although this has been disputed on the ground that comfort conditions for personnel are unnecessary except in order-picking and peripheral areas, and heat generated by crane motors combined with insulated cladding should keep the temperature above freezing – but this again depends on the temperature of the goods when they enter the warehouse. Goods from refrigerated lorries can lower the overall temperature by several degrees. Background heating to keep temperatures at approximately 7°C would reduce the possibility of condensation which can damage goods and electronic equipment, allow a wet charged sprinkler system to be used and keep packaging materials in good condition. Keeping the building near steady state will minimize rack and track movement. Owing to the height of these buildings, radiant panels have little effect; blown air is more useful. The blower units, which can also be used for extraction and for circulating fresh air in summer, and for some humidity control can be mounted as packages on the rack structure on the roof far away from expensive electronic equipment, thus freeing the floor area for handling plant.

24.02 There is also argument about whether light should be provided in high-bay stores except for maintenance purposes. As personnel are involved only in order-picking areas, general lighting is unnecessary. In-aisle order picking by picking tower is a closed system in that operators are not aware of any of the aisle excepting the bay they are picking from, so lighting can be local. An argument for lighting high rack areas has been that it might be needed in emergency. But in the event of fire, power would be cut at once and, if a crane breaks down, portable emergency lighting can quickly be positioned by maintenance staff. The need for lighting is psychological; warehouse users seem to need to walk into the high-bay area to see that everything is operating correctly – but this is dangerous and, in any case, malfunction is obvious from the control boards and printouts.

24.03 Daylight should definitely be excluded except in order-picking zones. An interesting case occurred in the high-bay automated warehouse for a Swedish company where cranes were stopping seemingly at random and restarting by the time maintenance engineers arrived. The fault was finally traced with the aid of a diary. The first stoppage was a few days before the winter solstice and the next a few days after it. It was found that on these two days a sunbeam had managed to activate a photo-electric sensor cell.

24.04 Rainwater down pipes can be a problem. Users are loath to allow these into the storage area for fear of leakage onto stock or electronic equipment, and so they are usually run outside the cladding. This is assisted by the narrow profile of these buildings.

25 Special services

25.01 Automated warehouses involve quantities of wiring and electrical supply services. This is one area where money should not be saved. Wiring includes the power supply for handling plant, primary and final positioning sensors, limit switch controls, and heat and smoke sensors at each bay. Return wiring for data feedback to the peripheral or central computer is also run from each rack bay, and from the main position switches. With mini-computer control, transistorized circuitry reduces the amount of wiring needed. In the use of local logic control units, each periphery has its own cabinet equipped with basic power handling devices and full system interlocks and sequence controls. An alternative is to return all primary signals to the central computer which then calculates control decisions, but wiring in these 'hard wire'

systems is complex; festoons of cable are a common sight, and finding a fault is laborious.

25.02 Control wiring and electrical supply has to integrate with other services when running up racks and in ducts. Care should be taken to prevent interference with control signals – a fault in some early installations. In order to keep floors clear for control cabling, wet services for environmental control units should be taken up to roof level and fitted with drip trays. There they are adaptable. Sortation conveyors also require control and supply wiring, and compressed air supply is often required for sortation machinery (Figure 5.41).

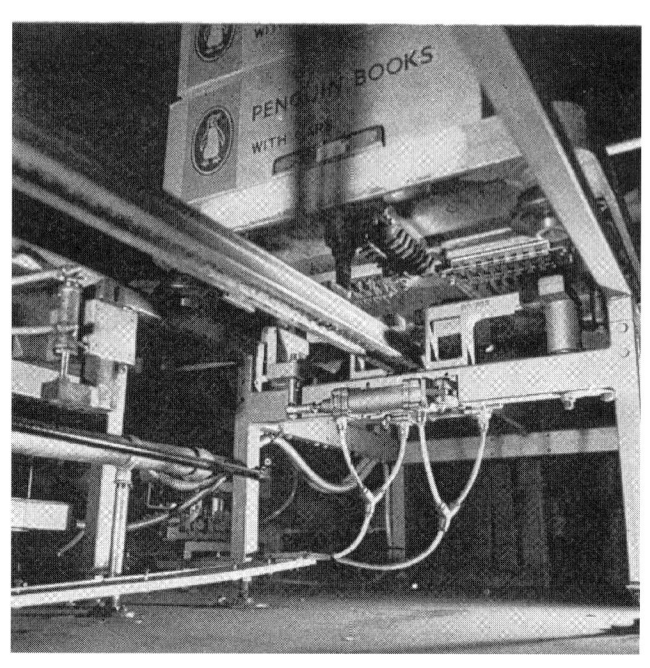

Figure 5.41 *Cartrac transporter used as a sorting machine: note pneumatic controls.*

25.03 Computers tend to require special air-conditioned environments, although some mini-computers work successfully in normal 'office' atmospheres. Check with the storage system manufacturer as to what is required and whether segregated compartments are necessary.

26 Building fabric

26.01 The high-bay zone of the warehouse can be clad in several ways:

cladding attached directly to racking
cladding attached to a sub-frame on the racking
cladding attached to a separate sub-frame
concrete integrated racking (as described in para. 22.01).

The choice is governed by height of building, prevailing wind, exposure and type of cladding used. In conditions of extreme exposure, cladding can be attached to an independent sub-frame, restrained from the roof and the ground and incorporating the intermediate stiffening and wind bracing.

26.02 In order to achieve steady state environment internally, cladding with an efficient insulator should be employed.

26.03 Both steel and proprietary sheeting have been used effectively. Fire regulations concerning hazards from, and fire resistance of, walls close to boundaries can result in a heavy cladding being required, involving an expensive, heavy-duty sub-frame.

26.04 Fire vents should be provided in the roof cladding (see para. 27.04); if packaged heater/ventilation units are roof-mounted then access hatches should be included. Catwalks are a good idea installed over rack runs, for maintenance of upper crane rails and access to sprinkler mains, wiring and heater units. But with integral rack structures, the rack frames are extended as roof support and accommodate the crane guide rails and services, so that there is generally little room for a catwalk without encroaching on storage space. Generally, upper level maintenance is performed from special personnel cage pallets from the cranes under manual control. Catwalks and escape stairs should be well marked and lit, and provided with emergency lighting. Contact also the local fire officer and factory inspector.

27 Fire control

27.01 The choice of fire prevention, detection and control equipment plays an important part in initial costing, as equipment sufficient for all contingencies is expensive but affects the present weighting of insurance premiums against this building type. Much is now known of fire characteristics from tests carried out by US insurers, the US Joint Fire Research Organization and the Building Research Station in the UK. The data on high-bay fire characteristics including evidence of very rapid spread of flame due to the 'chimney' effect of narrow aisles and high racking even with 'wet charged' in-rack sprinklers, makes some insurance companies weight these buildings heavily enough to impair seriously their cost-saving potential. The LPC provides a firm set of recommendations on fire protection and detection systems for use by insurers and designers alike but it is important that the client's insurer is contacted early in the design stage.

27.02 Regulations for means of escape are set out in the Building Regulations. The LPC Rules for Automatic Sprinkler Installations, have been replaced by the Loss Prevention Council Rules 1990, which give guidance on in-rack sprinkler clearances for high-bay stores. The complexity of detection and control equipment is based on the fire hazard rating of the goods stored; consult 'Classification of Goods in Storage', LPC Technical Bulletin TB17 1992, which replaced the FOC rules. As insurance costs vary according to the type of product stored, the choice of the correct detection method can save the user a great deal in premiums.

27.03 High-bay buildings can usually be classed under the Building Regulations as 'Single storey storage and general purpose', and may be subject to limits in compartment size. If in doubt take advice from specialist fire consultants. When peripheral sortation areas such as galleries and mezzanines are involved as elements of the structure, they can be required to have minimum periods of fire resistance. Between high-bay and sorting and order-picking areas there can be the requirement for a fire resisting compartment wall with four hours' duration: typically for floor areas over 3000 m². Insurers also tend to ask that the warehouse be divided into compartments. This can be achieved by compartmenting groups of aisles, but is often impracticable where there is a transfer aisle with conveyor feeds with automated high-bay stores. However, to date there is no firm policy, each being assessed on its merits.

27.04 Fire problems in high warehouses have been discussed (see Technical Study, Mechanized storage 2, para. 27). In a high-bay warehouse, the stack effect becomes even more pronounced. Arguments about venting continue, but it is suggested the loss of one rack load by fast vertical flame spread is preferable to ignition of the top of several racks by flames being forced across under the roof sheeting. The problems are those of conventional 'big box' buildings, but magnified. Pressure build–up can reach near-thunderstorm conditions; one warehouse in the USA had a large section of its roof blown off by the internal pressure. The problem with venting is primarily expense. The true effect of venting on sprinkler operation is known; there is a chance that if the vents open too soon, the sprinklers might not operate in time, and if too late, too many might open, damaging the goods. But it is unlikely that many sprinkler problems would occur with the new detection system produced recently by the Loss Prevention Council (see Technical Study, Mechanized storage 2, para 27). Another group has advocated shutting the warehouse off and letting oxygen starvation contain the fire, but smoke would prevent fire officers from finding the seat of the fire and the pressure build-up would be dangerous.

27.05 Whatever measures are suggested for extinguishing a fire, there is no substitute for immediate detection. If an extinguishing agent were applied 1–1.5 minutes after ignition, with substantial control after 3–5 minutes and total extinction in 8–10 minutes, damage by fire, smoke and water would be minimized. It is especially relevant in an automated warehouse that although water is still considered by insurers to be the most effective extinguisher, if applied with enough pressure and in sufficient quantities, it can severely damage stored goods and, more important, electronic components. Users also fear that water-charged sprinklers could leak onto stock. Shrink-wraps produce further complications, in that they deflect water and contain heat. When the wrap shrinks off allowing the heat to activate the sprinkler, the fire may already have taken a firm hold.

27.06 Because of these various arguments against water, other methods have been examined. One uses a stacker crane; fire control packs are placed in strategic positions in racking and fire is sensed by a linear sensor that follows the rack contours. The stacker crane is immediately put onto an emergency cycle, dumping its normal load, returning to pick up the extinguishing pack, and moving fast to the burning bay where it releases the contents of the pack. This might not be realistic in operating conditions; the first thing that is likely to happen in an area full of electronic equipment, especially as some fires are electrical in origin, is for the power to be cut.

27.07 Various extinguishing agents have been tried. High expansion foam with a 1000:1 water expansion ratio has been discussed. In high-bay operations, the volume to fill is even larger, and there is a greater chance through increased stack effect for the foam to chase the fire up the racks. Foam can still damage stock by damp. The 1 million cu ft/mm foam figure implies that a medium-sized high-bay installation would take 5–6 minutes to fill. It has been found that the fire tends to re-ignite unless the foam is topped up about every half-hour.

27.08 Carbon dioxide requires high concentrations to do an efficient job, but automated stores housing no permanent staff virtually eliminate the risk of people becoming trapped. To extinguish a fire with CO_2, the oxygen content would have to be reduced to between 12 per cent and 16 per cent for solids smouldering on the surface. For deep-seated smouldering oxygen content would have to be reduced further to 1 per cent to 2 per cent, in a 5 million cu ft warehouse, and this is a lot of CO_2. There is also a risk of pressure damage to the building fabric because, to be effective, no fire vents would have been installed, hence a blow-off valve should be fitted.

Automated storage – building function

27.09 A more promising gas is BCF. A 5 per cent to 10 per cent by volume concentration is sufficient for inhibiting combustion but this has to be directed at the seat of the flame, requiring a sprinkler type gas outlet in each rack supplied from a central pressure source. A zoned system with compartmentation has been suggested, whereby a multi-shot application of BCF would operate in the applicable racking zone with possibility of extending the operation to other areas as required. Total flooding capacity would have to be provided. The BCF would discharge on detection, and stop when the flame disappeared; injection being repeated until the fire brigade arrived. It is said that these gases would not damage goods, but check that stock will not be contaminated by gas.

27.10 The fire brigade is not enamoured of automated high-bay warehouses, for the following reasons:

1 Height of racks and risk of burning goods falling on fire officers.
2 In automated stores there are usually too few means of escape for fire officers and routes to them are often tortuous.
3 Inadequate access for fire engines except through the loading bay.
4 Insufficient water supplies for the size of the job involved.
5 The amount of electrical equipment and cabling, some of which might still be live and have had its insulation burned away.
6 Density of storage in automated warehouses and height of racks in relation to width of aisles makes water penetration from hoses difficult.
7 With integral rack-building structures, the fire problem is further increased by the risk of racks buckling and jeopardizing the whole structure. Crane rails will warp, and it is possible that a whole section of the warehouse would have to be cut out and rebuilt. It is likely that overall instability, especially under crane deceleration loading, would force a total shutdown during the work which, with rewiring and commissioning, would take well over a year. If the warehouse were a centralized distribution depot for a chain of supermarkets, a serious fire could quickly lead a company to near bankruptcy.

27.11 One suggestion to counter structural fire damage with integral racks is to use hollow, square section steelwork permanently filled with a water/glycol/rust inhibitor solution. Under-aisle piping would link the racks, when a fire is sensed, the solution would be circulated by natural convection, perhaps pump assisted, so keeping the steel below the temperature at which buckling takes place. This has been successfully applied in Switzerland at a white goods automated warehouse, Uster.

27.12 A high-efficiency zoned detection and sprinkler extinguishing system is expensive, but worthwhile compared with the typical losses described above.

27.13 Fire prevention in automated stores hinges basically on avoiding the risk, by compartmentation, fast detection, good design of the electronic and electrical supply systems, and on designers taking care to keep flammable sources out of the high-bay zone. Examples of excluded functions include battery charging, and repair of stacker cranes (often involving welding). A policy of good housekeeping should be instilled into the user, and planned maintenance and inspection cycle for the plant and all electrical apparatus built into the design proposal.

28 Security

28.01 In automated warehouses this is mostly concerned with malicious damage and pilfering of electronic equipment and copper wiring during construction. There is little chance of thieves scaling high-bay racks. One of the attractive features of fully automated control is the high security offered. However, computers can be tampered with and if wholesale theft is involved it is likely to have been carefully programmed. Agencies exist for checking programmes for such 'bugs'.

28.02 For peripheral areas and loading bay security, see Technical study, Mechanized storage 2, para. 28. With automated sorting, there is again little risk of pilfering, as the check scanner will record discrepancies at once on the stock printouts. Order-picking areas still require supervision, but again with bulk picking, especially with proof of pick scanning, discrepancies would quickly show up on the documentation. Closed-circuit television has been installed successfully in some large order-picking areas.

29 External works

29.01 High-bay warehouses are large enough to produce surrounding micro-climates. Careful siting is required: some installations generate dangerously high wind speeds. There was a case in the USA where a high-bay store was placed close to another large building in such a way as to form a high funnel (Figure 5.42). Wind already gusting near gale force, picked up a medium weight forklift truck, load and driver, and pushed them through the cladding of an adjoining building. High winds can have a slowing effect on truck marshalling areas, especially where high-sided vehicles are involved. Gusts are liable to blow dust back into the loading bay, shortening the life of sortation conveyors. Wind tunnel tests should be carried out on scale models to measure the effects of the warehouse orientation on surrounding buildings, considering local topography and the prevailing wind.

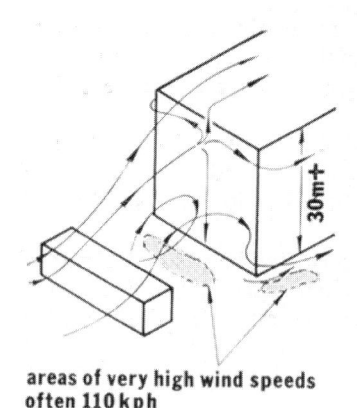

Figure 5.42 *Typical wind patterns round high buildings derived from tests performed on models by BRS.*

30 Structure-based plant

30.01 Conveyors and sorting systems have been covered in Information sheet, Mechanized storage 14, paras 8.01 to 8.07. A carousel is a slow conveyor for platten or pallet circulation used in order picking, typically running at 0.5 m/sec. Tilt tray sorters generally operate at 1.5–2 m/second, with shoe sorters operating up to 1m/second.

30.02 Transporter systems involve special elevators. These can have speeds up to 1.3 m/second and can take the form of conventional lifts or paternosters. Automatic interlocks are provided in the queueing mechanism, so

Automated storage – building function

transporters can flow smoothly onto the elevator as the plattens arrive.

31 Mobile plant

31.01 All plant can be fully on-line; this includes stacker cranes, order pickers or transporters. High-bay stacker cranes are heavy pieces of equipment. Single-masted types generally operate to heights of 20 m, and twin-masted units to over 30 m, although examples of both types both higher and lower exist (Figure 5.43). Tracks run at both high and low level. Order pickers follow a pattern similar to that of stacker cranes.

Figure 5.43 *Twin mast stacker crane.*

31.02 The trend in fixed path automated equipment is away from one-off plant, i.e. towards ranges of standard equipment, adaptable for special purposes and sharing common parts to simplify the problem of spares. Stacker cranes are now the core of packaged deal systems, the 'furniture of the workplace'.

31.03 Transporter systems are sophisticated inter-zone railways, with the added function of providing live storage. In general they offer reduced aisle areas, but do not provide immediate 100 per cent selectivity. One system employs a single type of transporter for all actions; another offers a basic carrier for live storage and in-aisle movement and a larger 'mother' transporter for inter-zone movement.

31.04 Automated guided vehicles, either as single or double pallet handling units or as robot tractor trains, have been operated successfully for horizontal travel. Although not as fast as conveyors and requiring individual loading of trucks, these can provide flexible transport to a large number of sortation stations (Figure 5.44). Robotugs and AGVs are battery powered, guided by wires buried 2 mm to 4 mm under the floor surfaces, or can be free ranging on grid, controlled via infrared updates, located by senser buttons in the floor surface. Automated guided vehicles

Figure 5.44 *AGV with container – note transfer P&D stations at right.*

can be 'smart', where the intelligence is in the mobile unit, or 'dumb', where the unit is a slave to a central controller: both are successfully in service. A further useful feature is their ability to send out feedback signals that can automatically open doors and turn traffic lights on cross-routes in their favour and to call the cranes with the next order. Speeds vary from 1–1.5 m/second depending on the load and the operating environment. The control system prevents collisions at junctions and head-on accidents, and can be set so that the tug always takes the shortest clear route to the discharge point.

31.05 The development of automated storage has been impeded by a history of premature failure of handling equipment: there are still examples of litigation for failed projects. These are usually due to poor communication within the project team, an insufficiently defined brief, and assumptions about suppliers' roles and capabilities. There is no substitute for system simulation as set out in the project implementation chart (Figures 1.2a/b Industrial Storage 1, Technical Study 1). Most manufacturers cannot afford to perform reliability trials at their factory before installing the plant unless these are clearly spelled out in the specification: problems can be aggravated by lack of testing with the integrated automatic control, but again this can be simulated. In the past, handling plant tended to be overcomplicated, but this is no longer realistic in the present competitive market. Designers should write durability into the user specification and ensure that manufacturers have tested their equipment with the control medium. This may increase tender prices but will reduce overall costs in the long run.

32 Integration of building and plant

32.01 This problem is especially severe in automated warehouses, where racking is an integral part of the structure, and stacker cranes are mounted on rails attached to racks or the roof and floor. Tolerances have been discussed in paras 22.01–22.11.

32.02 Care should be taken in planning supply and takeaway conveyor lines between high-bay store and sorting area. They will probably have to pass through fire compartment zones requiring fire shutters and control protocols for passing through the zone line.

33 Maintenance

33.01 The fabric of a high-bay warehouse should be designed to be maintenance-free: cladding materials such as plastic-faced steel sandwich panels ensure that the

Automated storage – building function

surface will be self-cleaning. With electronic equipment, it is essential to check for water leakage, and planned inspection cycles for roof and sprinkler lines should be treated as part of the building design. In a steady-state environment racking maintenance should be minimal, except for repairing damage by handling plant.

Maintenance of handling and control plant

33.02 This is more of a problem. The maintenance zone for stacker cranes should preferably be out of the high-bay area, in a segregated fire compartment. Hence the transfer carriage would have to pass through 30 m high fire stop doors, which would be costly. It is more realistic for maintenance contractors to dismantle the parts concerned in the warehouse, and provision should be made for operation of a hydraulic maintenance platform and a mobile crane. Catwalk access should also be possible to the accumulation conveyors in the high-bay area. Electronic sensors and limit switches require maintenance in the conveyor runs. Take advice from the suppliers. Automated warehouses must be treated as fully interlocked fenced enclosures to the satisfaction of the Factory Inspectorate in the UK, and the OSSHA in the USA. Full safety interlocks such as Kastell Keys should be built into the control system. Some unpleasant accidents have occurred where maintenance staff have been surprised by stacker cranes in narrow aisles, with little chance of escape.

Maintenance area for stacker cranes

33.03 This should have a vehicle entrance outside and should be equipped with a 5 tonne hoist or mobile crane. It is costly and disruptive to move components through the loading bay and sorting area: if restricted access makes this unavoidable, a maintenance gantry crane should be provided with unlimited access over the sorting plant to the maintenance zone. This can conflict with fire compartmentation.

33.04 As a rule, electronic equipment is taken off site for major maintenance and the contractors normally supply moving plant. Check with computer manufacturers that areas where units are positioned have adequate access. For maintenance of sortation plant, see Technical studies, Mechanized storage 2, para. 33.

34 Management

34.01 The project management of an automated warehouse is critical. The requirement for interaction between the handling plant and the racking, itself integral, and the factor of computer control, results in numbers of specialist design and installation teams being involved. The team should include staff from the existing facility, as management is seldom the user.

34.02 Construction contractors are loath to accept overall responsibility for automated high-bay warehouses unless part of a consortium with specialist suppliers involved: such packaged deal teams have been very successful. It is often the case that the construction contractor is a sub-contractor to the warehouse equipment supplier: this is sensible, as the programme for the sequenced installation of structural high-bay racking drives the slab and cladding. Well-planned and carefully installed site wiring is essential. Operators' experience of recent installations points to the value of employing the same contractor for electronic control and equipment wiring, so that the various integrating systems can be co-ordinated. It is virtually impossible to budget accurately for electrical work until the control system's design has been finalized and, so, is an integral part of the equipment tender. Wiring and controls are so important that this area should never be considered for financial savings.

34.03 The maintenance aspect is again important: with such complicated electrical work, protracted negotiation in an attempt to reduce costs is likely to be disadvantageous in that certain elements are liable to be skimped.

Building process

34.04 The building process of high-bay warehouses has to be carefully programmed. So many specialists are involved that the construction and commissioning programme can be as important as the design itself. The main difficulties experienced are where the programmes of various key groups, such as installation engineers and electronics personnel, conflict. Logical and clear responsibilities should be established between subcontractors by the lead supplier at an early stage, ideally as part of the tender submission. A strong co-ordinator/manager from the supplier team, able to visualize the total system continuously, is vital. During the construction phase, comprehensive operation and maintenance manuals should be prepared so that they are available some time before commissioning begins. These with the simulation results will be the basis for training clients' operational and maintenance staff. Designers should take care not to be forced into unrealistic construction and commissioning programmes by eager clients; this would cost both parties dearly later on. Eighteen months is a fast-track programme for an automated high-bay warehouse, 24 months if additional order picking and sortation are involved: 15 months has been achieved with 'off the peg' systems, but never underestimate the complexity of commissioning and 'settling' down. There is no point in deluding anxious clients that a three to six month settling down period will not be required. Good-natured commitments to commission just before a Christmas peak invariably lead to disaster!

34.05 When arranging the programmes from specialist subcontractors, assume that the installation of complex wiring and heavy cranes is bound to run into some difficulties. New systems will have to be tried and modified: the difficulty of commissioning computer systems to bring them on-line and to connect integrated sorting systems should not be underestimated. Remember also that there is usually a change of culture for the staff, and that redundancies may be involved. There is no substitute for staff visits to other installations so they can talk to real users parallel with their jobs – again, often grudged, but money well spent.

35 Personnel accommodation

35.01 In automated warehouses the general labourers and plant operators are of course reduced in number and replaced by a smaller number of supervisory and maintenance staff, many of whom are highly skilled and require high standards of accommodation; their union recently has proved particularly militant. The amount of office space required can be calculated from the staff generated by the control function, and for document processing. A separate traffic office is still required with the possibility of printout facilities for dispatch documentation. The offices which house data-processing machinery usually require air-conditioning, though mini-computers have been developed to work in normal environments.

36 Amenity

36.01 Personnel fall into three categories:
1. Maintenance staff and loading bay operatives, including forklift drivers and general machine supervisors.
2. Order-picking staff.
3. Control system clerical staff, management, and 'white collar' staff concerned with proprietary systems and plant.

It is the user's responsibility to choose whether segregated or integrated amenity facilities are required. Whatever the decision, a high standard throughout leads to an attitude of 'good housekeeping'.

36.02 The washing and toilet facilities for maintenance staff should provide for degreasing, and secure lockers for personal tools and equipment. Facilities should be bright, as psychological relief is necessary after working in high-bay areas with only maintenance lighting. Order-picking staff become dusty from handling plastics and cardboard packs and will also require visual relief after long shifts at the picking face. Fire precautions in high-bay warehouses, naturally preclude smoking or rest accommodation near storage. These activities are restricted to a segregated fire zone. Vending or beverage-making facilities should be provided, as should washing, toilet and restroom facilities, with a tea machine, for truck drivers. This area should not have direct access into the warehouse.

36.03 With the quantity of electrical equipment and fast-moving automatic plant, some accidents are inevitable. Staff will break safety regulations, however stringent, for their convenience; this is a fact of industrial life. A first-aid room should be provided with facilities for emergency treatment of electric shocks, burns and other injuries. The lighting system there should be capable of 600 lux at certain times, and a high level of ventilation should be provided. If the offices are air-conditioned, the system should be extended to the first-aid room. Ambulances should have easy and unhindered access to a loading bay or to vehicle access to office area.

37 Security and safety

37.01 The major problem is sabotage. With a centralized distribution facility serving a large chain of supermarkets or acting as a post-production store for a company's whole distribution system, a protracted breakdown could put the company out of business.

37.02 The sabotage of control equipment or tampering with the software would wreck the store's operation; although manual control should be built in, the warehouse would have been designed for high throughputs and the simultaneous handling of multiple orders. Manual control would not allow orders to be processed fast enough for the installation to operate economically. Access should therefore be strictly controlled. As sortation is automated, the loading bay zone can be segregated from the rest of the warehouse, with openings to allow pallets through, and personnel access closely supervised; this segregation will be necessary for fire control as well. The only other required accesses to the warehouse are to offices, the order-picking zone and maintenance area, which can be controlled by smart cards. The only common link between these areas is the amenity zone, so access between them can be segregated from the warehouse itself and this is also likely to be a fire requirement. The only personnel requiring access to the high-bay area are maintenance staff, again on zoned smart cards.

37.03 The grouping of control equipment into one area not only reduces the cost of environmental plant and services, but also allows supervision to prevent unauthorized access. The argument against placing all peripheral units together is that the whole system would be affected in case of fire. Mini-computers and plcs should be dispersed into the zones that they serve, and so only part of the system would be affected at one time.

37.04 Safety of personnel is not a difficult problem, as nobody except maintenance staff should have access to the high-bay or sortation areas. If a supervisor is required for palletizing and shrink-wrapping plant, the operating position should be well guarded. The route through the machinery to the operator's console should be clearly marked, and guarded along its length. Fail-safe stop devices (e-stops), should be positioned along conveyors, and in high-bay areas to protect maintenance staff; these positions should be lit, and routes to them clearly marked. The position of e-stop zones should be linked back to a mimic diagram on the main control board or through a SCADA system to the control screens, also with an audible alarm.

38 Circulation and parking

38.01 Delivery vehicle access and staff parking has been discussed earlier in this chapter. Parking should be provided for the external maintenance staff, and access allowed for heavy vehicles bringing replacement components.

38.02 Provision should be made in peripheral zones of an automated warehouse for circulation of maintenance equipment such as hydraulic platforms and mobile cranes. These routes should be lit and clearly marked. Catwalks should also be well lit, with guards and safety rails, and attachment points for safety harness – maintenance of high racks closely resembles mountaineering. Lifts and access stairs to catwalks should also be clearly marked. Emergency lighting should be provided on all these high-level routes, in case of central electrical failure.

Fire fighting and escape

38.03 Access routes should be provided for fire-fighting personnel and equipment. Planned escape routes are important, as there is a possibility of fires in high-bay stores getting out of control, with normal routes blocked by fallen burning pallets. Escape access could be in the form of cut-out panels placed at intervals along the base of the cladding, clearly marked on each side and equipped with an emergency light on the interior face.

INFORMATION SHEET

Automated storage 2

Automated horizontal transport systems

1 Free path systems

2 Fixed path systems

This sheet describes how fixed- and free-path horizontal transport systems can, in some cases, replace a system of stacker cranes and conveyors.

1 Free-path systems

Robotugs

1.01 The robotug driverless vehicle system has been used successfully in warehouses and factories throughout the world, and in some cases has superseded towline systems.

1.02 The robotug is a battery-powered tractor fitted with an electronic control system, enabling it to be guided along a route from signals supplied by a mini-computer through a wire buried 2 mm to 4 mm below the floor surface. Control can be integrated with stacker crane cycles for automatic loading and discharge, and with other materials-handling equipment. The tug's control mechanism can supply feedback signals through the guide wire to open doors automatically, change traffic lights in its favour if crossing other vehicle routes, activate unloading devices, or to calculate the quickest unobstructed route to the destination at the time. Up to 50 predetermined stations can be selected with a standard programme, but more permutations are possible if the control system is custom built. Contact the manufacturer as early in the project as possible.

Size and capacity

1.03 Towing capacity: the tug will tow a gross load of 8500 kg assuming a trailer rolling resistance of 23 kg/1000 kg over a smooth level surface.
Speed: 3 km/h maximum.
Size: see Figure 5.50a/b.

Space requirements

1.04 Turning circle fixed by track layout and determined by width of load and trailers (Figures 5.51 and 5.52). The aisle should be not less than 3.6 m wide at intersections.

Building needs

1.05 Tugs need level floors, and will negotiate only slight ramps under full load. Usually an off-track three-phase recharging point is required (trucks are driven to this point by a manual control handle). Maintenance facilities are also needed.

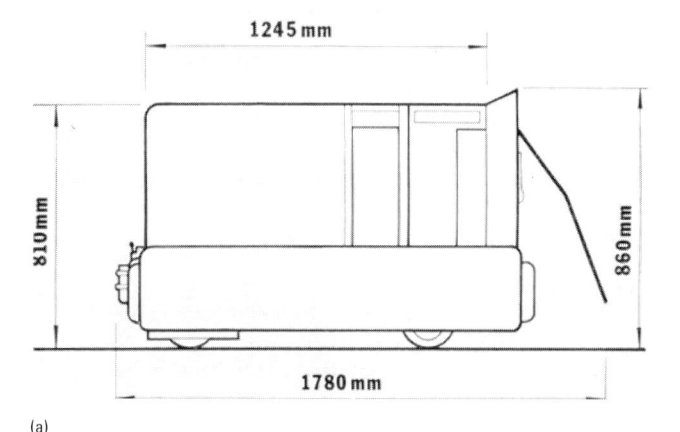

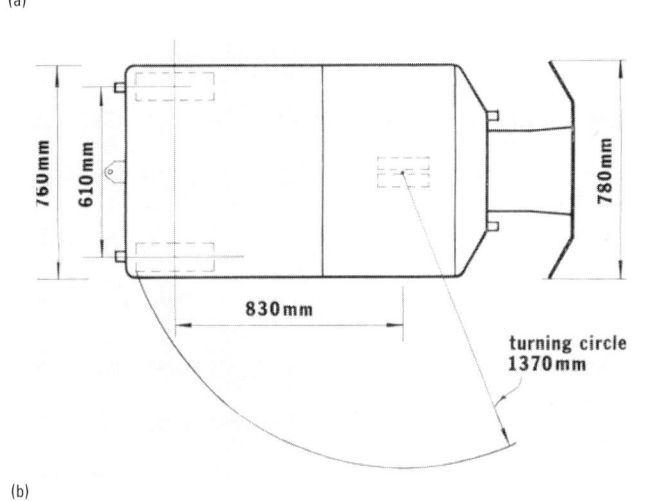

Figure 5.50 (a) *elevation of a Robotug;* (b) *plan of a Robotug.*

2 Fixed-path systems

Cartrac system: uses and limitations

2.01 The Cartrac system uses one transporter for all actions. It can turn through 90 degrees without stopping or changing the axis of the load, and so acts as an efficient live storage module, and can be used in ovens and freezing tunnels. For order picking the Cartrac can act as

Automated storage – automated horizontal transport system

Figure 5.51 *Two types of AGV in use in a warehouse. In the foreground AGV with direct load, behind articulated AGV towing a trailer.*

Figure 5.53 *AGV transfer station from conveyors in from loading bay. Chain conveyor lets pallets span across AGV with lifting bed.*

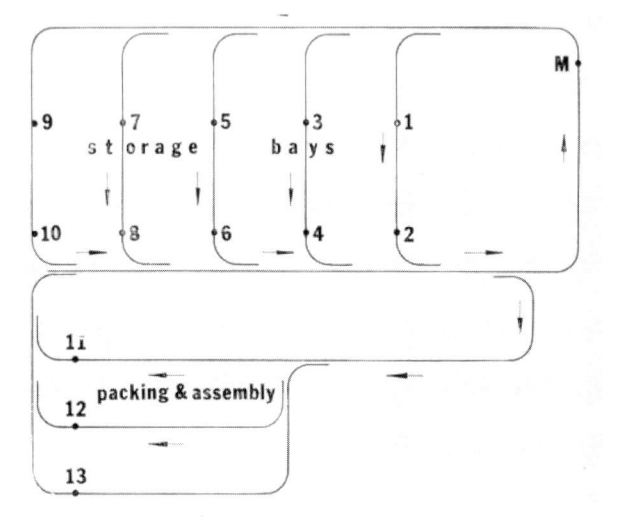

Figure 5.52 *Typical layout for robotug system with collection from production lines and delivery into storage and transfer to parking area. Routing from M direct to 13 would be through stations 1 and 2 or through any free line.*

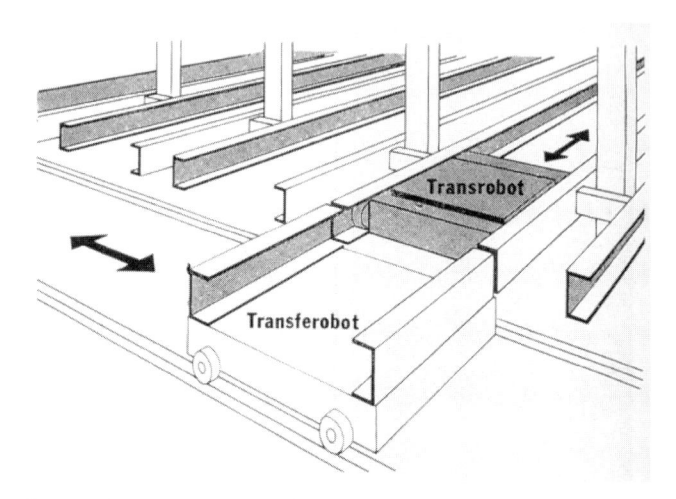

Figure 5.54 *Transrobot meeting Transferobot.*

a 'carousel' or pick whole pallets for immediate routing to the load accumulation zone.

2.02 Stopping is precise, with 0~8 mm tolerance in each direction. Queuing programmes can be supplied. The Cartrac can also be programmed to eject loads automatically at picking stations, or to phase in with stacker cranes, replacing roller conveyors at the transfer station.

Size and capacity
2.03
Capacity: light duty model will carry up to 500 kg, heavy duty up to 1500 kg.
Speed: 60 ml/minute average but faster on long runs.

Space requirements
2.04 Cartrac can turn through 90 degrees. Inside track widths are 500 mm (light duty) and 750 mm (heavy duty), but 100 mm building clearance and 25 mm machine clearance is required on each side (Figure 5.53).

Transrobot system: uses and limitations
2.05 The Transrobot system consists of a basic carrier for use in aisles and live storage (the Transrobot) and a second transporter for interzone movement, the Transferobot (Figure 5.54). The Transrobot system is integral with the structure. Both steel and concrete frames are available, with rail supports doubling as structure for storage of pallets.

Size and capacity
2.06
Capacity: 1000 or 2000 kg.
Speed: Transrobots move at 20 ml/minute, Transferobots at 90 ml/minute. Faster speeds are possible for long distances.

Chapter 6
Cold storage

TECHNICAL STUDY

Cold storage 1

Storage process

1 Introduction
2 Source of goods
3 Form of transport ISO containers
4 Control of transport
5 Receipt of goods
6 Form of goods
7 Unloading
8 Characteristics of goods
9 Sorting
10 Volume calculations
11 Turnover calculations
12 Variety and flow
13 Type of storage
14 Stock control
15 Stock withdrawal
16 Order picking
17 Picking area
18 Load build-up
19 Order and document check
20 Loading and dispatch
21 Additional data

This section (Cold storage 1) deals with the storage process. The second study (Cold storage 2) deals with the design of the building.

---

1 Introduction

1.01 Refrigeration slows down the deterioration of perishable products by microbal, chemical and enzymic means, though if putrefaction has already set in it will not prevent contamination of other products.

Types of cold store

1.02 There are three types of cold store:
- Public cold stores. These are contract facilities, and cater for a wide range of products, and for seasonal demands, e.g. frozen vegetables. Public cold stores tend to be multi-cellular to segregate products, and to lease areas economically.
- Specialist store, e.g. distribution centres for ice cream, chilled storage for dairy and perishable foods, or reception centres for imported meat products.
- Multi-product. Task specific cold stores, including chilled and deep frozen chambers for retail distribution operated by the retailer or their nominees.

1.03 The present trend is for chilled 'ready meals' reducing dependence on preservatives, and for pre-packed salads and vegetables. Low-density, high turnover, consumer packaging requires an increase in cold storage areas. Previously, capacities of 1500 tonnes were the norm. Common sizes now range from 3000 to 10,000 tonnes and, in the USA some very large cold stores are of over 10,000 tonnes capacity.

1.04 Specialist equipment manufacturers of chilled conditioning and freezing plant also supply insulation tailored to the environmental requirements of the cell. Some manufacturers offer a packaged deal including the building frame and floor construction.

User specification

1.05 Many distribution warehouses for retail food include refrigerated sections for meat, cheese and frozen foods. Architects will frequently be involved in the design of these, and of cold stores incorporated into food processing factories.

1.06 If extensive cold storage is part of a conventional warehouse, it should be established what proportion of the building it is to be, whether it will be a general purpose zone for seasonal trade, and what will be the development potential of frozen and chilled goods as opposed to dry goods. These factors affect the initial form of the building (Figure 6.1).

1.07 The user specification for a cold store must consider the trading potential of the product, which can be more varied than with conventional goods. Seasonal trade may demand a change from storing a low variety of products requiring similar temperatures to a wide variety requiring different temperatures and ripening rates, and subject to cross-contamination Some public cold stores have high peaks during the vegetable harvest season, and further peaks for pre-Christmas poultry. If meats are involved, check whether the brief requires frozen meat to be slowly defrosted under closely controlled conditions (i.e. moving through rooms of different temperatures) thus reducing the area available for general cold storage. Check whether it is necessary to construct cold rooms to cater for a wide range of temperatures, demanded by seasonal space requirements (adaptability in cold stores is very costly).

1.08 The user specification for a cold store is not a performance specification for the cold rooms, but a detailed operational one for each zone. Throughput and movement of products is more important than in other storage types,

Cold storage – storage process

Figure 6.1 *Building a cold store: foam glass insulation blocks are being installed.*

as this increases the chance of product damage, and cold loss through doors can increase the required capacity of refrigeration equipment.

1.09 A cold store is often used for activities other than purely storage. Typical uses:
- Cutting up meat carcasses into portions for supermarket sale. This involves shrink-wrapping and packaging. Meat processing takes place in a specialist store, is labour intensive and space-consuming.
- Packaging frozen vegetables. During the eight to ten weeks of the vegetable harvest, the product is frozen in bulk as quickly as possible to preserve the quality (Figure 6.2). These vegetables require packaging into saleable weights as they are withdrawn from stock, which involves wrapping, packaging and palletizing, and is personnel intensive.
- Cutting cheese from bulk blocks into saleable portions. Cutting, weighing, wrapping and label printing are all mechanized.

1.10 Any areas for activities peripheral to storage should be specified from the outset, as they are subject to public health regulations for food processing, and can require special floor surfaces and environmental control equipment. This also affects the choice of the number of cold chambers and their distribution in relation to processing and loading.

2 Source of goods

2.01 Frozen, ripening and chilled perishable goods arrive:
- from all over the world, and require continued temperature-controlled storage after transport, known as 'chilled chain integrity' and thawing facilities
- from local sources, requiring freezing facilities, or from a cold store acting as a distribution warehouse for seasonal products.

3 Form of transport ISO containers

3.01 Refrigerated ISO containers known as 'reefers' consist of two types: those fitted with integral cooling equipment, and those equipped with connection plugs for a central source (Figure 6.3). Most reefer containers are of the second type and are plugged into a cold air source on the dock at the port of entry, or are fitted with a clip-on individual cooler, operated by a donkey engine or from gas bottles. New specialist ships are in service that vary the type and characteristics of the cryogenic gas supplied to the containers to provide controlled ripening during transit.

3.02 Warehouses expecting large numbers of reefer containers where unloading may be delayed require a portable cooling centre (Figure 6.4). A typical centre can

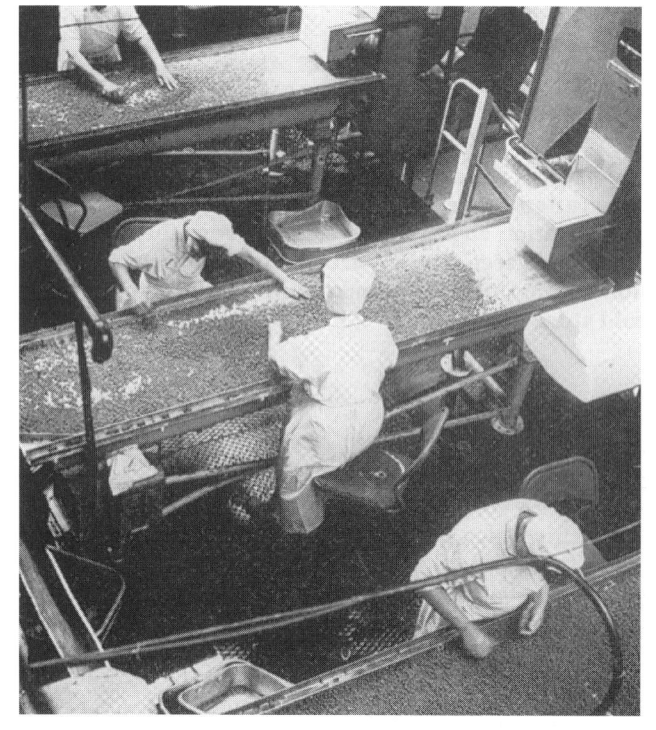

Figure 6.2 *Frozen vegetable processing.*

Figure 6.3 *Reefer container, which must be connected to cooling source (i.e. non-autonomous).*

Cold storage – storage process

Figure 6.4 *Portable cooler centre.*

Figure 6.5 *Refrigerated trailer with cooler on front.*

(a)

(b)

Figure 6.6 *(a) A well-planned parking/plug-in area. (b) A row of double lead drum units, showing weather protection and drainage channels. The wide concrete apron with deep kerbs around the plugs prevents reversing damage.*

handle 22 containers along a central spine which folds into three units of ISO container size when out of use. These ISO containers are efficient temporary stores, and in seasonal peak conditions it might be more economic to provide parking and portable cooling for containers than to build extra cold-rooms that might be only partially filled for most of the year.

3.03 Once ISO containers are removed from their skeletal semi-trailers or rail wagons, heavy and expensive handling equipment is required. The economic balance rests with the type of trade involved and the development potential.

Refrigerated trailers and demountable bodies

3.04 For trade over short sea-routes, or national transport, refrigerated trailers are popular. They are similar to reefers, but most have autonomous cooling equipment, either gas or donkey-engine powered (Figure 6.5). Demountable bodies bridge between ISO containers and trailers: they are widely used within the EU for chilled chain distribution, promoting multi-modal deliveries. (See Chapter 3.)

Fume build-up

3.05 Where trucks wait for long periods, cooler motors may build up fumes and contaminate products. Long, articulated vehicles cause less fumes as the cooler motor is usually outside canopy coverage anyway. Medium-sized inter-town vans and delivery vehicle bays cause more fume build-up.

3.06 Rather than extract fumes at canopy level, some companies run coolers off vehicle batteries during unloading or plug the vehicle into an electrical point at each dock position. In some vehicles the cooler is run entirely off batteries, recharged by the vehicle's motor, and banks of plug positions are provided in the parking area for when trucks are pre-loaded at night (Figure 6.6). If leads are fixed to the vehicle there is less damage if the driver forgets to unplug before moving, but these can easily be stolen. Fixed leads are safer and should be on spring-mounted drums to cater for variations on plug-in position. External plug points are equipped with heaters and strong spring-mounted cover plates to prevent icing. Gas connection points have also been used, the vehicle's insulation maintaining the temperature throughout the journey. Gas points and their storage tanks require clearance with the Factory Inspectorate. All plug positions should be clearly marked, fitted with guard rails and well lit.

Rail wagons

3.07 Rail wagons are inherently side loading. The STEF refrigerated fruit trucks from Europe have been a common sight on British railways for some time. Both refrigerated and insulated trucks are used depending on the product. (See Information sheet, Loading 6.)

Air cargo handling

3.08 A refrigerated air-cargo service is rapidly expanding for all season 'jet fresh' foods, flowers and for temperature controlled pharmaceuticals (Figure 6.7). The retail and air cargo industry has been quick to recognize the benefits of fresh foods providing all year round sales: chilled fruit and vegetables, packed directly into vendor packs on the farms and chilled down for loading into insulated air-cargo containers. Bellyhold containers are carried on conventional road vehicles, fitted with roller floors.

Figure 6.7 *Refrigerated air containers.*

4 Control of transport

4.01 As much refrigerated produce is imported, Customs facilities may be required. Large public cold stores carry their own Customs clearance, and international traffic must be segregated from traffic that requires no clearance. If the cold store is the first stop within the EU, it is likely to be designated, or the goods be pre-presented at, a border inspection post (BIP), that must provide EU standard inspection and quarantine facilities.

4.02 The measures taken to provide efficient traffic control depend on the type of store. As some include packaging or processing operations, vehicles other than refrigerated delivery trucks may use the site. For example for vegetable freezing, vehicles arrive direct from the fields and tip into a pre-freeze hopper (Figure 6.8). This should not interfere with the normal vehicle flow. Routes should be clearly marked, and, if it is possible, a separate entry provided for farm vehicles. Road vehicle peaks may coincide with local crop peaks (and a similar situation could occur as at groupage depots, where small vehicles constrict the movement of larger ones) bringing the flow to a standstill.

Figure 6.8 *Farm vehicles at freezing centre.*

Figure 6.9 *Dual-purpose loading dock in a cold store.*

Loading bays

4.03 Dual-purpose loading bays (i.e. one bay handling both incoming and dispatch goods) (Figure 6.9) may be necessary if economies allow only one door per cold chamber. Refrigerated vehicles seldom collect the same product from a contract store as it has delivered, so cross-bay circulation for loading goods for dispatch is often necessary. Some operators remove unloaded vehicles back to the accumulation area until a bay near the cold room for the dispatched goods becomes free. This not only reduces on-dock ice build-up, but allows time for refrigerated vehicles to be decontaminated (e.g. venting gas after carrying apples).

4.04 Cold stores serving supermarket chains have the problem of mixing small delivery vehicles with the trunk trucks. The operator may only use medium-sized trucks, but the supplier is likely to use the largest size possible. Many retail organizations receive fruit, meat and dairy produce direct from the Continent so European drive side (l.h.d) trucks must be planned for (see Technical study, Loading 1).

4.05 In mixed cold and dry goods stores large and small vehicles can be segregated. Maximum size vehicles deliver to the cold store section and the goods are dispatched in conventional delivery trucks in insulated roll pallets, or loaded into refrigerated delivery vehicles that are moved to a parking zone equipped with plug points. These should be segregated from parking zones for conventional trucks by road marking, e.g. use of the blue international refrigeration sign.

4.06 If rail wagons are mixed with road transport, their times should not coincide as shunting can block a roadway for some time. Contact the client and Railtrack concerning shunting tractors.

5 Receipt of goods

Rail wagons

5.01 The platform height for rail vehicles can be critical. With too high a platform certain insulated wagon doors will not be able to open. The height of the base of the doors of European rail wagons is 1.12 m (1.4 m in the USA). This dimension is affected by ground conditions, e.g. banked track (see Information sheet, Loading 6).

Road vehicles

5.02 Some reefer containers and refrigerated vans can side and end load (Figure 6.10a). Some cold store operators prefer to handle goods at ground level, using side doors, as the heights of refrigerated vehicle floors differ considerably and hand-unloaded carcasses can be dealt with by conveyor. But as cold store floors being insulated are likely to be above ground level, and as nearly all frozen produce is becoming palletized, end loading by forklift trucks should be planned for. Floor levels of insulated containers and vans are up to 100 mm higher than non-insulated and the ceiling 100 mm lower, so forklifts have 200 mm less clearance to work.

6 Form of goods

6.01 Meat: reefer containers from 'deep-sea' routes are loaded to maximum volume, carcass on carcass, and require hand unloading. Some meat products, e.g. frozen offal, are in blocks on pallets or in bins sized to insulated container dimensions. Where volume is less important than quality and the meat is chilled rather than frozen, the

Figure 6.10 *(a) Meat in reefer container. (b) Carcasses on pallet converter.*

carcasses are hung from rails mounted in the top of the van. A variation, popular in general purpose warehousing, is for carcasses to be hung from pallet converters, allowing forklift handling and five-high stacking (see Chapter 4, Information Sheet 4).

Fruit is normally boxed and palletized. Bulk raw fruit for jam-making, etc. can be handled in intermediate bulk containers and bulk bins.

Fats are pre-packed and palletized.

Poultry tends to be packed in cardboard outers for storage on pallets. Meat portions and processed meat tend to be stacked into 400 mm x 600 mm crates, stacked on pallets.

Vegetables are mostly pre-packed and stored on pallets. Bulk vegetables are stored in bins or in special pallet converters with plastic liners.

Fish products are pre-packed and stored on pallets.

Pharmaceuticals are packed onto pallets; some more delicate products like serums are packed into special expanded polystyrene canisters and shrink wrapped on to pallets.

Cold storage – storage process

7 Unloading

7.01 Refrigerated goods should be exposed to the normal atmosphere for the shortest time possible. This is known as 'chilled chain integrity'. Unloading procedure follows that of palletized goods, with forklift trucks shuffling in and out of vans.

7.02 Dock equipment may collect rime, which is water vapour in the atmosphere flash frozen when the cold metal surface comes out of the cold room or van. This can build up to dangerous deposits of ice on the dock surface, and is augmented by ice from the forklift tyres, collected in the cold rooms and from van floors. To lessen this risk, warm air curtains used on the dockside of the cold room doors will keep the cold air in (though some still escapes at the base). Some operators combine the curtain with scraper pads on the warm side to remove as much moisture from the tyres as possible. Heated dock surfaces and leveller plates have also been successfully used.

7.03 Due to the arrangement of cold room entrances and because products are segregated by temperature and not frequency of movement, the loading dock is liable to act as a cross-route. If inevitable, the cross-route should be planned with space for two forklift trucks to pass without encroaching on the manoeuvring space of unloading machines. In high-use cold stores modified sweepers can scarify the ice away but in the long term under-floor heating is more economic.

8 Characteristics of goods

8.01 Meat carcasses are awkward to handle, being a difficult shape and slippery when frozen. Pallet converters with meat hooks are an attempt to gain full volume (Figure 6.10b). Packaging for deep frozen products requires special consideration. Unpacked frozen goods should never be stored for reasons of contamination, dust and dehydration. Most goods are placed in a polythene inner lining to avoid air pockets which cause freeze burns.

9 Sorting

9.01 Refrigerated goods should not be left waiting for sorting as they can deteriorate quickly. The forklift should shuttle direct from the truck to the cold room allocated. If sorting into store sections is required for withdrawal speed as well as temperature, buffer space is required. It should be at a low temperature, to act as a lobby to the various temperature zones.

Pre-cooling and freezing tunnels

9.02 Some products, e.g. vegetables, are frozen prior to storage. Many refrigerated warehouses have tunnels for freezing goods in batches (Figure 6.11). The temperature is lowered quickly by high air velocity to –30°C or –40°C. Freezing tunnel efficiency is improved when the goods have been pre-cooled to 0°C in a pre-cooling chamber. Pre-cooled products are also of a better quality on arrival in the freezing tunnel, but the process is only economical if the products ripen or deteriorate rapidly, e.g. soft fruit and pears (apples need not be pre-cooled). Pre-cooling is achieved by high air velocity with controlled humidity (to avoid evaporation), or sprayed ice water or vacuum cooling. Pre-cooling allows the air in the freezing tunnel to be circulated with a uniform temperature, and is most important in a warehouse processing a variety of products to be packed in different-sized cartons.

Figure 6.11 *Freezing tunnel for frozen vegetables.*

9.03 The freezing tunnel usually uses overhead rails for carcasses and boxed goods are placed on pallets. Air circulation is either transverse, with several fans blowing perpendicularly to the main axis or longitudinally with one or two fans discharging parallel to the axis of the tunnel. Most fans are reversible, or are placed at either end to improve the homogeneity of the temperature. Freezing chambers of small dimensions are quicker to load and unload and air distribution with even temperatures is easier to achieve. The optimum capacity will be a compromise between the construction cost and the required throughput.

Freezing methods

9.04 These are as varied as the products themselves. The cold air stream is the most common method and is suitable for freezing every type of product, loose or packed. Belt or slat conveyors are used to take the products through the tunnel. Some materials are frozen through direct contact with a horizontal or vertical metal plate or by immersion or spraying with a fluid. Liquefied gases such as nitrogen are also used.

Location in store

9.05 Freezing tunnels are situated in a block of cells close to the refrigeration plant. Air locks link the chambers. If the cold store is part of a slaughterhouse, the pre-cooling chambers should be near the slaughtering process to reduce handling. Freezing tunnels often link production plant and cold store. The handling system should integrate the speed of production with packaging and grouping for transport through the freezing tunnel.

Weighing

9.06 Whether coming from the freeze tunnel or out of a container, cold store operators like to weigh goods before they are stored in the cold chambers. The weighing machine should not constrict the flow of handling plant. In one installation the weighing machine had been placed so that the forklift had to stop at 90° to the direction of travel across the main route, causing hold-ups. In-process weighing can be used at the end of the freeze tunnel, with roller conveyors equipped with sensor heads electronically recording the weight of each pallet it passes.

10 Volume calculations

10.01 Volume calculations will determine the number and size of the cold rooms. Larger, colder cells allow for greater flexibility. A large range of different products does not necessarily imply an equal number of cold rooms, although this is efficient and less subject to cross-contamination. As refrigerated warehouses cost approximately four times that of conventional warehouses, the volume must be planned accurately for the trade anticipated. Having determined the principal types of goods to be stored and if they require segregated chambers, examine what quantities of each are likely to be stored, their lead times and what daily requirements are likely to be met at different times of the year. Seasonal and daily peaks should be considered. If a freezing tunnel is involved, daily throughputs and allocation to particular cold rooms should be calculated.

11 Turnover calculations

11.01 Turnover calculation is similar to that described in Technical study, Mechanized storage 1, para. 11, except that with fixed walls the cold rooms can be considered as separate warehouses within a larger one. As a rough estimate, frozen foods can be calculated as 300 kg/m^3 and controlled storage above freezing for products like bananas, 160 kg/m^3. In the past, densities of 30 per cent were thought adequate with small rooms for special products, but this low efficiency is too costly today. A small number of large rooms is preferable.

11.02 Controlled meat thawing requires carcasses to move through chambers of rising temperature, spending several days in each. If the refrigeration plant is zoned for various temperatures, carcass thawing can add to the load.

11.03 The production or consumption throughput of frozen products can be seasonal. Vegetables have a steady consumption but input peaks, whereas a product such as ice cream has the opposite flow. Some products are withdrawn for repackaging and take up more space when replaced.

12 Variety and flow

12.01 The withdrawal characteristics of various sizes of packaged frozen goods differ. They are segregated by temperature, the need to avoid contamination and (within the cold room) by the speed each product is consumed. The products themselves have different speeds of flow according to season, package size and planned factors such as special offers.

13 Type of storage

13.01 Most products are block stacked on pallets with pallet converters, adding stability to crushable loads (Figure 6.12). These are stored up to five high and often seven to eight units deep, with gaps left for stock access and rotation. Drive-in racking has been used for refrigerated storage and live racking is effective for fast-moving products of similar temperature, where there is little risk of cross-contamination.

13.02 The floor should be marked out with pallet positions to avoid contact between walls and packages. Some operators specify a wide gangway right round the room for handling and air circulation.

13.03 Cold chambers should not be placed on both sides of a central corridor. Its walls and services may suffer from condensation and frosting, unless it is air-conditioned.

13.04 The pallet stacking method should allow cold air to circulate and goods to be accessible for quick stock checks. The relative amounts of carbon dioxide and oxygen affects

Cold storage – storage process

Figure 6.12 *Special carcass pallets stacked three high in a cold store. Carcasses can be packed more compactly when flat than when hung.*

Figure 6.13 *Reach truck being used in a cold store for bacon. Standard machines can be used after modifications to the electrical and hydraulic systems.*

Figure 6.14 *Turret truck used in cold store.*

storage life, especially with fruit. Chilled products can be spoiled by too dry air or too low temperatures.

13.05 If access is more important to the operator than filling to maximum volume, racking would be used, and the storage process would then be as for Technical study, Mechanized storage 1, para. 13.

13.06 Automated storage is also used for cold stores, thereby reducing personnel, an environmental and health and safety issue. Mechanical equipment has been well proven in low temperatures. Electronic equipment has been developed for this cold environment and is often trace heated.

13.07 Turret trucks are also used in several cold stores (Figures 6.13 and 6.14). Narrow aisles and high racks reduce volume wastage. Floors must be scarified intermittently to prevent ice build-up.

14 Stock control

14.01 In cold stores this is similar to that for conventional mechanized or automated dry goods stores. Refrigerated stock requires rotation depending on the product's characteristics and the depth of freeze. Planned stock rotation is necessary for all foods, and this is a further argument against deep block stacking, where an operator might overlook the cumbersome shuffling operation it requires.

14.02 Stock control can be complicated by additional repackaging of products such as vegetables. These tend to be withdrawn steadily, tipped out of bulk bins, packed into consumer packs, palletized and replaced in the cold room. Block-stacked bulk materials and drive-in racks of palletized loads of cartons, can give a high use of volume. The stock rotation of packaged goods and stock withdrawal is made much easier.

14.03 Stock control of refrigerated goods is less of a problem than with dry goods; the packaging has been designed for long periods of storage in cold conditions (see also para. 11.02).

15 Stock withdrawal

15.01 The pattern of stock withdrawal depends on the type of order picking, and the organization of the block stacks. But in cold rooms different products share the same temperature conditions, and the required air circulation space round stacks conflicts with the requirement to maximize volume, often resulting in small aisle widths and shuffling to reach pallets at the rear of a stack. In public cold stores receiving frozen goods from outside manufacturers, some goods are not at the low temperature required on arrival, and cannot be placed next to frozen products for fear of contamination and heat damage. Such suspect incoming goods are block stacked near the cooling plant, and moved into the main stack when freezing has been completed, dispatch and stock being withdrawn from the face away from the incoming goods.

15.02 A simulation of the operation of the cold rooms at design stage, with single product stacks and multiple stacks, would show how much space is lost through

Cold storage – storage process

leaving air space and circulation area round the combinations of block stacks. Check with the client that the size and shape of the cold rooms will be suitable for future storage patterns, e.g. different products with the same temperature but requiring segregation.

16 Order picking

16.01 Stock is usually removed from block stacks into racking for order picking. Some users prefer it to be in a special chamber, to reduce heat gain in the main store from frequent opening of the doors.

16.02 In cold stores serving supermarket chains, refrigerated goods must be picked into insulated roll pallets suitable for the delivery transport. The order picking of refrigerated stock is similar to that for dry goods, i.e. the lower two layers of racking are used for hand picking, and the upper levels for replenishment stock (see Technical study, Mechanized storage 1, para. 16). Live racking is useful for goods in cartons, combining the storage and picking function. Frozen food manufacturers pack the goods in carton sizes to suit the average shop freezer, and which hold convenient numbers of packets for ordering purposes.

16.03 Carcasses that have thawed are picked from hanging hooks either onto hooks on pallet converters, or are carried direct to the vehicle. Carcass handling is diminishing in favour of in-store processing into portion-sized packs. These are placed in cartons and are palletized and picked in the conventional manner.

16.04 Public cold stores and single product stores usually involve full pallet picking. The pallet loads are split into local orders at distribution centres nearer the markets.

17 Picking area

17.01 Because of the hostile environment of chilled and cold stores, automated order picking was introduced more than 20 years ago. Based on carton roll-through racking, cartons are separately released onto belts, leading to a tilt tray or 'shoe' sorter. This groups multiply released cartons into discrete orders. (See Chapter 5, Automated storage.) Layer picking from pallets using automated stacker cranes has also been employed, assembling pallets of mixed frozen or chilled stock. The rapid growth of the chilled ready-meals market has been responsible for a great increase in the variety of stock: brands, flavours, pack sizes, promotions. Because of the great variety, the trend is for manual item picking with guidance from audiovisual or pick-to-light systems onto belts leading to automated sorting. (See Chapter 4, Mechanized storage, para. 17.)

17.01 Safety requirements for personnel in cold stores are discussed in Technical study, Cold storage 2, para. 37.

18 Load build-up

18.01 Insulated roll pallets are handled as normal units and assembled either as part of a dry goods load, or grouped for transport in an insulated vehicle (Figure 6.15). Where cold space is precious, vehicle loads are not pre-assembled. Public cold stores shuffle goods to make the stock accessible, and then load directly into the refrigerated truck. The product should be exposed to the untreated atmosphere for the minimum possible time. Many delivery trucks are only insulated, and rely on the goods to withstand the

Figure 6.15 *Incoming empty insulated roll pallets being pushed out of the vehicle to the left insulated. Full dispatch units waiting for loading on the right. Channels are clearly marked, and loading bay door is insulated. Incoming units may constrict dispatch units in peak conditions in dual-purpose docks.*

journey time without deterioration. Most refrigerated goods are weighed before dispatch. The weighing machine need not constrict the flow of handling plant. One frozen food producer weighs forklift and load together, on a weighbridge positioned on the main route, rather than having to lower the pallet on to a weighing table each time. The economic requirement for a single door to each cold room congests weighing and cross–circulation in peak periods. Generous space provision in this zone is essential to ensure continuous operation in the cross–flow conditions dictated by the cold room design.

19 Order and document check

19.01 In cold stores, this check occurs at the same time as stock withdrawal and loading.

20 Loading and dispatch

20.01 Vehicles running in and out of cold rooms cause ice build-up on the dock and in the cold rooms. Scraper mats squeeze moisture from forklifts tyres and a dock shelter makes the waiting truck a homogeneous part of the cold store atmosphere. Pneumatic seals are also used to prevent ice build-up.

20.02 Icing will still occur as the truck pulls away from the dock, before the door built into the dock shelter has had time to seal the zone. The combination of a dock shelter with a pneumatic seal, a powerful cooler, a heated dock surface, and scraper mats would be costly compared to the cost of heating door equipment and intermittent scouring. Another method of avoiding ice build-up is to isolate cold room lift trucks, and deliver pallets to the loading bay by conveyor. The conveyor opening need only be one pallet high, plus clearance, and can be fitted with fast pneumatic sliding doors, activated by a sensor on the conveyor. The stuffer forklifts, also isolated, work in a normal atmosphere. Operators using this method claim that the icing problem hardly exists, and that short loading cycle eliminates product deterioration, as long as the van's refrigeration plant is kept operating.

21 Additional data

21.01 *Energy saving.* Cold stores are a major target for energy saving and environmental compliance. The gases in the chiller circuits have already been cleaned up (no CFCs): now the emphasis is on energy saving. Airlocks, though space-consuming and possibly cumbersome with forklifts, reduce temperature-loss between chambers. Solar power sources and chemical generators are being explored to produce autonomous chilled services.

21.02 *Health and safety.* Recent cases of legionaires disease has put the spotlight on heat exchangers exposed to the open air. Many cold stores have heat exchangers located round their perimeter to benefit from natural cooling. Whilst the incubation of the legionella virus is a water temperature and maintenance issue, advice should be sought from the public health authority and heat exchanger manufacturers concerning safe locations for siting heat exchangers in new cold stores, particularly if residential, sporting or other publicly accessible locations are nearby.

Technical study

Cold storage 2

Building function

22 Structure
23 Floor
24 Building services
25 Special services
26 Building fabric
27 Fire control
28 Security
29 External works
30 Structure-based plant

31 Mobile handling point
32 Integration of building and plant
33 Maintenance
34 Management
35 Personnel accommodation
36 Amenity
37 Security and safety
38 Circulation and parking

22 Structure

22.01 Before 1960, most cold stores were multi-storey, because the cube shape has a low surface-to-volume ratio and is thus most economical to refrigerate. This meant highly loaded floors, heavy structures and costly foundations. Now most cold stores are single storey (Figure 6.16) and the trend is towards higher rooms and lower temperatures. The present emphasis is on efficiency of insulation, which can be 15 per cent of the cost of the building.

Concrete frame construction

22.02 Concrete structures can be in situ or pre-cast, and concrete panels or cast walls provide a continuous surface for insulation. There are special problems with cold bridges through concrete structures, outside the scope of this section.

Steel frame construction

22.03 In Europe the steel structure is usually external and insulated cladding forms a sealed box with little risk of heat bridges. The alternative, and now more common method, is to use an internal structure with insulation placed round vertical and horizontal members, the cladding and insulation attached to a sub-frame, and flexible membranes forming corner seals to allow for movement. Some cold stores are constructed with a double frame, the outer forming the main structure, and the inner being buried inside the insulation to support it.

Foundations

22.04 Foundations should be designed by specialist structural engineers. They must have continuous insulation to stop cold bridges freezing the ground round the bases and causing frost heave that can displace footings and endanger the whole structure. One monolithic structure heaved sufficiently to dome both floor and RC roof slab.

22.05 Soil profiles and grain size distribution curves should be obtained from bore holes. The susceptibility of soils to frost heave depends on the uniformity of grain sizes, e.g. sand strata of 10 per cent granular material smaller than 0.02 mm are susceptible. Frost heave also requires water. In one cold store, grain size and a high water table combined with a cold bridge to freeze the ground to nearly 3 m below foundation base.

23 Floor

23.01 Cold store floors must keep the cold in, to stop soil freezing (causing frost heave). Insulation and sometimes sub-floor heating are required, and joints to columns and wall cladding require continuity of insulation. For rooms at 0°C and above (e.g. for fruit) the wall insulation is carried down to below ground level and a layer of subsoil forms a heat barrier, equivalent (it is claimed) to a layer of insulation.

23.02 To prevent frost heave on very low temperature buildings, either construct a basement, or heat under the slab. If the land is difficult to drain, the basement would be more attractive and should be force-ventilated.

Figure 6.16 *Nine metre clear height (manned) cold store with narrow aisles. Fully automated versions are built at three times this height.*

Cold storage – building function

Under-floor heating

23.03 There are several under-floor heating methods: heater mats can be used, or air passed through hollow core tiles, or a heated glycol solution pumped through polythene pipes in the sub-slab beneath the insulation. Typical construction of a solid floor is as shown in Figure 16.17:
- sub-slab plus heating method vapour barrier
- floor insulation (thickness depends on the material and the internal temperature range)
- top slab with a granolithic working surface which should continue at the sides to form a curb, to prevent ice forming between wall insulant and slab. Most operators require permanent thermocouples fixed at various points throughout the building to check subsoil temperature.

Floor finish

23.04 The floor surface should be carefully selected as repairs in a cold store are very expensive. It should be able to withstand scarifying machines and product spills, e.g. fruit juices and fats. Granolithic screed is acceptable for general purposes, but is not suitable for cold processing zones such as cheese cutting rooms and meat preparation areas. Jointless surfaces suitable for fatty and corrosive applications must still be efficient at low temperatures (some plastic-based products become brittle). Granolithic screeds should have non-slip finishes.

23.05 Damaged floors can be made accessible for repair without defrosting the whole cold room by placing a plastic 'igloo' over the damaged area.

24 Building services

24.01 Air in cold rooms can be contaminated by the products stored inside. Atmospheric segregation can be achieved by drawing external air in over a cooler coil,

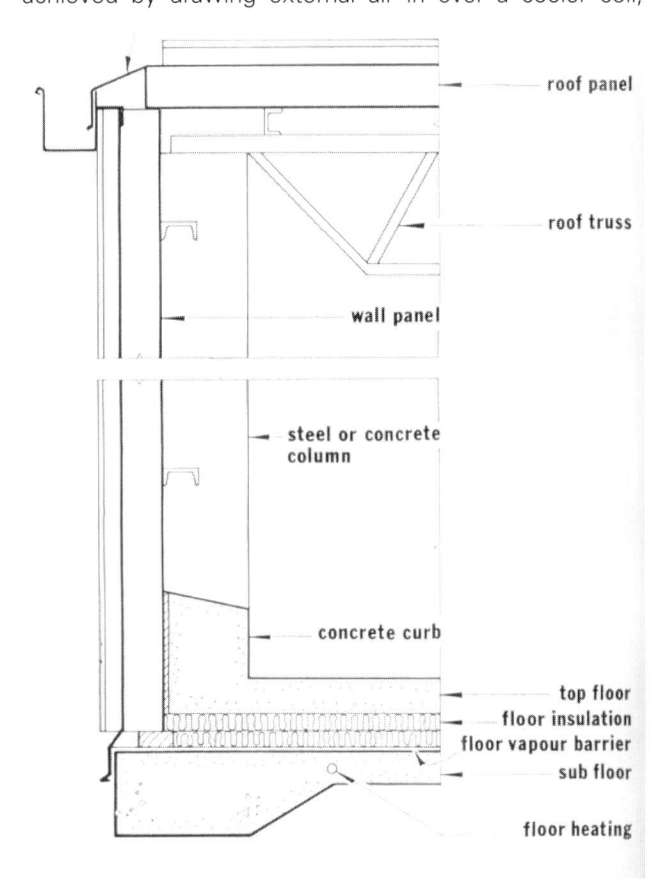

Figure 6.17 Section through typical cold store.

Figure 6.18 Cold storage palletising area for bacon products. Note cooling coils below ceiling.

which reduces the chance of odour intercommunication between cold rooms but does not guarantee fully filtered air (Figure 6.18). A central system is advantageous in that air can be put into the room at the same temperature and humidity at which it was expelled and at the same time cleaned and disinfected. The air distribution system must minimize condensation and frosting (Figure 6.19).

Lighting

24.02 Lighting is important for handling and to ensure absolute cleanliness. An overall level of 200 lux is suggested with 400 lux in processing zones and 500 lux in item picking areas. Up to 15 m height fluorescent tubes are recommended; above to 30 m height high-intensity discharge lamps. The efficiency of fluorescent tubes falls off rapidly at tube wall temperatures below 40°C. Special tubes are available, one with a double plastic sleeve for insulation. High-intensity discharge lamps will not normally give any problems in cold store environments. All corners of the cold store must be lit as this is where debris accumulates. Cold room door zones should also be well lit, but without glare as clear vision is essential.

24.03 Building services such as water pipes to amenity areas and electrical services should all be well insulated and detailed to avoid 'cold bridging'. Services should never be run under cold room floors.

25 Special services

25.01 In cold store design, the special service of refrigeration must be considered together with the building fabric (para. 26). The provision of chilling/refrigeration services is a specialist function with expert suppliers. The following paragraphs are a guide to the technology, but always involve specialist advice from the outset of the project.

26 Building fabric

Refrigeration systems

26.01 The most common system used is a central plant which supplies liquid coolant to individual cooler batteries

Cold storage – building function

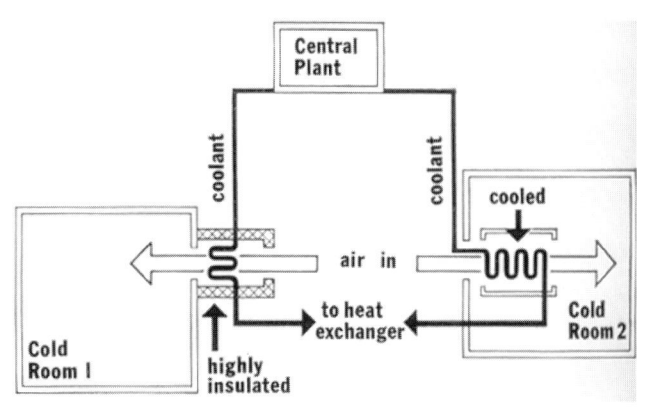

Figure 6.20 *Diagram of refrigeration system.*

(Figure 6.20), either mounted in the cold rooms at ceiling level or immediately next to the cold room, discharging through a grille, false ceiling or duct. As in a domestic refrigerator, air is drawn over coils by fans, and the heat that has been extracted from the atmosphere is circulated back to a heat exchanger. If cooler units are mounted in the store room at ceiling level, frost deposits tend to build up on the output side of the fans, drop off the ceiling cladding onto the floor or products and cause the cladding surface to spall away. Cooler units outside the room require a fully insulated plant space.

26.02 In large single-product warehouses, ducted cold air is supplied by one central conditioner, but in multi-product stores, several conditioners must be used to avoid cross-contamination.

26.03 Five air changes per hour are usual, less if ozone can be used as a purifier. Ozone is unsuitable for dairy products; activated carbon should be used, but this is unsuitable for fruit.

Types of refrigeration plant

26.04 Direct expansion cooling, produced by evaporation of the refrigerant, is used for cooling tunnels and freezing chambers. Fast temperature reduction is possible, but refrigeration ceases when the compressors stop.

26.05 Secondary liquid cooling cools antifreeze liquid down to the operating temperature, and then distributes it to cooler batteries (as in Figure 6.20). This is initially more expensive than direct expansion, requiring evaporators and circulation pumps, but allows reserves to accumulate, and is advantageous for multipurpose warehouses.

26.06 Direct expansion cooling requires reciprocating (Figure 6.21) or turbo-compressors. The former are very noisy (more than 92 dBA has been recorded) and their rooms should be sound suppressed. The use of one com-

Figure 6.19 *(a) Plastic faced plywood cladding spalled off by ice build-up. Ice accumulation can be seen on the output face. (b) Output side of cooler bank is badly positioned, near a corner and frequently opening door. Ice is spread into the corner by the fans, and down to cover electric trunking.*

Figure 6.21 *Typical reciprocating compressor room in large cold store.*

pressor per cold chamber is not common, even though it simplifies pipe work. Cold fruit smells as it does not act with ethylene. Air ducts can absorb smells and transfer them to other zones. Cold rooms are usually grouped together by function allowing plant to be positioned centrally to cater for various temperatures and for flexibility. Three different cooling circuits of 0°C, minus 10°C to minus 25°C, and 25°C and below, run to each chamber. Their compressors should be similar to simplify maintenance. Very low temperatures result in a rise in compression ratio, requiring multi-stage compressors with inter-stage cooling for the refrigerant.

Condensers

26.07 Condensers are used to dissipate heat. Open circuit condensers use large quantities of fresh water, or seawater if available, as a medium. Fresh water should not exceed 25°C and seawater 18°C. Closed circuit coolers use cooling towers or atmospheric or evaporative condensers. The latter need treatment to prevent calcium scaling. As condenser efficiency depends on the cleanliness of the water side of the exchanger surface, access for cleaning and precautions against algal growth are advised. Condenser fans are noisy and may cause annoyance if sited near housing.

26.08 If brine is used as the cooling medium, valves and pipes must be corrosion resistant. Alternative cooling solutions are calcium chloride, ethyl alcohol and ethylene glycol.

Relative humidity

26.09 Relative humidity influences the weight loss of the product during refrigeration and must be controlled to prevent organic growth. Low relative humidity levels can shrivel fruit and cause cold burns. The level can be controlled by varying air flow speed, and (more costly but effective) by combined heating and cooling. Grid type in-chamber coolers cool by natural convection, so that relative humidity remains high. This type of equipment is difficult to defrost.

26.10 Refrigeration designers must include heat gain figures for product and packaging, including pallet, handling equipment, lighting, cooler fan motors, door openings, personnel, defrosting equipment and, if applicable, sorting and repackaging machinery.

Insulation

26.11 Insulation is an integral part of the cold store fabric. BS CP 406:1952 (Mechanical Refrigeration, HMSO) states that insulation thickness should be equivalent to 25 mm of good quality cork for each temperature difference between the inside and the outside of 5.6°C.

26.12 Insulation materials are available in soft board or block form. Some are specially developed for cold stores, and are, of their nature, impermeable (though their joints are not).

Vapour barriers

26.13 Continuous vapour barriers are essential. Failure in walls can cause the insulant to deteriorate and frost to damage fabric and structure; failure in foundations will cause frost heave. An impervious material must be placed on the warm side of the insulant, or the cavity between the insulant and cladding must be vented with dry air with a dew point lower than that of the lowest temperature to be encountered in the building.

26.14 Both insulant and vapour barrier must withstand expansion and contraction without fracture. One contractor foams wall, ceiling and floor joints in situ to achieve continuity. If the insulation is in board form, all joints should be well lapped. Corner seals liable to differential movement should be of flexible membrane material.

26.15 The choice of insulant depends on the type of goods stored, and temperature ranges. It should be odourless, anti-rot, have a low linear shrinkage and be vermin resistant. For fire precautions see para. 27.

26.16 Rigid foamed glass blocks, protected by lightweight metal cladding combine insulation and the main wall structure. A typical installation used two layers of 120 mm thick blocks step-jointed to the roof and sealed with mastic.

26.17 Many aluminium and steel sheet insulating systems incorporate sub-framing and internal and external cladding. Internal walls are usually left unpainted, as some enamel and aluminium paints can retain water. Cladding sheets are often slightly corrugated to take up thermal movement and lessen insolation. Bonded sandwich panels are rigid, and need little wind bracing. One system joins panels externally by pressing the sheeting with a closure tool, and internally with a vinyl batten, and then integrates joints with in situ foamed polyurethane, forming a vapour resistant seal.

26.18 In situ or pre-cast concrete cladding systems whose joints are sealed by grouting are also available.

Drainage

26.19 Rainwater guttering and down pipes should be fixed to the exterior of cold stores, or be well isolated from low temperatures (Figure 6.22).

Doors

26.20 Doors to cold rooms should be considered as part both of the insulation and the building fabric, and should have the same thickness of insulation. Surface warmers round the frames combat ice jamming but require drains beneath (Figure 6.23a).

Figure 6.22 *Detail of cold store facade showing pipe penetration and gutter fixing.*

Cold storage – building function

Figure 6.23 *(a) Ice has built up round door runner and guide wheel of cold store door. Guard rail and post are well used, as both are badly scuffed. (b) Double sliding cold store doors (closed) showing pneumatic door gear, heavy-duty guard rail and set back pull control, activated from a forklift seat.*

26.21 Doors are nowadays electrically or pneumatically powered, activated by pull switches and induction pads. These should be easily reached by forklift drivers and pedestrians and should be timed to stay open long enough to allow a loaded truck to pass, with a safety margin (Figure 6.23b). Other activation devices include radio control and photoelectric cells. Some operators prefer one set of doors per chamber to reduce heat gain and floor icing. Airlocks, curtains and impact opening rubber doors can reduce air intrusion but no perfect solution has been found. Warm air will tend to flow in at the top of open doors where cold air seeps out at the bottom, and ice will form on the first cold surface that it strikes. A curtain of hot air blown on the warm side will prevent cold air leaving, but moisture can still collect under doors and cause snow build-up.

27 Fire control

27.01 Conventional water charged sprinkler systems cannot be used. Dry riser systems with fast pressurization are possible, but with a localized fire the system may become icebound before the fire is controlled. Gas extinguishing systems are available. Contact the insurance company before deciding on any extinguishing method and finalizing the refrigeration plant.

Fire control in high-bay cold stores

27.02 Multi-injection gas systems and liquid extinguishing systems using a strong anti-freeze solution are possible. Fires can start at very low temperature and immediate sensing, which must not be affected by ice build-up, is essential. (See Technical study, Automated storage 2, para. 27.)

Choice of insulant in fire control

27.03 Insurance companies are not convinced by claims that expanded plastic foams are as retardant as materials like fibreglass. Some foams smoulder and give off smoke and noxious fumes which damage concrete structures. They prefer traditional construction (cavity brickwork with foam filler or reinforced concrete) to panel systems.

27.04 Cold stores cannot be vented like conventional warehouses. In one recent case, single access doors to a cold chamber were shut to limit the air supply in an attempt to contain the fire, effectively barring entry to the fire brigade.

27.05 Cold store fires are often started by malfunctioning door heaters, whose wiring should be treated with extra care where it runs through insulation.

Fire control in cold store plant rooms

27.06 The insurance company should be consulted before the refrigerant is finally chosen. A 50 per cent coolant alcohol-water solution is flammable and in a secondary liquid refrigerant system thousands of gallons of it will be circulating through the building. Gas and alcohol tanks should be positioned outside the plant area, and as far from the storage zone as possible.

27.07 Contact the local fire officer at an early stage as the regulations vary between areas. In the Inner London zone, the brigade does not differentiate between cold stores and normal warehouses. If the area is over 23 230 m^2, Section 20 of the London Building Act 1939 applies.

27.08 Ammonia charged systems may explode if a burst or large leak occurs, and should have special emergency ventilation.

28 Security

28.01 Alarm systems must be provided for operatives shut in freezing tunnels and cold chambers. Alarms should be audible next to the chamber and shown on the control room display. Specify a door system that can be manually operated in case of emergency.

28.02 Ice build-up on floors can cause forklift and pallet trucks to skid, damaging racking and doors. Ice drops from ceiling cooler units builds up round door zones, and forms from moisture brought in on the handling plant. It is aggravated in public cold stores by 'frozen' goods arriving at higher temperatures than that of the cold chamber. Ice on floors can be scarified off from time to time. Whatever measures are taken to avoid ice dropping from coolers and building up behind doors, some is inevitable at low temperatures.

28.03 For security from theft see Technical study, Mechanized storage 2, para. 28. If drugs and pharmaceuticals are involved, alarm and detection systems are available. (*Building Services Handbook*, 2001, R. Greeno and F.E. Hall, Butterworth–Heinemann.) If delivery vehicles are parked overnight, bright light is a deterrent against wholesale theft. If the vehicles are attached to plug points, an alarm system can show the position of the intruder on a schematic plan in the control room. Many

Cold storage – building function

cold stores operate a night shift, and the security problem is then mostly internal.

29 External works

29.01 Stacking of ISO containers is described in Technical study, External storage 1. Plug-in points for vehicle and container cooling should be guarded and clearly marked (Figure 6.24a/b). If vehicles are parked back to back, to use grouped plugs, a walkway should give access to plug positions. Lighting blocked by closely parked vans should be at low level plug positions (or incorporated with guard bollards).

29.02 Some public cold store operators provide a wash-down bay to decontaminate refrigerated trucks. Flexible hose lines to reach van corners are necessary. Movable steps allow cleaners to reach trailer floors; a movable gantry gives easy access to autonomous refrigeration units; a platform 2.9 m high has proved effective. The area should be well drained and lit (spotlights ensure cleanliness). The hot water from the heat exchanger can be used in wash-down areas (Figure 6.25).

30 Structure-based plant

30.01 Roller, belt and slat conveyors are used in freezing tunnels and re-packaging areas. Roller conveyors should be galvanized as icing can cause rusting and deterioration. For pallet loads, roller or slat conveyors are used. Packeted goods, though usually moved on belts, may be moved by air conveyors, combining cooling with lift and forward motion. The conveyor surface, often specially developed for cold stores, depends on the product handled, e.g. steel band and vibration conveyors are used in freezing and re-packing areas. Vegetable re-handling is shown in Figure 6.26. Account for the heat given off by this plant when calculating cooling capacity.

30.02 Overhead and continuous conveyors are not recommended in cold rooms because of bulk, except for goods moved at regular intervals along the same route. Overhead conveyors are mainly used in single purpose stores. As long as the rail is gap-free, frosting can lower its surface friction.

30.03 Fire regulations often require conveyor lines passing through cold store walls to have fire stop doors with fusible link controls. These may ice and insurers might ask for low output surface heaters. Conveyor fixing to the structure must not form heat bridges.

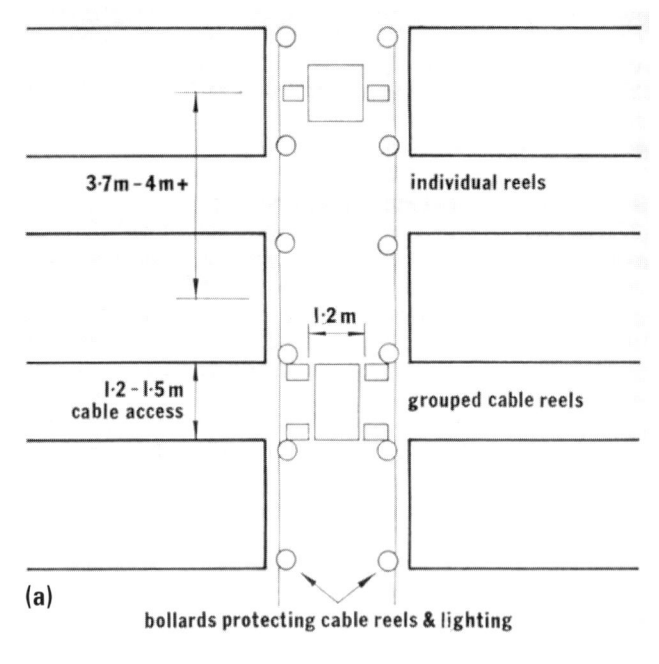

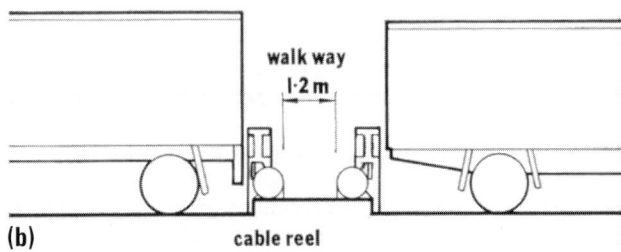

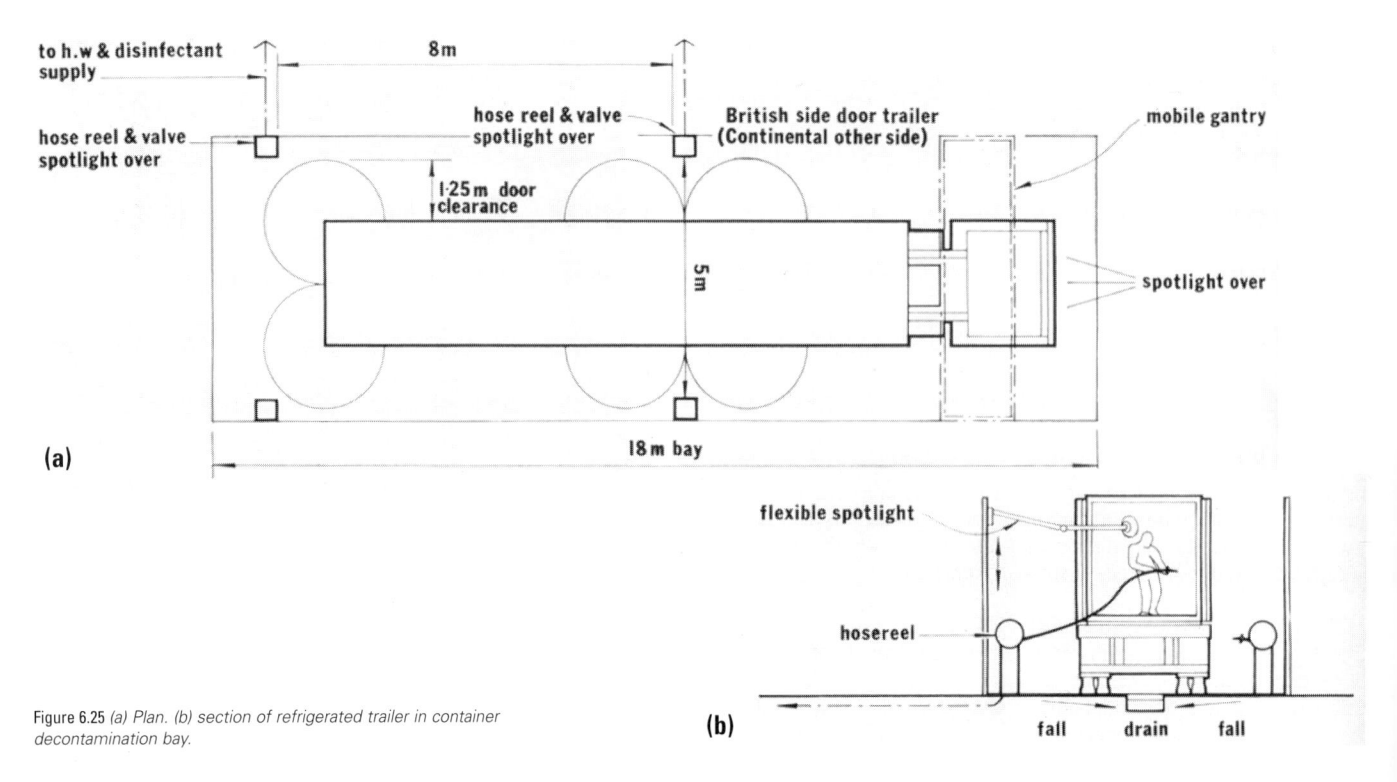

Figure 6.24 (a) Plan. (b) section through refrigerated vehicle park, showing electric plug positions and walkway.

Figure 6.25 (a) Plan. (b) section of refrigerated trailer in container decontamination bay.

Cold storage – building function

Figure 6.26 *For vegetable re-handling, bin tippers empty the bulk bins into an intermediate hopper, which distributes vegetables to a vibrating conveyor for sorting foreign bodies, and then to a packaging machine.*

31 Mobile handling plant

31.01 Handling plant used to suffer from metal fracture at very low temperatures, but has now been improved by use of sealed hydraulic systems, special hoses and wiring for cold store use. Turret trucks (Figure 6.27) and narrow aisle reach trucks, allow higher racking and therefore higher store capacity. Lift trucks moving in and out of cold chambers may ice through moisture collection.

31.02 Battery-charging maintenance areas should be well away from any foodstuffs. Gases given off during battery charging, if sucked into a cold chamber, can cause contamination.

Figure 6.27 *Forklift delivering frozen pallet from the truck dock to turret truck operating the narrow aisle warehouse.*

32 Integration of building and plant

32.01 Wiring has caused trouble in the past, usually because its insulation was unsuited to the very low temperatures. In automated stores control signals can be affected by icing. Some cabling has fluids in the sheathing to prevent brittle fracture.

33 Maintenance

33.01 Maintenance checks are essential, especially for foods, where contamination is very easy. In temperatures below 0°C heat exchanger coils become blocked with ice, reducing efficiency. Frost does not affect heat transfer unless air flow is blocked. Smaller cooling coils need more frequent defrosting. Primary refrigeration is defrosted by hot gas, secondary circulation systems by hot brine. Conditioner units have manual or automatic defrosting. Wet-type coolers are not defrosted but brine deposits must be cleared with ethylene glycol solution.

33.02 Floor cleaning avoids dirt build-up in corners. Industrial sweepers for cold stores are convertible into ice scarifiers. Forklift trucks can have sweeper attachments, useful as the lift allows cleaning of upstands and kerbs (Figure 6.28).

Figure 6.28 *Useful sweeper attachment to a forklift truck.*

33.03 Planned maintenance should be programmed from the outset. Refrigeration plant is now tending to be maintained on contract by specialist engineers. All structural joints should be examined at frequent intervals for moisture penetration, and metal surfaces should be galvanized or sheathed in plastic. Plant rooms should have vehicle access. Compressors are heavy and a chain hoist or space for a mobile hoist would be useful. Overhead hoists are often not practical as there is so much overhead pipe work.

Cold storage – building function

34 Management

34.01 The supply and fixing of insulation and refrigeration plant is usually by a nominated subcontractor who is a manufacturer of plant and material. Tenders should be obtained from an insulation and refrigeration plant contractor nominated before the main building contract goes to tender, to ensure co-ordination of all building requirements by the general contractor.

34.02 The nominated refrigeration subcontractor is one of the building team's most important members, with a specialized knowledge of refrigeration problems and particular knowledge of his own plant and insulation materials. There must be the closest working conditions throughout between the general contractor and the refrigeration subcontractor, because both have an important joint responsibility for the good working of plant and building.

35 Personnel accommodation

35.01 Cold store work needs heavy protective clothing (see Figure 6.26). Changing rooms should have large locker accommodation for padded clothing, and drying cabinets are needed.

35.02 Hot showers are advantageous as heavy clothing leads to perspiration and hot water is warming after a shift at very low temperatures.

Office accommodation

35.03 Office areas will vary with the type of cold store and the duty it is performing. Administration personnel and any expansion must be listed in the brief. Administration often requires a building separate from the cold store-perhaps attached to a processing area. For offices for store management and operatives see Technical study, Mechanized storage 2, para. 34.

36 Amenity

36.01 Men working in low temperatures require 10–15 minutes rest per hour or 30 minutes every two hours, and a maximum of a six-hour shift has been suggested. Rest rooms should be warm, away from the cooled zone and provide hot drinks. Working in very cold chambers is tiring and comfortable seating helps relaxation. Most accidents happen through carelessness due to fatigue. Rest and toilet accommodation should also be provided for truck drivers. If refrigerated trucks are expected from Europe there should be a separate parking area where drivers can sleep in their cabs and cook.

37 Security and safety

37.01 Cold chambers should have emergency alarms and also intercoms in freezing tunnels to ensure that operatives are not forgotten (see Figure 6.24b). Some operators place an axe in every cold chamber in case a power failure jams the door gear.

37.02 Some refrigerated products (e.g. apples) give off noxious gases requiring face-masks and oxygen packs. The refrigerant medium itself can leak dangerous gas accumulations. Plant rooms should be fitted with powerful extraction equipment, as gases from coolants like ammonia can quickly overcome operatives.

37.03 A first-aid room, outside the refrigerated zone, should be kept warm and equipped to handle cold burns, broken limbs, crushing and asphyxiation. Access for ambulances with a quick route to the first aid room should be planned. The loading bay is not suitable for emergency access in cold stores unless it is open to normal atmosphere.

37.04 Oxygen equipment and face-masks should be stored where in emergencies operatives can reach them quickly from most parts of the store – adjacent to the loading bay and cold chamber doors if possible. Similar equipment should be positioned in plant rooms.

38 Circulation and parking

38.01 Parking should be provided for store operatives, office staff and visiting maintenance personnel. Trucks must be able to drive into the plant area to unload heavy equipment close to the installation position. Access should be considered for the fire service, and the fire officer should be contacted. As access to cold chambers is limited, firemen might have to cut their way in from an outside wall. Parking for container handling equipment should be provided if it is used.

Chapter 7
Special storage

TECHNICAL STUDY

Special storage 1
Storage process

1 Introduction
2 Source of goods
3 Form of transport
4 Control of transport
5 Receipt of goods
6 Form of goods
7 Unloading
8 Characteristics of goods
9 Sorting
10 Volume calculations
11 Turnover calculations
12 Variety and flow
13 Type of storage
14 Stock control
15 Stock withdrawal
16 Order picking
17 Picking area
18 Load build-up
19 Order and document check
20 Loading and dispatch
21 Additional data

Previous chapters have examined the most commonly required storage types. But there are others which deal with a product requiring special storage conditions. Most of these would fall into the following categories:

- Sheet materials (metal, glass, asbestos, plastic).
- Tubular materials (metals, glass, paper, asbestos, plastic).
- Non-standard unit loads, e.g. air cargo.
- Easily damaged material.
- Bulk granular and liquid materials.
- Potentially dangerous material, e.g. radioactive material, explosives and high-security material.
- Combination of difficult shapes, large heavy units and fast turnover, e.g. vehicle spares.
- Material requiring specific method of handling, e.g. cable, wire.
- Combinations of large difficult shapes, low throughput and high selectivity, e.g. furniture storage.
- Inter-process storage in production buildings, i.e. varied throughout, outsize loads, small parts, or special environments.

These categories of storage are 'special' in that the ways and means of storing the product differ, but the basic principles (outlined in previous sections) remain the same. As an example of how these principles are applied in a specialist situation, this section studies in detail steel stockholding (paras 1–38), storage which is special because it has extra heavy loads, and very high throughput. Apart from these factors, which inevitably affect building structure and dimensions, a steel stockholding warehouse is designed on the same principles as a mechanized storage warehouse. Furniture and scenery storage for the performing arts is also briefly described in para. 1 as an example of large non-standard unit loads, with high volume and selectivity but low turnover. In the original version of this book, there was a whole chapter devoted to bulk handling: this is such a specialized subject in the hands of very few suppliers that it has been omitted from this edition except for some information sheets at the end of this chapter.

Special storage – storage process

1 Introduction

Furniture and scenery storage

1.01 Furniture and scenery storage is inherently space-consuming. Previously it was handled and stored in old buildings on the ground to a level as high as a person could lift. Since access gangways had to be left, the resulting volume efficiency was very low.

1.02 Furniture and scenery storage has now become containerized. Containers are fast and easy to handle, make greater use of volume and protect from dust, vermin and moths. But most existing furniture and scenery storage buildings and vehicles particularly are unsuitable for container use.

1.03 Warehouses for containerized furniture and scenery can be treated in the same way as those for block stacked goods using forklift trucks. One furniture removals and storage company uses 2.4 m x 2.4 m x 2.7 m containers, stacking two high. Containers are block stacked, or disposed either side of an aisle, depending on speed of stock movement. The Royal Opera House at Covent Garden, London, commissioned a dedicated palletized scenery-handling and storage system that has automated the process in the theatre, and which enjoys an efficient mechanized purpose-designed warehouse in Wales. There is no reason why containers of furniture should not be similarly stacked on fir tree racking by a sideloader as a low access repository function stored similarly in mobile racking, or handled into stacks by a gantry-slung stacker crane (some old crane-equipped machine assembly shops could get a new lease of life). (The scenery for the opera in Munich is stored on similar pallets to those of the Royal Opera House in a fully automated warehouse that uses air cargo handling techniques) (Figure 7.1). From past records and experience, removers can predict high user stock. They still must cater for the unplanned withdrawal of one particular piece of furniture from a large consignment.

1.04 Where furniture lots are too small for containers to be used economically, mobile racking is effective. Cantilever racking with adjustable bearers, wide shelves and mobile bases can store furniture to great heights and densities (Chapter 4, Information Sheet, Mechanized Storage 3). Some companies use standard pallets, and store furniture like normal packaged goods (in pallet racking). This is more realistic with new furniture, which is taken apart and packed into cartons. Removers do not like breaking down used furniture since they use the odd space for packing small objects, and so achieve compact loads in the containers.

1.05 Furniture depositories do not need temperature or humidity control, except to ensure that the stock is kept above dew point. Heating can create breeding conditions for moths and vermin. Scenery storage does require heating, as the intumescent coatings can grow mould if stored in damp conditions.

1.06 Fire is a major problem to depository operators. Storage in containers will reduce the risk from inside, but once a fire starts will hardly contain it. Most furniture containers are of timber and board construction. Sprinklers would be required in a new installation. Contact the user's insurers.

1.07 New furniture is usually dismantled and placed in cartons on pallets. If bulky, e.g. armchairs and settees, it is often shrink-wrapped. Demountable body systems are now widely used in the furniture manufacturing industry, allowing pre-loading and fast vehicle turnround.

1.08 Works of art and carpets require special temperature and humidity controlled storage conditions. Such a store should be treated as a sealed unit, e.g. as a cold store, to ensure freedom from vermin and high security. The design requirements are likely to come from the operator's insurers.

1.09 Design of a furniture or scenery warehouse requires care, and will inform and be informed by the whole logistics system, including the type of vehicle used, and the number of staff employed.

Metal stockholding

1.10 Metal stockholding is a supply service which, by virtue of its dealing with a basic commodity, is a highly competitive business. Success in this field depends on the ability to cope with orders, from a few kilograms to many tonnes, in a wide variety of materials at very short notice. The cost-effectiveness of plant and buildings is therefore critical.

1.11 The principle of stockholding as a buffer between the primary raw material producer and smaller consumers has been operative since the early days of manufacturing industry. This was essentially a basic wholesaling operation with simple block storage in low-cost buildings. However, realization by the producer mills of rolling programme economics within the last 20 years has tended to direct distribution of smaller orders to the

Figure 7.1 *Scenery pallet during factory acceptance test. Note heavy duty conveyor system which will become an automated storage and sorting system.*

Special storage – storage process

stockholders. The effect has been, notably in steel, for the larger stockholders to become production orientated and take over some of the final mill processes and services. This trend, starting in the USA, was closely followed by the UK, and must be ultimately accepted throughout Europe and the other major industrial nations. In the USA and the UK some 40 per cent of steel strip mill output passes through the service centres, as the stockholding operations have become, and of this nearly 75 per cent is processed in one form or another.

1.12 The basic stockholder buying-in material in finished form still remains, alongside the service centre, notably in non-ferrous metals. Such an operation normally requires only a simple racking or block stacking system. However, when processing is required, whether for flattening and cutting strip or sawing bars and profiles, more sophisticated handling systems are generally necessary: the more progressive companies demand plans for increasing automation and computer controls.

1.13 The facilities required by a company must be tailored to its closely defined market objectives, and experience has shown that it can be dangerous to generalize too much on the plant requirements of ostensibly competing organizations.

2 Source of goods

2.01 The bulk of steel and aluminium supplies still come from within the UK. However, developments in the continental European industry are already bringing about growth in imported material in addition to that regularly purchased from the Far East to mitigate against adverse UK production patterns. Space should be allowed for the removal of ocean packing.

3 Form of transport

3.01 Coils (Figure 7.2) are carried on special well-bodied articulated vehicles, one or two at a time. Tube and bars arrive in bundles on flat vehicles. Imported sheet and other forms of metal arrive in ISO containers, or in articulated trailers from Europe (from the USA in containers or as break-bulk cargo). Special half-height containers are now used for handling metals, with tilt tops and detachable sides for easy unloading (Figure 7.3). Standard ISO containers and box trailers have caused problems on arrival at stockholders, as they are not designed to be handled from the top or side, and without a dock, end unloading of metals is difficult and requires manual assistance. TIR-type 'tilt' trailers are time-consuming to unsheet, and block circulation within the store, vehicles usually being driven into the building for full weather protection. Ideally, a buffer space for unroping or unsheeting operations should be provided within the building, clear of circulation routes.

4 Control of transport

4.01 Vehicle peaks are common; check that the planned delivery pattern does not generate a loading peak when vehicles are likely to arrive from mills. Some truck parking should be provided, both for empty delivery vehicles and for large mill trucks that can arrive at periods when it is inconvenient immediately to unload them. Unlike conventional distribution warehouses, the number of loading doors should be kept to a minimum and unloading should be at ground level within the building. Each door reduces storage space and is an additional security hazard.

Figure 7.2 *Special semi-trailer for carrying metal coils.*

Figure 7.3 *Open, half height container used for carrying steel.*

5 Receipt of goods

5.01 Receipt of goods is as described in Technical study, Mechanized storage 1, para. 5.

6 Form of goods

6.01 Steel can arrive from mills in unit loads of up to 15 tonnes in the case of coil and up to 20 m long in the case of heavy sections. Use of coils weighing 25 tonnes will be a requirement of some larger companies, and encouragement by mills for acceptance of 35 tonne coils has been predicted, although such is unlikely to be profitable for all but a very few in the foreseeable future. Bars and tubes are usually bound into 1 or 2 tonne lots. Aluminium for sheet can arrive in coil form, but as yet is more often delivered from the mill in 0.5 and 1 tonne stacks of sheets packed in polythene-lined crates.

7 Unloading

7.01 For weather protection, trucks are driven right into the warehouse. Coils must be offloaded by overhead cranage, fitted with special grabs, C-hooks or slings, in view of the variation in the axial position of coils to be found on the incoming vehicles. Large profiles may be handled by sideloader, while much bar and tube material may also be handled by normal forklifts (Figure 7.4a–c). Overhead cranes can only operate efficiently on one section of track at a time, which limits unloading speed for multiple units, but does not affect the handling of heavy coils, as there are only one or two per vehicle. Heavy-duty sideloaders and forklift trucks require large manoeuvring areas. (See Information sheet, External storage 2, as machines are adapted from container carrying units). Where forklifts and sideloaders are to unload over the sides of trucks, a straight-through covered loading area at the perimeter of the building allows normal handling operations to continue undisturbed, and several vehicles can be handled at once (Figure 7.5). A buffer stacking area is required, accessible

Special storage – storage process

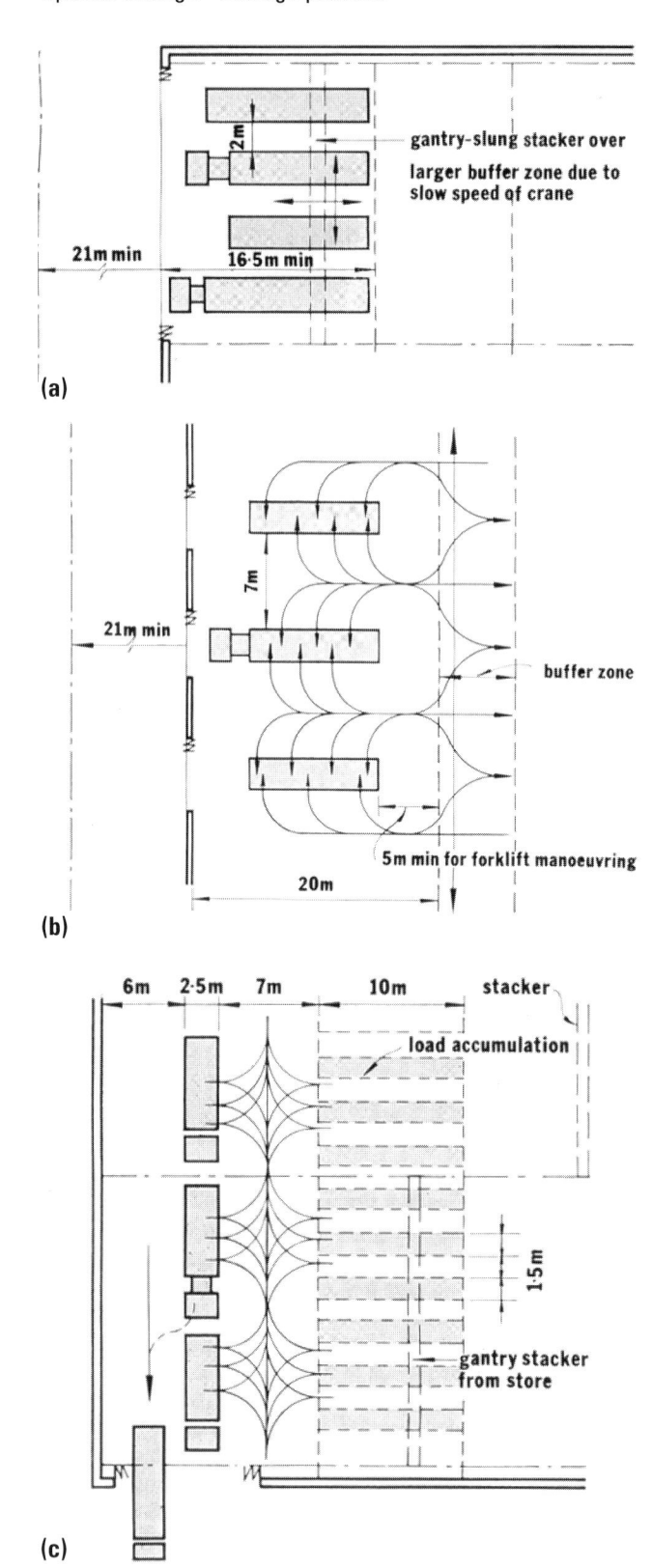

Figure 7.4 (a) Loading bay using gantry crane is slower than (b) but uses less area. (b) Loading bay using forklift trucks (load pre-assembly necessary). (c) High throughput straight-through loading bay using forklifts. Load pre-assembly necessary. Load accumulation depends on size of load and number of trucks. Forklift trucks need to pass between parked vehicles to unload both stacks.

to the unloading equipment and storage plant. The size and throughput of the installation will decide whether an island or peripheral straight-through loading area is the most suitable. Consider future extension possibilities and the chance of increasing throughput.

8 Characteristics of goods

8.01 Coils arrive from mills firmly bound. Tube and bar stock tends to 'whip' even when bound in bundles. Fork

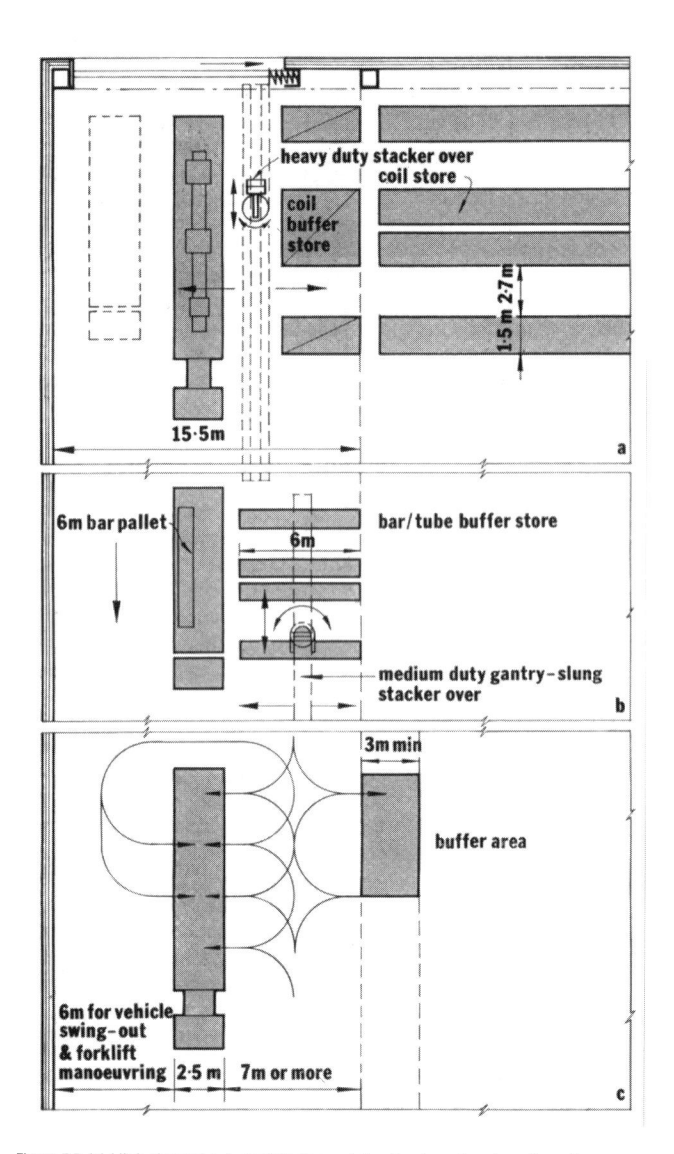

Figure 7.5 (a) High throughput straight-through loading bay showing alternative methods of loading a heavy coils by stacker crane. (b) Bar and tube by stacker crane. (c) sheet and bar by forklift. An island-loading bay is similar to this but has storage on both sides. Island bays tend to constrict plant movement. Where there is a single door, trucks reverse into the unloading bay. Unsheeting position should be nearest the door.

heads for handling bars are available. Special long pallets help bulk handling and order picking.

9 Sorting

9.01 Buffer space at input allows stacker crane schedules to be flexible. Coils are block stacked on frames on the floor, fitted with adjustable coil stops (Figure 7.6). The turnover and cranage requirements for supplying process machinery will determine whether separate handling plant is needed for unloading and the initial sorting function.

9.02 Buffer space should also be provided for bars, tubes, and sheet bundles and pallets. This could include full pallets awaiting storage and empty pallets awaiting transfer of goods from the delivery truck. These pallets can be 6 m or more long. Unpacked sheet crates require disposal or storage for collection. A skip positioned in this area can collect polythene liners, broken crates and general refuse. It should be sited where it will not obstruct handling plant, but can easily be collected by its carrier.

Special storage – storage process

Figure 7.6 *Block stacked coils in store.*

10 Volume calculations

10.01 See para 11, Turnover calculations.

11 Turnover calculations

11.01 Assuming that rapid handling systems in large-scale stockholding incorporating a processing line are used, the range of order lines to be produced and the replenishment period restrict the rate of stock turnover. Once the output/order mix has been defined, their relationship, plus a comparison of the cost of storage against bulk order discounts will define optimum and maximum coil sizes. The number of coils to be stored can then be calculated. The following should be quantified from the outset:
1 the required throughput for the product range
2 the gross return on capital expected as a result of trading.

The former will generate the basic specification for the processing plant, while the two factors combined will define the annual stock turnover to be achieved. The processing plant requires buffer storage zones between activities. The flow of material through the plant should be able to maintain a rate commensurate with the fastest conditions on the processing line.

11.02 The general metal stockholder must keep a very wide range of sheet and bar sizes both in steel and non-ferrous metals, which move at various speeds. Aluminium alone has 32 basic 'super standard' sizes, on which there are many variations. Turnover is also likely to expand as producers continue to rationalize output. A typical installation in the London area dealing in both ferrous and non-ferrous metals handles over 550 orders a day.

12 Variety and flow

12.01 Efficiency of the processing plant in a large-scale stockholding warehouse depends on:

1 the operational efficiency of the bulk coil store
2 the ratio of running time to down time of the processing line.

These are interrelated, and the overall performance laid down for the plant creates a design requirement for the bulk coil store. Even though volume efficiency is lowered as a result, every coil should be directly accessible. The loss of volume efficiency can be minimized by random coil storage.

12.02 Primary processing, i.e. conversion of wide strip coil into flat sheet or narrow strip, variously coated or formed. These can be continually processed. Primary is often automatic. A computer controlling stock movement can also programme processing machinery, and plan the storage of finished goods and dispatch pattern.

Secondary and tertiary processing, e.g. special finishes, grading, blanking, profiling, may also be assisted by a computer, but tend to be more labour intensive.

12.03 General purpose metal stockholders are faced with an ever increasing variety of stock. Some can be very fast moving, but accurate predictions are not easy, even for expert consultants; this is one of the reasons why some operators overstock.

13 Type of storage

13.01 Typical systems in operation with varying degrees of success are:
1 block stacking with overhead cranes (mostly for coils)
2 medium-height storage using overhead cranes, sideloaders, forklift trucks or four-way travel reach trucks, for coil, bar and tube stock
3 mobile racking for sheet, bar and tube (up to 160 tonnes per rack)
4 high-bay storage, with stacker cranes or special high lift sideloaders for bar and tube
5 specialized systems with varying degrees of automatic operation – many custom-built systems incorporate one or more of the former handling methods
6 "A" frame racks for plates
7 floor racks for large profiles.

Choice of hardware depends on space and labour-saving needs in relation to the range and turnover of stock held, and a consequent balance between storage density and speed of access to stock.

13.02 Block stacking with overhead cranes is the traditional method for handling coils. With such, random access is not possible and coil damage is increased by additional handling. Furthermore the system must be carefully designed to prevent coils slipping or springing out of position.

13.03 Medium-height storage (up to 6 m) is a common solution, and is as high as coils can go economically. If stock control, order planning and process machinery control is computer based, the coil storage area should be planned for eventual on-line control of the handling plant (depending on throughput and expenditure). Automation of a coil store requires careful design of the racking and plant so that it can be adapted with as little machine redundancy as possible. One such store (designed for later automation) using a manually controlled gantry-slung stacker crane to handle 15 tonne coils has an interesting rack construction. Special fir tree racking is designed with staggered peg positions. Coils slot into the spaces left by the units above and below. The pegs of the racking to support the coils are of double bar construction, to allow

Special storage – storage process

Figure 7.7 *Coil racking using overhead suspended stacker crane.*

the crane's peg to enter between them, and accurately position the coil. A closed-circuit television camera is mounted at the end of the stacker's carrier peg to help location. This rack design is the most efficient for combining volume efficiency, individual coil selection, and accurate handling (Figure 7.12).

13.04 The most commonly found form of coil rack is a 'pallet type', with the coils supported on cradles mounted in a rectangular frame. On considerations of volumetric efficiency this suffers from the 'round peg in square hole' concept and would be inefficient in a fully automated concept. Such racking can be supplied with adjustable cradle heights; a typical rack is 2.4 m deep and 5.5 m high, with a capacity of a 10 tonne coil on the top level, 2 x 15 tonne coils on the second and first levels, and a further coil resting on the floor.

13.05 Overhead, suspended stacker cranes are efficient for use in coil stores; a 2.7 m wide aisle can be used with 1.5 m wide coils, allowing full mobility (Figure 7.7). Sideloaders are also used, but are not so flexible, even with four-wheel steering, since they require substantial turning space.

13.06 Bar and tube stock is stored in special pallets. Fir tree racking with parallel pins is used, and both overhead stackers and sideloaders (Figure 7.8) are employed. Areas for bar and tube storage require more space at the ends of aisles for manoeuvring. With an underslung stacker, the turning area can be taken as the radius of the load from the centre of the mast. With a sideloader (Figure 7.9) swing-out with long bars can be considerable, and the curve complicated. Plant manufacturers supply turning diagrams. See also Information Sheet, Mechanized Storage 7 and Table 4.13.

13.07 Mobile racking has been used successfully for bar and tube stocks. Heavy-duty cantilever racking is mounted on motorized bases, and operates as conventional mobile racking, only one aisle at a time being open. This increases the volume efficiency without reducing access (important for bar stocks, as they generate very low spacial efficiency solutions). Sideloaders or an overslung stacker crane would be used with mobile racking. See Information Sheet, Mechanized Storage 3.

13.08 Cut sheet for individual sheet picking is stored in timber crates on shallow racking, or in special sheet pallets, thus achieving quite high densities. Bulk sheet tends to be block stacked in crates (a 1-tonne 2.4 m x 1.2 m lot of aluminium sheet is approximately 304 mm high in its crate). Clearance should be allowed in the racking for forklift manoeuvring of the sheet crates, and for order pickers to reach in to lift out sheets without fouling the racking structure (Figure 7.10). Aluminium extrusions can

Figure 7.8 *Narrow aisle sideloader picking from fir tree racking.*

Figure 7.9 *Heavy sideloader picking from fir tree racking.*

Figure 7.10 *Semi-automatic stacker crane for picking metal sheet. The work cycle is programmed into the control panel (centre) from a position at the end of the aisle.*

be stacked on end to save space, but in this situation mechanical handling is difficult. Aircraft industry approved stock is segregated from normal metal stock.

13.09 Partially or fully automated high-bay storage of sheet and bar is now widespread in the USA, but as yet relatively uncommon in Europe (Figure 7.11). One steelworks store in Germany employs a high-bay semi-automated configuration with the potential of full automation. Cantilever racking 18.6 m high supports special pallets carrying bar stock up to 6 m long. Stacker cranes are adapted to handle the extra-long pallets. There is considerable potential for high-bay storage for tube and bar stock, as this is inherently space-consuming.

13.10 Profiles over 6 m in length or large cross-sections are normally floor-stacked by overhead crane fitted with a spreader bar from which slings, clamps, or magnets are attached.

13.11 Plates can be stored in 'A' frame racks with overhead cranes fitted with clamps. Thicker material tends to be floor-stacked and handled with overhead cranes fitted with clamps, magnets, or vacuum lifters.

14 Stock control

14.01 Stockholding was previously considered to be keeping as much metal as possible to offset unpredictable deliveries from the mills. This is a costly gamble. By the careful monitoring of the market, and by realistically restricting the product range, a balance can be achieved between stored material and output.

14.02 There are two levels of stock control:
1. The main coil store, supplying steel to processing lines, must operate smoothly.
2. Further control is required between primary and secondary processing, as well as between final processing, packaging and loading delivery vehicles.

14.03 Manual stock control methods are still used successfully and should be employed unless staff are fully familiar with the disciplines of a computer. If such is the case, then computer stock control systems will offer considerable advantages to the larger companies.

15 Stock withdrawal

15.01 Heavy gantry-slung stacker cranes retrieving 15 tonne coils tend to 'crab' when loaded eccentrically. The drive and control method best suited to the application should be considered when the store is being planned.

16 Order picking

16.01 Special sideloaders with elevating picking-platforms can be used, as can fixed path stacker cranes. Bar and tube stock is either bound into packs or stored loose in pallets for order picking. Orders tend to accumulate on the picking unit before being dropped at the load build-up position. Often in the smaller installations, the order picking machinery loads vehicles direct.

17 Picking area

17.01 Bars and tube are available in such a great variety of sizes and grades that their order picking areas tend to waste space, as easy access to the stock and clearance between racks are required. Mobile racks for bars and tubes provide a solution to this problem, and a high-bay system has considerable potential.

18 Load build-up

18.01 Load build-up depends on delivery cycles and type of vehicles in service. Trucks must be kept moving for as much of the time as possible. Large orders of bulk stock can be loaded direct from the storage position and placed on the truck bed by overhead crane or sideloader. Small orders collected for an area delivery round can cause delay. Some operators load goods direct onto articulated trailers which are parked in strategic positions in the store. The tractor returns the empty trailer and immediately leaves with the full one. Demountable bodies are also used in this way. Other operators prefer to separate loading from general in-store handling, and allocate an area for load assembly. This can be space-consuming, as (unlike packaged goods and roll pallets) metal must be spread out on the floor to prevent snagging, and to build up a delivery pattern. A forklift truck or sideloader then loads the vehicles as quickly as possible. The accumulation area required will depend on the number of orders built up at a time and the size of the vehicles used.

19 Order and document check

19.01 This is similar to the process described in Technical study, Mechanized storage 1, para. 19.

20 Loading and dispatch

20.01 Vehicles are usually fitted with special bodies for carrying metal products. Trucks are driven into the

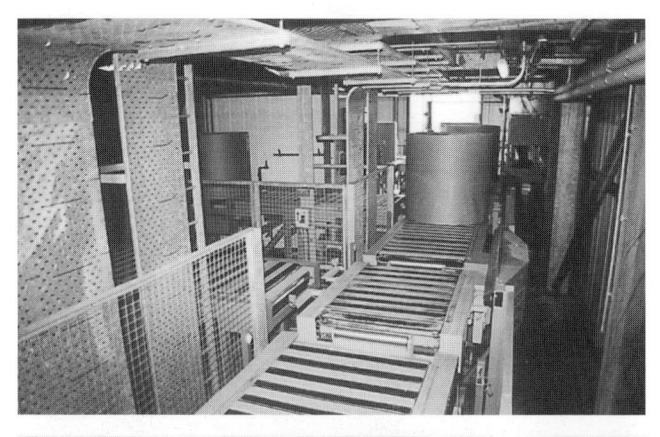

Figure 7.11 Reels of newsprint stored on end rather than edge to avoid flat spots. Apart from handling by heavy-duty forklift trucks with clamps to stack reels up to 9 m high, the automated storage process is similar.

warehouse. If trailers or swop bodies are pre-loaded, parallel parking is used. Space can be saved by loading with an overhead crane, although this is slower than using forklifts. If loads are accumulated prior to a vehicle's arrival, a straight-through loading bay is efficient, with trucks loaded over the side by forklifts. If a weighing machine is required at the loading area (to check picked stock), it should be accessible to loading bay plant without blocking circulation routes.

21 Additional data

21.01 *The use of radio frequency technology (RFI) for the identification of particular unit loads.* Special storage, such as pallets of furniture and scenery with a contents of many individual items offers a great opportunity for the use of radio frequency tag technology. Developed originally for the identity of farm animals, monitoring body weight gain and triggering feed quantities, these tags are effectively simple circuit boards encased in robust shell. Two generic types exist, both used increasingly in manufacturing; read-only where the identity and other useful data is encapsulated; 'I am order number x, so require green paint'. And read–write where the data can be updated after particular processes such as proof of the addition of a sub-assembly.

The benefit on specific unit loads of mixed material is to not only identify the unit load, but to carry the contents, a real time inventory. In special storage situations such as theatrical scenery and 'props', where for the best of reasons items are 'borrowed' for other productions, the ability to individually identify each item (by a barcode read-only RF tag) and be able to scan them in and out of the unit load, updating the master tag each time will ensure accurate stock management with complete stock 'transparency'. Although currently in the region of $20 (£12.50) per tag, for a closed circuit such as a furniture depository or theatre store these systems are economic and achievable.

TECHNICAL STUDY

Special storage 2

Building function

- 22 Structure
- 23 Floor
- 24 Building services
- 25 Special services
- 26 Building fabric
- 27 Fire control
- 28 Security
- 29 External works
- 30 Structure-based plant
- 31 Mobile plant
- 32 Integration of building and plant
- 33 Maintenance
- 34 Management
- 35 Personnel accommodation
- 36 Amenity
- 37 Security and safety
- 38 Circulation and parking

Technical study, Special storage 1 dealt with the storage process. This second study deals with the design of the building.

22 Structure

22.01 To carry gantry cranes handling 15 tonne coils, the structure must be substantial. Some operators sacrifice efficiency and the possibility of automation by using side-loaders which allow a lighter structure.

23 Floor

23.01 Floors in metal stockholding warehouses need to be very strong. Double-sided cantilever racking for coils can carry up to 90 tonnes per vertical bay, with an additional 30 tonnes resting on the floor. Block stacked coils also impose heavy weights, but with different distribution (Figure 7.12). Mobile racking has special problems; one installation that recently upgraded its storage capacity by placing cantilever racking on mobile bases increased the floor loading per bay from 300 to 640 tonnes. This was achieved for the rail support.

23.02 Foundations for metal stockholding must be designed by specialist engineers to take impacts from the heaviest coils, which can fall from machinery and 'pop' out of block stacks. Design for 5–6 tonne wheel loadings where trucks run into the store for loading. If heavy-duty side loaders or forklift trucks are used for coil handling, plan all plant circulation areas to their wheel loading, up to 15 tonnes, but check with plant manufacturer. The floor must be suitable for slitting and processing machinery, which may need special bases and foundations (Figure 7.13). In some warehouses the floor is divided up into bays of different capacities to save money initially. This also restricts flexibility of store organization and handling.

24 Building services

24.01 In storing metals, oxidization by the atmosphere must be prevented. Aluminium stockholders have special requirements for metals used by the aircraft industry,

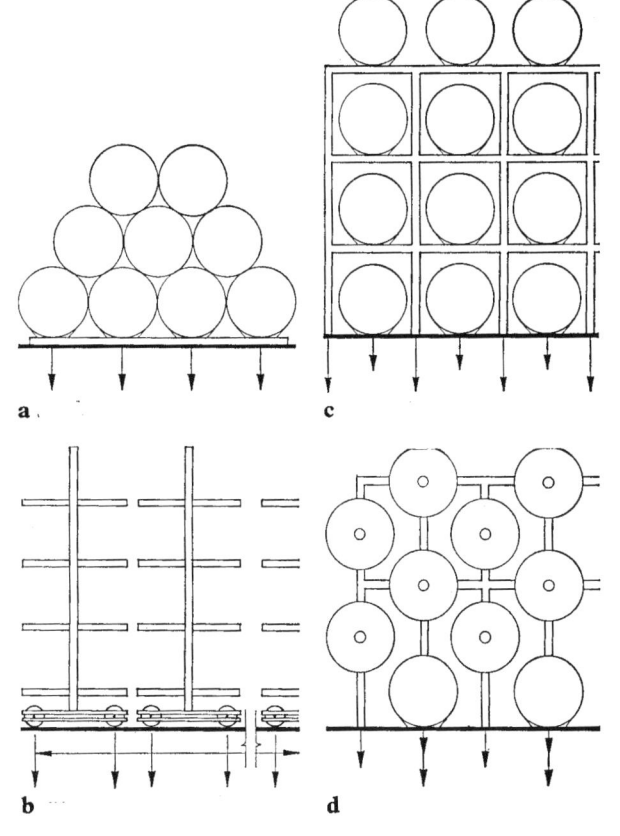

Figure 7.12 *Distribution of loads for foundations and floor in coil stores. (a) Block stacking. (b) Mobile fir tree racking. (c) Coil racking. (d) Fir tree racking with staggered pegs.*

which set standards for environmental control. These range from conventional blown air or radiant panel heating (to keep the temperature above dew point), to full humidity control. The level of control depends on local environmental conditions, and particular care has to be taken in maritime climates. A temperature level of 10–12°C is suggested.

Special storage – building function

Figure 7.13 *Advanced slitting line in use (coil shown right, with coil store in background.*

Figure 7.14 *Dual weighbridge (one incoming, one dispatch) with digital read out for rapid throughput. Cycles of one minute per vehicle are possible. Note strategic siting on circulation route.*

24.02 Consult the operator about temperature and humidity ranges. Air-conditioning in large-scale special-purpose warehouses can save money (e.g. car bodies stored between production and final painting can be left as bare metal, unprimed and ungreased, if air-conditioning is used, and greasing and degreasing cut out).

24.03 Suggested artificial lighting levels are 200 lux for general storage zones, and 400 lux or more for in-process and loading zones. Natural lighting can be used, as heat and light do not harm stock. If internal combustion handling plant is used, e.g. heavy-duty sideloaders, extraction should be installed to prevent fume build-up.

25 Special services

25.01 Three-phase power supplies are required for overhead cranes, and most processing machinery. If slitting lines are used, contact the plant manufacturer for his plant requirements.

26 Building fabric

26.01 Insulated cladding is advisable for metal stockholding. Some operators use the warehouse cladding as advertising, using metal sheet materials with striking external finishes. Waterproofing is very important, as metal, especially stacked sheet, deteriorates when wet. Stacked sheets of galvanized steel wet-stain very fast, and the plastic-lined crates for aluminium can contain moisture. For this reason, operators seldom allow rainwater down pipes to run through storage areas, and prefer flank glazing and ventilation to roof lights. If aisles follow the building perimeter, cladding should be protected from impact damage.

27 Fire control

27.01 This is dealt with in Technical study, Mechanized storage 2, para. 27.

28 Security

28.01 Internal security, such as theft by warehouse staff, often working with delivery drivers, may be a problem. Gatehouse security checks will prevent this, and also control traffic (Figure 7.14). However, storage of high-value metals, particularly when in the form of small fittings, may require special internal security enclosures. Weighbridges counter-check weighing during loading. A high fence, strong lighting and alarm systems fitted to doors and windows will deter intruders. Vehicles and handling-plant parking areas should not adjoin windows, as they act as a convenient stepladder. many stockolding warehouses operate at night, which reduces the external security problem.

29 External works

29.01 Some steel sheet, e.g. Cor ten weathering steels, can be stored externally. These areas should be drained, and surface water laden with oxidization products must not come into contact (by flow or splashing) with surfaces where staining would be unacceptable.

30 Structure-based plant

30.01 Heavy-duty gantry-slung stacker cranes (Figure 7.15) are very sophisticated, and movement controls can now position the crane in the racking very accurately. They can load and retrieve from fir tree racking and block stack coils, place coils onto processing lines, and unload coils from lorries. A gantry-slung stacker crane carrying a 15 tonne coil has considerable momentum, and there have been problems of mast whip and gantry crabbing.

Figure 7.15 *Large gantry stacker handling coil.*

Figure 7.16 *Large sideloader handling metal sheet.*

Figure 7.17 *Sideloader handling coils into racking.*

30.02 For tube and bar stock, a conventional gantry crane with a sling attachment is sometimes used, though a 3–5 tonne capacity gantry-slung stacker with extendable fork heads is faster. The latter can also remove piles of sheet from a cutting line and transport them to a pre-dispatch buffer store. If stackers are also used for loading lorries, the mast must be telescopic to at least 2.5 m above floor level, to clear the truck bed and load.

30.03 Primary processing lines for steel strip are normally for flattening and cutting to length, or for slitting into narrower coils. In either case, special foundations will be required and space allowed for a floor buffer store of two or three coils prior to the decoiler unit. The finished product is either a stack of flat sheets, palletized or unpalletized, or a batch of narrow coils which may be palletized 'eye horizontal', strapped to skids 'eye vertical' or simply strapped together 'eye vertical'. Stacks of sheet are not normally in units greater than five tonnes, while slit coil from a service centre is normally limited to unit loads of three tonnes maximum.

31 Mobile plant

31.01 Mobile plant includes sideloaders (Figures 7.16 and 7.17) normal and heavy-duty forklift trucks and special purpose free path order-picking machines. Heavy-duty plant is diesel powered, so fume extraction equipment must be installed. Low-pressure gas power is popular for normal forklifts and sideloaders as fume levels are low.

31.02 Special-purpose free-path stacker/order pickers allow narrow aisles as in conventional stores (Figure 7.18). With 5 tonne capacity order pickers, 1.8 m wide aisles between rack arms are possible. The operator's control platform rises with the fork head, and the base runs between guide rails at floor level. Some models have sliding masts, allowing stacking and picking at both sides of the aisle. One trend is for the use of automated guided vehicles for handling coil from store to machinery (Figure 7.19). Many of the heavy-duty machines for handling steel have little suspension, and solid-tyred wheels. This may cause extra vibration and should be accounted for when calculating floor loadings.

32 Integration of building and plant

32.01 For mechanized plant, see Technical study, Mechanized storage 2, para. 32.

33 Maintenance

33.01 Provision should be made for crane and mobile plant maintenance. If heavy processing machinery is not covered by overhead craneage, then access must be available for mobile craneage. Normal size forklifts are usually taken off site for maintenance, but large coil-carrying equipment is unsuitable for roads, and tends to be maintained on the premises.

33.02 Building maintenance is mostly repairing impact damage, e.g. a misplaced 15 tonne coil can buckle racking and cradles. Coils, if they get out of control, can smash through external cladding. Breakables, e.g. electrical controls, should be protected.

34 Management

34.01 If processing is involved, the integration of production and storage consultants is important.

35 Personnel accommodation

35.01 Locker accommodation should be provided for operatives. Working with metals can be dirty and washing and grease removal facilities should be installed.

Office accommodation

35.02 The amount of office accommodation depends on how much administration is handled from site. Several new metal stockholding warehouses have incorporated large offices. Offices for warehouse and process personnel are required on the warehouse floor.

Special storage – building function

Figure 7.18 *A useful machine for constricted premises: the Matbro swing lift reach truck incorporates a side reach mechanism for side loading in narrow aisles, and a rotating mast for conventional forklift use.*

36 Amenity

36.01 This is dealt with in Technical study, Mechanized storage 2, para. 36.

37 Security and safety

37.01 Safety is important in a metal stockholding warehouse. Personnel routes should be segregated from heavy plant, e.g. carrying coils. All processing machinery should be guarded and clearly marked (contact the Factory Inspectorate). A first-aid room equipped to handle crushing injuries should be placed out of the storage area, with easy access for ambulances.

38 Circulation and parking

38.01 Internal circulation is inherent in the planning of the storage area and the choice of the handling plant. Parking should be provided for operatives and administrative staff, and for empty delivery vehicles.

Figure 7.19 *Automated guided vehicle handling new print reel stripped of barrier wrap direct to press spider interface. Similar heavier duty machines are now used for metal coils to slitting lines.*

INFORMATION SHEET

Bulk storage 1

Conveyors for bulk materials

1 **Belt conveyors**

2 **Vibration or oscillating conveyors**

3 **Steel plate apron feeders**

4 **Screw conveyors and elevators**

5 **Other bulk conveyors**

This sheet gives information on belt conveyors, spiral conveyors, feeders and other types.

Bulk handling is a specialist topic and is generally professionally handled by the specialist contractors involved in providing loading and unloading equipment, storage hoppers, transportation pipe work and conveyors, many of which can be on a very large scale. The handling of bulk materials, including liquids, powders and granular materials, involves expert knowledge of flow characteristics, explosion hazards and relief, discharge characteristics in hoppers. Building designers, project managers and logistics and handling consultants tend to come across bulk handling as part of manufacturing processes built into production or storage facilities: they need to understand how the equipment and its support services fit, and the space/volume demands implied. In this second edition of this book, information sheets on typical bulk handling equipment are included in this special storage chapter for planning purposes: but any detailed work should be in the hands of specialists.

1 Belt conveyors

1.01 Belt conveyors for bulk materials differ from other conveyors (see Information sheet, Mechanized storage 14) as they have a troughed profile to contain granular material (Figure 7.20). Side rollers usually have 20° angles, although supports allow up to 60° angles at the edge of the trough to contain fluffy or light material. Belts of cotton or canvas construction are limited to angles of 30 degrees as the carcass is not flexible enough to trough at steeper angles without damage. Synthetic fibre carcass belts can trough at angles of up to 60°, and can carry a bigger load. Some materials can be carried up inclines with steeper angles, as the greater trough confines the load.

1.02 Most bulk handling conveyors run on closely spaced angled idler rollers (Figure 7.21). A wire rope system for supporting and driving long runs is used, which maintains sufficient tension for the fast transport of materials such as ores, but reduces the number of idler brackets.

1.03 Troughed belts can run at 3 m/sec, and can be formed into a near circular section for gentle (20 m radius) bends: they have been considered for baggage handling in airports. Allow 1300 to 1500 mm over belt width for overall width including catwalk.

Belt surface materials

1.04 Some surfaces are designed for abrasive materials, others for corrosives. Ribbed belts can convey certain materials up inclines. Belt manufacturers will supply information needed to determine suitable flow rates and maximum inclines for the product. Most troughed belts are electrically powered, using a three-phase supply. Some conveyors for external use and heavy-duty work are powered by hydraulic motors.

Figure 7.20 *Troughed belt conveyors supported by idler rollers at each side.*

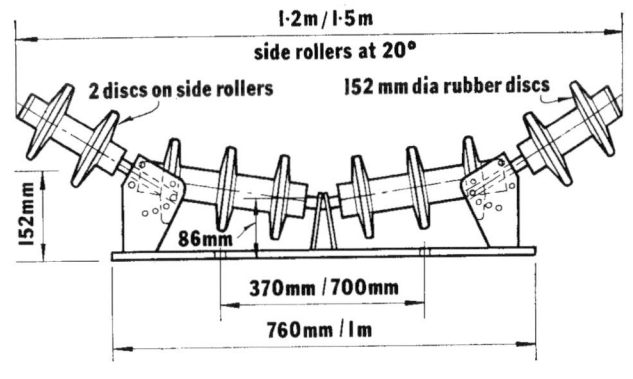

Figure 7.21 *Typical dimensions of rollers with discs, for belt conveyors.*

Bulk storage – conveyors for bulk materials

1.05 Some typical belting materials are listed below:
Polyester with polyurethane coating. For foodstuffs, grains, powders. Smooth surface, 1 mm thickness, weight 1.2 k/m². Resistant to humidity, dirt, putrefaction, all solids, oils, fats, and most chemicals and solvents. Not resistant to alkalis and acids.
Polyester with elastomer coating. 2 mm thick. For foods, pharmaceuticals, salts, grains, fats. Anti-static and resistant to dirt, wet, dryness, putrefaction, all solids, fats, petrol, most chemicals. Not resistant to more than 10 per cent concentration of caustic soda, 20 per cent of hydrochloric acid, 50 per cent of sulphuric acid. The same surface can be moulded into a heavy grip finish for clinker, scrap iron, glass, bricks, etc.
Nylon. 1 mm thick. For fast speeds of abrasive goods, broken glass, powders, gravel, clays, stone chips, fertilizer, etc. Resistant to humidity and dryness, all solids, fats and most chemicals and solvents. Not resistant to 5 per cent of acetic acid, phenol-derived products and mineral acids.
Nylon with profiled elastomer coating. 3 mm thick, weight 3.3 k/m². Specially made for troughed belts and inclines. Suitable for grains, powders, rock products. Anti-static and resistant to dirt, humidity, dryness, putrefaction, all solids, oils, fats, petrol and most chemicals and solvents. Not resistant to acids, alkalis and phenol-based products. The surface is slightly rough for inclines.

2 Vibration or oscillating conveyors

2.01 Vibration conveyors/feed hoppers with abrasive or sharp materials (Figure 7.22). Material is vibrated up inclines, requiring no belts or moving parts other than the vibration machinery. Power requirements are lower than for belt conveyors, but capacities are also lower, averaging up to 50 tonnes per hour for each unit. For in-plant operation, vibration conveyors are more compact than belt units, but may still constrict services and plant movement. Various tray profiles, sizes and duties are available to suit the particular product. For elevating bulk material in confined spaces, spiral vibration conveyors are efficient. These units are particularly suited for processing in transit, e.g. drying, cooling or moistening. They do not transmit vibration to the floor or structure.

3 Steel plate apron feeders

3.01 Feeders handle bulk materials in large lumps, such as quarry products. They are shallow hoppers, with heavy-duty plate conveyor bases, fed by tractor shovel or troughed belt. Feeder widths range from 452 mm to 3047 mm. Power units are electric, fed from three-phase supply. Heavy-duty versions feed household refuse and scrap metal.

4 Screw conveyors and elevators

4.01 These handle powdered and granular materials (Figure 7.23). Helix diameters range from 160 to 400 mm, but smaller and larger sizes are available. Capacity depends on the type of helix, its revolving speed, and the cross-sectional character of the material (free-flowing materials will fill 45 per cent of a helical section, abrasive products will fill only 15 per cent). A typical 305 mm helix with normal material turning at 80 rpm has a capacity of 30 m³/h. The pitch of the helix usually equals the diameter. Materials suitable for screw conveying are given in Information sheet, Bulk storage 4.

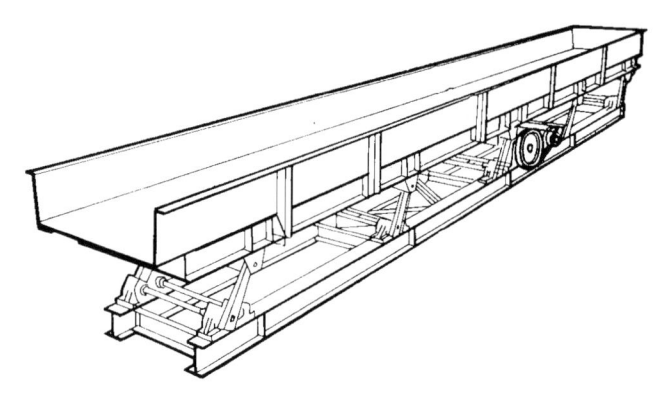

Figure 7.22 *Vibration conveyor, 1.3 m wide.*

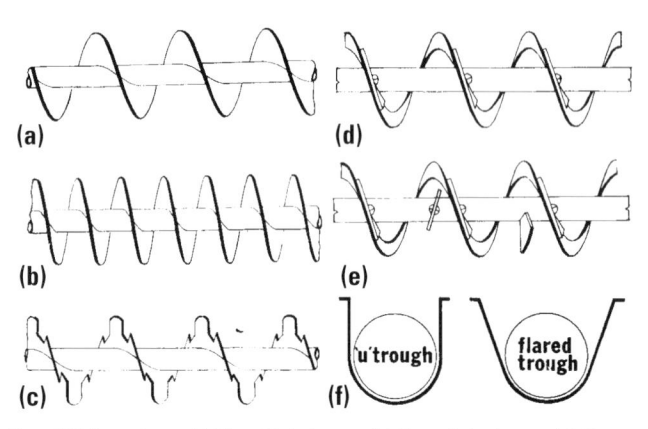

Figure 7.23 *Screw types. (a) Close bladed screw. (b) Short pitched screw. (c) Close bladed screw with notched blades. (d) Ribbon screw. (e) Ribbon screw with paddles.; (f) Troughs.*

4.02 Capacity of spiral conveyors decreases rapidly as the angle of inclination increases. A closer pitch and a tubular casing should be used for an angle over 20°. A vertical helix should be rotated at a much faster speed than horizontal travel, to give the particles centrifugal force. As friction is produced by the screw action, screw conveyors are unsuitable for fast conveying of abrasive materials.

Screw types

4.03
Close bladed screws are the most common. The pitch is equal to the outside diameter (Figure 7.23a).
Short pitched screw is recommended for inclines of more than 20° (Figure 7.23b).
Screw with notched blades has mixing action for fine granular or flaky materials (Figure 7.23c).
Ribbon screw is formed from a flat bar and attached to the axle by radial arms. It is suitable for sticky material that would adhere to a normal screw (Figure 7.23d).
Ribbon screw with paddles set at intervals on the shaft give resistance to forward movement; this stirs the material as it is transported (Figure 7.23e).
Troughs: the most usual form is a U-trough or flared trough. Cover plates fit flanges in the trough tops (Figure 7.23f).

4.04 As screw conveyors operate slowly, geared motors are used; they can be electric, hydraulic, or pneumatic for flame-proof areas. Allow 100 mm width over screw diameter for overall width. Screw conveyors can be top or base mounted. Suspension of 3000 mm standard lengths at 1000 mm centres is usual.

5 Other bulk conveyors

5.01 Drag link conveyors handle powder or granular materials in depths greater than the chain itself. Skeletal chains and push plates force the material along the casing.

5.02 Scraper conveyors scrape the material along a trough. They are simple in operation, and are used for materials such as animal feed stuffs and wood chippings, and in heavy-duty form for minerals in lumps; such as bulk ores.

5.03 Cased bucket conveyors have either centrifugal or positive discharge (tipping) (Figure 7.24). Rows of buckets are mounted on guide chains, and rise vertically or travel horizontally. The self-levelling action of the buckets enables the conveyor to move in complex patterns, incorporating vertical or steeply sloping sections, without spilling. They have been used effectively between bulk hopper truck unloading pits and storage hoppers, and from hoppers to the process. Being flexible they can be routed efficiently. Widths available are 304 mm to 914 mm buckets, but other sizes have been specified. Shaped buckets allow tight horizontal bends as well as vertical direction changes. Typical capacities are 10.8 m³/h at 18 m/min. Buckets are never filled more than 80 per cent. Allow 280 mm over bucket width for casing, 356 mm over the flanges. The conveyor depth for fitting into vertical duct should be 1100 mm over the casing, 1220 mm over flanges.

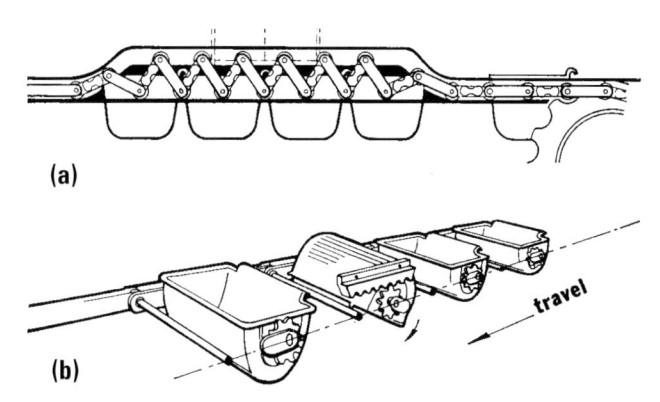

Figure 7.24 *Bucket conveyors. (a) At feed-in position. (b) At tipping position.*

INFORMATION SHEET

Bulk storage 2

Bag loading equipment

1 Use

This sheet gives dimensions of machines for loading bags and sacks. Three basic types of machine are illustrated; for end-loading trucks and containers, for sideloading trucks, and for loading railway wagons through side doors (Figures 7.25–7.30).

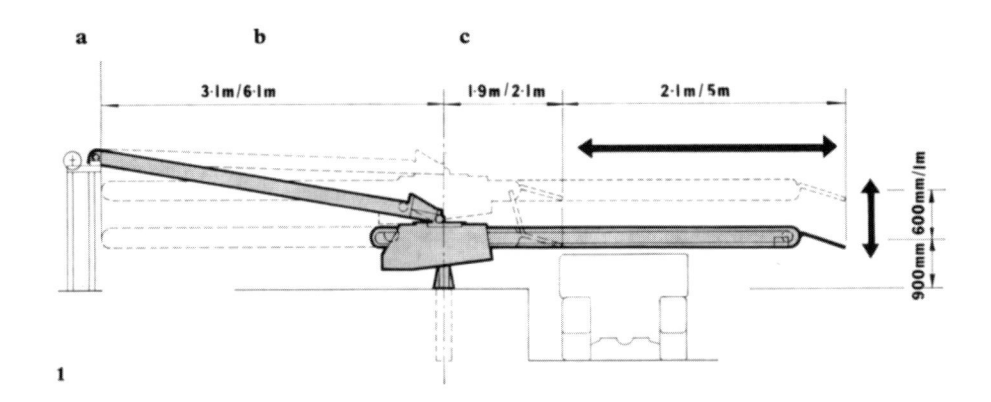

Figure 7.25 *Truck end or side loaded:*
(a) is fixed and has intermediate feed belt
(b), (c) elevates and is telescopic.

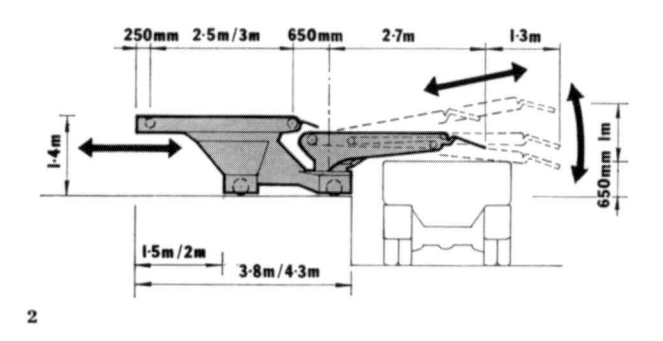

Figure 7.26 *Sideloader for trucks the whole unit advances across the lorry*

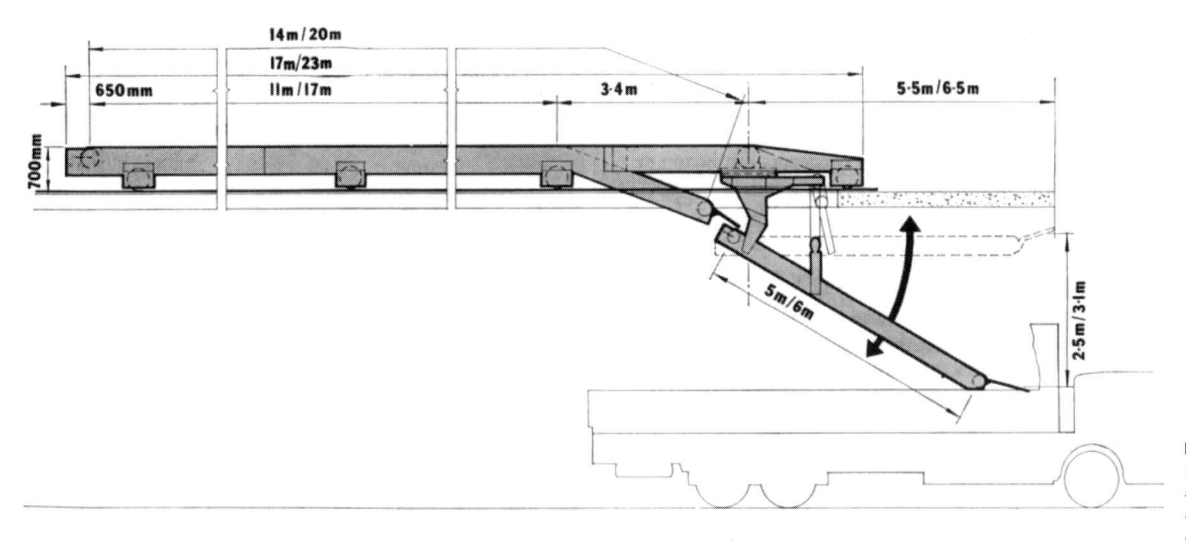

Figure 7.27 *Truck is tail-loaded by suspended, swivel mounted, adjustable height conveyor.*

Bulk storage – bag loading equipment

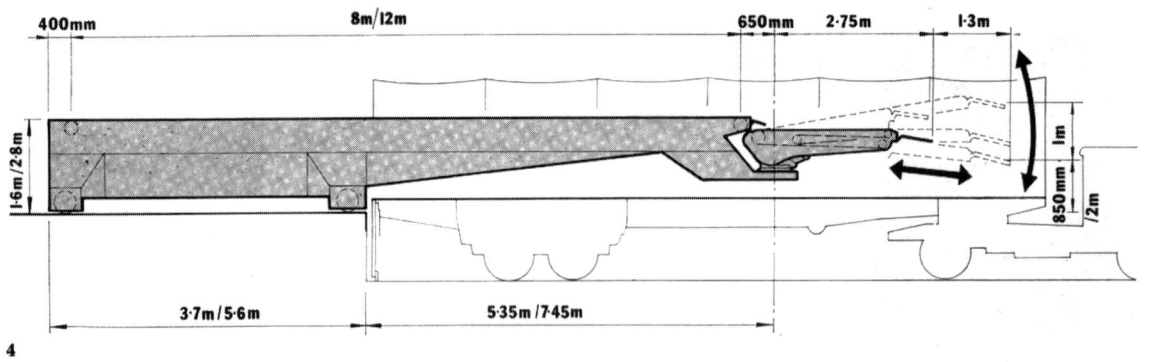

Figure 7.28 Truck is tail loaded by telescopic belt conveyor at dock level.

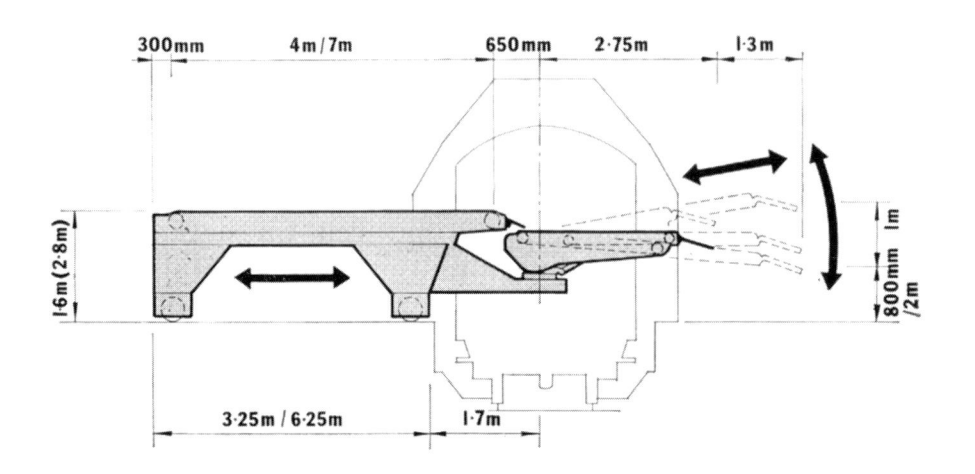

Figure 7.29 Railway wagon is side loaded by swivel-mounted telescopic belt conveyors.

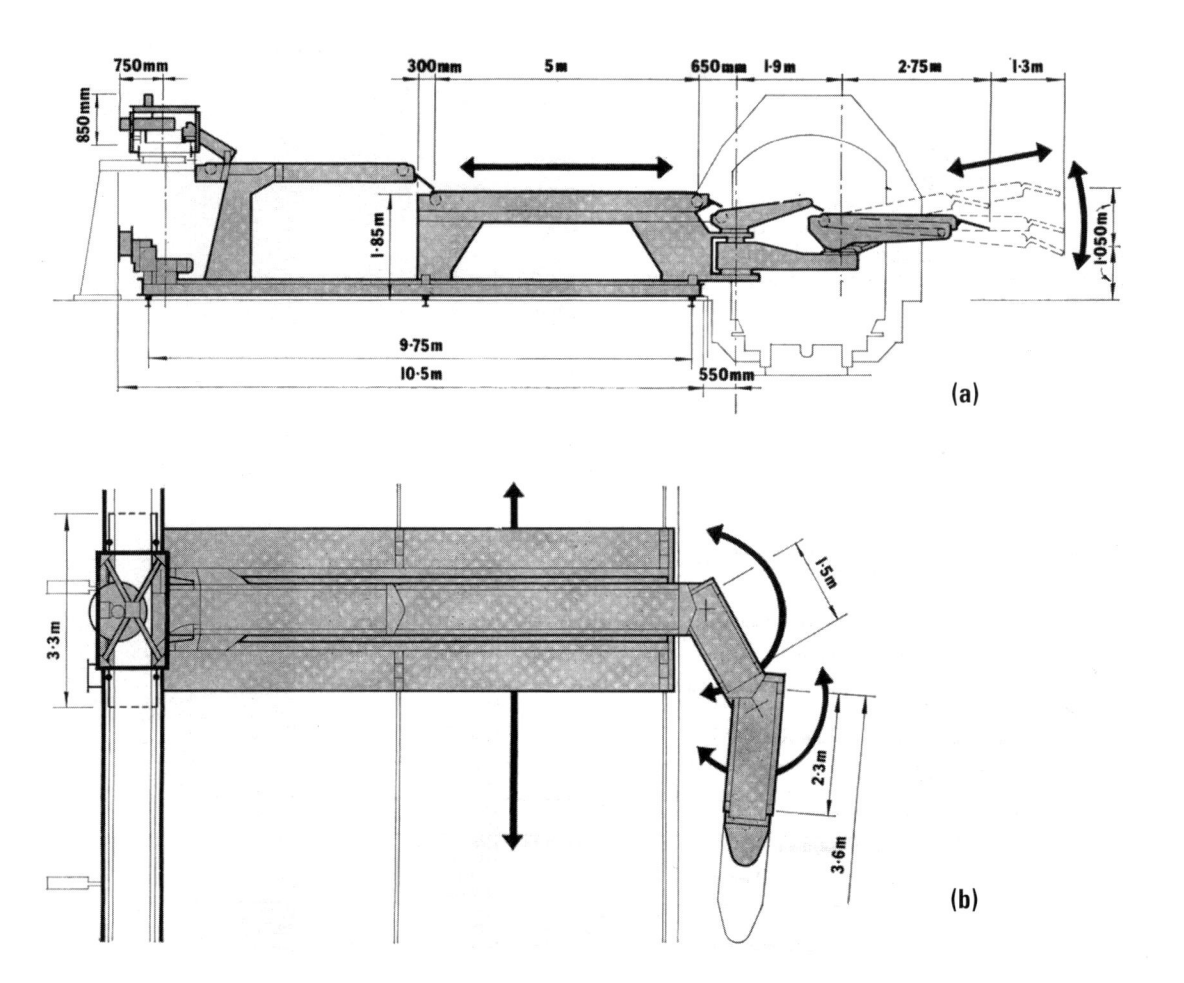

Figure 7.30(a/b) Railway wagon is side loaded by swivel-mounted telescopic belt, capable of lateral movement on rails. Sacks are ploughed from a continuous belt at 90° to the loading conveyor.

INFORMATION SHEET

Bulk storage 3

Mobile bulk-handling plant

1 Use

This sheet gives dimensions of typical tractor shovels and dumpers.

1 Use

1.01 Loader shovels can handle very high throughputs continuously. Small shovels are used in constricted production areas and for cleaning bulk barges and sea-going vessels. Table 7.1 gives data on large and small loaders for providing turning space and for suspended floors suitable for laden wheel loadings.

1.02 Dumpers range from strengthened commercial chassis to purpose-built machines capable of carrying 100 tonnes at a time. They are used in cement works, crushing and processing plants for quarry products, and ore-processing installations where the material is stockpiled in bulk and re-handled with loading shovels.

1.03 Forklift trucks with bucket attachments can move material from stockpiles into hoppers feeding process machinery, and clear spills of granular material. Although versatile, they are no substitute for loader shovels.

Table 7.1 Sizes, weights and capacities of mobile bulk handling plant

Type	Capacity (kg)	Total length (m)	Weight unladen (kg)	Max lift (m)	Max height (m)	Cab height (m)	Turning circle radius (m)
Loader shovel	1 000	3.9	4 040	2.3	3.6	1.9	2.8
	2 500	6.4	8 660	3.52	4.66	3.10	5.09
Dumper	15400	5.8	24385	na	5.8 (tipped)	2.9	15.25
	25000	7.5	39626	na	7.8 (tipped)	3.2	22.83
Forklift with bucket	2260	3.1	5 095	varies	4.4	3.3	3.55

INFORMATION SHEET

Bulk storage 4

Intermediate bulk containers

1 Size

2 Types

3 Equipment

This sheet describes types and dimensions of intermediate bulk containers.

1 Size

1.01 General purpose and special products containers are available. Base sizes are usually of standard pallet dimensions (see Information sheet, Mechanized storage 4, Table 4.9). Heights vary according to capacity of bin, and density or specific gravity of the solid or liquid. Sizes and general properties are shown in Table 7.2.

2 Types

2.01 Collapsible containers are used where storage space is limited and return transport is expensive. Aluminium collapsible containers for liquids can be fitted with disposable liners.

2.02 Disposable containers can be pallet mounted or fitted with slings (suitable for one trip only).

2.03 Metal containers are of welded construction. Mild steel units are subject to corrosion. Aluminium is widely used because of its high strength/tare ratio, but must not be used for acids, alkalis or caustic materials

2.04 Plastic containers are more resistant to corrosive materials and to impact damage by forklift trucks. Polypropylene is lighter than high- or low-density polythenes and is resistant to more chemicals. Polypropylene containers are fabricated, other plastics tend to be moulded.

3 Equipment

3.01 Vibrator frames can increase the flow rate of material being discharged from containers, or vibration motors can be clamped to the bin itself.

3.02 Automated discharge and handling systems, e.g. overhead conveyors and automatic tipper/weighers, are used in production buildings where containers feed directly into the process.

Table 7.2 Properties of typical intermediate bulk containers

Product	Construction	Capacity m^3	Dimensions L/H x W, mm	Method of discharge	Notes
Powders and granules	Aluminium alloy or steel with steel base frame	1.41 to 3.38	1219 x 1066 1651 to 3353	Base sleeve	Stackable
	Corrugated fibreboard	1.41 to 1.69	1066 diam 1905 to 2235	Slide-in base	Disposable Pallet mounted
	Pvc coated nylon Neoprene coated nylon or polyester	Up to 1.98	1168 diam 1320 to 1981	Slide-in base or sleeve	Collapses to 203 to 330 mm Tubular top frame Stack when full
Free-flowing powders and grain	Reinforced proofed paper	0.99	1066 x 762 1219	Slide or slitting base	Disposable Hoods for exterior use
Cohesive powders	Glass fibre	1.66	1219 x 1118 2032	Fluidizing chamber in base	In steel frame Stacks
Slow-flowing materials	Stainless steel	1.36	1219 x 1219 1168	Special base discharge Low angle cone	
Powders and liquids	Low-density polythene Moulded	1.98 to 2.54	1168 x 1168 2235 x 2819	Base sleeve or valve	60° cone angle Steel frame
	High-density spiral bound polythene or polypropylene	1.41	1219 diam 1219 high	Valve base or slide	Steel frame
Liquids; paints/inks, etc.	Glass fibre	1.13	1143 x 1143	Sump in base	Steel frame
	Polyester fabric or Neoprene sandwich	1137 litres Up to 1.98	1575 1219 x 1219 stability when full	Base valve Base valve	Collapsible Frame gives

INFORMATION SHEET

Bulk storage 5
Mass densities

This sheet lists mass densities of bulk goods and suggests suitable conveyors to handle them. Many of these materials can also be conveyed pneumatically.

Key

Classification of materials

Abrasiveness
A = non-abrasive;
B = mildly abrasive;
C = very abrasive.

Flowability
1 = very free flowing. Angle of repose up to 30°.
2 = free flowing. Angle of repose 30 to 45°.
3 = sluggish. Angle of repose 45° plus.

Size
4 = 100 mesh and under.
5 = fine; 3 mm and under.
6 = granular; 12 mm and under.
7 = lumpy; lumps under 12 mm.
8 = irregular; fibrous, stringy, etc.

Other characteristics
D = degradable or friable.
E = contains explosive dust.
F = fluidizes, aerates.
L = very light and fluffy.
M = matted – resistant to re-handling.
P = packs under pressure.
R = mildly corrosive.
V = very corrosive.
(Example: material that is non-abrasive, sluggish and contains lumps over 12 mm is coded A37; if it is mildly corrosive as well the code is A37R).

Conveyors and elevators

Ch = chain elevator up to 76 m/min.
B = belt elevator or conveyor faster than 76 m/min. (Both types have centrifugal discharge).
Pd = positive discharge. Slower speeds for fragile/sluggish materials.
Co = continuous overlapping elevator/conveyor.
S = screw conveyor/elevator; screws designed for the material handled.

Mass densities and classifications of commodities and conveyors suitable for handling them
Material
Mass densities (kg/m³)
Type of material
Suitable conveyor

A

Alum	– lumpy	800–960	A27	Ch
	– pulverized	720–800	A25	Ch
Alumina		960	C25	Pd, Co, S
Aluminium	– chips	112–240	A38M	Co
	– hydrate	290	A26	S
	– oxide	1970–1920	B14F	B, Co
Ammonium chloride (crystalline)		830	A25	S
Animal feed pellets		480–560	A25D	Pd, Co
Asbestos	– grit	960	C25	Co
	– shred	320–400	B37LP	S
Ashes, coal, dry 75 mm		560–640	B37	Ch, S
Asphalt crushed, 12 mm		720	A26	S

B

Bagasse		112–160	A38FLM	S
Bakelite, fine		480–640	A34	S
Baking powder		660	A24	Pd, Co, S
Barley		610	A15E	B, S
Ballast	– dry	1527–1727	B36	B
	– wet	1727–1926	B36	B
Bauxite, crushed 75 mm		1200–1360	C27	Ch, Co, S
Beans, caster, whole		580	A16	Ch, Co, S
Bentonite 100 mesh		800–960	B24F	Ch, Pd, S
Bicarbonate of soda		660	A24	S
Bonechar, 3 mm		435–640	B25	S
Bonemeal		880–960	B25	Ch, S
Boracic acid, fine		880	A25	S
Borax, powdered		850	A25	Ch, Pd, S
Bran		250–320	A25	Ch, Pd, S
Brewers grains	– dry	440–480	A36	Ch, S
	– wet	880–960	A36R	Ch, S

C

Calcium carbide		1120–1280	B27	S
Cast iron	– borings	2080–3200	B36	Co
	– chips	2080–3200	B36	S
Cattle nuts		610–640	A27D	Pd, Co
Cement	– Portland	1040–1360	B24F	Ch, Co, S
	– clinker	1200–1280	C27	Pd, Co
	– kiln, dust	560–640	C14	Ch, Co
Chalk	– crushed	1360–1440	B37P	Ch, Co
	– lumps	1360–1440	B37P	S
Charcoal	– whole	280–400	B37D	Pd, Co, S
	– pellets	400	B37D	Pd, Co
Cinders, coal		640	B37D	Co
Clay	– dry (ground)	1015	A24P	B, S
	– wet	1760–1909	B37P	Ch, B
Clay and gravel		1593	B38	Ch, B
Coal	– anthracite	960	B26R	S
	– slack	640–770	A36R	Ch, Co, S
Cocoa	– ground	480–560	A34P	Pd, Co
	– beans	560–640	B26D	Ch, Co
Coffee	– green beans	500	A26D	Ch, Co, S
	– ground	400	A25	S
Coke	– loose	370–500	C37DM	B, Co
	– petrol, calcined	540–720	C28M	B, Co
	– breeze, 6 mm	400–560	C36	B, Pd, S
Concrete	– cinder	1760	B36P	B, S
	– dry mix	1246	B36P	B, S
	– gravel agg.	2423	B36P	B, S
	– limestone agg.	2391	B36P	B, S
	– sandstone agg.	2325	B36P	B, S
	– stone agg.	2492	B36P	B, S
	– wet mix	2394	B36R	B, S
Copra	– cake, lumpy	400–480	A27	S
	– cake, ground	640–720	A25	S

Bulk storage – mass densities

Cork	– fine, ground	192–240	A35FL	S
	– granulated	192–240	A36	S
Corn	– seed	720	A16DE	S
	– grits	640–720	A25	S
	– Indian	720–770	A16	Ch, B
	– meal	640	A25	Ch, B, Pd, S
Cottonseed	– whole	480–560	A36	Ch
	– hulls	192	A35L	Co
	– meal	560–640	A25	Ch, Pd
Cullet		1280–1600	C27	Ch, B, Co
Crushed stone		1600	C27	Ch, B

D, E

Dolomite, crushed		1440–1600	B27	Co
Earth, damp, loose		1246	B37P	Ch, B
Earth and gravel	– wet	1926	B37	B
	– dry	1593	B25	B
Abonite, crushed 12 mm		1010–1120	A26	S
Epsom salts		640–800	A25	S

F

Feldspar	– ground 3 mm	1040–1200	B25	Ch, Co, S
	– powdered 100 mesh	1200	B34	Pd, Co
Ferrous sulphate		800–1200	B26	S
Fertilizer		960	B35V	Pd, Co
Fish	– meal	560–640	A35	S
	– scrap	640–800	A38	S
Flaxseed	– whole	720	A15E	B
	– meal	400	A25	Ch, S
Flour, wheat		560–640	A34	B, Pd
Fluorspar		1310	B36	S, Ch, Co

G

Gelatine, granulated		640	B25	S
Glass, batch		1440–1600	C27	Ch, B, Co
Glue	– ground 3 mm	640	B25	S
	– pearl	640	A16	S
Grains, distillery, spent dry		480	A28L	Ch, Co, S
Granite	– broken	1520–1600	C27	B, Co
	– chips	2656	C25	B, Co
	– tarred	1992	C36	B
Grass seed		160–192	A25EL	Co, S
Graphite	– flake	640	A26	S
	– flour	450	A14F	S
Gravel	– screened	1440–1600	B27	Ch, B, Co
	– dry	1678–1909	B27	Ch, B, C
	– wet	2000	B26	Ch, B
	– and sand, wet	1909	B37	Ch, B
Gypsum	– calcined 12 mm	850–960	B26	Ch, Pd, Co, S
	– raw 25 mm	1440–1600	B27	Ch, Pd, Co, S
Garbage, 75 per cent water content		755	B38R	Ch, B

H to L

Hemp seed		495	A25	Co
Hops, spent	– dry	560	A38	Ch, S
	– wet	800–880	A38R	Ch, S
Ice	– block	900	A17D	Co
	– crushed	560–720	A17	Pd, Co, S
Lead ore		1700	B37	Co
Lignite, air-dried		720–880	A27	Ch, Co
Lime	– ground 3 mm	960	A35P	Co, S
	– hydrated 3 mm	640	A25FP	Pd, Co, S
	– hydrated pulverized	510–640	A24FP	S
	– pebble	850–900	A37	Ch, Co, S
	– over 13 mm	850	A37	Ch, Co
Limestone	– agricultural 3 mm	1090	B25	Ch, Pd, Co, S
	– crushed	1360–1440	B27	Ch, Co
	– rock	4536	B37	B, Ch

M

Magnesium chloride		560	A36	S
Malt	– dry, ground 3 mm	350	A25EL	Ch, Pd, S
	– dry, whole	435–480	A26E	Ch, S
	– wet/green	960–1040	A36	Ch
	– meal	580–640	A26	Ch, Pd, S
Manganese	– ore	2000–2240	*	Pd, Co
	– sulphate	1120	C26	S
Marble, crushed 13 mm		1140–1520	C72	C
Mica	– ground	210–240	B25	S
	– pulverized	210–240	B25F	S
	– flakes	270–350	B15FL	S

Milk	– malted	480–560	A34P	S
	– dried	570	A35	B, Pd
	– whole, powdered	320	A35P	S
Mortar		1370–1900	C36	B, Pd
Muriate of potash		1230	C25	S
Mustard seed		720	A15E	Ch, S
Mud	– wet	1727	B25	B, Ch, S
	– dry	1444	B25	B

O

Oats	– whole	415	A16E	B, Pd, S
	– rolled	350	A26EL	Ch, Pd, S
Oatmeal		620	A25	Pd
Oxalic acid crystals		960	A35,	S

P

Peas, dried		720–800	A16D	Co
Peanuts	– in shells	240–320	A27D	S
	– shelled	560–720	A26D	Co, S
Phosphate	– rock	1200–1360	B27	Ch, Co
	– sand	1440–1600	C25	B, Co, S
Potash		720	B34F	Pd
Potassium nitrate		1220	B16R	S

R

Refuse, dry		399	B38	B, Ch
Rice	– polished	720–770	A15	S
	– rough	580	A25E	S
	– grits	670–720	A25	S
Rye		700	A15	B

S

Salt	– dry, fine	1120–1280	B25R	Ch, B, C
	– coarse	720–800	B25R	
Salt cake	– dry	1360	B27	
	– pulverized	1040–1360	B25	
Saltpetre		1280	A25E	S
Sand bank	– dry	1440–1760	C25	B, S
	– wet	1760–2080	C35	B
Sand	– dry, silica	1440–1600	C15	B, S
	– foundry	1440	C35/C27	B
Sawdust	– dry	128–205	A35	Pd
	– damp	320	A35	Ch
Shale	– crushed	1478	B26	S, B
	– solid	2757	C26	B, Ch
Silica		2169	C15, S	
Shingle		1280–1360	B27	Ch
Slag	– granulated	960–1040	C26	S
	– bank	1113	C27	B, Ch, S
	– machine	1527	C26	B
	– sand	880	B25	S
	– screening	1593	C26	B, S
	– shale	2590	C27	B
Slate	– ground 3 mm	1310	B25	S
	– crushed 12 mm	1280–1440	B26	S
	– dust	1600	B25	B, Pd
Soap	– flakes	80–240	A250	Pd
	– powder	640	A25	B, Pd
Soda ash	– light	320–560	B24L	Pd, S
	– heavy	880–1040	B25	Ch, Pd, S
Sodium nitrate		1150	*	Ch
Sugar beet pulp	– dry	190–240	*	Pd
	– wet	440–720	*	S
Sugar	– raw	880–1040	A35	Ch, B
	– refined	800	A35	Ch, B, Pd
	– granulated	800–880	B25D	S
Steel chips, crushed		1600–2400	C37	S
Sulphur, lumpy		1280–1360	A27	Ch, Pd
Superphosphates		960–1040	A25R	Pd

T

Talc		800–960	B24F	Ch, Pd
Talcum powder		640–960	B24F	S

V, W

Vermiculite, expanded		255	B36L	S
Wheat	– whole	720–770	A16E	B, S
	– cracked	640–720	A25E	Ch, B, S
	– germ	450	A25	S
Wood chips		190–320	A37	B, Pd

269

Bibliography and useful addresses

Heat, ventilation, lighting

American Society of Heating, Refrigeration and Air-conditioning Engineers (1987). *ASHRAE Handbook: Heating, Ventilation and Air Conditioning.* ASHRAE.

Chartered Institute of Building Services Engineers (CIBSIE) guides.

Dekker, I. and Janse, M. (1994). Warehouses. *International Lighting Review*, 2, 68–71.

Fire precautions and control

BS 5306: Part 2 (1990). Specification for sprinkler systems.

BS 5839: Parts 1–5 (1988).

Fire Precautions Order, 1989.

Loss Prevention Council (1990). *Rules for Automatic Sprinkler Installations.* 30th edition. Loss Prevention Council.

Loss Prevention Council (1992). *Categorization of Goods in Storage.* TB17. Loss Prevention Council.

Loss Prevention Council, Technical bulletins TB1–33.

Fire Prevention for Cold Stones by Oxygen Depletion with Nitrogen, 2000. D. Hurren, Institute of Refrigeration.

Transport and logistics

All the publications in this section can be obtained through the Institute of Logistics and Transport, PO Box 5787, Corby, Northamptonshire, UK, NN17 4XQ. Tel: 01536 740100. Email: bookshop@iolt.org.uk

Summaries of contents of the following publications are available through the website.

Brewer, A. M., Button, K. J. and Hensher, D. A. (eds) (2001). *Handbook of Logistics and Supply-Chain Management.* Pergamon.

Brooks, M. R. (2000). *Sea Change in Liner Shipping: Regulation and Managerial Decision-Making in a Global Industry.* Pergamon.

Christopher, M. (1998). *Logistics and Supply Chain Management: Strategies for Reducing Costs and Improving Service.* 2nd edition. Financial Times Pitman.

Freight Transport Association (2000). *How to Improve Warehouse Productivity.* Added Value Logistics Publications Ltd.

Harrison, A. and van Roek, R. (2002). *Logistics Management and Strategy.* Financial Times Prentice Hall.

IOLT (1996). *Guideline No. 8: A Guide to Locating Industrial Facilities.* IOLT.

IOLT (1999). *Guideline No. 7: Understanding European Intermodal Transport: A User's Guide.* IOLT.

Lowe, D. (2002). *The Dictionary of Transport and Logistics.* Kogan Page.

Rushton, A., Oxley, J. and Croucher, P. (2000). *Handbook of Logistics and Distribution Management.* Kogan Page.

Stranks, J. (2001). A Manager's Guide to Health and Safety at Work. Kogan Page.

Taniguchi, E. (2001). *City Logistics: Network Modelling and Intelligent Transport Systems.* Pergamon.

Useful addresses

Factory Inspector: address of Local Inspector obtainable from Factory Inspectorate Division, Baynards House, 1 Chepstow Place, Westbourne Grove, London W2 4TF.

Freight Transport Association, London Road, Southborough, Tunbridge Wells, Kent.

Fire Research Station, Station Road, Boreham Wood, Hertfordshire.

Petroleum Officer: see local authority.

Institute of Logistics and Transport. PO Box 5787, Corby, Northamptonshire, NN17 4X.

The Stationery Office (formerly HMSO) www.tso.co.uk, Tel: 0870 600 5522. A special service that informs of new legislation and delivers revised UK and EU statutory instruments/documents.